WOJTYŁA's WOMEN

How They Shaped the Life of Pope John Paul II

and Changed the Catholic Church

First published by O Books, 2008
O Books is an imprint of John Hunt Publishing Ltd., The Bothy, Deershot Lodge, Park Lane, Ropley,
Hants, SO24 0BE, UK
office1@o-books.net
www.o-books.net

Distribution in:	South Africa
	Alternative Books
UK and Europe	altbook@peterhyde.co.za
Orca Book Services	Tel: 021 555 4027 Fax: 021 447 1430
orders@orcabookservices.co.uk	
Tel: 01202 665432 Fax: 01202 666219	Text copyright Ted Lipien 2008
Int. code (44)	
	Design: Stuart Davies
USA and Canada	
NBN	ISBN: 978 1 84694 110 8
custserv@nbnbooks.com	
Tel: 1 800 462 6420 Fax: 1 800 338 4550	All rights reserved. Except for brief quotations in critical articles or reviews, no part of this
Australia and New Zealand	book may be reproduced in any manner without
Brumby Books	prior written permission from the publishers.
sales@brumbybooks.com.au	
Tel: 61 3 9761 5535 Fax: 61 3 9761 7095	The rights of Ted Lipien as author have been asserted in accordance with the Copyright,
Far East (offices in Singapore, Thailand,	Designs and Patents Act 1988.
Hong Kong, Taiwan)	
Pansing Distribution Pte Ltd	
kemal@pansing.com	A CIP catalogue record for this book is available
Tel: 65 6319 9939 Fax: 65 6462 5761	from the British Library.

Cover photo of Pope John Paul II, October 1979 © Martin Athenstaedt/dpa/Corbis
Photo of young Karol Wojtyla as a toddler with his parents Karol and Emilia Kaczorowska Wojtyla ©
Sygma/Corbis Photo of Pope John Paul II with Mother Teresa, Vatican City, May 1983. © Bettmann/Corbis

Printed in the US by Maple Vail

O Books operates a distinctive and ethical publishing philosophy in
all areas of its business, from its global network of authors to
production and worldwide distribution.
No trees were cut down to print this particular book. The paper is
100% recycled, with 50% of that being post-consumer. It's processed
chlorine-free, and has no fibre from ancient or endangered forests.
This production method on this print run saved approximately
thirteen trees, 4,000 gallons of water, 600 pounds of solid waste,
990 pounds of greenhouse gases and 8 million BTU of energy. On its
publication a tree was planted in a new forest that O Books is
sponsoring at The Village www.thefourgates.com

WOJTYŁA's WOMEN

How They Shaped the Life of Pope John Paul II

and Changed the Catholic Church

Ted Lipien

BOOKS

Winchester, UK
Washington, USA

Ted Lipien has written an incisive and penetrating book on the role remarkable women played in shaping John Paul II's outlook on important and controversial issues that defined his papacy. One of them was the Albanian-born nun and Nobel laureate Mother Teresa. Much of the ground that Lipien covers in his meticulously documented book is not familiar to students of John Paul II's papacy. He presents new information on the Pope's enduring relationships with women who had an enormous impact on his life, offers original interpretations, and makes a significant contribution in advancing the theoretical discussion on John Paul II's papacy. The greatest strength of "Wojtyla's Women" lies in the author's impassioned analysis of astonishingly complex issues and events. Lipien's landmark book opens new paths for other scholars and is essential reading for specialists as well as the wider public. **Dr. Elez Biberaj**, author of *Albania in Transition: The Rocky Road to Democracy*

Extremely detailed research into a heretofore unexamined aspect of the beloved Pope John Paul II's life. This book is worthwhile reading for anyone interested in the personal network of highly influential women who shaped John Paul II's attitudes, particularly on the debate of women's roles.
Dr. Nancy Snow, author of *Information War*

An important book. Few persons are as qualified as Ted Lipien to enlighten readers about Pope John Paul II's Polish roots — and the impact that they had on his views on women. Lipien provides a stimulating analysis of the Pope's ideas on gender roles and how John Paul believed the Church should deal with sexual issues. While he does not agree with many of the Pope's stands on women, Lipien makes a laudatory effort to understand — and explain — them. This book is a must-read for anyone interested in the relationship between feminism and Catholicism, a key issue of our times.
Dr. John H. Brown, former U.S. diplomat in Poland, editor of *Public Diplomacy Press Review*

CONTENTS

Acknowledgements 1
Introduction 7
Brief Outline of Polish History 32
Short Biography — Karol Józef Wojtyła — Pope John Paul II
(1920-2005) 38

CHAPTER ONE: Cared For by Women, Educated by Men 45
Wojtyła's Mother and Early Life 45
Life in Pre-World War II Poland 58
Passion for Theater 64
Male Role Models 67
Relationships with Girls during Student Years 86
Priest and Young Women 93
Talking to Male Students 117
Talking to Female Students 122
Women Taking Care of Wojtyła 126

CHAPTER TWO: Marxism, Second Sex and Wojtyła's
Feminist Philosophy 148
Feminist Theories and History 148
Liberal-Democratic Roots of Modern Feminism 150
De Beauvoir's Marxism and Feminist Scholarship 154
Wojtyła's Response to Marxist and Liberal Feminism 162
Liberal Critics of John Paul II 165
Feminist Reading of History and Criticism of
American Values 168
Post-Christian Feminists 175
New Feminists and Solidarity of Love 189
Liberal or Conservative Pope? 195
Wojtyła's Theological Argument Behind the Ban
on Women-Priests 199

Genocide and Abortion 203

CHAPTER THREE: Polish Roots 206
The Romantic Tradition 206
Women from Poland's History: Saint Jadwiga 226
Polish Descendents of Amazons—Powerful at Home 230
Wojtyła's Pacifism and Sense of Duty 237
The Positivist (Liberal) Tradition 240
Women in Communist-Ruled Poland 246
Commitment to the Family and Women's Role at Home 257
Wojtyła and Pro-Choice Feminists 268
Women and Social Solidarity 271
Focused on the Past—Explaining John Paul II to Westerners 278

CHAPTER FOUR: Significant Women, War, Genocide
and Abortion 284
Dr. Wanda Półtawska s and Karol Wojtyła's Views
on Love and Sex 285
Wojtyła on Female Orgasm 290
Celibacy Rules 292
Wojtyła and Dr. Półtawska Urge Paul VI to Ban
Contraception 295
Teaching Natural Birth Control
The Pill—Links between Contraception and Abortion 298
Fighting for Human Dignity 301
Saint Maximilian Kolbe 309
WW II Genetic Killings Key to Understanding Wojtyła's
Pro-Life Stands 324
Abortions in Nazi Concentration Camps 331
Suffering of Women in Soviet Camps 335
Polish Women as Fighters During WWII 336
Victims of War Crimes and Western Feminists—
Different Perspectives 338
Dr. Anna-Teresa Tymieniecka 339

Unsuccessful Dialogue with Western Women 350
Edith Stein (Saint Teresa Benedicta of the Cross) 351
John Paul II and Mother Teresa 359
The Cairo Conference and the Clinton Administration 362
John Paul II and Evangelical Religious Right in the U.S. 365
Abortion — the "Culture of Life" versus the
   "Culture of Death" 389
Black Genocide 398
Papal Impact on the Abortion Debate in the U.S. 401
Abortion and Death Penalty in the 2008 U.S.
   Presidential Elections 408

CHAPTER FIVE: Contraception versus Love —
   Agenda for Polish Women 1947-1978 414
Progressive within the Polish Church 414
Birth Control and Poland's Population Losses 418
Love and Responsibility 424
Family Counseling in the Kraków Archdiocese 430
Wojtyła s Contribution to Humanae vitae —
   Encyclical on the Regulation of Birth 433
Wojtyła Defends Humanae vitae 438
Wojtyła and Medical Profession 445
Help for Single Mothers 453

CHAPTER SIX: Women-Priests 462
Familiaris consortio — On the Family 462
Mulieris dignitatem — Dignity and Vocation of Women 464
Ordinatio sacerdotalis — Reserving Priestly Ordination
   to Men Alone 469
Conservative and Liberal Arguments on Women-Priests 474
The Infallibility Argument 489
Women and Priests in the Third World 491
Ludmila Javorová — First Ordained Catholic Woman-Priest 494
Women Clergy in Poland: Felicja Kozłowska 497

Polish National Catholic Church   500

Letter to the Beijing World Conference on Women   504

Appeal to Women for Forgiveness   513

"Different but Equal" and American Slavery   517

End of Dialogue?   519

Wojtyła's Theory of Gender Complementarity and
    Equal Dignity   530

Polish Friends Defend Wojtyła's Views on Women,
    Family and Feminism   531

Wojtyła's "New Feminism"   536

John Paul II's Views on Homosexual Marriages   540

Poland — Practical Applications of John Paul II's
    Ideas for Women   542

Havel, Gandhi and Alternative Views of
    Western Feminism   553

CHAPTER SEVEN: What to Expect from the New Pope   557

American Catholics and the New Pope   557

Dismissal of Western Liberalism   559

How to Evaluate John Paul II and Benedict XVI   566

Appendix: Sources and Communist Spy Scandal
    at the Vatican   589

SELECT BIBLIOGRAPHY   615

NOTES   624

To Deborah

ACKNOWLEDGEMENTS

I am deeply indebted to many people who have offered their ideas and otherwise helped me with research, writing and editing of *Wojtyła's Women*. Despite her busy law career, my wife Deborah Croyle, shared with me her insights and gave me much needed advice and support. I could not have written this book, which is dedicated to her, without her inspiration and love. My daughter Leokadia (Lodi) Lipien-Rohrer and her husband Dr. Douglas Rohrer helped me sort out facts and ideas and offered excellent suggestions. While taking care of Chloe, their beautiful infant daughter, Lodi read and re-read the manuscript pointing out errors and areas requiring further elaboration for non-Polish readers. After Chloe's birth, she has taken a break from her job of analyzing data on child abuse prevention and care for the elderly, while her husband continues his university research and teaching work in psychology. I want to thank them both for their enormous help.

I also received much encouragement and support from my mother Helena Maciaszek Lipień and my father Stanisław Bolesław Lipień, both of whom had passed away in 2006. In the *Appendix*, I describe their World War II experiences and how their remarkable stories shaped my own views of history and helped me write this book.

I would also like to thank all of my friends and colleagues — in the United States, the Czech Republic and Poland — who directed me to previously undiscovered documents and sources. Danuta Ciesielska shared with me her memories of her many days spent with Karol Wojtyła during hiking trips he organized for young women and men from Kraków's universities. In 1957, he presided over her marriage to Jerzy Ciesielski, one of his closest friends. After Jerzy's tragic death in a boat accident in Sudan, Karol Wojtyła promoted his beatification, a step toward eventual sainthood in the

Catholic Church.

Sister Zofia Zdybicka, a Polish philosopher specializing in ontology and philosophy of religion and the first nun to become a professor at the Catholic University in Lublin (KUL), spoke with me about her frequent discussions with Karol Wojtyła during a period of over 50 years. Cardinal Wojtyła helped to launch her academic career, and after he was elected pope, she would see him at least once a year at the Vatican, where they talked about philosophy, women and feminism.

Another one of Wojtyła's close friends, Dr. Anna-Teresa Tymieniecka, a Polish-American professor of philosophy who translated into English his book *The Acting Person*, also shared with me her unique insights. She was one of the few people close to John Paul II who had a good understanding of both Polish and American culture and could interpret his philosophical theories and his views on women. I want to thank her for agreeing to talk to me and for answering my questions.

I also want to thank Father Stefan Filipowicz SJ, a former head of Polish broadcasts at Vatican Radio, for sending me his article about communist secret police attempts to recruit him as a spy among persons close to John Paul II. His story is included in the *Appendix*.

My cousins in Poland: Justyna Maciaszek, Marta Maciaszek, Teofila Latoś-Kasprzyk and Marek Lipień were enormously helpful during the final phases of my research and writing. Justyna, who received her doctorate in sociology at the Catholic University in Lublin (KUL), offered sound advice in analyzing information from various Polish sources. She and Marta made great efforts to put me in touch with people who knew John Paul II and helped me arrange interviews. They also took time to send me books and articles written by Wojtyła's friends whenever I requested them. I am very grateful for their help.

My cousins, Teofila and Marek, spoke with me about our family's history. I also talked at length with my aunt Maria

Wołoszyn, asking her questions about political conditions in Poland at the time when Karol Wojtyła was beginning his lifelong campaign in defense of human life. The stories I got from my cousins and my aunt helped me present a better picture of Poland during wartime and under communist rule.

In collecting facts and information about Pope John Paul II's relationships with women and his views on many critical issues, I also received help from the staff of the Library of Congress in Washington D.C., the Hoover Institution at Stanford University in Stanford, California, the Library at the University of California at Berkley, Centrum Jana Pawła II in Kraków, and the sisters of the Order of Our Lady of Mercy in Łagiewniki, Poland. I relied on various biographies of John Paul II and numerous other books and memoirs, especially those written by his Polish friends and his students, many of them women.

Library of Congress
http://www.loc.gov/

Hoover Institution
http://www.hoover.org/

University of California at Berkley
http://www.lib.berkeley.edu/

John Paul II Center in Kraków
http://www.janpawel2.pl/

Order of Our Lady of Mercy in Łagiewniki, Poland
http://www.sisterfaustina.org/

Wikipedia
http://www.wikipedia.org/

FreeMediaOnline.org
http://www.freemediaonline.org/

While consulting and using many basic reference sources and materials, I was pleased to learn that Wikipedia has articles on almost every Polish historical and contemporary figure mentioned in my book. Wikipedia has been making an important contribution to the free exchange of information and ideas worldwide. I have also benefited from my association with FreeMediaOnline.org, a non-profit organization which supports independent journalism and promotes free flow of information.

Because the Internet has become for many readers a primary

source for getting instant information, I tried to include throughout the book web addresses of various sites dealing with religion, feminism and Pope John Paul II. But as with any information found on the Internet, it is highly changeable and there can be no guarantee of its accuracy or usefulness. Its inclusion does not imply any kind of endorsement, either from me or from these web sites, organizations and individuals.

I also want to thank Ms. Zofia Korbońska, a remarkable woman with whom I worked in the 1970s at the Voice of America (VOA) international broadcasting radio station in Washington, D.C. A great admirer of John Paul II and his message in defense of human rights and families, she inspired my interest in studying the relationship between journalism, religion and politics. During WWII, she risked her life each day to broadcast news and information from a clandestine radio station in Nazi-occupied Poland. Her husband, Stefan Korboński, was the last civilian head of the underground wartime government. After the war, both of them had to flee their country to avoid arrest by the communist secret police.

My longtime friend Enver Safir, also a former VOA broadcaster, urged me many times to get the book published sooner rather than later. I am also indebted to Dr. Nancy Snow, Dr. John H. Brown and Dr. Elez Biberaj for reading the manuscript and offering their comments. I also want to thank John Hunt, my editor Stuart Davies and the staff at O-Books for assisting me with getting *Wojtyła's Women* ready for publication. Without their dedication and professionalism, the book would not have been finished on time.

During the time it took me to write *Wojtyła's Women*, I was fortunate to benefit also from the advice and suggestions of many other individuals. I am grateful for their patience and willingness to share with me their time and their knowledge in countless discussions and exchanges of correspondence. Their help allowed me to develop and refine many of the ideas covered in this book. I want to thank all of my sources for providing me with access to such a rich history of women who shaped the life and views of Pope John Paul II. I am, however, solely responsible for any errors and omissions.

Dr. Nancy Snow

http://www.nancysnow.com/

Dr. John H. Brown

http://uscpublicdiplomacy.org/index.php/newsroom/johnbrown_main

O-Books

http:// www.o-books.com/

Pope John Paul II with Mother Teresa

Let me go to the Lord.
John Paul II[1]'s last words on the day of his death, April 2, 2005
spoken to Sister Tobiana, a Polish medical doctor and member of
his papal household.[2]

*In men, reason [and] intellect has a certain supremacy over the
heart, and this is why Christ entrusted responsibility for the
Gospel as idea to them.*
Karol Wojtyła, 1961

*... women have a great role to play in the Church, and in
Catholicism.*
Karol Wojtyła, 1961

*Throughout our history, our entire nation's debts to the Polish
woman: mother, teacher [of children] ... hero, are beyond measure.*
John Paul II, 1987

INTRODUCTION

Women played a surprisingly decisive role in the life of Pope John Paul II, and yet their story has not been well documented or told. It is true that Karol Wojtyła grew up in a largely patriarchal society of his native Poland and spent most of his life among men. Men were his teachers, his mentors and his closest friends.

Karol Józef Wojtyła – Pope John Paul II

Born: May 18, 1920, Wadowice, Poland

Died: April 2, 2005, the Vatican

Book: *Love and Responsibility*

Quote: "Promote a new feminism which rejects the temptation of imitating models of 'male domination,' in order to acknowledge and affirm the true genius of women." *Evangelium vitae*

www.vatican.va/holy_father/john_paul_ii/index.htm

But Polish women not only cared for him, but saved his life during the Nazi occupation and advised him on questions of sex and marriage. Their opinions and their unquestioning support for his pro-life and pro-family agenda profoundly affected the lives of millions of men and women and helped to bring about historic changes in the Catholic Church.[3]

These Polish women, however, and Karol Wojtyła himself were separated by history and culture from the growing number of far more liberal Catholics in the West. By the middle of the last century, well-educated and economically independent Western women began to identify en masse with the feminist movement and demanded equal treatment in all spheres of life, including ordination to priesthood and other leadership roles in religious institutions. Their demands went far beyond what seemed wise and acceptable to Karol Wojtyła and many other conservative Poles. As he began to offer the Polish model of gender relations to the rest of the Catholic world, John Paul II relied on the example set by the Polish women who nurtured him throughout his life. These women supported his vision of human solidarity and gender complementarity, as opposed to gender competition offered by Western feminists. He was not shy to confront his critics on gender and sanctity of life issues. But the confrontational approach to gender relations advocated by radical feminists, combined with what he perceived as their selfish individualism and lack of respect for human life, John Paul II viewed as fatal flaws in radical feminist ideology.

Betty Friedan (Bettye Naomi Goldstein)

Born: 1921, Peoria, Illinois, USA
Died: 2006, Washington, DC, USA

Book: *The Feminine Mystique*

Quote: "I want something more than my husband and my children and my home."

For the women surrounding Wojtyła and for himself, Polish traditions and Polish history resulted in a much different outlook on life, a different reading of history and a different view of gender roles than those commonly subscribed to by Western women. I first became intrigued by the near total lack of mutual understanding between the Polish pope and Western feminists after coming across Betty Friedan's description of what she saw as male oppression of women in the 1950s middle-class America.[4] While stressing that the American suburban home was not a German concentration camp and American housewives were not destined for extermination, Betty Friedan—one of the pioneers of the American feminist movement—nevertheless insisted in her seminal book *The Feminine Mystique* that there were similarities between the lives of middle class American women and the lives of inmates in Nazi concentration camps. Both, according to her, were forced to adjust to their "biological" role and to "become dependent, passive, [and] childlike." Only years later, Betty Friedan's biography by Daniel Horowitz revealed that for years she had kept secret her Marxist sympathies and her role as a radical labor organizer — details which might have contradicted the image of a bored and oppressed suburban housewife presented in *The Feminine Mystique*.[5]

Chapter Two: Marxism, Second Sex and Wojtyła's Feminist Philosophy explains John Paul II's response to Marxist, radical and post-Christian feminism and analyzes the progression of feminist ideas from Simone de Beauvoir to Betty Friedan and Mary Daly.

Uncovering hidden history also became a large part of writing this book as some of John Paul II's closest friends found themselves accused of spying on him for the communist secret police. In the *Appendix* listing information sources used for my book, I describe the Vatican spy scandal and my own contacts with Karol Wojtyła and his friends. I also try to explain the difficulty of communicating to younger generations of Western readers my own perceptions of World War II atrocities and the opinions I formed as a result of living in communist Poland. Memories of World War II and communism are absolutely essential for the understanding of John Paul II's views on abortion and a number of other issues, including his very negative assessment of Western liberalism and Western societies.

Simone de Beauvoir

Born: January 9, 1908, France

Died: April 14, 1986, France

Book: *The Second Sex*

Quote: "One is not born, but rather becomes a woman."

Having lived both in Poland and in the West, I understood Wojtyła's concerns based on his experience of totalitarian ideologies, but I developed a somewhat different view from his about the ability of liberal-democratic societies to protect human life and advance the rights of women. At the same time, I saw tremendous significance in his attempts to reach out to women and especially in his philosophical positions on individual human worth and dignity.

Chapter Four: Significant Women, War, Genocide and Abortion has perhaps the most crucial information on how war and genocide profoundly influenced John Paul II's views on abortion and protection of human life. This chapter also deals with his collaboration with Dr. Wanda Półtawska, the most important of Wojtyła's women who implemented his pro-life agenda. Albanian-born Mother Teresa was another important woman-ally whose support for John Paul II's pro-life campaign is described in *Chapter Four*.

John Paul II, who had actually experienced life under Nazi occupation, would surely find Betty Friedan's comparison between middle-class American housewives and Nazi concentration camp prisoners offensive to the memory of World War II victims. But the essence of her observation about women being reduced to their "biological and dependent" role did not seem totally off the mark — an observation Wojtyła himself would not necessarily dispute. Like Friedan and other secular feminists, Pope John Paul II also made frequent warnings against treating women as nothing more than objects of carnal desire. But he also concluded that secular feminism represented a grave threat to human life, families and women. He wanted to take the middle ground and be known instead as an enthusiastic supporter of *new feminism*, which he based on his somewhat novel interpretation of Christ's attitude toward women and the Biblical story of creation.

Mindful of the different traditions of tolerance for religious and social experimentation in Poland and in the West, I tried first of all to define conservative and progressive labels used to describe Karol Wojtyła and his pontificate and to unravel the mystery behind his philosophy of new feminism. What was his vision for women, marriage and family? What cultures and traditions did he rely upon or try to oppose in developing his philosophy of personalism and new feminism? Can he be called a feminist? How does his new feminism differ from Marxist, radical, socialist, liberal and libertarian feminism? How did he arrive at his concepts of *female genius, gender complementarity* and *different but equal*? What did he mean when he told a group of young women students in the early 1960s that "exterior emancipation and equality with men produce split personalities in women, especially those with professional training"? What was behind his observation that women are more likely to seek *a great Love* with capital "L," rather than just sexual love?

To answer these questions, I chose to write a slightly different story of Karol Wojtyła's life by paying more attention to his relationships with women and his decisions affecting women in the context of his own culture and his understanding of other cultures. Such an approach is not novel, but for various reasons it was rarely employed in the previously published papal biographies. Most books dealing with John Paul II's early life in Poland present an impressive number of facts and fiction. But since they had to cover a lot of ground, they rarely gave more than just a superficial treatment to gender issues. No book has documented how so many Polish women, relegated by tradition and custom to supportive roles, helped Wojtyła survive the war and communism and reach the peak of his church career.

Unlike his closest male associates, these Polish women, whom I introduce in *Chapter One: Cared for by Women – Educated by Men*, did not become archbishops or cardinals, but without their help Wojtyła might not have lived through the war to become a priest, and neither he nor the Catholic Church in Poland could function without them. I included their stories in my book. In his roles as a priest and a university professor, Wojtyła was also a mentor to many of these women. They loved and admired him for his openness, tolerance and his deep faith. In the 1980s, he asked one of the nuns, whose academic careers he helped to launch, whether feminism existed in Poland. He expressed to her his great pain that the world does not understand his deep respect for women. He was happy to hear her response that radical feminism had not taken root in his native country.[6]

Many of Karol Wojtyła's early relationships with women developed through his active personal involvement in promoting marriage counseling, sex education and natural birth control training. This experience of close collaboration with Polish women who embraced his ideas had a profound impact on his later decisions when he became a bishop and was elected pope. Dr. Wanda Półtawska, a Nazi concentration camp survivor and victim of Nazi medical experiments, was one of these women and, as noted earlier, she was by far the most important and the most influential among them. She had helped Cardinal Wojtyła convince Pope Paul VI to issue the anti-contraception encyclical *Humanae vitae* (1968), which alienated millions of women and continues to deeply divide the Catholic Church. Still active in the pro-life movement but avoiding media attention, this close friend of Pope John Paul II is virtually unknown in the West except among some pro-life organizations. But through her work with Wojtyła on birth control and because of their successful joint effort to

---

Dr. Wanda Półtawska

Born: 1921, Lublin, Poland

Concentration camp prisoner and victim of Nazi medical experiments: 1941-1945

Memoirs: *And I Am Afraid of My Dreams*

Quotes: "Today once again there are doctors who have been given life-or-death powers over the human embryo, yet no one stands in judgment of *them*."

"Use of contraception leads to neurosis."

"Feminists demanding the right to kill their own children are creatures without beauty and loving instincts similar to witches in tales for children."

influence Pope Paul VI's decision on artificial contraception, she has had an enormous impact on the status of women in the Catholic Church.

Those who have come in contact with Dr. Półtawska describe her as extremely tough and determined. She does not grant interviews and rejected my inquiries by saying that if anything should be known about her collaboration with the pope, she would write it herself.[7] But by consulting other sources, I was still able to bring together some of the unknown and lesser known elements of the incredibly influential role Dr. Półtawska and other women played in Karol Wojtyła's life.

One of the remarkable Polish women I spoke with was Dr. Anna-Teresa Tymieniecka, a Polish aristocrat living in the United States who was Wojtyła's friend for many years and translated into English his book *The Acting Person*. This philosopher-phenomenologist told me that at the outset of his papacy, John Paul II's conservative Polish friends fed him a lot of misinformation about America. She claims she was able to get him to modify some of his views. Indeed, a few of John Paul II's speeches at the beginning of his pontificate did

Dr. Anna-Teresa Tymieniecka
www.phenomenology.org

Books: *Phenomenology and science*
Translator: Karol Wojtyła's *The Acting Person*

Quotes: Wojtyła told me that in many respects women are superior to men."

"His conservative Polish friends, who tried to convince him that Americans were decadent, knew little about life in America."

include positive comments about American society, but in later years I saw a marked decline in the warmth of the pope's messages to Americans. More and more they began to reflect his exasperation with America, its liberal values and its growing influence around the world. American women in particular, including

Catholic nuns, publicly challenged many of John Paul II's assumptions and expectations about gender roles. While they were not able to change his views to any significant degree, their challenges prompted him to pay more attention to women's issues and to develop the theology behind new Catholic feminism. There was never, however, any meaningful dialogue between these rebellious American Catholic nuns and the Polish pope.

John Paul II believed there is an essential complementarity of the natures of men and women, with neither gender being superior and both enjoying equal dignity—a departure from classical Catholic theology based on Aristotle's view that women are less perfect than men. St. Paul preached that "man did not come from woman, but woman from man," and that "women should keep silent in the churches." This thought was later reflected in St. Augustine's view that the serpent tried his deception first on the woman, making his assault on "the inferior of the human pair," and St. Thomas Aquinas' conclusion that "woman is defective and misbegotten."[8]

Without disavowing the Church fathers and philosophers— which is one of the principle demands of post-Christian feminists—John Paul II asked for affirmation of "the true genius of

Aristotle 384BC-322-BC

Quote: "Women's nature is very similar to that of children."

Saint Paul the Apostle d. AD 64-67

Quotes: "Women should keep silent in the churches." I Corinthians 14:34-36
"There is not male and female; for you are all one in Christ Jesus."
Galatians 4:28-29

Saint Augustine of Hippo 354-430

Quotes: [Woman] "the inferior of the human pair." *City of God, Book XIV, Chap. 12*

Saint Thomas Aquinas c. 1225-1274

Quote: "Woman is defective and misbegotten." *Summa Theologica, Part I, Question 92* women in every aspect of the life of society" and called for overcoming all gender-based "discrimination, violence and exploitation." But where radical feminists perceived nothing but exploitation and competition, his goal was to offer human solidarity based on love and respect for human life.

I wanted to explore whether John Paul II's vision of women and family was indeed totally incompatible with the views of liberal feminists in America and elsewhere. I also wanted to understand what was behind John Paul II's message to women about their equal dignity with men while at the same time promoting their largely supportive roles as wives, mothers and nuns. What prompted him in 1961 to tell a group of young Polish male students that "we cannot leave the affairs of the Kingdom of God to women" and that "the Gospel as idea is primarily a male sphere"? What was the meaning of his remark to Polish nuns in 1979 that "the so-called social advancement of women has in it a little bit of truth, but it also has a great component of error"? I decided to investigate and try to explain the seeming disparity between his various views on gender issues.

John Paul II thought Western societies did not respect women and their hard work at home and in religious institutions. He took a position that the Western feminist culture reinforced by media messages purposely devalued the work of mothers and made women who want to be full-time wives and mothers feel ignorant and deficient. He himself showed great admiration for working women, both lay and religious, as well as for women who stayed at home to care for their families, but he insisted that women could not become priests. He did not agree with those who saw the Catholic Church's ban on ordination of women to priesthood as highly discriminatory. He also did not understand how some liberal women wanted to be priests but viewed the right to choose abortion as a sign of justice and emancipation. To Wojtyła abortion was murder, not dissimilar to murders committed in Nazi concentration camps, but he assigned most of the blame for abortions to men and secular ideologies. He blamed abortions and many other social ills on moral relativism and consumerism of affluent Western nations, where he believed almost everything was for sale, including human life—a disturbingly incomplete view of these societies. To justify his opposition to women-priests, he insisted that being a mother or a nun brought women closer to sainthood than being a priest.

These were some of the first observations that alerted me to the tremendous misunderstanding and antagonism between John Paul II and Western feminists. I knew from my earlier research that John Paul II was not nearly as socially conservative as his feminist critics in the West portrayed him to be. But I also realized that he did not fully understand much of the criticism leveled against him by liberal Catholic women and secular feminists. Neither he nor they were speaking from the same experience. Feminists who realized that history was written by men focused on rediscovering their own history but failed to see history as revealing far more than just the men's oppression of women. They had a particular problem understanding women and cultures that did not share their ideas. For many feminists, especially those teaching at American and European universities, political theories, most of them Marxist in origin, took precedence over the study of recent history. But as immersed in history as he was, or perhaps because of it, John Paul II also found it extraordinarily difficult to see the realities of life in Western societies through the minds of Western women.

In my book I try to explore historical events and interpretations of history that made John Paul II advance his particular theology of woman and his theology of the body. At the same time, I also present arguments that John Paul II's response to the challenges of traditional feminism may have been largely a product of cultural influences, political calculations and misunderstanding of foreign cultures—forces and circumstances that are subject to constant change in any period of history. This may help to explain why so many liberal Catholics and other Christians from more pluralistic and more democratic societies than Wojtyła's Poland did not agree with him on the gender issue and why many Christian churches, mostly in the West, now allow women-priests, tolerate birth control and accept gay clergy.

In the early and mid-20th century, Wojtyła's Poland did not have a wide diversity and tolerance in religion, politics and social life. Unlike the U.S. in the 1960s and 1970s, there were no large numbers of rebellious nuns in Poland who supported birth control, were tolerant toward homosexuals, demanded priesthood for women and otherwise challenged the male-dominated Church. If Polish women strayed from the established order, as in the case of the Mariavite nuns, they were suppressed and met with ridicule, intimidation and sometimes violence from intolerant groups of lay Catholics at a time when such intolerance was no longer common in the West. The only major challenge by Polish Catholics against the religious establishment in recent times occurred not in Poland but in the liberal-democratic environment of early 20th century America, where a group of dissident Polish immigrants led by a priest from Poland broke with Rome and established the Polish National Catholic Church. With far less democracy, cultural diversity and tolerance, people in 20th century Poland made distinctions between religious beliefs, good and evil, and right and wrong differently than in the United States, France or Great Britain. This may explain why Western feminists had such a difficult time understanding John Paul II, and why he in turn could not understand them.

Unlike Britain and the United States, Poland did not have influential women who would challenge the established religious order with any measure of success and wider social acceptance.[9] There was no successful Protestant movement in Poland to upset the primacy of the Catholic Church.[10] Unlike some other European countries, Poland also did not have powerful female monarchs. Polish aristocracy greatly despised foreign-born queens who were married to Polish kings and tried to exert their influence.[11]

> **Queen Jadwiga of Poland – Saint Jadwiga** 1374-1399
>
> http://www.poland.gov.pl/Jadwiga,of,Anjou,(1374-1399),1954.html

Polish traditions and culture would not allow women to emerge as secular or religious leaders. But Polish history still provided John Paul II with many examples of remarkable women, which he then offered the rest of the world as part of his vision of ideal female vocation. One of them was Queen Jadwiga (Hedwig of Hungary)— Poland's first and only female monarch in more than just a name—whom John Paul II greatly admired and canonized as a Catholic saint in 1997. According to 14th and 15th century historical records, Polish nobles would not let Jadwiga to rule on her own as a woman and a foreigner. But unaccustomed to having a queen even as a nominal ruler, they still crowned her as King of Poland— *Hedvig Rex Polonae*—before deciding whom she should marry. Even though the twelve-year-old girl was already betrothed to an Austrian Habsburg prince, Polish aristocrats ignored her wishes and married her off to another foreigner, Lithuanian Grand Duke Jogaila (Władysław II Jagiełło) who was twenty-three years older than Jadwiga. This marriage allowed Poland to consolidate the union between both countries, bringing Christianity to Lithuania and making the Polish-Lithuanian Commonwealth a major European power.[12]

As a traditional religious thinker and leader, John Paul II saw these historical events in somewhat different terms than how many political historians and liberal feminist theologians would interpret them now. What he was most impressed with was Jadwiga's sacrifice of her personal happiness to serve her adopted country. In 1974 he used the occasion of the 600th anniversary of her birth to extol the value of sacrifice and to warn against Western models for personal self-fulfillment. Presenting Jadwiga's life as an example of Christian virtue, especially for women, he warned his countrymen of the dangers of consumerism: "One must learn, that not everything in life depends on having more [material possessions]; which is characteristic of today's man." The greatness of man, he told Polish Catholics, is in being somebody: "Man becomes somebody through sacrifice, often made in the depths of one's heart."[13] (The Polish word for "man," *człowiek*, is gender neutral.)

Jadwiga's life, however, was apparently more complex than what John Paul II chose to emphasize about her. Despite her young age, she was her husband's intellectual superior, spoke many languages, conducted diplomatic negotiations, participated in military campaigns and liked to entertain. In advocating her canonization, Wojtyła understandably focused, however, on her charitable activities and her motherhood. He stressed that while "God did not grant her the joy of personal motherhood," Jadwiga left "a splendid legacy of motherhood in relation to communities and nations" by giving up her personal plans for marriage in order to serve the people of Poland and Lithuania.[14] Jadwiga died giving birth to a daughter who also died. Even after her canonization was assured, John Paul II chose to present her largely as a model of female Christian virtues of suffering, sacrifice and generosity.

Historical records show that in addition to her achievements as a diplomat and co-ruler with Jagiełło, Jadwiga's life was not as full of self-denial as one would be led to believe. At least initially, she apparently strongly resisted her marriage to the pagan Lithuanian prince. She loved lavish entertainment and imported large quantities of exotic expensive foods for use by her court in Poland.[15] Women's history can be read, interpreted and presented in various ways depending on who does the reading. As with most historical figures, however, both images of Saint Jadwiga — religious and deconstructionist-feminist — are probably each correct to some degree. It is always a question of emphasis or exclusive attention that results in a one-dimensional viewing of history.

Revisionist feminist historians would have offered a much

more critical and strikingly different interpretation of Saint Jadwiga's life. John Paul II felt, however, that modern women would benefit more from his traditional view of her womanhood. He assumed that today's women already have enough models that encourage life devoted to ambitious pursuits of personal happiness. At the same time, he was not overly concerned with feminist complaints that Christianity's focus on sacrifice and suffering assigns women to a life of menial work and helps men keep their privileged position. John Paul II saw his interpretation of Saint Jadwiga's life as a perfect example of Christian living. He was especially proud of the respect Polish men showed toward Polish women. There is more information about Saint Jadwiga and her importance for Wojtyła's vision for women in *Chaper Three: Polish Roots*.

Even after it became obvious that women in the West were questioning their status, demanding new rights and becoming alienated from the male Church hierarchy, Wojtyła and other Polish bishops tended to idealize the treatment of women in Polish society and believed that it could be a model for the rest of the world together with what they perceived as their country's superior piety and morality. During that period, Wojtyła's women, and Polish women in general, were not sending any strong signals that adjustments in the Church's position on gender issues were urgently needed. Unlike women in the West, Polish women were not becoming indifferent to religion and the Church. The need for change in the Church's approach to women could only be gathered by looking closely at statistical data on abortion, birth rates, alcoholism, domestic abuse and sex discrimination in communist Poland—data which often contradicted the rosy picture of traditional Polish Catholicism and Polish respect for women and for the unborn. But John Paul II was far more concerned by communist repression of religion and empty churches in the West than with demands of Western feminists. He may have assumed that if only Western women behaved like Polish women, religious faith in the

West would return and many social ills would be avoided.

Most of the information on Polish history, culture and traditions, how they influenced John Paul II's views on women and how they fueled misunderstandings between him and Western feminists, can be found in *Chapter Three: Polish Roots.*

Total Fertility Rate (births per woman)	Birth rates per 1000 population
Poland 1.26	Italy 9.2
Italy 1.29	Poland 9.5
Russia 1.39	Russia 10.7
UK 1.85	UK 12.0
USA 2.09	China 13.1
Israel 2.38	USA 14.0
India 2.81	Israel 19.7
Iraq 4.07	India 23
Afghanistan 6.64	Iraq 31.7
Somalia 6.68	Somalia 42.9
Source: CIA World Fact Book (2007)	Afghanistan 48.2
	Source: UN estimates for 2005-2010

As a journalist familiar with both East Central Europe and the West, I knew the optimistic assessment of Poland as a model Christian nation for others to follow was not at all realistic.[16] In fact, even today more American Catholics (54 percent) agree with John Paul II that abortion is always wrong than Catholics in his native Poland (46 percent).[17] Like American women, Polish women have rejected John Paul II's teaching on birth control, apparently in even larger numbers than women in the United States and Great Britain. Poland has one of the lowest fertility rates in Europe—lower than the U.S. and the UK and far below the replacement rate of slightly more than 2 birth per woman.[18] One of Wojtyła's closest friends predicted it was more likely that John

Paul II's theology of marital love and equal dignity of men and women would first gain wider understanding and acceptance in the United States and Western Europe rather than in Poland.

John Paul II's teachings on birth control having been universally disregarded—with Poland being no exception—I was convinced even more that a new book about the Polish pope and the historical and cultural forces that shaped his outlook on women could be useful to readers who may want to know why John Paul II held on to certain views throughout his papacy and left it as a legacy for his successors. I was also hoping to find some clues how the new pope, Benedict XVI (Joseph Ratzinger), is likely to deal with women and feminism. As a former close advisor to John Paul II, he did not think conservative Polish upbringing and life under fascism and communism made the Polish pope incapable of understanding Western cultures and Western women. He was convinced John Paul II had a unique ability to combine his vast experience, intellectual analysis, and faith to investigate with unprecedented human empathy "the nature of virginity, marriage, motherhood and fatherhood, the language of the body, and, thus, the essence of love."[19]

I found plenty of evidence of John Paul II's deep faith, as well as many examples of his unprecedented human empathy on a personal level, but even Cardinal Ratzinger admitted that "when the Pope speaks, he does not speak in his own name."[20] His personal empathy may not extend to matters that affect the whole Church if he thinks his public statements might encourage unwanted behavior. Cardinal Ratzinger also defended John Paul II from criticism that, being a Pole, he only knew "the sentimental, traditional piety of his country and hence cannot completely understand the complicated issues of the Western world." Ratzinger concluded that such a criticism is both "foolish" and "shows a complete ignorance of history." He pointed out that Poland has always been at the intersection of various cultures: Germanic, Romance, Slavic, and Greco-Byzantine.[21]

Interestingly, Ratzinger did not list specific modern philosophical and cultural movements that could have influenced John Paul II: the French and English Enlightenment, Anglo-Saxon individualism, libertarianism, pragmatism and liberalism. Whether John Paul II was able to understand Western women and apply the right kind of philosophical and historical analysis in assessing the contemporary Western culture should be vigorously debated. Unfortunately, strong ideological positions taken by both radical feminists and radical conservative elements within the Catholic Church make it difficult for scholars to engage in a probing and dispassionate debate. Such a debate is also made more difficult by John Paul II's bigger-than-life status as a great religious and moral figure with enormous accomplishments to his credit. Most books about Wojtyła rely on understandably biased Church sources portraying him as a saint who was omniscient and could not make a wrong decision. Books written by his ideological enemies distort his message and condemn him mercilessly. There is relatively little independent study and analysis on John Paul II's papacy, his philosophy, his theology, his knowledge of different civilizations and his decisions.

Many of the concerns and demands of Western feminists, including those within the Catholic Church, did not have too much in common with Wojtyła's own personal experience or with the experience of the vast majority of Poles of his generation. If anyone in pre-1989 Poland tried to portray the Church as an oppressive institution bent on subjugating women, such a person would be perceived as an enemy of Poland's independence and a communist sympathizer. Even Polish communists, also brought up in the patriarchal culture, did not truly believe that men inevitably sought to differentiate themselves from women by dominating them and treating them as "the Other." The question of whether Judaism and Christianity reflect traditions of a patriarchal world that is hostile and oppressive towards women was not on the minds of very many Poles. As far as most of them were concerned, the communist regime equally oppressed both men and women, although it could be argued that women fared much worse than the majority of men under the economic inefficiency of the communist system. Women were overwhelmingly responsible for creating and maintaining homes in an economy incapable of providing with any reliability the most basic consumer goods, while many were also holding full time jobs. Fortunately, or perhaps unfortunately for women, work in state-managed enterprises, particularly for office workers, was usually not very demanding. Many women could take time off during working hours to stand in long food lines.

For most Poles, the Church was their ally in the fight against the invasive and alien state, and the Polish family itself remained largely patriarchal, although many more women found themselves in the workplace both out of financial necessity and as a result of the communist regime's promotion of wide access to education. Before 1918, it was also the quest for national independence that took precedence over all other issues. Also then, the Catholic Church was the bastion of national traditions, although by the 19th century there were already some Polish women and men working at the grassroots level to advance the cause of women's rights.[22] The period between the two world wars was too short for the development of a true democratic culture in Poland, although Polish women made some gains, including winning the right to vote a few years before American women were able to cast votes in national elections.

Much of the information about life under communism in Poland and Wojtyła's collaboration with Polish women in promoting natural birth control can be found in *Chapter Five: Contraception versus Love: Agenda for Polish Women 1947-1978.*

Living in democracies and free from the sort of pressures experienced by women in the East, Western feminists coming from the Catholic tradition had, in contrast, both the energy and the space to discuss and expose the cultural sources of their traditional status as the second sex, both within the society at large and within the

Catholic Church. Although many Western feminists during the last century turned against capitalism and bourgeois democracy—and some initially put their hopes in communism—feminism not only developed as a system of ideas in states with long traditions of democracy and individual liberties but also led to substantial gains for women's rights precisely in those countries which had the most liberal political and religious cultures. Early feminists in the West were middle and upper class women who took advantage of liberal political systems and liberal traditions to pursue their struggle for equality through democratic institutions and legal reforms, while many of the later feminists, especially in Europe, started to identify with Marxism, socialism and Soviet communism. The trend among academic feminists in Europe and in America to promote Marxist analysis of gender issues became especially widespread after the publication of French existentialist Marxist Simone de Beauvoir's book *The Second Sex* (1949).

> **Ayn Rand** (Alisa Zinov'yevna Rosenbaum)
>
> **Born:** February 2, 1905, Saint Petersburg, Russia
>
> **Died:** March 6, 1982, New York , NY, USA
>
> **Book:** *Atlas Shrugged*
>
> **Quote:** "The essence of femininity is hero-worship – the desire to look up to man."

Only in recent years, new feminists, inspired by John Paul II's theology, and individualist feminists, following the teachings of liberal and libertarian philosophers—such as Russian-born American atheist Ayn Rand who introduced her philosophy of objectivism—are beginning to promote the rediscovery of feminism's liberal-democratic, Anglo-American and Christian roots.[23]

There is more information in *Chapter Two* on conservative and liberal feminist organizations active within the Catholic Church. I have also included throughout the book web addresses and other information which may help readers in doing further research on the subject of religion, feminism, Catholic Church and the life and philosophy of Pope John Paul II. I have tried to list the most representative and active web sites, but I am not suggesting that in all cases individuals and organizations behind them have a significant following or influence. I also claim no responsibility for views and information on these web sites.

With so much confusion about the cultural roots of feminism, few people in the West, whether they are social liberals or religious conservatives, had time to learn enough of the Polish cultural and historical background to fully understand the complexity of John Paul II's moral and social message. Despite his reputation as a great communicator, John Paul II was not very good at explaining his philosophy and his theology. Even his Polish friends said that reading his philosophical writings was equivalent to being in purgatory. Simone de Beauvoir's Marxist language was simple, clear, and supportive of women's sense of injustice, anger and hostility toward men. John Paul II's message for women was complex and seemingly full of contradictions. It imposed heavy demands of

---

Libertarian Web Sites

iFeminists http://www.ifeminists.net

Association of Libertarian Feminists – AFL

http://www.alf.org

The Women's Freedom Network – WFN

http://www.womensfreedom.org

New Feminism Web Sites

The New Feminism
http://www.thenewfeminism.net

Feminine-Genius
http://www.feminine-genius.com/

Women of Grace
http://www.womenofgrace.com/

love and sacrifice without identifying any enemies or goals for ending sex discrimination. It asked women to trust in the wisdom of a religious leader who was also a Central European male, who did not rely on experiences and opinions of Western women, and who was a beneficiary of the male-dominated system. It is hardly surprising, therefore, that John Paul II's message to women is frequently viewed with suspicion, sometimes intentionally mischaracterized and often misunderstood.

Wanting to capitalize on John Paul II's enormous popularity as a great moral figure, both conservatives and even some liberals try now to claim him as their spiritual ally. Yet, he held views that were often opposite of what each side wanted them to be. Many conservative Christian groups and individuals see much common ground with John Paul II's positions on women, marriage and family. In the United States, he is greatly admired by evangelical Christians. Yet those who view Karol Wojtyła as a great conservative religious leader might be disappointed if they were fully familiar with his political preferences.

If he were a politician dealing with moral issues, John Paul II would be a member of the most conservative faction of the Republican Party in the U.S. or the British Conservative Party and would have full political support of evangelical Christians. However, on economic and social policy issues – other than abortion, birth control and marriage – he would be a member of the most progressive wing of the Democratic Party in the U.S. or the Labour Party in Great Britain.

John Paul II was a moral conservative, but his admirers on the Right, including evangelical Christians, tend to overlook the fact that he strongly favored Left-leaning solutions to most political, economic and social problems, including the role of unregulated free market economy, immigration, national health insurance, the death penalty and U.S. foreign policy. He considered the American military intervention in Iraq a great tragedy and he saw America as "a continent marked by competition and aggressiveness, unbridled consumerism and corruption."

On the whole, however, on theological and moral issues John Paul II was much closer to the conservative viewpoint and far more reluctant to criticize religious conservatives when they strayed from his vision of the ideal social order. He strongly supported *Opus Dei*, an international organization of mostly conservative lay Catholics. In Poland, he avoided taking any decisive public action against Radio Maryja, an ultra-nationalistic and ultra-conservative Catholic radio station accused by liberal media of promoting anti-Western conspiracy theories and anti-Semitic propaganda. Even though John Paul II called anti-Semitism a sin, he did not use his power to force the station to moderate its political messages. A strong papal action against Radio Maryja might have alienated some of John Paul II's conservative supporters in Poland and elsewhere. They are still the most ardent defenders and promoters of his views on abortion and protection of family values.[24]

In 2007, it would be inconceivable for a major Catholic radio station in the United States—a country viewed with great concern by John Paul II—to air programs full of slurs against liberals, feminists, Masons and Jews. Similar attacks have not been heard or seen on major Catholic media outlets in the United States probably since the Roosevelt Administration forced a Catholic priest, Father Charles Coughlin (1891-1979), to stop his media activities during World War II.[25] In Poland, however, a sizable group of Catholics still feels free to express such extreme views on a major Catholic radio network. It was not until September 2007 that John Paul II's closest friend, Kraków's archbishop Cardinal Stanisław Dziwisz (b. 1939), finally issued a warning that Radio Maryja and its director should not be allowed to take over the responsibility for presenting the message of the Catholic Church in Poland.[26] But he is also afraid to confront openly Radio Maryja supporters. His warning was read at a closed meeting of Polish bishops and was made public only through leaks to Polish media. Not wanting to alienate the most conservative base of the Catholic Church in Poland,

Cardinal Dziwisz thanked Radio Maryja listeners for their prayers.

Conservative radicalization of the Catholic Church is part of the legacy of John Paul II's unwillingness and inability to understand Western liberalism and his refusal to engage in a meaningful dialogue with liberal women. But whether this is good or bad for the Catholic Church in a rapidly changing world is not yet a settled question. Had the previous pope reached out to liberal Catholics and made substantial concessions on moral issues and the role of women, it is likely that the Catholic Church might be now more tolerant and more inclusive but at the same time smaller, even more polarized and perhaps much less able to attract new followers, especially in the developing world.

Whether John Paul II's ideas of religion and morality were more beneficial or more harmful for most people during his particular time in history, as well as for future generations, is one of the most difficult questions to answer based on only what we know from recent events. I have no doubt that history will judge John Paul II as a great religious and moral leader who brought dignity back to millions of people, contributed to the fall of communism, reached out to Jews, Muslims and other religions and worked tirelessly to eliminate poverty and secure peace. It is still too early to know, however, how history will judge his decisions relating to women's rights, his assessment of Western secular culture and his views about America's global role as a liberal superpower. I can only guess that John Paul II's apparent lack of credibility among women on issues of birth control, ordination of women-priests and the role of women in society will continue to diminish the credibility of his larger message in defense of human dignity, human love and human life.

Rather than trying to answer these questions, my goal was to give readers a better understanding of what drove John Paul II to become one of the strongest opponents of abortion and a severe critic of Western and American liberal values. I also hope this book will offer some insights to those living in the West and elsewhere who, after September 11th, are puzzled how some non-Western cultures view the West and the United States. I try to show how important the issue of women's rights is in the eyes of those who feel insecure about their ability to protect their own traditional way of life. Shortly after the 9/11 attacks, John Paul II told Muslims in Central Asia that terrorism was "profaning the name of God," but he also told them that Western nations were showing "their deepening human, spiritual and moral impoverishment."[27] Talking about the Western world, John Paul II also said that "a civilization, which rejects the defenseless, deserves to be called barbarian, even if it has great economic, technological, artistic, and scientific achievements."

I hope this book will also help to explain the critical gap between the American and Western liberal approach to gender issues and John Paul II's much more traditional and more cautious view of the proper balance between women's rights and their duties to religion and community. Getting a true picture of John Paul II has not been an easy task for a journalist. Many writers, reporters and commentators have made sweeping conclusions about his legacy depending on their particular political or ideological outlook. I have tried to focus instead on Wojtyła's life by describing it primarily through his contacts with women in addition to analyzing his public statements and comments by those who knew him. Hopefully this in-depth look at his early life as well as an explanation of Polish history and culture will help readers better understand the richness and complexity of John Paul II's views, regardless of whether they ultimately agree or don't agree with his positions on some of the controversial issues he addressed.

Some of the possible outcomes of John Paul II's legacy for women and the Catholic Church are discussed at the end of *Chapter Six: Women-Priests* and in *Chapter Seven: What to Expect from the New Pope.*

It is important to remember that John Paul II was a Polish man who grew up with certain expectations about gender roles and formed his values and opinions under complicated and harsh historical conditions that few people in the West can fully grasp without extensive reading and study of history. I tried to dispel certain media myths and to look beyond news headlines and propaganda generated by John Paul II's opponents and his supporters. Much of the material in this book deals with the use of language and ideas to influence public opinion and to advance various agendas. In selecting information and sources, I tried to account for potential biases, including the accusations that a few of the pope's friends were spying on him for the communist secret police and may have contributed to the disinformation campaign run by the Polish communist regime and the Soviet KGB,

I hope some of the new material I collected about John Paul II and the role of women in his life will be of interest to the general public as well as to specialists studying the impact of his decisions on the Catholic Church and the situation of women worldwide. My ultimate hope is that this book will contribute to a better understanding of the choices facing John Paul II's most immediate successor Pope Benedict XVI as well as future popes. I realize that writing about a highly popular and to some a highly controversial religious leader is not an easy task for any journalist who has personal and professional ties to the people and events which are the subjects of his inquiry. I hope that in the end I have managed to maintain a sufficient distance, balance and clarity while documenting the largely unknown history of a group of remarkable women who shaped John Paul II's life and his papacy. Through him, they had a major impact on the Catholic Church and the status of women throughout the world. The story of how they implemented his vision of women, marriage and family, and ultimately changed the Catholic Church, deserves to be told.

San Francisco, California,
December 2007

Brief Outline of Polish History

966 AD – Polish prince Mieszko I accepts Christianity for himself and his kingdom. [1]

1386 – Poland and Lithuania unite under the Jagiellonian dynasty.

1410 – Poland defeats the Teutonic Knights (mostly German) at the battle of Grunwald. Poland becomes a major European power but eventually goes into a decline.

1795 – Poland loses its independence with the final partition by Prussia, Russia and Austria.

19th and early 20th century – Writers and poets of the Romantic period in Polish literature blame the loss of Poland's independence on excessive liberty and lack of patriotism among the Polish aristocracy and nobility. The Romantics question Western rationalism and portray Poland as a Messianic nation that would lead a spiritual rebirth in the world starting with Western Europe. The Polish Catholic Church helps to maintain religious and national traditions, especially among the peasants who are the majority of the population. The Poles rise several times against the occupying powers but the partitioning powers crush each military uprising. Some Polish aristocrats, especially those living in the liberal and largely Catholic Austro-Hungarian Empire, collaborate with the foreign rulers. The Roman Catholic popes generally support the occupiers in the interest of peace and stability in Europe. Despite this, popular support for the Church in Poland increases. Religious faith among the population and the patriotic stand of the Polish priests help to maintain the drive for independence.

1918-1939 – Poland again becomes an independent state. Polish women gain the right to vote, a few years earlier than American women. Authoritarian rule and conflicts with ethnic minorities predominate for most of the period before World War II.

August 23, 1939 – Germany and the Soviet Union sign the Ribbentrop-Molotov nonaggression pact which secretly provides for the dismemberment of Poland into Nazi and Soviet-controlled zones.

September 1, 1939 – Hitler's armies invade Poland. Poland's allies, France and Great Britain, declare war on Hitler but fail to come to Poland's aid.

September 17, 1939 – Soviet troops invade and occupy eastern Poland under the terms of the Berlin-Moscow pact.

1939-1945 – Poles form an underground resistance movement and a government in exile, first in Paris and later in London. Resistance against the Nazis in Warsaw, including uprisings by Jews in the Warsaw ghetto and by the Polish underground Home Army, is brutally suppressed by the Germans. In 1945, the retreating Germans destroy Warsaw. The Soviet regime imprisons and tries the key leaders of the Home Army and the anti-communist underground government. During the war, about 6 million Polish citizens are killed, 2.5 million are deported to Germany for forced labor, hundreds of

Soviet Foreign Commissar Vyacheslav Molotov signs the German-Soviet nonaggression pact; Joachim von Ribbentrop and Josef Stalin stand behind him. Moscow, August 23. 1939.

thousands perish in Soviet prisons and labor camps. Of the total number of WWII victims from Poland, about 3 million Polish Jews (all but about 100,000 of the pre-war Jewish population) are killed in death camps at Oświęcim (Auschwitz), Treblinka, Majdanek or are murdered or die from starvation in other locations. Some three million non-Jewish Polish citizens perished during the course of the war, over two million of whom were ethnic Poles (the remainder being mostly Ukrainians and Belarusians).

June 1941 – Germany invades the Soviet Union. Poland is

completely occupied by German troops. The Soviet Union recognizes the Polish government in exile.

April 1943 – The Soviet Union breaks off relations with the Polish government in exile after the German military announces the discovery of mass graves of murdered Polish army officers at Katyń, in the U.S.S.R. Moscow claims the Polish officers were murdered by the Nazis and objects to the Polish government's request for the Red Cross investigation. The U.S. State Department and the Voice of America try to suppress the evidence of Soviet responsibility for the massacre.[2] (Decades later the Russian government admits the Polish officers had been killed by the KGB on orders from Stalin.)

July 1944 – The Soviet Red Army enters Poland and establishes a communist-controlled regime.

1943-1945 – President Roosevelt agrees with Stalin to give to the Soviet Union large parts of eastern Poland. The move ignores his previous promises as well as wishes and concerns of the Polish government in exile. Most Poles view it as a cynical betrayal of a loyal ally in the war against Hitler. The big powers also agree to give Poland parts of German territories. Following the Yalta

Prime Minister Winston Churchill, President Franklin D. Roosevelt, and Marshal Joseph Stalin at the palace in Yalta, where the Big Three met and sealed the fate of Poland.

Conference in February 1945, a Polish Provisional Government of National Unity is formed in June 1945 and is recognized by the U.S. and Great Britain.

January 1947 – Although the Yalta agreement calls for free elections, they are controlled by the communist party. With Moscow's help, the communists use force and intimidation to crush their opponents.[3]

1947-1953 – The communists establish a regime entirely under their domination and start mass repressions against the former anti-Nazi fighters loyal to the government in exile and against the Catholic Church. The Polish bishops do not believe that the West would liberate Poland and assume the Soviet domination would continue. Poland's Primate, Cardinal Stefan Wyszyński, signs an agreement with the communists in an effort to protect the Church's legal position but refuses to be co-opted as the regime's supporter. Many Left-leaning writers and intellectuals initially support the regime. The communists expand educational and employment opportunities for women, workers and peasants, but fail to provide sufficient food and consumer items.

1953 – The communists imprison Cardinal Wyszyński, as well as several bishops and priests.

1953-1956 – Regime's attempts to control the priests are largely unsuccessful. The Catholic Church remains the only major public institution opposed to communism and supports the population's demands for freedom and respect for human rights.

October 1956 – The 20th ("de-Stalinization") Soviet Party Congress in Moscow and riots by workers in Poznań lead to a shakeup in the communist regime in Poland. To avoid bloodshed, Cardinal Wyszyński, who earlier had been released from prison, gives conditional support to the Władysław Gomułka regime.

1956-1989 – The Polish bishops see the legalization of abortion by the communists as one of many measures designed to weaken the Church's influence among Polish women. Shortages of consumer good persist including contraceptives. Doctors perform hundreds of thousands of abortions in communist Poland.

1956-1970 – While retaining loyalty to Moscow and communist ideology, the regime of First Secretary Władysław Gomułka liberalizes to some degree Polish internal life. Repression against the Catholic Church and political opposition soon resumes at full scale but without much of the violence characteristic of the Stalinist period.

1966 – The communist regime prevents Pope Paul VI from visiting

Poland for the celebrations of the Millennium of the country's acceptance of Christianity.

1968 – Student demonstrations are suppressed and an "anti-Zionist" campaign initially directed against Gomułka supporters within the communist party eventually leads to the emigration of much of Poland's remaining Jewish population.

December 1970 – Food price increases trigger protests and strikes in the port cities of Gdańsk, Gdynia, and Szczecin. Edward Gierek replaces Gomułka as First Secretary.

October 1978 – The Archbishop of Kraków, Cardinal Karol Wojtyła, becomes Pope John Paul II.

June 1979 – Pope John Paul II visits Poland and inspires demands for religious freedom, human rights and democracy.

July 1980 – The government announces increases in meat prices. Polish workers go on strike on the Baltic coast, in coal mines in Silesia and in other state enterprises.

August 31, 1980 – Workers at the Lenin Shipyard in Gdańsk, led by an electrician Lech Wałęsa, sign a 21-point agreement with the government ending their strike. Similar agreements are signed at Szczecin and in Silesia. The key provision of these agreements is the guarantee of the workers' right to form independent trade unions and the right to strike. A new national union movement— "Solidarity"—is formed.

December 12-13, 1981 – The regime of General Wojciech Jaruzelski declares martial law and uses the army and special riot police to crush the union. Virtually all Solidarity leaders and many opposition intellectuals are arrested or detained.

1981-1989 – The United States and other Western countries respond to martial law by imposing economic sanctions against the Polish regime and against the Soviet Union. Unrest in Poland continues for several years. John Paul II offers his moral support to Solidarity and repeatedly calls for the restoration of human rights in Poland. After an initial refusal, the regime allows John Paul II to visit Poland and meet with Lech Wałęsa. Many Catholic priests actively support the opposition movement led by Solidarity. Secret police officers brutally murder pro-Solidarity priest Father Jerzy Popiełuszko. Strikes, protests and economic collapse force the regime to enter into "roundtable" talks with the Solidarity-led opposition.

1989 – The regime agrees to partly open elections to the national assembly. Nearly all freely contested seats are won by candidates supported by Solidarity. President Jaruzelski asks journalist/Solidarity activist Tadeusz Mazowiecki to form a government. For the first time in more than 40 years, Poland has a government led by non-communists.

December, 1990-2007 – Lech Wałęsa becomes the first popularly elected President of Poland. After strong appeals by Pope John Paul II and lobbying by the Polish bishops, the Polish parliament and the courts outlaw most abortions. Parties claiming to support John Paul II's vision of women and family advance traditional Catholic and anti-liberal agenda. Political power changes between Right-wing nationalist/conservative Catholic parties, Left-wing social democrats (former communists), and socially conservative liberal and pro-business parties.

Short Biography—Karol Józef Wojtyła—Pope John Paul II (1920-2005)

(with events, statements and documents dealing with women)

John Paul II Photographic Exhibit at the Archbishop's residence in Kraków (2007).

May 18, 1920 – Karol Józef Wojtyła is born in the Polish town of Wadowice near Kraków to Emilia Kaczorowska Wojtyła and Karol Wojtyła Sr. His sister, Olga, died before he was born.[1]

June 20, 1920 – Karol is baptized in Wadowice's parish church.

1929 – Karol's mother dies.

1932 – Karol's eldest brother Edmund, a doctor, dies.

1938 – Karol Wojtyła graduates from Marcin Wadowita high school for boys in Wadowice, where he was active in theatre groups. The same year, he enrolls in the Jagiellonian University in Kraków to study Polish literature. While in high school, he appears in school plays with girls and develops a lifelong friendship with Halina (Helena) Królikiewicz (Kwiatkowska).

1939 – Hitler and Stalin occupy Poland. The Nazis close the Jagiellonian University.

1940-1944 – Karol Wojtyła's French teacher Mrs. Jadwiga Lewaj helps him find work as a laborer at the Solvay chemical factory in Kraków to protect him from being arrested by the Nazis. Older women look after Karol and teach him foreign languages. Karol is active in the underground "Rhapsodic Theatre." A fellow student actress Halina Królikiewicz risks her life carrying Karol's letters between Wadowice and Kraków.

1941 – Karol's father dies. Karol lives in the home of his friend Juliusz Kydryński and his wife and is taken care of by his friend's mother Aleksandra Kydryńska.[2]

1942 – Karol enters the clandestine seminary run by Cardinal Adam Stefan Sapieha.

February 25, 1944 – While walking home Karol is hit by a German truck. Mrs. Józefa Florek jumps off a tram and finds him unconscious. In an effort to get help, she stops a German car. A Nazi officer helps her get Karol to a hospital.[3] Mrs. Irena Szkocka and Mrs. Zofia Późniakowa take care of Karol during his recovery from the accident.

1944 – Karol stops work at the Solvay factory. Mrs. Irena Szkocka helps him avoid Nazi patrols and safely reach the Archbishop's palace.

1945 – Karol continues studies at the seminary and at the faculty of theology of the Jagiellonian University.

November 1, 1946 – Archbishop Sapieha ordains Karol Wojtyła to the priesthood.

1946 – Archbishop Sapieha sends Karol for studies in Rome.

1948 – Karol Wojtyła returns to Poland and works in various parishes and as chaplain to university students. He takes hiking trips with students, including young women, and discusses with them issues of love, marriage and sex.

April 1952 – Karol Wojtyła takes a group of five female university students on an excursion trip to Zakopane.

1953 – Karol Wojtyła defends his thesis at the Catholic University in Lublin (KUL) and later becomes professor of moral theology and

social ethics. He helps academic careers of several nuns.
December 1956 – Karol Wojtyła meets Dr. Wanda Półtawska, former Ravensbrück concentration camp inmate, who later becomes his chief advisor on sex and birth control methods. Wojtyła's and Dr. Półtawska's arguments help convince Pope Paul VI to issue the *Humanae vitae* encyclical confirming the Catholic Church's ban on artificial birth control.

1958 – Karol Wojtyła sponsors his first doctoral thesis at the Catholic University in Lublin (KUL) written by Sister Karolina Kasperkiewicz. He fails to help her secure a teaching position due to objections from other priests to having a nun as a university lecturer. Later, he helps to launch the academic career of Sister Zofia Zdybicka. She is the first nun to become a professor at KUL.

July 4, 1958 – Pope Pius XII appoints Karol Wojtyła auxiliary bishop of Kraków.

1958-1978 – With active assistance from Dr. Półtawska and other women, Karol Wojtyła promotes natural birth control training, sex and marriage counseling, and assistance to single mothers in the Kraków Archdiocese. He campaigns against abortion and promotes large families. At the same time, Karol Wojtyła defends religious freedom and human rights. He actively supports efforts to build new churches despite the communist regime's attempts to restrict such construction.

1960s – Karol Wojtyła meets Mrs. Alina Gryglowska and encourages her to write about her experiences in Soviet labor camps.

1960 – Karol Wojtyła publishes *Love and Responsibility*, a book on the meaning of Christian love and marriage. The book includes chapters on issues of sex in marriage written with Dr. Półtawska's help and with input from male and female university students.

1962 – Karol Wojtyła writes letters to Father Pio da Pietrelcina asking him for prayers to cure Wanda Półtawska's apparent cancer. She fully recovers without any medical intervention.

1962-1964 – Karol Wojtyła participates in Vatican Council II. He is the only speaker who specifically recognized and addressed the women-auditors who, for the first time in the Church's history, were allowed to listen to but not to participate in the Council's proceedings.

January 13, 1964 – Pope Paul VI appoints Karol Wojtyła archbishop of Kraków.

June 26, 1967 – Pope Paul VI makes Karol Wojtyła cardinal.

1968 (approx.) – Cardinal Wojtyła gives Pope Paul VI his and Dr. Półtawska's materials on birth control, parts of which were reportedly included in the *Humanae vitae* encyclical.

1970s – Cardinal Wojtyła works to lift the Vatican's condemnation of Sister Faustyna Kowalska.

1973 – Polish-American philosopher Dr. Anna-Teresa Tymieniecka visits Karol Wojtyła in Kraków. She translates into English his book *The Acting Person*.

1974 – Start of "Cardinal Wojtyła SOS" program for helping unwed mothers and mothers with large families.

October 16, 1978 – Cardinals at the Conclave elect Karol Wojtyła pope. He takes the name of John Paul II.

1978-2005 – Pope John Paul II makes 104 pastoral visits outside Italy and 146 within Italy.

June 1979 – Pope John Paul II thanks Mrs. Helena Szczepańska for helping his mother take care of him when he was a child. Mrs. Szczepańska is the only person granted a private audience during the pope's first visit to Poland.

October 7, 1979 – During his first visit to the United States, Sister Theresa Kane asks Pope John Paul II to include women in all the ministries of the Church.

Statue of Pope John Paul II in front of the Archbishop's residence in Kraków.

November 22, 1981 – John Paul II publishes his Apostolic Exhortation

Familiaris consortio on the Christian family in the modern world.

June 13, 1987 – In a speech to women workers in Łódź, Poland, John Paul II talks about Stanisława Leszczyńska, a Polish midwife who defied Nazi orders to kill newly born children of women inmates at the Auschwitz concentration camp.

August 15, 1988 – John Paul II publishes his Apostolic Letter *Mulieris dignitatem* on the dignity and vocation of women.

May 22, 1994 – John Paul II publishes his Apostolic Letter *Ordinatio sacerdotalis* confirming the Church's ban on ordination of women to priesthood.

1995 – John Paul II selects Mary Ann Glendon, a law professor at Harvard University, to lead the Holy See delegation to the U.N. Women's Conference in Beijing.

March 25, 1995 – John Paul II publishes *Evangelium Vitae* (*The Gospel of Life*) the Encyclical Letter on Abortion, Euthanasia, and the Death Penalty. He launches *new feminism*:

> In transforming culture so that it supports life, *women* occupy a place, in thought and action, which is unique and decisive. It depends on them to promote a **"new feminism"** [emphasis added] which rejects the temptation of imitating models of "male domination," in order to acknowledge and affirm the true genius of women in every aspect of the life of society, and overcome all discrimination, violence and exploitation.

June 29, 1995 – John Paul II publishes his Letter to Women with an apology for past discrimination:

> And if objective blame, especially in particular historical contexts, has belonged to not just a few members of the Church, for this I am truly sorry.

June 8, 1997 – John Paul II canonizes Queen Jadwiga (Hedwig), a Polish monarch who reigned from 1384 to1399.

April 30, 2000 – John Paul II canonizes Sister Faustyna Kowalska, a Polish nun belonging to the Order of Our Lady of Mercy whose visions in the 1930s included a call from Jesus to spread the devotion of the Mercy of God.

October 14, 2003 – John Paul II presides over the beatification ceremony for Mother Teresa at the Vatican.

April 2, 2005, 9:37 p.m. – John Paul II dies at the Vatican. He speaks his last words "Let me go to the Lord" to a Polish woman, Sister Tobiana, a medical doctor and his nurse.

Young Karol Wojtyła with his parents.

Man must be a servant [...]. Woman in a marriage is a servant of life [...]. Maleness, which has its natural drive toward domination, must be balanced by a willingness to serve.

We cannot leave the affairs of the Kingdom of God to women.

...the Gospel as idea is primarily a male sphere.
Karol Wojtyła, 1961

Faced with the abuse of power, the answer for women is to seek power. This process leads to opposition between men and women, in which the identity and role of one are emphasized to the disadvantage of the other, leading to harmful confusion regarding the human person, which has its most immediate and lethal effects in the structure of the family.
Cardinal Joseph Ratzinger, 2004 (Pope Benedict XVI)

CHAPTER ONE

Cared For by Women, Educated by Men

Wojtyła's Mother and Early Life

Karol Józef Wojtyła, future Pope John Paul II, was born on May 18, 1920 in Wadowice, a small town in southern Poland, and was baptized June 20, 1920. His parents came from families of small farmers and craftsmen, and while not poor, they were neither well off nor well educated. Neither of his parents had a university degree, although his father, Karol Wojtyła Sr. (1879-1941), who initially worked as a tailor, learned German and became a noncommissioned officer in the Austro-Hungarian army at a time when Poland did not exist as an independent state with its own armed forces. After the country regained independence in 1918, Wojtyła Sr. joined the newly-established Polish army and worked in a recruiting office, finally reaching the rank of captain—a considerable achievement for a man without money, property or family connections to the Polish nobility.

In his book, *Rise, Let Us Be on Our Way*, published in 2004, John Paul II referred to himself as coming from the "proletariat," but he used the term in a broad sense since it was usually applied by communists to industrial workers.[1] At the time Wojtyła's father was trying to find his way in the world several decades before communists took power in Poland, a person a noble background, as opposed to someone of a peasant or poor urban background, would have had a much easier time acquiring higher education and rising through the ranks of public service. Karol Wojtyła Sr. could not, however, be described as a person of a "proletarian" background in the Marxist sense of the term. He was not strictly speaking a blue-collar or industrial worker. (The future Pope John Paul II did work as an industrial worker during World

War II, but this was due only to the extraordinary conditions of the Nazi occupation of Poland.) These subtle distinctions may not mean much to Americans who are more accustomed to social mobility and do not look down on blue-collar workers as much as some upper-class and middle-class Europeans, but these distinctions were significant to many people in Poland, including the Wojtyłas. As with people in America who may have experienced persistent racial discrimination, such experiences early in life often leave a permanent mark on the way they think and act as adults. The future pope's father must have been a man of considerable intelligence and some ambition to overcome social barriers within Polish and Austro-Hungarian society. As a Pole entering the Austro-Hungarian military he had to deal with the language and ethnic barriers that would not have affected him had Poland been an independent country. Basically a foreigner, trying to advance in the imperial Austrian army, Karol Wojtyła Sr. undoubtedly experienced some discrimination and other personal difficulties, of which the younger Karol would have become aware in his childhood by listening to his father or other Polish men and women of his father's generation.

John Paul's lifetime sympathy for ethnic and other groups struggling for political and cultural rights, as documented by his strong support for both the Jewish state and the Palestinian state as well as the rights of immigrants and to some degree the rights of women, can perhaps be traced to his immense pride in national culture combined with glorification of Polish resistance to foreign domination and a sense of unjust humiliation. Karol experienced the intensity of these feelings first at home and later at school. His strong opposition to globalization of Western secular culture may also contain some traces of anti-foreign and anti-great power sentiments which permeated his nation's history in the 19th and the 20th century. Before that, Poland herself was a great power in Central and Eastern Europe. After the rise of nationalism in Europe, many nationalities within the former Polish-Lithuanian empire, including

Lithuanians, Belarusians and Ukrainians, considered Poles to be the oppressors of their native cultures.

It is also worth noting that Karol Wojtyła grew up in a family whose head earned his living from public service and believed strongly in its importance. Neither his father nor anybody else in his immediate family became wealthy from private business and investments. Economically underdeveloped, Poland did not have a strong business class. Polish nationalists at the time of his father's youth conveniently blamed their country's poverty on excessive profit taking and exploitation of the Poles by German, Russian, Austrian, Jewish and other non-Polish businessmen and foreign companies, as well as foreign governments, including those of wealthy Western nations. Although his father may have wanted him to have a comfortable and productive career as a military officer, he obviously did not encourage him to succeed by making a lot of money. Instead, Wojtyła Sr. instilled in his son the idea that public service was much more important than personal enrichment. That was a common attitude among the Polish middle class *intelligentsia* which looked down on business pursuits. Wojtyła's later ambivalent attitude toward Western capitalism, consumerism and economic globalization can perhaps also be traced to his family's history and the prevailing cultural Polish attitudes at the time of his youth.

Wojtyła's mother — Emilia Kaczorowska before her marriage to Karol Wojtyła Sr. — came from a large and traditional Polish family. She was born March 26, 1884, the fifth of nine children from his father's first marriage. Her father, Feliks Kaczorowski, a saddler, had altogether thirteen children.[2] Her mother, Maria Scholtz Kaczorowska (d. 1897) — the maiden name suggests German ancestry — came from a family of a poor shoemaker. It is quite possible that Wojtyła's maternal grandmother had German roots, since many German craftsmen, as well as Jews from Germany and other Western countries, settled in Poland throughout the centuries. Interestingly, Polish media has not explored the possi-

Emilia Kaczorowska Wojtyła

Born: March 26, 1884, Bielsko Biała, Poland

Died: April 13, 1929, Wadowice, Poland

bility that Wojtyła's family might have had partial non-Polish roots.

There is much less information about Wojtyła's mother and her family than about his father. Even his mother's birthplace is unknown. We know that the Kaczorowski family lived in Biała, a small town in the Wadowice region. Later the family moved to Kraków, the largest city in southern Poland and the country's former royal capital. Emilia was apparently educated in a convent, but there is no reliable information about where and how many years of formal education she had received. The date of her marriage to Wojtyła Sr. is also unknown. We also do not know where and how she met her husband, but they lived in Kraków before moving to Wadowice. As with many married Polish women at that time, Karol's mother worked at home, helping the family's budget by sewing in addition to her normal household duties. She was described as being in poor health and needed help from her neighbors with lifting heavy things, such as young Karol's baby carriage. Her first son, Edmund, 14 years older than Karol, was able to assist his mother, as did some of her women neighbors. Emilia and Karol Senior also had a daughter, christened Olga, who died in infancy. John Paul II often mentioned his sister when talking about his early childhood, but there is very little information about her from other sources. Some have suggested that the death of his sister at such an early age and the loss of his brother when Karol was still very young helped to shape John Paul II's opposition to contraception and abortion. After his brother's death, he was left without any brothers or sisters.

Karol's mother did not live long enough to play a significant role in his religious upbringing. She died April 13, 1929 at the age of forty-five from a heart and kidney failure when Karol was only nine years old. When Wojtyła became pope, biographers and other writers, particularly in the West, often speculated that the death of his mother when he was still very young may have profoundly affected his attitude toward women, making him more likely to idealize women as mothers and caregivers. But while the death of his mother and other psychological factors from his childhood undoubtedly influenced the development of Wojtyła's personality, it is much more likely that his view of women developed largely as a result of broader cultural conditioning. He was still very young when his mother died and most of his formative years were spent in the company of his father, his male school teachers and priests. He learned about the role of mothers and women in Polish homes by visiting the families of his friends and neighbors. Women in these homes provided him with food, care and other assistance, but he observed them only as a welcomed guest and did not experience living with close female family members. This may also explain his tendency to idealize women as caregivers. And, he certainly shared the general belief among Poles that mothers have a crucial patriotic role to play in the upbringing of children, teaching them to love God and their country and in maintaining other family traditions.

While Wojtyła himself grew up without a mother, he gave mothers most of the credit for encouraging young men to become Catholic priests. In a 1997 speech to a group of Polish-Americans in Detroit-Hamtramck, John Paul II noted that "there are today many priests who could confirm that their saintly mothers were above all responsible for their priestly vocation." Some accounts suggest that Emilia Wojtyła wanted Karol to become a priest, but this information cannot be confirmed. She had died before Karol received his first communion. John Paul II writes that his mother's contribution to his religious training "must have been great," although he admitted that he did not have a clear awareness of her role. When visiting Wadowice in 1991, he recalled how his mother used to put his small hands into hers to teach him to make the sign of the cross during prayers.[3] Helena Szczepańska, a former school teacher and a neighbor of Karol's mother remembered Emilia Wojtyła telling her that Karol "will be a great man some day," and saying it, according to Mrs. Szczepańska, with greater conviction than anybody else she had known. The close relationship between his mother and Mrs. Szczepańska and the help she gave her in taking care of him as a young boy were of great importance to Wojtyła. Mrs. Szczepańska was the only person granted a private audience during his first official visit to Poland in June 1979. As the 85-year-old woman approached him and wanted to kiss his ring, John Paul II tried to prevent her from kneeling down. She did it anyway. At that time, Mrs. Szczepańska may have already been the last person alive who had a close personal link with his mother.

After his mother's death, Karol spend most of his young life in the company of men, thus missing perhaps an influence that the love of a mother or another close female family member could have had on the development of his personality. While the loss of his mother and the deaths of the other members of his immediate family may have made Karol more sensitive, more melancholy and more spiritual than other boys, these losses apparently did not develop in him any strong desire to get married and establish his own family. None of his childhood friends mentions any special interest in girls or marriage during Karol's childhood and early adulthood. In many other ways, however, he was similar to young boys his age growing up in Poland: he liked to read books about American Indians, play soccer, swim in the river and go on hiking trips in the nearby mountains. At the same time he was different from the other boys: more sensitive, less aggressive, more religious, more tolerant, more disciplined, and above all a much better student. In high school, he had dreams of becoming an actor and made plans to go to college to study linguistics and Polish literature.

While the death of his mother did not seem to have had an immediate traumatic impact on young Karol, it may have been much more painfully felt later. The loss seems to have been compensated at first by the development of a very close relationship between Karol and his father, who by then retired due to poor health from his clerical position in the Polish army. Although it was common in Poland at that time for widowed men to find a new wife who would take care of young children, Wojtyła Sr. did not remarry. Instead, he took entirely upon himself the task of preparing Karol for adulthood. With the exception of cooking major meals, his father did almost all the housework, made school uniforms for Karol out of old military suits and helped him with his homework.[4] Wojtyła's friends, who knew his father, describe him as a rather stern man of few words, totally dedicated to the care of his young son but strict in his child rearing.[5] It seems that Karol's father did not place unreasonable demands on his son, but he expected him to stick to an established routine of daily tasks, such as breakfast, lunch, homework, exercise and going for long walks. Many of these activities they did together always at the same time according to a schedule established by his father. In his autobiography *Gift and Mystery*, published in 1997, John Paul II gives most of the credit for his priestly vocation not to his mother or a priest, but to his father, whom he described as "a deeply religious man."[6] He recalled that while waking up sometimes during the night, he would find his father praying on his knees.

According to one account, Karol learned of his mother's death not directly from his father but from his teacher when he was sitting in class. His father apparently did not go to school to personally deliver the tragic news and console him. While having a teacher inform the young boy of his mother's death may seem cruel by today's Western sensitivities, there may have been other reasons why the father could not tell him the news himself at that moment. But Karol's teacher apparently did not see anything wrong in what his father did. This was the way children were expected to be treated by their parents and teachers in 1920s Poland. Public displays of religious faith were common, but cultural norms discouraged young Polish men from showing their emotions and guided their development according to strict rules of discipline and devotion to their country. School discipline and teachers' authority over students were severe. Press reports suggested that Cardinal Joseph Ratzinger (b. 1927), now Pope Benedict XVI, grew up in a very similar environment in a small town in Germany and experienced similar discipline at school.[7]

Emilia Wojtyła's and Edmund Wojtyła's Tomb in Kraków's Rakowicki Cemetery.

According to his classmates, Karol did not cry at his mother's funeral. After Emilia's funeral, his father took both Karol and his brother Edmund on a pilgrimage to the Shrine of the Virgin Mary at Kalwaria Zebrzydowska, a place a few miles east of Wadowice, where all three of them offered their suffering to the Virgin.[8] A childhood friend, Eugeniusz Mróz, recalled that Wojtyła's mother's room was never used after her death, but Karol would sometimes take a break from his studies and go there to pray. One of the first poems he wrote as an adolescent was devoted to the memory of his mother and expressed his grief over her absence. Written during the spring of 1939, when he was 19 years old, the poem starts with the words: "Over this your white grave, the flowers of life in white — so many years without you — how many have passed out of sight?…" John Paul II carried with him a picture of himself as a young boy in his mother's arms wherever he went.[9]

Some writers suggest that the psychological impact of the death of his mother can explain the development of Wojtyła's deep devotion to the Virgin Mary. But the religious culture in Poland at that time, which promoted personal devotion to the Virgin, was all around him, and many other Polish boys of his generation also prayed regularly to Mary, possibly seeing a female figure as more accessible and less threatening than an all-powerful, male God and stern male authority figures in their lives. Polish nuns were not charged with being teachers of young boys, but they also had a reputation of being stern in teaching and disciplining girls and young women. Polish girls may have found the figure of Christ to be more appealing, as memoirs and other literature of the period seem to suggest. Such attitudes can be understandable among children brought up in homes in which both fathers and mothers frequently administered corporal punishment, but there is no evidence that such punishment was abused in Wojtyła's home or that his father was stricter with his son than other Polish parents of that period. Nevertheless, Wojtyła did grow up in a family and school environment of strict discipline and deep respect for authority figures, almost all of them males. He had no significant female teachers or other female role models in his youth other than women who helped his father in taking care of him.

The prevailing culture in Poland at the time of Wojtyła's childhood was definitely religious, patriarchal and patriotic. It was based on the authority of mostly male patriotic poets and writers, fighters for independence and male religious leaders. All of them preached devotion to the nation and often glorified the Polish military effort against the occupiers. Even the image of the Virgin Mary was employed by the Polish Catholic clergy to justify resistance to Poland's enemies. But while militaristic nationalism mixed with religion was the dominant cultural influence, there was also a feminine side to Polish nationalism, which may have been somewhat unique among nationalist movements in modern European history. This feminine characteristic of Polish nationalism was emphasized by the Catholic Church in presenting the Virgin Mary as the protectress of the nation and in the veneration of her images in numerous shrines throughout Poland, usually centered on important historical anniversaries. Partly because of this important tradition, Polish women were not entirely excluded from the liberation struggle and in some areas, such as education and social work, even played a decisive role. While religion usually makes nationalists more aggressive in pursuing their aims, the Marian devotion may have had an opposite effect in Poland at least in some cases. For patriotic Poles, the Marian devotion may have helped to suggest other, non-violent ways of working for Poland's independence. This message would have been particularly attractive to women and to more sensitive young men such as Karol Wojtyła. John Paul II alludes to this in his autobiography by explaining how the "Marian Thread" affected the development of his religious personality since early childhood and adolescence. He recalled how during those years he and his schoolmates would visit the chapel dedicated to Our Lady of Perpetual Help and pray there, both before and after classes. It was an experience of deep individual and group devotion that few Americans or other Westerners of later generations can identify with. While young Karol was naturally more sensitive and artistic, devotion to the Virgin Mary may have helped to strengthen and develop these qualities. Western feminists generally do not acknowledge that Marian devotion could have a moderating influence on male aggressiveness as they tend to focus much more on its alleged negative effects on developing societal views of women.

Many Polish boys of high school age were joining paramilitary nationalistic organizations, but Karol became a member of the Sodality of Mary.[10] It was a somewhat elite society devoted to forming characters of young men and developing their religious and intellectual potential as patriotic

---

Sodalities

Sodality of the Blessed Virgin and St. Patrick, Dublin, Ireland
http://www.sodality.ie

St. Monica Sodality
http://www.cantius.org/St-Monica.Sod.htm

St. Monica Sodality of Michigan
http://www.stmonicasodality.org/

The Sodality of the Most Holy Rosary (Anglican)
http://www.netsource1.com/Sodality/

Catholics. In Wadowice, there was also the Sodality of Mary for girls. These societies were run by priests whose job was to organize lectures, lead discussions, offer guidance and recommend books and magazines for young students to read. Famous Albanian Catholic nun, Mother Teresa, was also a member of Sodality in her home town of Skopje, Macedonia, before she joined her religious orders. In Poland, the overall focus of the Marian school societies was more on religious and community service than on individual spiritual development, but they were more moderate and more intellectual than other youth organizations devoted to physical exercise and paramilitary training. In 1935 Karol was selected to be the chairman of the Sodality of Mary for boys at his all-male high school and held this position until his graduation in 1938.[11]

Soon after his mother's death, 12 year old Karol experienced another loss in his family. His older brother, Edmund, a promising physician, died at the age of 26 from scarlet fever contracted from a patient. Father Kazimierz Suder, who knew young Wojtyła from his seminary years in Kraków, believes that Karol may have been even more affected by his brother's death than the earlier loss of his mother, since the two brothers had became very close.[12] With his father's death in 1941, when Karol was 21, he was left with no immediate family members. Some of Wojtyła's Polish friends speculate that the experience of losing his entire family at a relatively young age may have influenced his preference for large families and his firm opposition to contraception and abortion. While this is partly true, there were, however, other, much stronger factors that shaped his thinking on these issues. At the time of the loss of his father, Karol Wojtyła was already an eyewitness to the beginnings of the Nazi genocide and may have already heard the rumors about the experiments at the concentration camps on women's reproductive organs being conducted by the Nazi doctors. His conversations with Dr. Wanda Półtawska, herself a victim of Nazi medical experiments, who later became his closest advisor in Kraków on sex and birth control, confirmed and reinforced this crucial experience, which will be discussed in depth in later chapters.

There is little doubt that since the death of his mother, mostly men played a significant role in Wojtyła's life. This can be clearly seen from John Paul's own autobiography, in which he mentions numerous men, both lay and religious, with only a few minor references to women. When he does mention women, they are not professors or spiritual advisors, but usually mothers of his friends spending most of their time at home as housewives, but most of them are educated and active on behalf of social causes linked with the struggle for Poland's independence. It is not true, however, as some writers have suggested, that after the death of his mother there were no important women in Wojtyła's life and that he had no significant relationships with women. It is true that as a teenager and a young man he did not have a girlfriend with whom he would share romantic love. Most of the women he knew at that time were older women who took care of him, while male teachers were responsible for his education, and male priests watched over his spiritual development.

Again, this was a more or less a normal experience for a young boy growing up in Poland in the 1920s and the 1930s, but being raised from an early age by his father without any sisters or other close female family members was somewhat unusual and may have had an impact on his later views on women. Relying on women to worry about his physical well-being after the death of his mother may provide at least some explanation for Wojtyła's insistence on promoting traditional roles for women as mothers and homemakers. This is what he personally experienced and benefited from, but it was generally expected at that time in Poland that women should have the primary responsibility for such tasks as cooking, cleaning and making sure that men were properly taken care of. There is no evidence that Karol viewed the role of women, mothers and homemakers as less demanding, less difficult or not as important as jobs traditionally held by men. On the contrary, this experience may have convinced Wojtyła that homemaking is the most important job a woman can have, and he seemed troubled that Western societies do not value very highly this kind of work performed by women. Perhaps because he apparently appreciated such work, he may have assumed quite erroneously that most Polish men felt the same way. There is also plenty of evidence to suggest that Karol was far more sensitive than most Polish boys and young men of his generation. This too may have colored many of his views on gender roles for men and women.

Whether or not this can be attributed to the early loss of his mother or the traditional upbringing in Poland, which placed great emphasis on respect for women, Karol Wojtyła always had an exalted view of mothers, as it can be seen from many of his comments and statements over the years. In 1985, he told the wife of the mayor of Boston, Ray Flynn, that while both her husband and the pope had very important jobs, her job was much more important. Ray Flynn, who was later named the U.S. Ambassador to the Vatican, recalled that during a later meeting he and his wife had with John Paul II, the pope focused his attention on Mrs. Flynn, telling her that "the future of the world is with mothers" who raise children and give humanity peace and freedom. He assured Kathy Flynn that "like Mary, the Mother of Jesus, we need you the most."[13]

Mothers have always held a special place in Wojtyła's heart. He was surrounded by numerous women, often mothers and grandmothers of his friends, who felt it was their duty to feed and take care of him. Far from seeing it as a burden, these women derived a great satisfaction from being able to help a polite young man who showed them great respect and tried to help them himself by taking on tasks considered more appropriate for a Polish man. It is hard to say who benefited more from this arrangement, which later John Paul II was presenting as a model of gender collaboration and solidarity. When Wojtyła became a priest and later a bishop and a cardinal, women—most of them nuns—continued to cook and clean for him as they did for other Polish priests. The experience of American and West European nuns was already quite different in the period after World War II and some of them would later become outspoken critics of John Paul II's views on the role of nuns and women in the Catholic Church.

Life in Pre-World War II Poland

Karol's parents rented a small apartment consisting of one large room and a kitchen in a house near the church in the center of Wadowice. There was no separate bedroom for their two children, and all of them had to share a hallway bathroom with their neighbors. The house, owned by a Jewish couple Chaim and Rozalia Bałamuth, was itself not in the best condition; water was leaking from broken pipes and the exterior entrance and stairs were left unrenovated. The family lived very frugally, but according to their neighbors, they were always happy and full of hope.[14] Until the end of World War I, Wadowice was a provincial town in the Austro-Hungarian Empire and was also known by its German name as Frauenstadt—women's town—perhaps an ironic name for the birthplace of the pope who disappointed many liberals and pleased many conservative Catholics by confirming that women can never be ordained as Catholic priests.[15]

Being born and growing up in a small, provincial Polish town may have some significance for understanding Wojtyła's moral conservatism but does not explain his progressive views on many social issues. Social and moral attitudes in Poland are largely determined by where people live, although education and social class also play a role. Public opinion surveys have consistently shown that on women's issues and most other social questions inhabitants of large cities are considerably more liberal, more tolerant and less bound by religious traditions than people living in small towns and villages. Between the wars, Wadowice had between six and seven thousand inhabitants, about two thousand of them Jews—clearly a small provincial town. Karol Wojtyła lived in Wadowice from his birth in 1920 until 1938, when both he and his father moved to Kraków so he could study at the Jagiellonian University, the most prestigious university in Poland.[16]

Despite its typical small town atmosphere, Wadowice in interwar Poland had a rather lively cultural as well as religious life. In the era before television and before going to the movies became popular in Poland, the town had several active theaters, two of them sponsored by the Catholic Church. The Jewish inhabitants of Wadowice had their own cultural center with their own theater group.[18] Acting seemed to have been a major cultural activity in Wadowice of Wojtyła's youth and a way of expanding the horizons of young people, but while some Greek tragedies and a few of Shakespeare's plays were performed, the vast majority of roles were in plays by Polish playwrights focusing on the struggle for national independence. What may have started Karol's lifetime fascination with the theater was a friendship he developed as a sixteen-year-old high school student with a male drama teacher twelve years his senior. Eventually, he became involved with most of the theater groups in town. Also, while still living in Wadowice, Karol started to write poetry.

Karol Wojtyła's boyhood home in Wadowice.

Coutryard of Karol Wojtyła's boyhood home in Wadowice.

His connections with the town of his youth remained strong throughout his life. Partly because of friendships established while working as an actor in amateur theater, Wojtyła continued to stay in touch with his hometown friends, some of them women. Karol's religion teacher, Father Edward Zacher,

Main square and Wojtyła's parish church in Wadowice.

recalled that the future pope would return to Wadowice for a visit at least once almost every year until he left permanently for the Vatican. He then returned a few more times to his hometown as pope.

In 1926, at the age of six, Karol started his education at a Wadowice grammar school for boys. He was described as an excellent student and a good friend among boys his age. He was also very religious, becoming an altar boy at the Wadowice parish church and, together with his father and a group of boys from school, making his first pilgrimage to the Shrine of Our Lady of Częstochowa. After finishing grammar school, Karol started high school in 1931, again at an all-male school. Among more than 30 teachers who taught at Karol's high school, there were only three women.[19] In high school, he had three religion teachers, all of them priests. Most of his young school life was spent among boys and older males in an atmosphere of strict discipline, full respect for authority, and above all love of the fatherland and its tragic recent history. The discipline and a sense of duty, instilled in Wojtyła at an early age, never left him throughout his life. When he became a priest and a bishop, he was convinced of the need to develop the character of young people by exposing them to Catholic education from a very early age through the university and beyond. Under communism, it had to be done outside of the public schools through various Church-sponsored activities, which Wojtyła enthusiastically supported. His profound interest in young people and their moral education continued even after he became pope and assumed much wider responsibilities.

The atmosphere in Polish schools before the war was quite different from what most Americans attending public schools at

The Jagiellonian University
Kraków, Poland

Founded: 1364

http://www.uj.edu.pl/index.en.html

According to a medieval legend, a Polish woman named Nawojka may have barely escaped punishment when, she entered the Jagiellonian University in Kraków in 1415 dressed as a man and using a male name *Andrzej* (Andrew). When her real gender was accidentally discovered, Nawojka's life was spared, but she was locked up in a convent where she spent the rest of her life teaching nuns how to read and write. She would have been also the first female teacher in Poland.[17] Nawojka's existence cannot be proven with historical certainty, but the story illustrates quite well the tragedy of women who wanted to be educated and were forced to resort to deception to overcome the restrictions placed on them by the Church and society.

that time would experience. While discipline in American schools sixty or seventy years ago was certainly much stricter than it is now, it could not compare with what most students of Wojtyła's generation experienced in Poland. Corporal punishment was socially accepted and widely used. There was very little room for free exchange of views and ideas between teachers and students, and there was no separation of church and state. Even though the school Wojtyła attended was a state-funded public school, it was very much run by Catholic priests and teachers closely connected with the Catholic Church. Catholic values and ethics were simply assumed to be the correct ones, and students were expected to believe in them with no questions asked. While some students at Wojtyła's high school were Jewish and were allowed to study and practice their own religion, teachers did not encourage tolerance for diversity of values and opinions on religious and moral issues.

The most significant difference between pre-war Polish and American schools, however, was the overwhelming emphasis on developing in students a sense of duty and service to the nation, the Catholic Church and the community. School rules at the time Wojtyła was enrolled in high school required students "to be ready to take responsibility for [protecting] their own honor, [the honor of] the family and the school, to protect the weaker, and to react when others openly violate state and school rules." As one Polish historian noted after studying the records at Wojtyła's school, both the school authorities and the students were extremely serious about observing these rules.[20]

Most of the students, including Wojtyła, were very religious. School discipline and expectations to score well on exams were high, and students were required to go to church for daily prayers both before and after classes. John Paul II said during his first return visit to Wadowice as pope in 1979 that he and his fellow students prayed regularly to the picture of Our Lady of Perpetual Help. He also asked his audience a rhetorical question whether this practice continues, probably well aware that for the most part it no longer does in today's Poland.[21]

> **Halina Królikiewicz Kwiatkowska**
>
> b. 1921
>
> **Book:** *Wielki kolega*
>
> **Quote:** [Wojtyła] "never lectured. [He] always understood."

While Wojtyła went to all-boys high school and spent most of his free time either with his father or with other boys, he had some contacts with girls his age, largely in a school theatrical group that included students from a private high school for girls in Wadowice. One of them was Halina (Helena) Królikiewicz (Kwiatkowska) who after Wojtyła's election as pope was rumored in the media to have been romantically involved with young Karol. There is absolutely no evidence of any kind that there was any truth to these rumors. Halina Kwiatkowska recalled that while male and female members of a theatre group, to which they both belonged after enrolling at the Jagiellonian University in Kraków, would go to a local bar to have fun, Karol did not participate and would instead read books and study.[22] In fact, everything that is known about Wojtyła indicates that he did not develop any deep or romantic friendships with girls during his youth. The co-educational theatrical group in high school, in which Karol and Halina were the most active members, performed mostly patriotic plays by Polish Romantic writers. In his autobiography, *Gift and Mystery*, Wojtyła writes that through his participation in drama club activities he knew many girls and had many opportunities to be with other young people—a more or less normal experience of middle class Polish youth.[23] He admits, however, that in addition to his deep religious interests, his mind was almost entirely on literature and the theater and does not mention any strong personal attachments to young women his own age.

After graduating from high school in Wadowice, in 1938 Wojtyła enrolled at the Jagiellonian University in Kraków to study his beloved subject Polish literature with the intention of devoting himself to an artistic career as a poet, actor or theater director. His interest in acting led to probably the only serious disagreement in an otherwise harmonious relationship between Wojtyła and his father. According to Father Mieczysław Maliński, Wojtyła's father wanted young Karol to follow in his footsteps and to seek a career

---

Mieczysław Maliński

Born: 1923, Brzostek, Poland

Book: *Ale miałem ciekawe życie*

Quotes: "I was never a SB (communist secret police) agent."

"In 100 or 200 years, when true equality of women and men is achieved in the Third World, then women can become priests in the Catholic Church."

http://www.malinski.pl

in the military, but his son had absolutely no interest in becoming a military man.[24] (See the footnote about possible interpretations of Father Maliński's details from Wojtyła's early life.) Karol, according to Maliński, insisted on studying Polish literature and on pursuing an acting career. He may have already decided at that time that he was a Christian pacifist. Out of love for his son, Karol Sr. agreed. As a boy and a young man, Karol was extremely close to his father. Maliński wrote that despite Karol's love for the theater, time spent with his father was more important to him than anything else. Maliński also observed that Karol rarely talked about his father, but when he did, he spoke about him "with utmost respect, and even with uncharacteristic for him tenderness."[25] When his father died in 1941, Karol was devastated. Zofia Kotlarczyk remembered that while she and her husband were sharing Wojtyła's apartment in Kraków, he made regular trips to his father's grave at the Rakowicki cemetery.

At the university, Karol quickly joined an amateur theater group and worked alongside female students, but again did not develop any significant attachments with women. After his university studies were interrupted by the outbreak of World War II in 1939, he participated in a clandestine theater in German-occupied Kraków, where he also worked with women-actors, but again without any deep friendships with women.

Passion for Theater

Understanding of Wojtyła's passion for drama and literature in his younger years is essential for the understanding of his personality and the cultural milieu that shaped his personality. Theater was much more than entertainment in pre-war Poland. It was a place where national and social aspirations and concerns were expressed in order to raise the level of social awareness and to reform society with the ultimate goal of making the country strong and independent. Wojtyła also dreamed of using drama to make Poles more religious and more aware of Christian values. It was not the love of drama for drama's sake or for the sake of entertainment that attracted Wojtyła to an artistic career. Yet despite its social role, acting was still not a usual occupation for a young Polish male, and it was frowned upon by many Catholic priests. Karol's commitment to acting could be interpreted a sign of a more liberal mindset and greater than normal intelligence and sensitivity, but it seems that his strong dedication to the theater was driven primarily by a patriotic and religious desire to change people's perceptions and values. He wanted to express himself artistically as an actor and a poet, but he was drawn to the theater by his love of Poland's past. Almost all of the theater productions, in which Karol participated in Wadowice, dealt with Poland's history and glorified the struggle for national independence. These plays were not usually about young love or non-conforming lifestyles. Theater in Poland at that time served a specific social function as a platform for expressing patriotic feelings, and it became an important national institution.

It was in connection with his acting during his teenage years that Wojtyła started a pattern of establishing relationships with older male role models and mentors who gave him direction, guidance and encouragement in areas in which he developed passionate interest. Theater being his first strong passion, Wojtyła found his mentor in Mieczysław Kotlarczyk, a high school teacher of Polish and a drama director a few years older than Karol.[26] He and Kotlarczyk shared an appreciation for Poland's history and had a common vision of making their country greater and better through poetry and drama. During the war, they became such close personal friends that Wojtyła invited him and his wife Zofia to live in his small apartment in Kraków. From 1941 to 1945, the underground theater group put together 22 performances of seven or eight plays and had over 100 rehearsals. The plays performed most often were by Poland's Romantic writers: Juliusz Słowacki, Stanisław Wyspiański and Adam Mickiewicz, all of whom wrote about heroic characters from Poland's past struggling between individual desires and loyalty to the nation.[27] In nearly all of them, the nobility of sacrifice for the Fatherland takes precedence over personal and gender preferences while at the same time preserving basic gender distinctions.

This deep attachment to Poland's national traditions and a sense of duty to work for the betterment of his people can be seen from Wojtyła's early letters and reminiscences of his friends, some of which already reveal his attitudes toward women and Western liberal ideas. Sometime in the early 1940s, during the Nazi occupation of Poland, Wojtyła suggested to his friends that the Poles desire freedom, beauty, artistic expression and ultimately God more than anything else. He was dissatisfied with the Polish poetry of the interwar period, describing it as rarely reflecting the spirit of the nation. He complained that it was being more influenced by international Marxist humanism than by traditional Polish values.[28]

This very early comment by Wojtyła is significant, for it already indicates a clear preference for religious and traditional Polish solutions to social problems rather than solutions based on individualism and other Western liberal ideas. Already at that time, feminism was associated in Poland with Marxism and anti-religious liberalism, mainly of French origin. Priests, Polish nationalists and later communists perceived individualism and humanism as at least unpatriotic if not criminal. Even for Marxists, emancipation of women was to serve the interests of the communist party, the communist state and in some cases the nation — not interests of individual women.

Much of Wojtyła's later philosophy of life — his belief in tradition and suspicion of liberal Western ideas — can be found in some of his earlier writings and confirmed by reminiscences of his closest friends. Looking at his comments on the Polish inter-war poetry one can already see the origins of his relentless attempts to promote some of the traditional Polish values, first for the Poles and later for the whole world. Traditional gender roles were part of

Wojtyła's blueprint for a better society, and they were very much in line with what he saw as the best examples from Polish history and literature. They were not, however, of any great importance to those who gave priority to their own personal achievements and private gain. Wojtyła's real life experience, particularly in such areas as business, was limited, although he desperately wanted a better future for the Polish people. He thought, however, that solutions were to be found in great ideas uniting the whole nation rather than in pursuit of individual interests and profits. As Father Maliński described it, for both Karol and for his artistic mentor, Mieczysław Kotlarczyk, the goal was to make society better through beauty, poetry and drama.[29] According to Father Maliński's description, their theater performances were not mere entertainment. Inspired by the love of their country, Kotlarczyk's actors had a sense of mission. Acting represented a form of "priesthood" with the ultimate goal of "guarding and imparting the deepest truths of life." Theater was similar to a religion and an actor was a priest.[30] Kotlarczyk's goal was to make patriotic, religious and philosophical ideas accessible to common people. Another one of Karol's artistic mentors, the famous pre-war Polish actor Juliusz Ostrewa, asked Wojtyła to rewrite Sophocles' *Oedipus Rex*, so that the play could be fully understood — as he put it in his instructions — "even by female cooks."[31] Appreciation of female intelligence, especially among women from lower social classes, was not particularly strong among educated Polish men who were Wojtyła's friends. Wojtyła, however, would never make such a comment. I did not find a single quote from his letters, speeches and statements that would show anything but great respect for women.

Male Role Models

While Wojtyła had plenty of opportunities to exchange views with male and female students — all of them rather young and inexperienced in the matters of love, sex and marriage — there were few outstanding mature intellectual women among Wojtyła's mentors and role models in Poland during his formative years as a seminary student and a young priest. There were, however, many outstanding, patriotic Polish women who took care of him as a young man. He could observe them pursuing traditionally female occupations as mothers, teachers and caregivers, while male theologians and university professors were preparing him for priesthood.

Despite his involvement with the theater during the war under the artistic direction of Mieczysław Kotlarczyk, Wojtyła was also pursuing his spiritual development, devoting many hours to prayer and study of religious literature. One of his great spiritual role models was at that time Jan Tyranowski, an accountant who finished high school but, for reasons of health and in order to concentrate on the development of his spiritual life, worked as a simple tailor at his father's shop. Tyranowski was a mystic who with the blessing of the Church authorities devoted his spare time to working with young boys at the Kraków parish of St. Stanislaus Kostka. He was recruited for this job after the Gestapo arrested all the regular priests at the parish with the exception of one who was ill. Young Wojtyła met Tyranowski during the war when Tyranowski was about forty years old and invited Karol into a religious study group focused on building faith and character of young men. The boys under Tyranowski's care met with him once a week at his house or in the church for prayers, spiritual exercises, and discussions of religious and ethical questions. Wojtyła estimated that Jan Tyranowski's parish "school"

Mieczysław Kotlarczyk 1908-1978

Jan Tyranowski 1900-1947

Cardinal Adam Stefan Sapieha
Born: 1867, Krasiczyn, Poland
Died: 1951, Kraków, Poland

Jerzy Ciesielski
Born: 1929, Kraków, Poland
Marriage: 1957 to Danuta Plebańczyk
Died: 1970, Sudan

included at times about one hundred boys and young men between 14 and 25 years old.[32] Older boys, recruited and trained by Tyranowski, worked with younger ones as their spiritual counselors, and there was an element of competition in their struggle for spiritual perfection. Wojtyła and other older instructors were each assigned groups of fourteen young boys, known as "Roses," which formed the "Living Rosary." The instructors of the groups were required to devote one hour a week to each young man under their care.

At the time, the Nazis closed all universities in Poland and Karol had to find a job at the quarry and the Solvay chemical factory to support himself and to avoid being arrested or sent to Germany as a slave laborer. Since this job did not leave Wojtyła much free time, some of the boys would accompany him on the way to work or on the way home. During those walks, they would discuss with him their concerns and seek his advice. Karol would also visit their homes and talk to their parents who greatly appreciated his involvement with their children. Toward the end of the war, Jan Tyranowski also started organizing a "Living Rosary" for girls, but unlike his work with the boys, those activities are not well documented. Among several articles about Jan Tyranowski in a 1999 book chronicling Wojtyła's life in Kraków, there was only one sentence referring to Tyranowski's work with the "Living Rosary" for young women.[33]

There is no question that Jan Tyranowski had a profound influence on young Wojtyła and may have been the most important male role model he had before he decided to enter the seminary. Tyranowski introduced Wojtyła to mysticism and to a program of daily self-improvement, which formed an important part of Tyranowski's work to shape the characters of young men under his spiritual care. It was a carefully designed program based on the strong authority of the teacher and strict discipline. The boys were required to write down in special notebooks time devoted to prayer, meditation and study. These notes were then reviewed by Tyranowski.[34] Mieczysław Maliński, who also later became a priest, described one of the aims of Jan Tyranowski's spiritual development program as teaching young men self-control and responsibility for their thoughts and actions.[35] After Tyranowski's death in 1947, Wojtyła wrote that his spiritual mentor used every means to "tame his body" and sometimes spent up to four hours daily on mystic meditation.[36] But when they first started as members of Tyranowski's group, Maliński was much less impressed with Tyranowski than Karol had been, and even told him that he found their spiritual advisor intolerable. Others described Tyranowski as enormously lovable, shy and humble. Father Maliński's accounts of his first meetings with Tyranowski suggest that he did not understand or approve of Wojtyła's fascination with their teacher. In one of his books about John Paul II, Maliński referred to rumors that Tyranowski had been a psychiatric patient, but he could not confirm them and ultimately concluded that he appeared completely normal.[37]

Saint John of the Cross
1542-1591
Saint Teresa of Ávila
1515-1582

Before he finally changed his opinion of Tyranowski, Maliński disliked him almost as strongly as he liked his friend Karol. His initial impressions were that Tyranowski was a man belonging to another century: strangely dressed, using outdated language and being too eager in pushing his agenda. But Karol, while admitting Tyranowski's peculiarities, strongly defended him to his friend by stressing his great spiritual gifts as an educator of young men. He argued that it is less important how the man speaks or looks than what he represents and what he brings into their lives.[38] Apparently, Maliński changed his view of Tyranowski after he began to talk to him about Saint John of the Cross and Saint Teresa of Ávila, both 16th century Spanish mystics, in whom both he and Wojtyła shared a deep interest. The relationship both men had with their spiritual leader was intensive and focused heavily on mystic meditation. Wojtyła's interest in

New Sprirituality

Caroline Myss

http://www.myss.com/

Matthew Fox b. 1940

http://www.matthewfox.org/sys-tmpl/door/

Creation Spirituality

http://www.creationspirituality.info/Index.html

Saint Teresa of Ávila's mysticism, which John Paul II helped to popularize, is now inspiring New Thought and New Age spiritual leaders in the United States and elsewhere. A New Thought spiritual speaker and writer Caroline Myss has published a book *Entering the Castle: An Inner Path to God and Your Soul* (2007) which draws on Saint Teresa's mystical experiences.[39] But despite his own fascination with mysticism and perhaps even mystical experiences in his early life, John Paul II was known to oppose New Age religions on several grounds, including their alleged minimalization or denial of sin. In 1988, Cardinal Ratzinger (now Pope Benedict XVI) took action against American Catholic priest Father Matthew Fox who is a leading exponent of Creation Spirituality. In 1992, Father Fox was expelled from the Dominican Order and subsequently became an Episcopal priest. One of the reasons for the Vatican's harsh treatment of Dr. Fox may have been his advocacy of equal treatment of women in the Catholic Church. Fox accused John Paul II of taking action against feminist philosophers, preventing girls from serving at the altar and denying priesthood to women.[40] According to Dr. Fox, Cardinal Ratzinger called his work "dangerous and deviant."[41]

mysticism and his commitment to pacifism and belief in non-violence were also unconventional in mid-20th century Poland, as was his older mentor Jan Tyranowski. Many of Wojtyła's early theological views may have been formed under Tyranowski's unusual influence. When Wojtyła met him for the first time, Poland was under German occupation and many young men were joining underground armed struggle against the Nazis. Wojtyła and Maliński were opposed to the use of violence and tried to prevent young men under their care from becoming involved in military actions. They would most likely not discourage these young boys from becoming underground fighters if Tyranowski was not of the same opinion. Some of their friends believed that young Poles should sacrifice their lives in the fight for freedom and accused them of cowardice, but Wojtyła and Maliński argued that they were preparing young men to be ready to serve their Fatherland in future peacetime.

Although their own activities in the underground theater and in Tyranowski's "Living Rosary," were also illegal under the German occupation rules, in Poland — where young men were expected to fight foreign aggressors — their pacifist attitude and unofficial status as conscientious objectors may have seemed to some as unpatriotic. But Wojtyła was serious about the commandment to love one's enemies. This may explain at least partly why during the war he first wanted to join a monastery and later to become a priest. By taking religious vows he could prove that his commitment to non-violence was genuine and religiously motivated — the only acceptable excuse for a young Polish man for not wanting to fight Poland's enemies with more than just words. This may also explain John Paul II's strong opposition to U.S. foreign policy initiatives relying on the use of American military force — a stand which had won him a measure of admiration from his otherwise severe critics among Left-leaning Western liberals.

Many years later, John Paul II wrote that Tyranowski taught him "the elementary methods of fashioning my own character and introduced me to the works written by great mystics: St. John of the Cross and St. Teresa." He also credited Tyranowski for leading him to the priesthood: "I frequently recall with veneration this man, so providential in shaping a new vocation." In addition to his most famous student, Tyranowski's "Living Rosary" produced ten other priests. [42] Jan Tyranowski died in 1947 from blood poisoning while Wojtyła was studying theology in Rome and could not attend his funeral. Despite great pain and the amputation of his arm, Jan Tyranowski remained peaceful and gave encouragement to other patients and his friends who came to visit him at the hospital. According to Father Maliński, Wojtyła was greatly affected by Tyranowski's death and did not want him to be forgotten. [43] Jan Tyranowski is currently being considered for beatification and eventual sainthood in the Catholic Church.

According to Father Maliński, it was during the period of involvement in the spiritual group of Jan Tyranowski's boys when Wojtyła made a choice between the theater and the priesthood. Zofia Kotlarczyk, the wife of the underground theater director, recalled that one day Karol told her husband not to cast him in plays anymore because he wanted to become a priest. Kotlarczyk, according to Father Maliński, tried to convince Karol that he may end up somewhere in the provinces running a small parish and waste his enormous talent, but Wojtyła would not be dissuaded. He never entirely gave up his passion for literature and the theater, and continued to appear in some plays, but—having made his decision to become a priest—he used most of his free time from that point on for religious studies.

Perhaps under Kotlarczyk's influence and as a result of being a witness to war atrocities around him, Wojtyła initial desire to make Poland a better place through his work as an actor gave way to a conviction that he can be more effective as a priest helping ordinary people live their lives. Tyranowski's influence can be clearly seen in Karol's initial desire to improve his spirituality by joining the Carmelite monks. Wojtyła even talked to them about entering the order, but the attempt failed because the Nazis forced the Carmelites and other religious orders to close their schools to any new students. Instead, in 1942 when Poland was still under

Nazi occupation, Wojtyła entered a clandestine seminary run by Kraków's Archbishop, Cardinal Prince Adam Stefan Sapieha. The seminary was operating covertly at the archbishop's residence, since the Nazis also did not allow any new Polish priests to be educated. At a risk to his freedom and possibly life if his illegal studies were to be discovered, Wojtyła continued to work at the chemical plant while attending secret seminary lectures in his spare time. Toward the end of the war, he took an even greater risk by abandoning his place of employment and becoming a full time seminary student.

At that point all of Wojtyła's seminary teachers and spiritual advisors were men. After Mieczysław Kotlarczyk and Jan Tyranowski, Cardinal Sapieha became Wojtyła's next great male role model and mentor during his years as a seminary student and a young priest. Wojtyła also continued his close friendship with Maliński as they prepared together for priesthood. The war ended for both of them in early 1945 when the Soviet Red Army troops entered Kraków already abandoned by the German troops. After the end of the war, Wojtyła continued his studies at the Theology Faculty of the Jagiellonian University in Kraków, where the teaching staff was again composed entirely of men. Wojtyła names some of his university professors in his autobiography, mentioning among others, his confessor and spiritual director in Wadowice and later in Kraków, Father Kazimierz Figlewicz. As a young boy living in Wadowice, Karol would confess his sins to Father Figlewicz, but the two would also meet and talk outside of the church. When he was transferred to Kraków, Father Figlewicz invited Karol to participate in the Holy Week services at the cathedral. Father Kazimierz Suder, who knew Wojtyła immediately after World War II, described Father Figlewicz as the future pope's "idol."[44] (The communist secret police also listed Father Suder, Wojtyła's lifelong friend, as their informant from 1985 until 1989. Again, it is not clear whether Father Suder considered his conversations with the secret police as in any way compromising his friendship with Wojtyła or undermining his loyalty to the Church. He strongly denies that they did. Many priests who know Father Suder believe that he could not have been an informant.[45])

The description of being Wojtyła's idols can be applied to several other male role models, both priests and lay men, with whom he established a strong personal attachment as a young man. There were no similar powerful female figures at that stage in Wojtyła's early life. After he became pope, many journalists looked for evidence of any kind of romantic involvement with women or a strong emotional attachment to young women among his friends and fellow-students. There was no such evidence to be found. During his early adulthood, Wojtyła's close friendships were exclusively with men. Father Maliński was particularly upset by the erroneous media reports that John Paul II decided to become a priest after his fiancé had left him. The information about a fiancé and a priest was true, but—as Maliński pointed out—it was not Wojtyła but another priest from Wadowice.[46] Wojtyła and Maliński were two male priests who maintained a strong friendship and supported one another, but the concept of "the old boys' network" was practically unknown during Wojtyła's life in Poland. It may have not even occurred to John Paul II that men socializing and working together in an environment that excluded women could have produced a distorted sense of reality and views that would conflict with the wellbeing and interests of women.

While studying for priesthood, Wojtyła was clearly one of Cardinal Sapieha's favorite seminarians for whom the archbishop apparently had ambitious plans. Maliński wrote that he was devastated after he found out that Wojtyła had been selected by Sapieha to continue his studies in Rome while he had to stay in Poland.[47] When Wojtyła became a bishop, he helped Maliński get approval for travel to the West to study for an advanced degree in theology. He and John Paul II remained close friends for life. After Polish media reported that communist-era secret police files apparently listed Maliński as an informant, he claimed that John Paul II knew about his contacts with *bezpieka* officers and approved of his attempts to convert them. Father Tadeusz Isakowicz-Zaleski, the anti-communist priest from the Kraków Archdiocese, who prior to 1989 had been a victim of several beatings and other harassment by the secret police, revealed in a book published in 2007 that Maliński's alleged code name was "Delta." In addition to denying that he had been a communist secret police collaborator, Father Maliński also denied that he could be the person described in the communist-era secret police files as the agent "Delta," apparently a close friend of John Paul II who spied on him in Poland and at the Vatican.[48] Father Maliński suggested that there may have been several agents sharing the same code name. Early in 2007, he informed me that he would address these charges in a soon-to-be published autobiography (September 2007) and for the time being referred me to his personal web site, where he denies all accusations. (See *Appendix* for more information.)

I could not confirm these serious accusations at this time since the nature of various contacts between Polish priests and communist secret police officers was highly complex and open to many interpretations. While evidence shows that some priests had been full-fledged collaborators, these accusations also have a potential of unfairly tarnishing the reputations of others who may be totally innocent. Because of his close friendship with John Paul II, Father Maliński was a major source of information for numerous papal biographers, including Tad Szulc, Jonathan Kwitny, Carl Bernstein and Marco Politi, George Weigel, and this author. Maliński had access to practically all of Wojtyła's friends in Poland and in Rome. He has been such a helpful source to Jonathan Kwitny that he included his photograph in his book. I believe that at this time there is not enough evidence to make any final judgments about these accusations and Father Maliński's credibility. As I noted in the Appendix, John Paul II never questioned what Maliński had written about him. He also encouraged Maliński's writing career. The pope and his secretary Father Dziwisz apparently read at least some of his manuscripts before publication, made corrections and gave their approval.[49] John Paul II also praised the priest's books in the presence of others, including Father Dziwisz, who was also Maliński's close friend.[50] Maliński was invited to the Vatican for private meals with the pope sometimes several times a year — a clear sign of their close personal friendship. At one time, John Paul II even asked Maliński to organize a new Vatican television service — an offer he refused to accept. Father Maliński wrote in his latest autobiography that if indeed he were a secret police agent, he would have taken the television job as it would give him constant access to John Paul II.[51]

Cardinal Stanisław Dziwisz

Born: April 27, 1939, Raba Wyżna, Poland

Books: *A Life with Karol: My Forty-Year Friendship with the Man Who Became Pope*
Swiadectwo

Quote: "Karol Wojtyła always had in his heart great respect for women, especially women who are mothers to their families."

In the 1960s, Karol Wojtyła met Stanisław Dziwisz, another priest from southern Poland who became his personal assistant in Kraków and continued to occupy the same but much more important post at the Vatican as the pope's personal secretary.[52] Another one of Wojtyła's close male friends from Kraków was Cardinal Andrzej Maria Deskur (b. 1924) who had a stroke just before Wojtyła's election as pope. Wojtyła visited him at a Rome hospital during the first day of his pontificate. These were some of the most important relationships in Wojtyła's early life, and all of them were with men.

Wojtyła's outlook on life seemed to have changed considerably when he returned to Poland from his studies in Rome and started to work with university students. Despite his continued admiration for Tyranowski's ability to bring young men closer to God through prayer and self-denial, Wojtyła's contacts with young students after the war convinced him that Tyranowski, who never married, may have been insufficiently aware of the mystical nature of marriage and human need for creative work. After all, Tyranowski was a confirmed bachelor and spent most of his time in the company of males. It was the influence of another lay man Jerzy Ciesielski, whom Wojtyła met after the war, that directed the focus of his interests more toward the issues of marriage, family and love in human life. Ciesielski was also considerably younger than Tyranowski. Wojtyła never gave up Tyranowski's mystical approach to religion, but he was forced to develop his own theory of Christian marriage to deal with some of the real problems presented to him by young students whom he served as their spiritual advisor. The traditional Church teachings seemed inadequate in dealing with more educated young people, although as patriotic Poles who grew up in patriotic families, they were still far from being individualistic or liberal in their moral behavior. After theater and priesthood, marital love and family became the third area of intense passion in Wojtyła's life.

The aforementioned Jerzy Ciesielski, an engineer and an avid sportsman, became the next man who had a profound effect on Wojtyła's thinking about life and religion. The two met in Kraków in the early 1950s and developed a close friendship. Ciesielski became a frequent participant in Wojtyła's hiking and kayaking trips with students and gave him lessons to improve his skiing. Jerzy also impressed him as a deeply religious man, and as Jerzy found Danuta, the love of his life, he and Wojtyła started sharing views on the importance of family and marriage. As a lay person, Ciesielski may have had a decisive influence on moving Wojtyła's own thinking about the importance of the traditional marriage and family from religious into more practical concerns, although as an aspiring philosopher Wojtyła also continued to explore the deeper meaning of love and sexuality. A conversation with Jerzy, after he had made his decision to get married, apparently made such a deep impression on Wojtyła that he wrote about it in an article published in the Polish Catholic weekly magazine *Tygodnik Powszechny* shortly after Ciesielski's tragic death. In remembering his friend, Wojtyła wrote that from the moment of making his decision to get married, Jerzy was absolutely convinced that his life-companion had been given to him by God:[53]

I will not forget that evening, when he returned from Tyniec [a monastery near Kraków], where in prayer and concentration he was preparing himself for the great decision of his life. He understood cooperation with Grace very simply and very concretely: the choice of the path of his vocation, the choice of his life-companion — we went to consider all of this before God. He knew that one must allow God to act in one's heart, [reaching] the very depths of one's actions, plans and intentions. From that day on, he knew with complete conviction that it was his life-companion that God put on the path of his life; that God gives her to him.[54]

This passage is a good illustration that a Catholic marriage represented much more to Wojtyła than a legal contract between two people. One of Wojtyła's personal friends Father Adam Boniecki (b. 1934) pointed out that many of John Paul's biographers make a mistake of writing about him without considering his faith. Wojtyła truly believed in the divine nature of Christian marriage and the sacredness of life, as he believed that the Holy Spirit was working through him when in his capacity as pope he made pronouncements on marriage, family and sex. When Jerzy Ciesielski died in a ship accident in Sudan in 1970 together with two of his young children, Wojtyła recalled that because of his conversations with Jerzy about marriage, he became inspired to write his first major book *Love and Responsibility*. In later years,

Wojtyła stayed in close contact with Jerzy Ciesielski's widow Danuta and her remaining daughter and frequently visited them at their home. Another one of Wojtyła's close male friends, Kraków's former Archbishop, Cardinal Macharski (b. 1927), has started the beatification process, which can lead to Jerzy Ciesielski becoming a saint in the Catholic Church. The current Archbishop of Kraków, Stanisław Dziwisz, a man who was John Paul II's closest personal friend for many decades, is likely to push Jerzy Ciesielski's beatification process forward.

Maliński, who knew Karol during his young adult years perhaps better than anybody else, had no significant accounts in his books about Wojtyła's professional or personal friendships with women. Maliński painted a picture of a group of young men, mostly priests, who developed close personal and intellectual relationships and spent a lot of time together without having much contact with any women of equal professional or intellectual status. It seems that the celibacy rule rather than helping these Polish priests develop deep platonic friendships with women, created instead a close environment for men who enjoyed each other's company and the special status of authority and respect still accorded to Catholic priests in Poland. The Poles of Wojtyła's generation, and even today, would look with great suspicion at any close friendships between priests and women. Such societal attitudes may have greatly diminished Wojtyła's ability to have such friendships, although later he did develop a strong professional and personal relationship with Dr. Wanda Półtawska, his advisor on sex and birth control issues.

In his books and speeches, John Paul II often acknowledged that he tried to model his behavior as a priest and a religious leader after various historical figures, usually those from Poland's distant and more recent past. For the development of his deep attachment to the Virgin Mary, however, he gave credit to a Frenchman, Saint Louis Marie Grignion de Monfort (1673-1716), the author of *The Treatise of True Devotion to the Blessed Virgin*, which Karol read and

Adam Chmielowski – Saint Albert Chmielowski

Born: August 20, 1845, Iłomnia, Poland

Died: December 25, 1916, Kraków, Poland

The Albertine Brothers

http://www.albertyni.opoka.org.pl/english.html

The Albertine Sisters

http://www.albertynki.pl/index_usa.html

studied as a student. Wojtyła's religious vocation and his deep concern for the poor were also greatly influenced by the historical example of Saint Albert Adam Chmielowski (1845-1916), a 19th century Polish patriot, painter and eventually a monk who devoted the later years of his life to helping the poorest people in Kraków. The life-story of this historical figure appears to offer many clues for the understanding of Wojtyła's personality, his decision to choose priesthood over a career in acting, his strong belief in social activism on behalf of the poor, as well as his critical attitude toward capitalism.

Chmielowski's early life was typical of a patriotic Polish nobleman under foreign occupation. At the age of seventeen, he participated in the 1863 uprising against Russian rule and, after being wounded in battle, had one of his legs amputated below the knee. After the uprising, he studied painting, first in Warsaw and then in Paris and Munich, and became a known artist and art critic. Dissatisfied with his life and his artistic profession, he tried to join the Jesuits but had a nervous breakdown and was rejected. Later he found his own order of the Albertine Brothers and afterwards the Albertine Sisters. In a way, Wojtyła modeled his life after Chmielowski who, like Wojtyła, abandoned a promising artistic career to devote himself entirely to religious life and to serving the poor. The example of this religious man had such a profound influence on Wojtyła that after World War II he wrote a play about

Adam Chmielowski. The play, entitled *Our God's Brother*, explains Chmielowski's decision to exchange his middle class existence as an artist for what he saw as a much more meaningful service to the homeless and others at the very margins of the Polish society. Although in his play Wojtyła describes an artistic career as not entirely useless if art is used to promote appreciation of beauty and high values among the educated, being a monk allowed Brother Albert to serve those who suffered the most and whom society had forgotten.

The play was also a veiled commentary on the ongoing debate in Poland after World War II about the possible contributions of religion and communism to eliminating poverty and solving various social problems. By exploring the differences between a proto-communist, who saw the poor only as potential revolutionaries, and Brother Adam, whose service to the poor was based on Christian ideas, Wojtyła was arguing in his play that the Catholic Church by radically changing its attitude toward social reforms can be an effective ally of the poor peasants and workers. Wojtyła had always been in favor of radical economic and social change to help the very poorest, but he wanted to accomplish this through non-violent, Christian means; hence his later criticism of the consumerist West but also his consistent opposition to Liberation Theology in Latin America. Just as he worked hard to introduce Christianity into the socialist movement, he would later try with much less success to bring

Helena Modrzejewska (Helena Opid, Helena Modjeska)
Born: 1840, Kraków, Poland
Died: 1909, California, USA
http://www.ocparks.com/modjeskahouse

Susan Sontag (Susan Rosenblatt)
Born: 1933, New York, NY, USA
Died: 2004, New York, NY, USA
http://www.susansontag.com

Hannah Arendt
Born: 1906, Linden, Germany
Died: 1975, USA

Christianity to feminism and to merge feminism with Christianity. Significantly, women do not appear as a poor and an oppressed group or even as a separate class anywhere in *Our God's Brother*. All of the poor encountered by Brother Adam are men. But there is a female character, the famous Polish actress Helena Modrzejewska (1840-1909) who actively participates in a discussion on the need for social reforms to help the poor. Wojtyła was definitely expressing his approval for the involvement of women in the area of social work. Including an actress as a character in his play was also a sign of some courage for a young Polish priest, especially since Helena Modrzejewska (Helena Modjeska) was not known to have followed Catholic rules with regard to marriage in her personal life. Helena Modrzejewska life in the United States provided a plot for Susan Sontag's novel *In America*, published in 2000. Susan Sontag, a Left-leaning bisexual American feminist, was inspired by Modrzejewska's unconventional lifestyle. (In Sontag's book she appears as Maryna Zalewska.) As many of America's Left-leaning feminists, Sontag was inspired by communist social experiments in Cuba and North Vietnam, but she later described communism as a form of fascism—something that was obvious much earlier to Karol Wojtyła, Hannah Arendt, a Jewish refugee from Nazi Germany and author of *The Origins of Totalitarianism* (1951), and many people who experienced living under communism. Toward the end of her life, Susan Sontag became a campaigner for human rights in communist countries.[55]

In the 1940s and the 1950s, Left-leaning Christians in Poland did not see women's problems as critical or in need of radical solutions. In fact, the double threat of atheistic communism and Soviet domination was so overwhelming in Poland after the end of World War II that middle class concerns with feminism, appearing in the West after the war, were more or less meaningless. Seeing that poverty can lead to communism and oppression, Wojtyła became a strong supporter of radical economic reforms to help the poor in order to avert the threat of workers abandoning Christianity and the Church. There was no particular concern among educated Catholic Poles for women as a separate group. Wojtyła was also not alone at that time in believing that capitalist societies in the West were incapable of dealing with the problems of poverty and workers' alienation. In addition to true Marxists, many Left-leaning West European and American intellectuals also saw capitalism as incapable of self-reform, much less providing solutions to the world's problems or helping to strengthen individual dignity, human rights and personal freedoms. In the West, feminism was associated with Marxism and with other progressive Left-wing ideologies. Catholics in Poland also saw the same link between feminism and Marxism, but the Catholic Church hierarchy also saw a link between feminism and capitalism—a link that many radical Western feminists ignore or strongly deny.

Another important historical male figure worthy of at least a brief mention in discussing Wojtyła's role models, is Saint Stanisław, the first bishop of Kraków who was killed in 1079 by the Polish King Bolesław the Bold (1030-1079). The figure of the martyred bishop became especially important to Wojtyła after he became the bishop of Kraków and was forced to oppose the attempts of the communist regime to eliminate religion from public life. King Bolesław ordered the killing of Saint Stanisław for opposing his treatment of his subjects but also for condemning his immoral sexual behavior. Legend has it that the king was courting another man's wife. The model of a religious leader willing to speak out strongly and courageously in defense of basic freedoms and moral values is the one that Wojtyła began to follow as Kraków's archbishop and became even more committed to as pope.

As it can be seen by analyzing Poland's history, Karol Wojtyła grew up in a country in which the tradition of priests and bishops serving as important authority figures and engaging in moral education and social action has been much stronger in recent centuries than in the West. Starting with Cardinal Sapieha, priests, bishops and cardinals who spoke out against immoral behavior and human rights violations were important male role models for Wojtyła. Also extremely important in Poland was the tradition of the educated elite attempting to bring appropriate solutions to the masses of poor and uneducated peasants and workers, unfortunately often imposing them from above without much participation from below. Democratic traditions in Poland among classes other than the nobility were not very strong. When democracy functioned between the wars, it was deeply flawed and limited to a much smaller group of people than in most of Western Europe. Based on Poland's historical experience with the liberal rule of the nobility, which ended in the loss of independence at the end of the 18th century, most Poles saw excessive democracy and individualism as serious threats to the country's sovereignty and prosperity. In fact, Polish writers and priests blamed too much freedom enjoyed by the rich aristocracy for the loss of Poland's independence. Wojtyła grew up in a nation where an educated man and an important religious figure was expected to be not only a moral authority and a guardian against excessive liberalism of the rich but also be able to offer practical solutions to the less educated and the less privileged.

After World War II, the ability of Catholic leaders to affect social policy under communism became, however, much more restricted than in the West. Ordinary Catholics in Poland under communism could not easily organize and meet to discuss such topics as birth control or ordination of women. In any case, these were not seen as pressing issues. While Wojtyła was growing up in Poland, there were very few alternative female figures or role models he could rely on that could bring him closer to the mentality of educated Western women. Those women who could offer an example of a feminist lifestyle were usually on the extreme Left of the political spectrum and were therefore unacceptable to the Church leadership.

Relationships with Girls during Student Years

Despite many journalistic rumors after his election as pope, to which I alluded earlier, Wojtyła was not known to be romantically involved with women during his youth. Mrs. Zofia Kotlarczyk, who together with her husband worked with Wojtyła on the underground theater productions when Poland was occupied by the Nazis, told Father Maliński in 1979 that Karol always kept aloof from girls. She said that he once complained to her and her husband that a relative of theirs who was staying in the house kept looking at him and made him feel awkward. At that time Mrs. Kotlarczyk already suspected that Karol wanted to be a priest. She described him as good looking and fun to be around. From time to time girls took fancy to him but, according to Mrs. Kotlarczyk, he never paid attention.

For some reason, Father Maliński put a lot of emphasis on this aspect of Wojtyła's early life. Józef Krasuski, a fellow worker at the Solvay plant in Kraków, where Wojtyła worked from 1940 until 1944, remembered that Wojtyła's fellow workers, not aware of his intention to become a priest, tried to introduce him to a girl, but the attempt failed. According to Mr. Krasucki, Wojtyła "didn't want to hear about it, was very indifferent [toward the proposals], and avoided the subject." At that point, his coworker began to suspect that Wojtyła had plans to become a priest.[56] One of Wojtyła's many biographers suggested that he may have been romantically involved with a girl during his youthful years and that the relationship may have been more than platonic. Somehow, this information reached John Paul II. He wrote to the author chastising him for making such an unfounded claim and pointed out that it is entirely possible to live one's life even in youthful years without committing the sin of fornication.[57] This may also explain his impatience with what he perceived as Western and particularly American, self-indulgence and obsession with sex.

During his student years before going to college, Wojtyła went to schools for boys only, but while in high school he had some contacts with female students from a neighboring school for girls, some of whom were members of the same amateur theater group. One of these girls defeated him in a reciting contest in Kraków organized by one of Poland's famous actresses. The already mentioned Halina Królikiewicz was the daughter of the boys' high school principal, who was also Karol's tutor in Greek. Karol and Halina appeared together in many theater productions, often playing leading roles and both trying to be better than the other, but it was a rivalry between friends that did not develop into a romantic attraction. After Karol lost to Halina in the acting competition, he told her, "you won this time," and gave her a bouquet of flowers. During the war, Halina Królikiewicz risked her life carrying Wojtyła's letters to and from Kraków to his friends in Wadowice, including letters to his drama teacher Mieczysław Kotlarczyk.[58] The first baptism performed by Wojtyła ten days after his ordination was the christening of Monika Kwiatkowska, the daughter of Halina Królikiewicz and her husband Tadeusz Kwiatkowski whom she had met at the university in Kraków.[59] Halina and Karol stayed in touch after the war, and after he became pope, he would invite her many times to Rome for regular reunions with his school friends.

One former high school girl student who knew Wojtyła remembers him as a rather lonely figure who did not avoid the company of girls, but at the same time did not seek it.[60] According to various accounts of his student life after high school, most of Wojtyła's close college friends were men. Zofia Żarnecka, a fellow student who knew Karol during his university years in Kraków, described him as a modest, calm, poorly dressed peasant boy without social graces, but who possessed character and was well liked and respected among his close friends.[61]

Although Wojtyła's parents were not Polish peasants, his behavior and dress may have betrayed his origins from a poor lower-middle class family in a small provincial town. Next to religion and nationality, social class distinctions were considered important in 1930s Poland. The same fellow student remembered seeing Wojtyła frequently in the company of a Jewish female student, Anka Weber, whom Karol tried to protect from verbal abuse by ultra-nationalist Polish students. According to Żarnecka and his Jewish boyhood friend Jerzy Kluger, Wojtyła was openly critical of the nationalist student groups which engaged in verbal and physical attacks on Jews and other minorities. At that time, he already knew that open anti-Semitism at the Jagiellonian University in Kraków forced Regina Beer (called Ginka), a Jewish girl from Wadowice two years older than Karol, to interrupt her medical studies. She and Karol knew each other well from living in the same building and acting together in plays. He was apparently closer to her than to other girls among his friends.

Because of his friendship with a Jewish girl, Karol must have developed a much more personal and much deeper understanding of the ugly effects of anti-Semitism. Ginka, a top science student, had difficulty getting admitted to the university after it had imposed a quota on the number of Jewish students. It was a period of growing anti-Semitism, manifesting itself not only in Poland. Similar quota systems to limit enrollment of Jewish students were also adopted in the 1920s by major universities in the United States, but discrimination against American Jews did not have broad public support or federal government sanction and was success-fully challenged in courts.[62] Wojtyła's friend eventually won admittance to the university with the help of a patriotic Polish headmistress of the girls' high school she had attended in Wadowice, but she left the university after a few months and made a wise decision to immigrate to Palestine a few years before Hitler's invasion of Poland.

In the years preceding the outbreak of World War II, many Jewish university students in Poland were forced by some of their fellow Polish students to sit on separate benches. If Jewish students resisted, nationalist thugs among the Polish students would beat them up with the professors and university administrators usually turning a blind eye. In the years prior to the outbreak of World War II, however, such incidents of racial and ethnic violence were again not unique to Poland. In Nazi Germany, much more severe acts of violence against Jews in the 1930s ultimately led to the Holocaust. Segments of the population in many other countries in Western and Eastern Europe also participated in such violence. In the United States, ethnic and racial hatred never reached similar levels in the 20th century, but lynching of African Americans did not stop until the 1940s. It was also not until the 1960s before schools in the American South were forced to drop their segregationist policies.[63] But while Western nations were resolving some of these serious issues of discrimination through the democratic process, including discrimination against women, the Poles of Karol's generation had to live under the Nazi occupation and later the communist dictatorship with no direct experience with democracy and political compromise.

When Ginka Beer made her decision to leave Poland and came to say goodbye to Karol and his father, Karol was described as being so upset that he could not say a word. He was silent, but his face grew very red. His father, also very upset, managed to say that not all Poles are anti-Semitic. Years later, Ginka Beer wrote that in Wadowice "There was only one family who never showed any racial hostility toward us, and that was Lolek (Lolek was Karol's nickname) and his dad."[64] That comment, while highly complementary toward the Wojtyła family, did not reflect very well on all the other Polish inhabitants of Wadowice. It also illustrates that nationalist issues and anti-Semitism, in addition to anti-communist and anti-liberal agitation, dominated Polish social and political life during the interwar period. At the time, feminism itself was not a major or even a minor concern, but conservative Poles including Catholic priests associated feminist ideas with Jews, Masons, communists and others whom they viewed as Poland's enemies.

While in his youth Wojtyła apparently felt somewhat uncomfortable around younger women, he developed strong friendships with older women. Mothers and grandmothers of his student friends in Kraków served as mother figures for young Wojtyła. Among several women who took care of him during the Nazi occupation was the mother of Juliusz Kydryński, his close friend and a member of the underground theater group in Kraków. Karol called Juliusz's mother, Aleksandra Kydryńska, "Mom." Juliusz Kydryński also introduced Karol to Mrs. Irena Szkocka, an older schoolteacher and a typical middle class patriotic Polish woman who also took great interest in Karol's welfare. When he met Mrs. Szkocka during World War II, she was already in her sixties and showered him with grandmotherly affection. He in turn called her "Grandma" and became an almost daily visitor at the Szkockis' home. A neighbor described Mrs. Szkocka and her husband Leon Szkocki as a deeply patriotic couple, sensitive to the needs of others and sharing with Wojtyła their love of Romantic Polish poetry.[65] Mrs. Szkocka wrote two short stories, one of which was published, aimed at popularizing the works of two Romantic poets, Juliusz Słowacki and Cyprian Norwid. Their poems were frequently read and discussed in the Szkockis' home. She found in Karol someone who shared her deep interest in Polish poetry and an eager listener. The two had discussions on Polish cultural life and exchanged letters on topics ranging from literature to religion. The Szkockis did not have a son, which may explain why Mrs. Szkocka took a particular interest in the welfare of a poor, motherless young man. Of their four daughters, two had died, leaving her and her husband greatly affected by their loss.

As a middle class educated Polish woman, it was expected of Mrs. Szkocka to help young men who were making sacrifices for their country or facing other difficulties. Her patriotic activities during World War I took the form of opening her home and providing assistance to Polish soldiers fighting for Poland's independence. Like Karol Wojtyła, these young soldiers also saw her as a substitute "mother" and wrote moving letters to her from the front. Mrs. Szkocka was one of the women who took care of

Karol during the war when he temporarily lost consciousness after being struck by a German truck and had to spend several weeks in bed after leaving the hospital. She constantly worried about his health and tried to make sure that he was properly fed. She also may have saved his life when, toward the end of the war, the Nazis began to arrest large numbers of young Polish men on the streets of Kraków. As Nazi reprisals intensified, Wojtyła and other young Polish men who were studying to become priests at the underground seminary but continued to work and lead normal lives, were asked by their mentor, Cardinal Adam Sapieha, to hide at his residence in Kraków. To help Karol safely reach the archbishop's palace, Mrs. Szkocka served as his spy, walking ahead of him so that she could warn him about the movements of German police and soldiers. In bringing Wojtyła safely to the seminary, she was assisted by a priest, Father Mikołaj Kuczkowski.[66] According to Father Maliński, several other older Polish women helped other young seminarians including himself to walk safely to their destination by warning them about the movements of Nazi patrols.[67] It was relatively safer for Polish women than for Polish men to be walking in the streets, but it was never entirely safe. Polish women were willing, however, to take the risk of arrest and possibly even death so that they could help young men avoid being sent to Nazi concentration camps.

Polish women also risked imprisonment and possibly their lives by delivering food from the countryside to the cities in violation of strict Nazi restrictions. The Nazis limited the amount of food that Poles could legally buy, not only because Poland was a conquered nation, but also because they considered Poles racially inferior. Even harsher restrictions were imposed on selling food to Jews. Without women-smugglers and those willing to engage in black market trade, Poles living in cities   risked death from starvation. A Polish underground government leader, Stefan Korboński (1901-1989), marveled on how Polish women kept the population alive by managing to move "tons of foodstuffs in little bags sewn into their undershirts and blouses." Never before, Korboński related, had he seen "such over-sized busts as in Poland."[68]

Cooperation of Polish men and women during the Nazi occupation and later during the communist rule helped to promote a spirit of gender solidarity that may be difficult to understand in Western societies where gender relations are now characterized more by labor market competition than mutual assistance. Obviously, John Paul II preferred the latter to the former and worked hard to convince the West that the solidarity between men and women he experienced in Poland was a better way of managing gender relations. In a tragic and costly way, the Nazi occupation of Poland may have contributed to greater independence for Polish women, especially for those women who lost their husbands and fathers and had to assume full responsibility for themselves and their families. Their sacrifices gained them additional respect, which John Paul II saw as a proof of emancipation when he made comments suggesting that Polish women may have advanced further than Western women in the way they are perceived by society.

Another middle class Polish woman, who became Wojtyła's close friend, may have also helped him survive the Nazi occupation. Mrs. Jadwiga Lewaj, an older woman who was tutoring Wojtyła in French, used her contacts to get young Karol a job at the Solvay chemical factory in Borek Fałęcki near Kraków. This job, considered by the Nazis to be essential for the war effort, offered some protection against arbitrary arrest on the street and the threat of being sent to Germany to do forced labor. Those who worked at the plant carried a special identification document that could be shown to German patrols to avoid detention. Wojtyła worked there as a laborer during the war for four years, from 1940 until he became a full-time seminary student in 1944.

Wojtyła's English teachers were also women, Jadwiga Horodyska and Marta Jodko.[69] Wojtyła started learning English in adulthood and therefore he did not master it as fully as German and French. Even though he understood English and later spoke it quite well, his poorer comprehension of English may have prevented him from developing a deeper understanding of some of the seminal English and American writings on democracy and feminism. He may have read some of these texts only in Polish or French translation. It is usually true that fluency in a foreign language acquired early in life and consistent contacts and communication with people who speak it are necessary for the development of a deeper understanding of their culture and their way of thinking. Wojtyła's understanding of the Anglo-Saxon and American traditions of liberalism and pragmatism extending to tolerance of diverse views even on basic moral issues was rather weak judging by some of his statements about the United States and the West. He was much more familiar with French liberalism and Marxism. His knowledge of French and German was far better than his knowledge of English.

Priest and Young Women

Wojtyła's first extensive contacts with women, most of them very young, came after the war and after his seminary and university studies. Only after he became a priest, he befriended a great number of Polish university students, both male and female, who apparently had a significant influence on his thinking about women. At a minimum, they seemed to have been responsible for inspiring another lifetime preoccupation—interest in all aspects of human love and sex. Some of the students who were under his pastoral care recalled the young priest holding a retreat in 1951 on the subject of love for students at St. Anne's Church in Kraków. Another one of Wojtyła's retreats, in 1954, was devoted to women's vocation in life.

Wojtyła seemed to have learned a lot from his students about life and he gave them credit for helping him to write his first major book *Love and Responsibility*, which centered on love, marriage and sex. The book was largely based on individual and group discussions with students who shared their problems and questions during a great number of gatherings and hiking trips throughout Poland.[70] Between 1952 and 1978, there were nearly a hundred such excursions with students and his older friends, both male and female. He credited his circle of young men and women for introducing him to what he described as "the contemporary style of life." In 1953 alone, Wojtyła went on 11 separate trips, lasting from one day to more than two weeks of continuous, daily contact with young men and women.[71] Almost all such hiking, skiing, and kayaking expeditions included regular prayers followed by extensive discussions about love and relationships. Young women seemed to have been particularly impressed by their one-on-one conversations with Wojtyła. His last hiking trip in Poland with a group of former students and their children took place in July 1978, a few weeks before his election to the papacy.[72]

Danuta Rybicka, one of the women with whom Wojtyła spent time as a young parish priest, remembered how in April 1952 he took five female students on an overnight excursion trip to Poland's mountain resort Zakopane. Male students, who were expected to go on the trip, did not come because they were studying for exams and only five young women showed up Saturday night at the train station in Kraków. It would have been very unusual for a Catholic priest at that time to travel in the company of only young women. At first, Wojtyła suggested that the trip be called off, but seeing how disappointed the women were, he agreed to go forward with the excursion. In any case, the women had no place to sleep, since it was already late and the doors to their dormitory, which was run by nuns, would have been locked.[73] Wojtyła was wearing civilian clothes and the women got his permission to call him "uncle" in order not to shock other travelers or attract the attention of the communist police. One of the participants on that trip described Wojtyła's decision to get on a train with a group of five women as "almost insane" and certainly very courageous for those times.[74]

Wojtyła made sure, however, that nothing morally objectionable went on during these trips and apparently under his supervision nothing ever did. He took good care of his students, insisting that they get nine hours of sleep each night while he himself got up very early to pray. When a group traveling with Wojtyła included both male and female students, they always slept on the opposite sides of a room.[75]

The students who went on hiking trips with Father Karol started to call themselves *Rodzinka* (*Little Family*).[76] The name was more than appropriate, since many of the participants eventually married other students in the *Rodzinka* group. Their romantic attachments developed during these trips. Concerns they expressed to Wojtyła in private conversations and open discussions, convinced him of the need to provide his students with pre-marital counseling, both religious and practical. He performed many of their marriages himself and baptized their children. He often visited the young families at their homes and showed keen interest in their spiritual and material well-being. His deep commitment to the family and concern with such issues as selfless love, pre-marital counseling, family size, use of contraceptives and natural birth control date back to his involvement with his "Little Family" in the late 1940s and the early 1950s.

It was also known at the time that some of Wojtyła's superiors did not look favorably on his co-educational activities involving young female students. One of Wojtyła's students, who spoke about his mentor with Archbishop Eugeniusz Baziak (1890-1962) who was then in charge of the Kraków Archdiocese, thought that the archbishop was not greatly impressed with Wojtyła's status as a scholar-priest associating with young students. There were rumors among priests that Wojtyła's lectures for students on love, family life, sex and religion were heretical and would soon be terminated along with his university career.[77] That did not happen, although his activities as a marriage advisor on issues of love and sex were quite unusual for a Catholic priest in Poland at that time.

While carefully avoiding any overt political activities, Wojtyła was also taking various risks on behalf of his students vis-à-vis the communist regime. If he had been exposed as a Catholic priest wearing civilian clothes and traveling alone with women, it could have caused a major scandal among his superiors, other priests and conservative lay Catholics. There could have also been unpleasant consequences for Wojtyła from the communist authorities. While such Church-sponsored trips were not technically illegal in communist-ruled Poland, a Catholic priest who organized them would open himself, if found out, to possible harassment and blackmail from the police. According to Father Tadeusz Isakowicz-Zaleski, a Catholic priest who published a book about this subject, about 10 percent of Polish priests had succumbed to such blackmail and served as communist secret police informants. Some of them were spying on other priests and their potential anti-communist activities, but many were reluctant collaborators forced into this role by intimidation.

Before the young women who traveled alone with Father Karol to Zakopane started to address him as "uncle," some students belonging to his group called him *Sadok*, which is the name of the hero of a popular Polish novel about a pious and ascetic young priest. Some of the students did not even know Wojtyła's real name. During the early 1950s in communist-ruled Poland, it was safer not to disclose one's true name out of fear that activities and meetings unsanctioned by the authorities, even as innocent as choir practice, could lead to reprisals against both priests and students.[78] Wojtyła was also taking other risks during his hiking trips with groups of university students. He would frequently celebrate a holy Mass for them, even at such unusual and dangerous locations as a military guardhouse near Poland's border with Czechoslovakia, where his group once found refuge from the rain. The communists purposely tried to instill in the population fear of the authorities and hostility toward alleged Western spies or people trying to escape to the West. In addition to their own paranoia, they were driven by the real fear that Poles would try to illegally cross the border to escape to the West from the communist paradise. Consequently, the communist regime deployed many resources for the purpose of guarding the border areas. Celebrating Mass in a military facility near the border could have been very risky for both the students and the soldiers who allowed them to sleep in the attic. The soldiers may have not been aware that the students were praying and participating in a Mass or, if they knew, they chose to ignore it. Many of them were conscripts who came from Catholic families and were themselves prevented from attending Mass while on duty. Religious ceremonies in churches were tolerated during the communist period, but celebrating Mass outside of church buildings often lead to police harassment. One of the students who went on hiking trips remembered that Wojtyła had an unpleasant encounter with the authorities for allowing his group to spend a night in the border-zone in the Tatra Mountains that was off-limits to civilians during the hours of darkness.[79]

By organizing trips which included both boys and girls, Wojtyła opened himself up to criticism from other priests as well as his superiors that he might be facilitating sinful encounters between the two sexes. Criticism must have been strong enough to encourage Wojtyła to publish a letter in a Church periodical, in which he defended the practice of allowing young students of both sexes to go together on hiking trips under the supervision of a priest. One of the controversial issues was the way that boys and girls would dress during these trips. Wojtyła argued that uniforms are always appropriate for each sporting activity, including swimming, but otherwise young students and particularly girls must dress modestly. Making a comment that would outrage many Western feminists, Wojtyła stated in his letter that Christ's words about lusting in one's heart "apply more to women than to men: women must take care so that they do not become an object of men's desire." He added, however, that by bringing young men and women together on these trips women can get a better idea whether they can trust their partners.[80]

In his book, *Love and Responsibility*, published a few years later, Wojtyła showed more sophistication by observing that "very often a woman does not regard a particular way of dressing as shameless...although some men, or indeed many men, may find it so."[81] But in his 1957 letter to a religious magazine, he seemed to put nearly all responsibility for avoiding sexual temptation on women. Wojtyła claimed that his motivation was to protect women from being deceived by unscrupulous men. He explained that because of their much stronger sex drive, men are more likely to take advantage of the feelings of young women without being totally committed to the relationship. Wojtyła suggested that girls should first learn the extent of their partner's sincerity and argued that hiking trips, during which both boys and girls can experience religion more intensely, can be a good test of male honesty. He also stated that films and pictures in magazines can be much more "dangerous" than boys and girls hiking together under the supervision of a priest.[82]

Wojtyła's comments in the article, particularly that women are expected to wear modest clothing, may seem sexist by today's Western standards, but they must be viewed in the context of very strict attitudes toward sexuality among devout Catholics in 1950s Poland. Moral standards for men and women at that time were also quite different, with men enjoying much greater freedom in terms of behavior and dress. When one of the male students suggested that men and women should not be judged differently in terms of standards for sexual behavior, Wojtyła agreed that as long as such behavior is immoral there is no equality in sin. He also made it quite clear to his young friends that he expected boys to show total respect and honesty in their dealings with girls. One of his male students recalled how Wojtyła ordered him to go on an arranged date in order to apologize to a girl with whom he had previously flirted while having no serious intentions of developing a relationship that might lead to marriage.[83]

When Wojtyła became pope, his progressive views on female dress code were too much for some conservative Catholics. Their Tradition in Action web site criticized his meeting with "bare-breasted native women" in Papua New Guinea and published several pictures designed to show his inappropriate behavior.

Tradition in Action

http://www.traditioninaction.org/RevolutionPhotos/A016rcNursingWoman.htm

By the moral standards in 1950s Poland, Wojtyła could only be described as a radical progressive, particularly for a Catholic priest. He argued for example against puritanism and prudery in sexual matters—attitudes which were common among the older and conservative Polish Catholics. But in his usual way, he tried to strike a balance between the views and preferences of younger people, including his students, and the long-established social norms favored by the majority of older priests and lay Catholics. In *Love and Responsibility*, he concluded that "there is nothing immodest about the use of a bathing costume at a bathing place," but wearing the same costume while walking on the street would be "contrary to the dictates of modesty."[84] There were, however, clear limits to the application of a more liberal dress code. Wojtyła went swimming early in the morning when his young companions were still sleeping. A woman who went on hiking and kayaking trips with Wojtyła also observed that students, who were with him, wore swimming suits while in the water, but on shore they put on tops or t-shirts following the example set by their priest.[85]

During student trips supervised by Wojtyła, boys were usually put in charge of various sporting activities. On kayaking trips, a male student in charge of the expedition was sometimes referred to as "admiral" or "captain," while girls were usually called *majtki*.

Majtki is a Polish word that in its plural form can mean either "deck help" or women's "panties." According to Father Maliński, most of the kayak captains were men. Boys sat in the back of the kayak and steered, while *majtki*, mostly girls, sat in front.[86] Male students in Wojtyła's group had all the preconceived ideas about girls typical for Polish men of that generation. On one occasion they examined Danuta Ciesielska's backpack that appeared to them to be too heavy for a girl. As a student of physical education, Danuta preferred to carry a big backpack, just like the boys. She admitted that as a sportswoman she may have not felt "one hundred percent female." On another occasion, one of the boys secretly removed some of the heavy items from a girl's backpack to make it easier to carry. Danuta Ciesielska also described how her future husband, Jerzy, who was in charge of the group, asked her to give up wearing shorts insisting that shorts were inappropriate for girls. Danuta Ciesielska complained that for two weeks she had to wear heavy wool skirts during hot weather, while other girls were allowed to wear shorts.[87]

But another female student Danuta Rybicka remembered Jerzy Ciesielski arguing on a different occasion that women on hiking trips should wear shorts rather than skirts. This may have been after Wojtyła intervened and made his own views known to the group. According to Danuta Rybicka, initially the girls themselves refused to wear shorts fearing that it would be disrespectful and indecent in the presence of a priest. Wojtyła listened to their disagreements over the issue of female clothing for two days without saying a word. When finally asked to express his opinion, he responded that everything depends on the circumstances and the intentions of those who wear such clothing. Danuta Rybicka remembered that Wojtyła never gave his students direct instructions to do or not to do something but rather tried to analyze the issues. She saw him as teaching the students how to take responsibility for making decisions and showing respect for their individual free will.[88] This was one side of his personality that was entirely lost on his feminist critics, although once he became pope, he apparently felt that he was no longer able to suggest proper behavior but had to be direct, specific, and — in his opinion — uncompromising on many issues.

Danuta Ciesielska, who is now retired from her job as a physical education teacher and lives in Kraków, confirmed to me that Wojtyła had indeed very close fatherly-like relationships with young women and men and held with them open and honest discussions on many sensitive subjects. She also told me that at least some of the girls in their group strongly argued with Wojtyła about the role of women in the Catholic Church, questioning him about such subjects as the ban on ordination of women to priesthood. She herself would listen but rarely participated in these discussions and has never questioned the Church's teachings on women-priests and other issues. She also told me that all the male participants in the group were members of the Polish Boy Scouts movement and treated young girls and women with great respect. Danuta Ciesielska told me that the girls would indeed do all the cooking but pointed out that the boys would always wash dishes after each meal and would do all the heavy jobs in setting up the camp. She recalled that there was always one day during each trip, which they humorously called the "Day of the Tourist," when all the traditional roles would reverse. The group would rest and the boys would prepare meals. She admitted that these meals were not as elaborate and tasty as the ones prepared by girls. While some members of the group discussed with Wojtyła the topic of discrimination against women, this was not, according to Danuta Ciesielska, anywhere near the top of their concerns. She also pointed out that it was the women in the group rather than the men who in later years were more likely to write and talk about their encounters with Karol Wojtyła.[89]

By bringing boys and girls together, Wojtyła tried to break down some of the traditional barriers that existed between the sexes in post-World War II Poland. Most activities sponsored by the Church at that time were done in gender-segregated groups. One of his male students remembers Wojtyła integrating a group of female choir singers into an all-male church choir. This move initially upset the boys, but soon they realized that the girls rehearsed more, were better singers and contributed to the success of the combined choir. Without stating it outright, Wojtyła showed the boys that girls could be just as good, if not better singers, if both groups cooperated. Eventually, male and female choir members became close friends and were grateful to Wojtyła for bringing them together.[90]

Unlike many other Polish priests at that time, Wojtyła was willing to include both boys and girls in the same activities, spent a lot of time with young women and according to all accounts, treated female students with great respect and sensitivity. He did not, however, believe then, nor did he ever, in total equality of roles and opportunities for men and women. He saw women as being in many respects different from men and generally agreed with the cultural and moral norms of Poland at the time, although he interpreted them more liberally than most other Polish priests. The young women who knew Wojtyła in the 1950s remember him as a great friend to whom they could turn for advice and for help. He spent countless hours discussing their personal problems, visited their family homes, exchanged long letters, loaned them money, invited them on hiking trips, introduced them to young men, participated in their name's day parties and other celebrations, offered pre-marital counseling, blessed their marriages, and baptized their children. Female students whom he got to know closely as a young priest in Poland remained his loyal friends for life. They are also the strongest defenders of his approach to women's rights and his view of women's role in the Catholic Church and society.

One of Wojtyła's female students Maria Tarnowska remembered that at the age of seventeen she found in her "uncle" not only a spiritual father but also a substitute father who helped her deal with her family problems. She described Wojtyła as an ideal friend to a young person, as someone who had: "ability to listen, boundless patience, goodness and unbelievable gentleness. Each advice, comment, even criticism was presented by him in a form of a gentle, absolutely non-binding proposal, giving me complete freedom to respond and to make a choice." Maria Tarnowska was impressed by Wojtyła's ability to offer clear advice while at the same time respecting his students' personal freedom and dignity.[91] Danuta Ciesielska talked of his ability to connect with young married couples and convey such interest and concern that it was as if their marriage was the only thing in the world that mattered to him.[92] She realized later that there were many such married couples in Wojtyła's life. Danuta Ciesielska described Wojtyła as extremely careful in trying to influence the behavior of his students by offering proposals rather than giving orders. Many years later she asked him why he had not been more demanding. He

> **The John Paul II Catholic University of Lublin (KUL)**
> http://www.kul.lublin.pl/uk/

told her that he was in fact a very demanding person but wanted to respect other people's right to make a free choice.

One of his female students at the Catholic University in Lublin (KUL) Dr. Maria Braun-Gałkowska described Wojtyła's relationship with his students as one based on friendship and willingness not only to hold discussions with them but also to participate in their leisure activities despite his busy schedule. When he came to one of their parties after a long trip, she asked him whether this was not a waste of time. He was a little surprised by her question, but answered that he simply came to be with them. According to Dr. Braun-Gałkowska, the students felt loved by Wojtyła and each one may have thought that he or she was loved the most.[93]

Sister Klawera Wolska, who worked in a shelter for homeless girls and troubled youth while Wojtyła was the Archbishop of

Kraków, described how he made everyone feel loved regardless of who they were or what kind of serious moral transgressions they might have committed. According to Sister Klawera, he would never treat any matter brought up by the young women and men at the shelter as trivial or unimportant. The sister described how during one of the meetings with Wojtyła at the shelter, the cardinal became visibly moved when a young girl named Rose, who did not know her mother, spontaneously started to sing the Italian song "Mama." Wojtyła also showed a special interest in young couples who met and married while under the care of the sisters and tried to meet with them regularly. During such meetings, he played with their children and even allowed them to play with the special hat he wore as cardinal.[94]

Female students who knew Wojtyła as a young priest in Poland after the war confirmed that he felt comfortable in the company of young women. After the trip to Zakopane with a group of women he continued such excursions, for example, taking a group of female students from the Catholic University in Lublin (KUL) on a hiking trip which included religious studies. He would treat his female students affectionately, kissing not only boys but also girls on their foreheads — thus shocking some of the older Poles. Wojtyła also showed even very young women a great deal of old-fashioned respect. Even when he became a bishop, he would insist that young female students enter the room before him. At the request of the mother superior of the local monastery, every month he would also have special study sessions for nuns enrolled at the Lublin University. One such series of lectures for nuns dealt with the subject of life in chastity. As one of the nuns who had attended these lectures explained, Wojtyła described chastity only in general terms as "exclusive betrothal love of Christ."[95]

In 1957, Wojtyła led a weeklong religious course for women titled "Chastity of the Heart and Celibacy in the Scientific Analysis."[96] While in Kraków, his encounters were mostly with younger students. As a professor of theology and ethics at the

Catholic University in Lublin (KUL), Wojtyła, probably for the first time in his life, had frequent contact with slightly older and more mature women scholars. By all available accounts, Wojtyła was very much liked by all of his students, both male and female, and was particularly kind and helpful toward women. Sister Karolina Kasperkiewicz was the author of the first doctoral thesis he sponsored at the Catholic University in Lublin (KUL). The thesis' title was: "Friendship and Its Place and Role in the Aristotelian Ethical System."[97] After Dr. Kasperkiewicz successfully defended her thesis in 1958, Wojtyła tried to help her get a teaching position at the university. The attempt failed when the older priests-professors objected to a nun teaching classes that could also be attended by priests. It would not have been Wojtyła's style to resign in protest over such a flagrant case of discrimination or to make of it a public issue — he continued his successful academic career at the university — but Wojtyła encouraged Sister Karolina to pursue her scholarly work while she was assigned to other duties. She published another book on ethics in 1983 and for 20 years worked with Wojtyła on various projects in his archdiocese.

Dr. Kasperkiewicz described Wojtyła as a "man of goodness, kindness, simplicity and rare self-critical attitude."[98] He did not get angry when she came late for her first lecture in his class but instead gave her an encouraging smile. He was by her account a demanding but compassionate professor. At her master's exam, Wojtyła asked Sister Karolina to describe both differences and similarities between the moral norm of Saint Thomas Aquinas and Kant's categorical imperative. At first, she thought it was a difficult question but quickly managed to give a satisfactory answer. When she met Wojtyła in the corridor after the exam, he said to her: "Sister Karolina, forgive me, I don't know why such a difficult question came to my mind. I noticed it too late. But the whole time I was praying that Sister would answer it well; and that's what happened."[99] On another occasion, he gave her lecture notes to study, which she then shared with other students. The sister also remembers that he once asked his students to honestly tell him if there was anything they disliked about him, so that he could improve his teaching methods.

Karol Wojtyła was also responsible for launching the academic career of Sister Zofia Zdybicka, the first nun appointed as a professor at the Catholic University in Lublin (KUL) at the time when nuns teaching priests at a Catholic university were unheard of in Poland. Sister Zofia's religious superior in the Ursuline Order was not in favor of her teaching at the university, and she also had doubts whether an academic career was a proper choice for a nun. She consulted Wojtyła who told her that he did not share her doubts. He wrote a letter to Sister Zofia's superior and was able to convince her that scholarly work by a woman requires both humility and sacrifices and should be seen as a service to humankind. Unlike his earlier efforts on behalf of Sister Karolina, in this case he was successful. With assistance from Wojtyła, Zofia Zdybicka became the first nun to be appointed to a professorship at KUL.[100] Of course, as a promising young scholar, she would not have had such problems in obtaining an academic position if she were an ordained priest. Wojtyła also helped another nun to win approval for pursuing an academic career, even though he did not know her personally. Asked by another male professor and his close friend Father Tadeusz Styczeń (b. 1931), Wojtyła wrote a letter to the head of a religious order on behalf of Sister Teresa Wojtarowicz. In this case, her mother superior immediately agreed and proudly showed Wojtyła's letter while visiting various

---

Zofia (Maria Józefa) Zdybicka

Born: 1928, Kraśnik, Poland

Quotes: "Motherhood is a great gift and vocation for most women."

"Some Polish women, but fortunately not too many, are embracing Western-style feminism."

http://www.sjk.pl/index.php
http://www.kul.lublin.pl

houses of her order in Poland.[101]

In her description of Wojtyła's dealings with students at KUL, Professor Zofia Zdybicka also wrote how important confession was in the lives of Polish Catholics in the 1950s and how successful Wojtyła was as a spiritual advisor. When a fiancé of one of her female acquaintances was beset with moral and religious doubts and refused to go to confession prior to their wedding, she needed to find a "good priest" and turned for help to her professor. At her request, Wojtyła had a conversation with the young man and in just one conversation was able to persuade him to confess his sins. The young man and Wojtyła developed a friendship which lasted many years. Professor Zdybicka wrote that from that moment she felt a special link with Wojtyła.[102] His later attempts as pope to convince American and West European Catholics to go to confession proved, however, unsuccessful.

As someone who valued personal friendships, Wojtyła tried to keep in touch with his female students, expressed sincere interest in their personal lives and wrote letters to them requesting meetings if he had not heard from them in a long time. One of Wojtyła's students, Zofia Abramowicz-Stachura, who died in 1996, remembered how Wojtyła tried to find her when she was assigned to work in Mszana Dolna, a small town south of Kraków, where she felt isolated and lonely. He wrote to her parents asking that she get in touch with him so that he would know how she was doing. After a meeting with Zofia and a group of other former students in Kraków when Wojtyła was already a bishop, he offered to drive her back to Mszana Dolna, about 30 miles out of his way, so that she would not be late for work. He was aware that Zofia was coping with various personal problems and dilemmas, including a decision about her marriage. When he visited her parish, he spent over an hour talking with her, while other people including priests who also wanted to see him, had to wait.[103] Zofia Abramowicz-Stachura described Wojtyła as a priest who sought the company of young people and found it extremely easy to establish a close rapport. He was interested in everything that concerned their lives, studies, work, and their families. For Zofia, as well as other students, "uncle" was always pleasant, often playful and humorous. At hiking camps and other informal occasions, his students could not contain their laughter while listening to his monologues or conversations. He fascinated them and they felt very close to him, but according to Zofia Abramowicz-Stachura, he always kept a very discrete, almost unnoticeable distance.[104]

Young university students may have become for Wojtyła a second family to the one he had lost when he was a child and a young adult. As the group got bigger, the name changed from *Rodzinka* (The Little Family) to *Środowisko* (The Community). In his 1997 letter to *Środowisko*, John Paul II wrote that his contacts with young people allowed him to feel young again and to experience the thrill of participating in sporting and hiking activities— something he had not been able to do as a young man because of the war. It became plain, however, that in addition to hiking and other sporting activities, Wojtyła was deeply interested in the spiritual lives of his young friends, and particularly in their problems with love and personal relationships. In his letter, John Paul II stressed that marriage and preparation for marriage and family life were the most important goals of most members of the group.[105] One of the women remembered that Wojtyła brought a manuscript of his book *Love and Responsibility* to a summer camp for students and distributed sections of it to solicit their views. After they had a chance to read his manuscript, the students, sitting on the grassy edge of a lake, had a discussion on love, sexuality and marriage.[106] Wojtyła also had countless conversations with individual students, including many women who shared with him their most intimate problems.

Wojtyła's conversations about love and marriage were not limited to his encounters with students during holiday trips. The topic fascinated him so much that he incorporated it into his lectures as a professor at KUL. Sister Zofia Zdybicka remembers that love, described as the most important human act, was a frequent topic in Wojtyła's formal university lectures. According to Professor Zdybicka, Wojtyła presented the subject not only in theoretical terms. He spoke about love with great inner conviction but always in a calm and reflective manner. At the time, the young sister thought that only someone truly capable of great love could talk about it in such a convincing way. Professor Zdybicka also observed the idealism of Wojtyła's definition of love but considered it quite normal. As a young student, she was impressed with Wojtyła's argument that human love requires a person to make a gift of himself or herself to another person to the point of being willing to give up one's own life — a theme he would expand on in his later writings.

Professor Zdybicka's recollection of Wojtyła's line of reasoning about love may shed some light on the understanding of his position in cases when a woman is faced with a choice between saving her own life or the life of her unborn child. According to Professor Zdybicka, Wojtyła told his young students that in wartime, men show the willingness to give up their own lives to defend the lives and freedom of others. Similarly, a mother should be willing to sacrifice her own life if the life of her unborn child is at stake.[107] Another former female student who knew Wojtyła in the 1950s remembers him telling young university students a similar story about a mother who had sacrificed her life to save her child. In 1954, Wojtyła celebrated a mass in St. Florian's Church in Kraków on the occasion of one of the student's name's day. After the mass, a little girl approached Wojtyła and he patted her on the head. He told the students that her mother, who worked as a domestic helper for a convent and was married to a church janitor, became pregnant and was told by doctors that she needed an abortion to save her own life. The woman, who was physically handicapped, refused to get an abortion and told her husband that in case of her death he should marry her girlfriend, who was also working for the nuns. As predicted by doctors, the woman died, but her child was saved. Her husband married her girlfriend and since they had no children of their own, the girl was a great joy for her stepmother. Wojtyła finished his story by telling the students that "this girl is alive thanks to the heroism of her mother." According to Marta Podlaska, the Polish students were greatly moved by Wojtyła's story.[108]

The analogy between soldiers and mothers risking their lives for others may seem strange to Western liberal feminists, but for Wojtyła it was not without some historical foundation. He himself did not participate in the underground armed struggle during the Nazi occupation, but countless other young Polish men of his generation, as well as thousands of women, were killed in combat or suffered torture and execution for their underground resistance to the occupation. At the time, Wojtyła was somewhat safer from Nazi reprisals thanks to finding work in a factory producing materials for the German war effort. It is more than likely that because of that he felt a duty to honor those who had sacrificed their lives during the war. He had to justify in his mind his choice of non-violent resistance through the underground theater and enrollment in a clandestine seminary—acts which also carried significant risk but not the immediate threat of death faced by the young soldiers of the underground army. Wojtyła's justification for his choice of non-violent resistance to the Nazis was that Christianity imposes on each person an obligation to protect life even under the most dramatic circumstances. The memory of the young Poles of his generation who died fighting for their country must have placed a tremendous burden on Wojtyła to prove to the world that all human life should and must be protected in a non-violent way whenever possible. Judging by his frequent references to the genocide of World War II, his campaigns against abortion and euthanasia, as well as his strong anti-war position—all this seemed directly or indirectly related to his wartime experiences.

There is little doubt that Wojtyła believed that a woman who truly loves her unborn child should be willing to sacrifice her own life to save her child if such a choice has to be made. He made this argument to his students in Lublin on many occasions. Knowing Wojtyła's personal history and his views on the sanctity of life, we can assume that this kind of sacrifice by a mother would have to be voluntary. We do not know whether Wojtyła discussed the woman's responsibilities toward the rest of her family, including her husband. According to Professor Zdybicka, Wojtyła was simply trying to make a point to priests and nuns listening to his lecture about how much they should be ready to sacrifice for others in order to meet the ultimate objective of unselfish love.

Sister Zofia Zdybicka knew Wojtyła since 1956 when she became one of his students at KUL. She talked to him frequently in Lublin and Warsaw when he was still in Poland and he would invite her to the Vatican at least once or twice a year throughout his papacy. She told me that students at KUL were amazed by Wojtyła's kindness, openness and hard work. They were also impressed that he delivered his lectures without any notes. According to Sister Zofia Zdybicka, the students could not believe their ears when he told them that he was writing a book about love (*Love and Responsibility*) and wondered from where he could have gotten so much knowledge about this subject. Personally, the sister was most impressed seeing Wojtyła frequently immersed in prayer. She describes him as a great philosopher, thinker, lover of mankind and a person of great holiness. It was his great love of every individual which, according to Professor Zdybicka, would prevent him from ever agreeing that abortion should be tolerated.

Professor Zdybicka also told me that during one of her visits to the Vatican in the early 1980s, John Paul II surprised her with a question "whether there was feminism in Poland." She told him that fortunately Polish women did not want feminism as it was developing in the West. She also assured him that based on her own observations of Western societies, (She spent several months at Yale University in 1977/1978 and visited a number of West European countries.) women in Poland enjoyed much greater respect than women in the West. John Paul II agreed with this assessment. It was during that conversation that John Paul II assured her of his enormous love and respect for women and seemed greatly pained that some people, particularly in the West, did not understand his philosophy of love and gender relations.

Professor Zdybicka told me that feminism was not an important issue for KUL students in the 1950s. She did not recall any discussions among students about women-priests and said that even now Polish women have no desire to enter priesthood. She said that this is simply not part of Polish tradition. She gave me the example of Sister Faustyna Kowalska, a woman with barely elementary school education who held no important positions in the Church of any kind—as being now far better known and respected throughout the world than any ordained priest with the possible exception of the pope. She completely agrees with John Paul II that sainthood, whether it is officially recognized or not, is incomparably more important than any official Church position. She said that even though she did have an academic career, now that she is mostly retired from university life her academic titles do not seem to her very significant. She did acknowledge that some Polish women, but fortunately not too many, are now embracing Western-style feminism. Just like John Paul II, she blamed this on past discrimination and a wrong understanding of the different roles of men and women. Professor Zdybicka fully shares John Paul II's view that motherhood is a great gift and vocation for most women, but she has no problem with women who for various reasons may want to pursue a single life, as long as it is filled with love and service to others.[109] Most Western feminists would find such attitudes difficult to accept.

Because of their long and unique relationship, the closest one can get to understanding John Paul II's views about women and feminism may be through Professor Zdybicka's comments and articles. They are more direct and more revealing than Wojtyła's own writings on this topic while still fully reflecting his cultural conditioning, perceptions and conclusions. Professor Zdybicka is in complete agreement with John Paul II that there are different forms of feminism, some of which are worthy of praise and support while others are highly dangerous and harmful for women and society. Good feminism, which she described as "true" or "authentic," promotes women's desire for recognizing their dignity and equal rights while always protecting woman's vocation as a wife and mother and strengthening family values. Zdybicka speaks approvingly of women who have fought for their right to equal treatment. She and John Paul II believed that women should be able to receive the same education as men, not only to be able to enter the workforce on equal terms but also to increase their participation in economic, social, political and religious life. What they both strongly objected to was feminism which Professor Zdybicka describes as "false feminism" deriving from "extreme liberalism, socialism, Marxism, psychological theories of Sigmund Freud and post-modernism." Such feminism, according to Zdybicka, "undermines female identity and deforms social structures, primarily as a result of weakening family relationships and questioning the right to life of unborn children (abortion)."[110] Professor Zdybicka argues that while "authentic feminism" recognizes woman's specific nature, her nurturing "female genius" and natural differences between the sexes, "false feminism" instead of liberating has a destructive impact on women, especially in terms of morals. She accused radical feminists of trying to eliminate all differences between genders and pretending that they do not exist. She accused Marxist feminists of trying to promote conflict between men and women. Her claims that liberal feminists deny all gender differences and do not recognize most moral limits on sexual expression seem, however, somewhat farfetched to those who live in the West. John Paul II, who also did not have much exposure to ordinary life and attitudes of Western women, held similarly somewhat exaggerated opinions about views and morals of secular liberals and feminists living in the West. Neither of them would concede that Western liberal thinkers and activists, some of whom were motivated by their religious faith, were primarily responsible for many of the advances women have made so far. They both welcomed many of these gains for women without conceding that reforms that made them possible were strongly opposed initially by the Catholic Church hierarchy. From the perspective of most Western feminists, neither John Paul II nor Professor Zdybicka could provide a convincing argument as to why nuns, who forego their natural roles as wives and mothers, could not become priests.

During her university years, Zofia Zdybicka and other female students were greatly impressed by Wojtyła's lectures, his personality and his willingness to engage with them as a group and to hold one-on-one conversations about life, love and religion. His friendships with young women were so strong that in 1951 the students decided to organize a surprise name's day party for him at his apartment in Kraków. Name's day celebrations are just as important to Poles as birthday parties are to Americans. Everybody, including Wojtyła, sat cross-legged on the floor and ate cake, which the girls obtained from a nearby convent. The bed sheets, spread on the floor to serve as tablecloths, were also borrowed from the sisters. The male students gave Wojtyła a student cap as his name's day present. Danuta Rybicka described the atmosphere at the party as "fantastic." The following year, the girls organized Wojtyła's name's day party at the private apartment of a female dentist to avoid a confrontation with the maid at Wojtyła's apartment who strongly disapproved of his contacts with female students. The maid, Pani Marysia, had a low opinion of his young friends and was convinced that they were a bad influence on Wojtyła by distracting him from his studies. Remembering her with affection years later at a gathering in Rome, Wojtyła told his former students that Pani Marysia was to some degree right, although not entirely.

Undeterred by the disapproval with which some of the older

priests and older lay people viewed his pastoral activities, Wojtyła continued his close contacts with the students. In 1952, he partici- pated in a carnival ball at the dormitory for female students in Kraków run by the Sisters of Nazareth. Prior to the ball, both the students and the nuns were despondent after being informed by the communist authorities that the Church would have to turn over the facility to the government. Despite the bad news, Wojtyła encouraged the girls to proceed with the ball and told them not to lose hope. When one of the girls at the ball found herself without a male partner for the final "Polonaise," a traditional Polish marching dance, Wojtyła took her hand and they marched together down the stairs to the refectory for supper.[111]

The close relationship between Wojtyła and the women continued even after they completed their studies and left Kraków for jobs in other cities and towns. Many of the women returned to Kraków for occasional gatherings of his former students, during which they discussed with Wojtyła various spiritual, moral, psychological, educational and religious questions. If he was not able to talk to them in person, he communicated with them by writing letters. Danuta Rybicka noted that among various problems discussed in the letters were questions relating to the preparation for marriage.[112] One young woman Teresa Życzkowska received a letter from Wojtyła, in which he explained that his intention was not to help arrange marriages but to help them develop the power of selfless love:

> You see—a person lives above all through love. The ability to love determines most deeply one's personality—it is not by accident the most important commandment—it is not any great intellect, but precisely the ability to [achieve] authentic love, such a love that depends on moving outside of oneself, on some kind of affirmation of another person or people, on giving oneself [for the benefit] of a person, people, and above all God.

In another letter to the same woman, Wojtyła wrote that "after much experience and thinking, I am convinced that the (objective) starting point for human love is the realization that I am needed by another person." Wojtyła went on to explain that a loving relationship allows people to recognize and nurture positive traits in another person which could otherwise be lost. At the same time, a person who helps someone else become a better human being also benefits from a loving relationship.[113] Wojtyła was offering these ideas to young women rather than trying to impose them or to appear in any way overbearing. In his letter to Teresa Życzkowska, he introduced his comments by saying that he wanted to tell her a few things, but added that he also wanted her to share with him her views on the subject of love.

To many feminists John Paul II appeared as an unforgiving, authoritarian figure who arbitrarily made harsh rules and demands that had to be obeyed, at least by Catholics. This is not, however, how he is remembered by many of his former students in Poland, including young women who went with him on hiking trips in the 1950s and the 1960s. There seems to be a tremendous difference between the descriptions of Wojtyła in his personal encounters during his years as a priest in Poland and his public image among liberal Western Catholics and feminists after he assumed positions of leadership in the Catholic Church. On a personal level, he appeared to his friends as understanding, tolerant and compassionate, but as soon as he started speaking on behalf of the whole Church his public image drastically changed, particularly in the West. In his public pronouncements he seemed to be ruled by his feeling of tremendous responsibility for protecting the moral order and the interests of the Church as an institution. As pope, he was perceived by his liberal Western critics as dogmatic, inflexible and angry with those who saw themselves as tolerant and liberal. That assessment is quite different from how young women remember Wojtyła when he was still a young priest in Poland. It is also quite different from how most Poles see him now and how he is perceived by many Catholics and non-Catholics who share his views on abortion and ordination of women.

According to American writer Darcy O'Brien, who wrote a book about Wojtyła's boyhood friendship with a Jewish neighbor, John Paul was not driven by hostility to sex or to women but by respect for both.[114] The writer, who objectively dealt with another difficult topic, the Polish pope's attitudes toward Jews, observed that as a young priest in Poland, Wojtyła enjoyed a special relationship with Polish women: "Women students appreciated his treatment of them as intellectual equals and his admonitions to the young men that they must guard against the temptation to treat women only as sexual objects rather than as independent persons meriting respect."[115]

Talking to Male Students

A good illustration of Wojtyła's early views on women's role in the Church can be found in his talk at the 1961 retreat for university students in Kraków. Wojtyła spoke separately to male and female students, as it was customary in Poland at that time to hold separate religious retreats for men and women. Wojtyła's talks to Polish student represented an early indicator of his later attitudes on gender issues. In a talk to male students, he encouraged them to take a more visible and active role in the Church. Men were called by Wojtyła to assume a leadership role in the Church *"in accordance with our specific characteristics as men."*[116] He further explained his position with frankness, with which he would certainly not be able to speak after becoming pope, but which probably reflected his deeply held personal views. He told the students that, *"In men, reason [and] intellect has a certain supremacy over the heart, and this is why Christ entrusted responsibility for the Gospel as idea to them."*[117] He did add that "women have a great role to play in the Church, and in Catholicism," but he concluded that *"the Gospel as idea is primarily a male sphere."*[118]

Implicit in that statement is Wojtyła's belief that only males can become priests. Speaking to male students, Wojtyła explained that it would be impossible to leave "the affairs of the Kingdom of God to women." He told male students that, "Christ gave clear instructions in this regard when he told his Apostles: "Go therefore and make disciples of all nations" (Matthew 28:19). This, according to Wojtyła, meant, "Go and teach," which in turn meant that "we [men] must take responsibility for the Gospel as Truth!"[119] Further in his talk, he again addressed this issue in terms of men's "special responsibility with regard to spreading the concept of Gospel.[120] In order to remove any doubt about what it means for women, Wojtyła warned his male students: "...my Dear [men], we cannot leave responsibility for God's Kingdom to women. We cannot. We cannot because this is how Christ settled the matter. This is how Christ settled the matter. When [Christ] was saying: 'Go, therefore, and make disciples of all nations' (Mt.28:19), there were around him eleven men [and] not a single woman."[121] Wojtyła explained that both men and women are responsible for the Gospel as it relates to life, but when it comes to presenting the Gospel as idea and a way of life, he complained that "responsibility for the Gospel has been left far too much to women, and we must make sure that those who are growing up now recognize this."[122] Wojtyła told the male students that taking responsibility for the Gospel as a way of life and as an idea is "in accordance with male nature."[123]

Anyone who had read these words spoken in 1961 would have realized, even at the time of great excitement surrounding Wojtyła's historic election in 1978, that the first non-Italian pope in a few centuries was not likely to make any revolutionary changes in the Church on the issue of women's rights. Unfortunately, most of Wojtyła's writings on questions relating to women were in Polish and at that time available to only a handful of readers outside of Poland. In his 1961 talk to the male students in a Kraków church, Wojtyła expressed satisfaction that Polish Catholicism was acquiring more male characteristics and, consequently, becoming less feminine.

There was a common perception among Catholic priests in Poland at that time that due to various concessions to women, churches in the West were attended mostly by women and that men in the West have lost interest in leading the Church. Wojtyła was encouraged by large numbers of men in Polish churches and the large number of male students listening to his lecture. He told them that their presence in the church speaks very well of them as Christian men. At the same time, he admonished the male students for believing that it is only woman's role to teach young children how to say prayers. He conceded that teaching children the words of prayers may be suitable for women, but suggested that men should also take upon themselves the responsibility of teaching children how to pray and of developing in them a religious attitude.

Western feminists would see such words as misogynist, but in Wojtyła's case they probably reflected his understanding of how his own male-dominated society was functioning. This, combined with somewhat limited first-hand knowledge of the role of women in Western societies, led him to conclude that without leadership from men, the Church was likely to lose its influence. He suggested to the male students that they should reject the view that talking about religion is somewhat embarrassing and better left to women.

Otherwise, however, he did not have many positive comments about the male gender. He told the young men that they are by nature more inclined to be ruled by pride, less willing to give, and much more willing to conquer and dominate. He described men as being more like Nicodemus who visited Christ at night when nobody would see him but would not openly declare himself as his follower. Wojtyła used Nicodemus as an example to criticize male attitudes toward women: "We are reluctant to commit ourselves. We are just like that young man, who was very willing to take everything he could from Christ, in a spirit of conquest, but who went away when it came to committing himself."[124]

While both man and woman create life, Wojtyła pointed out

that afterwards the whole burden of carrying a new life falls upon the woman. This is where, as Wojtyła warned his male listeners, a frightening moral danger begins as the man can fall into the role of a primitive exploiter by denying his responsibility as a father and urging the woman to get an abortion and even offering to give her money:

> It is precisely when the man does not mature to the role of a father, we hear such words as: "Go see a doctor, I will give you money. Why did you allow this to happen? There are contraceptives." She, however, has the right to your fatherhood, to [your] responsibility, care, [and] the right to your tenderness.
>
> We definitively give too little effort to understand the psychology of the woman. Because of that, deep resentments set in and wounds are opened in the soul. [A woman] feels betrayed by someone closest to her, [feels] a sense of loneliness, and even destruction. And we are prevented by seeing all of this by our male pride; our attitude as a conqueror.[125]

Wojtyła told the male students that the Church is asking doctors around the world to find solutions in order to address economic and demographic issues related to fertility. He suggested, however, that the rhythm method, which he described as a great scientific achievement, is not the entire solution. He told the young men that they must be guided by a correct attitude toward love and suggested that expressing love does not always have to lead to pregnancy.[126] It was a clear suggestion that men should exercise self-control and express their love more often in spiritual ways.

Wojtyła's view on the role of men vis-à-vis women did not change much after he was elected pope. As time passed, he apparently became even more convinced that men are responsible for most abortions and the use of contraception. In a homily in early 1978, just before his election to the papacy, Wojtyła identified the root cause of abortion as stemming from the unbalancing of the male role model. He concluded that men in Poland were not doing enough to help women, although in this case he was not talking about housework. Wojtyła was concerned that Polish men were not willing to take responsibility for providing support to women whom they had gotten pregnant but instead were urging them to get an abortion. He told a group of Catholic family counselors in 1978 that "masculinity, which has its natural tendency to dominate, must be balanced by willingness to serve" following the example of Christ.[127] He was certain that woman's role in marriage was to be "the servant of life," as shown by the example of Mary who willingly accepted motherhood:

...this is her vocation. She is led to this by [her] femininity. And, this service, which is expressed in her whole femininity and in which [her] femininity matures, must have the support of a male servant. ... if a man does not want to be a servant—he destroys femininity; [he] destroys the female servant—Lord's servant—servant of life.[128]

In his 1978 homily, Wojtyła was not at all certain that marriages in which men and women share equally all the tasks and responsibilities, are the best solution for dealing with the pressures of today's world. In his opinion, equal division of all family responsibilities may be fine as long as it does not contribute to greater use of contraception and abortion. He seemed convinced that such partnership marriages are more likely to break Church rules on contraception and abortion:

Perhaps under today's social conditions, male role as a servant is more pronounced in some sense in marriages in which all responsibilities are shared. This matter, however, must be thought out to a final conclusion, especially in connection with those points, which are most significant for the ultimate responsibility of the male...[129]

This is not an overwhelming endorsement of marriages that are based on full partnership with both spouses combining outside careers with family responsibilities and practicing effective birth control. Wojtyła was definitely arguing here against the tendency of today's couples to limit the number of children. He seemed to show little concern for such practical matters as the growing need in more advanced societies to provide children with superior education in order to assure them a decent quality of life and to teach them to be at the same time tolerant, self-reliant and competitive. Under communism, many people in Poland assumed that providing education at all levels was the duty of the government and that self-reliance and competition were not absolutely necessary since the state would take care of most of their problems.

Talking to Female Students

Wojtyła's 1961 talk to female university students in Kraków contains all of the elements of his later pronouncements on women. At the beginning of his talk, he told female students that Christ has a special role for them and *"offers them different possibilities from those open to men."*[130] Wojtyła had a consistent position that women are better suited for some roles and functions, while others are better performed by men. At the same time, he always maintained and stressed that there are no differences in dignity between men and women or in the value of what they separately contribute to their families and society.

Christ, according to Wojtyła, enhanced the interior dignity of all women who had come in contact with him, even those who were "fallen women." When Christ tells the Samaritan woman that he knows about her many lovers, he does it in a way that does not humiliate her or cause her to fear him. Wojtyła told female students that the women who had come with contact with Christ discover their independence. He described Christ's mother as his "mature, independent companion throughout his life."[131] Wojtyła also made a strong point to female students that Christ did not consider women as slaves, even though they were treated as such by the Romans and the Jews. (He was only partly right on this point, since unlike Jewish women, free Roman women enjoyed considerable rights, including the right to inherit and hold property and to obtain divorce on favorable terms.) Women were Christ's promised brides and sisters, but Wojtyła concluded from his reading of the Gospel that *"a woman is above all a mother."*[132]

Even though Wojtyła was speaking to university women, there was nothing in his talk on the value of their education or the opportunities that their education can offer. This would have been the normal thing to say to university students in the United States, even if the speaker was a priest at a Catholic college. Instead, Wojtyła had a message for the young women about the dangers of the incorrect interpretation of "the concept of emancipation." He expressed his approval for equality between men and women, but only if such equality takes into consideration the roles and functions assigned to women in the Gospels. He then offered a warning to the university students about the dangers of gender emancipation that goes too far:

> Equality between men and women is basically correct as long as it is based on the woman's interior maturity and independence. Without a sense of being an individual and in charge of her own life and future, exterior emancipation will destroy a woman instead of improving her position. There is no doubt that quite frequently this exterior emancipation and equality with men produce split personalities in women, especially those with professional training. The tasks, duties and problems of their lives simply double, and conflicts are generated. One must add to this woman's specific interior character which is different than man's.[133]

This comment shows that Wojtyła was well aware of the Polish men's reluctance to help with household duties. Christ, according to Wojtyła, had a perfect understanding of woman's unique nature and how she is different from man. Wojtyła described women as "more feeling and intuitive" and more capable of total commitment:

Woman is more a person of heart, a person of intuition; [she is] more involved in all matters; ... involved more warmly, more completely.[134]

Because of that, according to Wojtyła, women need maturity, interior independence and support. In reference to the need for support, Wojtyła pointed out that in the Gospel, women are described as being "by Christ's side." Although he did not elaborate, Wojtyła was pointing out that women who followed Christ were not leaders or Apostles.

Wojtyła also told female students that they are more capable of experiencing total love which goes beyond a mere sexual attraction. Women, according to Wojtyła, are more likely to seek "a great Love" with capital "L," rather than just sexual love. This makes them more vulnerable and more susceptible than men to be exploited, or as Wojtyła put it, susceptible to "psychological conditioning." Wojtyła told the women that their faith in Christ can make them autonomous and independent, even to the point that they do not need men in their lives. But he urged them not to give up on true "Love," in which they can find their purpose in life and their vocation through motherhood.

The internal independence, which Wojtyła advised women to strive for, enables them to persuade men to see and treat them as persons, rather than objects of desire. Wojtyła concluded that "without the mediation of love, a woman remains an object for a man" to be used by him for his pleasure.[135] He stressed that women can only expect to receive from men full "Love," if they first achieve "internal emancipation" and "interior independence," as opposed to exterior independence, which he apparently identifies with seeking equality with men in professional lives.

When a woman marries, only this "interior independence" can guarantee that she will not become an object for her husband and will remain an autonomous person. Wojtyła told the young women that their basic task is to educate men to take responsibility for them and to prevent men from treating them as objects. He told the students that "marriage is not only ... a sexual institution." "If that is the case," he explained, "then both feel, but particularly the woman, that [the value] of everything has been lowered."[136]

Even in the so-called "True Love," Wojtyła saw women as having a more passive role then men. A woman, according to Wojtyła, is "first and foremost a mother."[137] Women find their true worth in motherhood, or as he described it, "with Christ women blossom as mothers." The possibility that the woman may become a mother, according to Wojtyła, should convince the man that she is a person of equal dignity. Because the mother's basic task, as Wojtyła saw it, was to educate young children and to share this responsibility with her husband, he cannot treat her as an object. Wojtyła also pointed out that Jesus Christ allowed himself to be educated by a woman. When Wojtyła talked about the woman's role as an educator of children or an educator of her husband so he would not treat her as a sexual object or a kitchen slave, he used such terms as "educating through intuition" or "educating with [her] heart." In his talk to women-students, he made no references to women using reason or their already acquired education, although this did not necessarily mean that he did not appreciate the value of reason or education. He simply did not mention it at that time when talking to these young university women.

Wojtyła's talk to a group of female students also included a strong warning against abortion. He told them that he intended to explain to male students that abortion robs women not only of their motherhood, but also of their dignity as persons. He acknowledged that women, when they become mothers, are required to give more of themselves than men, but motherhood is their great responsibility and duty which they have to take seriously. While he described the living conditions in Poland in the early 1960s as difficult, anybody who accepted abortion, according to Wojtyła, was not a Christian, even though they may claim to come from a Christian family. Wojtyła told the women that any solution to such problems, which does not recognize the personhood of a conceived child, cannot be considered Christian. This remained Wojtyła's consistent position after he became pope. John Paul II did not consider as full members of the Church those American Catholics and Catholics in other countries who are pro-choice. John Paul II would have preferred that any Church debate on abortion would absolutely reject any notions of compromise. This was his message to the Polish students in 1962 and it remained his firm position throughout his papacy. He found pro-choice arguments so abhorrent that he wanted total opposition to any compromise on this issue to be a major legacy of his pontificate.

Women Taking Care of Wojtyła

When after the war Wojtyła was traveling to Lublin from Kraków to give lectures at the Catholic University, nuns in Lublin provided him with a place to sleep and cooked his breakfasts and suppers. They remember Wojtyła as being grateful and described him as being especially kind to the sister who was cooking his meals.[138] Sisters, who took care of him in Kraków, noted that Wojtyła made a point of praying at the tomb of Sister Zofia Firley, who for many years had been in charge of the household staff at the archbishop's residence.[139] In his autobiographical book about priesthood *Rise, Let Us Be on Our Way*, John Paul II also mentioned Maria Gromek, who had been his cook for several years while he was finishing his advanced theological studies.[140]

In this book focusing on the importance of priestly vocations, John Paul II writes at length about scores of priests, bishops, cardinals, and other male teachers, mentors and role models. Women are rarely mentioned, although he does write about a few female saints, usually nuns who engaged in intellectual pursuits. And he did mention his personal cook in one sentence. But this and his other autobiographical books can hardly be used to support arguments that women who devote themselves to serving others as full-time mothers, cooks and housekeepers are recognized by society as just as important as men who become leaders of the Church or secular public figures. John Paul II must have known that this is not how society perceives women who cook and otherwise take care of priests' daily needs. Wojtyła's books conformed to their readers' expectations that intellectual achievements are more important. Of the more than 180 names of important individuals John Paul II mentions in *Rise, Let Us Be on Our Way*, only about a dozen belong to women. Most of the women mentioned engaged in performing some form of charitable domestic work to benefit others or in organizing such work.

As archbishop, Wojtyła liked to join other priests for dinner or to invite them to dine with him at his residence. Since he liked to entertain and had an increasing number of visitors each year, it put a strain on the nuns working in the kitchen. It was perfectly normal for priests in Poland at that time to have all of their meals prepared by nuns. According to one of Wojtyła's cooks in Kraków, he insisted that the sisters bake their own cakes for Christmas rather than buy them in stores. She recalled that they were constantly baking from just before Christmas until early February. She also confirmed that Wojtyła enjoyed his meals. She denied newspaper reports that he was refusing certain types of foods as a form of fasting or self-denial. She also could not remember any dish that he really disliked. According to Wojtyła's cook, everybody liked him for his goodness and his ability to deal with people.[141] After he was elected pope, Wojtyła asked some of the sisters who cooked for him in Kraków to come to Rome, where they continued to cook for him his favorite Polish dishes.

Expecting women to do cooking and cleaning was customary

for Polish men of Wojtyła's generation. When as a young man he was visiting his friend Mieczysław Maliński to help him study Latin, Mieczysław's sisters would prepare for them scrambled eggs or sandwiches.[142] After he became archbishop, Wojtyła made public appeals to nuns — without a similar appeal to members of the male religious orders — to help with decorating churches and cooking meals for visiting priests during important religious ceremonies. One such special occasion was the displaying of the copy of the Black Madonna of Częstochowa in the parishes of the Kraków Archdiocese in 1967 — a practice that greatly annoyed the communist regime to the point that they had the copy of the icon "arrested" by the militia to prevent it from being moved from town to town. In his letter to the heads of female religious orders, Wojtyła explained that religious retreats, which accompanied the movement of the icon from parish to parish, would mean a lot of work for priests and monks. He asked the nuns to pray and to respond to requests for help.[143] In the late 1960s, the Kraków archdiocese had about 1,500 diocesan and monastic priests and almost twice as many nuns.[144] While members of male religious orders could hear confessions, celebrate Mass and distribute communion, these duties were denied to nuns, as they still are today. With not enough male priests, even to take care of the functions reserved only for them, the nuns had to cook and perform other housekeeping tasks.

It was also not a common practice in Poland for nuns to lead religious retreats or to teach religion to adults. It was therefore not unusual that during an important religious event Wojtyła would ask nuns to pray and to help with cooking, cleaning and decorating. It should be noted that many nuns who had joined religious orders in Poland before World War II and even for some time after the war were not highly educated. In many Polish families during the interwar period, women were not expected to seek advanced degrees, but they were expected to take care of cooking and cleaning the house. Father Maliński described in his book how his two sisters were very curious what he and Wojtyła were studying behind closed doors, and they would look over their shoulders to see their books and notes.[145] After the two young men finished studying, Maliński's sisters would join the discussion, which often centered on the theater and literature, but it was seen as natural for women to first assume the role of hostesses and cooks and to serve breakfast for the two men who were only slightly older.

At that time Polish women did not generally see such domestic roles as subservient or in any way degrading. Putting the needs of their brother ahead of their own would not have been unusual for a young woman in a Polish family. In fact, sacrificing out of love to help a male family member, particularly in difficult times, would have been a source of great pride and a sign of a noble spirit. A brother would probably make similar sacrifices to help his sister financially or in other ways more acceptable for a Polish man. Such attitudes may be difficult to understand by pro-feminist women who grew up in the West in relative affluence, did not have to face any major threats to their physical or economic security, and therefore did not have to rely on other family members for life-saving help.

When it comes to today's women, especially younger working women in the U.S. and in other industrialized countries, John Paul II may have still seen the role of a wife and a mother in the light of his own experience but not without showing some sense of humor. When he met in 1995 with a group of middle aged mothers from Boston, who were friends of the wife of the U.S. ambassador, he told them jokingly that they must like being in Rome, because when they come to Rome they don't have to cook. Both the American women and the pope laughed at his joke, but these American women were of the

> **Maria Faustyna Kowalska – Saint Faustina** (Helena Kowalska)
> **Born:** August 25, 1906, Głogowiec, Poland
> **Died:** October 5, 1938, Kraków, Poland
> http://www.sisterfaustina.org

generation when many women did not work full time outside of the home.[146] On a more serious note, he also told them never to forget that being a mother is the most important job.

Polish nun Sister M. Beata Piekut, who worked closely with Archbishop Wojtyła on the beatification of Sister Faustyna Kowalska, described him as not only a person of noble spirit, full of goodness and kindness, but above all as someone open toward others and interested in their affairs and problems. Sister Faustyna belonged to of the Order of Our Lady of Mercy, which helps Polish women who are abused, use drugs or engage in prostitution.[147] Despite his slightly teasing manner toward this shy young nun — a picture which emerges from Sister Beata's description of several of their encounters — she wrote that she was able to overcome her fear of authority figures thanks to his friendly attitude toward her. Since she knew Wojtyła when he was still a young priest, she concluded that even after becoming an archbishop he remained a deeply humble person.[148] When after the death of John Paul I, Cardinal Wojtyła was getting ready to travel to Rome for the conclave, which elected him to be pope, he found a moment for one last meeting in Warsaw with Sister Beata. In the course of their conversation, he asked her how she was planning to return to Kraków and learning that she was taking the night train, he insisted on making his personal car and driver available to take her back to her convent. Sister Beata thought that his willingness to take time to make arrangements for her travel at such an important moment for him when he was obviously extremely busy and did not even have sufficient time to pack his own things, showed how deeply Wojtyła cared for others.[149] As a person of considerable authority and influence, Wojtyła dealt with both highly educated and simple nuns in a similar manner that obviously won him the admiration and respect of religious women in Poland with whom he came in contact. Both he and the nuns understood and accepted their respective roles. As pope, John Paul II was, however, unable to achieve the same level of intimacy and understanding with religious sisters in the West, especially with nuns in the United States.

Sister Beata's collaboration with Wojtyła proved successful only after he became pope. Sister Faustyna Kowalska, who left a diary of her many revelations attracting wide attention among Catholics in Poland and elsewhere, was beatified by John Paul II in April 1993 and canonized at a ceremony at the Vatican in April 2000. This would not have happened if Wojtyła, in his capacity as the Archbishop of Kraków, had not worked closely with the Sisters of Our Lady of Mercy in trying to rehabilitate Sister Faustyna after the Vatican condemned in 1958 a translated version of her diary as heretical.

Sister Maria Faustyna, born Helena Kowalska in a small rural village in Poland, was the third of 10 children, attended school for only three years and was practically illiterate.[150] She worked as a domestic servant in homes of wealthy families and was rejected by several convents before being accepted by the Sisters of Our Lady of Mercy in Warsaw and changing her name to Maria Faustyna. At the convent, she was charged with menial tasks as cook, gardener and porter. She continued her humble service while at the same time keeping a diary of her mystical experiences, which included visions, revelations and hidden stigmata. In one of her visions, she saw Jesus asking for a picture to be painted of him with beams of light, red and white, shining from his heart and with the inscription: "Jesus, I Trust in You." Three years before her death, Sister Faustyna commissioned such a picture from a painter in 1935. Her supporters claimed that the Vatican scholars, who initially had declared her writings to be heretical, received an inadequate Italian translation of her nearly 700-page diary, which Sister Faustyna wrote phonetically and without knowledge of Polish grammar. In order to reverse this ruling, Wojtyła requested a new translation of Sister Faustyna's diary and asked a Catholic scholar Professor Ignacy Różycki to analyze her writing. Initially reluctant to undertake this task, Father Różycki told Wojtyła after studying Sister Faustyna's diary that she was "a wonderful mystic."[151] As someone who all his life was interested in mystical experiences and may have had them himself, this is what Wojtyła wanted to hear. He had the new translation of the diary and the scholarly analysis delivered to Rome and asked for the ban to be lifted.

The Vatican rescinded the condemnation of Sister Faustyna's diary in 1978, just six months before Wojtyła was elected pope.[152] As the Archbishop of Kraków, Wojtyła was one of those who believed that Sister Faustyna's mystical experiences, focused on the message of God's mercy to each human being and to the world, offered hope to many people and deserved to be promoted. At her canonization ceremony in Rome, he described Sister Faustyna's life as "a hymn to mercy," stressing that her message of Jesus' mercy is also a message on the value of every person.[153] The problems with the Vatican bureaucracy over Sister Faustyna's diary and Wojtyła's response to them are also illustrative of the occasional misunderstandings and distrust between the Polish bishops and the Catholic hierarchy at the Vatican and generally in the West.

As with many Polish nuns before the war, Sister Faustyna was not well educated and like most of them was relegated to perform mostly menial tasks. As the archbishop of Kraków, Wojtyła was known for his support of expanding educational opportunities for Polish nuns, but eventually this may have had a negative impact on some of the traditional roles performed by the sisters, which surprised the male hierarchy of the Polish Church. Jerzy Kłoczowski, a professor at KUL, observed that after the fall of communism, there was a great demand for nuns in institutions taking care of the sick and the elderly, but the Polish Church could no longer find enough nuns who were trained and willing to undertake such duties. Some of this may have been caused by the communist regime which made it difficult for the Church to continue its humanitarian work. When communists consolidated their power in Poland, they took over hospitals and other Church-run facilities that had been providing social services to the most needy. At some of these facilities, nuns were allowed to stay, but in July 1962, at the insistence of the communist authorities, they had to leave 72 hospitals and 322 kindergartens.

Home for troubled youth in Łagiewniki (2007).

One of them was the home "for morally lost" girls run by Sister Faustyna's Congregation, the Sisters of Our Lady of Mercy, in Łagiewniki, a suburb of Kraków. As a bishop, Wojtyła often visited the girls under the care of the sisters. When it again became possible for nuns to do such work after 1989, it turned out that there were very few of them who had been trained as nurses and social workers or were even willing to accept such assignments. Pope John Paul II visited the home for girls in Łagiewniki again in 1997 and 2002 and urged the nuns to continue their work.

According to Professor Kłoczowski, during the communist period the Polish nuns started to specialize in other fields, such as religious education, and could no longer be recruited in sufficient numbers to work in hospitals.[154] Thus, communists may have indirectly contributed to the academic emancipation of Polish nuns by restricting their charitable activities, but most Polish men still think that some jobs, usually those requiring more sacrifices, are better done by women. For men, it is a very convenient view to have. While John Paul II strongly supported educational opportunities for some of his best female students who also happened to be nuns, it is evident that he believed most women are better suited for taking care of their families and, if they are nuns, for taking care of those most in need of help. He was, however, convinced that humble work in the service of others represents a great virtue. He did not specify the reasons as to why the most menial and difficult work of helping others has always been performed by religious sisters rather than priests. Even communists realized that the most difficult work of carrying for mentally ill patients or severely handicapped children is better left to Catholic nuns. After removing the nuns from hospitals and institutions for mentally handicapped patients, the communist regime was not able to find enough lay workers and consequently allowed a few nuns to continue working in some of these facilities while still preventing them from returning to work in daycare centers, schools, orphanages and regular hospitals, where their spiritual and intellectual influence could have interfered with promoting communist ideology. In 1972, Cardinal Wojtyła visited a home for mentally ill women in Bolechowice, where communists allowed a few nuns to continue their hard work. The same year he went to visit a home for elderly and terminally ill women in Kraków, celebrated Mass for those who could walk and visited others in their rooms.[155] Many of these facilities would not have been able to provide decent care to their patients if it were not for the Polish nuns' determination to stay on the job despite harassment from the communist regime.

Because of the nuns' willingness to work as household servants in parishes, Polish priests have become accustomed to the idea that such work is naturally more suitable for women. Priests and bishops in Poland in the decades before Wojtyła was elected pope and up to this day have benefited from household services of Polish nuns on a daily basis. It was considered perfectly normal that nuns should cook, clean, wash laundry and iron for priests of any age or position. As any other Polish priest or bishop, Wojtyła took advantage of this arrangement, although he was personally never particular about the appearance of his clothes and often gave away his jackets, sweaters, pants and shoes to friends and strangers who seemed to be in greater need of clothing. Such generosity was not a small sacrifice in communist Poland, where good clothes were expensive and in short supply.

At the time when Wojtyła was still in Poland, it is doubtful that many nuns resented their household duties or blamed the male

Church hierarchy for not allowing them to advance their education and to take on leadership positions. On the contrary, some of the nuns took great pride in their household work, which—at least in Wojtyła's case—was also greatly appreciated. One of Wojtyła's students, who invited him to his wedding in 1959 when Wojtyła was already a bishop, remembered that the nuns in Szczecin, where the wedding took place, strongly insisted that they be allowed to iron Wojtyła's clothes because it would have been unseemly for a bishop to appear in wrinkled clothing after a long train ride. In order to attend the wedding of his young friend, Wojtyła traveled all night by train from Kraków to Szczecin and his clothes were indeed in bad shape. His friend remembered that after talking with the nuns, Wojtyła smiled and told everyone that they would have to wait while his clothes were being ironed.[156] In another convent, where Wojtyła stopped with a group of students on a hiking trip, one of the nuns apparently tried to clean his shoes, but she made a mistake and cleaned and polished a pair of shoes belonging to one of the students.

Not all nuns in Poland, of course, had to perform household services for priests. Some clerical and administrative positions in the Kraków Archdiocese were filled by religious sisters, but the most important positions were still reserved for priests. While Wojtyła's secretary in the Kraków curia was a nun, she could not hold the title of personal secretary to the Archbishop of Kraków. That particular position went to a priest. Sister Jadwiga's most important function, according to Father Maliński, was keeping the diary of Wojtyła's official acts as bishop and archbishop and performing other secretarial duties. Wojtyła would provide Sister Jadwiga with his written notes, which she would then transcribe and enter into the official journal. In 1971, he gave Sister Jadwiga a religious picture on which he wrote a few sentences thanking her for secretarial help and for "trying to anticipate his thoughts."[157]

It was evident, however, that as a nun Sister Jadwiga had far less authority than most priests in his closest entourage and certainly much less influence than Father Dziwisz, John Paul's personal assistant and his official personal secretary since 1966. Stanisław Dziwisz, born in 1939 in Raba Wyżna, a village in southern Poland, followed Wojtyła from Kraków to the Vatican, where he was constantly at John Paul's side until the pope's death. He enjoyed Wojtyła's full confidence and had the authority to screen most if not all visitors who wanted to have an audience or a private meeting with the pope.[158] John Paul II made Monsignor Dziwisz a bishop in 1998, an unusual honor for a papal secretary but one that would guarantee him a secure position under the next pope. This indeed happened when after John Paul's death, Pope Benedict XVI named Bishop Dziwisz the Archbishop of Kraków in 2005 and made him a cardinal.

Caroline Pigozzi, one of the few female journalists allowed to observe John Paul II in his private moments, reported that Bishop Dziwisz almost never left the pope's side and was present during all papal meals. His private rooms were directly above the papal apartments, and the two usually ate supper alone. She described their relationship as a father-son friendship. In his own book published in 2007, Cardinal Dziwisz described his life with John Paul II in almost the same words.[159] When John Paul II made Dziwisz a bishop, he said to him, "We together faced problems and fears; [we] had common hopes. Today, in joy, be at my side."[160] No woman could ever expect to hear such words from John Paul II because the current structure of the Catholic Church would not allow a woman to be as close to the pope or to any male Church leader as Father Dziwisz was to John Paul II. After the pope's death, Cardinal Dziwisz made this touching tribute to his great mentor: "I was with him almost forty years, the first twelve years in Kraków and the next twenty-seven in Rome. [I was] always with him, always at his side. And now, at the moment of [his] death, he went alone. ... What disturbed me the most was that I could not accompany him on this journey ... At the other side, who will be with him?"[161] In his 2007 book, Cardinal Dziwisz does not say whether the Italian news channel *Sky Italia* information that he held the pope's hand as he died was true. He pointed out instead that John Paul II spoke his last words to Sister Tobiana.

In describing her attempts to gain access to John Paul II as a journalist for the French magazine *Paris Match*, Caroline Pigozzi characterized the Vatican as a world of men, in which not even the Virgin Mary would feel comfortable. She did not accuse the men who guard access to the pope of being misogynist, but noted that they have very little contact with the world of women other than the nuns who are usually assigned at the Vatican to do cooking, cleaning and answering telephones.[162]

It seems from Caroline Pigozzi's account that the Vatican administration under Pope John Paul II did not treat nuns differently than they were treated by priests and bishops in Poland. She identified five sisters brought from Kraków who were very close to the pope. Sister Tobiana was a medical doctor who watched after John Paul's health, but since her Polish medical degree was not recognized in Italy, she was usually described as a papal nurse.[163] Only in later years did Sister Tobiana begin to accompany the pope on his trips abroad, but all of the Polish sisters tried to stay out of sight and carefully avoided being photographed. It was Sister Tobiana who heard John Paul II's last words, "Let me go to the Lord." Sister Germana was in charge of the papal kitchen. Sister Euforozyna, a Polish Jewess who converted to Catholicism and speaks several languages, took care of the pope's private correspondence. Sister Matylda was responsible for the pope's clothing and from time to time did his manicure.[164]

Pigozzi described the nuns working at the Vatican as modest, barely visible and moving through the corridors as quietly as little mice.[165] But the Polish sisters in Wojtyła's household had at least some measure of power over those who sought a papal audience. They saw as part of their job to protect the pope from the outside world and treated all unfamiliar visitors with great suspicion. Caroline Pigozzi herself experienced this kind of intimidating treatment when she got lost in the pope's private apartments. She stumbled upon Sister Germana who, without looking at the journalist's official Vatican visitor's identification, asked a Swiss guard to escort her to the exit.[166]

Whether John Paul II was aggressively seeking to promote women to various positions within the Church outside of the priesthood is the subject of some controversy. Mary Ann Glendon (b. 1938), a law professor at Harvard University whom the pope selected to lead the Holy See delegation to the 1995 U.N. Women's Conference in Beijing, insists that John Paul II named an unprecedented number of lay and religious women to various councils and academies at the Vatican, but since the number was extremely small to begin with, his critics do not see it as a sign of any great progress. Professor Glendon believes, however, that these appointments of women provide an example for the male leadership of the Church throughout the world.[167]

When addressing both priests and nuns, John Paul II often stressed the concept of religious life as service to others, particularly to the nation and to smaller communities. Invariably, however, his statements to nuns tended to promote typical female occupations, even though nuns did not have to be wives and mothers and therefore could have devoted their time and attention to any number of causes. In a meeting with Polish nuns during his first trip to Poland after being elected pope, John Paul II told them in 1979 that the "so-called social advancement of women has in it a little bit of truth, but it also has a great component of error."[168] (In his 1995 "World Day of Peace Message," he referred to "the great process of women's liberation," but he again stressed that in addition to great accomplishments it also had its "share of mistakes.")

As one of the earliest statements of his papacy on the issue of emancipation of women, the comment made to the Polish nuns in 1979 revealed John Paul's rather ambivalent attitude toward many of the changes in social attitudes and legislation with regard to women's employment outside of the home in recent decades. He encouraged nuns to be among the people as witnesses of Christ's love, but he usually only dwelled on their service in taking care of the sick. There were no specific recommendations for nuns to play a greater role in running the Church other than his general advice that they should be "pushy" in making their experience more visible.

But what experience was John Paul II trying to promote? He was usually extremely vague when speaking about ideal occupations for nuns and lay women. In his 1979 speech to the Polish nuns, he observed that some young women saw religious life as an opportunity to fulfill their social ambitions of obtaining an advanced college degree, but he would not say specifically whether this was good or bad. He himself promoted academic careers of a number of nuns when he was a professor at the Catholic University in Lublin (KUL). But his comment made in 1979 seemed to be a warning that personal ambitions should not take precedence in religious life. Thus, he appeared to be retreating somewhat from his earlier support for intellectual pursuits by Polish nuns, perhaps under some pressure from the Polish bishops who began to realize that not all educated nuns wanted to work in hospitals and take care of the laundry.

If such a warning was otherwise warranted, it should have been applied equally to both men and women, but John Paul II made these comments only to the religious sisters. While calling on the nuns to spend more time among the sick, John Paul II made no similar appeals at the same time to the Polish priests. But since the Polish priests already controlled most of the intellectual and administrative functions within the Polish Church, ordinary domestic work might have distracted them from these duties. John Paul II may have simply assumed that men are not capable of taking care of the sick with the same devotion and efficiency as women. The pope confirmed that this is indeed what he believed when he told the Polish nuns that no one but they can perform such tasks because they require "heroic sacrifice."[169] To John Paul II, it may have meant that women are simply capable of being better Christians, but to feminists it means that they were being shoved into positions of perpetual servitude according to social norms determined for women by men.

Women whom Wojtyła met during his youth belonged overwhelmingly to the traditional model of Polish womanhood centered on the family and service to men, children, the elderly and the sick. During his brief period of study at the university in Kraków before the war, Wojtyła may have met women who had higher aspirations than those considered typical for women in smaller towns and rural communities. In fact, the number of women who were seeking higher education in Poland before the war was steadily growing as the country started to develop economically. The Jagiellonian University, which Wojtyła entered in 1938, had been accepting women with various initial restrictions since 1894.[170] Despite informal and sometimes official discrimination against women, in 1936, about 17% of lecturers and assistant professors were women, and in 1939 three women were tenured professors.[171]

After the war, the communist regime started to promote higher education for women and their number at the universities increased even further. Many of the college students during the post-war period came, however, from highly traditional small town and rural families. Far from being communist sympathizers, some of these students tended to gravitate toward young priests such as Wojtyła who worked semi-openly as pastors in academic communities. Despite being in favor of mothers spending more time at home rather than pursuing demanding careers, Wojtyła did support academic careers of several of his female students who were nuns and therefore had no family obligations. His statements made to Polish nuns after he became pope suggest, however, that he may have later developed some concerns about nuns wanting to pursue intellectual goals to the detriment of more "female" occupations. This concern may have become magnified after he experienced great resistance from much more educated and politically active Catholic nuns in the United States who complained to him privately as well as publicly about a number of issues, including ordination to priesthood, male language in liturgy, religious dress and, in some cases, even with the Church's position on abortion.

Sister Theresa Kane

The Sisters of Mercy

http://www.sistersofmercy.org

The Leadership Conference of Women Religious

http://www.lcwr.org

The first public challenge to John Paul II from a woman, in this case an American Catholic nun, Sister Theresa Kane, came during his first trip as pope to the United States in 1979. She complained that the Church was treating women as "second-class citizens" by denying them ordination. Sister Theresa Kane, then Administrator General of the Sisters of Mercy of the Union in the United States and President of the Leadership Conference of Women Religious, welcomed the Pontiff at the National Shrine of the Immaculate Conception in Washington, D.C. on behalf of about five thousand nuns who had filled the shrine on the morning of October 7, 1979. What she had to say was undoubtedly a great shock to Wojtyła, who throughout his life as a priest and a bishop in Poland would never dare to disagree publicly with his superiors. As an American woman used to expressing her views, Sister Theresa Kane was not diplomatic in reminding the pope about what she believed to be the injustice in the Church's denial of priesthood to women:

As women we have heard the powerful message of our Church addressing the dignity and reverence for all persons. As women we have pondered these words. Our contemplation leads us to the state that the Church in its struggle to be faithful to its call for reverence and dignity for all persons must respond by

providing the possibility of women as persons being included in
all the ministries of the Church.[172]

Sister Kane finished her short remarks by asking for the Church "to
respond to the suffering of women..." She was dressed in secular
clothing, a practice John Paul II was known to frown upon as sign
of secularism, and she did not kiss his ring when she shook his
hand. In fact, in his speech to the sisters gathered at the National
Shrine of the Immaculate Conception, John Paul II directly rebuked
Sister Kane and others like her by reminding them that "Two
dynamic forces are operative in religious life: your love for Jesus —
and, in Jesus, for all who belong
to him — and his love for you."
"All who belong to him" was a
clear reference to the unborn.
He also told American sisters
that their "consecration to God
should be manifested in the
permanent exterior sign of a
simple and suitable religious
garb." He added that this was not only his personal conviction,
"but also the desire of the Church, often expressed by so many of
the faithful."[173]

| Madonna Kolbenschlag 1936-2000 |
| The Catholic Order of the Humility of Mary |
| http://www.chmiowa.org/index.cfm |

Being directly challenged in a public forum by a nun was not an
experience John Paul II had much practice with in Poland, but
according to American Catholic theologian Richard P. McBrien,
there were hundreds of other sisters in America who would have
said exactly the same thing.[174] A similar view was expressed by
American feminist theologian Madonna Kolbenschlag (1936-2000),
a sister of the Catholic Order of the Humility of Mary. She
described Sister Kane's "respectful but unexpected plea" for a
greater role of women in the Church as "the 'original sin' that cast
United States women forever in the role of upstart 'Eve's reaching
for forbidden fruit."[175] Conservative Catholics criticized Sister

Kane for her remarks to the pope. Afterwards, she issued a short statement that it was John Paul II's openness that encouraged her "to express a concern experienced by me and many other women across the country."[176]

As Carl Bernstein and Marco Politi observed in their 1996 biography of John Paul II, women were almost always the ones to openly contradict the pope in front of large audiences and the world media. This had never happened to Karol Wojtyła in Poland, where the only public criticism he encountered came during the papal trip in 1999 from a Jewish-American rabbi protesting the placing of Christian crosses near the Nazi extermination camp in Auschwitz. All the encounters with women who publicly questioned or criticized John Paul II, as recorded by Bernstein and Politi, occurred in the United States and in Western Europe, but in every case John Paul II managed to avoid engaging in a dialogue with his women-critics. His mind was apparently made up: there were no longer any serious human rights violations against women in the Catholic Church.

This was, however not what he heard in 1980 from Barbara Engel, a young German woman in Munich, Germany, the capital of predominately Catholic Bavaria, who confronted him on the issues of priestly celibacy and sexual ethics. In Switzerland, once again a woman, Magrit Stucky-Schaller, told John Paul II that women are considered second-class citizens in the Church. During his 1985 trip to Holland, at the meeting of missionary organizations, Hedwig Wasser accused the Church leaders of assigning blame instead of giving help to those who need it.

> Catholic University of Louvain
> http://www.uclouvain.be/en-index.html
> Katholieke Universiteit Leuven
> http://www.kuleuven.be/english/

She criticized Church restrictions against divorced couples, homosexuals, married priests and women. She told the pope that many Catholics are forced to disobey Church authorities.

At yet another meeting, this time in Belgium, Veronique Yoruba, a young woman of Polish descent representing the students at the old Flemish university in Louvain, criticized Wojtyła's stands on contraception and Liberation Theology. One of the notable alumni of the Catholic University of Louvain was Gustavo Gutiérrez Merino (b. 1928), a Peruvian Dominican theologian and founder of Liberation Theology. With the students applauding and the pope's' supporters trying the silence her with shouts, "Long Live the Pope," Karol Wojtyła showed his parental respect by kissing the young woman on the head but did not respond directly to her complaints.[177]

An event that produced an even greater shock for John Paul II and most likely confirmed his worst opinions about the American Church was the 1984 advertisement in *The New York Times*, signed by twenty-four nuns and four priests, protesting Cardinal John O'Connor's (1920-2000) attacks on the Democratic vice-presidential candidate Geraldine Ferraro (b. 1935). The then New York Archbishop was known for his conservative views on abortion and homosexuality, but like John Paul II he was an outspoken supporter of labor unions and the poor. He was criticizing Geraldine Ferraro, who is Catholic, for her support of the pro-choice position on abortion. The signing of such a declaration by Catholic nuns and priests was an unprecedented challenge not only to Cardinal O'Connor but also to the pope.

The ad called for a debate within the Church on abortion: "Catholics—especially priests, religious, theologians and legis-lators, who publicly dissent from hierarchical statements and explore areas of moral and legal freedom on the abortion question—should not be penalized by their religious superiors, church employers or bishops." The ad also stated that "a diversity of opinions regarding abortion exists among committed Catholics" and that a "large number" of Catholic theologians believed that abortion "can sometimes be a moral choice." (This may explain John Paul II's and Cardinal Ratzinger's actions to remove liberal theologians from Catholic universities in the United States and Western Europe.) The Vatican reacted swiftly by pointing out that that anyone who procures an abortion incurs automatic excommuni-

Barbara Ferraro and Patricia Hussey
Covenant House, Charleston, WV
http://www.wvcovenanthouse.org/

cation from the Church and orders the signers to recant or face dismissal.

Within a few months, the priests admitted their mistake, but it took several years before most of the nuns who signed *The New York Times* ad submitted to Church discipline. Even then, the nuns did not agree to a full retraction of their views as expressed in the abortion ad, and most American congregations refused to cooperate with the Vatican in taking disciplinary actions against the sisters. Two nuns, Barbara Ferraro (no relation to Geraldine Ferraro) and Patricia Hussey, resigned in 1988 from their order of the Sisters of Notre Dame de Namur. They said that they had succeeded in making the point that "you can be a nun and be pro-choice," but decided to leave. Some of their colleagues ostracized them after they had taken part in public demonstrations in favor of abortion rights. Ferraro

Sisters of Notre Dame de Namur
http://www.sndden.org/

and Hussey said that they were leaving with sadness. Conservatives Catholics, however, greeted their departure as "a victory for all pro-life people in the United States." James Likoudis, president of Catholics United for the Faith (now president emeritus), actually commended the nuns for "the realization that their pro-abortion stand is incompatible with Catholic religious life and the Catholic faith." [178]

Even though the two sisters did not announce that they were leaving the Catholic Church and were working as lay Catholics at Covenant House, a shelter for the homeless in Charleston, West

Virginia, Likoudis's comment was in line with John Paul II's and Cardinal Ratzinger's views that it is better for the Church to be smaller than to tolerate ideas and behavior they considered intrinsically evil. The *National Catholic Reporter* listed the two sisters among 24 prominent theologians and others who had been silenced or subjected to various forms of papal discipline under Pope John Paul II and Cardinal Ratzinger. The list includes such names as: Fr. Hans Küng, Fr. Edward Schillebeeckx, Fr. Charles Curran, Leonardo Boff, Fr. Gustavo Gutiérrez, Fr. Karl Rahner (Wojtyła's friend Father Maliński's favorite teacher), Fr. Matthew Fox, a sister of Mercy Mary Agnes Mansour, the former archbishop of Seattle Raymond Hunthausen, Fr. Robert Nugent and Sr. Jeannine Gramick who ministered to homosexuals, a Brazilian Sister of Notre Dame Ivone Gebara and several others.[179]

James Likoudis, president emeritus of CUF
http://www.credobuffalo.com/

Catholics United for the Faith
http://www.cuf.org/

After leaving their order, Ferraro and Hussey have not ceased their social and political activism. In 1991, they launched Single Mothers' Program at Covenant House in Charleston, W. Va. In 2004, they published a newspaper commentary protesting the war in Iraq and President Bush's budget cuts, which they saw as hurting poor Americans seeking help at shelters such as Covenant House, where they are co-directors. The two former Catholic sisters also accused Christians and others identifying with the religious Right of supporting a similar ideology that drives religious fundamentalism and promotes terrorism abroad. According to them, these groups "support war and discrimination ...diminish women as moral decision makers and ...are intolerant of other positions or religions." Their commentary also said that "Bush's fever-pitched God talk and desire for a Christian theocracy are frightening" and that "Right-wing politics are blessed by religions that support these same ideologies."[180] The two former nuns suggested that when communities of faith abdicate their voices and leadership because they do not want to cause divisions in the congregations, they in fact

> *Dissent from the Magisterium...is not compatible with being a good Catholic.*
>
> Pope John Paul II

support injustice. Ferraro and Hussey are co-authors with Jane O'Reilly of *No Turning Back: Two Nuns' Battle With the Vatican Over Women's Right to Choose* published in 1990.

The story of these socially conscious and dedicated former nuns is perhaps a good illustration of how difficult it was for John Paul II to understand them and for them to understand him. After all they all shared a deep commitment to helping the poor and supported the idea of religious tolerance. They were equally critical of the Bush Administration's foreign policy in the Middle East. But they could not agree on women's rights issues and abortion. The answers as to why they could not agree may be found not only in their different experiences with history, as discussed in this chapter, but also in Marxist and communist roots of much of the radical feminist ideology. This topic will be explored in the next chapter before returning in *Chapter Three* to the story of Wojtyła's cultural roots and Wojtyła's women.

CHAPTER TWO

Marxism, Second Sex and Wojtyła's

Feminist Philosophy

Feminist Theories and History

In criticizing radical feminist scholarship in the United States, Camille Paglia, a leading American libertarian feminist scholar and author, observed that to achieve success in life and in their profes-

Camille Paglia
Born: 1947, Endicott, NY, USA
http://www.randomhouse.com/
pantheon/paglia

sional careers, women need to study military history, not feminist theory.[1] She is the author of a bestselling book *Sexual Personae* (1985), in which she criticized leaders of the American feminist movement for their alleged ignorance of history, outright rejection of gender differences and teaching women hostility toward men. Paglia, who claims to be an atheist who respects religion, has been roundly criticized by traditional feminists, while conservative feminists object to her libertarian pro-choice views and her tolerant attitude toward homosexuality and pornography.

From my own experience and perspective, the most revealing for judging political theories and for making comparisons between cultures has been the study of history of freedom, human rights and economic development. Evaluation of feminist and other political theories is best achieved by looking at and analyzing actual experiences of people who are subjects of ideological experiments. Something as simple as a study of refugee movements and immigration patterns can also be quite revealing. John Paul II favored a phenomenological approach by looking at personal experience, but all evidence suggests that in the end he did not quite grasp the strengths and advantages of liberal societies, and neither did Western feminist scholars.

I was intrigued by the descriptions of the life of Soviet women published by the iconic feminist leader and writer, French atheist Marxist and ex-Catholic Simone de Beauvoir, in her highly influential book *The Second Sex*. In

Sheila Rowbotham b. 1943
Rosemary Radford Ruether b. 1936
Daphne Hampson b. 1944
http://www.st-andrews.ac.uk/~dh1/ hamp1.html

Soviet Russia — she claimed — "the feminist movement has made the most sweeping advances."[2] Sheila Rowbotham, a Marxist feminist in Great Britain, wrote in the early 1970s that communism is "the solution to exploitation and oppression" of women.[3] An American feminist critic of Christianity Rosemary Radford Ruether argued in the 1980s that "collective laundries and kitchens," in addition to state-supported daycare centers, represent "a significant advantage for women in socialist societies in contrast to capitalist societies, which have resisted such efforts to alleviate women's domestic role by various appeals to the sanctity of the (patriarchal) family."[4] For many decades, scholars with strong Marxist, pro-Soviet, and far-Left sympathies dominated feminist philosophy and theology in the West.

I was aware that some of their assumptions and comments were totally at odds with the reality of women's lives under communism. I also came across more sophisticated arguments by a British feminist theologian Daphne Hampson, but ultimately even she agreed with de Beauvoir that "feminism represents the death-knell of Christianity as a viable religious option."[5] This observation reminded me of my pro-regime teachers in Poland who insisted that religion would soon disappear under communism. When told about such claims by his communist co-workers and bosses, one of my uncles suggested waiting another 2000 years to see if communism survived that long.

Liberal-Democratic Roots of Modern Feminism

John Paul II had a long-term outlook on matters of religion, gender and feminism and was not going to take at face value what Marxist feminists or radical American nuns were saying about the Church. Not all feminists, however, were Marxists, and not all American nuns wanted the Church to be run only by women. Anti-religious communists within the feminist movement in the West were a minority, although some like Simone de Beauvoir had enormous influence on generations of Western women who read, analyzed and discussed de Beauvoir's books. Most Western women, who were not feminist scholars but identified with feminism, were mainly concerned not with ideology and revolution but with sex discrimination and improving their status through social and legal reforms undertaken within a democratic process. Modern feminism had its strongest roots not in any revolutionary theories of violent class struggle but in the ideas of liberal democracy and human rights, which developed in the 18th and 19th century in a small number of Western countries, mainly among the British, French and American upper-middle class Christian and deist intellectuals.

One of the early modern feminists was a British writer and philosopher Mary Wollstonecraft (1759-1797) who in 1792 published *A Vindication of the Rights of Woman*, a passionate appeal for the education of women.[6] She had an unorthodox and unhappy personal life of love

Mary Wollstonecraft

Born: April 27, 1759, London, England

Died: September 10, 1797, London, England

Anne Hutchinson 1591-1643

Elizabeth Cady Stanton 1815-1902

Susan B. Anthony 1820-1906

Mary Baker Eddy 1821-1910

Antoinette Brown Blackwell 1825-1921

Virginia Woolf (Stephen) 1882-1941

affairs, illegitimate children and suicide attempts, but later feminist writers, including Virginia Woolf, saw her "experiments in living," as Woolf described it, as a possible model for modern women.[7] It was perhaps John Paul II's observations of the impact of the feminist lifestyle on women, children and families that led him to conclude that the "so-called social advancement of women has in it a little bit of truth, but it also has a great component of error." Someone born in the West might have reached a different conclusion that there was a little bit of error and a great deal of truth in feminism. Still, despite her departure from the traditional Christian moral code, Mary Wollstonecraft not only emphasized her religious faith and spirituality but also insisted that a woman's primary role is to be a mother. (Her daughter, Mary Shelley was the author of *Frankenstein*.) Many early British and American feminists, including Susan B. Anthony who fought for women's voting rights in the United States, were in fact strongly religious and opposed abortion; only much later did the movement acquire its antireligious and pro-abortion label.

America and Britain had many women who assumed leadership roles—more in churches than in politics—and who had a significant impact on religious debate and practice. Anne Hutchinson, the unauthorized Puritan preacher in New England, is regarded as a key figure in the development of religious freedom and the history of women in ministry. Another American female religious leader, Mary Baker Eddy, was the founder of the Christian Science movement. Elizabeth Cady Stanton, the primary author of *The Woman's*

The Church of Christ, Scientist
http://www.tfccs.org
Christian-Universalism.com
http://www.christian-univer-salism.com/churches
Unitarian Universalist Association of Congregations
http://www.uua.org
Friends General Conference Library
http://www.fgcquaker.org/library/welcome

Bible published in New York in 1895, expressed doubts concerning the doctrine of the virginal birth of Christ and its impact on the lives of ordinary women.[8] *The Woman's Bible* was widely read by American women.[9]

While social debate in Poland during the 19th and most of the 20th century focused on issues of national independence and the need for basic social reforms, it was much more socially acceptable for Western women to raise the issue of their own oppression. Not surprisingly, many of them, particularly those concerned with theology, moved beyond the failures of individual religious figures to focus on what they identified as a fundamental bias of Judeo-Christian religion and theology as a whole. It was also much easier for women in Western Europe and in America, particularly those who were exposed to the Protestant tradition of a personal relationship with God and individual study of the Bible, to begin questioning some of the long-held views about women and religion. They quickly observed that until recently Christian theology had been almost exclusively the purview of men and reflected, powerfully, a male point of view. Poland has had very few feminists in the Western sense of the word, but as one of them observed recently, the assumption that women should play a secondary role has been so deeply rooted in the culture, and so imbedded in the language, that the harm done to women often goes unnoticed.[10]

The tradition of religious tolerance and liberal culture based on individual liberty, inherited from Protestantism and the great English and French thinkers of the 18th century, allowed American women not only to preach, but even to form their own religions as exemplified by Mary Baker Eddy. In 1853, Antoinette Brown Blackwell, member of the Congregational Church and graduate of Oberlin College, became the first ordained woman minister in one of the major denominations in America. Antoinette Brown Blackwell was in favor of women obtaining education and seeking out masculine professions. In her articles and books, she asked men to share in household duties, even though she believed that women's primary role is care of the home and family. In her book *The Sexes Throughout Nature*, published in 1875, she argued that evolution resulted in two sexes that were different but equal. This is exactly the same argument as the one advanced by Pope John Paul II in support of new feminism, yet he would also use it to argue that Antoinette Brown Blackwell could not become a priest in the Catholic Church. In addition to the Congregational Church, a few other Protestant congregations, particularly the Quakers, also had unordained women ministers and preachers, as did the Pentecostal and the Unitarian or Universalist Churches.[11] The Society of Friends, known as Quakers, established in England in 1646 by George Fox (1624-1691), from its very beginnings appealed to women in Britain and America because of its claim of equal spiritual status of both men and women. Since the Quakers believed that the Spirit could move any person to speak, both men and women could lead the congregation in prayer and women preachers played an important role in Quaker communities in America.[12] These traditions of religious experimentation and individualism in Anglo-Saxon culture are barely known in Poland. But even American and British feminists, especially those on the far Left who promoted collectivism and collectivist solutions to gender issues based on Marxist and Soviet models, barely acknowledge the tradition of personal freedom, individualism and religious activism that gave rise to modern feminist ideas. As the scholar of feminism, Elizabeth Fox-Genovese observed in her book *Feminism Without Illusions*: "In many academic circles, the Western tradition, not to mention the idea of an American national culture, enjoys scant popularity today."[13] While acknowledging the importance of American traditions that value individual freedom, she in fact argued for more human solidarity in line with John Paul II's social teachings and more restraint in imposing middle-class feminist values on women who lack economic security and other advantages of middle-class lifestyle.

While it is true that Western feminists joined the liberal and socialist Left in great numbers because it offered a promise of social reforms, most were not seeking the establishment of a communist society. Whether they knew it or merely suspected it, feminism had almost no cultural equivalent in either pre-revolutionary or post-revolutionary Russia. Its society remained patriarchal even under communism, but there was no shortage of theoretical speculation by a segment of feminist writers and activists in the West that communal living arrangements and the elimination of religious restrictions in the Soviet Union were freeing Russian women from centuries of oppression. With such a wealth of ideas and ideological confusion about the roots and the goals of the feminist movement in the West, John Paul II was not the only person who found it difficult to understand its real nature or to appreciate its diversity.

De Beauvoir's Marxism and Feminist Scholarship

Elisabeth Schüssler Fiorenza b. 1938
Harvard Divinity School
http://www.hds.harvard.edu

Journal of Feminist Studies in Religion
http://www.fsrinc.org/jfsr

After coming to America, I met many Catholic women who had not rejected religion and wanted to remain in the Church, yet they also called themselves feminists and felt that the male hierarchy treated them like children and second-class citizens. They were angry at the pope for telling them which methods of birth control they could use and preventing them from making important decisions about their religious life. Some women wanted major reforms of the Church structures and teaching. Others, especially in the academic world, began to advocate a complete rethinking of the Catholic tradition and a revolutionary break with the past. Elisabeth Schüssler Fiorenza, a leading dissident Catholic feminist theologian, professor at Harvard Divinity School and editor of *Journal of Feminist Studies in Religion*, coined the word "kyriarchy" to describe "a complex systemic inter-structuring of sexism, racism, classism and cultural-religious imperialism that has produced the Western 'politics of Otherness.'"[14] She also coined the term "women-church."

"Politics of Otherness" was essentially a Marxist concept based on German philosopher G.H.F. Hegel's dialectic of the Master and the Slave and popularized in feminist scholarship and literature by Simone de Beauvoir. According to this theory, man is "the Absolute" who gets to define and

> G.H.F. **Hegel** 1770-1831
>
> **Karl Marx** 1818-1883
>
> **Jean-Paul Satre** 1905-1980

dominate woman as "the Other," relegates her to mindless domestic work and reserves creative work and all advantages for himself. Woman becomes alienated from herself and starts to believe in her inferiority. Simone de Beauvoir used some of the philosophical concepts of the French existentialist Jean-Paul Sartre, who was her lifelong companion. She made her theory of gender relations fit closely with Karl Marx's ideas of the alienation of the working class (being alienated from the product of their labor and their humanity with no control over their destiny) and revolu-tionary class struggle (capitalists vs. workers). When applied to women, de Beauvoir hoped these concepts could be used to mobilize women for class-warfare against capitalism, Western imperialism and all other aspects of Western bourgeois societies. In a 1976 interview she observed: "Most workers of the class world today are aware of the class struggle whether they ever heard of Marx or not. And so it must become in the sex struggle. And it will."[15]

Sartre visited the Soviet Union in 1954, and he and de Beauvoir went there again five times between 1962 and 1965. After his return from Moscow in 1954, Sartre wrote that "there was total freedom to criticize in the USSR" at the time when when Soviet prisons and labor camps were full of people accused of speaking out against the regime.[16] Claims that de Beauvoir's feminist theories went far beyond Marxism into existentialism, and were thus highly original and full of promise for women, are not supported by de Beauvoir's and Sartre's enduring political sympathies, and certainly not by any practical results of her ideas for women in countries like the Soviet Union, China or Cuba. In any case, John Paul II viewed existentialism—the rejection of God and giving individuals complete freedom to define their reality and morality—as equally dangerous for human life and dignity as Marxism and communism.[17]

No Marxist-feminist revolution ever took place in any nation with strong democratic traditions, but de Beauvoir's ideas influenced scores of feminist scholars and writers and helped to launch a feminist revolution in the United States and Western Europe. The 1969 paperback edition of *The Second Sex* sold seven hundred and fifty thousand copies in the United States. One of many American feminists inspired by de Beauvoir's ideas was Kate

> **Kate Millett**
>
> **Born:** September 14, 1934, St. Paul, Minnesota, USA
>
> http://www.katemillett.com

Millett, the author of another widely-read book *Sexual Politics* (1970), in which she explored the concept of male sexual domination of women. De Beauvoir wrote that Millett, with whom she developed a personal friendship, should have given credit to *The Second Sex*, because—as she pointed out—"that's where she gets all her theory."[18] Indeed, Millett took de Beauvoir's principal feminist idea that biological differences between sexes are not particularly important. She argued that giving birth and taking care of children does not make women much different from animals—a point John Paul II and conservative feminists strongly dispute. De Beauvoir also saw marriage and family as institutions designed to oppress women and considered her observation: "You are not born a woman; you become one."—as expressing one of the leading ideas in *The Second Sex*.[19] As an existentialist, de Beauvoir believed that all women are free to rebel against their biological and subordinate status. If children are born, they can be raised in state-run institutions, such as Soviet-type nurseries and kindergartens. Female subordination in all areas of life, including sex, according to both de Beauvoir and Millett, is a product of socialization and culture and thus can be changed.

John Paul II clearly understood the danger of de Beauvoir's ideas for his vision of women, marriage and family. He most likely inspired the release of the 1983 Vatican statement making it public

L'Osservatore romano
http://www.vatican.va/news_services/or/or_eng/index.html
America
http://www.americamagazine.org

knowledge that *The Second Sex* had been placed earlier on the Roman Catholic index of prohibited books.[20] In reporting this news, the Vatican newspaper *L'Osservatore romano* commented that de Beauvoir "considers the institution of marriage to be a hoax and defends free love." ("Free love" was a term frequently used by Wojtyła when discussing Western societies and feminism.) According to the Vatican paper, de Beauvoir's ideas were designed to "permit woman to flee the enslavement of motherhood." As such, the paper argued, they must be condemned by the Church as "immoral doctrines which trample underfoot the good character and sanctitude of the family." The practical result of the Vatican's announcement was a strong rise in sales of de Beauvoir's books. [21] As reported by *America*, a moderate-liberal weekly magazine published by American Jesuits, Hitler's *Mein Kampf* was reviewed by the Vatican but never banned. [22] One of the reasons cited for not banning Hitler's work was his legal ascent to power, but the main reason was probably fear of Nazi reprisals against the Catholic Church in Germany and elsewhere.

Kate Millett and Elisabeth Schüssler Fiorenza were among

Web Sites Critical of Radical Catholic Feminism

Catholic-Pages.com on Feminism

http://www.catholic-pages.com/dir/feminism.asp

Missionaries Under The Sun

http://www.missionsun.net/diss.htm

Our Lady's Warriors

http://www.ourladyswarriors.org/dissent/dissorg.htm

Catholic Culture

http://www.catholicculture.org/library/view.cfm?recnum=69

These Last Day Ministries

http://www.tldm.org/news6/dissenters.htm

The Feminist Threat to the Roman Catholic Church in the UK

http://www.catholic-feminism.co.uk/

Living Tradition: The Whole Truth About Catholic Feminism

http://www.rtforum.org/lt/lt53.html

many American feminist scholars who read *The Second Sex* and borrowed some of de Beauvoir's existentialist analysis and Marxist language. Millett was familiar with her French friend's political sympathies, but most Western feminists probably did not understand de Beauvoir's political agenda or were fully aware of her strong rejection of religion and her initial support for Soviet communism and other totalitarian regimes. Unlike de Beauvoir, Schüssler Fiorenza did not claim to be an atheist and did not advocate abolishment of religion. She was concerned with eliminating misogyny, oppression and patriarchy in the Catholic Church and in religion in general. In the passage in her book about "Politics of Otherness," she was merely arguing that the Catholic Church needs to abandon all forms of patriarchal sexism, which she saw as the main obstacle to the access of women to priesthood. "As long as women cannot represent Christ in the Eucharistic celebration," she wrote, "our participation at the table of the Lord remains a perversion of the eucharistic community intended by Jesus."[23] "Missionaries Under The Sun," one of several conservative Catholic web sites which name dissident Catholics organizations, describes her, however, as a "Catholic in name only," and points out that she had been one of the signers of the *New York Times* ad which called for an open debate in the Catholic Church on abortion.

Marxist analysis was useful in pointing out contradictions and weaknesses in patriarchal and capitalist societies, but—as it turned out—it was based on simplistic and incorrect assumptions about liberal democratic capitalism, about actual experiences of women and men and about human nature. Despite Marx's firm belief to the contrary, democratic capitalism in countries with liberal traditions was capable of reform. Many of de Beauvoir's assumptions in *The Second Sex* about feminism also did not pan out. Not all women saw themselves as being deceived, defined and oppressed by men. Even if they accepted the idea of being oppressed, not all women shared the same goals for their emancipation or wanted to tell women of different cultures, races, ages or classes what exactly they should do to improve their lives. More importantly, radical political regimes de Beauvoir supported turned to be historic failures. She eventually admitted that she had "often cherished hopes that have come to nothing" and that her high expectations of socialism in the USSR, in Cuba and in Algeria have not been fulfilled.[24] She was genuinely concerned when the Soviet regime imprisoned dissident Marxists and human rights activists, but she did not make a link between these arrests and her radical Marxist ideology. Neither did scores of middle class American and Western European feminist scholars who found de Beauvoir's theories of feminist revolution and confrontation far more appealing than the liberal-democratic traditions of the early British, French and American feminists. These feminist scholars grossly misinterpreted history, ignored liberal traditions and embraced philosophical and political theories of a group of French intellectuals whose main preoccupation was to deconstruct and expose the evils of Western civilization.

By the mid-20th century, this current of feminist scholarship had little in common with the experience of most American and other Western women who were successful in their struggle for greater equality largely because they benefited from democratic capitalism and liberal traditions. American columnist Sally Quinn concluded in 1992 that "feminism has failed to address the needs and problems of most women and has become an ineffectual fringe movement."[25] While it is true that radical feminism, both within the Catholic Church and in society at large, has become a fringe phenomenon, more than 54 percent of American women surveyed in 2003 still said that "being a feminist is an important part of who they are."[26] Many new currents emerged in the women's movement, and feminism is by no means dead. Equity feminists stress equality of the sexes before the law and may demand more government action to curb sex discrimination, while libertarian feminists reject the portrayal of women as victims, defend free speech and argue for less government intrusion. New Catholic feminists try to combine feminism with traditional Catholic values. Most American women self-identify as feminists, and the term has lost much of its radical meaning except for for the most conservative Catholics and evangelical Christians.

Liberal societies have been able to absorb, reject or transform radical Marxist ideas and even found some of them useful in debates about social reforms, as did John Paul II and many other progressive social thinkers and activists. During a 1993 trip to Riga, Latvia, the pope said that there was "a kernel of truth" in Marxism, just as he had acknowledged earlier that there was a kernel of truth in feminism. But radical Marxist and feminist ideas proved to be disastrous when implemented in less developed nations with strong authoritarian and patriarchal traditions. These countries had no cultural and institutional restraints on state power or the tyranny of the majority. It was in these societies where ideas of class struggle, class hatred and forced social experimentation have cost millions of lives and produced the greatest harm. Still, John Paul II did not think that liberalism was the complete answer to dictatorship. He believed that in the long run radical liberal and capitalist ideas could be just as harmful to non-Western cultures or for that matter to any culture or nation. He had his own ideas, and so did liberal Catholic theologians who disagreed with him. Nearly everybody made a mistake that their ideas could be good for people of different cultures at different levels of development, and many refused to consider other ideas as legitimately feminist or legitimately Catholic and Christian.

Dr. Schüssler Fiorenza, a white Christian woman living in the United States and educated in Germany, did not see a contradiction between her condemnation of white Euro-American imperialism and her advocacy of the global *ekklesia* of women—a worldwide "rainbow" alliance or sisterhood of women engaging in a discourse about struggling against patriarchal relations of oppression. Anyone at all familiar with societies and women in the Third World or in countries like Poland is aware that women in traditional societies are more likely to embrace more conservative feminism (feminism based to some degree on moral, religious and some liberal traditions) than feminism derived from Marxist or postmodernist analysis. Dr. Schüssler Fiorenza, however, dismissed the conservative women's movement that arose in the United States in response to liberal feminism as a political manipulation—an attempt by the political and religious Right to make women submissive to their husbands and male Church leaders. [27] The idea of sisterhood envisioned by Schüssler Fiorenza did not include conservative women who identified with the pro-life Christian Right but still considered themselves feminists. According to this American feminist scholar, the political and religious Right in the United States perpetuates the oppression of women by advancing the very ideas which represent the foundation of John Paul II's new feminism. One of these ideas is the divinely ordained gender roles and gender complementarity— ideas categorically rejected by Simone de Beauvoir and other radical feminists.

Wojtyła's Response to Marxist and Liberal Feminism

Even though I have emphasized the dominant role of Marxist ideology in Western feminist scholarship, I am not sure whether John Paul II realized that Marxist terminology was used rather loosely by feminist activists in the West, many of whom were not in fact true Marxists, even if they appeared highly ideological. Even as late as the 1960s, many political and religious thinkers in the West and in the Soviet block still saw Marxism and communism as highly viable and took seriously many of their ideological claims. In arguing that the Catholic Church should come to terms with the social advancement of woman, progressive Belgian prelate Cardinal Leo Jozef Suenens (1904-1996) quoted from Lenin in his 1962 book about the future of female Catholic orders. Suenens, who was responsible for many of the Vatican II reforms and opposed *Humanae vitae*, included as a warning Lenin's observation that "the success of a revolution depends on the degree of participation of women." Suenens was concerned how women in Africa and Asia would respond to the changing gender roles in the West, where he saw women as having both a positive and an evil impact on the Christian civilization. Despite his progressive views and approval for public roles for women, he perceived great dangers in noisy feminist campaigns in favor of abortion, divorce and birth control.[28] On the whole, however, Suenens was far less afraid of communism and feminism than Wojtyła.

John Paul II saw secular feminism in much stronger ideological as well as moral terms. For him, secular and radical feminism not only contained Marxist ideas but was also a product of Western secularism, as was—in his opinion—communism and fascism. He saw feminism as being equally promoted in different form by liberals, capitalists and communists, with each group advancing its own separate agenda for women. At the same time, he did not see all Marxist analysis of class and gender oppression as wrong and all feminist ideas as bad. He embraced some feminist demands for reforms as much needed responses to gender discrimination. He was even willing to criticize to some degree how the Church had treated women in the past. But he also saw in feminism many dangerous elements, especially harmful to women and families in traditional religious cultures. Excessive individualism, the breakdown of traditional morality, and above all abortion were by far the greatest dangers which he associated with liberal and Marxist feminism. The theory of gender competition advanced by ideological feminists reminded him of millions of victims of other confrontational political theories that turned deadly, such as the Marxist concept of class struggle and Nazi claims of ethnic and racial superiority.

As far as protecting the dignity and value of individual human life, Wojtyła did not see a great philosophical difference between Marxism and liberalism or between radical feminism and Marxism. For Marxist materialists, a person was just a collection of atoms and therefore an insignificant part of the universe. Marxists could only see significant value in broad classes of people united in a struggle against capitalist or imperialist oppression; the collective was far more important than the individual. But according to Wojtyła, individualism and liberalism when taken too far could be equally dangerous for human life and human dignity. If all the rights are vested in each individual, he or she is free to make decisions that destroy human life, encourage others to act likewise and allow using other people to advance selfish ends. It is not surprising that Wojtyła would respond to Marxism, existentialism and liberalism by embracing and expanding the philosophy of personalism, which placed the absolute value on each human person who is endowed with dignity and freedom by God. Such a person is not concerned by the pursuit of individual happiness but collaborates with others to bring the gift of God's love to his or her spouse, family and community.

By stressing the link between each person, the sexual act and the divine, Wojtyła defined every human life as sacred from the moment of conception. He insisted that each person created in the image of God is given the right to life that no other person has the power to take away. He strongly promoted Immanuel Kant's (1724-1804) ethical rule against "using" human beings. In his book *Love and Responsibility* (1960), he argued that in all aspects of life, including sexual morality, individual freedom carries with it serious responsibilities toward God, the co-creator of all life, as well as toward a partner in marriage and the larger community. In *Love and Responsibility* he anticipated many of the arguments advanced in such feminist manifestoes as *Sexual Politics*. Wojtyła's "personalist norm," which became a key element in his theology of the body, stated that individualistic pursuit of pleasure, which allows for using other persons, must be replaced in sexual relations by human love as a special gift from God unselfishly shared by a married couple. George Weigel, an American Catholic writer with close connections to the Vatican, described John Paul II's theology of the body as "one of the boldest reconfigurations of Catholic theology in centuries" but practically unknown among today's

---

Theology of the Body and Personalism Web Sites

Theology of the Body International Alliance
http://www.tobia.info/

Theology of the Body Times Square Discussion Group
http://www.catholicculture.com/ToB_blog/

Love and Responsibility Foundation
http://www.catholicculture.com/

God of Desire
http://www.godofdesire.com/

The Personalism Library (includes Andrzej Potocki's English translation of Wojtyła's The Acting Person)
http://www.personalism.net/

Catholics. He predicted that Wojtyła's teaching on human sexuality may re-emerge at some point in the twenty-first century or perhaps even much later as "a kind of theological time bomb."[29]

Liberal Critics of John Paul II

Not all American Catholic theologians share George Weigel's positive assessment of John Paul II's gender theories and moral teaching. According to WomenPriests.org, the largest international web site supporting female ministry, eight out of ten Catholic scholars in the world support the ordination of women.[30] These dissident theologians, who are the majority, believe John Paul II focused too much on abstract ideas. (Wojtyła was a professor of philosophy in Poland.) Father Charles E. Curran, who was

| Charles E. Curran b. 1938 |
| http://www.smu.edu/theology/people/curran.html |

accused of being too liberal and was fired from his teaching position as a Catholic theologian by the Catholic University of America on orders from John Paul II and Cardinal Joseph Ratzinger (now Pope Benedict XVI), believes the previous pope took "several major strides backward" on issues of human sexuality and the rights of women.

Father Curran sees in Wojtyła "a claim to too great a certitude," too much emphasis on the universal and the unchanging, extending divine law too far, and "a failure to recognize historical development and historical consciousness." He concluded that "educated women in the West were very upset with John Paul II," none more so than Catholic nuns. Other than the issues of sexuality, women's rights, and democracy within the Church, however, Curran approved of John Paul II's social teaching (economy, poverty, death penalty, war and peace) and described it as "a very positive contribution to Catholic social ethics."[31]

John Paul II understood the power of ideas and took them seriously, perhaps too seriously according to some of his critics. As

Web Sites Promoting Ordination of Women

WomenPriests.org

http://www.womenpriests.org

"Eight out of ten Catholic scholars in the world support the ordination of women."

"We love our family, the Catholic Church. We fully accept the authority of the Pope. We respect his personal integrity as an outstanding spiritual leader. But we are convinced that the Pope and his advisors in Rome are making a serious mistake by dismissing women as priests. We feel obliged in conscience to make our carefully considered reasons known, fulfilling our duty to speak out as our present Pope has repeatedly told us."

Roman Catholic Womenpriests

http://www.romancatholicwomenpriests.org/index.htm

"We believe:

1. Women and men are created equal by God and can therefore equally represent Christ;

2. Jesus offered an example of inclusiveness and respect of persons that led, in the early Church, to the practice of ordaining women and men from all states of life as deacons, priests, and bishops;

3. We affirm that no intrinsic connection exists between priesthood and mandatory celibacy;

4. We are called by the Holy Spirit from within our communities to follow Jesus as our model of empowerment and generous service, rejecting all forms of domination and control;

5. We are called to live as a community of equals, inclusive and respectful of differences;

6. We are called to transform hierarchical structures by creating new, community-based structures for discernment and the recognition of the gifts of all;

7. We are called to a model of ministerial priesthood that is grounded in our common Baptism, in prophetic obedience to the Spirit, in a teaching authority

based on Scripture and Tradition, and in 'reading the signs of the times';
8. We are called to renew Theology, Liturgy, and Pastoral Practice to better
reflect the spirit and teachings of the Second Vatican Council as expressed in
Gaudium et Spes."

a victim of fascism and communism and as a critical observer of
liberalism and capitalism despite his limited exposure to life in the
West, he may have overestimated the impact of rigid political
theories on post-World War II democratic societies. As he
evaluated Western democracies as an outsider from a potentially
distorted perspective of someone forced to live under an
oppressive one-party dictatorship, he may have underestimated
their capacity for change and for tolerating extreme ideas and
diversity. He saw major threats to the dignity and value of human
life in democratic capitalist societies, even as millions of people
were trying to flee to these countries to escape oppression and
make their lives safer and more successful. Communism, which he
had known first-hand, was one of the most ideologically-driven
political systems and one of the most incapable of reform. But
despite his first-hand observations of life under communism,
Wojtyła did not believe in a quick collapse of the Soviet system.
While he contributed greatly to the fall of communism in Poland,
his assessment of the strength of communism turned out to be
wrong.

A strong ideological focus and lack of solid information may
have prevented John Paul II from seeing the feminist movement as
a broad range of constantly evolving ideas, which pluralistic and
democratic societies were free to accept, reject or modify. I was
repeatedly amazed by vastly exaggerated, stereotypical and often
ill-informed opinions about the United States, feminism and
American women expressed by some of Wojtyła's closest Polish
friends. They were well educated priests, university professors and

journalists with whom John Paul II frequently consulted during private dinners at the Vatican. One exception was Dr. Anna-Teresa Tymieniecka, a Polish-American philosopher and translator of his book *The Acting Person*, who confirmed my observations about the views of some of the pope's Polish associates. Unlike Wojtyła's Kraków friends, she has spent many years living and teaching in the United States. She tried to correct some of John Paul II's ideas about America, but her influence was limited and temporary.

Feminist Reading of History and Criticism of American Values

Unsophisticated reading of history and culture or being blinded by political theory and ideology are neither uncommon nor restricted to Wojtyła's Polish friends. It can be said in their defense that these individuals lived in a country which was subject to dictatorship, political oppression, censorship, propaganda, and other impediments to the free flow of information and ideas. Looking at more recent history, the same excuse cannot be used for President Bush's neoconservative advisors who successfully pushed for a military action in Iraq. The best and the brightest of the Kennedy and Johnson administrations also failed to take history, culture and nationalism into account when making judgments about the Vietnam War and the expansion of communism in Asia. For decades, Marxist analysis was one of the dominant currents in feminist studies in the West, but it was used without much effort to combine it with a critical and broad reading of history.

Anybody with some knowledge of Polish history would have known that there was very little room for a dialogue between John Paul II and those radical feminists who believed that religion only oppresses women and the right to abortion liberates them from male domination. Even Stalin observed that trying to impose communist ideas in Poland was like trying to put a saddle on a cow. Fascination with Marxism and Soviet communism undermined the credibility of radical feminists in the eyes of people like Wojtyła who had experienced life in the Soviet bloc. If Marxism, communism, atheism and the Soviet Union offered solutions to the oppression of women—while Christianity, capitalism and the United States represented the forces of female enslavement—then why did the Red Army soldiers, who were brought up on communist ideology, brutally rape hundreds of thousands of German women at the end of WWII? (Between 95,000 to 130,000 rapes in 1945 in Berlin alone according to estimates from two city hospitals.)[32] The American feminist Marilyn French (b. 1929) became notorious for her claim that "in their relations with women, all men are rapists, and that's all they are," yet there were no reports of mass rapes by American and British soldiers in their occupation zones in Germany.[33] These soldiers were brought up in a capitalist, liberal and individualistic culture, which feminist critics described as highly exploitative, blindly religious, racist, imperialist and dangerous for women.

94 million individuals killed or starved to death by communist dictatorships were also largely overlooked in feminist writings. This figure, estimated by French scholar Stéphane Courtois in collaboration with researchers from several countries, has been a subject of some controversy, but even if the estimated number is too high, the number of victims of communism is most likely still higher than the number of deaths caused by the Nazis. *The Black Book of Communism* (1997), in which the estimate was included, was defended among others by a British historian and author Tony Judt (b. 1948) and Anne Applebaum (b. 1964), an American journalist and Pulitzer Prize-winning author of *Gulag: A History*, which also documents Lenin's and Stalin's crimes. Most Western feminist leaders and scholars who praised the advances of women under communism failed to ask questions about the real status of women and human rights in Soviet Russia. Few pointed out that the Soviet system created substandard child care facilities, not so much for the purpose of liberating women from the menial tasks of parenting and cooking, but for getting their cheap labor to

strengthen the communist state. The drudgery of factory work was added to the drudgery of household work, which Russian men still expected and demanded from women. Even under the best conditions, the Soviet Union and communist Eastern Europe were in one sense a large concentration camp for women (and men). Only very few had permission to leave or could escape to the West. John Paul II may have been a critic of capitalism and a strong supporter of social justice, but he knew life under communism. It also seems likely, however, that when he applied his first-hand knowledge of totalitarian ideologies to his analysis of Western liberalism and capitalism, his phenomenology, or ability to determine the most essential characteristics of the system about which he lacked direct knowledge and experience, may have failed him. His perception of modern women, feminism, democracy and liberal economic systems became to some degree distorted by the misery and suffering he experienced around him.

But Marxist and radical feminists in the West were incomparably far more mistaken in their interpretation and observation of history and could not claim the lack of freedom as an excuse. From the perspective of someone living in communist Poland, Karol Wojtyła had no reason to be impressed with liberal Catholics who used Marxist and feminist language to demand a major break with Catholic tradition. He would never permit legalized abortion and contraception because he viewed them as violating the universal truths and the unchanging divine laws and plans. He would point out that the first country to legalize abortion was the Soviet Union (1920); the second was Iceland (1935). In his view, contraception and abortion diminished the value and dignity of human life, which was already under serious threat from other communist-supported political and social reforms.

But John Paul II found it difficult to understand fully some of the real complaints coming from Western feminists—not all of whom were Marxists or held radical views on morals and sexuality. Life in Poland before the fall of communism did not offer the full range of opinions, political dialogue and compromise found in countries with liberal democracies. At that time, Polish priests and bishops still did not yet see Western feminism as a serious cultural challenge to the traditional Church worldwide, but they were fully aware that the communist regime was responsible for legalizing abortion and tried to draw Polish women away from the Church.

Many Western feminist scholars who embraced de Beauvoir's Marxist analysis of female oppression knew very little about Russian history and everyday life of women in Poland and the Soviet Union. Without understanding the nature of communism, nationalism and their own cultural traditions, they tried to apply a simplistic theory based on an already failed ideology to explain a highly complex and changing situation of women from various nations and cultures. At least the pope knew enough about free-market capitalism to realize that most women in communist Poland would gladly exchange their lives for the life of an American middle class housewife. Under communism, working Polish women had to stand for hours in lines to find scarce food and other basic necessities. But even with that knowledge, John Paul II still did not see American-style economy and radical feminist ideas as a great improvement. He became convinced that America was "a continent marked by competition and aggres- siveness, unbridled consumerism and corruption," and he saw Americans as deeply unhappy despite their material wealth. His close advisor and successor, Cardinal Joseph Ratzinger (Benedict XVI), had a similarly low opinion of Americans. In a 1984 interview, Ratzinger suggested that being rich is a measure of one's worth in North America and "the values and style of life proposed by [American] Catholics appear more than ever as a scandal."[34] If in the 1920s and 1930s German Catholics and theologians were not afraid of scandal and were more outspoken in challenging the prevailing Catholic teaching on how to relate to Jews, perhaps there would have been more tolerance and fewer Germans would have supported Hitler's rise to power.

Having lived in the United States since 1970, I was intrigued by some of Wojtyła's and Ratzinger's views. Despite John Paul II's and Benedict XVI's bleak comments, I thought that most Americans were exceptionally, generous, tolerant, optimistic, and committed to the idea of personal dignity. Otherwise, why would so many Jews, Cubans, Vietnamese, Cambodians and other oppressed groups seek refuge in America? I also saw certain intriguing similarities between references by feminists to American racism and cultural-religious imperialism and John Paul II's condemnation of American consumerism, racism and aggressiveness. How could they agree that capitalist America and the expansion of Western culture created a grave danger for women, especially in the developing world, but could not agree on much else? Could it be that both sides focused too much on philosophical theories and ideology rather than on the real history, lives and desires of women? I saw moderate feminist ideas being spread most effectively from the West to more traditional societies in the East and in the South, including the communist nations, not the other way around. If there had been cultural-religious imperialism, as claimed by Schüssler Fiorenza, or cultural-secular imperialism, as claimed by John Paul II, both helped to advance the reform agenda developed in most part by politically liberal middle-class Western women, many of them practicing Christians and Jews.

As an immigrant from communist Poland, I also could not overlook the fact that despite their isolationism and reluctance to go to war, Americans helped to rescue democracy in Europe or parts of it at least three times in the 20th century—during WWI, WWII and the Cold War—and more recently in Bosnia and Kosovo. I observed how America, a largely Christian nation, defended Bosnian and Kosovo Muslims threatened with genocide and rape by the Serbian regime controlled by former communist leader Slobodan Milošević (1941-2006) and his ultranationalist forces. These European Muslims lived in small enclaves with no economic significance to Americans. I could think also of no other country that would allow over ten million immigrants to illegally cross its borders and not make every effort to catch and deport them. I knew that other nations would not be nearly as tolerant and generous toward millions of poor workers knocking on their doors. Most of these immigrants and refugees were fleeing from countries which had weak economies, traditional religious cultures and severe restrictions on women's rights. In what other country could foreign-born men and women—Henry Kissinger (b. 1923), Zbigniew Brzezinski (b. 1928), and Madeleine Albright (b. 1937) — become secretaries of state or top national security advisors to the top political leader? Two of them were Jewish: Kissinger and Albright, although Albright's parents converted to Christianity, while Brzezinski was a Polish Catholic who did not change his ethnic-sounding Polish name after becoming a U.S. citizen. They were refugees from continental Europe as it was being taken over by totalitarian ideologies of fascism and Marxist communism.

Perhaps John Paul II and Benedict XVI are right that Americans tend to abuse their freedom, but when in the 1930s several Catholic nations in Europe embraced fascism, including Benedict XVI's Germany, and large segments of their populations supported communism, the vast majority of Americans and Britons resisted the appeal of totalitarian ideologies. Still both Pope John Paul II and Benedict XVI persisted in their belief that Western societies are decadent because they lack hope, which in turn makes them reject family values. In his message for 2008, Benedict XVI called the family the primary means for assuring peace. And he warned that any negation of family rights threatens the foundations of peace: "everything that serves to weaken the family based on the marriage of a man and a woman, everything that directly or indirectly stands in the way of its openness to the responsible acceptance of a new life, everything that obstructs its right to be primarily responsible for the education of its children, constitutes an objective obstacle on the road to peace." He also criticized the West for what he called its lack of hope—a theme frequently advanced by Pope John Paul II. Benedict XVI concluded that "even in Rome one feels this deficit of hope and faith in life that constitutes the dark evil of modern Western society." He added that the lack of hope leads many people to seek sexual gratification instead of practicing faith and protecting family values:

Millions of immigrants, however, seem to contradict the views about Western society held by John Paul II and Benedict XVI. Visitors from the West to the Soviet-block countries were struck by the lack of smiles on people's faces on the streets of Warsaw and Moscow. But even then, John Paul II believed that Americans were deep down very unhappy and deprived of true love. Nevertheless, after the fall of the Berlin Wall, Great Britain, Ireland and the United States still attract large numbers of Poles seeking work and more opportunities for themselves and their families. Some are also attracted by freedom from strong social restrictions and prejudices. By some estimates, there are at least 700,000 Polish immigrants living in Great Britain and 200,000 in Ireland. There are estimated 10 million Americans of Polish descent. While economic opportunities have been the main reason for these migrations, most Polish immigrants do not have problems adjusting to the more liberal culture in Britain, Ireland or in the United States. They seem more hopeful about their future than people who live in more traditional societies.

Far from considering America as a good model for others to

Polish Organizations in Great Britain, Ireland, and the U.S.

Federation of Poles in Great Britain
http://www.zpwb.org.uk/eg/index.php

Polski Dublin
http://www.polskidublin.com/

Polish Information & Culture Center in Dublin
http://www.polishcentre.ie/en/

Polish American Congress
http://www.polamcon.org/

follow, however, John Paul II was appalled by its growing cultural and political influence in the world, especially after the 1960's sexual revolution, the Vietnam War and the *Roe v. Wade* U.S. Supreme Court decision legalizing abortions (1973). After a visit to the U.S. in 1976, Wojtyła wrote in a letter to the Polish Catholic youth, in which he observed that while the advances of technology and civilization may have made life "easier, more comfortable and more pleasant," they do not satisfy "the deepest human hunger, which is the hunger for love." That's why—he continued—everywhere in today's world, both in America and in Poland, "there is a great need for people who are capable of real love."[35] He had the same message in a radio interview I conducted with him at the end of his 1976 visit to the U.S.[36] He stressed that the modern, progressive world increases man's hunger for love and that man is being increasingly denied love and separated from it. I had no doubt that behind "real love" he meant also the love of the unborn, and behind "denying love and being separated from it" was America's acceptance of casual sex and abortion. I also detected in his answers some measure of disappointment in how Polish immigrants were absorbing what he considered negative aspects of American culture.

Post-Christian Feminists

Wojtyła believed that only faith in God and strict observance of Christian morality can bring people authentic hope, happiness and real love. He also believed that authentic respect for life derived from religion can eliminate abortion, prevent war and genocide and help moderate discrimination

Mary Daly

Born: October 16, 1928, Schenectady, N.Y., USA

Book: *The Church and the Second Sex*

Quote: "Simone de Beauvoir's position on the role of Christianity in the oppression of women is in large measure justified"

http://www.marydaly.net

against women. Many early feminists in the West agreed instead with Simone de Beauvoir who, as a convinced Marxist, saw religion as a powerful weapon of oppression in the hands of men. "Legislators, priests, philosophers, writers, and scientists" — she wrote in *The Second Sex* — "have striven to show that the subordinate position of woman is willed in heaven and advantageous on earth. The religions invented by men reflect this wish for domination." [37]

Some American Catholic feminists similarly concluded that Christianity is bad for women and cannot be reformed. Mary Daly made this a central argument in her 1973 book *Beyond God the Father*. Declaring herself "post-Christian," she moved away from the Catholic Church. Her earlier book *The Church and the Second Sex* (1968) already had a major impact on countless American Catholic women, including many nuns who had become radicalized after being exposed to feminist ideas.[38] As the title of Daly's book

---

Sister Margaret Traxler 1924-2002

The School Sisters of Notre Dame
http://www.ssnd.org/

The National Coalition of American Nuns
http://www.ncan.us/

The Institute of Women Today
http://www.instituteofwomentoday.org/

Maria Shelter
http://www.instituteofwomentoday.org/iwtPrograms.php

Sinsinawa Dominican Sisters
http://www.sinsinawa.org/

suggests, it was her attempt to introduce de Beauvoir's ideas to American Catholics, including nuns. Judging by relatively large numbers of socially conscious American nuns and liberal Catholics who had embraced her conclusion that de Beauvoir's Marxist criticism of the role of Christianity in the oppression of women was "in large measure justified," Daly can be considered a major figure responsible for the current state of American Catholicism.[39]

Sister Margaret Ellen Traxler of the School Sisters of Notre Dame is perhaps the most famous among radical American nuns who admit to being influenced by feminist ideas in Betty Friedan's and Mary Daly's books. Sister Margaret was a founder of the National Coalition of American Nuns, an organization that works on issues of justice in church and society. Still politically active, the NCAN has called recently for the impeachment of President Bush and Vice President Cheney, accusing them of lying to Americans about the war in Iraq. (The dissident NCAN represented only about two percent of all American nuns, but its ideological influence was deeply felt. In 1982, NCAN took a position in support of women's rights to choose abortion.[40]) Sister Margaret also founded the Institute of Women Today, a secular, nonprofit group of Protestant, Jewish and Catholic women, which runs shelters for homeless women and children. She also co-founded the Interreligious Conference on Soviet Jewry, for which she received an award from Golda Meier (1898-1978), Israel's female prime minister. Sister Margaret Traxler is also remembered in Chicago for her work on SisterHouse, a rehabilitation facility for women-prisoners seeking work, and her involvement with Maria Shelter and Casa Notre Dame, which provide help to women who are poor, homeless or victims of domestic violence [41]

In the 1960s, Sister Margaret marched with Dr. Martin Luther King, Jr. in Alabama demanding equal rights for African Americans. In the early 1970s, she began to campaign for ordination of women to Catholic priesthood. In 1984 she was one of the Catholic nuns who signed an ad in *The New York Times* expressing doubts about the Church's official stand on abortion. The ad did not question that abortion was morally wrong but advocated a pro-choice approach. Later, due to pressure from the Vatican, most of the signatories, including Sister Margaret, signed vaguely-worded retractions. This did not stop her in 1994 from going to Rome with ten other radical nuns to stage a protest under the windows of the pope's apartment against restricted participation of religious sisters in a Vatican conference on religious life. (Nuns represent the majority of the religious in the world, but the Vatican invited only few sisters to the meetings.) The protesting nuns did not wear religious habits and were detained for an hour by the Vatican police.

Cheryl L. Reed, an investigative reporter for *The Chicago Sun-Times* newspaper, wrote in her book *Unveiled: The Hidden Lives of Nuns* (2004) that Sister Margaret stopped attending church regularly in the 1980s because she could no longer tolerate some of the practices of the institutional Church. She also told the reporter that "the Pope, despite all his talks to the contrary, despises women." But in her last interview before her death in 2002, Sister Margaret said that despite being angry, she will not give up the Church. The Church, she said, "was given to me, and I will stay in and chide the men as often as I have the chance. The Church is mine. I am in the Church. I will die faithful."[42]

Much of the feminist dissident movement within the American Catholic Church in the 1960s and 1970s was centered in Chicago, a city with the largest population of people of Polish descent after Warsaw. Polish American nuns belonging to such congregations as the Felician Sisters, and Polish

Felician Sisters
http://www.feliciansisters.org/

Felician Sisters Chicago
http://www.felicianschicago.org/index.htm

Polish Roman Catholic Union of America
http://www.prcua.org/

American Catholics in general, did not join the religious feminist movement in any large numbers.[43] The Polish Roman Catholic Union of America, one of several Polish American fraternal organizations with close ties to the Catholic Church, granted its women members equal rights in 1873 with support from the local Roman Catholic clergy.[44] Undoubtedly because of historical and cultural reasons, however, ordination of women has not been a particularly divisive issue in Polish American parishes and among Polish American religious sisters. But Chicago, with its large Catholic population of many ethnic backgrounds, gave birth to several dissident Catholic organizations which began to challenge the local hierarchy, the U.S. Conference of Catholic Bishops and the pope. Chicago Catholic Women, formed in 1974 and dissolved in 2000, had worked tirelessly for the cause of women's ordination. On May 13, 1981, one of the dissident feminist leaders, Sister Donna Quinn, a member of the Sinsinawa Dominican Sisters, and fourteen other women disrupted an ordination ceremony for male priests conducted by Chicago's Archbishop Cardinal John Cody (1907-1982). When the cardinal asked the last one of the fifteen men whether he was ready to be ordained, all fifteen women stood up and shouted "we are ready." Cardinal Cody proceeded with the Mass and shortly after the protest he received a note, which he then read to the congregation. The note said that Pope John Paul II has just been shot in Rome. According to Sister Donna, people glared at the protesting women as if they had pulled the trigger.[45] Sister Donna Quinn has been active on behalf of many other causes, including actions against racism and support for pro-choice legislation, but ordination of women has always been one of her main concerns. "They understand it when it comes to race," she said in an interview. "All colors are called to leadership in the Church—provided you are male. Why don't they get it when it comes to gender discrimination?"[46]

Another well-known and outspoken dissident Catholic nun is Sister Joan Chittister of the Benedictine Sisters of Erie,

Sister Joan D. Chittister b. 1936

"Men who do not take the woman's issue seriously may be priests, but they cannot possibly be disciples. They cannot possibly be 'other Christs.' Not the Christ born of a woman. Not the Christ who commissioned women to preach him. Not the Christ who took faculties from a woman at Cana. Not the Christ who sent women to preach resurrection to apostles who would not believe it then and do not believe it now."

The Benedictine Sisters of Erie, Pennsylvania

http://www.eriebenedictines.org/

Pennsylvania. She has also focused her criticism of Pope John Paul II and the Vatican on the issue of women's ordination. In June 2000, she attended the first Women's Ordination Worldwide (WOW) Conference in Dublin, Ireland despite a specific order from the Vatican issued to her and another Catholic nun to stay away. (The other nun was Sister Myra Poole of the Notre Dame de Namur Sisters in London, who initially stayed away from the conference but attended a session on women in developing countries, which she had helped to organize.) Sister Chittister received sustained applause and cheers when she said at the conference that "men who do not take the woman's issue seriously may be priests, but they cannot possibly be disciples." The prioress of the Benedictine Sisters of Erie, Sister Christine Vladimiroff, was openly angry with the Vatican and defiant in declining to carry out its request. Of the 128 members of the Benedictine community in Erie, 127 signed a letter in defense of Sister Chittister's right to speak out on issues of concern to Catholics. A frequent quest on television programs and a regular columnist for *The National Catholic Reporter*, Dr. Chittister has authored many books, for which she received seven Catholic Press Association awards. She continues to maintain her association with a number of dissident Catholic organizations supporting women's ordination.

Liberal Catholic media defended Sister Chittister's defiant

stand against the Vatican. Matrin Browne, Dublin correspondent for *The Tablet*, a Catholic weekly in Britain, warned that "intimidating those...who belong to religious

> **The Tablet**
>
> http://www.thetablet.co.uk/

congregations will hardly serve any purpose other than to create pain, harden attitudes and deepen division."[47] But conservative Catholics have an entirely different perspective on Chittister's activism and the support she enjoys in her religious community in Pennsylvania. One of their organizations, The Catholic Culture, has rated the web site of the Benedictine Sisters in Erie as theologically suspect. Conservative Catholics accuse Sister Chittister's order not only of defying the Vatican but also of promoting a "New Age mentality" and not being reflective of the true Benedictine tradition.

Sister Margaret Traxler, Sister Donna Quinn and Sister Joan Chittister stayed within the Catholic Church, but as British post-Christian theologian Daphne Hampson observed, some feminists found they could no longer be associated with a religion, which they believed was harming women, even though some still wanted to retain religion in their lives.[48] Hampson argued that it would be pointless to blame the early Christians for creating and perpetuating anti-female myths. They did so according to their view of the world and their limited and largely mistaken scientific knowledge. Some post-Christian feminists blame today's Church leaders for not trying to correct some of the mistaken views and for refusing to offer a sincere apology to women combined with meaningful reforms. Hampson, who has concluded that Christianity is "neither true nor moral," does not believe that such reforms are possible. She points out that feminism, unlike many other crises successfully weathered by Judeo-Christian faiths, fatally undermines their insistence on representing God as male.

Early in her academic career, Professor Hampson came up with an interesting argument in support of ordination of women in the

Anglican Church based on her study of the response (or lack thereof) of Christian churches to the rise of fascism in Nazi Germany. In an analysis that could also be used to attack John Paul II's views on women-priests, she asserted that just as honest religious leaders could not consider the churches in Germany truly Christian if they supported a repressive Nazi regime, the Church of England also could not be seen as truly Christian until it accepted the idea that women were full human beings and demonstrated its sincerity by ordaining them as pastors. But official Anglican and Catholic theology no longer describes women as less perfect than men and no major Catholic leader in recent decades has suggested that women should be deprived of civil rights or exterminated like the Jews in Nazi-occupied Europe. Hampson's argument, however, had a strong propaganda impact on the debate about women's priesthood, and that may have been her objective.

Like most other post-Christian theologians or radical Catholic nuns, Hampson has been associated with disarmament and peace movements. At least in this area, she had something in common with John Paul II's lifelong abhorrence of war even if, unlike most Left-wing Western feminists, he did not see the Soviet Union as working for peace and progress. Still, in drawing analogies between Nazi Germany and the denial of priesthood to women, Hampson's arguments were more subtle than somewhat similar comments by Betty Friedan. While appreciating propaganda value of Friedan's and Daly's rhetoric, Hampson chose to use more scholarly arguments to prove her point that feminism and Christianity were incompatible.

Daphne Hampson concluded that Jesus was undoubtedly "kind to women" but that he was neither a feminist nor a misogynist.[49] In his 1995 *Letter to the Women of the World*, John Paul II made a similar point: "Transcending the established norms of his own culture, Jesus treated women with openness, respect, acceptance and tenderness."[50] As a post-Christian feminist, Hampson does not believe, however, that Jesus Christ was divine, describing him only as "a very fine human being." She also inisist that despite some unconventional attitudes about women, Christ was indeed culturally conditioned and largely followed the Jewish tradition. He did not include women among the Apostles since under Jewish law women were not considered reliable witnesses and therefore could not "go out and bear witness to Jesus." Women who discovered the empty tomb were advised to go and tell the men, and Christ then proceeded to show himself to the traditional Apostles.[51]

On the question of exclusively male priesthood, Daphne Hampson points out that there is no evidence of any direct connection between the twelve Apostles and the Church ministry that grew in the non-Jewish world. In that sense, St. Paul was not ordained and, according to Hampson, "would not have known what the term connoted."[52] She also challenges the view that Christ himself was a radical feminist. Hampson, observed, that there are 170 references in the Gospels where Jesus calls God "Father," and not a single reference to God as "Mother."[53] Ironically, on this point at least, she and John Paul II may be in agreement. John Paul II also did not see Christ as promoting feminism in its modern-day definition, but he interpreted his teachings quite differently than feminist theologians.

Hampson conceded that judging from the writings of Christ's male disciples, he may have allowed women to be among his students, but she points out that there is no record of Christ suggesting that men take over some of the household chores associated in the Jewish society only with women. She also noted that Christ's parables do not challenge the privileged legal position of males in the Jewish society or directly challenge the oppression of women. Christ also did not question the idea that property can only be divided among male-children. She also points out that all authority figures in Christ's parables are male, and that, at least in his recorded sayings, Christ never suggests that women should be allowed into the main part of the synagogue or that they should follow the same obligations for prayer as men.

For feminist scholars like Dr. Hampson, there was little doubt that Christ was not divine and that he reflected and largely conformed to the culture of his times—a point hotly disputed by John Paul II, who chose to use some of the same recorded teachings and actions of Christ to show his kindness toward women while justifying denying them ordination as priests. John Paul II preferred to see Christ as stressing the dignity of women and their specific but restricted role as mothers. He believed that Christ's behavior encouraged acceptance of differences between women and men as a natural and desirable reflection of God's divine plan for humanity. But since Hampson's studies led her to conclude that Christ was merely human and did not even intend to establish a new religion, there was no good reason—according to her—why twenty centuries later, women should model their behavior based on the views of a first century Jewish man and his male disciples, even if he were a remarkably gentle and tolerant person for his times.

Conservative Christians vehemently disagreed with such post-Christian feminist analysis. Catholic journalist Donna Steichen, in her 1991 book *Ungodly Rage: The Hidden Face of Catholic Feminism*, attacked these views as the work of enemies of religion and the Catholic Church. She described "Women-Church"—being promoted by Sister Donna Quinn, Sister Margaret Traxler, Dr. Rosemary Radford, Dr. Elizabeth Schüssler Fiorenza and others—as primarily a forum for advancing feminist agenda items: "abortion, homosexuality, [pagan] spirituality and revolutionary politics."[54] Steichen identified these women scholars and theologians as especially dangerous and argued that they should not be allowed to speak on behalf of the Catholic Church.

While it is difficult to make accurate assessments of popular support for various movements, it does not appear that these dissident Catholic scholars and their organizations still have much of an impact among Catholics in the United States after nearly 30

Lavinia Byrne b. 1947

Sister Lavinia Byrne, author of the influential book *Woman at the Altar* (1994), has been one of the most outspoken promoters of sacramental priesthood for Catholic women in the UK. In 2000, she left the Institute of the Blessed Virgin Mary, also known as the Loreto Sisters.

http://www.laviniabyrne.co.uk/

The Institute of the Blessed Virgin Mary

http://www.ibvm.org/

Not to be confused with Sisters of Loretto, another progressive community established in the 19th century in the United States, the Loreto Sisters is a religious order founded in 1609 by an Englishwomen Mary Ward (1585-1649). Mary Ward was an early proponent of socially active orders of uncloistered nuns free from the jurisdiction of male diocesan priests. She also believed that women were equal to men in intellect and should be educated accordingly. Her ideas were, however, too revolutionary for the 17th century Catholic Church. Church officials declared her a heretic. Mary Ward was imprisoned and her community was suppressed. She was not recognized by the Church as founder of IBVM until 1909. Focused on education, the Loreto sisters run a number of schools in several countries.

Loreto Sisters Australia

http://www.loretosisters.org.au/

Loreto India

http://www.loreto.in/

The Loreto Ireland

http://www.loreto.ie/

IBVM Loreto Sisters UK

http://www.ibvmloreto-uk.org/

IBVM US

http://www.ibvm.us/

years of John Paul II's papacy and increased ideological challenge from moderate and conservative Catholic thinkers. Many of the radical post-Christian feminist web sites are not being regularly updated. Some of these organizations have aging and declining membership and other characteristics of a fringe and divided community. Many of the ideas initially advanced by radical post-Christian feminist theologians, however, have already become, in more moderate forms, a permanent part of mainstream American Catholicism, which continues to be much more liberal than John Paul II and his successor would have liked.

Early in John Paul II's papacy, some Catholic feminists were still hoping for a change in the Church's stand on women, homosexuality and celibacy for priests. In a petition circulated in November 1980, two years after his election as pope, Christian women theologians called upon him to enter into a dialogue with members of the women's liberation movement and to "better acquaint himself with the actual concerns of this movement." They described its primary purpose as "a just and necessary corrective to the long centuries of subjugation of women to secondary participation in human development."[55]

Most radical Catholic feminists, however, quickly gave up any hopes for a change in the pope's attitudes on women. Writing in her 1984 book, *Pure Lust*, Mary Daly rejected expectations of change in the Vatican as completely unrealistic. "Their mistake," she wrote about women hoping for a positive change, "lies in failing to confront the fact that they are dealing with dealers of Biggest Lies, from whom there is no hope of rationality."[56] Daly described any hopes of a dialogue with John Paul II as "exercises in self-abasement and absurdity," comparing the 1980 petition of women theologians to the pope to "petitioning hard-core porn peddlers to acquaint themselves with the actual concerns of the women's movement and enter into dialogue about the ethics of their multi-billion-dollar industry."[57]

Comparing John Paul II to a hard core porn peddler was a sure

WATER

http://www.his.com/~mhunt/index.htm

Mary E. Hunt

http://www.his.com/~mhunt/marye.htm

Diann L. Neu

http://www.his.com/~mhunt/diannneu.htm

One of the Woman-Church feminist organizations still showing some activity on their web sites is WATER—the Women's Alliance for Theology, Ethics and Ritual in Silver Spring, Maryland, USA. Its co-founders and co-directors are Mary E. Hunt and Diann L. Neu. WATER is described as a feminist educational center offering publications and workshops, counseling, spiritual direction and liturgical planning which help people actualize feminist religious values in the service of social change. The WATER web site describes Hunt and Neu as partners raising a daughter and identifies Hunt as a Roman Catholic. Nothing about WATER or its web site suggests that it is a mass movement of Catholic women. (New feminism and conservative Catholic women's organizations appear more active, but they also lack widespread influence among generally liberal American Catholics.) Author and editor of numerous books and articles on religion and feminism, Dr. Hunt is an advisor to the Women's Ordination Conference, a member of the advisory boards of the Center for Lesbian and Gay Studies in Religion and Ministry at Pacific School of Religion and of the Lesbian Gay Bisexual Transgender Religious Archives Network. Together with Elizabeth Schüssler Fiorenza, Hunt established Feminist Theologians Liberation Network. She expressed a strong belief that John Paul II's papacy caused serious problems for women worldwide in numerous ways. Dr. Diann L. Neu is a feminist liturgist and psychotherapist as well author of several books on feminist liturgy, including *Return Blessings: Ecofeminist Liturgies Renewing the Earth* (2003).

Dissident Catholic and Woman-Church Web Sites

Federation of Christian Ministries
http://www.federationofchristian-ministries.org/

Southeastern Pennsylvania Women's Ordination Conference
http://www.sepawoc.org/

Future Church
http://www.futurechurch.org/

God Talk
http://www.godtalktv.org/

Women's Justice Coalition
http://www.sepawoc.org/

Catholics Speak Out
http://cso.quixote.org/

Spiritus Christi Church
http://www.spirituschristi.org/

sign that the most radical feminists among current and former Catholics were not interested in a dialogue with him. On the other hand, he also did not seem interested in having a serious dialogue with radical feminists, even if in personal encounters he treated every person, including communist leaders, with great respect. Whether their demands were indeed too radical and whether the "radical" label should be used at all is, of course, debatable. But John Paul II clearly saw them as being radical and their demands as misguided and harmful. They in turn saw him as an arch-conservative pope who was out of touch with the modern world when in fact his background was far closer to the life experience of the vast majority of people worldwide than the life experience of Western feminists. Dr. Schüssler Fiorenza observed that some of the American cardinals and bishops, as well as the "Right-wing Catholic press" took their cue from Pope John Paul II and Cardinal Ratzinger in making the term "radical feminism" into "a scare word for many church women."[58] Using de Beauvoir's analysis of what it means to be "the Other," she accused the Christian Right of applying the label of "dangerous outsiders" to "groups such as blacks, socialists, terrorists, Jews, gays, or feminists"—a partly debatable claim at least in light of the Evangelicals' strong support for Israel and some of their attempts to win over to their cause conservative African American Christians.[59] Each side was convinced that its model of gender relations was best and neither was willing to entertain the idea that perhaps no single and rigid model could possibly meet the needs and desires of women living under vastly different economic and social conditions.

Mary Daly and others who had rejected Christianity as fundamentally biased against women and were seeking other forms of spiritual expression have not been successful in proposing a new religion attracting any substantial following. Their ideas once had a powerful impact and fundamentally changed the Catholic Church in America, but their "ungodly rage" is no longer a serious threat as described by Donna Steichen in her 1991 book by the same title. Catholics who have drifted away from religion altogether represent now a much more serious problem for the Catholic Church. In terms of active practicing members, the American Church is now smaller and more conservative. At the same time, a large group of liberal Catholics simply ignored the rules imposed by the pope, the Vatican and their conservative bishops. They began practicing within the Church their own form of liberal and tolerant, and as some critics would say, self-indulgent "supermarket" Catholicism. Some liberal and moderate Catholics, who have not become totally indifferent, are still hoping the Church will change its views on women, perhaps under a new pope.

New Feminists and Solidarity of Love

Conservative and some liberal Catholics who remained in the Church began to promote John Paul II's "new feminism" as an alternative to the traditional feminist movement. With his death in 2005, the movement lacks, however, a single significant spokesman or an influential theologian. Unlike Simone de Beauvoir and Mary Daly, theorists and theologians of "new feminism" — such as Elizabeth Fox-Genovese, the author of *Feminism Without Illusions: A*

Elizabeth Fox Genovese 1941-2007

Book: *Feminism Without Illusions*

Quote: "Feminism, as the daughter of individualism, carries the potential of bringing individualism back to its social moorings by insisting that the rights of individuals derive from society rather than from their innate nature."

Critique of Individualism (1991) and Michele M. Schumacher, the editor of *Women in Christ: Toward a New Feminism* (2004) — have not yet achieved much influence or even wide name recognition.

They are all proponents to various degrees of difference feminism, a philosophy which stresses that men and women are different versions of the human being and points out fundamental biological, emotional, psychological or spiritual differences between the sexes. Their message is certainly not as clear and as direct as Simone de Beauvoir's appeal for the struggle against patriarchy. As treacherous as they were, de Beauvoir's ideas were catching enough to help push forward a feminist revolution that produced significant gains for women, as well as created some serious new problems. Fortunately, liberal traditions in the West mitigated some of the negative impact of de Beauvoir's theory that was based essentially on exploiting antagonism and hatred between human groups. The results were, however, disastrous in some of the communist nations with few liberal protections and traditions. But somehow even in the West, Marxist slogans calling for gender competition seemed more straightforward than calls to promote gender solidarity through love and sacrifice combined with long explanations as to why women and men are different but equal. A simple message of love and gender solidarity combined with a call for ending discrimination might have worked better. Unfortunately, John Paul II was also trying to excuse the ban on women holding leadership positions within the Church and defended the male hierarchy's exclusive right to dictate birth control methods and most other significant decisions affecting women. This did not go too well with many people. But even though many Catholics and non-Catholics are still pro-choice, his "culture of life" versus "culture of death" message against abortion, euthanasia and the death penalty had a definite resonance and impact because of its powerful emotional content and straightforwardness.

As women have become more sophisticated and the Soviet Union collapsed, radical and Marxist feminism has also lost much of its earlier appeal. In the West, the feminist movement has become more diverse and mainstream, with women choosing between many different ideas, including those of Catholic feminism in its conservative and liberal forms. John Paul II's new feminism, however, is still waiting for someone who can explain it. "Gender complementarity," "different but equal," "female genius," "personalism," and "love and responsibility" do not seem to be particularly catching slogans, while "new feminism" has such broad meaning that most people do not even associate it with John Paul II. "Female genius" is probably the best slogan to describe new feminism, but many will question whether it is not simply a cover for keeping women in the kitchen. If offered seriously, "female genius" evokes patronizing irony. It sounds too far-fetched to be believable to skeptical, educated women scared by centuries of male-generated propaganda and discrimination.

To be successful in advancing a new movement that would appeal to more than just socially conservative Catholics and other conservative Christians, John Paul II's message to women may have to be presented in its most essential elements of human dignity, love and solidarity in a language that is understandable to people who grew up in liberal societies without war, repression and poverty. The cultural assumptions behind Wojtyła's gender philosophy relating to his Polish background and his nation's history would have to be either explained or excused as too rigid for modern men and women. Above all, to be successful, John Paul II's message would have to be greatly enhanced with a true commitment to removing discrimination and exploitation of women, starting with the Catholic Church. New feminists who want to promote his theology of woman have a formidable task before them. They may want take an example from John Paul II's homeland and use such terms as "solidarity between genders" and "human solidarity" – although the word "solidarity" has socialist connotations which may be alien to modern women. "Human solidarity" shows that men and women indeed share a common history and must work together to achieve their common goals and their common future. Elements of love – divine, human, or both – can be inferred from both of these terms or combined in "solidarity of love" between genders.

Barring a major historical upheaval, it seems unlikely that a single vision of gender relations will ever again dominate the feminist movement or win the hearts and minds of the majority of women. But in the United States, in Britain and in most of the Western world, liberal and post-Christian theologians still set the tone for the debate on feminism and religion. In an article on the on the history of American Catholic feminism in *Reconciling Catholicism and Feminism?*, a book of essays published in 2003, Rosemary Radford Ruether discussed such early feminist and dissident organizations as the Grail, the Women's Seminary Quarter, the Christian Family Movement, the Leadership Conference of Women Religious, the Women's Ordination Conference, the Women-Church Convergence, Chicago Catholic Women, Catholics for a Free Choice, and WATER (Women's Alliance for Theology, Ethics, and Ritual.

In her article, Rosemary Radford Ruether did not include any information about new feminism and its pro-life scholars and organizations, such as Feminists for Life (FFL), Concerned Women for America, Women Affirming Life, The Feminism and Nonviolence Studies Association, Susan B. Anthony List, Women for Faith and Family, ENDOW, and Women of the Third Millennium. In Northern California, the California Catholic

Additional Liberal Catholic, Women Priests and Feminist Liberation Web Sites

The Grail

http://www.grail-us.org

The Christian Family Movement (CFM)

http://www.cfm.org/home.html

The Leadership Conference of Women Religious (LCWR)

http://www.lcwr.org

The Women's Ordination Conference (WOC)

http://www.womensordination.org

"Eliminate all forms of oppression against women.

Support and affirm women's talents, gifts and calls to ministry."

The Women-Church Convergence (W-CC)

http://www.women-churchconvergence.org

Chicago Catholic Women (CCW)

http://www.luc.edu/wla/pdfs/Chicago_Catholic_Women.pdf

Catholics for a Free Choice (CFFC)

http://www.catholicsforchoice.org

Call to Action (CTA)

http://www.cta-usa.org

"CTA believes that the Spirit of God is at work in the whole church, not just in its appointed leaders."

School of Theology – The University of Auckland

http://www.theology.auckland.ac.nz/

Center for Feminist Theology and Ministry in Japan

http://cftmj2000.cocolog-nifty.com/

Circle of Concerned African Women Theologians

http://www.thecirclecawt.org/default

Women's Forum reports that since 2005 its members have been unraveling Pope John Paul II's Apostolic Letter to women *Mulieris*

Dignitatem on the dignity and vocation of women. Despite an abundance of Catholic groups that have embraced new feminism, Rosemary Radford Ruether used the term Catholic feminism to describe only those individuals and organizations which have been in some way in opposition to the Vatican and Pope John Paul II.[60]

Liberal feminists, who have actively promoted the idea of sisterhood, generally do not recognize pro-life Christian feminists as legitimate participants in their movement. Similarly, conservative Catholic organizations denounce liberal Catholic feminists as anti-Catholic and demand their excommunication. But most feminists in the United States, whether they are pro-life or pro-

---

Pro-Life and New Feminism Web Sites

Feminists for Life (FFL)

http://www.feministsforlife.org

"The early feminists, some of whose names are very familiar to you, and others whom you have yet to meet, were overwhelmingly pro-life."

Concerned Women for America

http://www.cwfa.org

Women Affirming Life

http://www.affirmlife.com

The Feminism and Nonviolence Studies Association

http://www.fnsa.org

Susan B. Anthony List

http://www.sba-list.org

ENDOW (Educating on the Nature and Dignity of Women

http://www.endowonline.com

"Unfortunately, in the past, traditional feminism divided and categorized women. ENDOW brings women together, to unite instead of divide."

Women of the Third Millennium

http://www.wttm.org

The California Catholic Women's Forum (CCWF)

http://www.ccwf.org

choice, are not radical. Feminists for Life received media attention in 2005 when news reports revealed prior to the confirmation hearings for the U.S. Chief Justice John G Roberts, Jr. (b. 1955) that his wife Jane Sullivan Roberts is legal counsel to the organization and a former Executive Vice-President.[61] She can hardly be described as a radical. Patricia Heaton (b. 1958), an Emmy Award-winning American actress best known for playing Debra Barone on the CBS television sitcom *Everybody Loves Raymond*, is honorary co-chair of Feminists for Life. Another FFL co-chair is actress Margaret Colin (b. 1957) who appeared in the soap opera *As the World Turns* and in a number of movies including *Independence Day* (1996). *As the World Turns* is probably one of the best portrayals of an unacceptable Western lifestyle and would be harshly condemned by John Paul II, yet a former soap opera star can easily become a spokesperson for an organization with a serious pro-life message without offending too many Americans. According to *The New York Times*, Patricia Heaton, who comes from an Irish American Roman Catholic family, supports gay rights and is in favor of using most methods of birth control even though she campaigns against abortion, embryonic stem-cell research and the death penalty.[62] John Paul II and his conservative Polish friends would probably find Heaton's views on birth control and gay rights and Colin's acting roles difficult to reconcile with their pro-life feminist label. Huge capacity for tolerance among Americans of all faiths may explain why the pope found it difficult to communicate with liberal American Catholics and could not quite grasp the diversity of American feminism. He felt strongly, however, that by setting clear rules he was doing his job and, in the long run, helping Americans reach a higher moral standard.

Liberal or Conservative Pope?

It took some time after Wojtyła became pope before liberal Catholics in the United States and other Western countries began to see him as the enemy of progress and reform who would not change his views on women. Many people were initially impressed by his youthfulness, energy and charisma. Call To Action (CTA), a leading liberal Catholic organization founded in Chicago in 1978, tried to engage the pope in a dialogue. Eventually, however, the organization accused John Paul II of repeatedly dashing "hopes for any liberalizing during his lifetime" and preparing for the future "by appointing as bishops only men who upheld his views on contraception and the ordination of women."[63] One of the bishops appointed by Pope John Paul II, Bishop Fabian Bruskewitz (b. 1935) of Lincoln, Nebraska, excommunicated CTA members in his diocese.

Andrew M. Greeley
Born: February 5, 1928, Oak Park, IL. USA
http://www.agreeley.com

In 1978, Father Andrew M. Greeley, a liberal American Catholic priest and author, also had high hopes that John Paul II — an intellectual, a poet and a liberal during the Second Vatican Council — would turn out to be a liberal pope.[64] Wojtyła was indeed a liberal Catholic bishop, which he had demonstrated during Vatican II by his advocacy of reconciliation and better relations with other religions — some of them far less liberal toward women than Catholicism — but he was liberal when measured against Polish historical and cultural norms, and much less liberal by American and West European standards of the 1970s and beyond.

Those who knew John Paul II well before he became pope — his Polish friends and the late Polish-American Archbishop of Philadelphia Cardinal John Krol (1910-1996) — were more realistic in their initial assessment of Wojtyła's potential for promoting radical reforms with regard to women. In 1979, Cardinal Krol quoted from Wojtyła's article "Crisis in Morality," published ten years earlier: "It is one thing to be understanding in the spirit of Christ, but quite another to remove the limits between good and evil within the context of the same principle."[65] John Paul II consistently applied this rule throughout his papacy to any controversial issue. By stressing it, he showed his unwillingness to compromise on the basic principles of traditional Catholic morality and religious practice, which he considered well-established and well-tested. He was willing to reject some traditional beliefs, such as anti-Semitism, antagonism toward other religions and some forms of discrimination against women. It should not have been surprising to American Catholics, however, that he differentiated between good and evil and determined what was good and bad for the Church and for women largely according to his own cultural assumptions and expectations. After all, even in a country like the United States with a common history and basic common values, there are strong cultural differences between "red" and "blue" states, as there are between conservative evangelical Christians and liberal Christian churches. Depending on their level of education, income, urban or rural lifestyle, ethnic background and regional culture, Americans hold vastly different views on many important issues dealing with morality and the role of women in churches and families.

As many Americans realized after the terrorist attacks and the war in Iraq and Afghanistan, these differences are far greater between religions and between nations with even more distinct cultures and vastly different histories. Resorting to war by a largely Christian superpower to establish a liberal democracy in an under-developed Muslim country was, in John Paul II's view, a tragic mistake. He was not against democracy, but he saw desirable democratic change as a long-term process that should not be imposed on a Muslim country by an outside military force of a largely Christian but morally deficient nation, even if that nation had previously saved Europe from fascism and to some degree also from communism. Despite vague suggestions by the Bush Administration officials of historical analogies between Adolf Hitler's Germany and Saddam Hussein's Iraq, John Paul II believed that there were no such analogies, and if there were any, they did not justify a military action by the United States. John L. Allen Jr. (b. 1965), the veteran Vatican correspondent for the *National Catholic Reporter* and author of a book on Cardinal Ratzinger, *Cardinal Ratzinger: The Vatican's Enforcer of the Faith*, and another book on *Opus Dei*, observed that the Holy See simply does not think the U.S. is fit to run the world.[66] In 1999, John Paul II said: "After the fall of the Soviet Union, the United States remained alone. I don't know if this is good or bad, but this is how it is."[67] Abortion, birth control, and radical feminism and their global spread were part of John Paul II's severely negative evaluation of American democracy in addition to any geopolitical factors. In dealing with non-Western countries, the pope was particularly sensitive to placing too much emphasis too quickly on expanding women's rights, especially in matters dealing with sexual morality and religion. He did not want this issue to upset the Catholic Church's dialogue with the Orthodox Churches and Islam — a dialogue which he greatly desired.

What perhaps makes John Paul II difficult to understand is that he was neither a Westerner nor a typical East Central European male, neither a true conservative nor a true liberal; neither an enemy of feminism nor its unquestioning supporter, neither a blind admirer of democracy nor someone who rejected democracy. He did not quite fit the definition of a misogynist shaped by Western imperialist culture. Wojtyła was not born in the West — something he often stressed in claiming, as a Pole, a special respect for women and a special understanding of the concerns of people in the developing world and the concerns of other religions. At the time of his election to papacy, Poland was still in the Soviet block and part of the so-called "Second World." He would have been much more likely to agree with radical feminist views on women's rights if he had been born in the West and educated by liberal American and West European theologians.

Wojtyła's Theological Argument Behind the Ban on Women-Priests

It is understandable that as a religious leader who did not want to make a radical break with tradition and was horrified by the excesses of Western liberalism, John Paul II saw gender at its core as an unchangeable expression of God's design rather than a product of a specific culture at a given historical moment. Once he decided that he would not allow women to become priests, he had to take a theological position to defend his decision. (Christ was a male; he did not choose women as apostles; women cannot represent male Christ; the pope and the Church have no power to question Christ's design for male priesthood; men and women are different but equal.) In the Western cultural context of freedom, equal rights and liberal democracy, only a theological argument for not treating men and women equally could have even the remotest chance of being considered, and then perhaps only by those who strongly believe in God and tradition and are not inclined to question religious authority.

This theological argument against women-priests is now one of the key features of "new feminism"—a movement which John Paul II helped to launch but which has not yet caught the imagination of vast numbers of women probably because of such arguments. A theologian of new feminism Michele M. Schumacher observed that John Paul II used the term "new feminism" for the first time in his 1995 encyclical *Evangelium vitae* (*The Gospel of Life*). The encyclical dealt primarily with the value and inviolability of human life.[68] Its focus was on abortion, which remains one of the central issues that new feminists address using John Paul II's teaching. But if history of Western liberalism and expansion of human rights offers any guidance, it will be extremely difficult if not impossible for theologians of new feminism to come up with new convincing arguments in favor of John Paul II's theological position that women cannot be priests because they do not resemble Christ or because Christ did not want them to be priests. In the West, the majority of people no

Women for Faith and Family

http://www.wf-f.org

Affirmation for Catholic Women

Because of the assaults against the Christian Faith and the family by elements within contemporary society which have led to pervasive moral confusion, to damage and destruction of families and the men, women and children who comprise them;

Because we adhere to the Catholic Christian faith as expressed in Holy Scripture, the Nicene, Apostolic and Athanasian Creeds, in the ecumenical Councils of the Church, and in the continued deepening of the understanding of the revelations of Sacred Truth to the Church by the Holy Spirit through the teaching authority of the Church and of the Successors of Peter, Apostle;

Because we wish to affirm our desire to realize our vocations and our duty as Christians and as women in accordance with these authentic teachings, following the example and instruction of Our Savior Jesus Christ, and the example of Mary, His mother;

Because we are cognizant of our obligations as Christian women to witness to our faith, being mindful that this witness is important to the formation of the moral conscience of our families and of humanity, we wish to make this affirmation:

1. We believe that through God's grace our female nature affords us distinct physical and spiritual capabilities with which to participate in the Divine Plan for creation. Specifically, our natural function of childbearing endows us with the spiritual capacity for nurture, instruction, compassion and selflessness, which qualities are necessary to the establishment of families, the basic and Divinely ordained unit of society, and to the establishment of a Christian social order.

2. We believe that to attempt to subvert or deny our distinct nature and role as women subverts and denies God's plan for humanity, and leads to both personal disintegration and ultimately to the disintegration of society. Accordingly, we reject all ideologies which seek to eradicate the natural and essential distinction between the sexes, which debase and devalue

womanhood, family life and the nurturing role of women in society.

3. We affirm the intrinsic sacredness of all human life, and we reject the notion that abortion, the deliberate killing of unborn children, is the "right" of any human being, male or female, or of any government. Such a distorted and corrosive notion of individual freedom is, in fact, inimical to authentic Christianity and to the establishment and maintenance of a just social order.

4. We accept and affirm the teaching of the Catholic Church on all matters dealing with human reproduction, marriage, family life and roles for men and women in the Church and in society.

5. We therefore also reject as an aberrant innovation peculiar to our times and our society the notion that priesthood is the "right" of any human being, male or female. Furthermore, we recognize that the specific role of ordained priesthood is intrinsically connected with and representative of the begetting creativity of God in which only human males can participate. Human females, who by nature share in the creativity of God by their capacity to bring forth new life, and, reflective of this essential distinction, have a different and distinct role within the Church and in society from that accorded to men, can no more be priests than men can be mothers.

6. We recognize and affirm the vocations of women who subordinate their human role of motherhood and family life in order to consecrate their lives to the service of God, His Church and humanity. Such women's authentic response of consecrated service to the physical, spiritual and/or intellectual needs of the community in no way diminishes or compromises their essential female nature, or the exercise of inherent attributes, insights and gifts peculiar to women. Rather, it extends the applications of these gifts beyond the individual human family.

7. We stand with the Second Vatican Council, which took for granted the distinct roles for men and women in the family and in society and affirmed that Christian education must impart knowledge of this distinction: "In the entire educational program [Catholic school teachers] should, together with the parents, make full allowance for the difference of sex and for the particular role which Providence has appointed to each sex in the family and

in society." (Declaration on Education, Sec. 8, paragraph 3, from Vatican II Documents, ed. Austin Flannery, 1981)

8. We pledge our wholehearted support to the teachings of Pope John Paul II concerning all aspects of family life and roles for men and women in the Church and in society, especially as contained in the Apostolic Exhortation, *Familiaris consortio*; and we resolve to apply the principles contained therein to our own lives, our families and our communities, God being our aid.

longer accept such reasoning. Poland, however, is one of the few European countries where those opposed to the ordination of women-priests are still in the majority.[69]

Despite his reputation as a defender of Catholic dogma, John Paul II was not incapable of questioning and changing the Church doctrine. As one of the Vatican II reformers, he was definitely aware of the influence of the liberal German theologian Father Karl Rahner, SJ (1904-1984) who observed that "many Church doctrines, which were once universally held, proved to be problematic or erroneous."[70] (Wojtyła supported academic training of Father Maliński when his friend decided to write a doctoral thesis on Rahner's religious philosophy.) For many centuries, the Catholic Church and most lay people thought that slavery and the divine right of kings to rule over their subjects were natural and normal, and few questioned these ideas. Eventually, however, these ideas were exposed as unjust and quickly rejected. John Paul II himself contributed to the demise of some of these doctrines and beliefs. It will be interesting to see whether in a few decades from now, John Paul II's positions on birth control and women-priests will still be debated or whether the institutional Church will also discard them, as many Catholics have done so already. Whether the institutional Church will continue to put as much emphasis as John Paul II did on different and restrictive role models for men and women (Jesus Christ and Virgin Mary) is also a question waiting to be answered.

There are, however, many other elements in John Paul II's teachings with regard to women, gender and moral theology that are perhaps more original and also worthy of careful watching and continued analysis. His writings that emphasize inviolability of human life and human dignity, his personalistic concept that no person can be used merely as a means to advance other people's ends, his ideas of social and gender solidarity, and his concept of love as a free "gift of self" for the good of another person, and his entire theology of the body will likely continue to inspire serious discussions.

Genocide and Abortion

As important as Polish traditions and culture are for the understanding of John Paul II's views and ideas, his country's recent history may have played an even greater role in shaping his approach to gender issues, particularly with regard to birth control and abortion. Of course, history and culture are always closely linked, and Wojtyła had the misfortune of living during one of the most tragic periods in Poland's history. Although not indifferent to the problem of discrimination against women, John Paul II was much more concerned about something quite different from the demands of American and West European feminists. After experiencing the Nazi occupation of Poland and life under communism, he wanted to know what could prevent future generations from destroying life on the scale of the Holocaust and Joseph Stalin's *gulags*.

Andrea Dworkin

Born: September 26, 1946, Camden, NJ, USA

Died: April 9, 2005, Washington, D.C., USA

Books: *Intercourse, Life and Death*

Quote: "I want rapes documented, the brothels delineated, the summary murders of pregnant women discussed."

http://www.andreadworkin.com

For John Paul II, love, God, human dignity and respect for life were the same thing. If humanity wanted to avoid another

Holocaust, it could not tolerate abortion. He concluded rather early that contraception leads to abortion and that without God, man is capable of committing new acts of genocide.

A truckload of bodies of prisoners of the Nazis in the Buchenwald concentration camp at Weimar, Germany. The bodies were about to be disposed of by burning when the camp was captured by troops of the 3rd U.S. Army. Photo by Pfc. W. Chichersky, April 14, 1945.

Most Western feminists did not see any direct links between abortion and a decline of respect for human life, and if they did, they would not admit it out of fear of depriving women of their hard-won right to make reproductive decisions on their own. Andrea Dworkin, who accused the pro-choice movement in the U.S. of ignoring the issue of pornography in crimes of violence against women, while at the same time raising the issue of "hate speech" as contributing to terrorist attacks on abortion clinic doctors, did not draw any significant comparisons between abortion and threats to human dignity or between abortion and genocide. But in her book *Life and Death* she complained that the Holocaust Museum in Washington, D.C. ignored the experience of women in the Nazi concentration camps.[71] The Nazis forced women prisoners to have abortions and killed their

> **The U.S. Holocaust Memorial Museum**
> http://www.ushmm.org/
> **Remember the Women Institute**
> http://www.rememberwomen.org/

newborn children, but Dworkin did not mention this in her long list of Nazi crimes against women and children. For her, Nazi pornography was apparently a more important indicator of the German fascists' hatred for women. Even though she chose not to address the dilemma of abortion and dignity of life, at least Dworkin focused on the issues of genocide and history. She and John Paul II had almost identical positions on the impact of pornography on women and shared a deep concern that the Nazi killings of mentally handicapped persons, Gypsies, homosexuals and Jews should be a constant warning for future generations. Most feminists who grew up in affluent and safe societies, however, were rarely concerned with such issues — issues, which had profound importance for John Paul II.

CHAPTER THREE

Polish Roots

The Romantic Tradition

One of the keys to understanding Wojtyła's mind is the power of the Romantic movement in Poland which sprung up in the 19th century and to this day continues to influence generations of young Poles as they study some of the most widely read Polish Romantic poems and novels. Developed following the loss of national independence in 1795, when the country was fully divided between Russia, Prussia and Austria and ceased to exist for over 100 years, the Romantic movement, fueled by its poets and fighters for independent Poland, produced an ethos of devotion to national causes and to military service. Men as well as women of character were expected to sacrifice their personal ambitions for the greater cause of national rebirth, a view constantly reinforced by both the Romantic writers and the Catholic Church.

As an impressionable young boy who wanted to be an actor, Karol Wojtyła read, studied and could recite from memory many of the Romantic poems and plays. Wojtyła's deep interest in literature and theater as a high school and university student and the subsequent development of his ideas suggest that the Romantic poets profoundly shaped much of his personality and beliefs. He grew up performing their works. Their poems and plays formed the minds of several generations of young Polish men and women and do not really have an equivalent example in the West. The only American book that comes even close in its power to influence attitudes and mobilize a large segment of society to action could be *Uncle Tom's Cabin*. Later examples of powerful writing, but which influenced mostly women already inclined to support feminist causes, might be Simone de Beauvoir's *The Second Sex* and Betty Friedan's *The Feminine Mystique*. None of these books, however, managed to shape attitudes, behavior and the future of an entire nation, as the Polish Romantic poets did so successfully for many generations. The Romantic poets subscribed to several beliefs which, as Polish historian Oskar Halecki (1891-1973) pointed out, centered on Poland as the nation chosen by God. While the country fought for its independence, patriotism and the so-called Polish values and traditions were elevated to the role of national religion with the encouragement of the Catholic clergy and the Polish patriots. These values were especially present in the poetry and drama of the Romantic writers whose works Wojtyła read and performed as a young actor. A historian of Polish Christianity Jerzy Kłoczowski observed that "Polishness...was becoming the highest moral ideal and value for which one should accept every sacrifice, including the loss of one's life, taking example from ... national martyrs."[1] The Romantic patriots saw Poland as a martyr and a messiah of nations and considered themselves to be different and somewhat better than people in the East as well as in the West. They were fighting not only against the Russians and the Prussian Germans but also against the alien religions of Russian Orthodoxy and German Protestantism. Such attitudes may appear melodramatic to Western observers, but as Jerzy Kłoczowski pointed out, Polish religious Messianism must be seen in the light of a serious threat to national survival. Polish Messianism included a romantic notion of the noble Poles bringing their superior moral vision to the corrupted Western societies and fighting for the liberation of oppressed nations. John Paul's severe criticism of secularism in the West and his passionate crusade against abortion certainly had historical precedents in his country's past. His only highly significant break with the Romantic tradition was over the issue of glorifying military power and the use of violence in the defense of freedom. John Paul II was a determined pacifist and believed that suffering combined with the power of prayer is a better way to peace than waging war.

Just what history and Romantic literature meant to John Paul II could be seen from his deeply emotional reaction when he viewed the Polish movie, *Pan Tadeusz* (*Master Thaddeus*), based on the epic poem by the most well-known Polish Romantic poet, Adam Mickiewicz. In January 2000, the pope made a point of taking a break from his busy schedule to attend a private screening of the movie at the Vatican, despite some apprehension on the part of the film's Polish director Andrzej Wajda (b. 1926) that watching the movie might be a waste of time for someone as busy as John Paul II. The pope's response to the director was that "it is not a waste of time to remember the roots of your country." One of the actors present at the screening reported that "the Pope was in tears and repeated some of the expressions in the film," which he remembered from his days as a young theater actor in Poland.[2] The movie, which presents the painful history of the Poles in Lithuania as they fought for independence on the side of the French during Napoleon's invasion of Russia in 1812, was a huge box-office success in Poland, but the story would be largely incomprehensible to those unfamiliar with Polish history and evokes no strong emotions in a Western reader.

Polish Romantic Poets and Writers

Adam Mickiewicz 1798-1855

Juliusz Słowacki 1809-1849

Zygmunt Krasiński 1812-1859

Cyprian Norwid 1821-1883

Henryk Sienkiewicz 1846-1916

Stanisław Wyspiański 1869-1907

English Translations from Polish literature:

http://info-poland.buffalo.edu/

Unlike *Quo Vadis*, a novel by another Polish writer, Henryk Sienkiewicz, which was widely read outside of Poland and turned into a MGM film starring Robert Taylor, Deborah Kerr and Peter

Ustinov, Adam Mickiewicz's Romantic epic is virtually unknown in the West, although it has been translated into English and French. Its message is only familiar to those who care deeply about Poland and its history. The only American literary example that even comes close to having a similar impact could be Henry Wadsworth Longfellow's *The Midnight Ride of Paul Revere* (1860), but this poem could only carry the same emotional content if the Americans lost the Revolutionary War and for the next 150 years had to fight a guerilla war against the British. Missing in the American poem are strong elements of moral superiority, suffering and sacrifice, which are essential for the understanding of how the Poles, both men and women, see themselves vis-à-vis each other, their country and other nations. As one Polish scholar observed, Adam Mickiewicz convinced generations of Poles that "Poland was a Christ among nations, crucified for the redemption of corrupt European peoples who had reverted to idol worship."[3] One can certainly see this pattern of thinking in many of John Paul II's comments about the West and the United States.

There is very little doubt that Karol Wojtyła absorbed and accepted much of Mickiewicz's theology of nationhood and as pope made it part of his attempt at what he described as "re-evangelization" of the West. He used this term because he believed that the West had lost its religious faith and must regain it or continue to slide into pagan barbarism. In *Quo Vadis*, Henryk Sienkiewicz's novel also widely read by Wojtyła's generation, the author repeatedly contrasts the immorality of the imperial Rome with the sexual virtues of the Christians, particularly the Christian women. Sienkiewicz repeatedly describes non-Christian Roman women as sexual predators and sees frequent divorces initiated by women as one of the causes of the Roman Empire's decline. Other Polish Romantic writers also made frequent comparisons between the fall of Rome and Poland's loss of independence in the 18th century, attributing both to the decline of morals and patriotism among the ruling elites while extolling the moral virtues and simple faith of the common people. The common people, particularly the Polish peasants, were compared with the Roman Christians and presented as the defenders of traditional moral values. Wojtyła, for whom Latin, which included the study of Roman history, was one of his best subjects and who tutored other students in Latin, was familiar with these arguments.

The Polish Church's attacks on the immorality of the West and a belief that common people in a poor country such as Poland are morally superior had definite roots in the Romantic Polish reaction to the loss of independence. Most blamed the loss of independence on too much freedom among the Polish nobility, and Catholic priests used examples from Imperial Roman and Polish history to condemn the French Revolution, immorality and liberal ideas coming from the West. As a population more greatly affected by history than Americans, Poles are much more likely to see the present through the eyes of the past. In 2001, a Right-wing Polish politician offered an opinion that the current civilization is at the same stage as Rome was 50 years before its fall. He was commenting on the proposal to give Polish men an option to take paid leave after the birth of a child, so far available only to women. For him, a natural environment for children was in the company of their mothers.[4]

Polish Romantic literature helped to shape views of several generations of Poles and undoubtedly influenced Wojtyła's attitudes toward the West as well as his desire, perceived as a religious and moral duty, to reform Western societies. A Polish Romantic poet, Zygmunt Krasiński, believed that "each individual nation—instrument of the Divine Will—had its own mission to carry out in the harmonious whole of this plan, to the benefit of all the others."[5] Wojtyła studied and performed the works of both Mickiewicz and Krasiński, but his favorite Romantic poet was Cyprian Norwid a religious mystic who, like Wojtyła, was fascinated by the idea of the Christian God influencing the course of Poland's history through the acts of morally and religiously motivated individuals. Norwid is the least known and the most difficult to understand among the Polish Romantic poets, but his deep interest in religious mysticism attracted Wojtyła's attention. Norwid was also very focused on the struggle for national independence, but he showed more interest than others in individuals and their personal struggles and suffering. Wojtyła probably viewed the world very much the same way, giving priority to national duty and honor but not forgetting the individual. Norwid was also more concerned with the ways that God reveals himself through history than the other Romantic poets and thinkers. His conclusion was that history should be judged by moral progress of humanity rather than the acts of rich and powerful nations or individuals.[6]

Again, this view was fully adopted by John Paul II who believed strongly in the dignity of each person but saw nations and their traditions as more important. John Paul II wanted equality of all nations and was highly critical of wealthy countries in the West for exporting immorality and rejecting their duty to assist the less fortunate and the weak. But, as with other Romantic Polish poets, Norwid was convinced that the suffering of Poles under foreign occupation had a deep spiritual meaning for the more powerful nations. He believed that the suffering presented his countrymen and women with a challenge to achieve greater moral strength and to help other nations achieve the same level of moral perfection. Just as Norwid saw the Poles as the victims who were morally superior to the nations that oppressed them, Wojtyła also tended to view history as a struggle between the weaker and less powerful but morally superior nations and individuals, and those who are rich and successful but are morally corrupt.

Norwid was also one of the first Polish writers to criticize anti-humanitarian aspects of the early capitalism. Under Norwid's and probably also Wojtyła's interpretation of economic history, nations could not become rich simply through hard work and observing higher moral standards than their less successful neighbors. If there was capitalism, there had to be an element of exploitation to explain the successes of some and the failures of others. Marxists, socialists and later progressive Church leaders such as Wojtyła accepted this analysis as totally or partially valid.

Norwid's skeptical view of the materialistic Western civilization and his desire for a moral revolution which could transform human history are frequently reflected in John Paul's comments about the West. In many ways, John Paul II also subscribed to Norwid's view that a true victory is achieved by leaders who are actually ready to lose battles and be defeated as long as their ultimate aim is the defense of the moral good. Norwid believed that ultimately such leaders would be vindicated by God and history.[7] John Paul II certainly saw himself as such a leader as he firmly defended his beliefs on such issues as contraception and abortion despite humiliating setbacks and frequent criticism, even in his own country.

This kind of heroic resistance was reflected in Poland's 1935 Constitution, which stated that the president of the republic was responsible only "before God and History," and the interwar Polish leader Józef Piłsudski (1867-1935) supposedly said: "To be defeated but [remain] unconquered, that is a victory."[8] Norwid's Romantic notion of a lonely moral leader who defies conventional morality in defense of the ultimate good explains much of John Paul's stubborn resistance to criticism from Western liberals and feminists. In his zeal to point out and condemn the moral failings of the West, John Paul II was a modern-day Romantic moral revolutionary. Whether the majority of Westerners are indeed less moral than, for example, Poles or Russians, or whether societies more likely to agree with John Paul II's morality are indeed more just in their behavior than Western nations practicing democratic capitalism is, however, a difficult proposition to prove. My personal travels and contacts in the West and in the East, as well as some of the social research I have seen on such issues as treatment of women and minorities and even attitudes toward abortion, have not convinced me that an average person would have been better off living in a highly religious and traditional society, especially if such an individual were a woman, an immigrant, a handicapped person, a person from a lower social class, a homosexual, a Jew, or a member of an ethnic or religious minority. But John Paul II was absolutely convinced that sooner or later—even if it had to take several centuries—history will show that he was right and his Western critics on such issues as contraception, abortion and secularism were mistaken.

Specifically reflected in the Polish Romantic literature was not only the moral deficiency of Western societies but also a dim view of material progress that was achieved in the West as a result of the Enlightenment, the Industrial Revolution and the introduction of market capitalism. Mickiewicz warned his countrymen not to be impressed with nations which grow fat in prosperity: "For if a nation which eats and drinks well is most to be respected, then respect those people among you who are fattest and healthiest. ...even animals have these virtues, but for a human being this is not enough."[9] (This was written obviously before health benefits of low-fat diets were discovered.) Sacrifice and suffering in the face of oppression were necessary in Mickiewicz's view. He wrote that like Christ, Poland "suffers for the salvation of the world to redeem the sins of all the nations so that they may become worthy of freedom."[10] As one Polish scholar living in the West observed, such a historical vision can appear absurd or even blasphemous to men of pedestrian temperament who can be described as rational and Western, but it made perfect sense to millions of Poles deprived of liberty and national independence and gave them great spiritual strength in the face of great suffering. In somewhat different but nevertheless profound ways, it influenced both Polish men and women, giving each a sense of self-worth, dignity and purpose.

Not surprisingly, most of Wojtyła's objections to Western secular morality, or lack thereof, centered on women, their sexuality and their interactions with men and society, but he was not blaming just women. John Paul II was a severe critic of "consumerist" societies, in which—he believed—everything can be bought and sold, including human life. He was not persuaded by arguments that countries practicing capitalism combined with constitutional democracy usually provide their citizens far greater protection against death, violence and political oppression than any other political and economic system, including theocracies.

The Romantic poets in Poland also drew inspiration from the mother of Christ and offered the Virgin Mary as a symbol of noble sacrifice. For Wojtyła and many Polish believers of his generation, the vision of the Virgin formed in the national consciousness by the Polish Romantics fighting for Poland's independence, became the model which John Paul II was also trying to promote throughout his pontificate. This is hardly surprising considering the powerful presence of the images and symbols representing the mother of Christ in the Polish Romantic literature and used by the Polish Church in the pro-independence activities of its clergy. Adam Mickiewicz's poem *Pan Tadeusz* starts with homage to the Fatherland under the protection of the Virgin Mary. Growing up in Poland reading Romantic poets and participating in religious and patriotic observances, Karol Wojtyła was constantly exposed to the idea that in the difficult moments of Poland's history, the struggle for national survival was always connected with the veneration of the Blessed Virgin. National legends credited her with protecting the nation from foreign invaders on numerous occasions.

Black Madonna of Częstochowa
Jasna Góra Monastery
http://www.jasnagora.pl/
The National Shrine of Our Lady of Częstochowa in Doylestown, Pennsylvania, USA
http://www.czestochowa.us/home_us.php

John Paul II often reminded his fellow Poles that the Jasna Góra's Icon of the Black Madonna, as the painting is known in English due to its black coloration, helped them survive as a nation after Poland lost its independence at the end of the 18th century.[11] Speaking at Jasna Góra in 1977 still as the Archbishop of Kraków, he pointed out that pilgrimages to the Shrine of the Black Madonna from various parts of Poland under Russian, German and Austrian occupation helped to unite all Poles at a time "when an attempt was made not only to erase the name of 'Poland from the map of Europe, but also to deprive Poles of their [national] characteristics..."[12] The Black Madonna became the primary symbol of national unity, independence and the preservation of Catholic values. Poles also began to see the Virgin Mary as a spiritual ally in their struggle to protect their language and culture. Karol Wojtyła's association with Dr. Półtawska that turned out to be so crucial for millions of Catholic and non-Catholic women started during a pilgrimage to the Shrine of the Black Madonna.

This clash of cultures was particularly evident due to the pressure of the German-speaking population in western and northern parts of Poland. In 1877, in the ethnically mixed town of Gietrzwałd in north-central Poland, which at the time belonged to Prussia, Poles claimed that the Virgin Mary appeared speaking in Polish rather than German.[13] By insisting that she addressed them in their native language, Polish Catholics were claiming their spiritual and moral superiority

Black Madonna of Częstochowa.

vis-à-vis the Germans and were trying also to emphasize their status as an oppressed group putting their faith in the protection of the Virgin Mary. Her icons in Częstochowa, Gietrzwałd and in other locations became powerful reminders of resistance against foreign influences that could undermine the faith, morals, and patriotism of Polish families. Marian devotion also had a powerful influence on the development of gender relations in Poland.

The veneration of the Black Madonna of Jasna Góra in Częstochowa, more than any other religious activity in Poland reinforced the image of an ideal patriotic woman, modeled after the Mother of Christ, and placed it at the center of national and family life. It had a major impact on how the Catholic Church in Poland and the Polish society viewed and treated women. By addressing their appeals for protection and help primarily to the Virgin Mary, rather than directly to Christ, the Church helped to instill and develop patriotic feelings among Polish women and to activate them as a group for the cause of national independence. The Polish women responded by willingly accepting great sacrifices for the cause of Poland's freedom. They became involved in various underground educational and social activities, but most importantly, they did not object when their sons and husbands sacrificed their lives in the struggle for independence. They themselves occasionally risked their lives and took on many traditional male roles when male family members were either killed or imprisoned. Their role, however, was not to participate in the armed struggle but to support it when necessary through conspiratorial and social work.

By linking the struggle for national independence with the cult of the Virgin Mary, the Polish Church initially helped to advance the status of Polish women within the society. Many Catholic women, including nuns, became socially active in now traditional female occupations, particularly as educators, nurses and social workers. Most others stayed at home or combined their home duties with other work convinced that their sacrifices had a higher national and religious purpose. They were respected for their sacrifices and for being active co-conspirators with men in the struggle for independence, but at the same time the Catholic Church assigned Polish women a specific role at home and insisted that any social activity should not undermine their duties as wives and mothers. It would be impossible to understand Wojtyła's constant promotion of traditional family models, centered around an ideal mother-figure, without taking into account the history of Polish religious nationalism of the 19th century and the influence that the Romantic tradition had on his generation.

The Polish Romantics paid a lot of attention to women, certainly not as much as to the goal of national independence, but with sufficient intensity to influence the attitudes about women of several generations of Poles. The center of attention, however, was not women alone. The Romantic writers were more concerned with the emancipation of Polish peasants who represented the vast majority of the population and were therefore seen as the key to strengthening the nation for the eventual military conflict with the occupying powers. The emancipation of women albeit within the national tradition was, however, also very much a part of the Romantic agenda, and had both positive and negative impacts on the situation of Polish women. The Romantics offered their own version of female liberation that was designed to promote the goal of national revival by using women in such fields as social work and education. Their views were to a large degree similar to Wojtyła's vision of women as wives and mothers who, when necessary, could be capable of great sacrifices for their families and their country but remained essentially focused on their traditional feminine roles. They were expected to be strong and noble, socially active, but play a supportive role to men.

John Paul II's explanation to justify the ban on the ordination of women by claiming that being a nun is superior to being a priest because it represents a greater commitment to sacrifice and service may also be rooted in Polish Romanticism. Adam Mickiewicz believed that sacrifice and suffering on behalf of the nation could be the key to the emancipation of Polish women.

In a 1842 lecture at College de France in Paris, Mickiewicz described the "ideal Polish woman" as a patriotic female who can combine chaste female feelings with strength and courage, as "a daughter close to her father, a wife ready to follow her husband into the fire."[14] Women could gain their right to freedom through suffering. Mickiewicz also claimed that a Polish woman in the mid-18th century "has greater freedom than anywhere else, is more respected, and feels as a man's companion." These views match very closely opinions expressed more than a hundred years later by Wojtyła and other Polish priests and bishops. Wojtyła would probably also agree with Mickiewicz's statement that "women will gain importance in society not by talking about women rights or proclaiming wild theories, but through sacrifice."[15] In fact, ultimately this was John Paul II's message to women as well as to the poor in the Third World. He was, of course, a defender of their rights, but would stop short of advocating a radical change that could possibly result in violence or, as he suspected, irreparable harm to society. In his view, suffering, sacrifice and nonviolent struggle for human rights would, in the long run, produce better results than radical feminism, Marxism or Liberation Theology. John Paul II strongly believed that one's own suffering can appeal to the essential humanity of an adversary and can awaken his conscience. This was the essence of Wojtyła's theology of suffering and non-violent resistance.

Princess Wanda
http://www.kresy.co.uk/wanda.html

Princess Grażyna

Maria Walewska 1789-1817

Emilia Plater 1806-1831

The Virgin Mary was the ultimate model, but there were also mythical heroines, promoted by the Romantic Polish writers, who likewise served as powerful models for many generations of Polish women. In his lecture in Paris, Mickiewicz gave the example of the Polish heroine from his own epic *Grażyna* who in the Middle Ages led the fight against the Teutonic Knights, viewed by most Poles as the mortal enemies of

Poland. When Grażyna suspected her husband of entering into an alliance with the Germans, seen as being against her nation's interest, she felt compelled to put on her husband's armor and under this disguise led his troops into the battle to prevent him from betraying his country. Shamed by the discovery of what had happened, *Grażyna*'s husband joined the fight. While it was too late to save her life, with her husband's help the Germans were defeated. The mythology of this story for Polish women was rather clear and in some ways more progressive than what would be expected in more traditional patriarchal societies. In this story, Poland's interests came even before a woman's duty to obey her husband.

According to the Romantic tradition, under extraordinary circumstances Polish women were required to make extreme sacrifices, even if it meant betraying their duty to their husbands and families. In the end, however, a contemporary Polish woman-writer noted that different roles for men and women were clearly conveyed in Mickiewicz's epic. The military victory was achieved only after the husband joined the battle and the woman conveniently dies without having to face the consequences of her actions.[16] The woman is presented, however, as the guardian of morality who is expected to make the ultimate sacrifice for the good of her family and her nation.

Mickiewicz also recalled the sacrifice of Emilia Plater who, supposedly dressed as a man, joined the fight against the Russians during the 1830-1831 uprising. Born in Lithuania to an aristocratic family, she became involved in various underground activities against Tsarist Russia. When the uprising broke out, according to some accounts, she formed a partisan group of local peasants and fought in several battles

Emilia Plater 1806-1831.

gaining the rank of an infantry captain. Other reports described her as unsuccessfully trying to join various military units and being told by the male-commanders to return to traditional female occupations. In any case, the strain of the military life proved too much for the young woman. She died at the age of twenty-five. Mickiewicz immortalized her in his poem, "The Death of the Colonel," in which he refers to the young woman as "the virgin-martyr."

Legends about Polish women willing to make sacrifices for their country helped to shape the image of a patriotic female who is strong but essentially still feminine. One of the oldest Polish myths describes Wanda, a daughter of Krak, the prince of Kraków in pre-Christian Poland who after her father's death governed the province with the consent of the nobles. According to one version of the myth, written in the early 13th century by Kraków's bishop, Wincenty Kadłubek, a German prince attempted to take over her lands, but amazed by the beauty of the princess, his army refused to fight and the German prince committed suicide. The former Primate of Hungary, Cardinal József Mindszenty (1892-1975) was so impressed by this Polish patriotic myth that in his book, *The Mother*, devoted to the supremacy of the motherly vocation, he quoted from a Polish source the last words of the German knight: "Wanda shall reign over heaven and earth, over land and sea. [...] I yield myself to death, so that Poland's children and her children's children may enjoy the dominion of this woman."[17] According to this version of the legend, however, Wanda remained a virgin for the rest of her life—a woman could not successfully combine the duties of statehood with motherhood. The fact that this patriotic, anti-communist Hungarian prelate, who believed that woman's place was primarily at home, would present Wanda as an example of an exceptional woman proves that religious nationalism in Poland and in Hungary did in fact nobilitate in the eyes of the Catholic Church some public roles for exceptional women as long as they served the nation and the community.

A careful reading of Wojtyła's writings on women conveys the same attitude. According to a different, more popular version of the same myth, written in the 15th century by another Polish priest-historian, Jan Długosz, Wanda, unwilling to marry the German prince, threw herself to her death from a steep bank of the Vistula River. Tradition has it that Wanda is buried in a large Wanda Mound (*Kopiec Wandy*). Wojtyła's favorite poet Cyprian Norwid visited the Mound in 1840 and was inspired to compose the narrative poem *Wanda* in honor of the ancient princess.

19th century painting of Princess Wanda by Maksymilian Piotrowski.

Both versions of the myth present Wanda as a beautiful and wise virgin who was able to become at least a token ruler despite her gender. This part of the legend of Wanda offered a positive message to women. But, while Wanda was able to govern, it was only with the consent of the city nobles and the approval of the people of Kraków. The legend also made it quite clear that Wanda remained a virgin and that she could not defend the city as a conventional military leader, thus reinforcing the idea, still accepted by the vast majority of Poles, that only a man could be a successful warrior. By killing herself, Wanda made the only sacrifice a woman was capable of in order to save her country from a German invasion. The myth underscores not only the value of sacrifice for the fatherland, but also cultural restrictions on the role of women as well as a deep suspicion of foreigners, particularly the Germans. Even today, German tourists, visiting the Wawel Castle in Kraków, are sometimes told the story of Wanda "who did not want to marry a German," but less frequently now that Kraków's economy depends more on international tourism—perhaps a positive example of changes caused by economic globalization.

Countless generations of Polish women and men have been exposed to this legend in numerous poems, plays, romance novels and articles. Wanda became the first model of an ideal Polish woman who defends her virtue and is willing to make the ultimate sacrifice for her nation but will not challenge the traditional division of gender roles. Karol Wojtyła, first as a bishop and cardinal in Poland and later as pope, was likewise trying to promote as models of ideal female behavior the example of women from Polish history whose lives were marked by sacrifice, service to the Church and the nation, and defense of moral values. His emphasis, however, was definitely on motherhood and familial duties rather than any leadership roles for women.

Women presented as models by the Romantic poets were not exactly ordinary, family-oriented females concerned only with their children. They were in many ways exceptional women, a clear departure from the traditional patriarchal models. But under the influence of the Church, the 19th century Polish woman also acquired additional duties as a defender of family morality and a contributor to the nation's strength through motherhood. Described as the "patroness of Polishness," the Polish woman came to be seen as the primary defender of the Polish family from alien influences, usually from the secular West. Jan Karol Kochanowski (1869-1949), a Polish historian and a promoter of Romantic ideas, in a book published in 1925, wrote about a Polish woman as a selfless guardian of the Catholic faith and national values who is capable of any sacrifice, including giving up her life for her country. Her faith is so strong that it puts her close to God. Nearly half-divine, a Polish woman uses her body on earth to multiply life. She is a "temporary tool in the service of the highest ideals."[18] The same writer described all Poles as the guardians of the faith against the barbaric nations of Eastern Europe as well as against the aggressive expansionism of the West and the Western ideas which undermine the traditional faith in God, attack freedom and weaken the family. If one eliminates from this description the historic antagonism toward Russia, which John Paul II tried very hard to turn into a spiritual alliance between traditional Catholicism and Russian Orthodoxy, what emerges is John Paul II's position on what Europe needs to survive.

Another Polish scholar of Romanticism, Artur Górski (1870-1959), wrote in a book, published in 1938, that during the darkest period of lost independence, the Polish woman, the priest and the Polish soldier guarded national dignity. The Polish woman was described as using her hands to build the fortified foundation of Polishness, which was the family home. Keeping an eye on young and older children, she was responsible for forming the moral character of the nation and guarded the purity of their behavior. She was helped in this work by her parish priest. At the same time, the Polish soldier was defending God, the fatherland and his honor.[19]

Faithful to the Romantic tradition, Polish women representing the noble classes and the *intelligentsia*, had an important role to play, both at home and through their patriotic and educational activities. A Polish sociologist living in the West observed that Polish women "were not only romantic companions but also, and more importantly, the sacred centers of family life."[20] They were required to be both hard-working housewives and "patriotic missionaries." "While men were fighting, or in hiding, or missing, the burden of raising children, maintaining the household, and maintaining links with existing patriotic organizations fell into the hands of mothers (matrons). There emerged a particular image of the Polish woman-patriot." Not surprisingly, the Polish Church promoted the cult of the Virgin Mary which "served to reinforce the strength of overburdened women."[21]

But encouraging women to put the needs of their country above everything else sometimes took grotesque forms during Poland's struggle for independence and violated the very principles upon

Maria Walewska
1786-1817.

which the Polish Christian family was to be based. In the early 1800s, Polish Catholic noblemen put considerable pressure on a young Polish aristocratic woman Countess Maria Walewska to become Napoleon's lover after the French Emperor took a liking to her during a chance encounter in Poland. Even though Maria Walewska was married (to a Polish aristocrat several decades her senior), Polish noblemen became convinced that her affair with Napoleon would serve their country's interests and urged her to submit to his advances and to lobby Napoleon on behalf of Poland's independence. Convinced of her duty to her country, Walewska became Napoleon's mistress. She followed him to France and bore him a son, giving him her legal husband's last name, although it was common knowledge that he was Napoleon's child. Her son, who took on French citizenship, would later become a diplomat and a French foreign minister.

Maria Walewska's sacrifice for her country did not produce any lasting results for Poland, since the French Emperor was soon defeated and imprisoned. But despite the fact that her behavior violated religious norms, Poles viewed Maria Walewska with admiration and respect since her affair with Napoleon was undertaken for the highest purpose of winning Poland's independence.

Wojtyła was the product of the Polish Romantic tradition, moderating only its call for armed struggle, in which the Polish patriots engaged throughout Europe and in the United States under the slogan "For Your Freedom and Ours." He also rejected their hostility toward Russia and the Russian Orthodox Church and was strongly in favor of reconciliation with Germany. Like the Romantic Polish poets, Wojtyła believed that Poland could return to its glorious past only through moral and social reform undertaken according to the most demanding Christian standards. With such lofty goals and enormous stakes, and with the use of history and tradition as the guides for action, women did not have much of a chance to achieve equal status with men as defined by today's Western feminists, liberals and others who reject traditional gender roles. Karol Wojtyła, however, did not see these Western standards of gender equality as either appropriate or good for women.

It is probably safe to conclude, however, that thanks to the Christian idealism of the Polish Romantics and the cult of the Virgin Mary, Polish women had been given greater respect than in most other patriarchal societies at a similar level of development. Marian devotion in Poland probably tended to moderate the most extreme forms of sexist and patriarchal behavior, while at the same time strengthening some cultural and institutional discrimination of women and their relegation to largely domestic functions. John Paul II was convinced, however, that this form of popular piety can also work to the benefit of women in more developed societies. He also believed that most women in the world had more in common with experiences of Polish women than with women in the West. Feminists saw the papal emphasis on Marian devotion as yet another attempt by the patriarchal order to keep women under male subjugation; John Paul II and many Polish women saw it quite differently.

Polish women who did their duty vis-à-vis their religion, nation and family did indeed enjoy higher respect and admiration, particularly among the nobility and the educated elite. While Western Europe was moving away from religion in the 18th and the 19th centuries and toward greater reliance on individual rights with scientific skepticism and rationalism dictating more and more public policy choices, religion in Poland actually grew much stronger as a result of the merging of patriotic and religious themes and symbols. In the hierarchy of Romantic values, religion came very close to the exaltation of the Fatherland with its historical heroes, traditions, culture, and the emphasis on the group rather than the individual. Wojtyła was trying to modify to some degree the Romantic theology of the nation by introducing themes combining appeals that stressed duty to the country and the family with the theology of personal dignity. This may explain why Wojtyła was one of the few Polish bishops who actively promoted natural birth control for overworked women, but ultimately he opposed other forms of birth control and in his public statements still urged Polish women to have large families. His ultimate focus was ultimately on the nation rather than the individual. Each person's dignity, according to Wojtyła, had to be protected and there could be no justification of violence, but individuals had to achieve their worth by following in the footsteps of their glorious and heroic forefathers.

Women from Poland's History: Saint Jadwiga

While there could be exceptions for truly outstanding and intellectual women, such as Poland's 14th century Queen Jadwiga (Hedwig), whom John Paul II canonized during his papacy, most women, according to Wojtyła, should be wives and mothers staying at home to take care of their families or at least avoiding those careers that could prevent them from being good mothers and wives. Even exceptional women, according to John Paul II,

possessed "female genius" that made them different from men. For Wojtyła, Queen Jadwiga became a special example of such a woman who above all wanted to serve her people and desired to be a mother. She was Poland's first and only ruling female monarch, although Polish historical and literary sources do not emphasize this fact.

18th century drawing of Queen Jadwiga of Poland 1374-1399 by Jan Matejko.

Jadwiga of Anjou (Hedwig of Hungary) was the third daughter of King Louis the Great of Hungary and Elisabeth of Bosnia. Through the tangled dynastic diplomacy of the period, Jadwiga, despite her gender, inherited the

Polish throne in the 14th century. After King Louis' death, the Polish throne under a prior arrangement with King Casimir the Great of Poland was to be given to one of his sons. Since Louis had no sons, the Polish nobles, powerful enough to veto the deal, agreed to accept his youngest daughter, Jadwiga. In 1384, at the age of 10 or 11, she was crowned *Rex* or King of Poland rather than being called Queen. Polish nobles insisted on the annulment of her betrothal, already made to William of Habsburg, son of Leopold III of Austria, and instead decided to marry her off to Jagiełło, the pagan Grand Duke of neighboring Lithuania, who had agreed to accept Christianity in return for effective control of Poland. An alliance with Lithuania was considered to be more advantageous for Poland, which at the time was under considerable pressure to the North and the West from the German religious order of the Teutonic Knights. William, the Austrian prince, came to Kraków to claim his fiancée, but Polish nobles would not allow him to enter the royal castle. According to some historical accounts, Jadwiga at first rebelled against the idea of marrying a barbarian pagan prince more than twice times her age, and demanded that she be allowed to join her childhood companion and her lawful fiancée. There were accounts of secret meetings between Jadwiga and Wilhelm at a monastery in Kraków, but they may have been just a romantic legend. Eventually, Jadwiga married Jagiełło. In the view of influential Polish historian, Oscar Halecki, deeply religious Jadwiga realized the advantages of converting Lithuania to Christianity and strengthening Poland vis-à-vis the Germans and the hostile nations in the East.[22] But one could question the influence Jadwiga had in the matter, particularly since Wilhelm had been forcibly shown the door by her new "subjects." Whether willing or not, her apparent sacrifice of personal happiness for the benefit of the nation has been strongly emphasized and praised by patriotic historians and the Polish Church, even though the nation as we understand it today—a cultural and political body with common ethnic, linguistic and historical past—did not exist in the minds of most

14th century aristocrats. They were much more concerned with preserving their personal power and control over their lands.

The desire to declare Jadwiga a saint became an important goal for Wojtyła when he was still the Archbishop of Kraków. Like many other Poles, Wojtyła was convinced that Jadwiga's contributions and sacrifices as a Christian woman for the benefit of her adopted nation deserved recognition. He was uncomfortable with the Vatican's reluctance to recognize her unique qualities. This reluctance may have stemmed from the unusual circumstances surrounding the annulment of her lawful engagement to Wilhelm of Austria and, as some Poles suspected, to the influence of the German-speaking churchmen in the Roman Curia. It would not have been unusual for some Polish priests to suspect the pope's reluctance to elevate Jadwiga to sainthood to the machinations of the anti-Polish German lobby. Cardinal Wojtyła took upon himself the task of proving to the Church that Jadwiga was indeed a saint by trying to resolve all the historical questions surrounding her marriage to Jagiełło and her short reign. For that purpose, he engaged the help of Polish historians, archeologists and other specialists who met and conducted research under his direction and guidance. At the same time, Cardinal Wojtyła continued to stress the example of Jadwiga's personal sacrifices and her contributions to the Polish culture. Keeping the issue of Jadwiga's sainthood alive also served to counter the communist propaganda, which tried through various distortions to minimize the importance of the Church in Poland's history. Jadwiga died at the age of 25 shortly after the birth of her daughter, who also died a short time later.

In a letter issued in 1974 for the 600th anniversary of Jadwiga's birth, Wojtyła chose to link the theme of sacrifice with her unrealized motherhood. In his letter, he stressed that while "God did not grant her the joy of personal motherhood," Jadwiga left "a splendid legacy of motherhood in relation to people and nations" by giving up her personal plans for marriage in order to serve the people of Poland and Lithuania.[23] He also took the opportunity of the 600th anniversary of her birth in 1974 to warn the Poles against the dangers of materialism and consumerism and the importance of sacrifice exemplified by Queen Jadwiga: "One must learn," he told parishioners, "that not everything in life depends on having more [material possessions]; which is characteristic of today's man...The greatness of man is in being somebody. Man becomes somebody through sacrifice, often made in the depths of one's heart."[24]

Queen Jadwiga may not have been, however, a perfect model of sacrifice and self-denial as Polish churchmen like to present her. Some historians believe that there may have been two sides to Jadwiga. The young queen may or may have not been unhappy in her marriage to Jagiełło, but she was definitely passionate about food and lavish entertaining, importing large quantities of exotic ingredients, such as almonds, and introducing Western cuisine at the Polish court. Almonds, from which almond milk was made that could replace cow's or sheep's milk, were essential for bypassing strict Church restrictions on using animal products during Lent. When Jadwiga dined with Polish noblewomen, she served simple Polish dishes, but otherwise she preferred to enjoy fine French and Hungarian dishes prepared by her own personal chef who may have come from Hungary as part of her marriage settlement.[25] As a result of Jadwiga's marriage to Jagiełło, Poland was transformed into a multi-ethnic European power. At the time of her marriage in 1386, Jadwiga would have been twelve or thirteen years old. Unlike her husband, who at his baptism took the name Ladislav, Jadwiga was educated and literate woman who spoke many languages and, according to Polish historical accounts, was a virtual co-ruler with Jagiełło until her death.[26] She became a supporter of the intellectual elite in Poland, providing money for the rebuilding of the Jagiellonian University in Kraków. Far from being a passive wife, she involved herself in diplomacy striving successfully for peaceful compromises with the Teutonic Knights and other European rulers.

Queen Jadwiga was finally canonized by John Paul II in 1997. As a Catholic saint, she has become a role model, and her life of public service was offered by the pope as an inspiration to women. At her canonization mass in Kraków, however, John Paul II did not speak specifically of her intellectual and diplomatic skills as a role model for women, but instead focused on her religious faith, her personal sacrifices for the benefit of her adopted nation and her support for the Jagiellonian University, with which he himself was closely linked. John Paul II did not mention that even with her royal status, Jadwiga, as a woman, would not have been able to study at the university from the time it was established in the Middle Ages until the early 20th century. In the Middle Ages, the usual penalty for any woman trying to study at a university disguised as a man would have been death by burning, although one Polish woman, who had tried this, apparently was spared the death penalty after being discovered.

Polish Descendants of Amazons — Powerful at Home

The Polish nobility hated two of Poland's Western European queens, the Italian Bona Sforza d'Aragona (1494-1557), and the French Marie-Louise Gonzaga (1611-1667), both of whom, instead of devoting themselves to good works and prayers, became involved in politics and wanted to force reforms designed to strengthen their husbands' power.[27] Polish nobles were not accustomed to queens playing politics and did not look favorably on Western women trying to introduce new ideas that challenged the patriarchal order. Bona Sforza was a woman, a foreigner from Western Europe, and a political queen. This combined with her attempts to enrich her family at the expense of Polish nobles, made her very unpopular.

But some Poles, especially the educated aristocracy, saw her Western origins and ideas as having a positive influence on life in Poland. She invited to her court in Warsaw many Italian artists and was an active promoter of Italian Renaissance culture. She also introduced Poles to the joys of Italian cuisine, importing and gardening many exotic vegetables previously unknown in Poland, such as savoy cabbage and cauliflower. Conservative Polish nobles did not care much for delicate Italian cooking or for ambitious women. At one point, they rebelled briefly against the king, partly because of their annoyance with the Italian queen and her political and financial intrigues. Polish respect for the institution of royal rule remained, however, quite strong, even though the gentry believed that they had the right to elect their kings. Keeping women restricted to home and insistence that a male king should be in charge without interference from women were part of the same Polish patriarchal tradition. Despite Bona's provocative behavior, the rebellion ended in a compromise with the king.

In 1575, the Polish nobility elected Bona Sforza's daughter, Anna Jagielonka (1523-1596), the only remaining royal descendant of the Jagiellonian dynasty, as king of Poland, but as it was the case with Saint Jadwiga, also named king by Polish nobles, there was never any question that either of them would be able to rule entirely on her own. Women rulers were not part of Polish tradition, and queens had to have suitable husbands who could exercise power. While Jadwiga was able to become in fact a ruling monarch, Anna did not. First, the Polish nobles secured a promise to marry Anna from a French prince, Henry Valois, as a condition of electing him king of Poland, but he successfully avoided taking marriage vows with the homely Polish princess. As soon as he heard of the vacancy at the French throne upon his brother's death, he fled Poland in the middle of the night to become king of France as Henry III. His desertion of the Polish throne was one of the early examples of humiliating Western betrayals of the Poles' fascination with the West and Western culture.

After Henry Valois's escape, annoyed Polish nobles did declare Anna Jagielonka king of Poland, but immediately found her a husband, this time much closer to home, in the person of the Prince of Transylvania, Stephen Bathory (1533-1586), who did keep his promise to marry the Polish princess. Anna herself had no strong political ambitions. A deeply religious woman, she did not challenge any social conventions. Her main public role was to give strong support for the Catholic Church's actions against Protestants. At the time when Elizabeth I was an undisputed ruler in England, the tradition of keeping women away from politics and most other areas of public life was still very much part of the Polish culture.

Polish aristocratic women exercised, however, considerable authority at home, and Polish magnates, including some fierce military leaders, were known to have been somewhat intimidated by their wives. Women were exalted in public for their piety, fidelity, frugality and devotion to the family, but they had no legal rights and were often repressed at home by tyrannical fathers and husbands. This kind of duality, according to a Polish feminist writer Maria Ciechomska, persists to some degree to this day.[28] When John Paul II and others talk about a special Polish way of treating women and their important role as wives and mothers, they are defending a tradition that was already very well established in the 16th century and rarely challenged since.

Challenges, when they did occur, usually came from Western women, such as Bona Sforza, Marie-Louise Gonzaga, and King John III Sobieski's wife, Marie Casimire de La Grange d'Arquien — all of whom were familiar with more liberal rules of behavior for aristocratic women in the West and all of whom were deeply involved in politics. Marie-Louise Gonzaga, combined political ambitions and promotion of French customs with attempts to educate aristocratic Polish women. She invited to Poland two religious orders of nuns specializing in educating young girls. She met, however, with strong opposition from the Polish nobility when she tried to open special homes where nuns could train and rehabilitate prostitutes. This was a common activity for female religious orders in Western Europe, but the idea of nuns mixing with prostitutes was too much for the conservative Polish gentry. They also objected to Marie-Louise's attempts to introduce French customs at the royal court, being particularly appalled by women wearing revealing dresses. Marie-Louise Gonzaga, according to Maria Ciechomska, succeeded, however, in emancipating some aristocratic Polish women and by doing so helped to spread the idea of emancipation to the other segments of Polish society.[29]

Romantic love was a rarely mentioned topic in aristocratic Polish homes. John III Sobieski's letters to his wife, Marie Casimire, whom he affectionately called Marysieńka, are one of the very few confirmations of explicitly erotic element in Polish marriages in that period. According to Polish scholars, most marriages in old Poland were based on economic considerations and respect and even friendship between the spouses rather than eroticism. As noted by Polish historian, Maria Bogucka, Poland "lacked the tradition of troubadours and courtly love which has left permanent traces in the culture and mentality of Western Europe."

Another Polish king, Sigismund-Augustus, Bona Sforza's son, was so greatly in love with an aristocratic Polish woman, Barbara Radziwiłł, that it lead to a conflict with his mother and caused a great scandal in Poland. Polish nobles waited three years after Sigismund Augustus' marriage before they allowed Barbara Radziwiłł to be crowned as queen. Maria Bogucka observed that such a passionate love was so completely strange in 17th century Poland that it met "with general misunderstanding and condemnation."[30] It may be useful to remember that when John Paul II writes and speaks about love and marriage, he is much more likely drawing on the old Polish tradition of marriage based on respect and friendship than marriage that is primarily focused on erotic love. Tradition is still a powerful force in a country like Poland, placed between East and West, and still trying to find its own religious and cultural identity. Western ideas usually came to Poland with considerable delay and had to be adapted to local conditions which were not always the same as in Western Europe.

The influence of Western-born queens and Western culture was responsible for the golden age of Polish Renaissance in the 16th century, a few centuries after it developed in Western Europe. A large part of the Polish nobility, however, was opposed to new ideas of greater freedoms extending to all social classes and was definitely not in favor of greater roles for women in public life, although admittedly public roles for women were a minor issue. The Polish nobility, convinced of its superiority, believed that only they and no other class or group should enjoy unrestricted freedoms. This ideology, called Sarmatism because of its obscure oriental roots, was characterized by a belief that Poland, as the "bulwark of Christendom," was politically and socially superior to other nations. Sarmatism, which fully developed in the 17th century, carried with it contempt for Western ideas and other political and social systems and encouraged isolation from other nations, turning often into xenophobia.[31] Parts of this tradition have also survived in Poland with some modifications, particularly among the most conservative Catholics and nationalists, although anti-Western sentiments have never become predominant.

According to the norms of behavior of the Polish nobility, women exercised a lot of authority but only at home and were not expected to participate in politics or to engage in business or travel.[32] Such activities were largely reserved for men. While the nobility represented about 10 percent of the population, they set the cultural norms for the rest of the society, including the peasants. The largely agrarian Polish nobility, *szlachta*, traced its roots to the ancient Sarmatians, Indo-Iranian nomads who may have come to southern Poland from the Baltic Sea region early in the third century AD. Toward the end of the second century AD the Roman emperor Marcus Aurelius (121-180) defeated another group of Sarmatians, the Iazygians, and resettled some of them in northern Britain as Roman soldiers. They ended up in the area of Ribchester.[33]

Polish archeologist Tadeusz Sulimirski made several discoveries which seemingly confirm the Sarmatian roots of some of the Polish noble families, but many of the claims about Sarmatian culture were largely based on myths developed much later to reinforce *szlachta*'s claims of superiority and privilege. These Sarmatian myths also helped to support the Polish nobility's suspicion of foreigners and non-Catholics, as well as the rejection of foreign ideas, particularly those of Western origin. One Polish custom, which Sulimirski traced back to the Sarmatians, was what he described as the uniquely Polish attitude toward

Polish noblemen in Sarmatian costumes.

women, including such customs as kissing a woman's hand as a sign of respect. Even young unmarried women had their hands kissed on each social occasion.[34] In his excellent book about the people of the Black Sea region, British journalist Neal Ascherson reported Sulimirski's observations that Sarmatian noblewomen in prehistoric times were powerful and respected. They may have been the mythical Amazons as there is archeological evidence that some Sarmatian women in prehistoric times participated in battle. Sulimirski argued that "Polish gallantry toward women, which amazes foreigners," as well as the strong role of women within families and even in social life, may have had their roots in Sarmatian matriarchal society many centuries earlier.[35]

Until well after World War II, *szlachta*'s conservative-agrarian way of life determined what should be the ideal model of the Polish woman, mother and wife. The Polish Church fully accepted and promoted this model. Contemporary Polish writer, scholar and politician, Professor Wiesław Chrzanowski (b. 1923), believes that John Paul II's writings on the importance of national culture and identity may bother some intellectuals who, after World War II, thought that the era of national movements had passed. The pope, according to this Polish writer, understood very well that this was not true and had the courage to talk about it.[36] Chrzanowski maintains that "a nation plays an important function in defense of man against the threat of social displacement, isolation ... atomization and disintegration encouraged by modern civilization."[37]

The negative ideas coming from the West, against which the Poles had to defend their national values, ultimately included Marxism and capitalism, as well as secularism, feminism and liberalism. Even though many Poles placed a high value on freedom, they combined it with a sense of duty, commitment to the nation and devotion to the family. Therefore, some Poles viewed liberal ideas of individualism in moral choices and feminist-supported social reforms with great suspicion. In promoting personal freedom and personal achievement, liberalism and free-market capitalism undermined the sense of duty, solidarity and community which, as an oppressed nation, Poles valued very highly. Generations of Polish historians blamed the loss of Poland's independence in the 18th century on the abuses of freedom and lack of social responsibility on the part of the Polish nobility. In this case, Polish historians agreed that the Sarmatian traditions of excessive individuality were harmful. Wojtyła fully accepted this assessment. He undoubtedly used it to formulate his own criticism of the West and particularly the American society, which he viewed as being also excessively individualistic and dangerous for the rest of the world, just as the excessive freedoms of Polish *szlachta* and aristocracy had led to Poland's decline in the 18th century.

It was also Wojtyła's firm belief that every nation should have the right to defend its own superior moral culture against powerful outside influences, even if they came from nations considered scientifically and economically advanced. While such a stand is perfectly understandable for someone from a country under foreign domination and forced to accept an alien ideology, it does tend to promote resistance to foreign ideas and makes it less likely that traditional attitudes about women in less developed societies can change. Traditional ideas about the treatment of women are usually deeply rooted in national cultures, and most of the new ideas, which feminists embrace, are products of liberal, bourgeois societies in the West despite claims of Marxist scholars and Soviet propaganda that these ideas have revolutionary proletarian origins. Many Western Left-wing liberals, including many feminists, bought the propaganda claim that women's rights were better protected in communist countries and in Third World nations fighting Western imperialism. Wojtyła had no illusions about communism, but he was a rather uncritical admirer of traditional societies. His deep belief in the importance of protecting national values and his public pronouncements on this issue in the developing world were not particularly helpful to those who wanted to overcome some of the strong cultural barriers to gender equality using largely Western models.

Wojtyła's Pacifism and Sense of Duty

In *Crossing the Threshold of Hope* Wojtyła wrote that devotion to duty vis-à-vis the nation and willingness to make personal sacrifices for a higher cause was the basic tradition in which he grew up as a boy. He also observed that young people today, while in his mind still idealistic, tend to express their idealism "mostly in the form of criticism, whereas before it would have translated more simply into duty."[38] Wojtyła's sense of duty to the nation and the Church in upholding national and religious traditions was much stronger than most people in the West who had not been exposed to ideas promoted by Poland's Romantics can easily comprehend. John Paul II was never likely to suddenly become critical of the Church's position on women. He would first consider the impact of such criticism on people who, like himself, have a different view of women's role in society and rely on the Church to provide them with moral guidance. The Catholic Church, which in Wojtyła's view was not only guided by God but also served the cause of Poland's rebirth after the loss of independence, could not be all wrong on the issue of how it treated women from the beginning of Christianity until today. History and tradition, in Wojtyła's view, could not be changed to conform to popular trends which may be no longer fashionable in a few decades from now. This was his view at least on such issues as artificial contraception, abortion, the ordination of women as priests, priestly celibacy and divorce. As for John Paul II's views on another controversial issue which divides liberal and conservative Catholics—the Church's position on homosexuality and gay marriages—they may have also been influenced by the strong prejudice that characterizes the Polish society's view of homosexual unions and homosexual acts. In a public opinion survey conducted in 2002, only 15 percent of respondents in Poland were in favor of legalizing homosexual unions while 76 percent were against it.[39]

Those who doubt the power of the Polish Romantic tradition can also look at the more recent history. John Paul II was deeply impressed and moved by the heroism of the World War II generation of young Poles. Some of the fighters in the underground Home Army during the Nazi occupation of Poland were boys and girls as young as 14. Wojtyła had concluded that he himself could not kill another human being, even in self-defense. He participated in peaceful underground activities for which he and others could have been sent to a concentration camp. Wojtyła's friends who became involved in military actions against the Nazis argued that it was the duty of every Pole to shed blood for freedom. They accused Wojtyła and his friend Mieczysław Maliński of cowardice, stupidity and middle class mentality. The two, however, insisted that they were preparing a young generation of boys under their care for service to the fatherland when Poland regained her independence.[40]

The attitude of Wojtyła's friends who joined the underground Polish army was more typical of the prevailing Romantic ethos in Poland than engaging in passive resistance. But while Wojtyła and Maliński decided not to fight the Nazis because of their somewhat different understanding of Christianity, they saw their own work with young Polish boys as a form of service to the Fatherland. (The word "Fatherland" is always capitalized in Polish.) After the war, Wojtyła realized, however, that the times were changing and that the younger generations may not share his idealism or a sense of patriotic duty. In *Crossing the Threshold of Hope*, he observed that in the past, "the younger generations were shaped by the painful experience of war, of concentration camps, [and] of constant danger."[41] He recalled that in the Warsaw Uprising in 1944, many young Poles died in a heroic struggle against the German occupation army and credited "the heroism" of his contemporaries with helping him to define his "personal vocation."[42] Today, however, he saw that the young people "live in freedom, which others have won for them," and to Wojtyła's dismay, "have yielded in large part to the consumer culture."[43] "Consumer culture" and "consumerism" were the terms John Paul II often used to criticize and condemn Western societies for their lack of idealism and for their focus on material goods rather than spiritual faith in God.

Unfortunately for more liberal Catholic women today, Wojtyła did not see their struggle for equality in the same way as he saw his country's struggle for independence. The idealism of Western women and feminists demanding an equal role in the Catholic Church while insisting they be given the right to destroy unborn life seemed to offend his sense of the relative importance of various human rights. For Wojtyła, this was not the same type of idealism and struggle as the fight for a nation's independence, battling the communists for religious freedom or securing the right to strike for Polish workers. In fact, John Paul II seemed to view secular, pro-choice feminism as a product of Western liberalism and excessive self-indulgence. For John Paul II, pro-choice ideas represented a form of attack on the Church and its traditions—an attack on the same basic values which, in his mind, could save the world from the suffering caused by Nazism, Marxism, communism and increasingly capitalist materialism. It would have been impossible to convince John Paul II that there was no significant difference between the Solidarity workers, who were struggling for basic human rights and democracy in Poland, and American women demanding a legal right to abortion.

During the workers' strikes in Poland against the communist regime in the early 1980s, one of the popular posters reproduced the words of an anonymous poem that became popular during the anti-Russian uprising in 1830. The poem, *Farewell, My Lass, Our Country Calls Me Away*, reminded Polish women of the need to put the interests of their nation ahead of their personal concerns. The poem ends with the words: "Poland's liberty is your rival."[44] It could be argued that the same tradition of Polish women making tremendous sacrifices for their nation made it much less likely that John Paul II would see some of the concerns of Western feminists in the same light as the concerns of oppressed nations or workers fighting for their right to organize. It would be wrong to conclude, however, that John Paul II did not support many of the same demands for giving women greater equality—he just did not support all of feminist demands and not with the same intensity.

The Positivist (Liberal) Tradition

Romanticism was not the only intellectual movement which shaped Polish culture and social attitudes. Positivism is the name which Poles use to describe cultural and economic trends developed in Poland in the 19th century as a reaction to the unsuccessful, bloody and costly uprisings against the occupying powers. This tradition grew under the influence of liberal and capitalist ideas coming from the West and appealed mostly to the emerging middle class, often described in Poland as the *intelligentsia*. In that respect, Polish Positivism resembled Western rationalism and liberalism, although in Poland it still focused on the issue of regaining national independence and did not advocate a radical break with religion and tradition.

Instead of the armed struggle, the Polish Positivists stressed the ultimate goal of independence through self-improvement, education, scientific and economic progress and hard work. They were the 19th century promoters of globalization in East Central Europe. Although many of them considered themselves patriots, they too encountered opposition for introducing alien economic and cultural concepts. Polish bourgeois Positivists were perhaps less individualistic than their liberal upper and middle class counterparts in the West, but they had an equally positive impact on women's rights due to their emphasis on education and economic development. Some Positivists became vocal advocates of the need for the emancipation of women. Even though most of the gains in women's rights in the 19th and the early 20th centuries were limited to upper and middle class Polish women, some Polish Positivists were also very much concerned with political and social reforms aimed at improving the lives of poor Polish peasants and workers. Revolutionary Polish thinkers and activists, including radical socialists and communists, emerged from the ranks of Polish and Jewish middle class *intelligentsia*.

While willing to accept some of the Positivist goals, particularly when they applied to education, work ethic and non-violence, Wojtyła developed a deep suspicion of the Positivist tradition because of its liberal Western materialistic roots. He shared the concern of many Polish bishops that the Western emphasis on promoting personal freedom, personal achievement and individual pursuit of happiness can undermine traditional religious and moral values and would ultimately weaken any nation. Wojtyła was always very critical of Western liberal thought going back to Descartes and the French Revolution. During his years as a professor of philosophy in Lublin, he delivered lectures

René Descartes 1596-1650
John Locke 1632-1704
David Hume 1711-1776
Jeremy Bentham 1748-1832

(1954-1955) criticizing and rejecting rationalistic and utilitarian theories of the two British philosophers, David Hume and Jeremy Bentham, who together with John Locke helped create the philosophical foundations of Western liberalism. Wojtyła was particularly critical of Hume's utilitarian theories accusing him of removing ethics from philosophy by giving priority to human reason and the maximization of pleasure rather than to permanent moral norms.[45]

Wojtyła rejected liberalism as an intellectual tradition that gave rise to democracy, free market economies, human rights and the emancipation of women as incompatible with Christianity and dangerous for human dignity and the sanctity of human life. Concerned as he was with the protection of the dignity of human life in the aftermath of the horrible crimes against humanity during World War II, he would not forget that democratic political systems, based on liberal ideas and majority rule, have permitted abortion and now included calls for the legalization of euthanasia and gay marriage.

When someone with such deep sensitivity and this type of mindset was faced with the statistics showing 41.6 million

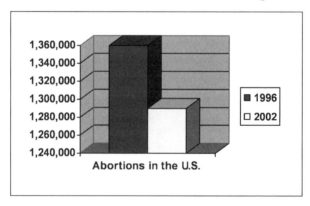

Source: The Alan Guttmacher Institute

abortions each year (2003) around the globe, an estimated 1.29 million in just one year (2002) in the United States and an estimated 39 millions U.S. abortions since 1973 through 2000, no wonder John Paul II saw abortion as a form of genocide.[46] He would be likely to compare the more than forty million abortions performed worldwide each year with the estimated number of 41 million Europeans killed during five years of World War II.[47] Blame had to be assigned, and the guilty party was the secular, liberal elites in the West. Artificial contraception was seen as the root cause of the further evil of abortion, euthanasia and genetic experimentation. John Paul II's conservative supporters in Poland would claim in Radio Maryja programs that even now Germans imperialists were trying to use abortion and contraception to biologically weaken the Polish nation.

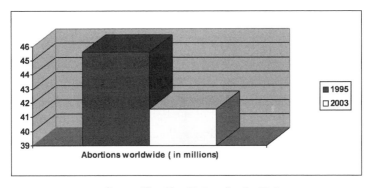

Source: The Alan Guttmacher Institute

But John Paul II's primary objection to liberalism seemed to focus on its perceived marginalization and in some cases rejection of religion in public life and its apparent technological and material rather than spiritual focus. He became convinced that by rejecting God and religion and putting all the emphasis on man, science and reason, Western liberal thinkers provided the intellectual basis for communism and fascism. He closely identified liberalism with secularism, consumerism and ultimately moral decay. In his 1994 *Letter to Families*, John Paul II specifically warned against accepting a "Positivist," i.e. liberal, materialistic and strictly scientific point of view:

> Positivism, as we know, results in agnosticism in theory and utilitarianism in practice and in ethics. In our own day, history is in a way repeating itself. Utilitarianism is a civilization of production and of use, a civilization of things and not of persons, a civilization in which persons are used in the same way as things are used. In the context of civilization of use, woman can become an object for man, children a hindrance to parents, the family an institution obstructing the freedom of its members. To be convinced that this is the case, one need only look at certain sexual education programs introduced into the schools, often notwithstanding the disagreement and even the protests of many parents; or pro-abortion tendencies which vainly try to hide behind the so-called right to choose (pro choice) on the part of both spouses, and in particular on the part of the woman.[48]

There was yet another aspect of the Polish Romantic tradition with a strong impact on the situation of Polish women. The glorification of the nation and its past can lead people to feel convinced of their own country's superiority in areas where it does not exist. John Paul II, however, apparently thought that it was his Western liberal critics who had a superiority complex. According to his closest friend Cardinal Dziwisz, accusations that John Paul II was a traditionalist because he was Polish are simplistic and highly offensive. He blamed them on a "superiority complex" among certain Western groups. According to Cardinal Dziwisz, some Westerners thought that "nothing good can come from the East because people living there are inferior."[49] Dziwisz argued that Wojtyła was a very modern man whose focus was on the person rather than groups when such a focus was warranted while being traditional on issues that required a traditional approach. In his first book *Love and*

Responsibility John Paul II showed what a very modern man he was, according to Dziwisz. His former secretary said that in this book Wojtyła "presented a personalistic concept of love, [and] covered the issue of sexuality in its most controversial aspects, such as the exchange of pleasure between husband and wife in a sexual act, the shame of nudity, [and] female frigidity, which is often caused by male selfishness." This in Dziwisz's view was proof of Wojtyła's courage and progressive thinking.[50]

There seems to be plenty of evidence that John Paul II never accepted the feminist view of how Polish society was treating its women as proof of inferiority in social development. Someone totally devoted to serving his nation in such a conservative institution as the Catholic Church was also less likely to be open to revolutionary ideas that tend to conflict with one's assessment of his nation's superior moral position vis-à-vis others. The ordination of women was one such revolutionary idea that originated not in Poland but in the West. The only social revolutionaries in Poland at the time were the communists and, of course, they were indifferent to the idea of reforms in the Catholic Church, which they wanted to destroy. By taking pride in his country's past and traditions, Wojtyła dealt extremely well with communist ideology and communist tactics. Such a struggle required sticking to the principles without any significant compromises. There were negotiations between the Church hierarchy and the communist regime. But they only required the Church leaders to be flexible in preserving the Church's existence and some freedom of action. From Wojtyła's point of view, the purpose of these talks was to allow priests and bishops to do their job of defending the very principles that the communists wanted to undermine. There was very little room left for experimenting with revolutionary ideas on how to run the Church when religion itself was under a constant threat from the communist regime and communist ideology.

Women in Communist-Ruled Poland

The majority of Polish women in post-World War II Poland came from peasant and worker families in which patriarchal traditions were particularly strong. Wojtyła's superior in Poland, Cardinal Stefan Wyszyński, was known to distrust the *intelligentsia* and suspected its members, quite correctly in many cases, of experimenting with Marxism or Western liberalism. Poland as a nation was Wyszyński's primary concern. He put his faith in the masses of religious peasants and workers, not in the intellectuals who tended to support Left-wing and liberal causes. Wojtyła, by contrast, was identified more closely with a small group of Catholic writers, journalists and university students in Kraków and Lublin. Still, both Wyszyński and Wojtyła were considered progressive social thinkers by the conservative standards of the Catholic Church at that time. Wyszyński had strong socialist leanings in his younger years, and Wojtyła may have been even more interested in how some of the Marxist ideas could be reconciled with Christ's teachings of love, brotherhood and concern for the poor. They were both interested in how socialism and Christianity could be combined and used to improve the living conditions of the poor. Both believed that the capitalist system, which existed in Poland before the war, was grossly unjust. But they were equally opposed to communism as an atheistic ideology. Interested in making the Church more open to social reform, they wanted to counter Marxist influence with progressive Catholicism. As far as Wyszyński and Wojtyła were concerned, limited socialism was fine as long as Christian and national values were preserved.

Overall, there were not any substantial differences between Stefan Wyszyński and Karol Wojtyła in their views on women. Both men came from very similar backgrounds and were brought up in the same tradition of treating women with courtesy, but assigning them to mostly domestic and always nurturing roles. The Polish *intelligentsia*'s views on women, particularly among those with socialist or communist sympathies, were far more radical than what either Wyszyński or Wojtyła were willing to tolerate. Already during the interwar period, contraception, divorce, career in preference to marriage or children, and partnership living arrangements had become acceptable among small segments of the Polish elite, mostly on the Left of the political spectrum. Neither Wyszyński nor Wojtyła came from such backgrounds. Unlike the Left-leaning intellectuals, however, the vast majority of the Polish population remained faithful to the Church's teachings on marriage, divorce, sex and the role of women. Yet, peasant and worker families did not offer the same kind of respect and freedom enjoyed by educated bourgeois women in the homes of the *intelligentsia*. Violence against women and verbal degradation through name-calling of a most colorful and humiliating sort combined with exploitation of their domestic labor was the norm. The supposed respect shown by Polish men toward women, the existence of which John Paul II truly believed, was largely a myth, particularly outside of the upper class circles Wyszyński eyed with such suspicion. This myth developed over time along with other patriotic myths designed to glorify and uplift the nation during the dark period of foreign oppression and was accepted as true and convenient by the Polish Church as well as by most Poles.

Wyszyński and Wojtyła both likely realized, although they would not want to admit it openly and directly, that if Polish women embraced contraception and started to have only one or two children, the impact on the Polish Church and culture could be profound. The number of Catholics would fall making Catholic Poland less able to resist pressure from the local communists, the Soviet Union and the liberal West. That is clearly the case now after the fall of communism, as Poland has one of the lowest birthrates in Europe, well below the replacement rate, but it is too early to conclude what impact this will have on religious faith. Obviously, Polish women are not using only the rhythm method of birth control, and it would be reasonable to assume that mothers of only a few children would show less support for their sons' possible ordination as priests.

Until recently, most Polish priests came from large, usually peasant families. Although both Wyszyński and Wojtyła were supportive of higher education for women, they also must have realized that educated women were more likely to use contraception and would be far less likely to steer their sons toward priesthood. Both chose to blame not the experience of education and greater sophistication of women themselves but directed the blame at the West and communism for introducing ideas that made contraception more acceptable among the educated Poles. During his years as priest and bishop, Wojtyła was convinced that through hard pastoral work among students, physicians, nurses and other professionals, the Church still had a chance to counter the negative influences of communism and Western liberalism even among the educated elite.

Both leaders of the Polish Church strongly believed that gender differences were real. The brutalizing of male behavior, according to Wyszyński, was against nature, since every man was born of a woman who usually nurses and takes care of him as an infant. Wojtyła repeated almost the same arguments years later as pope in advising women to accept differences between men and women, while at the same time criticizing developed societies, particularly in the West, for ignoring the contributions of women as mothers, teachers and wives. Wyszyński repeatedly told Polish women not to try to be like men, not to dress like men, and not to behave like men at home, at work or in other public places. He also told men, but much less frequently, that they should not behave like women, although he believed that men could benefit greatly if they acquired certain "feminine" characteristics of care, compassion, gentleness and pragmatism.

Cardinal Wyszyński told Polish women to model their behavior after Mary not only in accepting sacrifice, but also in doing so with tact, moderation of expression, quiet dignity, even a sense of humor, but without drawing too much attention to themselves. He was telling Polish women to behave exactly in ways which, according to feminists, tend to perpetuate, even facilitate the exploitation of women and make them less able to protest their inferior position at home, in school and at work. Judging from Wyszyński's and Wojtyła's comments, the greatest danger to women in Poland in the 1960s and the 1970s was not discrimination, exploitation or even domestic abuse, but rather the threat of their masculinization. At the same time, the two Polish Church leaders seemed convinced that most of the discrimination against women in Poland had already been adequately addressed.

Wyszyński's opposition to women taking on traditionally male jobs in heavy industry, construction and sanitation, however, must be understood in the context of post-World War II politics in Poland. The communist regime was trying to promote such occupations for women, partly to alleviate labor shortage and partly to break up the traditional Church-oriented family structures and to fill the letter of utopian Bolshevik promises for women's emancipation, which were passed along with May Day and Women's Day celebrations. The communist propaganda immediately after the war encouraged women to become socially and politically active in support of the communist state by massively seeking education and employment outside of the home. As one communist writer described it, "employment was accepted as one of the basic principles of socialist democracy and an element of liberating women from male domination." The communists had concluded that "equality of the sexes can only be achieved if women became financially independent from men" — a view shared by many of today's feminists, but definitely not by John Paul II. The same writer admitted that the communist government was also interested in hiring women to alleviate the labor shortage and to keep real wages down by forcing more family members to leave home and work for the state economy.

One way to accomplish this was by encouraging young people to move from the countryside to the factories, offices and schools in the cities. Between 1952 and 1955, the number of new female workers grew faster than the number of new male workers. But when the economic situation worsened only a few years later, the communists changed their strategy and began to discourage women from seeking jobs. After 1954, the government propaganda used the Catholic Church's arguments in showing the negative sides of outside employment for women. Now, according to the communist media, women working outside of the home could be responsible for breaking up of families and delinquency of their children.[51] The swings between promoting and discouraging employment of women continued throughout the entire period of communist rule in Poland, discrediting communist feminism and making Polish women rightly suspicious of the regime's real motives.

Just as the communists were unable to create a prosperous economy with or without women's help, they also failed in their effort to alienate Polish workers and Polish women from the Catholic Church. Their failure became quite apparent in Wojtyła's own archdiocese, when workers in the steel mill town of Nowa Huta started to press for building new churches. Nowa Huta was deliberately located and developed in the 1940s and the 1950s near Kraków, the city viewed by the communists as the stronghold of Polish conservatism. As the Archbishop of Kraków, Wojtyła for many years lead the fight to obtain church building permits in the face of opposition and active persecution from the communist state. Eventually, the struggle for religious and civil rights replaced to some degree the activities centered on the family as Wojtyła's foremost pastoral concern. He encouraged his parishioners to organize, conducted open air masses in bitter cold to underscore the government's rejection of his applications for building permits, paid fines levied against priests who ignored the government's ban on building churches, and wrote countless protest letters to the communist authorities.

In June 1966, when the police arrested Father Władysław Kajzer, the pastor of a small village church in Wróblowice near Kraków, Wojtyła arrived at the church the next day to celebrate Sunday Mass and announced to the stunned parishioners that he would temporarily assume the duties of the pastor until the authorities released their priest. Ten days later, Rev. Kajzer, who was charged with tax evasion in retaliation for his relentless attempts to secure official permission for building a parish house, was released from prison.[52] Wojtyła's defense of the priest's right to preach and to be among his parishioners was strong and successful. He treated it as a human rights issue and was not afraid to speak out and to stage a public protest.

This experience, however, did not sensitize Wojtyła to the feelings of women who desire to be priests but are prevented by the Church from fulfilling their calling, probably because while in Poland he never experienced any significant desire by Polish women to assume such roles. Many Catholic women in the West do see attempts to prevent them from celebrating Mass as a human rights issue. John Paul II never accepted any analogies between the actions of the communist regime against religion in pre-1989 Poland and the Church's refusal to ordain women. For John Paul II, both radical feminists, because of their support of abortion rights, and communists, have shown profound lack of respect for human life and human dignity. He did not see the ordination of women issue as being in any way related to human rights concerns.

But there was much in Wojtyła's struggle for human rights in Poland that today's women could still use to persuade his successors in Rome to grant them greater rights within the Catholic Church. In order to apply this model to the current struggle of Catholic women for greater recognition within the Church, however, the pope would have to first acknowledge that the Church continues to be fundamentally unjust in its treatment of women. As a human rights pope, John Paul II probably would not oppose efforts by those wanting to have a dialogue on this issue as long as they did not include demands for the right to abortion. But since most of them did include such demands, there was really no true dialogue between John Paul II and secular and Catholic feminists who support legalized abortion.

The regime's attempts to draw the population away from the Church were fairly constant during the communist period in Poland. Part of that strategy was to encourage the employment of women not just in any profession but specifically in construction and heavy industry. Aware of this trend, Cardinal Wyszyński described in one of his sermons a conversation he had in Warsaw with a woman-construction worker, a mother of two young children, who had been assigned to do a job which both she and he found to be too strenuous for a woman. In his sermon, Wyszyński observed that the effort to make everything and everyone equal ignored both the strengths and the weaknesses of each sex. A woman, according to him, should not be forced "like a dog" to do a job for which she is not "psychologically" or "physically" prepared.[53] He was concerned that such work would prematurely destroy women's health and—as he pointed out—make them unable to bear children. At that time, the Polish Church was still very much in favor of compensating for Poland's wartime population losses by encouraging Poles to have large families. Wojtyła may have realized, however, much faster than Wyszyński that the communist economy was not capable of supporting large families. This may have been one reason for Wojtyła's involvement in natural birth control education, something that Wyszyński never fully embraced.

Neither Wyszyński nor Wojtyła were opposed to access to higher education or professional jobs for women as long as this kind of emancipation would not prevent them from becoming mothers and assuming responsibility for raising children. In fact, Wyszyński welcomed educated women in new professional roles, as well as their greater involvement in the Church, hoping that such participation by women would have a positive and moderating effect on their male colleagues and priests. Women, according to Wyszyński, tend to be not only less aggressive and more sensitive but also more practical and more optimistic in dealing with life's difficulties. Wyszyński would even describe women as being in some cases better able to lead a family and solve family problems. Although both were strongly opposed to abortion, it was Wojtyła, not Wyszyński, who spoke out more forcefully and was much more publicly focused on the issues of sex. It was also Wojtyła who took the initiative to organize in his archdiocese a relentless public campaign against artificial birth control. While Wyszyński focused on national issues and the confrontation with the communist regime, initially Wojtyła devoted much of his time and resources to expanding marriage counseling and promoting the rhythm method of birth control in his archdiocese.

Both Polish Church leaders shared the basic view that women are more suitable to be helpers rather than leaders. Stefan Wyszyński saw the Virgin Mary as a helper given to Jesus by the Divine Father.[54] He had no problems asking women to make sacrifices without making similar demands on men. Speaking in 1970, Wyszyński called on Polish women to be helpers for "their husbands, their children, their elderly parents, their extended family, their neighbors" and anybody else who is poor, lonely and needs care and kindness.[55] He made this appeal to women who, by his own admission, were already required to carry the double burden of raising families and working outside the home. It may not have occurred to him to ask men to help, or he may have concluded that appealing to men would not have produced the desired results in a traditional male-oriented society.

Since the vast majority of Polish men of Wyszyński's and Wojtyła's generations would not touch "woman's" work for fear of being feminized, such attitudes are a far better indicator of women's status in society than a thousand glowing poems, novels or sermons. At the time, lay women did not play much of a leadership role in the Polish Church. It was simply assumed by nearly everybody that male priests had the authority and knowledge to speak out on issues dealing with women's daily lives. This may explain some of John Paul II's confidence when he made numerous pronouncements on women during his papacy without making direct references to opinions expressed by women. In the United States, where women play a much greater role in the Church and different views are more tolerated, most Catholic priests today would probably be ashamed to discuss in any great detail how women should structure their daily life or what professional careers they should seek. In communist-ruled Poland, this was not unexpected or unusual. Both Wyszyński and Wojtyła grew up in Poland at a time when it was the average woman's duty to cook for the family, clean the house, do the laundry and, if necessary, take care of her grandchildren and elderly parents. Cardinal Wyszyński would even comment that the world needs not only women carefully listening to Christ's words, but also those who would see to it that everything is clean and the food is on the table.[56]

Wyszyński and Wojtyła both blamed first capitalists and later the Polish communists for drawing women away from the home. Polish women, however, were apparently also embracing outside employment for their own reasons. A 1983 study showed, for example, that while 49% of Polish women who wanted to work outside of the home were motivated by a desire to improve the financial situation of their families, 24% wanted to expand their social contacts and 32% wanted to be financially independent.[57] Among younger and childless women, more than 70% wanted financial independence. Nine percent of Polish women said that they did not work because their husbands would not approve of their working outside of the home.[58] Wyszyński believed, however, that it was capitalists who first created the conditions for outside employment by women in order to take advantage of their cheap labor.

This idea, ironically borrowed from the Marxist analysis of early

The strength of our fatherland, as with every other country and nation, comes from the family. Much too little is being done to keep this strength. Much too much has been done to weaken the unity of marriage and family! Help is needed for the individual, for the marriages, and for the families: the state and a strong society exist for the purpose of helping the family.

Karol Wojtyła, 1969

Employment of wives and mothers should not be engaged...at the cost of family life.

Karol Wojtyła, 1971

As in all the churches of the saints, the women should keep silence...for they are not permitted to speak, but should be subordinate, as even the law says. If there is anything they desire to know, let them ask their husbands at home. For it is shameful for a woman to speak in Church.

I Corinthians 14:33b-35

capitalism, seemed convincing to Wyszyński and probably also to Wojtyła. Wyszyński was also convinced that communists promoted the idea of working women for precisely the same reasons as capitalists—to exploit them as cheap labor and also to draw them away from the Church. He was right as far as the communists in Poland were concerned, and he was probably right about the profit motivations of early capitalists without, however, taking into consideration the benefits of outside employment for women themselves. A communist propaganda book for women, published in 1950, described domestic work as "unbelievably unproductive, unbelievably barbaric, unbelievably hard labor." The propagandists conceded that even under full legal equality, guaranteed by the communist state, unfair division of labor at home still persisted, but the book promised that employment of women outside of the home would guarantee their full emancipation. At the same time, the communists pointed out that women were still silenced in the Catholic Church, where "only men rule, and women can at best perform the role of servants."[59] The hypocrisy of communist propaganda soon became obvious to Polish women. The communist media encouraged Polish women to find employment in factories and offices and to have more children while at the same time communist censors blocked media articles that advocated measures aimed at making women's lives easier. The regime feared that even spelling out such policies would raise expectations for "real new gains for women with children." Communist censors also blocked articles arguing for improving women's position in the workplace and calling for a better balance between work and other human needs.[60]

For Wyszyński and Wojtyła, an economic system based on the pursuit of economic self-interest alone led to the destruction of human solidarity. This view of capitalism, focusing largely on its early abuses, was strongly reinforced in Poland by communist propaganda. For tactical reasons, the Polish Church wanted to score points with the population by criticizing both capitalism and communism and by drawing comparisons between the two systems. Neither Wyszyński nor Wojtyła had much first-hand knowledge of how capitalism had developed and worked in the West after World War II. Since they did not see women achieving economic independence as a worthwhile goal in itself, they did not fully comprehend enormous advances made by Western women precisely because of the rights and freedoms obtained by them thanks to the economic advantages of democratic free market capitalism. They also had limited knowledge of government regulations in Western countries aimed at preventing exploitation of workers, corruption and other abuses. If anything, Wyszyński and Wojtyła saw the luxury of life in the West as a real threat to the Church and to Polish women. Both Stefan Wyszyński and Karol Wojtyła accepted the traditional Polish model of an ideal woman who is pious, quiet, modest, resourceful at home, and above all willing to sacrifice for the good of the family, the Church, the community and the nation.

Commitment to the Family and Women's Role at Home

Protecting the Catholic family in Poland was a constant goal of Wojtyła's activities as a bishop and a frequent theme of his sermons. His efforts to limit abortion and artificial contraception were all designed to protect, strengthen and enlarge Polish families. Wojtyła referred to Poland as "the family of the nation," when recalling in 1966 the oath taken by Tadeusz Kościuszko (1746-1817), the Polish general and a hero of the American Revolution who promised to liberate his country from the Russian occupation.[61] A commitment to the family also meant for Wojtyła providing shelter for the homeless as exemplified by Father Albert, another 18th century Polish fighter for independence and someone who took care of the neediest people in Kraków. Wojtyła's commitment to the family can also be seen in his pastoral work as priest and bishop focused on the groups in Poland that could have the greatest influence on such issues as abortion and birth control. These included students, nurses, physicians and lawyers.[62] Journalists, on the other hand, did not participate as frequently in Wojtyła's retreats, lectures and seminars as other professional groups. The vast majority of the Polish media was under communist control and, at that time, beyond much hope for reform. Wojtyła met frequently, however, with a small group of progressive Catholic journalists in Kraków centered around a weekly opinion magazine *Tygodnik Powszechny*.

The population losses and brutalities of World War II also undoubtedly influenced Wojtyła's thinking on the importance of family and the protection of human life. In a 1967 sermon, speaking about the unsuccessful effort of Pope Paul VI (1897-1978) to visit Poland for the millennium anniversary of Polish Catholicism, Wojtyła compared Poland to "a family of special significance with one thousand years of history and Christianity."[63] This perception of Poland as a Christian family was strengthened, in his view, "after World War II and the terrible [Nazi] occupation." As he advanced in the Catholic hierarchy in Poland, Wojtyła continued his efforts to bring families and married couples closer to the Church, included them as members of various Church committees, organized special Church celebrations for wedding anniversaries and recruited couples to promote his pro-family agenda.

The glorification of the Polish nation, Poland's past and the Polish family became an even more important part of religious life in Poland under communism than before World War II. As one scholar observed, "Polish religiosity blended with traditional Polish culture and customs."[64] Patriarchal traditions blended with religious traditions and reinforced each other. This made it difficult for people like Wojtyła to identify, criticize and reject those customs that became part of the religious tradition even if Western feminists find them highly oppressive and offensive. It cannot be said, however, that Wojtyła advocated blind acceptance of all historical traditions. He was, after all, a strong opponent of excessive nationalism and all forms of anti-Semitism. He also never embraced the Polish military tradition. During one of his frequent trips to Poland, John Paul II observed that "being truthful to one's roots does not mean mechanical copying of models from the past."[65]

But in offering his vision of women's role in the modern world, John Paul II was clearly looking far more at Poland's history than at new feminist ideas coming form the West. In his speeches in Poland, he did not talk about such basic and mundane issues of importance to women as Polish men's refusal to do more housework. Instead, he often gave Polish women credit for their contributions to preserving national traditions and working for Poland's independence, usually by stressing their roles as mothers, as he did in a speech to women-textile workers in Łódź in 1987:

> The Polish woman has made almost incalculable contributions in our [country's] history, especially in the most difficult

periods. Throughout our history, our entire nation's debts to the Polish woman: mother, teacher [of children] ... hero, are beyond measure.[66]

While John Paul II often stressed the value and uniqueness of each person, including those not yet born, his sermons and speeches in Poland left an impression that the nation, the society and the family are in many ways more important than personal life-choices of individual women or men. Opposition to contraception, abortion, and professional careers that prevent women from devoting sufficient time and energy to the upbringing of their children can be clearly seen in Wojtyła's early warnings and appeals to the Poles:

> The family lies at the base of all values of every nation. A nation in a way expresses itself in the family, since it is the family that forms the people and a new generation in the [national] spirit. The family passes on [to new generations] the national culture. (Starting with the language.) And, after the language, there are all the themes and values which constitute the entire culture of every nation. In that sense, a nation lives in the family and depends on it for its biological and spiritual survival.[67]

Wojtyła's pro-family activities, including his strong opposition to divorce, abortion and artificial birth control methods, were definitely influenced by the unusual and pivotal role of the Polish family home in the country's struggle for independence since the late 18th century. The term "Polish Home" has a special meaning in Poland. It does not only mean the family and family values, but it also signifies the place where national identity can survive and young Poles can be brought up as true patriots under the watchful eyes of Polish women.

While growing up as a child, Wojtyła observed the marital relationship between his parents only at a very young age. But since his mother died when he was only nine, his father never remarried and there were no sisters, in this respect Wojtyła had less experience with marriage and women during his formative years than most Catholic priests in Poland who usually came from very large families. He did, however, live for several years with a married couple, the theater director Mr. Kotlarczyk and his wife. The Kotlarczyks' two daughters were born in his small apartment in Kraków, which during the war he offered to share with his married friends.[68]

From his childhood and throughout his formative years, Wojtyła was surrounded by women who worked at home or in convents as cooks, cleaners and housekeepers. After his mother's death, Wojtyła's father took care of his young son and gave him a lot of love and attention. But like many Polish men of that generation, he apparently did not know how to cook. He was able to prepare breakfast and supper, but for lunch which is the main meal in Poland, father and son ate out in a local eatery run by a woman Maria Banaś. Their holiday dinners were prepared with the help of a female relative of Wojtyła's father who would visit them at their rented apartment in Wadowice.[69] Later, young Wojtyła ate hot meals cooked by other female relatives or women in the households of his friends. When he started to prepare for the priesthood, some of his meals were served by nuns who continued to cook for him when he became priest. Other theology students and priests who had studied with Wojtyła, both in Poland and in Rome, remember with gratitude meals prepared for them by Polish nuns. Lay women and nuns were not permitted to study theology at that time.

Brought up in the environment in which women cooked and took care of the home, Wojtyła never gave up his belief that the man should be the primary breadwinner and that it is better for women to devote most of their attention to being mothers and homemakers. In his sermons in Poland he often called on the communist authorities to provide greater economic opportunities for Polish workers so that they could support their families. In part it was the condemnation of the communist system, but it also reflected his displeasure that more and more women had to work outside the home. Living conditions in communist Poland were very difficult, particularly for women who had to hold jobs to help support their families. But many Polish women found work outside the home not only economically beneficial but also fulfilling. In his many sermons and speeches dealing with women, when he was still in Poland, Wojtyła never extensively commented on women seeking personal fulfillment through their careers. It was not the direction in which he wanted them to move. At the same time, he had limited experience or knowledge of more affluent societies, where technological advances and a more efficient economy made housework much less time consuming and gave women even more time to pursue careers and other activities in addition to their work at home.

While solidarity between genders in Poland was strong, especially against the communist regime and in support of the Church, treating men and women as two separate groups in terms of many social and religious activities was still the norm. Gender segregation in Poland extended not only to the division of labor but also to many religious customs and observances. Gender segregated religious pilgrimages are quite common in Poland even today. Although it is not always the case, young women, young men, even husbands and wives, would go on pilgrimages to the Shrine of Our Lady of Częstochowa at Jasna Góra in separate groups. This enabled Wojtyła and other bishops and priests to offer separate messages to men and women, as well as to young boys and young girls. During one such pilgrimage in 1971, Wojtyła spoke to a group of adult men about their responsibilities:

Economic conditions are important in family life. They are primarily the responsibility of the father, but now it is also the concern of the wife and the mother. Employment of wives and mothers should not, however, be engaged in at the cost of family life. Jasna Góra is a special place for considering family issues because of the presence of the Mother of the Holy Family. The duty of Catholic men is to create such a family atmosphere in which God and God's issues are at the forefront. A nation based on strong families will be a strong nation. At the present time, family life exists under difficult conditions. Catholic men should be able to influence their change.[70]

It was clear from this sermon that the example of Christ's mother was a powerful symbol used by Wojtyła to promote what he considered to be appropriate roles for men and women. The Virgin Mary was not the right model only for women. Also very early in his priesthood, Wojtyła started to identify with the Virgin Mary as the spiritual mother of all male priests. At a workshop for priests in 1954, Wojtyła urged them to behave as sons who are worthy of "Mary's motherhood."[71] In his presentation to the young priests, he focused almost entirely on Mary's motherhood to the exclusion of nearly every other aspect of her life. He concluded his speech by saying that "a priest is linked with God's Mother through a link with her motherhood."[72]

This focus on Mary's motherhood remained a central theme of John Paul's messages for men and women, but it had much

Catholic Web Sites for Men

Dads.org
http://www.dads.org/

Effective Fathers Ministries
http://www.effectivefathers.com/home.htm

National Fellowship of Catholic Men
http://www.catholicmensresources.org/

e5men
http://www.e5men.org/

FatherDaugtherDance.com
http://www.fatherdaughterdance.com/

Knights of Columbus
http://www.kofc.org/un/index.cfm

KEPHA
http://www.kepharocks.org/

PornNoMore.com
http://www.pornnomore.com/

more relevance for women. Quite early into his priesthood, Wojtyła started to identify women with motherhood and domestic duties and made frequent references to this theme in his sermons. At the same time, he was relatively silent about promoting any specific roles for men. In 1954 he told university students that love could make women devote themselves more fully to their children and husbands. Later into his priesthood he also spoke a few times about the special responsibilities of men, but his comments about male roles were much weaker, much less specific, and above all much less frequent.[73] (Internet searches show dozens of Catholic web sites targeted specifically to women but very few targeted to men with instructions about their family responsibilities.)

In a special message about the duties of fathers written in 1971, Wojtyła did not specifically name a single one. He simply stated that "men who are working have their duties as fathers—and they should not be deprived of time, strength and material means to fulfill these duties."[74] It was an appeal to the communist authorities to give men a break, but Wojtyła did not specify which jobs within the family belong to fathers. On the other hand, Wojtyła left no doubt that the father plays a central role in the family. As he explained in a 1977 sermon in Kraków, in his mind, a family is not complete without a father:

> A father is a foundation of a family. If it has a father, it is a family. The father is the person who brings together all members of the family in a unit which is called a family.[75]

When speaking to or about women, Wojtyła was always much more specific about what he considered to be their duties vis-à-vis their families. And throughout his papacy, John Paul II remained a firm believer in maintaining differences in family and social roles between men and women, between a mother and a father, as well as between nuns and priests.[76] Women, according to Wojtyła, should not aspire to the same functions in the Church as men. He was also convinced, however, that while these functions for men and women may differ, they are equally valid and valuable.

It is on this issue that many feminists vehemently disagreed with John Paul II. To them, talking about equal dignity in doing unequal work was like adding insult to injury. It was something that John Paul II simply could not understand: how could humility and service—two traits both exhibited and highly valued by Christ—be any less important than being a priest? They could, in fact, be more important from Christ's perspective and a purely Christian point of view. What Wojtyła could not fully understand from the feminist criticism was that this idea may have been espoused by men because it was simply more advantageous for them rather than more Christian.

The argument can be further extended that perhaps women, if given a chance, would agree with the proposition that holding Church positions is not necessarily as spiritually important and rewarding as other activities. But under Wojtyła's interpretation of what Christ intended, they may never be given that chance because they cannot hold positions of authority within the Church. Of course, other Christian Churches have already accepted female priests and granted leadership positions to women and do not see this as contrary to what Christ intended.

If one were to characterize the basic elements of Wojtyła's religious personality, it would be difficult to agree which were the most important: mysticism and direct personal relationship with God through prayer and meditation, veneration of the Virgin Mary, a concern for the unborn, a concern for the poor and those who are suffering, a desire to serve the Polish Church and the Polish nation, or his interest in marriage and families. There is little doubt that Wojtyła was above all a man of deep religious faith with a personal relationship with God, but he was also a strong believer in national and cultural Catholicism. In his writing on women, marriage and sexual ethics, Wojtyła made frequent links between the nation and the family. In a manuscript published in 1958, he stated that for achieving the ethical goals of families, there is a need for close cooperation between married couples, the Church and the State. Although Wojtyła was not specific in what he meant in this case, he undoubtedly wanted the government to ban abortion in addition to providing legal and material incentives for married couples to stay together, while making divorce more difficult or even impossible to obtain. He also stated that the nation "constitutes a certain good which must be taken into account by each individual as well as the community."[77] After the fall of communism, his use of analogies between the family, motherhood and the nation became even stronger, particularly during those occasions when he was trying to convince his fellow countrymen to abandon contraception and abortion and to show greater respect for motherhood and for women. His address to the faithful during his first trip to Poland as pope in 1979 was full of references to Poland and motherhood:

> In the name of our common Mother-Fatherland, I would like to once more pay homage to every Polish mother, my own mother, every Polish girl, [I would like to] pay homage to motherhood. [I would like to] pay homage to womanhood, pay homage to virginity! If there were no physical or spiritual motherhood, there would be no nest, there would be no cradle, there would be no family, there would be no nation!
>
> Let us do everything so that woman would enjoy greatest respect on the Polish soil, [let us do everything] so that motherhood would enjoy greatest respect on the Polish soil. Let us do everything so that virginity would enjoy the greatest respect on the Polish soil![78]

In the same speech in 1979, John Paul II stressed the importance of motherhood for women and the nation by comparing the Polish word *gniazdo* (a nest) with the name of the first Polish capital, Gniezno:

We say "Gniezno" — this means the "nest"! The nest of the nation, the cradle. A woman, mother always leans over the cradle. I would like to pay homage to Polish mothers living on our Fatherland's soil.[79]

After saying these words, John Paul II apologized to priests, seminarians and all men listening to his address in Gniezno for speaking in this instance exclusively to women and about women, but he stressed that Polish women deserve this. His later speeches in Poland dealing with women were more directly focused on the issues of contraception and abortion, but he continued to make frequent comparisons between nationhood and motherhood and between personal responsibility within the family and the strength of Poland as a nation. In 1991, John Paul II was visibly pained and almost shouted to the crowd as he tried to justify his highly emotional appeal to Polish families for "responsible love," which is "open to life" while stressing the maternal nature of his links with Poland:

Perhaps I speak this way because this land is my mother! This Fatherland is my mother! These are my brothers and sisters! Those of you, who carelessly deal with these issues, should understand that I could not be indifferent to them, that they cause me pain! They should also cause you pain! It is easy to destroy; it is more difficult to rebuild! The destruction lasted for too long! It is necessary to undertake intensive rebuilding! One must not carelessly destroy![80]

This highly emotional appeal was all about abortion and contraception, but even John Paul II found it difficult to use the words knowing that many among his audience probably had no intention of heeding his advice. The reference to his country being his mother and references to motherhood, however, were not accidental. Poland is a somewhat unique country in Central Europe in terms of its traditions and beliefs with regards to the role and treatment of women. Some scholars attribute this to the highly developed Cult of the Virgin Mary, both as a religious figure and the symbolic protectress of the nation. Cardinal Stefan Wyszyński was a tireless promoter of the Marian cult and believed it to have a positive effect on Polish men's attitudes toward women. He was convinced, as he stated in a 1966 sermon, that the Polish nation is famous throughout the world for "exceptional tact and delicacy" in dealing with women.[81]

Such a statement is, however, difficult to prove or disprove. Most Western women who visit Poland would probably not agree that they are more respected and their rights are better protected than in the United States or in Great Britain. In fact, many feminists who spent some time living in Poland were appalled how Polish women were treated by men and the society in normal everyday situations. Some Polish men may be exceptionally tactful in dealing with women, but physical and verbal abuse of women and their exploitation by men and families are common. Most Polish men, especially of the older generations, have no qualms in demanding that their dinner be served everyday without offering any help with domestic chores. Fortunately, some of these attitudes are slowly changing among the younger generation of Polish men, particularly those men who have been influenced by women and by Western ideas of gender equality.

Conservative Catholics in Poland argue that a strong religious and patriotic cult of the Virgin Mary encouraged by the Polish Church has had a moderating effect on Polish men in their treatment of women. Having grown up in the environment of deep respect for women, John Paul II found it difficult to understand the complaints of Western feminists. They disagreed that Polish women were better off and were better treated by men because of Polish religious traditions, including the cult of the Virgin Mary. They point out that Polish women had to deal with additional social pressure to work hard at home and to be engaged in various patriotic and social projects while often also holding regular jobs outside of the home. Such sacrifices would be understandable if they were equally shared by men and women. Unfortunately, this was not the case in Poland. It is true that more men then women died fighting for the country's independence, but it was women and children who had to bear the long-term consequences of armed conflicts and underground activities in support of the country's independence.

Wojtyła and Pro-Choice Feminists

Some pro-choice secular feminists may wonder why Wojtyła did not join them in their struggle considering his strong record of defending the oppressed and underprivileged, particularly his involvement with the Solidarity trade union in Poland. There are several explanations for Wojtyła's limited interest in the pro-choice and secular feminist agenda. The most important reason for keeping a distance from feminists is that he undoubtedly associated Western feminism with the defense of abortion and birth control. He also did not share the feminist view that men and women can basically aspire to the same goals in life, although he strongly defended the dignity of women as defined by his own view of their special roles. Another important reason for his opposition to feminism was his conclusion that radical feminist ideas tended to undermine social solidarity, which he considered to be far more important for humanity than competition between men and women — something he would regard as destructive for individuals and families.

Many other human rights issues were much more important for John Paul II's concept of social solidarity than those favored by secular feminists. The primary one was the defense of what he considered to be the most defenseless members of society, the unborn who face the risk of abortion. Wojtyła was described by one of his close Polish friends as a priest who was always preoccupied with the fate of those who are at the margins of the society and who are the most weak and vulnerable.[82] With the same determination and energy, which characterized his peaceful struggle for freedom and dignity of his countrymen living under communism, John Paul II chose the protection of the unborn as one of the main goals of his pontificate. The others were: fighting poverty, strengthening Catholicism in the Third World, seeking reconciliation with other faiths, opposing Western secularism and promoting re-evangelization of the West. For him these were much more urgent and important tasks than focusing attention on the treatment of women within the Christian tradition or the complaints of Western feminists, some of which he viewed as legitimate and others as potentially dangerous.

While opposed to reinterpreting history and radically changing the Church's position on professional careers for women, Wojtyła in many ways supported the social agenda favored strongly by feminists in the West. It should be pointed out, however, that in most cases his support was limited to issues affecting traditional families and women fulfilling traditional roles as wives, mothers and homemakers. When he was still the Archbishop of Kraków, Wojtyła urged that mothers staying at home to take care of children "should be treated as working people with a right to the pension."[83] He was also active in promoting various social programs and proposals designed to help families with children, such as part-time employment, more flexible working hours for mothers, better orphanages, adoption of unwanted children, and better housing for young families. Some of the ideas discussed by committees he created in his archdiocese betrayed a paternalistic bias, such as the proposal to totally ban night work for women. But, considering working conditions under communism and lack of prospects for any meaningful career for women, such ideas were both well-intentioned and not entirely without merit.

Other issues, however, such as domestic violence against women, sexual harassment at work and job discrimination, received little or no public attention from Wojtyła, both in Kraków and later at the Vatican. Some feminists, who have examined Wojtyła's record in defense of human rights and his attempts at reconciliation with the former enemies of the Catholic Church or the enemies of his native country, were extremely frustrated by his lack of willingness to treat their grievances with equal seriousness. By rejecting Christianity and religion altogether, most secular and pro-choice feminists, however, made a mistake in thinking that religion, the Catholic Church and Pope John Paul II were largely irrelevant for their cause.

When Wojtyła was first exposed to feminism, he and many Polish priests around him saw it much less as an expression of legitimate grievances and much more as yet another liberal idea born in the West and designed to undermine the traditional piousness of the Polish Church. Radical feminism, in Wojtyła's eyes, also undermined solidarity between genders and national cohesiveness. It is not surprising that one of the most frequent comments which Wojtyła and other Polish priests make about the West has to do with the empty churches in the Western world. Some of them often mistakenly put the United States at the top of the list without realizing that the number of regular churchgoers and practicing believers in the U.S. is actually very high—much higher, for example, than in such former communist-ruled countries as Russia, Czech Republic or Hungary—certainly much higher than in Western Europe, although not as high as in Poland. The common perception among Catholic priests in Poland, however, is that the vast majority of people in the West, and certainly in the United States, do not believe in God and do not go to church. Again, they are quite wrong about religious faith and religious practices of Americans. During his papacy, Wojtyła believed that the future of the institutional Church was in Poland, in countries with similar cultures and traditions and in the developing world. For Wojtyła, the empty churches in Western Europe signified not only the disappearance of religious faith but also the growing selfishness and the lack of human solidarity.

Women and Social Solidarity

Human solidarity promoted by John Paul II was primarily solidarity with the poor and the poorest nations in the Third World. Because of his Polish background, John Paul II always claimed to have a special understanding for nations and groups suffering from discrimination. In a

> *...a continent marked by competition and aggressiveness, unbridled consumerism and corruption.*
>
> John Paul II in *Ecclesia in America* (*The Church in America*), 1999

speech in Nigeria in 1982, he said that it is easy for him to identify with people and nations suffering from discrimination, lack of freedom and denied social justice, because he himself comes from a country which "had difficult history."[84] John Paul II felt that it was his duty not only as a Christian but also as a Pole to speak out on behalf of the poor and the oppressed. Solidarity was a concept directed equally against communists and capitalists. It also encompassed protecting the rights of the unborn, whom John Paul II considered the most defenseless members of society.

In the 1993 interview with Polish-born journalist Jaś Gawroński, published by the Italian newspaper *La Stampa*, John Paul II claimed to have a special understanding of the exploitation of "the poor, disinherited, oppressed, marginalized and defenseless" because he had lived "in a country subject to the aggression and influence of its neighbors." He often pointed out that because of his Polish background, he felt especially close to the people of Africa and other Third World countries. He also complained of being misunderstood and even disliked by "the powerful ones of this world." This last statement, however, may be somewhat misleading. It would be more accurate to say that John Paul II was disliked by many men and women in the West who consider themselves radical liberals and feminists. On the other hand, conservative men and women, who represent an important part of the powerful elites in Western nations—including American neoconservatives and affluent evangelical Christians—generally greatly admire Wojtyła and agree with his strong moral stands while ignoring his severe criticism of U.S. foreign policy, U.S. military interventions, unregulated capitalism, economic globalization, the death penalty and lack of concern for immigrants, the poor and the environment.

John Paul II definitely saw Western feminists, who defend the right of women to obtain abortion and have access to contraception and divorce, as also belonging to "the powerful" class. He had little sympathy for these women, seen by him as living prosperous lives and trying to impose their ideas on poor women in the developing world. Judging by his writings and pronouncements, he was much more bothered by the liberal ideas of free choice than by the cultural and religious subjugation of women in more traditional societies. Oppression of women by the fundamentalist religious forces, such as the Taliban regime in Afghanistan, received far fewer public statements from John Paul II than abortion practices in the United States or Germany. The same can be said about the tribal violence in largely Catholic Rwanda, female mutilation and sexual promiscuity of males who infect African women with HIV. He would, of course, condemn in general terms attacks on human dignity in any country, either developed or underdeveloped, but it was the West that bore the brunt of his most severe public criticism on almost any significant moral issue.

Whether such selective criticism focused on the West and relative silence on the internal causes of many problems in the Third World were actually good for the poor, whom Wojtyła was trying so hard to help, is open to question. Some have argued that by focusing his criticism on the West and by not addressing the acute internal shortcomings of some of the Third World societies and the countries in East Central Europe and Eurasia, John Paul II may have missed a chance to promote the necessary reforms and may have made them more difficult to achieve.

Abortion was undoubtedly one of the main reasons, most likely the main reason, for the extreme harshness of Wojtyła's assessment of the West and the United States. He may have not been fully aware, however, of the full extent of the practice of abortion in Eastern Europe and the Third World, and if he were, he probably still blamed it on Western ideas, imperialism and Western influence rather than local traditions and cultures. As John Paul II explained in the *La Stampa* interview, foremost among the basic human rights, which he felt obliged to defend, was the right to life.

Compared with the right to life for the unborn, a woman's right to control her body and her right to privacy were not as important to John Paul II and could not be used to justify abortion. It was not clear whether he was wrongly convinced that the number of abortions was far greater in the West than in the developing world including Eastern Europe, but he did see the West with its ideas of "free choice" as representing a much more serious threat to human rights and human dignity than outbreaks of violence in the Third World or Islamist fundamentalism, which he saw as a reaction to Western, largely American, political and cultural imperialism. If the large numbers of abortions in the former Soviet block including Poland were mentioned at all in papal statements, they were usually blamed on the legacy of communism. Overall, John Paul II saw abortion as a much greater danger than traditional patriarchal institutions and customs that contribute to the oppression of women in the developing world. He did not consider these traditions and customs as designed to exploit and oppress women but rather as necessary for the survival of these societies and nations and for the preservation of morality at their level of development. John Paul II rarely spoke critically about any Third World regime or fanatical religious leader.

John Paul II may have also overlooked the fact that many women in the developing world, including many in his native Poland when it was still under communist rule, would have preferred to live in the West and enjoy the rights and freedoms which were denied to them by their own cultures or regimes. It is no secret that some women in Eastern Europe, particularly in the economically poorer countries, go into great lengths to find and marry a Westerner. Many of them are motivated largely by the economic benefits of living in Western Europe or in the United States, but presumably at least some would not seek Western husbands if men in their own countries treated them as well as men brought up in the consumerist culture of the West.

While being less effective in expanding human rights in the developing world, John Paul II made major contributions to the promotion of human rights in East Central Europe, particularly during the struggle of the Solidarity trade union movement in Poland in the 1980s for the recognition of workers' rights to organize and strike. Father Maliński captured the essence of Wojtyła's spiritual link with his nation when he wrote that during his trips to Poland he said things that the Poles felt but were unable to talk about. Basically, as Father Maliński observed, the pope "brought back dignity to the Polish nation." But workers have always received much more attention from John Paul II than women or any other group that could be characterized as oppressed or disadvantaged. In some way, Wojtyła's interest in the working class was most likely a reaction to the imposition of communism in Poland and a desire to find an alternative explanation for some of the initial successes of communist ideology in Russia and in East Central Europe. Wojtyła was seeking alternative ways of turning the workers away from communism and bringing them back to the Catholic Church, but he had also become convinced that a socialized economy, although not one that is centrally planned as under communism, is far more humane and far better for any society than the totally free-market model. Even as a young priest, Wojtyła was already preoccupied with workers' rights and trade union issues. He himself worked as a laborer in a factory during World War II and after the war spent time with families of workers in France and Belgium. He was also studying the trade union movement in the West. Group and class solidarity meant much more to John Paul II than any collective action undertaken by women, especially if such action would undermine the family or solidarity of men and women.

Rather than blaming the imposition of communism in Poland entirely on the military power of the Soviet Union, Wojtyła also saw communism as a reaction to unrestricted capitalism, poverty and exploitation of the workers and peasants in Poland during the interwar period. While rejecting communist solutions, Wojtyła was willing to accept some elements of the communist explanation of the discontent of the working class and no doubt applauded some of the social and economic programs introduced by the communists. He was keenly aware that these programs came with a heavy price in terms of freedom of conscience and human dignity, but he was not willing to declare a totally free-market economy as a much better model because for him such a model lacked the essential element of social solidarity.

It is possible that Wojtyła never fully understood the links between extensive government intervention in the economy and the threat of diminished individual liberty. Obviously, as with everything else, there is a proper balance between the two, which may be different in multi-ethnic and multi-cultural countries such as the United States, where more freedom is needed, than in more culturally and ethnically homogenous countries of Western and East Central Europe, where there is greater consensus of opinion on what constitutes acceptable social policy. Wojtyła for sure did not understand the nature and the functioning of the American economy and the American society, viewing them largely as engines of "unbridled capitalism" and excessive and aggressive individualism. In fact, he often used the harshest language to describe the American society and American positions on abortion and poverty in the Third World. He did not fully explain many of his conclusions about America, but they did reflect the prevailing views among West European Left-leaning intellectuals, conservative European clergy and to some degree the views of American bishops who at times are more critical about the United States than even the most liberal American media. It is also possible that to some degree American bishops were responding to and reinforcing John Paul II's own prejudices about America. Ultimately, American individualism clashed with Wojtyła's preferred model of social relations based on solidarity. This prevented him from seeing America in a better light or from giving Americans greater credit for their voluntarism at home and for securing peace in Europe and protecting freedom around the world.

Jude Dougherty, dean of philosophy at the Catholic University in Washington, D.C. who met Wojtyła during his 1976 visit to the United States, remembers him speaking about "the impoverished state of the Church in America."[85] According to Jude Dougherty, Wojtyła also expressed his conviction that the American bishops should do more to discipline such Catholic theologians, such as Father Charles E. Curran who publicly disagreed with Paul VI over the birth-control encyclical.[86] When Wojtyła became pope, he insisted that Father Curran be fired from his teaching position at Catholic University in Washington, D.C. after he refused to stop his criticism of the Church's official views on sexual ethics. In justifying his removal from his university position in 1987, the Vatican explained that Father Curran could not teach Catholic theology in the name of the Church at a Catholic university while at the same time disagreeing with the Church's official teaching. Father Curran sued the university for a breach of contract, but the court rejected his claim.[87]

George Weigel b. 1951
http://www.eppc.org/scholars/scholar
ID.14/scholar.asp

While most of John Paul's statements suggest a strongly negative view of the American society and the American Catholic Church, some Americans who knew him personally argue that this was not the case. George Weigel, the author of papal biography *Witness to Hope* who while doing research for his book had unprecedented access to John Paul II, maintains that the pope was actually "very bullish on the Church in the United States" and understood that "there is a vibrancy to Catholicism in America."[88] John Paul II's Polish-American friend, Dr. Anna-Teresa Tymieniecka, told me that Wojtyła had moderated his initial negative assessment of Americans. If that was indeed true, then John Paul II was very effective in hiding his optimism about America and the American Church. George Weigel wrote a friendly biography and by his own admission did not find anything about the pope that would be less than admirable. Even Wojtyła's critics who knew him personally vouch for his personal decency and sanctity. Since he was a very private man who did not share his true feelings and opinions easily, particularly with foreigners, it is difficult to judge with absolute certainty what John Paul II really thought about America. Accounts of his conversations with his Polish friends as well as many of his public statements suggest, however, that the pope's view of the American culture was generally extremely negative and that he may have had a different understanding than what most Americans think how their society functions around the principles of tolerance and pragmatic compromise.

Because of the dangers that John Paul II perceived in the American model for the rest of the world, he seemed especially concerned that the end of the Cold War left the United States as the only superpower. This position had given Americans more influence in the world than he thought they deserve. In an interview aboard the plane during his 1999 trip to Mexico and the United States, John Paul II made a rather startling observation: "After the fall of the Soviet Union, the United States remained alone. I don't know if this is good or bad, but this is how it is."[89]

This was a stunning statement coming from someone whose native country regained its independence thanks to U.S. leadership during the Cold War and still depends heavily for protecting its security on U.S. willingness to intervene in case of a serious threat. John Paul II must have been so displeased with America that he decided to ignore this geopolitical and historical fact. (The West

Europeans have repeatedly shown that they are both unwilling and incapable of taking strong action against any aggressors. In 1939 they abandoned Poland to Hitler's and Stalin's armies despite their treaty obligations to come to Poland's defense. This betrayal of Poland was well documented in a recent book *A Question of Honor* by Lynne Olson and Stanley Cloud.[90]) Responding in his weekly radio address on April 9, 2005 to the news of John Paul II's death, President Bush said that "the Pope held a special affection for America." He did, but it was an affection diminished by serious doubts and a lack of understanding of what Americans are really like. George Bush was much closer to the truth when he said in the same address that John Paul II "challenged America always to live up to its lofty calling." These rather restrained comments may suggest that George Bush had read and properly interpreted secret CIA intelligence reports and State Department cables from the Vatican describing what Pope John Paul II really thought about the United States and the Bush Administration's foreign policy. The pope was horrified by the U.S. decision to invade Iraq and tried everything in his power to prevent it. As someone who understood the power of nationalism, anti-imperialist grievances and strong religious faith, John Paul II knew that the invasion could radicalize many Muslims and significantly change relations between Christianity and Islam.[91]

Focused on the Past — Explaining John Paul II to Westerners

Explaining John Paul II to those unfamiliar with oppression or struggle for national, religious or cultural identity is no easy task. Polish filmmaker Krzysztof Zanussi (b. 1939), who in the early 1980s directed in the West a biographical film about Karol Wojtyła, struggled to find a way of bringing his famous Polish compatriot's personality closer to Western viewers, particularly those in the United States. He concluded that the key to a better understanding of Wojtyła's mind may be found in different perspectives of history.

Westerners, particularly Americans, think differently about the past. As the Polish filmmaker explained, something that happened 200 years ago would seem like only yesterday to the Poles, while to the Americans it would be the whole history of the United States. He noted that while Americans look more toward today, Poles "look very much backward...and...try always to think how similar situations had been resolved in the past."

Liberal American Catholics may, for example, see the ordination of women as something requiring immediate action to correct a grave historical injustice. They are not likely to dwell on why and how the Catholic Church in the United States grew tremendously without women-priests, while John Paul II was more likely to view the same issue from the historical perspective and experience of many centuries. He would not only conclude that this arrangement, which has worked since almost the beginning of Christianity, cannot be all wrong, but he may have also looked at several centuries of still unsuccessful attempts at reconciliation between Catholicism and the Orthodox Church and wondered how ordaining female priests might affect the relationship between Christians in Poland and in Russia or between Christians and Muslims. The Orthodox Churches and Islamic religious leaders are far more firmly opposed than the Catholic hierarchy to allowing female priests or imams.

John Paul II may have been also concerned how such a move might affect the future of the Catholic Church in the developing world. People from countries under oppression and in poverty, or those who are unable to control their own destiny, often focus most of their attention on the past, both distant and more recent, and on their current struggles, which they link closely with the past. In the long-run, this usually spells trouble for women, but it is certainly not viewed in those terms by those who place the highest value on national or religious identity or even those who only seek religious freedom and national independence without wanting to oppress others.

But it is not just a different perception of history that made John Paul II different from many liberal Western religious leaders. Poland's history of the last two centuries fueled the development of a moral culture which was much less tolerant than the political and moral culture of some of the more religiously and culturally diverse Western societies. Moral and cultural inflexibility was seen by many Poles as beneficial and essential for the preservation of national identity and kept the Catholic Church in Poland much stronger as an institution than the Catholic Churches in the West. A strong moral stand was expected from Polish Church leaders as they attempted to identify and expose the dangers of Marxist and Western materialism. They also had to convince Poles of their moral and cultural superiority in contrast with the alleged weaknesses of the national and religious cultures of their Russian and German occupiers.

John Paul's passionate rejection of abortion and Western secular liberalism are largely explainable from the historical perspective and, of course, by religion and traditional Catholic moral teachings. The struggle against foreign dominance made John Paul II much more passionate about morality and other significant issues affecting women than what would have been expected from a less historically-minded Western religious leader accustomed to pluralistic values and not threatened by powerful enemies such as a communist regime bent on weakening and destroying the Church. John Paul II had stronger opinions and was much more passionate than almost any Western religious leader about such controversial topics as birth control, abortion, homosexuality, and what he viewed as the U.S.-led cultural globalization.

Comfortable, middle class consumer-oriented life in the West may have brought women unprecedented rights and opportunities, but this is not how Karol Wojtyła saw the situation of Western women. In this area, his pessimistic outlook had much in common with the Marxist and other Left-leaning feminists with their wholesale condemnations of bourgeois societies. They also thought that women in the West were oppressed but, unlike Wojtyła, they imagined that communism in the Soviet Union was on the right path to female emancipation. Patriotic Polish Catholics like Wojtyła who had experienced communism first-hand, saw it quite differently as far as communism was concerned, but they agreed with liberal critics in the West that capitalism and bourgeois lifestyle were bad. In that respect, Wojtyła's misconceptions about the West are easier to understand and excuse. As Krzysztof Zanussi explained, taking a stand and making sacrifices, even to the point of giving up one's own life for a just cause, made Wojtyła what he was and were important factors in what he expected from Catholics around the world:

> ...I would say this is an experience of suffering, of struggle, of religious conviction that has a price and the price may be measured. So, it's not just a ritual. It is an essence of life. If you pronounce yourself a Catholic, you will have different biography because you have no equal rights [under communism]. So, this was a dramatic vision of religion, and our feeling even today is that the weakness of the Christianity of the West is connected to the fact that life of rich, Western countries is not dramatic enough...[92]

Christians in the West, particularly in countries with strong Protestant Churches, see religion increasingly as a personal matter about which individuals can make their own choices. In Poland, religion in the last few centuries has played a much more unifying public role in the lives of People than in any Western country other than perhaps Ireland. Religion and remembrance of the past allowed Poles to survive foreign oppression without losing their desire for freedom or making any significant compromises with the occupying powers. In countless sermons and speeches in Poland and in addresses to Poles living abroad, John Paul II reminded them of the link between the struggle for Poland's independence and the support given to this struggle by the Polish Catholic Church. Before he became pope, he stressed in a 1967 sermon that "the unity of the Church with the nation has had and continues to have basic significance" and reminded the listeners how Polish bishops and priests saved the Church from falling under the Russian influence in the 18th and the 19th centuries.[93] With the same determination, he later tried to save the Church from being overcome by Western secular, liberal, and consumerist values and ideas.

John Paul II was well prepared for such a struggle. Both history and his personal experience pushed him in the direction of taking uncompromising stands against moral evil. It is possible, however, that excessive reliance on historical precedence of the Polish kind made John Paul II view the threats in Western liberalism and secular feminism as perhaps far more serious than they really were. This could have caused him to see dangerous historical analogies where few may have existed, or at least not to the extent that he perceived them to be. At the same time, he may have been ignoring significant contributions that liberal democratic nations, particularly the United States and Great Britain, have made toward securing freedom, democracy and peace for themselves and for many other people around the world. A later chapter will explore the question why most Poles did not see the Anglo-American contribution to the defeat of the Nazis in World War II as particularly significant or as a proof of the strength of liberal democracy that would be worthy of praise.

By equating Polishness with Catholicism, the Polish priests helped the Poles to preserve their national identity and to regain independence, but such close linking of religion and nationalism also had its negative side. While some Catholics and most certainly Wojtyła himself would have argued that patriotic Catholicism moderated Polish nationalism and mistreatment of women, others claim that it made oppression of ethnic minorities and exploitation of women much more severe. Jews living in Poland were especially fearful of Polish nationalism fanned by Catholic fervor. There is little doubt that nationalistic statements by Polish Catholic clergy contributed to the growth of anti-Semitism in Poland when Wojtyła was growing up. As Czesław Miłosz (1911-2004), the late Polish poet of Lithuanian origin who won the Nobel Prize in literature, observed, "when the line between national and religious behavior is erased, religion changes into a social power; it becomes conservative and conformist."[94] This can have a negative effect on both ethnic and gender relations. If John Paul II shared Miłosz's opinion even slightly, he was not likely to voice his doubts publicly knowing that such criticism would offend many patriotic Poles. Judging by John Paul's numerous comments about the heroic role of the Catholic Church in Poland, any reservations that he may have had about misogynist behavior of some Polish Catholics remained well hidden and, if they were ever expressed, it was done in very general and subtle ways. While being very sensitive to the feelings of conservative Polish Catholics, John Paul II was far less reluctant to criticize Westerners for what he perceived to be their significant moral failures.

CHAPTER FOUR

Significant Women, War, Genocide

and Abortion

Two Polish women, both highly educated, one a psychiatrist and the other a philosopher, had a unique opportunity to influence Wojtyła's thinking on some of the most important issues in his life: human dignity, sexuality, women's rights, and attitudes toward Western liberalism.

One of them confirmed his own basic beliefs and succeeded in convincing him to accept her vision of human sexuality and women. The other represented a more Western outlook and her more liberal opinions were largely ignored when they clashed with Wojtyła's firmly-held beliefs. One was a witness to World War II Nazi genocide and medical experiments on women. Her war experiences deeply affected Wojtyła's positions on contraception and abortion. As a scientist, she provided him with what he accepted as scientific confirmation of his religious and ethical stands on human sexuality. The second woman left Poland in 1946 and resettled in the West. Although she came from a similar ethnic and religious background and in many areas agreed with Wojtyła's philosophical, religious and ethical thinking, she developed significantly different views on at least some of the issues affecting women. She also had a different perspective on Western democracy. Both women had extensive contacts with

> *America needs no words from me to see how your decision in Roe v. Wade has deformed a great nation. The so-called right to abortion has pitted mothers against their children and women against men.*
>
> Mother Teresa, 1994

Wojtyła and more opportunity to engage him in intellectual discussions than any other women in his life with the possible exception of Sister Zofia Zdybicka, with whom he also discussed the challenge of feminism. A woman whose personal tragedies, education and career more closely matched Wojtyła's own life experiences emerged as one of his most influential advisors. Her impact on women's lives through her influence on John Paul II has not yet been properly appreciated or assessed.

The life of another woman, a Catholic nun born in Germany who was a convert from Judaism and was murdered by the Nazis in Auschwitz, also inspired Pope John Paul II. Her influence on John Paul II's thinking about religion and gender issues was made more significant by the fact that she was one of the early Catholic scholars who came out in favor of Catholic feminism.

There was also a fourth woman, an Albanian-born nun, whom John Paul II consulted regularly in developing his strategy for dealing with abortion and other women-related issues. Her views were very closely aligned with his. She is widely admired throughout the world.

Dr. Wanda Półtawska's and Karol Wojtyła's Views on Love and Sex

Dr. Wanda Półtawska (b. 1921), a psychiatrist working in Kraków, a mother of four daughters, and a former Nazi concentration camp inmate, had a more profound influence on Pope John Paul's views concerning sexuality, contraception and abortion than perhaps any other person.[1] Yet very few people know her name and are aware of the importance of her collaboration with Wojtyła. Her wartime experiences caused her to develop a lifelong interest in sex and religion and apparently provided her with strong credibility in the eyes of Karol Wojtyła. From 1941 until 1945, she was one of many women imprisoned at various concentration camps and forced by Nazi doctors to undergo medical experiments, some of which focused on controlling fertility through sterilization. After the war, she became one of Wojtyła's closet advisors.

When the former head of the Poznań Archdiocese in Poland, Archbishop Juliusz Paetz (b. 1935), came under suspicion a few years ago of sexually molesting young seminarians at his diocesan seminary, concerned conservative Catholic activists in Poland reportedly turned to Dr. Półtawska to break the news to the pope and ask for the archbishop's removal.[2] After the pope's death, one Polish newspaper, *Głos Wielkopolski*, and Italian newspaper *La Stampa*, accused John Paul II's friend and personal secretary Cardinal Dziwisz of not informing him about sexual scandals in the Catholic Church.[3] In February 2007, a spokesman for the Kraków Archdiocese said that Cardinal Dziwisz did not hide from the pope accusations of sexual abuses and that reports in both newspapers are totally false. But perhaps as a result of Dr. Półtawska's intervention, John Paul II dispatched an investigator to Poznań and the archbishop resigned, although he strongly proclaimed his innocence and insisted that his spontaneity was misconstrued as sexual advances. The case was especially sensitive since it became public at the time of increased media reporting on the sex abuse scandal in the American Church. Archbishop Paetz was not only nominated to his position by John Paul II, but from 1976 to 1982 he served in the papal household as a "prelate of the ante-camera," escorting important visitors to meetings with the pope.[4] Polish media reported that during that time he had contacts with the Polish communist regime's intelligence officers in Rome, but the purpose and the extent of his collaboration is unclear. At one time, his communist handlers suspected him of passing on misinformation at the inspiration of the Vatican, but overall they found him to be a valuable source of intelligence.[5] As in many similar cases of Polish priests suspected of sexual crimes or of being communist regime informants, the insular culture of the Polish Church under the communist dictatorship and communist disinformation make it difficult for journalists to establish the facts.

Whenever sensitive issues of sex and sexual ethics were at stake or John Paul's reputation or judgment was questioned, Dr. Wanda Półtawska was always at Wojtyła's side as his primary advisor and confidante, providing him with her professional advice as a psychiatrist specializing in sexual disorders but also advising him on much broader issues of Church policy. As it turns out, she was instrumental in helping Wojtyła develop arguments, which convinced Pope Paul VI to issue his highly controversial birth control encyclical *Humanae vitae*, which alienated vast numbers of Catholics and caused a major crisis within the Church. She almost never grants interviews except to a few pro-life publications and she rejected my request by saying that if anything needs to be said about her relationship with Pope John Paul II she would write it herself.

Dr. Wanda Półtawska met Father Karol Wojtyła more than ten years after the end of World War II during a pilgrimage of Catholic physicians to the Shrine of Our Lady of Częstochowa. Because of her great desire for protecting her privacy, her close personal and professional relationship with Wojtyła has never been widely publicized and hardly anyone in the West, or for that matter in Poland, knows who she is or was aware of her extremely close relationship with John Paul II. Mary Craig, a British writer who translated Dr. Półtawska's concentration camp memoirs into English and had greater access to her than other papal biographers, reported that a lifelong friendship between Wojtyła and Dr. Półtawska started in the late 1950s, when she sought his help in caring for a pregnant unmarried girl.[6] Afterwards, a close personal friendship also developed between Wojtyła and Dr. Półtawska's husband, Dr. Andrzej Półtawski, a professor of philosophy at Warsaw's Theological Academy whom she married in 1947.

Because of their academic background and shared interests, the two men liked to discuss philosophy, theology and history, but Wojtyła's relationship with Wanda Półtawska seemed to have been much deeper. Even after he became pope, the Półtawskis remained close to Wojtyła, spending their vacations with him almost every year and very likely discussing the same issues that brought a young woman-psychiatrist and a young Polish priest together more than fifty years ago. It was a relationship based not only on shared views and common interests, but also a relationship that progressed into intensive collaboration between Karol Wojtyła and Wanda Półtawska almost from the very beginning. They worked closely together on joint projects dealing primarily with women and their sexuality. It was also a relationship, about which surprisingly very little has been publicly known or written, even though their work had the most profound impact on the Catholic Church and its faithful.

While it may seem that much of Wojtyła's relationship with Dr. Półtawska centered on issues of sex and birth control, the primary and initial motivation for both of them was their desire to help young people who had found themselves in difficult situations due to sexual activity. At about the same time when Wojtyła met Dr. Półtawska for the first time in the 1950s, he became deeply interested in problems of sex among his students and among the young married couples under his pastoral care. Dr. Półtawska was a psychiatrist specializing in treating sexual disorders and focusing her practice on young Nazi concentration camp survivors, sometimes referred to by her as her "Auschwitz children." Papal biographer, Jonathan Kwitny (1941-1998), described the encounter between Wojtyła and Półtawska in Częstochowa as "a chance conversation that would touch the world."[7] It was also a friendship that would continue for many years.

Even before her meeting with Wojtyła, Dr. Półtawska was working with a group of other women in the Kraków Archdiocese as an active Church campaigner in promoting strict Catholic ethics in sex education and curbing abortion along with the use of artificial contraception. She so impressed Wojtyła with her pro-life activities, which included help for unwed pregnant mothers, that after becoming Kraków's archbishop he immediately made her his principle assistant in developing and managing programs of marriage and sex counseling and organizing family and health care ministry in the archdiocese. She apparently had no problems convincing the newly appointed archbishop that she was far better qualified for this position than some of the priests who were dealing with such issues. In his book *Love and Responsibility*, Wojtyła acknowledged that priests, while fully qualified to speak and advise authoritatively on the issue of sexual ethics, may lack the necessary education and professional experience needed for such practical tasks as advising women on natural birth control methods. In Dr. Półtawska he found a lay expert who was deeply religious, ethically orthodox, shared his interest in sexual ethics, and was able to offer him professional advice as a medical doctor and psychiatrist. She also agreed with him on almost every issue, including a deep distrust of Western materialistic societies.

Trying to organize Church-sponsored sexual counseling was not an easy task in communist-ruled Poland. But as soon as the communist authorities briefly relaxed their controls after 1956, Dr. Półtawska established the first home for unmarried pregnant women in the Kraków Archdiocese. She and other women kept the home open in a small town of Słomniczki near Kraków from 1957 until 1965, when they were forced to close it due to renewed harassment from the communist authorities.[8] It was a time when helping unwed mothers or engaging in other Church-sponsored charitable or teaching activities required considerable personal courage. By interrogating those involved in Church-sponsored marriage and sex counseling programs, the police and communist administrators tried hard to intimidate Dr. Półtawska's volunteers. The aim was to force them, usually by the use of threats and blackmail, to abandon their work or to become police informants.[9] While some succumbed to such pressure, Dr. Półtawska was described as being quite fearless and would not be deterred unless put in a position in which the authorities gave her absolutely no other choice.

The vast majority of volunteers whom she recruited to promote

Wojtyła's pro-life programs were religiously devout women. She organized and trained them to advise other women on matters related to sex and birth control, while Wojtyła supervised religious, spiritual and ethical training of female volunteers working as marriage and sex advisors. Dr. Półtawska and Karol Wojtyła were convinced that sex, as God's gift to humanity, cannot be separated from its spiritual or religious dimension and, therefore, cannot be left only in the hands of professional health care workers who do not have any religious training or do not want to mix religion with their profession. Motivated by this belief, Dr. Półtawska and Karol Wojtyła organized numerous conferences and training programs for medical students, doctors and nurses in an effort to broaden their knowledge of ethnical and religious issues connected with the practice of their professions.

Because of her specialization in treating sexual disorders, Dr. Półtawska was Wojtyła's chief scientific advisor as he began to write his major work on sexual ethics, *Love and Responsibility*. She may have been the one to convince Wojtyła, when he was still a young priest in Poland, that when contraception fails, couples who do not want to have children tend to resort to abortion. Together they coined the term "contraceptive mentality," which John Paul II used throughout his papacy to describe attitudes of people living in liberal Western societies who accept contraception and do not criminalize abortion. Wojtyła and Półtawska were convinced that it was the acceptance of contraception in communist Russia and later in the West that led to the acceptance and legalization of what they described as murder of unborn children. They convinced themselves and tried to convince others that contraception is one of the primary causes of abortion and possibly mass murder.

Wojtyła on Female Orgasm

Dr. Półtawska may have been also responsible for developing Wojtyła's interest in human sexuality in areas that until then were completely ignored by conservative Polish clergy. Wojtyła was probably the first Polish bishop to depart from the idea of sex as the breeding ground for sin and instead present it as something positive, but always in the proper context of marriage and love strengthened by religious faith. Some attribute to Dr. Półtawska's influence Wojtyła's unusual for the times endorsement of female orgasm. Most likely no other Catholic priest in Poland in the 1960s would have dared to write about such issues. Wojtyła asserted in *Love and Responsibility* that lack of orgasm in women can lead to neurosis and blamed it on male selfishness.[10] But while feminists could see the discussion of female orgasm as a progressive step on the part of a major Church leader, Dr. Półtawska's papers also frequently referred to neurosis in women caused by the use of contraceptives, one of Dr. Półtawska's many conclusions about sexuality which Wojtyła accepted as valid.

Dr. Półtawska's endorsement of the importance of orgasm was not unconditional. While approving of it in a loving marriage, she generally condemned what she described as "the hedonistic attitude," which puts orgasm at the very center of Western preoccupation with sex.[11] In Dr. Półtawska's view, which was fully shared by John Paul II, orgasm is a good thing only within a conventional marriage and only if it truly strengthens love between two individuals. It must also facilitate or at least keep open the possibility of procreation. Therefore, a culture that focuses too much attention on different techniques for achieving orgasm, which both Dr. Półtawska and John Paul II associated with Western societies, produces individuals who are "dominated by their physiological mechanism," unable to control them, and therefore much more likely to violate the Church rules on chastity, contraception and abortion.

Both of them believed that liberal thinkers in the West, as well as communists in the former Soviet Union, managed to persuade many people including many Catholics that sexual urges can never be fully controlled and therefore certain compromises such as contraception, abortion and de-stigmatizing of sex between consenting adults are desirable and necessary. Dr. Półtawska and Karol Wojtyła believed that this is exactly what was wrong with liberal and Marxist thinking, as well as with Catholics and other religious believers who had been fooled into accepting these ideas. Dr. Półtawska often quoted Wojtyła's words found in his books *Love and Responsibility* and *The Acting Person*, that "what differentiates us human beings from the animals is our ability to control our own reactions," including human libido.[12]

The standards, which both Dr. Półtawska and John Paul II believed were extremely important to uphold, were also extremely high but generally in line with traditional Catholic teachings on sex prior to the sexual revolution of the 1960s. Apparently both of them were able to achieve total sexual self-discipline or, as she described it, the degree of maturity which Karol Wojtyła calls "self-possession." In her war memoirs, Dr. Półtawska wrote with some pride how her religion and traditional Polish upbringing helped her to reject sexual advances of lesbian prisoners and, shortly after the liberation from the concentration camp, offers of sex and marriage from the Red Army soldiers. It was apparently also during the war that young Karol Wojtyła, who by then had lost his father and practically every other member of his family, made his vow of total chastity, even before he started to study for the priesthood.

Celibacy Rules

Both Cardinal Wojtyła and Dr. Półtawska apparently believed that the Catholic Church, particularly in the West, had already compromised too much on sexual ethics, confusing the believers and causing even greater problems such as sexual abuse of minors by priests. Their assumption was that such problems were much less common in the past when the Church's positions on sex were clear rather than simply being overlooked or swept under the rug. Rather than blaming the problem of sexual abuse of minors by Catholic priests on celibacy and secrecy of the Church leaders, they saw it largely as a manifestation of the rapid process of weakening of the Church's moral teachings under the pressure of liberal, communist and other atheistic ideologies. Some of the more liberal Church leaders in the West, including Wojtyła's friend and former Archbishop of Vienna Cardinal Koenig, considered such views as unnecessarily harsh and unforgiving, but by the standards of the Polish Church and the majority of its clergy in the 1950s and the 1960s, Wojtyła may be easily described as open-minded, remarkably progressive and even tolerant on issues of sexuality.

In a paper widely read within the Vatican circles due to the revelations of sexual abuse by some Catholic priests, Dr. Półtawska strongly defended the celibacy rule, warning that its abolition could have the opposite effect by appearing to sanction fornication, whether heterosexual or homosexual, even for priests.[13] Both she and the pope believed strongly that instead of a more permissive attitude, the Catholic Church needed more celibacy to combat sexual abuse within it. In her paper she noted with some regret that the Catholic Church no longer required candidates for the priesthood to be virgins. As she pointed out, "those who have committed the sins of fornication or masturbation find the obligation of celibacy all the more difficult to observe."[14] In Dr. Półtawska's view, "increasingly widespread permissive ethics" have encouraged Catholics and others to expect definite changes in the Church's teaching on priestly celibacy and other requirements dealing with sex. She believed, however, that this kind of uncertainty, which John Paul II tried very hard to dispel by continually reaffirming strict moral standards, made respect for chastity among lay people and priests even harder. She and Wojtyła agreed that uncertainty on moral issues was not a good thing and both seemed to be fully confident that they knew quite well the true answers to such moral questions. Such confidence can be explained in part by the peculiar conditions which existed in Poland for quite some time. Unlike Western Europe and the United States, Poland did not have a tradition of major religious dissidence or questioning of moral standards. While a large number women in the West started using the pill in the 1960s, Dr. Półtawska spearheaded Wojtyła's campaign to promote natural birth control methods in Poland and to oppose artificial contraception, including the pill. Both she and Wojtyła were fully confident that they would be successful.

Wojtyła's relationship with Dr. Półtawska may have been strengthened even more by her apparently miraculous recovery from cancer, which Wojtyła attributed to prayers by an Italian charismatic Capuchin monk, Father Pio da Pietrelcina (1887-1968), whom he met in 1947 during his student years in Rome. When Wanda Półtawska was diagnosed with what appeared to be a case of terminal cancer in 1962, Wojtyła had been reported to have written two letters in Latin to Padre Pio who was already famous as a stigmatic and a religious healer but, at that time, regarded with some suspicion by the official Church. In his letter, Wojtyła referred to her as "a certain mother of four young girls, who lives in Kraków, Poland ... [who during] the last war ... spent five years in a German concentration camp."[15] Soon after the letter with a request for prayers for Dr. Półtawska was sent, the presumably cancerous tumor rapidly disappeared and she fully recovered from her illness.[16]

John Paul II beatified Padre Pio on May 2, 1999 and made him a saint on June 16, 2002. His beatification, which drew 300,000 pilgrims, was the most widely attended in the history of beatifications held in Rome.[17] Father Pio himself suffered from many illnesses, and at the age of 31 the marks of the stigmata, the wounds similar to the wounds of Christ, appeared on his body. He was the first priest in the Church's history to be stigmatized. (Most stigmatics have been members of female religious orders. Some Catholics, particularly those who are educated view the alleged supernatural origin of the stigmatic wounds with some suspicion and even embarrassment.) Father Pio survived on minimal amounts of sleep and food, worked 19 hours a day saying Mass and listening to numerous confessions, never took a vacation, never read a newspaper or listened to the radio and warned the faithful against watching television.[18]

At the time of her illness, Wanda Półtawska did not know about the letters written by Wojtyła to Father Pio and accepted the doctors' conclusion that the tumor, suspected of being cancerous, may have been a simple inflammation. In 1967 she traveled to Rome and was able to attend a Mass celebrated by Father Pio. An encounter with Father Pio convinced her that she owed her life to his prayers and the intervention of Archbishop Wojtyła:

> ... I knew he recognized me. In this moment I also knew that it wasn't because of a wrong diagnosis that I found myself suddenly well several years earlier, but because this monk had come into my life in such an extraordinary way because the Archbishop of Kraków had asked for it.[19]

Wojtyła and Dr. Półtawska Urge Paul VI to Ban Contraception

The significance of the personal and professional relationship between Wanda Półtawska and Karol Wojtyła went, however, well beyond their joint efforts to promote Church-sanctioned family planning programs in the Kraków Archdiocese. Together with Wojtyła, she may have been directly responsible for initiating one of the greatest crises in the Catholic Church in the 20th century over the very issue of birth control. It appears quite likely that explanations of Dr. Półtawska's medical and psychiatric theories forwarded to the Vatican by Wojtyła persuaded Pope Paul VI to reject the advice of his Western experts who favored limited use of contraceptives by married couples. It is very likely that it was Dr. Półtawska who provided Pope Paul VI with what she billed as irrefutable scientific arguments against artificial birth control in any form. According to some of Wojtyła's associates, the then Archbishop of Kraków included Dr. Półtawska's ideas on contraception in the written materials sent to Pope Paul VI before the publication of the birth control encyclical *Humanae vitae*. Papal biographer Jonathan Kwitny goes even further by claiming that Dr. Półtawska's ideas and in some cases her exact words can be found in the text of the controversial 1968 encyclical.[20]

An enthusiastic supporter of *Humanae vitae* at the time of its publication and until his death, Cardinal Wojtyła turned to Dr. Półtawska to develop the program of marriage counseling and sex education for married couples in the Kraków Archdiocese in an attempt to publicize and implement the papal directives on birth control.[21] Dr. Półtawska was also at Wojtyła's side when he established the Family Institute in Kraków as an academic research arm of the archdiocese on family issues. Set up four years after the publication of *Humanae vitae*, the institute was charged with preparing uniform training materials for family ministry and organizing lectures for priests and lay marriage counselors. Dr. Półtawska was herself the author of a number of textbooks, including ones with such titles as: "Marriage—Our Future, Goal and Task,"[22] "Marriage Guidebook" and "Love Endangered."[23] She also presented papers at numerous special seminars and conferences, many of them organized and attended by Cardinal Wojtyła. At one such seminar, held in 1972 for counselors preparing university students for love, marriage and family life, Dr. Półtawska presented a paper on "Reconstruction of the Ideal of Virginity and Chastity in the Consciousness of Youth Counselors and Pastoral Workers."[24]

Teaching Natural Birth Control

Always looking for ways to establish broader contacts with the Polish youth and to bring to them the message of Christian marriage and sexuality, Cardinal Wojtyła also put Dr. Półtawska in charge of preparing teaching materials for high school students dealing with such topics as psychological difficulties during adolescence, first love, choosing a marriage partner and, significantly, "contraception [as] a sin against life and love."[25] Dr. Półtawska was also in charge of organizing meetings between physicians and students despite a cool reception from some doctors who opposed the Church's activities designed to limit access to abortion and contraception. She was more successful in organizing joint seminars for students of theology and medicine, known as "Kler-Med," which dealt with such topics as situational and sexual ethics, human love in marriage, but also contraception and responsible parenthood.[26] Extremely hardworking, she also received patients at a psychiatric clinic of Kraków Medical School, worked in a special outpatient advisory center at Kraków's Jagiellonian University, and ran a psychological and psychiatric counseling center.[27] With a number of priests and lay activists, she also shared responsibility for training female family counselors whose main job was to advise women on using natural birth control methods.

PORADNIA RODZINNA I DLA NARZECZONYCH			
		Poniedziałek.	9.30 – 10.30
		Wtorek	12.00 - 13.00
Porady dot. życia małżeńskiego rodzinnego, problemów wychowawczych z	Pracownik	Środa	12.00 -13.00
dziećmi itp. Porady dla narzeczonych przygotowujących się do małżeństwa	Poradnictwa	Czwartek	12.00 -13.00
		Piątek	15.30 - 16.30
		Sobota.	16.00 -18.00
INDYWIDUALNA NAUKA METOD NATURALNEGO PLANOWANIA RODZINY			
		Poniedziałek.	11.00 – 12.00
		Wtorek	16.30 – 18.30
Nauczyciel metod naturalnego planowania rodziny		Środa	15.00 – 17.00
		Czwartek	10.00 – 11.00

Marriage counseling and natural birth control training announcement at a church in Kraków (2007). Very few churches in Poland publicize such activities and even fewer display information about offering help to single mothers.

When the College of Cardinals elected Karol Wojtyła to the papacy in 1978, there were 82 family counseling centers in the Kraków Archdiocese, 25 of them in Kraków alone.[28] Their creation was largely a joint effort by Cardinal Wojtyła and Dr. Półtawska. More significantly, she trained many of the women who ran the

counseling centers. Without Dr. Półtawska's leadership, her enthusiastic support, her training efforts and the sacrifice of hundreds if
not thousands of women-volunteers who worked at these centers
despite harassment from the communist authorities, Wojtyła's
plans for teaching Polish women natural birth control methods
would have had no chance of being implemented. To this day, the
Kraków Archdiocese still has the highest church attendance and the
highest birth rate in Poland — but on the whole, the practice of birth
control among Polish women is so widespread that Poland now has
one of the lowest birth rates in Europe, well below the replacement
rate and below the birth rate in the United States. Cardinal
Wojtyła's ambitious plans for birth control for Polish women were
not successful.

Jonathan Kwitny, the author of perhaps the most insightful
biography of Pope John Paul II, described Dr. Półtawska as a
convinced believer in Catholic teachings on sex and marriage: no
sex before marriage and no artificial contraception except for the
rhythm method in limited circumstances. According to this papal
biographer who spoke with Dr. Półtawska's husband, she
considered all artificial methods of contraception as medically
harmful and believed that every sexual act must be at least open to
the possibility of procreation. In Dr. Półtawska's view, *coitus interruptus*, also known as withdrawal or the pull out method, while
more natural than other methods, can still lead to neurosis, female
frigidity and male impotence. She believed that only the rhythm
method was acceptable, and then only under limited circumstances
when it is practiced by married couples. What made this method
acceptable in Wojtyła's and Dr. Półtawska's view was its less than
full reliability, thus leaving open the possibility of conception.

The Pill — Links between Contraception and Abortion

Dr. Półtawska was also actively publicizing in Poland and in other
countries the alleged harmful medical effects of the pill and other
modern contraceptives — something that Western experts who

support the use of artificial contraception by women have described as harmful misinformation. In their view, Dr. Półtawska's medical theories on the alleged harmful effects of contraception may have succeeded in persuading some women to forego using the pill, but at the same time they may have also contributed to increasing the number of abortions in a country such as Poland, where until the early 1990s abortion was by necessity an alternative method of birth control and was more frequent relative to the size of the female population than in the United States or in any other Western country. However, both John Paul II and Dr. Półtawska consistently promoted the view that contraception and abortion were largely a problem created by Western societies. They both accused Western countries of trying to force contraception and abortion on less developed nations through the combined power of globalization, media and marketing.

In presenting his wife's views in an interview with Jonathan Kwitny, Dr. Półtawska's husband echoed Wojtyła's firmly held belief that contraception becomes the first step to abortion. This same view was reflected in the chapters of Wojtyła's book *Love and Responsibility* that deal specifically with sex and birth control and were most likely written in close cooperation with Dr. Półtawska. Wojtyła concluded, for example, that "contraceptives are of their nature harmful to health" and that chemical means, such as the pill, are "cellular poisons" and therefore must be "physically harmful." *Coitus interruptus* is less harmful, according to Wojtyła, but denies woman an orgasm and causes psychological damage.[29] Dr. Półtawska was actively promoting the same views over many years in her lectures, articles and books. There is little doubt that most of the ideas on sex, birth control and abortion, expressed by Wojtyła in his books and later in his papal sermons, were originally developed in his discussions with Dr. Półtawska while he was still a young priest.

Wojtyła also seemed to have fully accepted Dr. Półtawska's

argument that contraception leads to an increase in the number of abortions. Despite all the evidence pointing to the exact opposite relationship, Dr. Półtawska's claim that contraception encourages women to resort to abortion more freely was frequently repeated by John Paul II and in Church-sponsored publications designed to warn women about physical and psychological dangers of using the pill. A common theme of these articles was that the medical profession and feminists are engaged in a massive conspiracy designed to suppress evidence about the alleged harmful effects of the pill and other contraceptives. These publications also attempt to convince women that in many cases the pill works by stimulating a spontaneous abortion in the earliest stages of pregnancy. In one such pro-life article, Dr. Półtawska was quoted that in countries in which "the contraceptive mentality prevailed, abortion would be the logical outcome of contraceptive failure." The same words were used frequently by John Paul II in condemning contraception, particularly in the West. According to Dr. Półtawska reasoning, the acceptance of contraception for general use led to the increase in abortions forcing authorities to make them legal. "This second green light," according to her, "escalated the number of abortions to millions and millions each year."[30]

Dr. Półtawska also claimed in her lectures and publications that "the use of contraception leads to neurosis" by causing women to become depressed and aggressive toward themselves and their sexual partners. She also argued that abortion causes permanent changes in woman's personality and leads to mental illness manifesting itself in hysterical behavior.[31] In a paper published in 1977 she insisted that such reactions are very common and occur even in societies that do not have strong religious objections against terminating a pregnancy. As an example she cited Japan, where— according to data presented in her paper—73.1 percent of women felt guilty after having an abortion and some became paranoid. But while religion may not have had a strong influence on these attitudes in Japan, patriarchal views that put a great value on the birth of male children may have played a decisive role in how Japanese women react to abortion. In a later paper written in defense of priestly celibacy, Dr. Półtawska again argued that women whose desire for married life and motherhood are thwarted may suffer from "bouts of psychic depression." She maintained that the tendency toward depression among people who cannot marry is more common in women than in men.[32]

Dr. Półtawska's educational credentials are beyond question. She received a degree from one of the best medical schools in Poland and practiced and taught psychiatry for many years. But Jonathan Kwitny noted in his biography of John Paul II that he could not find any scientifically accepted proofs of Dr. Półtawska's claims or any references to her research in serious scientific journals. He pointed out that apparently all of her articles appeared in obscure publications put out by Church groups opposed to contraception and abortion.[33]

Excerpts from Dr. Półtawska's articles were often quoted by pro-life activists in Poland who were aware of her close connection to John Paul II. Some of these activists also received advanced scientific degrees from Polish universities. At a Church-sponsored academic conference in Poland in 1994, which focused on John Paul's *Letter to Families*, another Polish medical expert Dr. Maria Ryś extensively quoted from Dr. Półtawska's research to support her contention that abortions may cause psychotic behavior in some women. Dr. Ryś also argued that secular sex education eliminates a sense of shame among young people and encourages "positive attitudes toward masturbation, homosexuality, pedophilia, and even zoophilia."[34]

Fighting for Human Dignity

Western feminists and other women living in the West, as well as many younger women in Poland, may find difficult to understand the reasons behind Dr. Półtawska's views and her pro-life activism, just as it is difficult for them to understand what really motivated

Pope John Paul II when he made categorical pronouncements about sex. Perhaps the most useful for comprehending Dr. Półtawska's philosophy of life is the admission of her husband that she developed her traditional views on sex as a result of her experiences during World War II. It is not coincidental that John Paul II also frequently referred to World War II in justifying his positions on abortion and the need to protect human dignity. Dr. Półtawska and John Paul II were also very similar in how strongly they both believed in the importance of preserving the core values of Catholicism, particularly under extreme situations, and how closely they both linked them with their national traditions and the suffering of their own countrymen and women during the last world war. They both viewed most of today's moral choices largely through their war experiences — something that seems very difficult to understand by those who have never personally experienced the tragedies of war and genocide.

Wanda Półtawska's war experiences were more tragic than even the experiences of most other people who had lived through and survived World War II and the Nazi occupation. Arrested by the Gestapo in Nazi-occupied Poland in February 1941 at the age of only 19 and charged with helping the underground Polish resistance movement, she was sent together with about 130 young Polish girls to the Ravensbrück concentration camp, some twenty miles north of Berlin. (The youngest of the girls was only fourteen.)[35] At the camp, Nazi doctors performed medical experiments on Wanda and other Polish women, as well as women of other nationalities, Gypsies and mentally ill inmates. Before her arrest by the Nazis, Wanda wanted to study Polish literature and become a writer — an ambition similar to what slightly older Karol wanted out of his college education. But the Nazi occupation of Poland and the closing down of all Polish universities forced both of them to postpone their plans. Instead, Wanda, a daughter of a post-office clerk in Lublin, became involved in helping war victims, providing first aid and working in soup kitchens.

As a highly patriotic Polish woman brought up in the tradition of fighting for her country's freedom, she also joined the underground Polish resistance movement against the Nazis. Her job, usually assigned to young women, was to be a courier carrying letters and orders between male leaders of the underground resistance units. Arrested and initially imprisoned by the Nazis at the Lublin Castle, which was turned into the local Gestapo headquarters, she underwent numerous interrogations and beatings lasting several months before being sentenced to death in secret and without being told of her sentence. Death sentences were also imposed on several other women for being members of the resistance movement. Instead of carrying out all the executions immediately, the Nazis send some of the women-prisoners to concentration camps, perhaps already with a plan to use them for medical experiments.

Dr. Półtawska's husband told an interviewer that since the time spent as a Nazi prisoner, his wife had been "fighting for her human dignity."[36] In her desire to help other victims of Nazi crimes, Wanda decided after the war to study medicine and to focus on juvenile psychiatry and sexual dysfunctions. According to the British translator of Dr. Półtawska's concentration camp memoirs, Wanda's motivation in studying psychiatry was to help the individual "to become a mature person who is aware of his or her humanity" that was so terribly tested during the war and the Nazi occupation of Poland.[37] As a practicing psychiatrist immediately after the war, Dr. Półtawska was able to help deeply traumatized children and young people who were born or spent their formative years in Auschwitz and in other concentration camps and were among the very few lucky ones to have survived. She also tried to prevent these young people from making wrong moral choices with regard to their sexuality and to help those, especially unwed mothers, who found themselves abandoned and ostracized by their families and society.

Wanda Półtawska's journey from a provincial town in East-

Central Poland to become a powerful advisor to the Archbishop of Kraków and later the pope led through four years of unbearable suffering and heroic resistance in the face of humiliation and a constant threat of death. The Ravensbrück camp, where 92,000 women and children perished during the war, became infamous for medical experiments on healthy women, which involved injections of bacteria into bone marrow and removal of bones and skin. Some of the victims were as young as 15 years old and many died or became invalids for life as a result of these medical procedures. Wanda was one of the lucky women who survived and were not severely crippled by the experiments, but she suffered terrible pain as her legs became swollen from infection caused by injections of bacteria. In some of the women who died, their legs became black and so swollen that they expanded to four times their natural size.[38] One of the youngest girls, Basia Pietrzyk, whose dream was to be a ballet dancer, had a large section of her leg bone removed and then the rest of her leg was injected with bacteria.[39] The most horrific were experiments on women's reproductive organs, including forced sterilizations of Gypsy women and forced abortions. British Special Operations Executive (SOE) female agents, who had been captured by the Gestapo in France, were also held at the camp toward the end of the war and four of them were executed.[40]

Wanda was lucky not to be subjected to the most extreme procedures. Also helping her to survive was her strong religious faith and national pride combined with courage and stubbornness. At the concentration camp she discovered "the suicidal courage of people who could act as they chose today because they [knew] that by tomorrow they would be dead."[41] She was also helping other women-prisoners, devoting herself to protecting Krysia, a young and innocent Polish girl whom she helped to survive life in the camp.

Wanda Półtawska's war memoirs show her to be a proud Polish woman with virtues and prejudices quite typical of many other Polish women of her generation. She described women prisoners from Russia and other Slavic nations as more courageous and nobler than for example women from some of the Western countries, particularly from liberal France. She wrote in her book about Ravensbrück how Polish, Czech and Russian women at the camp would disrobe each morning and take cold showers, while French women, fully dressed, refused to wash and instead painted their faces with beetroot juice. She admitted that after this experience, the expression "French wash" became forever part of her vocabulary.[42] She also described her stay in a block occupied by lesbian prisoners as "purgatory," only slightly less terrifying than being in a block for prisoners who were subjected to medical experiments. She pointed out that the letters, "LL," which at the camp stood for "lesbian love," acquired for her "a hideous, inhuman reality" from which she was trying to protect her young and innocent friend Krysia.[43] According to Półtawska, lesbian prisoners not only terrorized other women but also stole their possessions. Some of the victims of alleged sexual harassment and molestation, who "at first had recoiled in disgust" eventually gave up to the demands of lesbian prisoners in, what Wanda Półtawska described, as an unequal struggle.

Not all Polish women who were at the Ravensbrück concentration camp shared Wanda Półtawska attitudes and prejudices, but they were in a minority. One remarkable exception was Countess Karolina Lackorońska. An aristocratic woman and a professor of art history, who had a German mother and a Polish father, she was arrested for being

> **Karolina Lackorońska** 1898-2002
>
> **Memoirs:** *Michelangelo in Ravensbrück*
>
> **Quote:** "Honorable people who are unable to imagine *Evil* can be very dangerous."

a member of the Polish underground army and her open hostility to the Nazi occupiers. Because of her highly placed international family connections, she was not subjected to medical experiments and received privileged treatment from the Nazis, a special status which she did not seek and to which she strongly objected. When the Nazis ignored her protests to treat her like any other Polish woman, she used her special status to help other prisoners by sharing with them her food packages, working as a nurse and giving lectures in art history. She also helped obtain medical leave for those who wanted to avoid work for the German war industry.[44] Like Wanda Półtawska, Lackorońska was a devout Catholic and Polish patriot, but as Eva Hoffman, author of *Lost in Translation*, wrote in the preface to Lackorońska's recently-published war memoirs *Michelangelo in Ravensbrück*, "her love of her homeland was untainted by nationalism, if that suggests a belligerent or insular attitude." "She abhorred discriminatory provincialism, claims to racial superiority, and ethnic stereotyping that went on even in the desperate world of Ravensbrück."[45] Her religious devotion, "compatible with genuinely enlightened views and encompassing sympathies," would make her a Catholic liberal,

Female prisoners at the Ravensbrück concentration camp. The chalk mark on their back showed that they had been selected for transport by the Swedish Red Cross buses at the end of World War II. The picture is courtesy of the Swedish Red Cross. Karolina Lackorońska was one of the evacuees from the camp at the end of the war.

but she came from a much more privileged and cosmopolitan family than Wanda Półtawska. She was also more educated and older. After the war, Karolina Lackorońska chose to live in exile in Italy rather than to return to communist-ruled Poland.

Wanda Półtawska's views of ethnic differences and gender roles were more typical for many Polish Catholic women of her generation. When she returned home after the war, she could not fall asleep without suffering terrible nightmares of being imprisoned in the concentration camp. She acknowledged that sharing her problem with a family member or a close friend might have helped her, but she did not want to burden her elderly parents with her camp stories or to talk about it with her sisters. In her memoirs, she wrote that she had wished she had brothers, then perhaps she could have talked about her problem with "a strong man."[46]

This frame of mind may be completely alien to a modern woman, particularly a woman who grew up in the West, but again it was not at all unusual for a Polish woman of Wanda Półtawska's generation brought up in the tradition of idealizing strong men as protectors and defenders of women, their families and their fatherland. In describing how women typically behaved at the camp, Półtawska concluded that "a woman's capacity for fantasy is boundless" and probably without limits.[47] She admitted that when she and other Polish women first came out of the camp after the liberation, they had "a horror of women and an exaggerated idealism about men," but they quickly changed their opinion after fending off numerous rape attempts by soldiers and former male prisoners. After a few days of being free, the women "were frightened of all men, no matter who they were; soldiers, civilians, Poles or Russians."[48]

Reading Dr. Półtawska's memoirs and her other books offers an interesting insight into some of Wojtyła's own statements and opinions about differences in national character, human dignity, women, sexuality and abortion. Almost every one of Wojtyła's strongly held beliefs is reflected in Wanda Półtawska's writings: nobility of the Poles, idealism of the youth, hysterical mothers forcing young women to get abortions, naïveté of young girls, the suffering of women who miscarry, young people destroying their lives as a result of sexual promiscuity, and men seen as sexual predators. Półtawska's book *Stare rachunki* (*Old Charges*), published in Poland in 1969, has a number of short stories about women and men who were victimized during the war and carried the war scars with them after the liberation or passed them in some way onto their children.[49] Speaking in 1986 at an international conference of anti-abortion activists in Hadamar, a German town where at the psychiatric hospital the Nazi doctors had murdered ten thousand mentally ill patients, Dr. Półtawska warned against doctors who, as she put it, have once again been given "life-or-death powers over the human embryo" and who perform experiments on living embryos. She stressed that what she saw and experienced as a human guinea pig at the Ravensbrück concentration camp made her extremely concerned about how human life and human dignity are viewed and measured by the post-World War II generations.[50] Bogna Lorence-Kot, a Polish history teacher living in California, wrote in her review of Wanda Półtawska's wartime memoirs that it was "national pride, group solidarity, commitment to the welfare of another, the realization that for Christians all life is preparation for death, all these wove the psychic shield which kept Półtawska intact."[51] The reviewer concluded that much of Wanda Półtawska's mental resilience "appears to have stemmed from her identity as a Polish woman."[52]

In 2003, Dr. Półtawska said in a lecture that women cannot be easily understood but should be accepted as they are. She pointed out that there have been many women throughout history who like Eve had allowed themselves to be seduced by Satan, as well as those who model their behavior after the Virgin Mary. To Dr. Półtawska, Eve and Mary represent the two extremes of female personality: foolishness and disobedience on one side and absolute confidence in God and obedience on the other side. Motherhood is something that both types of women have in common. Mary, according to Dr. Półtawska, accepts motherhood as the essence of obedience toward God and the essence of her life as a woman. Those women, who for some reasons cannot be mothers, express their motherhood by caring for other people. Dr. Półtawska also observed that instead of being independent, women want to be admired by men and are afraid of being alone. Many men abuse this need by seeing women as objects of desire instead of approaching them with selfless love. Women, according to Dr. Półtawska, are capable of much greater love and have nothing to gain from bringing themselves down to the level of men and trying to be like men. She said that "feminists demanding the right to kill their own children are creatures without beauty and loving instincts similar to witches in tales for children." She described feminists as "full of aggression, allegedly discriminated against." She added that there is nothing more important for women than motherhood, but observed that legalized murder of the unborn around the world shows that contemporary women are rejecting this great "gift." She commented that since God created women as protectors of life, abortion is the greatest charge leveled against them. Dr. Półtawska also said that at the other extreme, women who seek artificial fertilization are also committing an act of disobedience against God. She is, however, not entirely without hope. Dr. Półtawska believes that "new feminists," who defend human life, work to help the poor and want to change the world for the better, offer hope for bringing more dignity to men and women and for bringing humanity closer to God.[53]

Saint Maximilian Kolbe

Karol Wojtyła was one of the strongest supporters of the beatification and canonization of Father Maksymilian Kolbe, a Franciscan who offered his life in Auschwitz to save another Polish-Catholic prisoner from execution. There may have been many reasons why Wojtyła wanted Father Kolbe to become a Catholic saint and called him "a patron of our difficult century." Kolbe's death showed that Polish priests and nuns also died at the hands of the Nazis in defense of their religion and country and shared in the suffering of their fellow-Poles as well as Jews. People in Poland have always felt that they suffered during the war almost as much as anybody else and that their suffering and their contribution to the victory over the Nazis were not being recognized, particularly in the West. Father Kolbe's death also offered a heroic example of an extreme

Maksymilian Maria (Rajmund) Kolbe –
Saint Maximilian Kolbe

Born: January 8, 1894, Zduńska Wola,
Poland

Died: August 14, 1941, Auschwitz-
Birkenau, Nazi-occupied Poland

Canonized by Pope John Paul II: October
10, 1982 — The patron saint of drug
addicts, political prisoners, families,
journalists, prisoners, and the pro-life
movement.

http://www.kolbe.pl/english/index.php

sacrifice by a Catholic for another human being.

But another important fact for Wojtyła, which he also noted a number of times, was that Father Kolbe volunteered to take the prisoner's place after the prisoner Franciszek Gajowniczek pleaded to spare his life because he had a wife and a large number of children. While this may have not been the primary reason for Wojtyła's support of sainthood in this case, the fact that the pope was always a strong advocate for the family probably played a major role. Unbelievably, the Nazi guards at Auschwitz accepted Father Kolbe's offer and allowed the married prisoner to live. The Franciscan was killed by an injection of poison into his heart after spending two weeks in extreme suffering without food or water in

Entrance to the Auschwitz concentration camp.
The German sign above the gate says: "Work Will
Make You Free."

a tiny cell where he comforted nine other prisoners who were also condemned to die.

Dr. Wanda Półtawska, who had influenced some of Wojtyła's other controversial decisions, may have also played a role in convincing him that the manner of Father Kolbe's death and his sacrifice deserved recognition and sainthood. We know that many examples given by Wojtyła to justify his opposition to abortion and contraception came from Dr. Półtawska's medical practice. Some of these examples were related to her own experiences during the war and to her psychiatric practice with victims of concentration camps. In one of her books, she described her own experience that was very similar to what happened between Father Kolbe and the Polish prisoner whose life was saved. While she was being held at the Ravensbrück concentration camp, another prisoner tried to help her survive by willingly risking her own life. The offer was made toward the end of the war after the accounts of medical experiments on women-prisoners and the names of the victims had been secretly smuggled out of the camp and broadcast by BBC from London. This precipitated a frantic search by the Nazis trying to find those identified in the radio programs and destroy the evidence. Wanda Półtawska found herself facing an increased threat of death. At that point, a rebellion among the women— probably the only successful rebellion in a Nazi concentration camp—made the search difficult as fellow-prisoners tried to hide the women who were being sought.

As the Nazis got closer, an older Polish woman, in an effort to protect Wanda, offered to assume her camp number and identity. The woman, whom Dr. Półtawska identified in her memoirs only as Władka, argued with Wanda that while she was already near the end of her life, Wanda was still young. She also insisted that Wanda's survival was more important as a witness and a direct victim of the Nazi medical crimes, and she even lied to Wanda that she was suffering from a terminal cancer. After Wanda refused to make the exchange of camp numbers—the system used by the

Nazis to identify prisoners—Władka later assumed the identity of one of Wanda's friends, also in an attempt to help another woman's chance of survival.[54]

Considering the close relationship between Dr. Półtawska and Wojtyła, it is almost certain that the two discussed this story at length as well as religious and moral implications of such heroic behavior. Both obviously felt that such an extreme sacrifice by a Pole for another human being deserved to be recognized and offered as an example to others. It is quite possible that Wanda Półtawska's story may have strengthened Wojtyła's resolve to pursue Father Kolbe's controversial canonization.

John Paul II made Father Kolbe a saint despite the evidence that before World War II his order published anti-Semitic propaganda and that he himself was responsible for some of the anti-Semitic and numerous anti-Masonic writings. Anti-Semitic propaganda was widely distributed by his order in Poland before the outbreak of the war in various Church publications including a daily paper *Mały Dziennik* (*The Little Daily*). Polish-Jewish historian Lucjan Dobroszycki described the paper edited by the Franciscan monks under Kolbe as one of the popular anti-Semitic publications in Poland during the 1930s.[55]

The current defense of Father Kolbe by Wojtyła's friends centers on the fact that during the 1930s Kolbe spent several years as a missionary in Japan and was not directly responsible for the publications put out by his order. Some of his own writings, however, certainly expose him as being at least a passive, if not active endorser of anti-Semitic sentiments. In one of his open letters addressed to Masons and Jews, Father Kolbe accused the Masons of being manipulated by a "cruel Jewish clique" and blamed a "small group of Jews" of causing suffering at the service of the devil. He also called on Jews to convert to Christianity.[56] While such sentiments were common within the Polish Church at that time, including probably the vast majority of lay Catholic Poles, they were not by any means universal. There were many ethnic Poles, both Catholics and non-believers, who actively opposed anti-Semitism. They in turn became targets of attacks in Father Kolbe's publications.

Father Kolbe was not a simple monk whose anti-Semitism could be blamed on the lack of education. He had earned two doctorates in Rome where he studied from 1912 until 1919 after being sent there by his superiors because of his outstanding intellect. But he was not prepared for the life in the West and the freedom with which the pope and religion itself could be attacked and even ridiculed. He was greatly affected by anti-papal demonstrations and particularly distressed by the lack of respect for the Virgin Mary. I again heard "a terrible blasphemy against the Blessed Virgin," he wrote in his diary.

Not unlike Wojtyła's revulsion when he first saw pornography in the West, Kolbe was also appalled by the anti-clericalism of the Italians and even called them "a nation of blasphemers."[57] It was in Rome where he developed a life-long hostility toward the Masons and made a vow to devote his life to opposing their influence and trying to win them back to Catholicism. In 1917, under his leadership, seven seminarians studying in Rome formed The Militia of the Immaculate, an organization devoted primarily to converting the Masons under the care and intercession of the Virgin Mary. Such a mission statement may now appear odd, but the movement's founders were convinced of a deadly serious threat to religion and the Catholic Church. After finishing his studies abroad, Father Kolbe brought the organization with him from Rome to Poland, where—not unlike the focus of Wojtyła's pastoral care—he also concentrated his activities on working with the Polish youth, which he considered to be particularly vulnerable to being corrupted by liberal Masons. Jews were also added to the mix. To counter what he saw as their dark force influence in the cinema, theatre, literature and art, he launched the publication of *The Little Knight of the Immaculate* which targeted the very young readers.[58]

Father Kolbe order's activities before World War II were not only directed against Jews and Masons, but also against any liberal member of the Polish intelligentsia. The Polish Nobel Prize winner in literature Czesław Miłosz attributed his forced departure from a position at the Polish public radio station in Vilnius to attacks on him in newspapers run by Father Kolbe. In the period between the wars, Vilnius with its mixed population of Poles, Lithuanians, Jews and other minorities belonged to Poland. Father Kolbe's newspapers reported that Miłosz and others were allowing Jews to take part in radio discussions on religion and demanded that this practice be stopped.[59] Miłosz, who was born a Catholic in a region which is now part of Lithuania, was far too liberal for nationalist Catholics of Father Kolbe's persuasion who would naturally suspected him of being a Mason, a Jew or a communist sympathizer. After the war, Czesław Miłosz did work briefly for the communist regime as a Polish cultural attaché in Paris and Washington, D.C. before defecting to the West and making a public break with Marxism in *The Captive Mind,* his now classic book on the dangers of communist totalitarianism. The book became famous as possibly the best expose of how Left-wing intellectuals deceived themselves and others by choosing to support the so-called progressive ideas of communism despite evidence of its murderous ideology.

Because of Father Kolbe's publication activities, Cardinal Wojtyła called him in 1972 "the apostle and the pioneer of modern mass media." [60] (After his canonization Father Kolbe became known as the patron saint of journalists.)

Militia of the Immaculata

http://www.consecration.com/index.html

It is difficult to say whether at the time Wojtyła was completely aware of the strong anti-Semitic messages in Father Kolbe's publications, but he must have had at least some idea even if he did not know the full story. Before the war, Father Kolbe's magazine, *The Knight of the Immaculate* had hundreds of thousands of readers. The military reference in the title suggests a desire of waging a verbal war for the minds and hearts of the Polish people. Father Kolbe's order also published more than 250,000 copies of *The Little Knight of the Immaculate* written specifically for children, in addition to more than 130,000 daily and 250,000 Sunday copies of *The Little Daily*. These publications may have been read in Wojtyła's home and were widely distributed in churches. Father Kolbe also established a radio station and was thinking about using television.[61] His anti-Semitic messages were not unlike those heard in the radio broadcasts of the American Catholic priest, Reverend Charles E. Coughlin (1891-1979), who in the late 1930s and the early 1940s blamed Jews for exploiting American workers, supporting communism and various other crimes. In the early 1940s, Father Coughlin, sometimes described as "the father of hate radio," was finally silenced by his bishop when his broadcasts became even more virulently anti-Semitic and the Roosevelt Administration accused him of being sympathetic to Nazi Germany.

Wojtyła seemed to have been impressed by Father Kolbe's ability to use the media for spreading the Gospel and may have modeled his own media activities after the Franciscan communicator. There is no paranoia in Wojtyła's statements and obviously no attacks on Masons and Jews, but the militant tone of his criticism of liberalism, capitalism, consumerism, globalization, radical feminism, abortion and the West, is not significantly different from the tone of Father Kolbe's anti-Masonic and anti-Jewish warnings. There is a history of militancy of Church-led public discourse in Poland that is quite different from the general tone of public discourse in more recent decades in the West. Father Kolbe claimed that his use of such words as "Knight," "Militia" and "struggle" were not incidental, because they meant a war of ideas and a war to remove the perceived enemies of the Church from positions of power and influence. Father Kolbe maintained that it was not war with guns but a true struggle, in which the primary weapons were not guns but prayer. Nevertheless, some Jews and others who disagreed with him were removed from their jobs or prevented from studying at universities.

Apologists for Saint Maksymilian Kolbe claim that despite using strong language, he did not demonize his opponents. John Paul II was conducting a similar war of ideas with liberalism and the West but on a much more sophisticated level. Nevertheless, his tone of criticism of the West may also be seen as militant. The question remains whether the enemy was really so dangerous that such a tone was needed and whether a more moderate tone and dialogue would not be more beneficial. The verdict of history so far seems to be that Father Kolbe's militancy did not achieve much except for turning a large portion of the Polish Catholic population against Jews and leaving them even more defenseless in the face of Nazi atrocities.

Wojtyła's concern for Jewish sensitivities, which could have stopped him from declaring Father Kolbe as the patron of mass media, did not develop until much later when he was already at the Vatican. The same could be said about his sensitivity about issues of concern to Western women. It both cases, it took a long period of contacts with people of different backgrounds outside of Poland before we see a change in Wojtyła's language and before he even starts mentioning certain controversial and sensitive subjects.

Speaking in 1965 on the 20th anniversary of the liberation of Auschwitz by the Soviet Army, Wojtyła did not mention Jews by name as the main victims of extermination at the camp. He talked mostly about 400,000 Poles who went through at Auschwitz, of whom only about 60,000 survived, and pointed out that some of them were Catholic priests and professors from his *Alma Mater*, the Jagiellonian University in Kraków. After focusing on the suffering of ethnic Poles, only in a brief sentence he noted that "in addition, about 4 million people went directly from trains to their deaths in gas chambers and crematoria."[62] He did not identify them as Jews.

Wojtyła also did not say anything about the millions of Jews killed at Auschwitz and at the nearby Birkenau camp when he spoke there again in August 1972 before the first anniversary of Father Kolbe's beatification. At that time he invited all those who had survived the Nazi concentration camps to participate in the religious observances in memory of Father Kolbe, which were to take place at Auschwitz two months later.[63] He probably still had no idea that Jews might find such an invitation offensive.

Wojtyła and other Polish bishops were also largely silent during the communist party crackdown in 1968 directed against its Jewish members and other Jews, most of whom were eventually forced by the communist authorities and the climate of public hostility to leave Poland. There was speculation that Wojtyła and other bishops may have considered the events of 1968 as an internal communist party affair and were uncertain what was happening. Despite pleas from some of his friends at *Tygodnik Powszechny*, Cardinal Wojtyła made no immediate public statement after a small group of students, who were protesting the anti-Semitic campaign, were beaten up in Kraków not too far from his

Jewish civilians led by German soldiers to a certain death. A German photograph taken during the destruction of the Warsaw Ghetto, Poland, 1943.

residence.

But after he had time to reflect upon these events, they may have become for him a major turning point in his public attitude toward the issue of anti-Semitism in Poland. Nearly a year after the Polish communists started the anti-Jewish campaign, he visited the Kraków synagogue—a move apparently designed to compensate for his earlier silence. It was a visit that at the time did not attract much publicity, certainly not from the communist media. Public defense of Jews and Left-wing intellectuals would not have been a very popular cause for a Catholic archbishop in Poland, but Wojtyła made a strong statement by his visit to the synagogue.[64]

Prior to this point, Wojtyła apparently felt no need to deal with this issue head on in addressing Polish Catholics. When speaking about the war while he was still the Archbishop of Kraków, most of his comments were focused on Father Kolbe and the suffering of ethnic Poles including Catholic priests. It was only after Wojtyła was elected to the papacy that he publicly started to mention Jews as the primary victims of the Nazi extermination campaign. The real turning point came in 1979, when returning to Auschwitz for the first time as pope, John Paul II publicly referred to Jews as "the nation, whose sons and daughters were destined for complete extermination."[65]

But even in that speech, he again offended some Jews by comparing Father Kolbe with Sister Edith Stein, a Carmelite nun who had converted to Catholicism from Judaism and was also killed in Auschwitz. It was still a slow beginning for Wojtyła. He made no public mention of his Jewish neighbors and colleagues when during the same trip in 1979 he visited his hometown Wadowice and reminisced about his youth. Only during his second return trip to Wadowice, which took place in August 1991, did John Paul II refer to his Jewish colleagues from his high school who—as he put it—"are now no longer with us," and he noted that the Jewish synagogue in Wadowice located near the school building also no longer exists. He then quoted from a letter he had written to his Jewish friend, which he had asked him to read at an earlier unveiling of a special plaque commemorating the place where the Wadowice synagogue once stood.

In this letter, John Paul II stated that the Catholic Church stands united with the Jewish people because of their suffering. He also pointed out that the suffering and extermination of Jews should be a warning to "individuals, nations, and humanity," which he himself wants to express. He also said that as a pope from Poland, he has a special outlook on this issue because "together with you [he] has in some way lived through all of this here, in [his] fatherland."[66] Some Jews may have again been offended by this comparison of his experience during World War II as an ethnic Pole with the experience of Jews who were exterminated. His intention was probably to point out that as someone who had been an indirect observer of the Holocaust (he grew up near Auschwitz), he has a special right to warn against the dangers to human dignity and human life.

During the German occupation, Wojtyła had to be aware of the plight of Polish Jews, but he never elaborated on the extent of his knowledge of the Holocaust at that time. There were accounts suggesting that he may have been at least marginally involved in efforts to save a small number of Jews from extermination by the Nazis, but this has not been documented or confirmed by John Paul II. Some Polish Jews, in a desperate effort to change their identity and obtain false documents, chose to convert to Christianity. One of Wojtyła's friends, Feliks Zachuta, who studied with him to be a priest, was executed by the Germans in 1944 for preparing Jews for baptism.[67] But John Paul II never suggested that he had been involved in any direct efforts to help Jews during the war. According to Marek Halter, a Polish Jew who asked Wojtyła whether he had done something for the Jews during the war, his response was "I don't believe I – no. No."[68]

During his historic visit to Israel in March 2000, John Paul II did meet a Jewish woman, Edith Zirer, who attributes her survival in the last months of the war to the help she received from him when he was a young seminarian studying to be a priest. Even though the Soviet Army liberated the camp in Skarzysko-Kamienna, where the 13 year old Jewish girl was imprisoned for three years, she was so weakened by tuberculosis that she was unable to walk. She told journalists that it was Karol Wojtyła who found her, gave her a sandwich and a cup of tea and then carried her in the snow on his shoulders for almost two miles from the concentration camp to the railway station, where she joined the other survivors. She was the only member of her family to survive the Nazi massacre. In 1951 she immigrated to Israel where she married and had two children.[69] But there have been no accounts of Wojtyła actually helping to hide Jews during the Nazi occupation, nor did he claim that he had risked his life to provide such help. This fact combined with the history of anti-Semitism within his own Church in Poland may have caused him tremendous pain and guilt—something that could explain his later determination to bring about a lasting reconciliation between Catholicism and Judaism.

According to various reports, during the Second Vatican Council Wojtyła was one of the bishops working on the *Nostra Ateate* (*In Our Time*) Declaration on relations with non-Christian religions, which condemned anti-Semitism and affirmed that Jews are not to be blamed for Christ's death. *Nostra Ateate*, signed in 1965 by Pope Paul VI and the bishops participating in the Second Vatican Council, did not address, however, the question of the Church's blame for promoting anti-Semitism. It took thirty years from the publication of *Nostra Ateate* before the Catholic bishops of the Netherlands issued a statement saying that the Catholic Church shares part of the responsibility for the murder of Jews during World War II. Similar statements were issued earlier by the Polish and German bishops. The French bishops apologized to the Jews in 1997. Such statements would not have been possible without John Paul II's moral leadership.

But as his papacy unfolded, John Paul II directed his campaign in defense of human dignity not against extreme nationalism and xenophobia—although he had on many occasion condemned both—but primarily against abortion, euthanasia and sexual revolution. These were not issues that drove the Nazis to murder Jews. Also, the main focus of his constant criticism have not been nations where extreme nationalism is rampant but mainly Western nations, where he saw a great danger to human life from what he described as "the culture of death" and "consumerism." Examination of Wojtyła's sermons and statements shows that it took decades before he started to speak publicly at length about the Holocaust, and even then he made some decisions and comments that many Jews found offensive. His actions were certainly not intended to offend, but they prove that it was very difficult for Wojtyła to overcome some of the cultural barriers to understanding how Jews feel about Christianity and the behavior of some Catholic Poles during the war.

Father Kolbe was by far one of the most controversial figures in Polish-Jewish relations, yet it was obvious that Wojtyła was determined to bring him to sainthood despite any damage that such a move would cause to developing a better understanding between the Catholic Church and Jews. Proud of being a Pole and proud of how the vast majority of Poles behaved during the Nazi occupation, the pope was not going to accept the argument that by directly or indirectly promoting hostility toward Jews, Father Kolbe could be held responsible for creating an atmosphere of indifference among some Catholic families in Poland during the war to the suffering of Jews. Many Jews, who could have otherwise counted on receiving help from their Polish neighbors, may have gone to their deaths as the result of Father Kolbe's publishing activities before the war.

While the majority of Catholics in Poland and in other countries may have believed in the anti-Semitic Church propaganda before the war, some Catholic and non-Catholic Poles including Wojtyła himself were definitely not anti-Semitic even by the cultural standards of pre-World War II Poland. As a Polish patriot and someone who had no negative feelings about any nation or race, except perhaps the consumerist West, John Paul II may have found it difficult to understand why Jews perceive Father Kolbe as a particularly dangerous anti-Semite and viewed his ability to influence so many Catholics through his pre-World War II publications.

Before and after the canonization, the Vatican officials were making every possible attempt to prove that Father Kolbe was not anti-Semitic. American author Darcy O'Brien, who wrote a book about Wojtyła's life-long friendship with Jerzy Kluger who was his Jewish neighbor in Wadowice, repeats the Vatican's claim that a careful examination of Father Kolbe's own writings showed that he personally was not an anti-Semite.[70] This claim, however, has been repeatedly challenged by various scholars. In a 1999 PBS *Frontline* program on John Paul II, a Polish-Jewish journalist Konstanty Gebert described Father Kolbe's pre-World War II publication *The Knight of the Immaculate* as "an anti-Semitic rag that spilled hatred and venom, poisoned the minds and hearts of thousands upon thousands of Catholics who believed in his teaching of hatred, [and] teaching of contempt, because it came from the institutional Church, indeed from the Franciscan monks, the very example of love."[71]

Cardinal Edward Cassidy, while not defending Father Kolbe's magazine, pointed out in the same program that Kolbe was probably writing what most Catholics were feeling at that time. He can still be a saint due to his sacrifice and martyrdom at the end of his life even though he may have committed great sins. Other Catholic saints had also been guilty of great sins. Before his conversion to Christianity, St Paul, himself a Jew, persecuted Christians, but Father Kolbe engaged in his anti-Semitic propaganda as a Christian and a Franciscan. Konstanty Gebert conceded that Father Kolbe may have changed his mind in Auschwitz when he saw the logical consequences of his anti-Semitism, but for Gebert this does not change the fact that many Jews in Poland were denied help in hiding from the Nazis because some Catholic Poles believed what they had read in *The Knight of the Immaculate*. By bringing him to sainthood, John Paul II chose to ignore such concerns and deeply offended a great number of Jews.

Father Kolbe was not the only person in Poland who had sacrificed his life for fellow prisoners during the Nazi occupation. Janusz Korczak, a Jewish writer of children's books, physician and teacher, made a decision to go to the gas chambers of the Treblinka death camp to share the fate of about 200 of his young students from a Jewish orphanage, even though he had a reasonable chance of escaping. He made his decision wanting to ease the terror of the children's last journey by being with them to the very end. Such a sacrifice, however, could not qualify Janusz Korczak for Catholic sainthood because he was Jewish and only Catholics or those who convert to Catholicism can be declared saints. But John Paul II mentioned Janusz Korczak, which was the literary pseudonym of Dr. Henryk Goldszmit (1878-1942), in one of his speeches later in his pontificate and one of pope's close friends, Father Maliński, called the Jewish doctor a saint.

There is also some evidence that an ethnic Pole Marian Batka, a physics teacher in Silesia, made a similar sacrifice as Father Kolbe, but his case has not received much attention from the Catholic Church because it was not clear whether he was a religious man.[72] The prisoner whose life Father Kolbe had saved was an ethnic Pole, but Polish Catholics also sacrificed their lives to save Jews. The official commission for the investigation of war crimes in Poland documented the cases of 704 ethnic Poles, the vast majority of them Catholics and some as young as seven months old, who were murdered by the Nazis for sheltering Jews.[73] The Nazies often killed entire families if the adults were hiding Jews.

Many other Catholic Poles, whose cases have not been fully documented, were also killed for helping Jews, but the Polish Church and John Paul II decided to honor a Catholic monk who, despite his heroic sacrifice and horrific death, may have realized the harm of his anti-Semitic views only after he had been sent to a concentration camp. Had the Polish Church and John Paul II admitted openly that this was the case and proceeded with the canonization offering it as an example of how Christians can overcome their mistakes, such a move could have been accepted by at least some Jews as an attempt at reconciliation. Instead, the Vatican has tried hard to minimize Father Kolbe's anti-Semitic record and to divert attention away from this issue.

This kind of reaction is, however, not unusual when the Vatican is faced with a controversy. A similar attitude has been seen in the Vatican's handling of controversies dealing with priests who sexually abused children and with the response to misogynistic statements by various historical Church figures. Just as John Paul II frustrated many women with his ambivalent statements and actions, he also frustrated many Jews. He met Austrian President, Kurt Waldheim (1918-2007) at an audience at the Vatican after Waldheim had been accused of involvement in war crimes. On the other hand, John Paul II made it very clear on a number of occasions in much stronger terms than any other pope that anti-Semitism is a sin. A Catholic priest told Konstanty Gebert that since the pope had made his statement on anti-Semitism, people going to confession were expressing guilt for making anti-Semitic comments. For Konstanty Gebert, a Polish Jew, this is a major achievement of John Paul's papacy. Father Kolbe is now the patron saint of families, journalists, and the pro-life movement.

WW II Genetic Killings — Key to Understanding Wojtyła's Pro-Life Stands

Because of his experiences in Poland during the war and his acquaintance with women imprisoned in the Nazi camps, sterilization and euthanasia were particularly disturbing to John Paul II. Wojtyła also had first-hand knowledge of the fatal medical experiments performed by the Nazis and the killing of physically and mentally handicapped persons. The Nazi sterilization law, imposed in 1933 with the purpose of "uplifting the race" and eradicating "inferior hereditary traits," applied to all German citizens, not just Jews, Gypsies, and others considered by the Nazis to be inferior. Its first victims were German citizens, many of them ethnic Germans, who were sterilized for signs of feeble-mindedness, schizophrenia, epilepsy and manic-depressive disorder. Of about 400,000 sterilizations, half were done on women, but women represented about 90% of those who died as a result of these procedures.[74] When some of the women who were selected for sterilization became pregnant, the Nazis introduced an abortion law in 1935, which allowed abortions for the same eugenic reasons as sterilization. This measure was followed by Hitler's order, signed in September 1939, calling for "mercy killings" of certain categories of psychiatric, handicapped and chronically ill patients considered unsuited to live. German doctors again participated in the selection of victims and administered the killing procedures, which included starvation, lethal injections, and finally the use of poison gas. Some of the same doctors would later become involved in the Holocaust murder of Jews and in other mass murders of non-ethnic Germans.[75]

After almost two years, the so-called euthanasia program was officially ended in Germany in 1941, most likely as a result of opposition from Christian Churches and German families, but some killings of unfit individuals continued secretly. There were no restrictions on killings of Jews and other "inferior races." As far as abortion and contraception for healthy German women were concerned, Hitler was unequivocally opposed to such procedures and to birth control. He believed the use of contraceptives to be "a violation of nature, a degradation of womanhood, motherhood, and love." When used by healthy and racially pure Germans, the Nazis considered contraception to be tantamount to "racial treason." They used the same expression to condemn sexual relations between ethnic Germans and Jews, Poles or people of "colored races." Education about pregnancy prevention was punishable by imprisonment. After 1943, the death penalty could be imposed for providing abortions to German women.[76]

The Catholic Church in Germany, which except for a few courageous priests did not officially protest the persecution of Jews, was nevertheless vocal in opposing sterilization, abortion and mercy killings when these were used against ethnic Germans. The Bishop of Münster Clemens August Graf von Galen openly called on Christians to oppose the taking on human life even if it meant their own death.[77] Before the pressure of public opinion in Germany forced the Nazis to discontinue the "mercy killings" of ethnic Germans, from 1939 to 1941 up to 100,000 patients in psychiatric institutions in Germany lost their lives. But even after the "euthanasia" project was officially ended, many more of the so-called "useless eaters" were killed through ordinary starvation, including about 5,000 children.[78] Also, from 1942 onward, over twenty thousand inmates in German prisons were transferred to the police for "annihilation through labor." Classified as "asocial," most of them ended up in concentration and labor camps, where at least two-thirds were killed or died from physical torture and malnutrition.[79]

Considering the Nazi killings of "asocial" individuals, criminals and prostitutes, and limited forced sterilization of mentally ill patients in the United States before World War II, John Paul II would have been particularly concerned by the results of a study showing that legalizing abortion in the U.S. in the early 1970s led to the reduction of crime in later decades. For John Paul II, this news would represent yet another proof that even a democratically elected government might be tempted to use abortion for the purposes of social engineering. Tens of millions of abortions in the United States since their legalization also have had an impact on the future of the social security system in the United States, which currently does not have enough workers to support future retirees. The same problem is also being observed in Poland and in Western

Europe. Few argue, however, that supporters of legalized abortions want them primarily for reasons of social-engineering. If anything, the same people who support abortion rights in the U.S. are also in favor of government programs to help the poor and approve of amnesty for illegal immigrants, while evangelical Christians and other religious conservatives generally oppose such programs. In Poland, however, conservative Catholics who oppose abortion are strongly in favor of government-mandated social spending.

Still, before the practice of forced sterilization and abortion for socially undesirable individuals was discovered and definitely outlawed, the United States had its own shameful incidents of medical experimentation on patients considered by some doctors as racially and socially inferior. From 1932 until 1972, 412 men, all uneducated African Americans, participated in a medical study of syphilis without knowing the nature of the experiment or being told that a cure for their illness was available. Twenty-eight men who participated in the Tuskegee Syphilis Experiment died from effects of the illness. Of the hundreds of medical personnel who supervised the study, including an African American nurse who received a government award for her work, only one individual questioned the ethics of the experiment. The fact that such abuses were eventually discovered and condemned in democratic countries is, however, one of the advantages of democracy and free media. In 1997, President Clinton apologized to the survivors of the syphilis experiment.[80]

The Nazi genetic experiments received a lot of attention in Poland after the war. While the communist propaganda did not specifically emphasize the Nazi extermination of six million Jews, including women and children, communist media widely publicized Nazi crimes in general, particularly those directed against Polish women and children. The charges were true, but they were also useful in helping the communists to bolster their propaganda attacks against American support for West Germany and that country's membership in NATO. Widely reported was the plight of about 30,000 Polish children from the Zamość area in east-central Poland who, together with their parents, were forced out of their homes to make room for German settlers. Some of the children who had blue eyes and possessed the right racial features were separated from their parents and sent to Germany to be brought up as Germans. While the trains carrying the children were moving through Poland, Polish women waited for hours at railroad stations hoping to help them or to take them home, and some were in fact ransomed from their German guards. Some of the children who did not pass the racial test were sent to Auschwitz, where they were killed with injections of phenol into the heart.[81]

After the war, Wojtyła and other members of the Polish Church hierarchy concluded that legal changes in the West giving individuals the power to prevent or terminate life, either through contraception or abortion, were an equally powerful sign that the West was also turning away from God and that the Western civilization was in deep crisis. Even Israel, which according to John Paul II's line of reasoning should be particularly concerned about protecting the value of human life, allowed abortion in cases of rape, incest, fetal impairment, and when necessary to save the woman's life and her physical health. Although more restrictive than abortion laws in Western Europe and in the United States, the laws regulating abortions in Israel are much more liberal than in Muslim countries. In addition to the Middle East, the most restrictive abortion laws are found in Africa and Latin America, where societies are highly patriarchal, predominantly Catholic (in Latin America) or both. Under Israeli law, women can obtain abortions if they are unmarried, under marriage age, older than 40, and for reasons of mental health.[82] The inclusion of the last category means that abortion is widely available in Israel despite opposition from conservative religious Jews. Most Jewish religious scholars agree, however, that Judaism, while putting various restrictions and penalties on abortion under most circumstances, ultimately does not regard it as murder. Probably because of this religious tradition going back thousands of years, most Israelis have not significantly changed their view of abortion as a result of World War II atrocities, which seemed to have had such a great impact on Wojtyła's thinking on this issue.

Together with some but not all Poles of his generation, John Paul II became convinced that the mentality which accepts abortion, euthanasia and contraception may eventually sanction genocide. Dr. Półtawska encouraged him to accept this view. For someone who suffered through Nazi medical experiments, it is not implausible to conclude that sterilization and other forms of contraception can undermine respect for life and possibly lead to much greater abuses. It is also understandable that Dr. Półtawska would fear such abuses could happen again. Whether this was a reasonable fear as far as her assessment of Western democracies was concerned is a different question, which perhaps cannot be answered immediately. To feminists and most Western liberals, drawing analogies between the Nazi genocide and the support for legalized abortion in the West seems rather far-fetched, especially if compared with many other problems in less developed countries in the Middle East, Eastern Europe and elsewhere.

World War II shaped Karol Wojtyła's view of the West, but post-World War II social changes in Western Europe and America also greatly influenced his thinking. The introduction of the contraceptive pill and the sexual revolution did not help to change his negative view of the secular West. The image of the West in the pope's eyes as the civilization opposed to life was made worse by the legalization of abortion in most Western countries in the 1960s and the 1970s. More recent attempts to legalize and use euthanasia in some Western countries probably confirmed his worst fears. John Paul II became deeply concerned that legalizing euthanasia may lead to the acceptance of the view that people who are a burden to their families and draw on the resources of society should be encouraged to terminate their lives. Based on what he saw and experienced, he may have feared that such elderly people may be even at risk of being put to death against their will. He believed that this risk would increase with the aging of the world's population in the 21st century. As part of an effort to prevent legal acceptance of euthanasia, he actively supported scientific research of issues relating to aging.[83]

Because of these deep concerns, both Wojtyła and Dr. Półtawska saw and promoted the concept of the dignity of a woman and man expressed in sexual intercourse which is always open to life. They both believed that parents who use contraception adopt an anti-child attitude. The alleged link between contraception and forced sterilizations performed by Nazi doctors is crucial to the under-standing of Wojtyła's pro-life positions. In his view, anything that even hints at being against life can ultimately lead to forced steril-ization, euthanasia and even genocide. It was the opinion of a person who saw the cruelest side of mankind and did not have much faith in liberalism and democracy when it comes to protecting the lives of unborn children or, for that matter, any life at all except the lives of the rich and the powerful in the West. He included pro-choice Western feminists in that group.

Unlike John Paul II and Dr. Półtawska, few Westerners are willing to acknowledge that there is any direct link between contra-ception and genocide. For them, blaming democracy and liberalism for allowing abortion may be similar to blaming Christianity for not preventing the Nazis from committing their crimes. Wojtyła had taken a consistent line that the Nazi genocide, including the murder of millions of Jews, was the work of non-believers and neo-pagans. Yet, it could be argued that prior to 1945, the Germans were much more Christian, nationalistic and conservative than atheistic, liberal and democratic. Most Germans and most Nazis strongly opposed abortion. According to a survey conducted in 1939, ninety-five percent of Germans indicated that they belonged to a Christian Church, and forty-three percent declared themselves Catholic. This, together with the presence of hundreds of Christian chaplains who ministered to German soldiers in the occupied territories, did not stop the mass murder of innocent civilians.[84] Conceivably, it could have been stopped had there been a well-established liberal democracy in Germany with effective constitutional protections against dictatorship and excessive nationalism. John Paul II would sometimes point out that democracy during the Weimar Republic (1919-1933) did not prevent Hitler from gaining power. Others have argued, however, that in the 1930s Germany did not have a true liberal democracy and, unlike Great Britain and the United States, did not have a long tradition of democratic rule. The most powerful traditions in Germany at that time were Romanticism, nationalism and radicalism of all types, including communism.

Abortions in Nazi Concentration Camps

It should come as no surprise to anyone familiar with World War II atrocities that the powerful influence of Poland's tragic history is always in the background when John Paul II talks about the need to protect the rights of the unborn and in defining his vision of motherhood and the role of women. He knew from first-hand accounts that pregnant women, the vast majority of them Jewish, were sent to the gas chambers immediately upon arrival at the Nazi death camps. He also knew that at the Auschwitz-Birkenau concentration and extermination camps, the Nazis ordered prisoner staff to kill newly born children of those women-prisoners who survived the initial selection. One of those who tried to save women's lives by performing abortions was Dr. Gisella Perl, a Hungarian-Jewish doctor sent to Auschwitz in 1944.[85] She described these abortions as the cruelest choice that many women and health care workers among prisoners had to make. Many infants born at the camp were drowned in buckets of cold water by midwives or doctors who helped the mothers with delivery. Their bodies were then put into the piles of other corpses sent to the crematorium. If the Nazi guards discovered a live baby, it would mean a certain death not only for the infant but also for the mother, as well as for any other person who may have helped conceal the pregnancy.

Despite such tremendous risks, some inmate doctors and midwives refused on religious grounds to perform abortions on women-prisoners or to actively assist in killing newly born babies. If a baby survived delivery, these doctors and midwives made every attempt to hide and protect it for as long as possible, although their efforts were mostly unsuccessful. These are the people whom John Paul II wanted to present to the world as models of noble behavior. Many feminists see themselves as engaged in protecting women's basic rights, but John Paul II would never consider a defense of woman's right to control her body through the legalization of abortion a noble act.

Countess Karolina Lackorońska was one of the persons responsible for informing the outside world about the Nazi practice of forced abortions and murdering infants in concentration camps. Because of her privileged prisoner status and contacts with the Polish underground, she was able to sent letters with coded messages from the Ravensbrück concentration camp. She learned the details of the Nazi crimes from a German nurse whom she had befriended for the purpose or gathering information. The nurse, who would smother infants and throw them into the main central-heating boiler, told Lackorońska that since under Nazi law no child could be born in a concentration camp, "the child had to be deprived of life before or directly after normal birth." The conversation took place in 1943, about the time when the Germans had experienced their first major military losses. In the winter of 1944 regulations with respect to pregnant prisoners were changed. Women were no longer required to undergo forced abortions, usually in the seventh or eighth month, or to see their newborn children strangled to death. The nurse was relieved that "the unpleasant job of disposing of the bodies was no longer necessary."[86] But most of the newborns died anyway since the Nazis sent the mothers to work without allowing them breaks to

> **The Doctors Trial**
>
> http://www.ushmm.org/research/doctors/index.html
>
> "At the end of February 1943, Dr. Oberheuser called us and said, 'Those girls are new guinea-pigs'; and we were very well known under this name in the camp. Then we understood that we were persons intended for experiments and we decided to protest against the performance of those operations on healthy people". *Testimony of Władysława Karolewska, a Polish female prisoner subjected to medial experiments at the Ravensbrück concentration camp.*

feed the babies. Of the 120 babies born in January and February 1945, 80 died, mostly from starvation. There was also a testimony at the trial of the Ravensbrück guards after the war that in March 1945 over one hundred babies and pregnant women were gassed to death in a railway wagon.[87]

At the Nazi doctors' trial in 1946-1947, the only female defendant charged by the American prosecutors was the Ravensbrück camp physician Herta Oberheuser (1911-1978). She was sentenced to 20 years for performing medical experiments on prisoners, without the subjects' consent, and participation in the mass murder of concentration camp inmates, including killing of babies with oil and evipan injections. One of the notorious female guards at Ravensbrück was Hermine Braunsteiner who after the war married an American citizen and immigrated to the United States. Discovered in 1964, she was extradited to West Germany and sentenced to life imprisonment. One of her crimes involved killing women by stomping on them, but an Austrian court also had accused her earlier of infanticide. Her nickname was the Stomping Mare (*kobyła* in Polish). She was not the nurse who gave information to Lackorońska about the killing of children, but witnesses at Braunsteiner-Ryan's trial told of her seizing children by the hair and throwing them on trucks to take them to the gas chamber at the Majdanek extermination camp, where she had been a guard. She was also accused of whipping women to death.[88]

Countess Lackorońska was one of the Polish women who told Pope John Paul II about what they had seen and experienced in Nazi concentration camps.[89] When she died in Rome in 2002 at the age of 104, John Paul II sent a message to be read at her funeral, in which he acknowledged her WWII suffering and service to others. "The tragic experience of war, arrests, a concentration camp, fighting in General Anders' army, and finally her emigration far away from her homeland had a tremendous impact on her life. In all those harsh experiences, Lanckorońska always knew how to find enough courage to help the oppressed and those in need."[90]

After the war, Karol Wojtyła also became familiar with the story of Stanisława Leszczyńska, a Polish midwife-prisoner at the Auschwitz concentration camp who helped with the delivery of babies at the camp and made every possible effort to save them in defiance of the Nazi orders. Born in a working class family in Łódź, Stanisława studied in Warsaw to be a midwife and returned to Łódź in 1922 to practice her profession. In 1943, she was arrested with her children by the Gestapo for resistance activities and sent with her daughter to the Auschwitz-Birkenau camp. Her two sons ended up at the Mauthausen-Güsen camp and her husband was killed in the Warsaw Uprising in 1944. The rules imposed by Dr. Mengele and other Nazi overseers at Auschwitz-Birkenau required pregnant women to conceal their pregnancies and to have their newborns killed. Despite an enormous danger to herself, Stanisława Leszczyńska assisted women-prisoners with delivery. She then baptized the infants since the Catholic Church allows lay persons, including women, to perform baptisms under extraordinary circumstances. She tried to keep the infants alive by hiding them from the camp guards and arranging for food and medical

Stanisława Leszczyńska

Born: May 8, 1896, Łódź, Poland

Died: March 11, 1974, Łódź, Poland

Book: *Midwife's Report from Auschwitz)*

supplies.

Out of more than 3,000 babies she helped to deliver at Auschwitz-Birkenau, only about thirty lived long enough to see the liberation of the camp by the Soviet Army in 1945. After the war she returned to Łódź and resumed her career as a midwife. Her book, *Raport położnej z Oświęcimia* (*Midwife's Report from Auschwitz*), published in Poland in 1957, realistically described the fate of pregnant women and newborn infants at the camp. She also issued appeals against abortion, in which she reminded the Poles of the killings of defenseless infants in Auschwitz shortly after their birth. In 1983, the Kraków School for Midwives was named after her. Her face is also engraved on the "Chalice of Life" placed by Polish Catholic women in 1982 at the Jasna Góra Shrine to Our Lady of Częstochowa. In a speech to women-textile workers in Łódź, Poland in 1987, John Paul II presented Stanisława Leszczyńska as a Christian heroine and the model wife and mother.[91]

Suffering of Women in Soviet Camps

Karol Wojtyła became familiar with many stories of immense suffering of Polish women under both Nazi and Soviet occupation. Many Polish women also lost their children in Soviet prisons and work camps, where they delivered their babies under terrible conditions. Russian, Ukrainian, Jewish women, as well as women of many other nationalities, experienced a similar fate. While Soviet prison and camp commanders did not order killings of babies, many infants were born dead or died shortly after birth due to insufficient food and medical care. In some cases, the Soviet authorities also separated Polish mothers from their children, sending the children to orphanages to be brought up as Soviet citizens. Russian children, whose mothers were accused of crimes against the state, suffered a similar fate. Especially horrific were the stories of mothers who gave birth in prisons and camps and whose children died shortly after birth.[92] Many of these women became mentally ill, some committed suicide and others were psychologically scarred for the rest of their lives. Karol Wojtyła was familiar with many of these stories and they had a definite influence on the development of his view on contraception and abortion.

One Polish woman who was jailed in a Soviet prison and survived was Mrs. Alina Gryglowska, whom Wojtyła met in Kraków in the 1960s.[93] As a young woman, she was active in the underground anti-Nazi resistance movement in Poland. Because she was a member of an organization that was opposed to communist rule, she was arrested by the Soviet secret police in March 1945, interrogated in a Kraków jail and then taken with German prisoners of war to Central Asia, where she remained for some time before being allowed to return to Poland. During a long conversation with Cardinal Wojtyła, she described to him her experiences as a prisoner in the Soviet Union and he was deeply moved by her story. He urged her to write it down and then read her manuscript with great interest as it was being written, regretting that it could not be published as a book while the pro-Soviet regime was still in power in Warsaw.[94]

Polish Women as Fighters During WWII

During World War II, Polish women of all ages were members of the underground Home Army and a great number of them were killed or wounded. Women carried messages and ammunition, gathered military information and nursed male soldiers. They ranged in age from schoolgirls to grandmothers and came from all social classes but mostly from the *intelligentsia*. And while they received training in the use of arms and sometimes participated in military actions with great courage, for the most part they were not fighters or leaders, although they were exposed to horrendous risk, especially when carrying messages between leaders of various underground units. The commander of the underground Home Army, General Tadeusz Bór Komorowski (1895-1966), wrote in his memoirs that "in fulfilling this highly responsible and dangerous task, the Polish women gave proof of the utmost devotion and self-sacrifice." One of his personal messengers, Halina Stabrowska, was arrested and interrogated by the Gestapo, yet despite the use of torture, she did not betray him. She was eventually executed. Usefulness of female messengers was enhanced since the Germans were initially less likely to suspect women of being engaged in the underground resistance.[95]

Polish patriotism promoted greater emancipation of women than conservative Germans could at first anticipate. Eventually, however, even the Nazis realized the importance of these women, known as "liaison girls," for the underground Home Army. If caught with underground messages and letters, these women faced the same treatment from the Gestapo as a man caught carrying a gun. Several hundred Polish "liaison girls" died as a result of torture, execution or combat.[96]

Participation in conspiratorial activities and in some combat roles during World War II further strengthened the social position of Polish women. During the 1944 Warsaw Uprising, women who were members of the Home Army were not issued arms, since there were not enough weapons even for men, but special female patrols specialized in mine-laying and setting explosives to blast passages among the ruins. After observing both men and women during the uprising, the Home Army commander concluded that psychologically the women had shown far greater resistance than the men.[97] After the war, the communists imprisoned and tortured some of the same women who fought the Nazis because as members of the Home Army they were linked with the anti-communist Polish government-in-exile. Many of those women who survived became active in Church and underground anti-communist organizations. The vast majority of these women were religious, patriotic and highly independent, and most of them did not identify themselves in any way with Western-style feminist causes.

Victims of War Crimes and Western Feminists — Different Perspectives

Stories of women like Alina Gryglowska and many others who fought the Nazis and then were jailed in Soviet and Polish communist prisons may have convinced Wojtyła that Polish women did not have much to learn about emancipation from Western feminists. As far as Wojtyła was concerned, these Polish women had demonstrated by their heroic actions that they were already emancipated and just as capable as Polish men who were their partners in the fight against the Nazis and the communists. Many men who were active in the anti-communist movement shared a similar fate as women, although many more men were politically active and therefore more likely to be tortured or executed. This was quite a different perspective from that of Western feminists who were rarely put in a position of having to risk their lives together with men for a common cause. To Polish women and men of Wojtyła's generation as well as those born shortly after World War II, their common goal of fighting for free Poland and democracy appeared much greater than any differences between them based solely on gender. The story of Alina Gryglowska and those of countless other Polish women who went through Nazi and Soviet concentration camps convinced Wojtyła that nothing can be as important as the struggle for human dignity and for human rights against secular ideologies. Whether it was fascism, communism or Western liberalism, all of these ideologies to various degrees accepted and often encouraged abortions.

For some women who experienced the death of their children in the Nazi or Soviet camps or for people like Wojtyła, who talked with these women, abortion may have a different meaning than it does to a Western feminist concerned primarily with protecting a woman's legal right to control her body. Dr. Gisella Perl, while willing to perform abortions on pregnant women in Auschwitz, saw her actions as destroying life but justified it as necessary to save the lives of mothers. "I loved those newborn babies not as a doctor but as a mother," she wrote, "and it was again and again my own child whom I killed to save the life of a woman."[98] The debate among most Western feminists on the issue of abortion does not focus on the possibility that terminating a pregnancy undermines the value of human life to the point that it can make killing of certain categories of humans much more likely in the future. If anything, most secular and even some religious feminists see the right to choose as an essential protection for women who find themselves in extreme situations and as a protection against the power of the state which can be used to deprive citizens of other rights. The anthology of women's experiences in concentration camps written from a feminist perspective, *Different Voices: Women and the Holocaust*, published in the U.S. in 1993, documents numerous fertility experiments on women-prisoners as well as forced and voluntary abortions at Nazi hospitals and concentration camps, but it does not explore whether abortion in free democratic societies undermines respect for human life. The presumed link between abortion, contraception and genocide became, however, an overwhelming concern for Dr. Półtawska, Stanisława Leszczyńska and for John Paul II.

Dr. Anna-Teresa Tymieniecka

After *Love and Responsibility*, Karol Wojtyła wrote another book, *Osoba i czyn (The Acting Person),* also translated as *(Person and Act).* While his first book focused on preserving human dignity through love and marriage, in *The Acting Person* Wojtyła concentrated on the significance and the dignity of work and participation in public life. As with *Love and Responsibility*, his new book was also closely related to Wojtyła's experiences and concerns in Poland. He had observed the exploitation of workers by the communist system and wanted to counter the Marxist philosophy with his own view of work as providing worth and dignity to the individual. By that time, he had also developed a strong dislike of the capitalist system as he understood it to function in the West. The book, written from a phenomenological perspective, a branch of philosophy that stresses the importance of experience, caught the attention of Dr. Anna-Teresa Tymieniecka, a Polish-born aristocratic woman, at the time a philosophy lecturer at St. John's University in New York.[99] She visited Cardinal Wojtyła in Kraków in July 1973 and offered to edit and translate his book into English. Cardinal Wojtyła agreed, and for several years he and Dr. Tymieniecka became intellectual partners, exchanging letters and visits while she worked on the English translation of his book. *The Acting Person* required considerable editing and rewriting, as Wojtyła's writing style was far from being reader-friendly. Dr. Tymieniecka and Wojtyła communicated by letter and spent many hours together discussing his views during the four years of their collaboration on getting the book published in English. While on a visit to the U.S. in 1976, Cardinal Wojtyła stayed with Dr. Tymieniecka and her husband; she also visited him in Kraków and in Rome and helped to organize a number of speaking engagements for him in the West.

The English translation of *The Acting Person* produced by Dr. Tymieniecka was significantly different from the Polish original and, in the opinion of some experts, a much better book. The Polish friends of the pope, including, Dr. Wanda Półtawska's husband Dr. Andrzej Półtawski, accused Dr. Tymieniecka, however, of significantly changing Wojtyła's text and infusing it with her own ideas.[100] The whole controversy erupted after Wojtyła was already elected to the papacy. Unwilling to deal with the matter himself, John Paul II appointed a commission of three Polish theologians and philosophers, all men and two of them priests, to check Dr. Tymieniecka's translation of his book. They suggested a number of corrections, which she refused to accept, insisting that only Wojtyła himself could make such changes. Dr. Tymieniecka went ahead and published the book in 1979 without the approval of Wojtyła's Polish friends. The preface to the English edition included Cardinal Wojtyła's comments giving Dr. Tymieniecka full credit for clarifying and improving his original text and acknowledging that she had made some changes "with the full approval of the author."[101] Whether Wojtyła gave Dr. Tymieniecka full rights to the English translation of his book became a point of contention. The Vatican administration challenged her copyright claim and tried to stop the publication of her version of the book. Even though the book received a glowing review from the Vatican official newspaper, L'Osservatore romano, the Vatican bureaucrats launched a campaign in the Catholic press accusing her of injecting her own ideas into Wojtyła's original work and removing from the English translations his explicit references to Saint Thomas Aquinas. In addition to theological concerns of how the book would be perceived, the Vatican may have also tried to counter the possible embarrassment that a woman had a close personal, albeit professional relationship with the pope and may have influenced his philosophical thinking. Dr. Tymieniecka felt personally betrayed by the pope's silence during this controversy and even considered filing a suit against copyright infringement, but eventually she and the pope apparently reconciled. She continued to insist that her version of the book remains the definitive English edition.[102]

Dr. Tymieniecka told me in May 2007 that the controversy with the Vatican was still unresolved but that she and John Paul II remained friends and continued their contacts and philosophical discussions until his death in 2005. Dr. Tymieniecka is now president of the World Phenomenology Institute which publishes philosophical journals Analecta Husserliana and Phenomenological Inquiry. In previous years, she taught philosophy at the University of California at Berkley, Pennsylvania State University and Bryn Mawr College. In her 1962 book Phenomenology and Science she argued for reconciling science with spirituality using similar arguments as John Paul II against studying human existence and human using only scientific and psychological methods. "The philosophy of existence," she wrote, "begins by reinstating the concept of the soul because ... neither empirical processes nor mental activities exhaust the truly distinctive spiritual functions."[103]

She left Poland in 1946 after completing her undergraduate education at the Jagiellonian University in Kraków under Roman Ingarden, a well-known Polish phenomenologist who also had influenced Karol Wojtyła's philosophical interests. She then studied at the Sorbonne in Paris and received her Ph.D. from the University of Fribourg. She has been living in the United States since 1954.

> **University of Fribourg**
> http://www.unifr.ch/
>
> **Notable Alumni and Faculty**
> Anna-Teresa Tymieniecka
> Józef Bocheński
> Mary Daly
> Tariq Ramadan
> Michele M. Schumacher

Dr. Tymieniecka was probably the only woman with whom Karol Wojtyła had extensive contacts and who was his intellectual equal. She was also probably the only woman in Wojtyła's pre-papal period who spent most of her adult life in the United States and could judge his understanding of the West. Dr. Tymieniecka and her husband, Harvard professor Dr. Hendrik Houthakker (b. 1924), a Dutch-born Jew who spent time in a Nazi internment camp, shared their impressions of Wojtyła with Carl Bernstein for the papal biography he and Italian journalist Marco Politi published in 1996. Dr. Tymieniecka told Mr. Bernstein that in personal encounters, Wojtyła came across as a modest and a warm individual who showed total interest in the person with whom he was talking. But she also described him as a person of iron will who was not dissuaded by obstacles and, while interested in new ideas, not likely to change his mind.

Father Mieczysław Maliński, who knew him since both of them were young men, made a similar observation but from a different perspective. He described Wojtyła as very calm person who was never known to raise his voice or insult anyone, but he also saw him as a very dynamic, even fiery individual who was "hard and stubborn"—a personality closer to that of Dr. Półtawska's than Dr.

Tymieniecka's. A document from the communist secret police files based on information from an agent who spied on Wojtyła described him as having "a very strong will and well-developed convictions."[104] According to Father Maliński, Wojtyła rejected anything that might have detracted him from his life's goals or that might have taken his energies away from being a priest and later a professor, a bishop, an archbishop, cardinal and finally pope. Wojtyła liked to travel, meet people and engage in sports, such as hiking, skiing and swimming, but otherwise he did not have any hobbies, did not collect anything, had very few personal possessions, ate modest meals and slept only a few hours each night.[105] This may explain how Wojtyła was able to achieve many of his goals, including his successful defense of religion in Poland under communism, but it also explains his stubborn determination to promote his views on contraception, abortion, women-priests and the role of women in society. According to one American observer, the pope's compassionate sternness confused Americans who want to be loved and desire approval.[106]

John Paul's positions on many issues did not come close to what liberal Catholics in the West would consider as a sufficiently compassionate attitude toward the shortcomings of individuals and groups. He may have, for example, expressed compassion for homosexuals or priests who had left the priesthood but would under no circumstances tolerate homosexual behavior, homosexual marriages or the relaxation of the celibacy rule for priests. His unwillingness to modify or bend the Church rules alienated him from many liberal Catholics and gained him the reputation among his critics of being super-conservative and lacking compassion.

But only stubborn determination could have allowed Wojtyła to triumph in his struggle against communism. According to Dr. Tymieniecka, he was equally stubborn and determined when it came to many of his views about the Western world. As reported by Jonathan Kwitny, particularly disturbing to her and her husband were what they considered to be Wojtyła's erroneous impressions of life in the West and his lack of knowledge of how Western democracies function. Before John Paul's first papal trip to the United States in 1979, Dr. Tymieniecka visited him at Castel Gandolfo and discussed with him his proposed speeches, some of which may have been drafted in part by Dr. Półtawska. Dr. Tymieniecka told me in 2007 that she did not review the texts of papal speeches but held discussions with John Paul II about what kind of messages would resonate well with Americans. She confirmed that his initial ideas, which his conservative Polish friends had suggested, were way off the mark as far as the realities of life in the United States were concerned. But she said that she had managed to talk John Paul II into making drastic changes in his speeches to Americans and was gratified to hear that he had taken her advice.

Dr. Tymieniecka takes partial credit for some of John Paul II's first words on American soil after his arrival in Boston on October 1, 1979, where he said that he came "with sentiments of friendship, reverence and esteem" and "as one who already knows you and loves you." According to her, these words set the tone for his first apostolic visit to the United Statesn, but his message could have been much different if the pope accepted the advice of his conservative Polish friends. Dr. Tymieniecka told me that while John Paul II's initial views about America may have been uninformed, she said that this was quite normal at that time for any person living in communist Poland. She also told me that she not only had persuaded the pope to adopt a more moderate tone in speaking to Americans during his first visit in 1979 but that in subsequent years his opinions of Americans, American society and the American Catholic Church became drastically more positive.[107] However, my own analysis of John Paul II's later speeches to Americans shows a definite trend toward a much more critical attitude.

When Karol Wojtyła first visited Dr. Tymieniecka and her husband in the United States in 1976, Dr. Houthakker's initial impression was that he considered all Americans to be "money-grabbers" who are not interested in anything else.[108] According to Dr. Houthakker, Wojtyła also seemed to overestimate the strength of the communist system and at the time was not confident that communism would be defeated. This view has been contradicted by some of Wojtyła's Polish acquaintances who claim that he had always known that religion and human rights in the Soviet Bloc would prevail. Polish-born Dr. Zbigniew Brzezinski (b. 1928), who was the National Security Advisor in President Carter's Administration, agreed that Wojtyła had a long-term perspective, but when the two men met in Washington in 1979, the pope indicated to him that it may take a long time, perhaps a hundred years, before democracy is restored in Eastern Europe.[109] American journalist Jonathan Kwitny reported in his 1997 biography of John Paul II that Wojtyła's assessment of communism's longevity seemed too long to Dr. Brzezinski. But in fairness to Wojtyła, no well-known Western expert or any CIA analyst had predicted in 1979 that it would take only ten more years for communism in East Central Europe to disappear. President Ronald Reagan (1911-2004) may have been one of the few Americans who believed that communism could not survive

Pope John Paul II with President Reagan in Fairbanks, Alasaka (1984). Photo courtesy of Ronald Reagan Library.

for long, but I remember how his calling the Soviet Union "the evil empire" horrified most of the U.S. diplomats I talked to during the 1980s. They thought such words were too provocative and could harm communist reformers within the Soviet block. As a religious leader, John Paul II used different words than Ronald Reagan, but his message about human dignity and human rights was no less provocative and no less effective.

By precipitating the fall of communism, John Paul II did more for the protection and expansion of women's rights in his own country and around the world than any other world leader. He is rightly given credit together with Ronald Reagan and Mikhail Gorbachev for contributing to the fall of communism. Even such a seemingly minor consequence of increased economic competition and commercialization of life in Eastern Europe and Russia after the fall of communism as a decrease in alcohol consumption among men produced a drop in violence against women. Spousal abuse had been a major problem in alcoholic households in the Soviet Union and in other countries including Poland where communist regimes could not provide sufficient consumer goods and entertainment but made buying alcohol relatively inexpensive.

While parliaments in some countries such as Poland outlawed abortion after the fall of communism, women for the first time could make their own voices heard and were able to help build a civil society and advance their agenda through the democratic process. If there are no major setbacks, in time the women of East Central Europe will be able to organize their societies and their lives according to their wishes. The fall of communism and the fall of the Soviet Union, which John Paul II helped to bring about, also largely removed Marxism as an ideology and an attractive model for dictatorial and nationalistic leaders in the developing countries, thus giving many poor women a better chance of advancing their economic and social status. This assumes, of course, that their political elites decide to follow the free market-democratic model instead of Marxist and heavily socialist models promoted earlier by the Soviet Union and still favored by some on the far-Left in the West. The credit for defeating communism with a message of preserving human dignity and workers' rights understandably goes to John Paul II, although he would not be supportive of blindly applying all Western solutions to problems of workers, women and economies in the Third World. Many of these he considered highly dangerous on both moral and economic grounds. He also made it clear that he found some positive elements in communism as well as in capitalism.

While the fall of communism was due in part to John Paul's outstanding leadership and his powerful message in defense of human rights, evidence of his initial doubts about the ability of the West to resist and defeat communism may indicate that Wojtyła did not fully understand strengths and advantages of Western democracy. Dr. Houthakker told Carl Bernstein that while communists were still in power in Poland, Wojtyła "was not aware of the power of the Western system" and "had no real appreciation of the virtues of democracy."[110] Dr. Tymieniecka and her husband tried to introduce Wojtyła to the American way of life during his two visits in the 1970s to their house in Vermont and to persuade him that not everything in America was immoral and decadent.

Judging by the pope's later statements addressed to Americans, his comments about the American society and his views of capitalism, their efforts were less than successful. But in an interview with me, Dr. Tymieniecka strongly disputed this assessment. She insisted that while Wojtyła's initial view of America may have been quite negative, probably as a result of the lack of sufficient contacts with Americans and misinformed opinions of some of his conservative Polish friends, her numerous conversations with him, as well as his other encounters with Americans, eventually turned him into a great admirer of America and American Catholicism. According to her, John Paul II became greatly impressed by the intellectual quality of American priests and by American spirit of voluntarism. She even suggested that

John Paul II saw the future of the Catholic Church largely in America, meaning both North and South. She did admit, however, that during his visit to the United States in 1976, Wojtyła tended to gravitate toward conservative American priests and Catholic intellectuals and was quite taken by their old school conservative activism. At one point, Dr. Tymieniecka questioned some of what Kwitny, Bernstein and Politi had written about her and her husband's comments. She described their versions of what she had told them as not entirely consistent with what she meant to convey, but in my conversation with her I did not get an impression that their reports were substantially wrong.[111] She conceded to me that John Paul II had a very negative view of the West's materialistic culture but insisted that he did not think the United States was the worst among Western nations. In her view, in later years John Paul II had high hopes for America and began to realize that Americans are very religious. She also conceded that some of the pope's later statements, which had been highly critical of the U.S., were probably written for him by American bishops.

Dr. Tymieniecka believes that Wojtyła's conservative Polish friends, including Dr. Wanda Półtawska who tried to influence his views about the United States, had a very limited knowledge of life in America. She had been friends with Dr. Półtawska's husband and visited the couple in Kraków before Dr. Półtawski questioned her translation of Wojtyła's book. She also told me that it is very unlikely Wojtyła would have passed on to Pope Paul VI Dr. Półtawska's materials on birth control. She conceded that he might have discussed the issue with Dr. Półtawska and that she was certainly actively involved in running his birth control and marriage counseling programs, but as a serious scholar — according to Dr. Tymieniecka — he would have reached out to a number of academic experts before submitting any written materials to Paul VI. But since she admitted that she had not discussed this topic with Wojtyła and was not interested in it, the accounts of Dr. Półtawska's crucial involvement with Paul VI's birth control encyclical still seem highly credible. However, Dr. Tymieniecka's observation that Dr. Półtawska would not have been the only person consulted by Wojtyła on this issue is true. She was only one of several members of the commission established by Wojtyła in Kraków to advise him on the birth control controversy, but her access to him and her influence were significant.

My conclusion was that Wojtyła's personal relationship with Dr. Tymieniecka, a Polish woman who grew up in the West, apparently did not change much his opinions about the West or Western women. Dr. Tymieniecka admitted to me that her conversations with Cardinal Wojtyła and later Pope John Paul II did not focus at all on feminism. She also told me that she had never discussed with Wojtyła at any length the subject of human sexuality. She did say that as a female academic in the U.S. in the early 1960s she was one of the initial supporters of the feminist movement, although she quickly became disillusioned by feminist attacks on religion and their views on moral issues. Carl Bernstein and Marco Politi suggest that there may have been sexual attraction between the two, which both of them had sublimated, but Dr. Tymieniecka told them that falling in love with a middle-aged priest would have been inconceivable for her as a married Catholic woman.

As for Wojtyła, there is nothing we know about his life that would even remotely suggest any attitude toward women other than one of reverence, warm, non-sexual affection and total respect. Dr. Tymieniecka was one of many women who told me this was indeed John Paul II's entire attitude. She recalled a conversation she had with Wojtyła in 1974 in Naples, Italy, where he impressed her by his thoughtful analysis of the role of women in religion. She remembered him telling her that in many respects women are superior to men and gave the example of Mary Magdalene who was the first to see the risen Christ and was chosen by him to be the messenger of his resurrection to the male disciples. She said that she has been always impressed by Wojtyła's respect for women. When Anna-Teresa Tymieniecka learned of the pope's final illness, she flew to Rome from her home in New Hampshire and was there when John Paul II died on April 2, 2005.[112] She would not say whether she saw the pope shortly before he died.

Unsuccessful Dialogue with Western Women

Dr. Anna-Teresa Tymieniecka was not only Wojtyła's intellectual equal, but as a highly educated woman who could easily bridge the cultural gap, she had the necessary knowledge to explain the differences between the mentality of women and men Poland and men and women in the West. She may have had a unique chance to provide John Paul II with some insights into how women in the West saw themselves and what they thought about feminism and other issues that concerned them. She claims that she was successful in at least changing some of John Paul II's perceptions about the United States. But I found no other indication that she had managed to change in any substantial way Wojtyła's thinking about Western societies and the role of women or that her Central European background made her arguments more credible to Wojtyła.

Another woman of Central European background, Muska Brzezinski, a sculptress and the wife of Dr. Zbigniew Brzezinski, had a similar experience in talking with Wojtyła about American women. When John Paul II visited the United States in 1979, she urged him in a private conversation to "listen to the prayers of American women" for a greater role in the Church. As the wife of the man who was one of the architects of the Carter Administration's policy of promoting human rights, Mrs. Brzezinski expressed the opinion of many American women who felt that the Church did not grant them equal rights with men. According to a papal biographer, Jonathan Kwitny, she received an ambiguous answer from the pope that he respected "the reality of womanhood."[113]

While such an answer may have been difficult to interpret at the beginning of his papacy, it became clear in subsequent years that

John Paul II had no intention of allowing the ordination of women. It also became obvious that he had not altered his views on gender issues as a result of his conversations with women who shared his cultural background but spent many years living in the West. Had John Paul II listened to Dr. Tymieniecka and Mrs. Brzezinski—two highly-educated women who came to the United States from Central Europe and who wanted to help him understand Western women—he probably would have had far fewer problems with Western women in the later years of his papacy and could have recruited them to help him rejuvenate the Catholic Church in the West.

As it turned out, John Paul II lost a chance to reach out to liberal and highly educated Western women and use their considerable talents and energies to save the Catholic Church in Western Europe and the United States from its slow but steady decline. This was both tragic and ironic because Wojtyła was always convinced that women play an extremely important role in preserving customs and traditions and in encouraging priestly vocations.

Edith Stein (Saint Teresa Benedicta of the Cross)

The delicate and controversial nature of the relationship between the Catholic Church and feminists as well as between the Catholic Church and Jews was a constant factor during John Paul II's papacy. A controversy flared up in 1998 with the canonization by John Paul II of Edith Stein, a Jewish woman born in Germany who had become a Catholic Carmelite nun and was murdered by the Nazis at Auschwitz. Because before her

Edith Stein – Saint Teresa Benedicta of the Cross

Born: October 12, 1891, Breslau, Germany (now Wrocław, Poland)

Died: August 9, 1942, Auschwitz-Birkenau, Nazi-occupied Poland

Canonized by Pope John Paul II: October 11, 1998

Book: *Essays of Women's Sins*

http://essays.quotidiana.org/stein/

death Edith Stein wrote extensively on the vocation of women in the Church and in society, her canonization was also seen as the Vatican's attempt to win points with moderate feminists by presenting a Jewish-Catholic philosopher as an early advocate of women's rights. The publicity given to Edith Stein's feminism by some Vatican officials was not unusual given John Paul II's support for "new feminism" or "Catholic feminism." The cause of controversy was Edith Stein's Jewish background and her death at the hands of the Nazis. John Paul II offended some Jews by raising to sainthood a Jewish woman who had converted to Catholicism but was murdered by the Nazis because she was a Jew. They claimed that her canonization in October 1998 was offensive because it implied martyrdom for the faith, whereas in their view Edith Stein was not a martyr for her new faith but was killed simply because of her Jewishness. They also saw her canonization as a gesture that diluted the unique nature of the Holocaust as a Jewish tragedy and attempted to divert attention from the responsibility of the Catholic Church for helping to create the climate of anti-Semitism. John Paul II saw the canonization of Edith Stein, however, as a gesture of reconciliation and a reminder to Catholics that millions of "Jewish brothers and sisters" were exterminated during the Holocaust. At the canonization ceremony, the pope made a passionate appeal to prevent this kind of crime from happening ever again against any ethnic group or race. He also pointed out that like the Virgin Mary, Edith Stein was a daughter of the Jewish people.[114]

Perhaps as an attempt to counter Jewish criticism, soon after the canonization the Vatican spokesmen described Edith Stein as one of the 20th century's early feminist scholars. Born into a Jewish family in Breslau, before the war a city in Germany and now known as Wrocław in Poland, she received a doctorate in philosophy and became an assistant to the phenomenologist Edmund Husserl (1859-1938) — a philosopher who also inspired Karol Wojtyła during his student years and academic career. Edith Stein converted to Catholicism after reading the biography of Saint Teresa of Ávila, the same saint who was one of Wojtyła's most favorite saints, and later entered the Carmelite convent in Cologne taking the name Theresa Benedicta of the Cross. During World War II, her order had moved her from Germany to a convent in the Netherlands to save her from the Nazis, but she was nevertheless arrested by the Gestapo and deported to Auschwitz with her sister, who had also become a nun. They were both killed in a gas chamber on August 9, 1942.

During the Vatican-sponsored international congress under the title "A New Feminism for a New Millennium" held in Rome in May 2000, Father Abelardo Lobato, the rector of the Pontifical Roman Academy of Saint Thomas, described Edith Stein as "one of the most illustrious women of the 20th century" together with Simone de Beauvoir and Simone Weil. It was an unusual comparison considering Simone de Beauvoir's Marxism and her great hostility toward Christianity for perpetuating the oppression of women. Father Lobato declared that because of Stein's intellectual achievements and "her attention to the question of woman," the Vatican is considering naming her a doctor of the Church. Only three other women have received this recognition: Saint Catherine of Sienna, Saint Teresa of Ávila, and Saint Therese of Lisieux. Father Lobato announced that this proposal had enthusiastic support of Pope Wojtyła.[115]

John Paul II was undoubtedly familiar with Edith Stein's writings on women, which in many ways resembled his own ideas. Using her knowledge of Hebrew and Jewish tradition, Stein applied the same scholarly analysis as the one John Paul II used later to argue that originally God made woman equal to man, and only after the Fall their pure partnership of love was corrupted by sin into "a relationship of sovereignty and subordination" distorted by sex. In fact, some of John Paul's statements on the subject mirror almost word for word what Edith Stein had written in her essays on women. It would not be at all surprising that in his own writings on gender issues he had borrowed heavily over the years from Stein's views on women and feminism. Edith Stein rejected for example some of Saint Paul's restrictions on women's behavior and dress in the Church as applying to a particular time and place and without a wider significance. John Paul II had the same view on this subject. Edith Stein ultimately decided that while the ordination of women is not forbidden by dogma, the fact that Christ came to earth in the form of man speaks of "the pre-eminence of man" and seems to indicate that God "wished to institute only men as His official representatives on earth." This view more or less corresponds with the position taken by Pope John Paul II, although he was more emphatic that women can never become priests, or more precisely that he has no authority to order ordination of women to Catholic priesthood. But like John Paul II, Edith Stein argued that God ennobled the feminine sex by virtue of Christ being born of a human mother and having a more intimate relationship with her than with any other human being. For Edith Stein, the most sublime vocation for a woman was to be the Spouse of Christ by becoming a nun. She described shame and sex as one of the consequences of the Fall of Adam and Eve. Man was punished by having to struggle to feed his family, while woman was punished with suffering while giving birth and being under the power of her husband. Sin, shame and sex were introduced into humanity which must now guard against them. Here, Edith Stein was very much in agreement with John Paul II and his strong defense of celibate life for priests and nuns as a sign of desire for the original perfection of God's plan for humanity and an attempt to emulate Christ's example. That is why it was so important for the early Christians and for John Paul II to insist that Christ was born of a virgin, that Mary had no other children or sexual relations with her husband and that there was no sex in Christ's life. Edith Stein saw Christ as embodying the ideal of human perfection, uniting both the masculine and feminine virtues and eliminating the weaknesses of each gender. She believed that only by imitating Christ can men and women overcome the natural limitations of their sex, pointing out that this may explain why holy men show "a womanly tenderness and a truly maternal solicitude for the souls entrusted to them, while in holy women there is manly boldness, proficiency, and determination."[116] John Paul II could not have agreed with her more, and in fact in the early 1980s presented more or less the same interpretation in a series of weekly teachings on the creation of Man, the original sin and the differences between the genders.

John Paul II and Edith Stein had a misfortune of being born at the time of heightened nationalism, when liberalism and democracy were under severe attack throughout Continental Europe. They both tried to come up with a theological explanation that would confirm woman's full dignity as a human being in opposition to previous Catholic tradition. Interestingly, both embraced the Romantic nationalist tradition of their own countries and tried to prove their orthodoxy by presenting their ideas as being in opposition to the liberal tradition. Edith Stein's analysis of the 19th century European feminism was similar to his. They both believed that early feminists were too individualistic and went too far in denying the feminine singularity of women. Edith Stein pointed out that the views of the early feminists were accepted only by the extreme Left. When mentioning the early feminists and sometimes guardedly praising them for their achievements, neither one of them would give any credit to English and Continental liberalism for starting the feminist movement. While Edith Stein strongly applauded the struggle for women's right to vote and opening up of educational and professional opportunities for women, she concluded that in the heat of battle the Suffragettes went too far by denying that women are different from men. Her criticism of individualism of the early feminist movement seems ironic as it was made in Germany shortly before Hitler's rise to power.[117] Obviously, she did not know what was to happen in later years. In her paper "The Significance of Woman's Intrinsic Value in National Life" she expressed a moderately nationalistic agenda for German women, but since nationalism was then sweeping across Continental Europe, such sentiments were not unusual. What seems significant is that even after the experience of Nazi fascism and communism, both of which had their special agenda for women, John Paul II still saw liberalism and individualism as the two grave sins of feminism and continued to describe liberal societies as being on the verge of collapse from the lack of values. Edith Stein's criticism of pre-Hitler, democratic Germany, which was still far from being liberal, sounded almost exactly like the pope's later warnings to the West. The German people were suffering from "the great sickness of our time, [...] an inner disunion, a complete deficiency of set convictions and strong principles, an aimless drifting." Since the more or less democratic Weimar Republic collapsed under the pressure of Hitler's Nazis, perhaps it was not after all a wrong description of the German society at the time, but the Nazis used similar words to criticize democracy and also condemned individualism. The question remains whether more rather than less individualism and liberalism were needed to preserve freedom, or whether it could have been preserved at all. Germany lacked liberal traditions that could have protected it from the aftermath of World War I and the economic depression that followed. As a religious person and apparently not immune to nationalistic propaganda, Edith Stein became convinced, however, that individualistic feminism and liberalism were bad for the German nation. No doubt, she wanted Germans to embrace her version of ideal Christian feminism. Instead, the Nazis grabbed all of the conservative Catholic ideas of how women can best contribute to the society and rejected the religious component.

By stressing procreation, motherhood and wife's place at home, Catholic feminism was attractive to all sorts of nationalist movements, some of them opposed to Christianity, as in Nazi Germany, and some very much Catholic, as in Spain, Croatia, Poland, Slovakia or Hungary. Jews suffered badly in all cases;

women not as much, but they were also innocent victims of the political failure of extreme nationalism, especially in those countries where it was replaced by fascism and communism. (Marxist feminists would argue that communism was good for women.) Edith Stein concluded that in imitating Christ as "the archetype of all personality and the embodiment of all value," women should be above all mothers. By pursuing their vocation as mother and helping others, women "create healthy, energetic spores supplying healthy energy to the entire national body." Wives were to create a pleasant atmosphere at home so that husbands would not seek sinful diversions. Mothers who are able to let go of their children and allow them to enter public life were "the most important agents for the recovery of the nation." Edith Stein expressed many such religious and nationalistic objections to the individualism of the early feminist movement. While she mentioned teaching as another truly feminine vocation, she basically argued against open discussion in classroom and urged women teachers to be firm in preventing confusion in young minds from dangerous reading. She also saw a place for at least some women to pursue their vocation in medicine, politics and in academia, although she had some doubts about hard sciences.[118]

Wojtyła's and Stein's views on feminism are almost identical, particularly in their critique of individualism and their support for subordinating women's freedoms and activities to national, social and religious agenda. While women will always remain part of some larger community, it is always the degree of subordination of their freedoms that presents a dilemma for those trying to find the ideal situation. It comes down to a question whether male religious leaders, male politicians or even Catholic nuns know better what is best for women, or whether women together with men can best determine their future individually and collectively if they live in a truly liberal, pluralistic and democratic society. Edith Stein and John Paul II would argue that without some ideal model and religious guidance, the choices that women and men will make could easily end in a disaster for themselves and the society. They both seemed more afraid of too much freedom than not enough of it. While before Hitler's rise to power it would have been difficult for Edith Stein to predict what fate too much obedience to the national cause would have for her and other Jews in Nazi Germany, John Paul II had far more hindsight knowledge of history. Yet his version of feminism also put a premium on duty and pursuit of national objectives while discounting choice and individualism. He may have been convinced that if everyone follows the Christian ideal, everything would turn out fine. It is not so much what Edith Stein, John Paul II and other religious leaders had said in advocating the ideal but how their theories, flawed or not, have been abused and distorted by others. When we look at the Catholic Church's treatment of Jews and women, or for that matter at how other religions have been treating these two groups, a little skepticism and a little more of pluralism of views and individualism may not seem as such a bad idea.

Was Edith Stein a feminist? This highly educated and religious woman was undoubtedly a feminist considering the Catholic Church's official teachings on women. Her background, however, was in Judaism and in German Romanticism, both of which had definite visions of the role of women vis-à-vis the family and the nation. The fact that she was able to overcome some of the religious and cultural restrictions and presented her own view of Catholic feminism while contradicting some of the conventional Catholic thinking at the time speaks highly of her intelligence, creativity and determination. There is little doubt that John Paul II borrowed from her ideas in presenting his own vision of Catholic feminism. His canonization of Edith Stein in 1998 may have been his attempt to reach out to both feminists and Jews, but he seemed to have satisfied neither. The historical wounds were simply too great to be put aside by such gestures without a profound re-examination of the Church's historical treatment of both groups. Allowing women to be ordained as priests — something Edith Stein had considered as only as a remote possibility—could greatly hamper the expansion of Catholicism in the developing world and the Church's dialogue with Islam and other more traditional religions.

John Paul II and Mother Teresa

A woman who became one of John Paul II's strongest allies in his public anti-abortion campaign was the highly respected Albanian-born nun Mother Teresa. John Paul II quoted extensively from Mother Teresa's speech when in 1997 he gave a clear a warning to his countrymen to be on guard against the view that abortion, and particularly birth control, can improve the quality of life for men and women alike. John Paul II was convinced that "the struggle between the civilization of life and the civilization of death continues."[119] In a homily in Kalisz, he read a passage from Mother Teresa's anti-abortion speech to the 1994 U.N. Conference on Population and Development to prove his point that abortion is a form of genocide:

> I repeat it many times—and I am certain of this—that the greatest danger threatening peace today is abortion. If a mother can kill her own child, what can prevent you and me from killing each other?" "A nation which kills its own children is a nation without a future."[120]

Albanian-born Mother Teresa, winner of the Nobel Peace Prize in 1979, also made another statement, which captured the essence of John Paul II's strong opposition to abortion. In receiving the Nobel Prize, she accepted it "in the name of unborn children." She was quoted saying that "Any country that accepts abortion is ... teaching its people ... to use any violence to get what they want."[121] Her views about the Western civilization were also remarkably identical to similar statements about the West from John Paul II. They were both born at about the same time in less developed

---

Mother Teresa (Albanian: Agnes Gonxha Bojaxhiu) – **Blessed Teresa of Calcutta**

Born: August 26, 1910, Skopje, now Republic of Macedonia

Died: September 5, 1997, Kolkata (Calcutta), India

Beatified by Pope John Paul II: October 19, 2003

Quotes: "A nation which kills its own children is a nation without a future."

"Any country that accepts abortion is ... teaching its people ... to use any violence to get what they want."

"No one has been a better priest than Our Lady."

Mother Teresa of Calcutta Center

http://www.motherteresa.org/layout.html

Lay Missionaries of Charity

http://laymc.bizland.com/

Mother Teresa – The Path of Love

http://home.comcast.net/~motherteresasite/mother.html

Missionaries of Charity Fathers

http://www.mcpriests.com/

---

countries on the eastern edge of Europe. She once observed that "the spiritual poverty of the Western world is much greater than the physical poverty of our people." Using almost the same words as Wojtyła did in my interview with him in 1976, she said that millions of people in the West suffer from "terrible loneliness and emptiness" and feel "unloved and unwanted." They are not hungry in a physical sense, she noted, but long for a relationship with God.[122]

Mother Teresa, the founder of the Missionaries of Charity, who spent most of her life taking care of the poorest people in India, was not in favor of ordaining women. During her 1987 trip to the United States, she described abortion as "the greatest destroyer of love, the greatest destroyer of peace," and she urged women who do not want to keep their children not to destroy them but to give them up to her missions. In 1994, she commented on Roe v. Wade, "America needs no words from me to see how your decision in Roe v. Wade has deformed a great nation. The so-called right to abortion has pitted mothers against their children and women against men. It has sown violence and discord at the heart of the most intimate human relationships. It has aggravated the derogation of the father's role in an increasingly fatherless society. It has portrayed the greatest of gifts — a child — as a competitor, an intrusion, and an inconvenience."[123] Asked about women-priests, she responded, "No one has been a better priest than our Lady. The role that a woman has no man can fill. Every woman has something special."[124]

Mother Teresa was a tireless campaigner against abortion. A veteran Vatican observer John Cornwell claimed that John Paul II and Mother Teresa shared "a perverse notion that feminism was equivalent to promoting abortion."[125] As proof, he quoted from Mother Teresa's message to the Beijing conference on women in which she said that "those who want to make women and men the same are all in favor of abortion." It is highly unlikely these two religious figures really believed that every feminist approved of legalized abortion or abortion in general. But looking at the Clinton Administration and prominent American feminists like Hillary Rodham Clinton, they suspected that most feminists in the United States were promoting abortion rights for women. John Paul II was aware that American women who embraced new Catholic feminism were against abortion, but he probably did not fully realize that many other American women who identified with feminism in some way had diverse and nuanced views on abortion. He and Mother Teresa did not think that one could have a nuanced opinion about abortion when human life was being threatened. During the years when Hillary Rodham Clinton was the American First Lady, Mother Teresa repeatedly asked her in personal encounters and in dozens of notes and messages to change her position on abortion. In her autobiography *Living*

History, Mrs. Clinton wrote that Mother Teresa's never lectured or scolded her but delivered her plea in a loving and gentle manner. She explained that she had the greatest respect for Mother Teresa's opposition to abortion but would not change her own view that abortion should be legal or her belief that it is dangerous to give any government the power to enforce criminal penalties against women and doctors. In her book she mentioned communist China and Romania as examples of what can happen when governments have this kind of power over women. Unable to change Hillary Clinton's views on abortion and birth control, Mother Teresa managed to convince her to sponsor a home for infants who are being given up for adoption. They both agreed that adoption is vastly better than abortion in case of unplanned or unwanted pregnancies. Mrs. Clinton attended Mother Teresa's funeral in Calcutta in September 1997.[126]

According to Cardinal Dziwisz, John Paul II and Mother Teresa shared a deep friendship and mutual understanding. They met for the first time in the early 1970s before he became pope. (They used to sing religious hymns together.) John Paul II was greatly pained by her death in 1997 and ordered a speedy beatification process to make her a saint.[127] In 2003, he presided over the beatification ceremony for Mother Teresa. John Cornwell accurately observed that except for his remarkable association with Mother Teresa, John Paul II did not have such a close personal friendship with anybody outside of the group of his most trusted Polish associates.[128]

The Cairo Conference and the Clinton Administration

In 1994, Pope John Paul II became overwhelmingly concerned that the U.N. conference in Cairo, scheduled for September of that year, might approve abortion as a means of birth control. There was an all out effort on the part of the Vatican diplomacy to forge an alliance between the Catholic countries of Latin America, the Islamic countries and a few sympathetic nations in Europe, Africa and Asia to fight against what was described as "the demographic colonialism" of the West aimed at reducing the birth rate in the Third World. The Clinton Administration was the primary focus of the Vatican's criticism for supporting pro-choice language in discussions leading up to the Cairo conference.

As part of his efforts to lobby world leaders before the Cairo conference, John Paul II asked the U.S. Ambassador to the Holy See, Ray Flynn (b. 1939), to arrange a telephone call with President Clinton so that he could personally present his deep concerns. Despite opposition from the strongly pro-choice members of the Clinton Administration who did not want the president to telephone the pope, Ambassador Flynn was able to prevail on President Clinton to make the call. But a subsequent meeting between Pope John Paul II and President Clinton at the Vatican in June 1994 did not go well. On the morning of the meeting, the semi-official Vatican newspaper, L'Osservatore romano, ran a commentary which mentioned different kinds of imperialism, including "anti-conception imperialism." After the meeting, Ambassador Flynn described the pope as having "a stony expression on his face," and the president as looking "a little stunned."[129]

Just before the start of the Cairo conference, the pope's spokesman Joaquin Navarro-Valls (b. 1936) made an unprecedented personal attack on Vice President Al Gore who was the head of the American delegation.[130] In an attempt to calm down the controversy, Vice President Gore made a statement that the United States had never sought an international right to abortion. A few days later, the papal press secretary Joaquin Navarro-Valls, an Opus Dei member and fierce critic of the United States who was never known to make a controversial public statement without the pope's blessing, in effect called the Vice President a liar when he declared that "the draft population document, which had the United States as its principal sponsor, contradicted in reality Mr. Gore's statement.[131] For John Paul II it was beyond comprehension that radical pro-choice ecofeminists and Vice President Gore could show great concern, even reverence, for all living things in the environment but saw nothing wrong with supporting legislation allowing doctors to perform abortions on demand. John Paul II respected the environment. (He spent weeks on hiking trips with young students in the Polish mountains.) But he gave priority to human life.

Due to John Paul's relentless campaign and their own opposition to abortion, several prominent Muslim women, including Turkish Prime Minister Tansu Ciller and American-born Queen Noor of Jordan, decided to boycott the Cairo conference. Another prominent Muslim woman Pakistani Prime Minister Benazir Bhutto attended the conference but described the U.S.-supported conference's document as being seriously flawed and "striking at the heart of a great many cultural values" of both developed and developing nations as well as values of Christianity and Islam.[132] These were Muslim women leaders who profoundly disagreed with the Clinton Administration over the abortion issue. The Vatican began to court them in trying to gather support for its position, while at the same time also reaching out for support to the religious Islamic states. After numerous protests and delaying tactics, the Vatican delegation was successful in getting the Cairo conference to reaffirm opposition to abortion as a means of birth control. The final Cairo document stated that "in no case should abortion be promoted as a method of family planning." A proposal calling specifically for unrestricted access to legal and safe abortion was also rejected, but the conference approved the principle of a medically safe abortion in countries where it is legal.

It was not a complete victory for the pope nor was it a total defeat for the Clinton Administration. Ambassador Flynn, whose personal views on this issue were more in line with the Vatican than with the administration he represented, believed that the Clinton team alienated some of the Third World nations, the pope and the Catholic Church to please what he described as "a small, but vocal, minority of liberal and feminist groups." He admitted, however, that future events proved him wrong when the support of the very same groups kept President Clinton in the White House despite Republican efforts to impeach him over the Monica Lewinsky sex scandal.[133]

According to papal biographers, Carl Bernstein and Marco Politi, the Vatican's alliance with the Islamic countries ultimately broke down because Islamic law does not forbid abortion when the mother's life is in danger.[134] However, the Catholic Church also forbids abortion to save a mother's life, the difference is in how Catholicism, Judaism and Islam look at the personhood of the fetus in the very early stages of development. The conference did approve the principle of making abortion safe in those countries were it is legal, thus recognizing the practice of terminating unwanted pregnancies. Carl Bernstein and Marco Politi believe that as a result of the opposition encountered at the Cairo conference and the defeat of the anti-abortion and pro-Church parties in parliamentary elections in his native Poland, the pope was forced to reevaluate his tactics in dealing with abortion and with women in general and changed his public diplomacy strategy. If that were the case, there can be no doubt that it was only a tactical change aimed at improving the Vatican's public relations efforts and the pope's image among women rather than a sign of any weakening of John Paul II's absolute opposition to abortion.

John Paul II and Evangelical Religious Right in the U.S.

It would not be fair to suggest that John Paul II, the evangelical religious Right, Islamic religious figures and some of the Third World political leaders have much in common or are the only critics of the United States on moral issues. There are plenty of such critics in the United States and elsewhere in the Western world who did not agree with John Paul II on the death penalty, U.S. military interventions, or the benefits of free-market economy with minimal government controls.

Evangelical Christian Web Sites
National Association of Evangelicals
http://www.nae.net/
Southern Baptist Convention
http://www.sbc.net/
Concerned Women for America
http://www.cwfa.org/main.asp
Christian Coalition of America
http://www.cc.org/
Pat Robertson b. 1930
http://www.patrobertson.com/
Jerry Falwell 1933-2007
http://www.falwell.com/
James C. Dobson b. 1936
Focus on the Family
http://www.family.org/
Promise Keepers
http://www.promisekeepers.org/
Beverly LaHaye b. 1929
http://www.beverlylahayein-stitute.org/bli/

Some of those who have voiced serious concerns about the high rate of divorce, abortion, and attempts to legalize homosexual marriages include many conservative American Catholics, such as George Weigel, Pat Buchanan and William J. Bennett, although some of them may not have agreed with John Paul II on some of the fine points of social and Church policy. On the issue of abortion and gay marriages, John Paul II was very close to them as well as to some of the leaders of the conservative evangelical Christian movement in the United States. They are all equally strong critics of the current moral state of the American society, and express their views some-times even much more bluntly than John Paul II ever did.

Speaking on Pat Robertson's Christian Broadcasting Network's television show "700 Club" shortly after the terrorist attacks of September 11, conservative religious leader, Jerry Falwell (1933-2007), described them as probably a deserved punishment for such sins as secularism, abortion, feminism and gay and lesbian rights in America.[135] "When we destroy 40 million little innocent babies, we make God mad," declared Rev. Falwell. (40 million is an estimated number of abortions in the United States since the Roe v. Wade Supreme Court decision.) It is doubtful that John Paul II would ever put into one category, as Jerry Falwell has done, "all the pagans, and the abortionists, and the feminists, and the gays and the lesbians," especially in the context of the September 11th terrorist attacks, but John Paul II had

Pat Buchanan b.1938

http://www.buchanan.org/blog/

William J. Bennett b. 1943

http://www.bennettmornings.com/

used the word "pagans" to describe pro-choice non-believers in the West. The program's host, Pat Robertson, initially agreed with his guest. After a storm of criticism and a statement from President Bush describing Rev. Falwell's comments as inappropriate, the minister apologized and retracted his remarks.

Evangelical Christian activist in the United States Dr. James C. Dobson, founder of a nonprofit organization Focus on the Family has remarkably similar views on marriage and family as Pope John Paul II. Dr. Dobson believes women are not inferior to men because both are created in God's image and he recommends that married women with children under the age of 18 focus on mothering rather than work outside the home.[136] He believes this provides a stable environment for the children to grow up in. Dr. Dobson has supported Christian men's organizations such as Promise Keepers who advocate similar views. Concerned Women for America, a conservative Christian group in the United States has a program very similar to the pro-family activities of the Polish women who worked with Pope John Paul II. One interesting fact about Concerned Women for America is that it is an organization created in response to the challenge form radical feminists. It was founded in 1979 by Beverly LaHaye, wife of Christian Coalition co-founder Timothy LaHaye, as a response to activities by the National Organization for Women (NOW) and a 1978 Barbara Walters interview with noted feminist Betty Friedan.

But if one were to compare John Paul II with the leaders of the American religious Right, there are some obvious similarities but also important differences. The Evangelicals share similar

Pro-Choice Organizations

National Organization of Women (NOW)
http://www.now.org/

Feminist Majority Foundation
http://www.feminist.org/

MS Magazine
http://msmagazine.com/

NARAL Pro-Choice America
http://www.prochoiceamerica.org/

Planned Parenthood
http://www.plannedparenthood.org/

Religious Coalition for Reproductive Choice
http://www.rcrc.org/

Republicans for Choice
http://www.republicansforchoice.com/

Choice USA
http://choiceusa.org/

views on the importance of the family and oppose abortion and homosexual marriages. They also effectively use the media, particularly television, to promote their views. John Paul II, however, had much different priorities when it comes to social policies. He strongly supported redistribution of wealth and government intervention to fight poverty, both domestically and abroad. The American religious Right has different ideas on these issues as well as on a few others, including U.S. foreign policy, use of contraception, acceptability of divorce (under some conditions), global warming and other environmental concerns, immigration, gun control and the death penalty. Because of abortion and what he saw as a liberal attack on the family, however, John Paul II would much rather identify with the evangelical Right than with the liberal Left, even though the liberal Left shares his views on most other social issues. There are some social liberals in the United States who champion John Paul II's pro-life and anti-abortion views but they are clearly not in the majority. Democrats for Life of America (DFLA), a pro-life organization, is attempting to steer the Democratic Party toward taking pro-life positions

Democrats for Life of America (DFLA)
http://www.democratsforlife.org/

and wants to change how the American Left responds to abortion. DFLA members also oppose euthanasia and the death penalty.

John Paul II certainly understood the evangelical Right's concerns about the state of morality within the Western civilization. Visiting Kazakhstan only thirteen days after the 9/11 attacks, John Paul II warned the largely Muslim population of the dangers of "slavish conformity" with the Western culture. He left absolutely no doubt that he condemned hatred, fanaticism and terrorism as "profaning the name of God" but did not suggest that Western liberal democracies should be the model worthy of emulation in Central Asia and in the rest of the developing world. He told the Kazakhs instead that Western nations are showing "their deepening human, spiritual and moral impoverishment."[137] (This papal statement about "deepening" moral impoverishment of the West made in a Muslim country surprised me, since a few years earlier Western nations protected the Muslim population of Bosnia and Kosovo from genocide — something the West Europeans did not do for Poland in 1939.)

The West was, in John Paul II' words, "a civilization of many errors and also transgressions against man, exploiting him in various ways." While admitting that the Western civilization has had many achievements, the pope nevertheless saw the secular West as the enemy of Christianity. Using very harsh language, he accused the West of employing "the structures of power and violence, both political and cultural (especially the mass media) in order to force these errors and transgressions upon the whole humanity." For Karol Wojtyła this represented "the struggle against God" and "the systematic elimination of everything

Christian."

John Paul II also liked to point out that it was the West that had given birth to Marxism, fascism and communism. It is equally true, however, that Western liberalism has also produced parliamentary democracies, unprecedented political freedoms, economic prosperity and feminism—at first mostly in non-Catholic countries. It could be further argued that communism never managed to take hold in Western Europe but was first introduced in 1917 in still partly feudal Russia, where Christianity was at the time the dominant religion.

As for the intellectual roots and acceptance of fascism, Germany, which gave the world the widely read and variously interpreted works of Hegel and Nietzsche, was a country on the edge of Western Europe without any strong liberal and democratic traditions. Germany, like Poland, can be more accurately described as Central European nation. Hegel and Nietzsche came from Protestant backgrounds and have been blamed for everything from putting man before God and promoting individualism to glorifying nation-states and racial superiority. But Hitler's movement got started in Munich, in the southern state of Bavaria, which was predominantly Catholic, and the German Catholic bishops initially strongly supported Hitler's nationalist agenda. Spain and Italy, both Western countries that became fascist, were also predominantly Catholic. The fascist movement in Spain even referred to itself as Catholic, and some of its leaders were members of the right-wing

---

Radical and Anarchist Feminists

Redstockings

http://redstockings.org/

Radical Women

http://www.radicalwomen.org/

No Status Quo

http://www.nostatusquo.com/

anarcha

http://www.anarcha.org/

anarkismo.net

http://www.anarkismo.net/index.php

lobcom.org

http://libcom.org/

Catholic organization *Opus Dei*, which always enjoyed strong support from John Paul II. The fascist government in Catholic Slovakia during World War II under the protection and control of Nazi Germany was led by a Catholic priest Father Jozef Tiso (1887-1947). There was also a fascist government in Catholic Croatia, and the last Polish government before World War II also embraced many fascist ideas.

While John Paul II was right that ideas that gave birth to Marxism and fascism originated among thinkers who lived in Western countries, his attempt to blame the West for originating these ideologies seems somewhat far-fetched and designed mainly to make a rhetorical point. After all, it was the liberal West, mainly the United States and Great Britain, which defeated both fascism and communism. In fact, countries with the strongest traditions of liberalism and individualism — the United States, Great Britain, Canada, Australia, and New Zealand — were practically the only ones where Marxism and fascism did not develop any significant following. Former British Prime Minister Margaret Thatcher was probably more correct in stating that during her lifetime "most of the problems the world has faced have come, in one fashion of other, from mainland Europe, and the solutions outside it."[138] Like John Paul II, she was also referring to Nazism and Karl Marx, although Marx wrote *Das Kapital* in London, taking advantage of England's liberal system. Like the pope, Mrs. Thatcher also had great misgivings about the European Union and believed that Britain's national traditions need to be preserved, but unlike John Paul II, she is a great believer in Anglo-Saxon individualism and largely unregulated free-market capitalism. Her views on many economic and social policy issues were mostly opposite of what John Paul II would advocate.

When offering his severe criticism of the Western civilization, John Paul II was probably trying to make the point that not all ideas coming from the West were good for the West and for the non-Western cultures, but the same can be said about any other

Liberal Feminist Web Sites

Women's eNews
http://www.womensenews.org/index.cfm
AlterNet
http://alternet.org/
Broadsheet
http://www.salon.com/mwt/broadsheet/index.html
The F-Word Ezine
http://www.thef-wordzine.com/welcome.html
BushTelegraph
http://www.bushtelegraph.uk.com/
National Organization for Men Against Sexism
http://www.nomas.org/
Femina
http://www.femina.com/
Feminist.com
http://www.feminist.com/

civilization. Using the same logic, the entire Islamic world could then be blamed for the September 11th attacks on the United States, which would be a wrong and simplistic conclusion. John Paul II liked to make such generalizations about the West because he saw the West as producing most of the flawed ideas and as having more power to impose them on other civilizations. He believed that only those ideas rooted in Christianity are good and can save the world, therefore any philosophy or political theory that, in his view, rejected or undermined religion—whether it was fascism, Marxism or liberalism—must be in the long run bad for humanity.

Not too many Westerners would agree that women's rights are less protected in Western liberal societies than in traditional societies or in overwhelmingly Catholic countries, such as Poland.

Similarly, very few would argue that those living in undemocratic but highly religious and largely traditional societies enjoy greater rights and freedoms and that their lives are generally safer and more fulfilling than the lives of people in the West. This became much more obvious when after the September 11th attacks, Western media and politicians started to focus on the treatment of women by the Taliban regime in Afghanistan and in other religious Islamic states. Few would deny that women in the West are more economically independent and freer to choose between careers and family life than women in other parts of the world. They are also less exposed to domestic violence and better able to escape from abusive relationships. Finally, the West, particularly the United States and Western Europe, attract millions of Third World immigrants looking for a better and freer life.

John Paul's critics argue that his idealization of traditional societies and his severe criticism of the West have not been very helpful in promoting the necessary reforms in the developing world considered indispensable for raising the standard of living of

> **U.S. State Department Human Rights Country Reports (with sections on women's rights)**
>
> http://www.state.gov/g/drl/rls/hrrpt/

women. Many feminists believe that the key to improving the economies in the developing nations lies in empowering women so that they can reject traditional cultural restrictions and develop their full creativity. Feminists also believe that women need effective birth control to achieve this goal.

John Paul II remained convinced that the Western civilization wallows in selfishness. It is the "civilization of death" based on utilitarian principles of using things and people, and using people as things. What John Paul wanted to propose instead is the "civilization of love" and "peace in solidarity" based on altruism and personal sacrifice for the benefit of others. Freedom, according to John Paul II, should not be a license to do as one pleases; it should be "a gift of self" to other individuals, the community and the nation. In Wojtyła's view, human beings and entire nations, all of whom share a common humanity, should not treat each other as real or potential competitors.

Wojtyła's strong emphasis on a person's responsibilities and duties vis-à-vis his or her country may have been guided by Poland's historical experience with democracy. The conventional view of Polish historians holds that the loss of Poland's independence in the 18th century resulted from excesses of freedom enjoyed by the Polish nobility, particularly through *liberum veto*, the right of any Polish nobleman to veto legislation desired by the majority. Speaking in 1960 in connection with the 100th anniversary of one of Poland's uprisings against the Tsarist Russia in the 19th century, Wojtyła argued that Poland's history is full of examples of sinful abuses of freedom which led to the loss of independence and the need to fight to bring freedom back to the Polish people.

In 1964, Wojtyła delivered a lecture at the Catholic University in Lublin in which he again warned that liberty can be threatened by too much liberty, since true liberty demands seeking true goodness. In his lecture, he gave examples of Polish national shortcomings such as drunkenness, promiscuity, carelessness, quaralnessness and selfishness.[139] National independence — the greatest treasure for a Polish patriot next to religion — was lost because of the abuse of the principles of freedom and tolerance. This is what Polish children of Wojtyła's generation were taught at home and at school. While the foreign powers that had invaded Poland were always seen as primarily responsible for the country's loss of independence, the conventional view among Poles has also been that the abuses of freedom by the Polish nobility, their individualism, and their lack of concern for public good weakened the country and made it vulnerable to foreign invasions. For someone as sensitive and as concerned with the welfare of his people as Wojtyła, such views had a powerful influence on his way of thinking.

It is not surprising that John Paul II saw similar signs of the abuse of freedom in the West, particularly promiscuity and selfishness, with much greater alarm than most Westerners. However, even most Poles would be reluctant to draw such extreme historical analogies. John Paul II was particularly concerned that people in the West have divorced freedom from responsibility for seeking the truth and from responsibility toward others. Because Westerners have enormous freedom, but—in Wojtyła's view—lack reflection and a sense of what is good and moral, they have adopted a lifestyle based on consumption and exploitation of others.

Wojtyła seemed convinced that his concept of "personalism" was in direct conflict with the Western and particularly American idea of "individualism." He assumed that Western individualism "presupposes a use of freedom in which the subject does what he wants, in which he himself is the one to 'establish the truth' of whatever he finds pleasing or useful."[140] Speaking in 1988 to the parliamentary assembly of the Council of Europe in Strasbourg, John Paul II observed that "the person as the unique subject of rights and duties has often been replaced by the individual, a prisoner of his own selfishness, who thinks he is an end unto himself." In the same speech, he did admit, however, that "the exaltation of the group, nation, or race has led to totalitarian and murderous ideologies."[141]

The question that needs to be answered is whether an individual living in the West has too much freedom and insufficient sense of duty and responsibility or whether there is still not enough Western-style freedom and individualism, particularly in nations driven by nationalism, fundamentalist religion, or both. Wojtyła believed deeply in human solidarity, both at the individual and national level. John Paul II did not agree with the liberal idea of individual pursuit of happiness, particularly if it leads individuals and nations into competition and excludes God and religion as the final arbiters of what is good and evil. At the personal level, Wojtyła believed that an individual achieves his or her full potential in a community with another person, particularly when he or she makes a complete gift of himself or herself to another person in a loving marriage or through religious vows.[142] Same-sex relationships are excluded. In the 1994 *Letter to Families* John Paul II goes as far as to contrast his civilization of love with "free love" — yet another product of the Western civilization. He describes "free love" as "particularly dangerous because it is usually suggested as a way of following one's 'real' feelings, but it is in fact destructive of love."[143]

John Paul II was also convinced that the East Europeans, who for many decades had been forced to live under an atheistic system, have a much stronger attachment to religion than people in the West. In the mid 1980s, John Paul II published the encyclical *Slavorum apostoli* in which he presented a vision of a unified Europe with the traditional values of the Slavic nations and Eastern Christianity being incorporated into a common, Christian based European culture.[144] In a 1993 interview, he further elaborated his view that the East Europeans are more willing to accept the idea of God as the "ultimate and absolute" source of human dignity:

> The Easterner has realized this, the prisoner in the Gulag realized it, Solzhenitsyn realized it. In the West, man does not see this so clearly. He sees it up to a certain point. His awareness is to a large extent secularized. Not infrequently, he sees religion as something alienating.

What the Russian writer Alexander Solzhenitsyn (b. 1918), whom John Paul II mentioned, said about the West in his commencement address at Harvard University in June 1978, corresponds closely to the pope's own beliefs, although it may appear less convincing to those who are familiar with the conditions of life in pre-communist Russia, the Soviet Union, and in the West. Solzhenitsyn concluded that "through intense suffering" Russia has achieved "spiritual development of such intensity that the Western system in its present state of spiritual exhaustion does not look attractive." Solzhenitsyn observed further that many people living in the West are dissatisfied with their own society, and even despise it for not being sufficiently spiritual. According to Solzhenitsyn, "destructive and irresponsible freedom has been granted boundless space," and Western societies "appear to have little defense against the abyss of human decadence, [...] misuse of liberty for moral violence against young people, motion pictures full of pornography, crime and horror." Solzhenitsyn also complained about too much personal freedom and too much legalism in the West, making an interesting comment in 1978 that "when a government starts an earnest fight against terrorism, public opinion immediately accuses it of violating the terrorists' civil rights." Solzhenitsyn described his remarks about the West as "bitter truth," but he assured his Harvard audience that he was speaking not as an adversary but as a friend. He concluded that human beings in the West are weakening, while in the East they are becoming firmer and stronger, although at that time they were still being oppressed by communist regimes.[145] John Paul II also believed that the struggle against Marxist totalitarianism had made Eastern Europe religiously more mature. After Alexander Solzhenitsyn returned to Russia in the early 1990s from his exile in the United States, he continued to support a religious revival in Russia and remained highly critical of the West. The two men met in October 1993.

Solzhenitsyn's prediction that the Western way of life is not likely to become the leading model for the rest of the world has been largely ignored by most middle class Russians and Central Europeans. Still, neither Solzhenitsyn nor John Paul II altered their belief that the Western model poses tremendous dangers for the spirituality of people in the East. Asked in 1993 which part of Europe, the East or the West, has more to gain from the proposed reunification, John Paul II expressed fear that Eastern Europe faces a greater danger of losing its identity. Both John Paul II and Alexander Solzhenitsyn had made great contribution to the cause of human rights. The author of *The Gulag Archipelago* exposed the enormity of communist crimes in the Soviet Union, making Western readers aware of what life under communism was really like. Yet his address to the Harvard University class of 1978 showed a misunderstanding of what life is like in Western liberal societies. The same can be said about John Paul II. Suffering under communism and fascism, even when combined with a long period of living in the West as older adults—in both cases in semi-isolation from normal everyday life—did not make either man a fan of Western liberalism.

Abortion laws in the West became the main issue for the pope and the Polish Church during Poland's transition to democracy in the 1990s. A profound desire to keep a strict ban on abortion made Pope John Paul II and the Polish bishops somewhat ambivalent about plans to include Poland in the European Union. On the one hand, they wanted Poland to regain its "rightful place" in Europe and, on the other hand, they did not want Poland to become like any other Western country, where abortion is legal, separation of church and state enforced and children receive secular sex education. Bishop Józef Życiński (b. 1948), considered a liberal in the Polish Church and one of Wojtyła's close friends, expressed a common concern among the Polish bishops that the integration of the East European countries into the European Union would require them to accept without any exceptions the laws and the legal framework of the dominant West European partners. John Paul II and Bishop Życiński did not want Poland to have the same legislation as in Western Europe with regard to abortion, euthanasia, genetic experimentation, religious education, and in general the role of religion in public life. Most of the East European countries, however, with the exception of Poland, already allow abortion, sometimes with fewer restrictions than in Western Europe.

More moderate friends of John Paul II in Poland argue that he was not anti-Western or an opponent of democracy, but because he appreciated the benefits of Western democracy, he tried to prevent the West from self-destructing through moral relativism and rejection of religious values. The opponents of Poland's integration with Western Europe, on the other hand, interpreted the pope's frequent criticism of the West as a clear sign of his support for their position. As the pope's friend Polish bishop Tadeusz Pieronek observed in a July 2000 interview with the Italian newspaper *Avvenire*, "the idea had spread that entry into the West and integration in European structures would endanger Poland's national and religious identity. ... At a certain point it seemed that all traditional values would be displaced by a wave of materialism and permissiveness."[146] It would be fair to say that the pope's repeated warnings about the West contributed substantially to the development of a siege mentality among at least some segments of conservative Polish Catholics. While John Paul II was certainly not in agreement with their xenophobic agenda, he was also not an admirer of Western European societies as an ideal model for Poland to be adopted in its entirety.

Despite their frequent criticism of the West, however, the practical advantages to Poland of joining the European Union were difficult to ignore by the pope or the majority of the Polish bishops. After years of harshly critical statements, a delegation of Polish bishops agreed to accept an invitation to visit the headquarters of the European Union in Brussels in November 1997. This was interpreted as a belated gesture from the Polish Church to at least show an open mind about Poland's membership in the West European economic and political institutions. Considering the pope's well publicized fears, it was not surprising that even the most liberal Polish bishops, such as his close friend Bishop Życiński, were afraid that the integration with Western Europe would allow the dominant Western countries to impose their form of secular ideology on their economically and militarily weaker partners in

Eastern Europe. Bishop Życiński was also concerned, as was John Paul II, that the West European ideology of integration would be based on the idea of extreme individualism and moral relativism rather than the Christian ideal of social solidarity and the love of one's neighbor.[147]

Despite these misgivings, Bishop Życiński remained one of the strongest supporters of Poland's reintegration with the West, as did most of Wojtyła's closest friends in Poland. John Paul II also wanted Poland to be a full member of the European community of nations, but he wanted Europe to remain faithful to, what he calls, "its Christian roots." In welcoming Hanna Suchocka Poland's new ambassador to the Vatican and its former first female Prime Minister, John Paul II warned in December 2001 that by becoming a member of the European Community, Poland "must not lose any of its spiritual properties, which generations of our ancestors defended at the price of blood." He specifically mentioned the danger of perceiving the membership in the European Union exclusively in its economic and political aspects and warned against uncritical acceptance of "a model of consumerist life." Poland as a state—he declared—must have "its own spiritual and cultural face" and "its own historical tradition inalienably linked to Christianity from the dawn of its history." "If we want the new unity of Europe to be lasting, we must build on those spiritual values, which were once at its foundation, keeping in mind the richness and diversity of the cultures and traditions of each one of the nations," John Paul II concluded.[148] During her tenure as the first female Polish prime minister, Hanna Suchocka supported the passage of the 2003 highly

---

Hanna Suchocka b. 1946

Prime Minister of Poland: 1992-1993

Supported 1993 anti-abortion law

Appointed by Pope John Paul II to the Pontifical Academy of Social Sciences: 1994

Minister of Justice: 1997-2000

Serving as Poland's Ambassador to the Holy See: since December 2001

restrictive anti-abortion law. Although she did not belong to Wojtyła's circle of close collaborators when he was still in Poland, she can also be described one of Wojtyła's women who supported his vision of marriage and family.

John Paul's vision of the future of Europe called for re-introduction of Christian ideas, which, he believed, had been lost in the West European societies. He made no attempt to acknowledge any of the contributions and benefits of secular ideologies or liberal societies or to point out that to achieve greater prosperity, freedom, tolerance and cooperation, they had to give up some of their sovereignty and nationalistic prerogatives and to restrict the role of religion in public life. It would seem from the pope's words that Europe's distant, pre-Enlightenment past—the period that saw religious genocide, torture and burning of heretics and witches, religious wars, the Crusades and conflicts between Christian rulers and nations—was somehow much happier and purer than the post-World War II period of unprecedented peace, freedom and economic prosperity. (John Paul II would argue that fascism and communism prove that he was right about the greater dangers of atheistic ideologies, and that the jury is still out on post-World War II secular democratic order in Europe. He saw history in much longer terms than most of today's liberal thinkers.)

John Paul II believed that great human values such as the dignity and inviolability of the individual, freedom of conscience, the dignity of work and workers, and the right of each individual to a secure and dignified life would not have been "affirmed in people's consciences" without "the Christian message." In other words, John Paul II seemed convinced that without Christianity there would have been no respect for human rights. He deeply regretted that Christianity in Western Europe has been relegated to the sphere of private life or even "removed from the map of Europe." He called this process "anti-historical" and "offensive" to those who first had a vision of a unified Europe.[149]

Convinced that the post-communist countries have much to

offer Western Europe in spirituality, John Paul II was hoping that the Slavic nations would not be forced to accept everything that the West proposes. Even some of the strongly pro-Western Poles agree with Wojtyła's bleak assessment of the consumerist societies in the West. But the pope also seemed to share the view of Jan Nowak-Jeziorański (1914-2005), a former director of the Polish Service of Radio Free Europe who for many years lived in the United States and advocated strong ties between Poland and the United States and Western Europe. Nowak-Jeziorański argued that without Western capital, Poland would remain poor and technologically backward.[150]

Bishop Tadeusz Pieronek (b. 1934), Wojtyła's close friend and one of the most liberal members of the Polish episcopate, believes that the Polish bishops' initial doubts about Poland's membership in the E.U. have been overcome. According to Bishop Pieronek, "many evils have already entered Poland," but he concluded that "it is most certainly not the European Union's fault."[151] Still, some Catholic groups in Poland, particularly those associated with Radio Maryja, continued to attack Poland's ties with the West. Radio Maryja's Director, Father Tadeusz Rydzyk, kept warning that membership in the European Union will bring E.U.-sponsored sexual education, which—as he contended—destroys the morality of young children and teenagers and allows the sale of Polish land to foreigners.[152] John Paul II, whom Father Rydzyk quoted extensively in support of his arguments about the dangers of the European Union membership, would certainly agree with him on the first point. Attacking Masons, communists, and the liberal media, Father Rydzyk argued that only Radio Maryja provided Polish Catholics with the opposite point of view on the issue of Poland's E.U. membership. Most Poles, however, were in favor of Poland's entry into the European Union. In a survey conducted in November 2001, 61% of respondents declared their support for the E.U. membership while 39% expressed their opposition.[153] The highest support for the E.U. membership was registered in Karol

Wojtyła's former Kraków Archdiocese, which has both a high birth rate and a tradition of economic emigration to the West, especially to the U.S.[154] Many young Poles saw the E.U. membership as an opportunity to study and work in Western Europe.

Cautiously positive views on Poland's ties with Western Europe expressed by some of John Paul II's friends were still considered as too liberal by the conservative Catholics in Poland centered around Radio Maryja and political parties which identify themselves as Catholic. In the early 1990s, they dismissed plans for European integration as "a utopian project" that would never be realized and warned that Poland must never give up its sovereignty. They insisted that the Polish nation must be protected in the changing world and lashed out against Western liberalism.[155] Most of the Polish opponents of Poland's membership in the E.U. almost always listed the pope's primary objections against the liberal societies in the West, starting with the legalization of abortion in Western countries. Antoni Maciarewicz, member of the Polish *Sejm* (the Lower House of the Parliament) from the League of Polish Families (*Liga Polskich Rodzin, LPR*)—the party whose name was inspired by John Paul's frequent defense of family values—warned that "the European Union builds a secular civilization without God supporting the killing of the unborn, euthanasia, and homosexual unions."[156] What Poland wants—he argued—is "a civilization of love, not a civilization of death," again words borrowed from John Paul's statements.

The League of Polish Families, strongly supported by Radio Maryja, received more than 6% of votes in the 2001 parliamentary elections and won 36 seats in the 460-member Sejm. Interestingly, almost twice as many women as men voted for this anti-abortion, anti-European Union party, whereas the votes for other parties were more or less evenly split between the genders. Also, almost one third (27%) of the League of Polish Families legislators elected in the 2001 elections were women, which seems to confirm that the party has been attracting a large number of highly-motivated, conservative Catholic women activists. Only one other party, socialist, strongly pro-choice on abortion and otherwise socially liberal Union of Labor, had a higher percentage of women deputies (31%). The party ran on the platform making fun of the idea of an ideal Catholic Pole for whom having a large number of children is a "primary patriotic-religious duty." Thus, two small parties, positioned at the opposite sides of the political spectrum, managed to elect the highest proportion of women deputies relative to the overall size of their respective vote count.

> Open Society Institute & Soros
> Foundations Network
>
> http://www.soros.org/

The overall number of women in the Polish in the Lower House of the Polish Parliament after the 2001 elections went up to 20%, a sign of continued political activism and emancipation of Polish women after the fall of communism, but a significant minority of these women were strongly religious, anti-abortion, pro-nationalist and anti-liberal. This may be yet another indication that political and social emancipation of women in Poland may be proceeding in a somewhat different pattern than in the West. Most of the 90 women (17%) in the U.S. Congress in 2007 are liberal pro-choice Democrats, including speaker of the House Nancy Pelosi who is Catholic.

As in Western Europe and in the United States, the political Left in Poland was more likely to support at least some feminist ideas. Most women politicians in the Polish Parliament elected in September 2001 belonged to the former communist party, which now tries to model itself after West European socialist parties. They are moderately liberal on social issues but still far from being feminist in the West European or American meaning of the term, thus reflecting a generally conservative nature of the Polish society. Most Polish women are not politically active. In the 2001 parliamentary elections, only 40% of women voted as opposed to 50% of men. Thus, Catholic women who successfully ran on the League of

Polish Families ticket with the support of Radio Maryja and women voters, may be a good example of Christian patriotic-feminism promoted by John Paul II. In dismissing feminist protests in the West, a frequent female commentator on Radio Maryja uses such sarcastic comments as "the torment of women who feel a priestly vocation."[157]

In one of her commentaries, she compared American left-wing playwright Lillian Hellman (1905-1984) to former Polish communists and praised the American South for preserving tradition and moral order.[158] Other Radio Maryja commentators regularly present the European Union, the World Bank, the Soros Foundation, the spread of American culture, abortion and homosexual marriages as the greatest threats to Poland since the end of communism.[159]

This kind of rhetoric, however, has been losing support among Polish voters in recent years. In the 2005 elections, the League of Polish Families did better than in 2001, receiving 8 percent of votes, but it saw its seats reduced from 38 to 34. In the 2007 elections, however, the conservative nationalist party suffered a major voter backlash and failed to gain the five percent of votes required to enter the Sejm. It has lost all the seats it previously held. Civic Platform (*Platforma Obywatelska, PO*), a Christian-democratic, liberal-conservative political party won the largest number of seats with nearly 41 percent of the votes, while the right-of-center Law and Justice Party (*Prawo i Sprawiedliwość, PiS*) received only 32 percent. The Left and Democrats Party (*Lewica i Demokraci, LiD*), which includes former communists, received 13 percent. Overall, the October 2007 general elections ended in a defeat of the Right-wing coalition. The Polish voters showed they are no longer easily swayed by xenophobic, nationalistic and radical religious slogans and would rather see their future as a nation with close ties to Western Europe. The 2007 Polish election winners, however, are more socially conservative than for example the liberal wing of the Democratic Party in the United States or the Labour Party in Great

Britain.

Political culture in Poland, however, is still considerably more liberal, diverse and pro-Western than in neighboring Russia. Legislative elections in December 2007, described as by most Western observers as marred by Soviet-style manipulations, gave President Vladimir Putin's United Russia Party 64 percent of the vote, the Communist Party received nearly 12 percent, and the Vladimir Zhirinovky's Liberal Democratic Party (rather than being liberal, the party is ultranationalist) eight percent. Liberal, pro-Western parties did not receive enough votes to win seats in the Russian *Duma*, the lower house of the legislature. National TV channels in Russia are controlled by forces loyal to Mr. Putin, who is a former KGB operative. He enjoys, however, strong support among the conservative Russian electorate, which does not seem to mind his authoritarian style and in February 2008 elected Putin's annointed successor Dimitri Medvedev, to be Russia's next president..

From the early 1990s until his death in 2005, John Paul II very rarely, if ever, talked about the advantages of the West European model of liberal-democratic capitalism which, after all, brought the West Europeans unprecedented freedom and economic prosperity with equally impressive gains for the protection of women's rights. He almost never commented on how liberalism and democracy in the West helped to diffuse many ethnic and racial conflicts that still plague most of the world. After all, despite racial, ethnic or religious tensions and even occasional ethnic violence in some of the most developed Western countries including the United States, Great Britain or France, there have been no major wars between Western democratic nations or massive violations of human rights in recent decades. On very rare occasions, John Paul II would admit that Western Europe "fortunately shared many of the values which it had developed over the years," but he usually tempered any positive assessment with the observation that Europe "has not always given its best in the encounter with other civilizations" —

unfortunately not an inaccurate observation, but perhaps it was at the same time an indirect admission that Western Europe also had offered some positive models to other nations and civilizations.[160]

If one agrees with the proposition that too much emphasis on group rights at the expense of individual rights and on duties and responsibilities rather than freedoms tends to weaken the status and rights of women, then John Paul's concept of social solidarity needs a much better definition to become acceptable to feminists. Those liberal feminists, who are also socially concerned, would probably fully agree with some of the pope's calls for greater social responsibility on the part of the Western nations and for much greater sharing of resources with the poorer nations of the Southern Hemisphere. Even in his criticism of capitalism, John Paul II was not calling for any radical changes in the way free economies function. He believed that the right of individuals to accumulate private property should be respected within certain limits. In that sense, John Paul II was not opposed to the concept of a free market economy as long as other important values were protected. In his January 1st, 2000 message to the world, he pointed out that his principle of solidarity does not delegitimize private property; instead nations and individuals must properly manage private property "to the advantage of the common good and in particular the good of society's weakest members."[161] At the same time, he again criticized the West for not doing enough to help developing nations and again condemned the practice of birth control in the West. While describing "the persistent and growing gulf" between the West and the developing world, John Paul II pointed out that the North with all its wealth is "increasingly made up of older people," while the great majority of younger people now live in the South.[162] John Paul II saw the refusal of Western women to have large families as a sign of their selfishness rather than a rational decision to provide those children who are born with the best possible upbringing and education. Some liberal feminists criticized him for refusing to acknowledge the link between poverty in the developing world and overpopulation, which they blame on cultural and religious restrictions preventing many women in poorer nations from effectively controlling their fertility. But to admit this link would mean that the official teachings of the Catholic Church on birth control are partly responsible for the suffering and poverty in the Third World. This is something that John Paul II would never do having devoted almost his entire life and enormous amount of time and energy to convincing women that artificial birth control is intrinsically evil.

Polish friends of the pope, while generally pro-Western, also express strongly negative views of the West. Jerzy Turowicz, the late editor of Kraków's independent Catholic weekly, *Tygodnik Powszechny* and a close friend of Wojtyła, used such terms as "practical materialism of the consumerist civilization" to describe social processes in the West, which in his opinion are leading toward secularization, de-Christianization and the loss of values.[163] In his opinion, the West has moved from atheism and anti-clericalism toward complete indifference with regard to metaphysical and religious issues. He may have been right that many liberals and feminists have become indifferent toward the Church, although many may have also become indifferent as a result of the Catholic Church's positions on contraception and the role of women. But Turowicz's pessimistic view of the West, which was shared by Wojtyła, went much deeper. He saw extreme liberalism in the West creating moral relativism and permissiveness even among the Catholics who chose to accept some but not all tenets of faith and morality.[164] But even with this kind of "supermarket Catholicism," John Paul II was not totally without hope for the future of the West. He believed that a religious awakening and the search for truth and the purpose of life was already underway. Jerzy Turowicz attributed such positive signs at least partly to Wojtyła's message and his charismatic personality. John Paul II was convinced that the youth, even in the West, wants more than just a good life.

But is the Polish Church the model for Catholic Churches in the

West? Jerzy Turowicz did not think so. According to him, until 1989 the Polish Church had been under too much pressure from the communist regime to make changes that would bring to it the spirit of Vatican II. He was wondering in 1993 whether such things as "opening to the world" and "readiness to dialogue and to compromise" were really present within the Polish Church. He concluded that the lack of sufficient reforms were understandable given the historical conditions under which the Church in Poland had to operate until 1989 and suggested that there was a lot to be done. He described the Polish Church as still "relatively traditional" and "relatively clerical," but pointed out that it had very courageously resisted external pressures and enjoyed very strong support and loyalty of the population. The Polish Church could be judged objectively, according to Jerzy Turowicz, only with the understanding of its difficult and courageous history. But because historical conditions under which it had to operate were so vastly different from those in the West, he was not convinced that the Polish Church could be offered as a model for Western churches or churches in other countries. Speaking in 1993, he was nevertheless optimistic that the necessary changes would be implemented to make the Polish Church more in line with Vatican II reforms.[165]

Abortion—the "Culture of Life" versus the "Culture of Death"

Most Catholics in the West simply did not understand Wojtyła's thinking on the issue of birth control and his attempts to link birth control with abortion. He was never able to explain successfully his theology of sexuality and love, but it is well established that at some point in his early life he

> ...contraception and abortion are often closely connected, as fruits of the same tree.
>
> ...the pro-abortion culture is especially strong precisely where the Church's teaching on contraception is rejected.
>
> John Paul II, *Evangelium vitae*, 1995

apparently concluded that there could be no real love between two people if they do not want to have children and resort to using artificial contraception. He was convinced that artificial birth control inevitably leads to abortion. This is how he tried to explain his point of view to skeptical Catholics in Poland during his 1991 trip:

> The world would change into a nightmare if married couples facing financial difficulties would see in a conceived child only a burden and a threat to their stability; while in turn married couples, who are well off, would see in a child unnecessary and costly addition in their lives. For this would mean that love no longer has any value in human life.[166]

In his homily during his 1991 trip, John Paul told the Poles that they must change their attitude toward conceived children, even if a pregnancy is unexpected. He argued that a conceived child can never be considered an "intruder" or an "aggressor" — terms used by some feminists to justify abortion. As a human being, a conceived child deserves to live, even if — as he pointed out — it may require a special sacrifice on the part of the parents.

Most Catholics in Poland and the West, who regularly use contraceptives, may have had only a vague idea what John Paul II was trying to say in philosophical and theological terms, but they disagreed with him on the practical issue of controlling their fertility. They saw nothing wrong with trying to limit the size of their families for whatever reason and wanted to use the most reliable means rather than the Church-approved rhythm method of natural birth control.

While fighting artificial contraception was very important for John Paul II, it was abortion that became for him an overwhelming, all-consuming concern. As the Archbishop of Kraków, Wojtyła told the faithful in 1977 that according to the Fifth Commandment, "Do Not Kill," man is not the ultimate master of his own life and cannot take his own life or lives of others. He pointed out that there are similarities between suicide and murder. Describing life as "the ultimate gift from God," Wojtyła stressed that believers can never accept the argument that human life can be stopped during pregnancy because the embryo is not a human being and therefore abortion is not murder. If the embryo is not human, how come—he asked rhetorically—from this conceived "non-human," a human person is born? Speaking of the "demographic threat to our Nation," Wojtyła noted that "this threat comes ultimately from the lack of respect for each individual human life, which was conceived in the womb of woman-mother on our Polish soil."[167]

One could argue that abortions became common in communist countries because communism did not place much value on individual human life. Wojtyła would most certainly agree with this assessment. Western demographers offer an additional explanation. According to them, the abortion culture in Poland and in other communist states developed mainly because women had no access to other methods of reliable contraception.

Despite its low reliability rates, *coitus interruptus* was the major method of pregnancy prevention under communism. When this method failed, as it often did, it was backed by abortion. The communist authorities rarely encouraged the use of modern contraceptives and their supplies were always limited, but they did provide free or low-cost abortions through the socialized health care systems. True abortion rates may have been even higher due to inaccurate reports of the health risks associated with the use of modern contraceptives being circulated by some Catholic physicians and repeated by Catholic priests. Modern contraceptive methods were also rarely introduced during sex education classes in schools. In Poland, only 19% of urban and 9% or rural schools discussed methods of preventing pregnancy with students.[168] One expert studying demographic trends in East Central Europe concluded, "for many couples, the one-event abortion appeared cheaper and more reliable than dependence on irregular contraceptive supplies."[169]

Another expert, Czech demographer Libor Stloukal, blamed the abortion culture in East Central Europe on the protective capacity of the paternalistic state. By providing free or cheap health care and unlimited access to abortion, the communist state deprived individuals of motivation to take responsibility for their sexuality or to show initiative in resolving their fertility questions.[170] Stloukal, concluded that while rationality and responsibility for individual behavior is increasing in Central and East European countries as a result of the slow introduction of market economies, the transition from abortion to contraception still remains an incomplete process.[171]

Despite this, many countries in the region have already experienced substantial decreases in legal abortion rates after the fall of communism. At least in this area, greater exposure to Western materialism and Western ideas on sexuality, so much feared by John Paul II, have not produced negative results. On the contrary, abortion rates per 1,000 women age 15-44 fell by nearly half in the former German Democratic Republic (not including East Berlin), from 11.1 in 1990 to 6.0 in 1996. In the Czech Republic, where abortion continues to be legal, the abortion rate fell from 12.6 in 1990 to 8.8. in 1996.[172] Poland experienced a much more drastic reduction in legal abortion rates, but this fall is attributed largely to the post-communist legislative ban on most abortions. By comparison, in the United States the number of abortions per 1000 women aged between 15 and 44 was 23 in 1996. It went down to 21 in 2000. It was 16 in 1973 when abortion was first legalized.[173] Overall, the number of abortions in Eastern Europe per 1000 women aged 15 and 44 dropped from 90 in 1995 to 40 in 2003, but that number is still much higher than in Western Europe, where it was 12.[174]

Demographic experts are convinced that the only effective way of ending the abortion culture in East Central Europe is through the transition from abortion to contraception. John Paul II did not see it that way, nor did he accept the argument that having too many children impoverishes families and nations. Concerned with the abortion culture and the falling birth rates in his own country, John Paul II refused to describe overpopulation in the developing world as a "demographic threat" and a major cause of poverty. Also, despite all the statistical evidence to the contrary, he continued to insist that contraception leads to abortion, although he was probably referring more to his observation that individuals who accept contraception are more likely to accept abortion rather than any statistical connection between the two. His public statements on what he thought of this connection are not entirely clear, but he certainly saw contraception as a precursor of abortion.

Much of Wojtyła's campaign against abortion centered on the rights of children. In a pastoral letter written in 1970, he asked the faithful to show special charity toward each unborn child who, as he pointed out, "already needs love, and often needs charity of [his or her] own parents..."[175] During his 1991 trip to Poland, the pope's homilies against birth control and abortion, proved controversial even among Catholic Poles. Using very graphic language, John Paul II spoke about "the cemetery of the unborn" who were unaware of the mortal danger and tried to defend themselves against aggression. He told the Poles that he had viewed a film showing an unborn child hopelessly attempting to save itself in a mother's womb against death through abortion. John Paul II said that he cannot imagine a more terrible human and moral drama and to this day cannot forget what he had seen. He again made a link between acts of genocide during World War II and human attempts to take away from God the power over life and death. This kind of mentality, he warned, allows those who are privileged to decide whether an individual can live or die.[176] John Paul II considered abortion on the same level as murder with the added aggravation of what he perceived to be an attack of the powerful on innocent and defenseless lives—a blatant violation of human dignity and human rights. Former First Lady Senator Hillary

Rodham Clinton is probably the best example of the tremendous gap of mutual hostility and misunderstanding between John Paul II and pro-choice feminists. Being pro-choice, she is also a strong advocate of children's rights.

Birth control and abortion became the most divisive issues for women within the Catholic Church in recent decades, particularly in the West. But statistics show that abortion has also been widely practiced by Catholic women in less developed countries, including the pope's native Poland, where for various political and cultural reasons open questioning and criticism of papal positions on these issues has been much more muted or nearly non-existent. Considering the depth of his abhorrence of abortion, some Catholics may have hoped at the beginning of his papacy that John Paul II would modify his position on birth control. This, however, did not happen, even despite strong arguments and statistical evidence that contraception helps to reduce the number of abortions. The strength of John Paul's opposition to artificial birth control at the end of his papacy was nearly the same if not greater as it had been in 1960 when he had published his book *Love and Responsibility*.

In the 1995 Encyclical *Evangelium vitae* (*The Gospel of Life*), John Paul II acknowledged that the Catholic Church may be accused of promoting abortion by attaching a moral stigma to contraception. He even conceded that many couples may be using birth control to avoid a later need for abortion. He concluded, however, that using artificial birth control, as opposed to natural methods, which he approved of under limited circumstances, simply strengthened the "contraceptive mentality" and increased the temptation to get rid of an unwanted child.

According to Antoni Pospieszalski, a Polish journalist who had lived in Great Britain, John Paul II failed to prove that contraception indeed leads to increased use of abortion. Pospieszalski observed that John Paul II may have had a mistaken belief that de-legalization will actually limit the number of abortions. He echoed the warnings of the proponents of giving women access to legal abortions that de-legalization will simply force desperate women to be exposed to the dangers of illegally obtained abortions. In Poland, however, where abortion had been severely limited, the number of officially registered abortions dropped significantly without reports of any mass deaths from illegal procedures. That is not the case in many less developed countries where abortion is illegal and good health care difficult to obtain. More affluent Polish women still have an option of obtaining a legal and safe abortion in some of the neighboring countries. Antoni Pospieszalski concluded that the tone of John Paul's encyclical *Evangelium vitae* made it difficult to conduct a productive dialogue with those who disagree with the pope's position.

Pospieszalski also questioned the effectiveness of the pope's tactics in choosing to attack abortion in a much more open and vocal way than it was being done by some of the other Christian leaders and churches. In his criticism of the encyclical, Pospieszalski also noted the lack of any compassionate references to women who are victims of rape and brought up John Paul's suggestion that Bosnian women, who had been raped by Serbian soldiers, should give birth and love to the child conceived as a result of rape. After international media reported this story, the Vatican pointed out that this was not a direct papal appeal to the Bosnian women, as some press reports suggested, but a letter from the pope to the archbishop of Sarajevo. In the letter, John Paul II strongly condemned the rapes and those guilty of committing them, but at the same time he pointed out that innocent human beings who were conceived as a result of rape bear no responsibility for the crimes and should not be punished. He stated that under no circumstances could innocent unborn children be considered as aggressors. John Paul II called on the community to take care of the women and their families in helping them "to turn an act of violence into an act of love and openness to life."

This last statement unleashed a furry of criticism, even in

Poland. Catholic commentator Halina Bortnowska expressed her shock at the pope's appeal and his choice of words. While acknowledging that love can conceivably heal such an enormous injustice, Bortnowska stated that only God could call on women for a sacrifice of this magnitude. She concluded that the papal appeal was not helpful. Many found the pope's use of the term, "openness to life," especially unfortunate in this context, since he had used such words often in the past in support of his opposition to contraception. Some of his Polish defenders, however, were pointing out that John Paul II was not putting any moral pressure on the Bosnian women or condemning them if they chose abortion.[177] It is hard to imagine, however, that the pope did not expect his statement to be reported by the media and could not have expected that his words would indeed be seen as an attempt to put moral pressure on women who had to make these painful decisions.

John Paul's argument that a rape did not justify an abortion may have won some limited support in the West, although the vast majority of Westerners supports abortions in cases of rape or incest. Feminists for Life in the United States, an organization actively supporting pro-life views, published an ad featuring a woman who was conceived in rape and is now a lawyer and a mother. In an ad aimed at college students, she asks, "Did I deserve the death penalty?"[178]

While John Paul II never specifically condemned any woman for choosing abortion in a case of rape or to save her life, there is no doubt he personally believed that women, who had been victims of rape, should accept their pregnancy. He considered all life to be sacred from the moment of conception, even life that had resulted from rape. John Paul II apparently also believed that women should consider avoiding abortions even if their lives were in danger. Although he did not call directly on any woman to make this choice, in 1995, he beatified an Italian woman and a pediatrician Gianna Beretta Molla who insisted that her life should be sacrificed to save her unborn child. At the time she was suffering from terminal uterine cancer. John Paul II canonized her as saint of the Catholic Church in 2004. A practicing doctor and a mother of three children, she refused to consider an abortion to save her own life. She died in 1962 a few days after her third daughter, Gianna Emanuela, was born. Her husband Pietro and her children attended her beatification ceremony in 1994. By beatifying Gianna Beretta, John Paul II was certainly sending a message to women and all the faithful that the

Gianna (Francesca) Beretta Molla – Saint Gianna Bereta Molla

Patron Saint: mothers, physicians, and preborn children

Born: October 4, 1922, Magenta, Italy

Died: April 28, 1962, Magenta, Italy

Canonized by Pope John Paul II: May 16, 2004

Quotes: "If you must choose between me and the baby, no hesitation; choose—and I demand it—the baby, Save him!"

"Also in suffering, let us say: Thanks be to God."

sacrifice of one's life in the defense of life is a great virtue. Feminists, however, also saw a hidden message in the pope's decision. Frances Kissling (b. in 1943 into a Polish-American Catholic family in New York), president of Catholics for a Free Choice, an organization based in Washington, D.C. which supports abortion rights, suspected that John Paul II was also indirectly telling women that any other choice in Gianna Beretta Molla's situation would have been less than good:

I respect that choice: I would equally respect a woman who chose to live. I have a nagging suspicion, however, that in beatifying Gianna Beretta, the Pope is instructing us in the difference between a good mother and a bad one: a good mother will give her life for an unborn child: a bad mother might think that preserving her life would better serve her family and community. And only a very bad woman might think that she deserved to survive even if she had no family.[179]

Frances Kissling found it ironic that the Vatican State, which has few women and children as permanent residents, claims the right to make significant decisions about their lives. The official Church, however, does not recognize Catholics for a Free Choice as a Catholic organization speaking as an authentic Catholic voice on such issues as "the respect and protection due to defenseless unborn human life." The National Conference of Catholic Bishops has accused CFFC of being "funded by a number of powerful and wealthy private foundations, mostly American, to promote abortion as a method of population control" — a charge strongly denied by CFFC.[180]

Black Genocide

Some African American activists in the United States talk of "Black genocide" — an alleged conspiracy of White liberals to use abortion to reduce the population of black Americans. John Paul II and the Vatican diplomats were making a somewhat similar argument accusing the Western nations of trying to export "contraceptive mentality" to the Third World to exploit its resources. It is a fact that an estimated 13 million U.S. abortions since 1973 have been performed on African American women, leading some to charge that the legalization of abortion was engineered in part by the White liberal elites to promote "Black genocide." Some saw it as a preventative death penalty producing a reduction in crime rates. According to Alan Guttmacher Institute, black women in America are more than three times as likely as white women to have an abortion.[181]

BlackGenocide.org

http://www.blackgenocide.org

Although black women constitute only 6% of the population, they comprise 36% of the abortion industry's clientele.

Between 1882 and 1968, 3,446 Blacks were lynched in the U.S. That number is surpassed in less than 3 days by abortion.

3 out of 5 pregnant African American women will abort their child.

Article II of the Convention on the Punishment and Prevention of the Crime of Genocide, approved by the United Nations in 1948, defines genocide as "acts committed with intent to destroy, in whole or in part, a national, ethnical, racial or religious group," including "imposing measures intended to prevent births within the group." The BlackGenocide.org web site compares the high rate of abortions among African American women to genocide and criticizes a number of prominent African Americans for being pro-choice, naming such community and political leaders as Rev. Jesse Jackson and U.S. Senator Barak Obama. The web site quotes Dr. Martin Luther King, Jr., who in his letter from a Birmingham jail during the 1960 civil rights struggle wrote that "the early church brought an end to such things as infanticide." BlackGenocide.org asks: "What would Martin Luther King say to the church today?" Pope John Paul II was a great admirer of Dr. Martin Luther King, Jr. and his philosophy of nonviolent moral protest.

African American women's rights activist Loretta J. Ross claims, however, that the issue of African American women and abortion is more complex and cannot be seen only from the perspective of Black genocide. She argues that African American women supported and used birth control and abortion as part of their struggle against racism, sexism and poverty. She also pointed out however that some white feminist women who led the early movement for birth control in the U.S., including Margaret Sanger (1879-1966), became involved with eugenics. Loretta J. Ross charged that both wittingly and unwittingly the early feminists gave support to the growing number of racists "who were concerned about the rising population of African Americans."[182]

John Paul II used the opportunity of his brief visit to the United States in January 1999 to speak about the suffering of African Americans under the grips of slavery and racial discrimination. He also drew comparisons between abortion and denial of certain rights based solely on race and made references to slavery and racism in support of his arguments against abortion. Obviously,

John Paul II did not consider limiting priesthood to males only to be in any way comparable to racial discrimination. Commenting on the 1857 U.S. Supreme Court Dred Scott ruling that slaves were property and did not have rights as citizens, John Paul II described this decision as an attempt to put an entire class of people outside the protection of the law. He drew a comparison between those who before the Civil War denied freedom to African Americans and those Americans who today are in favor of abortion and euthanasia. Using his frequent theme of "the culture of life" versus "the culture of death," John Paul II described the conflict "between a culture that affirms, cherishes, and celebrates the gift of life, and a culture that seeks to declare entire groups of human beings — the unborn, the terminally ill, the handicapped, and others considered 'unuseful' — to be outside the boundaries of legal protection." Those familiar with Wojtyła's past are not surprised by this analogy, which may seem overwrought otherwise. During World War II, he himself experienced what it meant to be deprived of legal personhood, downgraded from a member of society to an object by the Nazis, who considered all Poles, as non-Aryan Slavs, to be subhuman — useful labor, nothing more.

It is not clear whether John Paul II saw abortion in the U.S. as a form of racial violence, but even though more abortions are being performed in the developing world and in some of the current and former communist countries, he still blamed the West for intro-ducing and spreading the idea of abortion and contraception. He believed the largely white and — in his opinion — powerful Left-wing liberal forces in the West were primarily responsible for what he considered to be a new form of genocide and "contraceptive imperialism" being forced on the Third World. Since secular and some religious feminists like Hillary Rodham Clinton were part of or closely identified with this group, their standing with John Paul II was never very high. Because John Paul II genuinely honored and admired women who conformed to his assumptions, he felt hurt and misunderstood when faced with frustration, rejection and even

Pro-Life Organizations

March for Life	**UK Life League**
http://www.marchforlife.org/	http://www.uklifeleague.com/
American Life League	**Society for the Protection of**
http://www.all.org/	**Unborn Children**
	http://www.spuc.org.uk/
Stand True Ministries	
http://www.standtrue.com/	**Voice for Life, New Zealand**
	http://www.voiceforlife.org.nz/
Rock for Life	
http://www.rockforlife.org/	**Christian Voice UK**
	http://www.christianvoice.org.uk/
Student LifeNet	
http://www.studentlifenet.co.uk/	**Precious Life**
	http://www.preciouslife.net/index.
LIFE	asp
http://www.lifecharity.org.uk/	

rage from women who did not agree with him that abortion was the same as murder and being pro-choice was the same as tolerating murder. He blamed the media for misinterpreting what he considered to be his positions in favor of women's rights and felt absolutely frustrated that the West did not see abortion and euthanasia as the greatest possible evils.

Papal Impact on the Abortion Debate in the U.S.

After many years of constant statements and warnings, toward the end his papacy Wojtyła's views were beginning to have an impact on the public discourse in the U.S. and the UK over the issues of abortion and euthanasia. While there still is almost no broad support for his positions on contraception, women-priests and priestly celibacy, pro-life activists and commentators are beginning to use some of his terminology and arguments against abortion and getting their message across to the American public through the media and through such pro-life organizations as March for Life, American Life League and Stand True Ministries. American Life League has launched Rock for Life project whose young members use some of John Paul II's pro-life messages about abortion, infanticide and euthanasia in appealing to America's youth through music and ministry. In the UK, pro-life organizations that have used John Paul II's anti-abortion concepts and messages include LIFE, UK Life League, Society for the Protection of Unborn Children, Christian Voice (UK), Voice for Life (New Zealand), Precious Life (Ireland and UK) and Prolife Alliance. Student LifeNet is a national coalition of pro-life UK students who defend human life from the moment of conception until natural death and have chapters at numerous universities.

In 1998, Peggy Noonan, a former speechwriter for President Ronald Reagan, wrote a commentary in *The New York Times* entitled, "In an Abortion Culture That Dulls Conscience."[183] "The culture of death" was an often-used phrase by John Paul II when referring to the way the American public views abortion. Peggy Noonan, like John Paul II, wondered what harm the public acceptance of abortions on demand has done to the minds and morality of American children. She wrote that the use by the media of such phrases as, "protecting the right to abortion," may have confused and morally dulled many of America's children to such an extent that a teenage American girl at a prom went back to the dance after delivering a baby in a bathroom and leaving it to die. President George W. Bush, in a phone call made in January 2002 to the March for Life president Nellie Gray, stated that a compassionate society will defend a moral proposition that "life should never be used as a tool, or a means to an end." Again, almost exactly the pope's words when he discussed abortion and the need to defend the dignity of human life. President George W. Bush also promised that his Administration will continue to speak out on behalf of "the most vulnerable members of our society," meaning the unborn, and defend the rights of everyone, "not just the healthy or the strong or the powerful." He declared himself to be on the side of "the unwanted" and called for setting a national goal that "unborn children should be welcomed in life and protected in law."

The U.S. President used concepts and phrases taken almost word for word from statements and warnings by John Paul II. George W. Bush made, however, an important acknowledgement seldom found in Wojtyła's public speeches. He noted that the abortion issue deeply divides the American society and that abortion opponents should treat those with whom they disagree with respect and civility. He called for overcoming the bitterness and rancor and for finding common ground.[184] The big difference between the position taken by President George W. Bush and many other Western leaders on one side, and Pope John Paul II on the other side, is that most Westerners accept the position in favor of abortion as a legitimate one for debate in a liberal society even if they do not agree with it, while John Paul II did not accept a pro-abortion viewpoint as legitimate and viewed defenders of the women's right to abortion almost as apologists for premeditated murder. That is why we saw frequent comparisons in the pope's speeches between abortion and the Nazi genocide.

Such comparisons have always been commonly used by abortion opponents in Poland, but more recently they are also becoming more common in the West, no doubt largely as a result of John Paul II's use of his strong language against abortion. In a letter to the editor of *USA Today*, a reader compared the Nazi crimes exposed at the Nuremberg trials after World War II to "inhumane medical procedures" called abortions, arguing that they are done for "selfish reasons" because individuals do not want to clutter their "living space" with unwanted children. In the opinion of the *USA Today* reader, this attitude is not much different from what the Nazis did during the war when they justified declaring some people to be sub-human and killed them to gain more *Lebensraum* (living space). The reader wondered when Americans will have their own Nuremberg trials.[185]

A pro-life activist in the U.S., Susan Carpenter Mcmillan, often describes abortion in her media commentaries as "America's Holocaust." Such comments do not go unchallenged, especially from the Jewish community. When a Catholic priest, John Joseph Powell, SJ published a book on abortion in 1981 titled, *Abortion: The Silent Holocaust*, some Jewish leaders in the U.S. regarded the analogy as offensive. He was defended, however, by an American rabbi Byron L. Sherwin, vice-president of the Spertus College of Judaica in Chicago, who conceded that Father Powell may have had the right to make such a comparison since his own grandfather had lost his life in Auschwitz. But in a 1992 interview with the Polish Catholic magazine, *Więź*, Rabbi Sherwin was opposed to making general comparisons between the Jewish Holocaust and abortion or the discrimination against women. He pointed out that such universalization of the Holocaust, when anyone who has been abused can speak about her or his own Holocaust, can be very dangerous: "The situation that a woman is in when she receives lower pay because of discrimination cannot be compared to the fate of people sent to concentration or death camps."[186]

Some Jewish survivals of the Holocaust also argue that one simply cannot compare the removal of an undeveloped fetus with the deliberate killing of living human beings, both children and adults with their past lives, hopes and dreams for the future. They were killed by the Nazis simply because they were Jewish. The strongest opponents of abortion in Poland, the U.S. and elsewhere do not accept such distinctions and continue to use John Paul's language and arguments to draw these comparisons. In Poland, however, most of the comparisons have not been with the Jewish Holocaust but rather with the Nazi killings of ethnic Poles. When discussing abortion, Catholic politicians in Poland used such statements as "Himmler's policy of national annihilation" [of the Polish nation], "anti-Polishness," and "desire to murder [Polish] children."[187] Mainstream commentators and political leaders in the U.S. almost never make direct references to genocide when discussing the issue of abortion, but unlike John Paul II and some of the Polish lawmakers, their life experiences did not expose them to indiscriminate killings of human beings on a mass scale. Karol Wojtyła and some of his supporters in Poland may claim to have a different perspective.

Comparisons between genocide and abortion are also a particularly sensitive issue in Germany, where a federal court declared in May 2000 that pro-life demonstrators could use the slogan "Holocaust then, Babycaust now" in their protests in front of abortion clinics.[188] German feminists complained that the verdict brands women as murderers, but this is exactly what John Paul II wanted the public to think about abortion, even while acknowledging that women seeking abortions are also victims. This important point, frequently made by John Paul II in his numerous appeals for extending help to pregnant women who are contemplating abortion, is often ignored by his most aggressive supporters. According to one Catholic observer, understanding of the drama of a woman seeking to terminate her pregnancy was lost among some churchmen during the abortion debate in Poland in the early 1990s. With the exception of one Polish bishop, Józef Życiński, who was Karol Wojtyła's close friend, the leadership of the Polish Church did not disavow comparisons between abortion and Nazi-perpetrated genocide.[189]

John Paul's outspokenness and activism in defense of life may have significantly contributed to recent changes in the American public's perception of abortion. Organizations, such as Feminists for Life, are active on college campuses advising women about alternatives to abortion. According to Serrin M. Foster, president of Feminists for Life, "one out of five abortions in the United States is performed on a college woman."[190] John Paul's message about abortion seems to be getting through to the American public more frequently now than when he was elected pope in 1978. More than a quarter-century after the legalization of abortion in the United States, overall support for abortion among Americans is declining. According to *The Los Angeles Times* poll, conducted in June 2000, 43 percent of survey respondents expressed support for legal abortion, compared with 56 percent in 1991. Americans, however, still continue to hold a more nuanced view of abortion than John Paul II—a position reflected in President George W. Bush's comments to the 2002 participants of the annual March for Life in Washington, D.C. *The Los Angeles Times* poll showed continued opposition among Americans to a constitutional ban on abortion. Of the 57 percent respondents who considered abortion to be murder, more than half believed that ultimately a woman should have the right to terminate her pregnancy. According to Susan Carroll, a researcher at the Center for American Women and Politics at Rutgers University in New Jersey, some Americans may view abortion as murder, but they do not want to impose their view on other people.

Support for Same-Sex Civil Unions	**Opposition to Legal Abortion**
Poland (2002) 15%	
U.S. (2007) 55%	Poland 40%
	U.S. 43%
Opposition to Same-Sex Civil Unions	**Support for Capital Punishment**
	Poland (2007) 63%
Poland (2002) 76%	U.S. (2006) 65%
U.S. (2007) 43%	
	Opposition to Capital Punishment
Support for Legal Abortion (2007)	Poland (2006) 31%
	U.S. (2007) 32%
Poland 50%	
U.S. 55%	Sources: CBOS (Poland), ABC News (U.S.)

She believes that "most Americans are in favor of letting people make their own individual choices."[191] This seems to be the main difference between liberal and traditional societies on this divisive issue.

John Paul's relentless anti-abortion and pro-life campaign may have contributed to some change of attitudes in the 1990s and beyond, but more recent public opinion polls still show that most Americans believe abortion should be legal. According to a November 2007 ABC News poll, 55 percent of Americans support legal abortion and 43 percent oppose it. In 1995, 60 percent favored legal abortion. Americans are considerably more liberal than Poles on homosexuality and gay civil unions. The same ABC poll in November 2007 also shows that the majority of Americans supports gay civil unions (55 percent — an increase from 40 percent in 2003), while 43 percent oppose such unions. In 2002, only 15 percent of respondents in Poland were in favor of gay civil unions, while 76 percent opposed them. On the abortion issue, differences in opinions between Poles and Americans are not as dramatic, even though most abortions in Poland are now illegal while abortion remains legal in the United States. In a poll conducted in August/September 2007 by CBOS, 50 percent of adult Poles expressed support for a woman's right to a legal abortion in the first weeks of pregnancy, while 40 percent opposed it. A differently worded question as to whether abortion should be allowed by law produced 47 percent of responses in favor of legalization and 45 percent against it. Some Polish respondents, who support woman's right to legal abortion in principle, do not support abortions under all circumstances, i.e. abortions on demand, but only those for which there is a sufficient justification. Therefore, comparing U.S. and Polish responses is difficult.

Opposition to abortion in Poland is much greater among people who regularly go to church, support Right-wing political parties and live in villages and small towns. Contrary to John Paul II's teachings, 63 percent of Poles support the death penalty and only

31 percent oppose it. Capital punishment has been outlawed in Poland since 1998 and no one has been executed since 1988. These numbers are not much different than in the U.S.: 65 percent were in favor and 32 percent were against the death penalty, according to a June 2006, ABC News/Washington Post poll.[192] Support for the death penalty in West European countries, however, is much lower than in the U.S. or in Poland.

On the question of legalizing abortion, John Paul II did not share a more tolerant outlook because for him it was not only a moral issue but an issue of inalienable human rights, and ultimately an issue of life and death. He believed that tolerating abortion now can have most profound implications for the future of society and he based his belief not only on the Bible but also on his personal knowledge of the Nazi extermination of Jews, the sterilization experiments and the murder of physically and mentally handicapped persons. He was convinced that abortion represents the most dangerous precedent that can in time invite further attacks on human life.

Abortion and the Death Penalty in the 2008 U.S. Presidential Elections

The former U.S. First Lady Hillary Rodham Clinton, who is well known for her pro-feminist views, made an indirect reference to possible comparisons between genocide and abortion in her now-famous 1999 comment of "keeping abortion safe, legal and rare into the next century."[193] Her position is that being pro-choice does not mean being pro-abortion, but her comment betrayed a possible recognition of a moral and religious dilemma in liberal stands on abortion. Unlike John Paul II, she believes that keeping abortions legal and protecting other rights of liberal societies would prevent re-emergence of genocidal regimes. In her 1996 book *It Takes a Village* (a highly revealing title), Hillary Clinton argued passionately for the rights of children but failed to deal with the physical and moral impact of abortion on children or the idea that "the village," especially in the less developed regions of the world, is often quite hostile to women, children and personal freedom. John Paul II would argue that the current feminist-dominated liberal "village" culture in countries like the United States tolerates and even encourages abortion and therefore contributes to the death of millions of unborn children and, as he put it, "turns parents against their children." In her book, Mrs. Clinton supported giving teenagers access to birth control and better sex education to prevent abortions. This approach was also anathema to John Paul II, but he would undoubtedly agree with most of Hillary Clinton's other left-of-center views on social issues, especially her attempts to introduce universal health insurance for Americans.

As a liberal and a moderate Christian feminist, Hillary Clinton might have been an ideal candidate to engage in a dialogue with John Paul II in an attempt to find common ground, but even she could not hide her deep hostility toward stands on women taken by the pope and the Vatican, and he in turn was quite vocal about his opposition to the Clinton Administration's positions on birth control and abortion, especially in the Third World. Mrs. Clinton has the support of EMILY's List, a political action committee (PAC) in the United States that aims to help elect to public office pro-choice Democratic Party women. (A pro-life equivalent of EMILY's List is Susan B. Anthony's List.) Hillary Clinton is hardly, however, the only pro-choice candidate among Democratic as well as Republican contenders for U.S. presidency in the 2008 elections. One of her main rivals for the Democratic Party presidential nomination, U.S. Senator Barak Obama (b. 1961) from Illinois, a member of the

---

Hillary Rodham Clinton

Born: October 26, 1947,

Chicago, Illinois, USA

www.hillaryclinton.com

Quote: "Keeping abortion safe, legal and rare into the next century."

EMILY's List

http://www.emilyslist.org

United Church of Christ, is also strongly pro-choice. Another former candidate, Republican Alan Keyes (b. 1950), while running for the U.S. Senate in 2004 against Barak Obama, said that "Christ would not vote for Obama" because of Obama's pro-choice stand. Obama and liberal media commentators criticized Keyes, who is Roman Catholic, for making this kind of comparison in a political context.

Both Obama and Keyes are African American Christians, yet they have vastly different views on abortion. A former Democratic contender, U.S. Senator Christopher Dodd (b. 1944) from Connecticut, another Roman Catholic but strongly pro-choice, has criticized the Vatican for condemning Catholic politicians who are pro-choice. Another Roman Catholic, Senator Joe Biden (b. 1942), a Democrat from Delaware, is a strong supporter of *Roe v. Wade* Supreme Court decision legalizing abortion, although he said that he is prepared to accept the Catholic Church teaching that life begins at conception. Yet another Catholic politician, Congressman Dennis Kucinich (b. 1946), a Democrat from Ohio, had been against abortion on demand earlier in his political career but changed his position before the 2004 elections and is now pro-choice. Unlike most other candidates who are Catholic, Kucinich is against the death penalty, so at least on this issue he agrees with Pope John Paul II. Democratic Governor of

---

Contenders for U.S. Presidency in 2008 (Roman Catholic)

Pro-Life

Sam Brownback (D)

Alan Keyes (R)

Pro-Choice

Joe Biden (D)

Christopher Dodd (D)

Rudolph Giuliani (R)

Dennis Kucinich (D)

Bill Richardson (D)

Only Senator Sam Brownback (D) and Rep. Dennis Kucinich indicated their opposition to the death penalty on moral and spiritual grounds.

New Mexico, Bill Richardson (b. 1947), a Roman Catholic of Hispanic background, is also pro-choice. Former U.S. Senator John Edwards (b. 1953), a North Carolina Democrat and member of the United Methodist Church, is pro-choice, as is former U.S. Senator from Alaska Mike Gravel (b. 1930) who is a member of the Unitarian Universalist Church.

Pope John Paul II would have been appalled that nearly all contenders for U.S. presidency in 2008 who are Roman Catholic are also pro-choice. Almost all of them are also in favor of the death penalty under certain limited circumstances. Pro-choice Democrats, however, are more likely than pro-life Republicans to support social welfare programs strongly favored by the previous pope. Sam Brownback (b. 1956), the Republican U.S. Senator from Kansas, is strongly pro-life, but he has withdrawn his candidacy and now supports Senator McCain. In October 2007, Brownback told *Christianity Today* that he sees abortion "as the lead moral issue of our day, just like slavery was the lead moral issue 150 years ago." Pope John Paul II also made this comparison. In speaking out against the death penalty during a Senate hearing in February 2006, Senator Brownback used the "culture of life" term frequently mentioned by the pope: "If use of the death penalty is contrary to promoting a *culture of life*, we need to have a national dialogue and hear both sides of the issue. All life is sacred, and our use of the death penalty in the American justice system must recognize this truth."

One of the major Republican contenders, former New York City mayor Rudolph Giuliani (b. 1944), said that he "hates" abortion but believes in "woman's right to choose." Giuliani, also a Roman Catholic, has been divorced and remarried. Another former Republican contender W. Mitt Romney (b. 1947), who is a Mormon, is now pro-life, but earlier in his

Religion, Politics, Abortion

The Pew Forum on Religion & Public Life

http://pewforum.org/

political career he was pro-choice. One of the contenders with the strongest anti-abortion record was Republican Duncan Hunter (b. 1948), a Southern Baptist from California. He has sponsored a bill in Congress which would have guaranteed unborn children all legal rights of personhood from the moment of conception. He also sponsored the Unborn Child Pain Awareness Act of 2006, which would have required abortion providers to inform women that a fetus feels pain after 20 weeks and offer anesthesia for the fetus. The expected Republican presidential candidate, U.S. Senator from Arizona, John McCain (b 1936), who is a Baptist, also has a strong anti-abortion record and supports overturning *Roe v. Wade*.

Another Baptist, Republican Congressman Ron Paul (b. 1935) from Texas, who is also a medical doctor, believes that the fetus is a human being with full rights from the moment of conception. Ron Paul was the only major pro-life candidate who in addition to opposing abortion also strongly opposes the death penalty. As reported in *The Pew Forum on Religion and Public Life*, Paul praised the late Pope John Paul II in 2005 for being an "eloquent and consistent advocate for an ethic of life, exemplified by his struggles against abortion, war, euthanasia and the death penalty." Former Republican U.S. Senator from Tennessee and television actor Fred Thompson (b. 1942) is a pro-life member of the Church of Christ, but he once expressed an opinion that abortion should not be criminalized. Tom Tancredo (b. 1945), a Republican Congressman from Colorado, who is an evangelical Presbyterian, believes that "abortion compromises the sanctity of human life" and he has called *Roe v. Wade* "a scar on the moral and intellectual history of the country" — opinions that Pope John Paul II had expressed using very similar language.

Governor Mike Huckabee (b. 1955), a Baptist, is anti-abortion, but this Republican politician from Arkansas has said that even though he strongly supports pro-life advocacy, he believes some people in the pro-life community are putting too much focus on the gestation period rather than being concerned with the welfare of

Oprah Supports Obama

Religion and politics are closely connected in America, but not always in conventional ways. Pro-choice Obama has won the endorsement of popular African American television host Oprah Winfrey. She was described in the *Christianity Today* magazine as one of the most influential spiritual leaders in America—a postmodern figure who combines Christianity with other religious and spiritual traditions. Winfrey is also known for her support of education for women and other philanthropic activities worldwide. According to *Christianity Today* writer LaTonya Taylor, "to her audience of more than 22 million mostly female viewers, she has become a postmodern priestess—an icon of church-free spirituality."[194] Her official web site (http://www2.oprah.com/) has a special section called "Spirit and Self," and she has had on her show various figures representing spirituality and mysticism of New Thought, New Age, Zen Buddhism and Hinduism. Among those appearing on her show were: Deepak Chopra, Gary Zukav, Caroline Myss, Marianne Williamson and Iyanla Vanzant. But John Paul II was known to oppose New Age religions or any kind of spiritual experimentation and merging of religious traditions that allows individuals to establish and follow their own moral code on such issues as abortion.

children throughout their lives—a position that would have been highly applauded by Pope John Paul II who was responsible for launching programs to help unwed mothers in his Kraków Archdiocese. But had he lived longer, the Polish pope would have been deeply disappointed to learn—although perhaps not surprised considering his low opinion of American Catholicism— that almost all contenders for the U.S. presidency in 2008 who are Catholics are pro-choice and that, with the exception of Alan Keyes, the only committed pro-life candidates were mainstream Protestants and Evangelicals.

CHAPTER FIVE

Contraception versus Love – Agenda for Polish Women 1947-1978

Progressive within the Polish Church

Although by most Western standards, John Paul II was very conservative on most moral issues and on the question of more openness in governing the Church, but by the standards of the Polish Church, Karol Wojtyła could be easily described as a socially progressive priest and bishop.

He was not afraid to break with some of the traditions, which

> *... a civilization, which rejects the defenseless, deserves to be called barbarian, even if it has great economic, technological, artistic, and scientific achievements ...*
>
> Karol Wojtyła, 1997

he considered unworthy of Christianity, even though he would never take a confrontational stand against the Church or against his conservative supporters. More than other Catholic priests in Poland before and after World War II, Wojtyła consistently promoted religious tolerance and a dialogue with other religions. He also supported establishing a dialogue with the Left-wing atheists who turned against communism and at one time sought support from the Polish Church. John Paul II was the first pope to establish diplomatic relations with Israel. Even though he was brought up in a largely patriarchal tradition, in later years he embraced at least some of the less radical demands of feminists. He was the first Archbishop of Kraków and the first pope to visit a synagogue. And while his wartime experiences in Poland may have made him a conservative on moral issues, they also made him an ardent defender of human dignity and religious tolerance. He was a strong promoter of better relations between the Catholic Church and other religions.

Wojtyła was also an early supporter of increasing the role of the lay Catholics within the Polish Church. At one of the meetings of the Second Vatican Council dealing with lay Catholics, Wojtyła was the only speaker who specifically recognized and addressed the women-auditors who, for the first time in the Church's history, were allowed to listen to but not to participate in the Council's proceedings.[1] Even before he became bishop, Wojtyła worked hard to reform some of the outdated customs among Polish priests. Prof. Irena Sławińska, who taught literature at the Catholic University in Lublin (KUL), remembers being invited by Wojtyła to address a group of priests in the mid 1950s on the need to change some of their terminology in communicating with the faithful. She made fun of such terms as "beloved little children," "pious young man," and "Christian virgins." According to her, Wojtyła tried to tone down her biting humor and to calm down the angered priests, but at the same time he strongly defended the need to change the language of priestly sermons to make them more appealing to a younger audience.[2]

Despite his progressive leanings, Wojtyła did not consider himself to be a religious innovator. While progressive on a number of issues, especially when compared with the vast majority of his fellow Polish priests, he remained a staunch conservative on the basic tenets of Catholicism, including celibacy for priests, keeping women out of the priesthood, and maintaining a strong position against divorce, abortion and contraception. Wojtyła stressed his conservative religious roots when he spoke during his formal entrance to the Wawel Cathedral in Kraków after becoming archbishop: "There is nothing original in this program—it is simple and ancient. Ancient issues—God's issues—are the most simple and deep; it is not necessary to create new programs; one must only enter into this ancient program in a new way."[3]

Father Maliński described Wojtyła as a strong supporter of preserving traditional beliefs and saw this as the most characteristic feature of his personality. He pointed to Wojtyła's sermon after his nomination as the archbishop of Kraków, in which he declared that he had no desire to be an innovator. On the contrary, he promised to preserve all the old values which the Poles had accepted for centuries. In 1974, he instructed the priests in his archdiocese to continue to wear clerical clothes in public as a sign of opposition against the process of secularization. He also told the priests to insist that they should be addressed as "Father."[4] According to Father Maliński, Wojtyła believed that there was nothing to be uncovered, discovered or changed in what is already contained in Scripture. The Church's message needs to be instead implemented, adhered to, and lived by. Maliński described Wojtyła as a defender of "old dogmas, values and truths."[5] (This was another aspect of Wojtyła's personality which Maliński emphasized in his many books about John Paul II. I found plenty of other evidence to support these observations, but Maliński's descriptions sometimes seem somewhat exaggerated. Maliński was a more liberal priest than Wojtyła and despite their friendship, John Paul II did not offer him any higher Church titles or positions.) If there was anything new in what Wojtyła recommended to the believers, it was that they should try to experience the old values more deeply.

Maliński warned, however, that Wojtyła's apparent conservatism should not be interpreted as anti-intellectual. Wojtyła was a deep thinker who, to the maximum extent possible, tried to reconcile reason with religious faith and philosophy with theology. He was after all for many years a university professor and wrote quasi-scientific books on love and sex. He believed, however, that reason alone cannot explain God or be a substitute for faith. He would not challenge what he perceived to be God's revealed truths. At the same time, Wojtyła was never an overly aggressive promoter of faith nor tried to impose his views on others, except for a few issues he cared most deeply about, such as abortion, euthanasia, promotion of peace, and what he perceived as fatal moral failures of the West. He respected his opponents and their right to hold their own views, but after the fall of communism in East Central Europe, he did everything he could to defend the Church from what he thought were attacks of secular and liberal Western forces on the Church's most traditional values. He was also not reluctant to promote those values and to constantly remind Catholics how the Church expects them to behave.

While most media accounts of Wojtyła's papacy tend to simplify his views and describe them as extremely conservative, John Paul II is not easy to categorize. As a young priest and later a bishop in Poland, Wojtyła expanded his activities beyond the normal scope of religious and patriotic duties and became interested in issues of love, marriage, sex and family life. Father Maliński noted Wojtyła's active participation in drafting the reforms of the Second Vatican Council, particularly his efforts in promoting reconciliation and dialogue between Catholicism and other religions. One of Wojtyła's papers presented to the bishops at the Second Vatican Council was on the subject of ecumenism. In a speech to the bishops he also addressed the subject of religious tolerance which, as Father Maliński observed, was not a favorite topic with the other bishops at the time.[6] Maliński was most likely referring to the Polish and West European bishops, since the idea of ecumenical dialogue and reconciliation with other religions enjoyed strong support among some of the American bishops and was strongly promoted by Father John Courtney Murray, SJ (1904-1967) and other American theologians.

Wojtyła also repeatedly spoke out against anti-Semitism and all forms of discrimination, including discrimination of women. His open and tolerant attitude toward other religions did not extend, however, to radical feminism and those who support abortion rights for women. John Paul II generally did not see the complaints by women against the Catholic Church in the same light as the discussion of religious or racial intolerance. As for the treatment of women, he was willing to reject some but not all parts of the Catholic tradition and doctrine going back to the Church's very roots. His openness and tolerance had much stricter limits in this case. Feminism and calls for the ordination of women also tended to complicate for him the dialogue with the other major religions, all of which, to lesser or greater degrees, with the exception of some the more progressive Protestant churches in the West and some liberal Jewish congregations, promote a subservient role for women. Overall, Wojtyła was a radical defender of human life, an ecumenical progressive and a conservative on some but not all issues affecting women. Maliński also suggests that at some point during the Second Vatican Council and as a result of his travels in Western Europe, Wojtyła concluded that Vatican II reformers went too far and that extremists were beginning to exert too much influence. But like Joseph Ratzinger, John Paul II's future right-hand-man, enforcer of Church dogma and future pope, Karol Wojtyła was seen during the Second Vatican Council as one of the more liberal bishops.

Birth Control and Poland's Population Losses

The historical perspective of Poland's tremendous population losses during World War II and as a result of the communist regime's repression against the armed underground and other political opponents immediately after the war determined to some degree Wojtyła's opposition to abortion. About three million ethnic Poles were killed by the Nazis or died as a result of war. Hundreds of thousands of patriotic Poles were killed or died in the Soviet Union, and thousands perished after the war during communist repression. After the war, communist media gave much publicity to the practice of kidnapping of Polish children by the Nazis and their forcible Germanization in institutions and private homes in Germany. After the war, both the communist media and the Church condemned the kidnapping of Polish children as an attempt to biologically weaken the Polish nation while increasing the strength of Germany.[7] In addition to deriving economic benefits from sending young Polish men and women of reproductive age to Germany for forced labor and restricting their sexual relations, the Nazis also hoped to stop and reverse the growth of the Polish population.[8] Polish slave laborers in Nazi Germany were forbidden to have sexual relations with other Poles, and a Pole having intercourse with a German was subject to the death penalty.

The Nazi sexual and genetic policies had a definite impact on how Karol Wojtyła and the Polish Church viewed various issues connected with sex and procreation after the war. They were widely discussed and condemned in Poland as an attack on the biological existence of the Polish nation. The communist regime, while supporting abortion, also made the attacks on the Nazi genetic experiments part of its propaganda campaign against West Germany, NATO and United States. The Church saw the "demographic threat" as a powerful weapon to be used against the regime in sermons on abortion, contraception and even alcoholism. The bishops presented population growth while opposing contraception and abortion as a patriotic duty in addition to being a moral and religious obligation. Wojtyła's sermons and letters to the faithful as the Archbishop of Kraków reflected this attitude. He often urged Poles to have larger families while warning of "demographic threats" to the nation. In 1964, he asked Polish nuns for special prayers so that modern parents would overcome their fear of children.[9] In his 1968 Lenten message, he wrote that "Our demographic situation is bad, and the number of unborn children who have been deprived of their lives in their mother's womb [is] frightening."[10] The same theme appears Wojtyła's speech to families in June 1977:

> ...I can't but express sorrow that in families, which claim to belong to the Church, children are dying in their mothers' wombs. ...But this is the issue for the whole Nation. It cannot be

left alone. We cannot go blindly into the future when a new human being is missing. The old becomes new through man. ...One must bow before each mother in Poland who conceived a new person, a new Pole; one must bow with worship, not with a surgeon's scalpel. One must not say: this will be taken care of with a procedure. For the nation must not weaken. The nation must not cause its own death. It has been destroyed enough during our distant and recent past... Too many irresponsible people, heartless people have been created in Poland. This type of person is even to some degree being promoted. One must respect his father and his mother because this is the issue of our future.[11]

Preventing population losses in Poland was also a theme in his 1970 letter to newlywed couples in which Wojtyła called on them "to love even now their future children, to want give children to one another, [and] to want to give children to the Fatherland and the Church."[12]

Wojtyła was not deterred by any obstacles, especially those put up by the communist regime. He would appeal to the communist leaders' sense of patriotism by calling on the communist authorities "to create all [necessary] conditions" so that "the Polish family could produce new people." He also offered prayers that Poland would not experience a shortage of people.[13] In 1970, Wojtyła told newlywed couples that "while for a married couple, children are the confirmation and crowning of their marital and familial love, for the Church and the Fatherland, they are the fulfillment of the society's future."[14] He told the newlyweds that they should already feel love for their future children and not limit their number due to purely material considerations and a desire for comfort. He appealed to them to give children to each other and to the Fatherland and the Church.

The same year, Wojtyła told the faithful in his archdiocese that "giving life within a family guarantees the life of a larger society, above all [the life of] a nation, which can find its members only in families. If [a nation] wants to live, [it] must support life, and not condemn to death [its] children, even those not yet born." Wojtyła also warned that the break-up of families would lead to the break-up of society. In 1971, Wojtyła asked the nuns in his archdiocese to pray for a stop to "immoral methods of escape from procreation."[15] The following year, he asked the nuns to pray for an end to "rape and violence even against the unborn."[16] Already in the 1970s, Cardinal Wojtyła warned that the failure of marriages constitutes a moral weakness of modern societies regardless of the level of their political, technological or social advancement.[17]

Tragic events in Poland, such as the killings during workers' demonstrations in 1956 and 1970, continued to influence and reinforce Wojtyła's unshakable opposition to abortion and birth control. The communist repression was a continuing reminder of the threats facing the nation that had always been part of his life in Poland. Speaking in 1970 after the publication of the official number of people killed during workers' demonstrations, Wojtyła stressed that these events "have caused us to offer a special prayer for the Fatherland, and brought before our eyes the basic value that is the value of human life."[18] In his Lenten pastoral letter, issued in February 1971 after the massacre of the Polish workers in Gdańsk, Cardinal Wojtyła made numerous arguments in defense of the fifth commandment. He again spoke of the "biological threat to our society" and extended his appeal to show respect for human life by including the lives of severely handicapped persons.[19] There were many other similar appeals to patriotic feelings and warnings about "a demographic threat to the nation...":

Let's not forget that ultimately this threat comes from not respecting each and every life which was conceived in the womb of woman-mother on our Polish soil (...) In Poland, we are all—believers and unbelievers—faced with enormous historical threat, which is linked with enormous historical moral challenge. This is the challenge of rebuilding the sense of life's value and society's respect for parenthood: fatherhood and motherhood.[20]

Alcoholism was yet another threat that concerned Cardinal Wojtyła. He saw alcoholism as a problem creating situations in which abortion became more likely. He may have also seen the link between alcoholism and domestic abuse but did not choose to focus exclusively on the issue of violence against women. In a 1968 address to men, Wojtyła told them that rejecting alcohol requires sometimes greater heroism than hand to hand combat with an enemy.[21] Also in 1968, he reminded the faithful that people in Poland were consuming 130 million liters of alcohol a year and that between 600,000 and 800,000 persons in Poland get drunk every day.[22] In 1978, he warned Poles that excessive drinking by their ancestors contributed to the loss of Poland's independence.[23] He acknowledged that alcoholism also contributed to sexual promiscuity, abortion, the fall of marital morality and breakup of families, but he would not make a specific link in his public statements between alcoholism and physical abuse of women. For him, abortion remained the primary factor undermining Poland's strength as a nation in addition to being a moral sin. Alcoholism

Home for single mothers in Kraków (2007).

contributed to the weakening of the nation, because it encouraged both sexual promiscuity and abortion.

In 1974, Cardinal Wojtyła started a special fund to help single mothers and mothers with many children. This program became known as "Cardinal Wojtyła's SOS." Calling abortion "undoubtedly, the most painful wound for the Church and the Catholic society in Poland...," Wojtyła continued to intensify his appeals to the patriotism of the Poles.[24] In his sermons he stressed that abortion raises "fear for the future of the entire Nation, which throughout the years lost millions of its sons and daughters due to the violations of the fifth commandment."[25]

Speaking about the Church's campaign against abortion and contraception, he called in 1972 for a "great Christian effort" to prevent the dying off of Poland's population.[26] At the same time, he blamed the communist regime for "years of fatal anti-conception propaganda, dictated by economic plans," which undermined the ethical foundation of the society.[27] For Wojtyła, "people who do not worship God" will sooner or later show that they will not respect another human being.[28]

"Window of Life" at the home for single mothers in Kraków.

Neal Ascherson (b. 1932), a British journalist who has reported extensively on Poland for over 40 years, described Wojtyła's close personal interest in a young Polish girl whose mother was subjected to medical experiments by Dr. Josef Mengele (1911-1979) in Auschwitz. Her ovaries were irradiated without any anesthetic, but by a miracle, the woman survived the camp. After the war, she married and made desperate attempts to reverse the results of Nazi medical experiments in order to have a child. Finally, after many operations she gave birth to a beautiful, intelligent girl. The daughter of the woman, who had suffered so terribly in Auschwitz, became for Wojtyła a living proof of the miracle of life and the victory of life over death. Wojtyła took her under his personal care, spending time with her and giving her skiing lessons even when he was already a cardinal. As Neal Ascherson observed, the story of this young Polish girl and her mother may help some people in the West understand why Wojtyła arrived at his strongly held views about contraception, abortion, and euthanasia, even if they ultimately do not agree with his conclusions.

Neal Ascherson believes that Wojtyła opposed contraception and abortion for reasons that go well beyond his obvious natural inclination to uphold religious dogma.[29] He was an eyewitness to the murder of the Jews and realized that the Poles could be the next victims of mass extermination by the Nazis. Protecting life of individuals was a matter of keeping alive the entire nation. As a patriotic Pole, he was going to do everything possible to ensure the survival of his people, their language and their culture. In Neal Ascherson's view, it was Wojtyła's personal experience rather than theology and religion that determined his attitudes on sexuality and reproduction.

Love and Responsibility

In 1960 Wojtyła published *Love and Responsibility*, a pioneering book on personal morality, which reveals the core of his beliefs on human dignity, love, personal responsibility, sex and marriage. Anyone who reads this book, which was first published in English in 1981, can see that John Paul II used the same basic arguments against artificial birth control and abortion that he used later in his writings as pope. He also continued to employ the same reasons for justifying his belief that birth control and abortion are closely linked. After developing these ideas as a result of his talks with young Polish men and women in the 1950s, Wojtyła never modified them after moving from Poland to the Vatican. In his mind, artificial birth control and abortion were both designed to interfere with the natural law. While the book deals with human sexuality, the main theme of Wojtyła's philosophical and theological analysis centers around the protection of human dignity. In *Love and Responsibility*, Wojtyła tried to show that Christianity is incompatible with treating persons as objects to be used for sexual pleasure or economic gain without considering first the other person's well being.

One of the most striking characteristics of his book is the depth of Wojtyła's opinions on the subject of sex and the strength of his convictions. As an ardent defender of human dignity, he saw numerous and serious dangers of sexual exploitation.

> *A person may not acquire another person: a person must always remain a gift for another person.*
>
> Cardinal Wojtyła at a wedding ceremony in Poland, Nov. 7. 1970

Artificial birth control, sex for pleasure, sex without love and sex outside of marriage—Wojtyła strongly condemned all of these as attacks on human dignity. In the book, he also developed his ideas on different family needs and roles for men and women. He even attempted to analyze sexual dysfunctions and their possible cures while taking issue with some of the professional practices of psychiatry based on Freud's theories which, in his view, failed to include the spiritual dimension of human sexuality.

In the introduction to *Love and Responsibility*, Wojtyła strongly defended the right of priests, who like himself lead a celibate life, to speak out on the subject of sex despite, what he admitted, was their lack of direct personal experience. According to Wojtyła, priests who do not marry or have sexual relations are nevertheless fully qualified to discuss and analyze sexuality because of their vast second-hand experience through pastoral work. In fact, in his opinion, priests may be better qualified to speak on the subject because of their concern with the principles of sexual morality, whereas medicine and psychology can only make a secondary contribution. Science, according to Wojtyła, does not deal with love and responsibility, which for him were the essential elements of a good marriage. Wojtyła argued that these two elements should be of primary importance in relationships between men and women.

Wojtyła's assertion that as a priest he was fully qualified to write about sex and love has been challenged by many feminists and other critics, including one of his former collaborators Dr. Anna-Teresa Tymieniecka. She described Wojtyła to American journalist Carl Bernstein as a modest man in supreme command of himself who knew very little about love and sex. According to the account of this conversation in Bernstein's and Politi's book, she saw Wojtyła as sexually innocent and naïve, but otherwise extremely wise in protecting the Church from the communist regime.[30] In a conversation I had with Dr. Tymieniecka in May 2007, she questioned whether Mr. Bernstein had adequately described her comments about Wojtyła's knowledge of love, sex and marriage. She insisted that she did not have discussions about this topic with Wojtyła because this was not something that interested her. (Bernstein and Politi reported that Dr. Tymieniecka was responding to what she had read in Wojtyła's book *Love and Responsibility*.) She said that the focus of her discussions with Wojtyła was phenomenology. She also said that what she was trying to tell Mr. Bernstein was that Wojtyła's primary concern was preserving the divine gift of love and life within a union between a man and a woman—something Wojtyła was, in her view, certainly competent to talk about. She said that unfortunately too many people see John Paul II's comments about sexual morality in too narrow terms and do not grasp that because of his deep love for all mankind, the pope was mainly concerned with broader questions of how people should treat their partners.[31]

In developing the philosophical argument in *Love and Responsibility*, Wojtyła observed that unlike animals, man possesses a spiritual life which allows him to seek out truth and goodness and to make moral choices. People use things and animals for their own benefit all the time, but is it permissible—Wojtyła asked—to use a person as a means to an end? His answer was an unqualified "no." "Anyone who treats a person as the means to an end does violence to the very essence of the other, to what constitutes its natural right."[32] Wojtyła pointed out that even God did not use a person as the means toward an end, since he gave man a free will to think and to make moral choices. Wojtyła concluded that only love for another person can eliminate the possibility that a woman or a man could be viewed with a utilitarian or consumer-like attitude and be treated only as a source of enjoyment or sexual pleasure.

A utilitarian approach to life, in which individuals are concerned with maximizing pleasure and minimizing pain is—as Wojtyła observed—"characteristic of modern man's mentality and his attitude to life."[33] Wojtyła applied this view largely to Western societies. Rather than viewing them as practical, pragmatic and based on compromise and liberal ideas of individual freedoms, for Wojtyła the utilitarian attitude represented "the greediest kind of egotism."[34] He advocated instead the personalistic norm of behavior, which claims that "the value of the person is always greater than the value of pleasure."[35] Thus, a person must always be treated "as the object of love, not as the object for use."[36]

In the area of sexuality, Wojtyła believed that men and women are capable of rising above the instinct of sexual urge for pleasure only. This means being able to achieve their existential goal of bringing about new life in respect and love for the other person. He postulated further that undermining the proper purpose of sex, by using such means as artificial birth control, damages love and respect between persons. He also maintained that life not only begins at conception, but also that both body and soul are united by God at the moment of conception as "God Himself takes the supreme part in the creation of a human person in the spiritual, moral, [and] strictly supernatural sphere."[37] Man and woman, in his view, are not the creators of life but merely co-creators of it with God.

Unlike some of his more recent papal predecessors, Wojtyła

rejected the negative view of sex and sexual desire as something nearly always sinful or at best only necessary for procreation. In his book, he promoted romantic love and underscored its enormous importance in human relationships. Some may have seen his views on sex as naïve, but as one papal historian noted, John Paul II "is probably the only pope in history who's actually written about a female orgasm as a good thing."[38] In his book *Love and Responsibility,* Wojtyła concluded that "it is necessary to insist that intercourse must not serve merely as a means of allowing sexual excitement to reach its climax in one of the partners, i.e. the man alone, but that climax must be reached in harmony, not at the expense of one partner..." He was most likely using information provided to him by Dr. Wanda Półtawska, his chief advisor on sex. In the same book Wojtyła advised his readers that "arousal in woman is different from that in man—it rises more slowly and falls more slowly." He urged that "[T]he man must take this difference between male and female reactions into account... ." He stated further that "[I]f a woman does not obtain natural gratification from the sexual act, there is a danger that her experience of it will be qualitatively inferior, [and] will not involve her fully as a person." Probably also as a result of advice received from Dr. Półtawska, he added that the lack of orgasm "makes nervous reactions only too likely, and may for instance cause secondary frigidity."[39] Orgasm is a good thing, however, only in the context of a loving marriage which is open to procreation and in which neither of the spouses sees the other as only the object of pleasure.

Wojtyła definitely disagreed with the traditional Church concept that sexuality and marriage are only good because they lead to procreation. Intercourse, according to Wojtyła, "is necessary to love, not just to procreation," otherwise procreation in the absence of love also leads to treating a person as an object for use.[40] He pointed out further that there can be two kinds of love: love as desire and love as goodwill. Love as desire is necessary for the attraction between man and woman that leads to procreation, but it is not sufficient in itself. A person must above all be concerned not with one's own well being, but with the well being of the other person. Wojtyła warned that "it is not enough to long for a person as good for oneself, one must also, and above all, long for that person's good."[41] In this context, Wojtyła saw any attempt to exclude the possibility of conception by artificial means as changing the emphasis of a relationship from love to enjoyment, and therefore again making the person an object for use. But he failed to explain why people who use contraceptives are more likely to objectify their partners than those who do not. He was only willing to accept the natural method of birth control, i.e. the rhythm method, which does not directly interfere with fertility. Even then husband and wife, according to Wojtyła, must be totally willing to accept the possibility of pregnancy.

Wojtyła's views were clearly in opposition to various Western philosophies, including liberalism, utilitarianism and existentialism, which put much more stress on the individual in the development of his or her own personal morality. Marian Jaworski (b. 1926), a fellow priest in Kraków and a dean of the Theological Department at the Jagiellonian University, described Wojtyła's writings as a counterpoint to Sartre and the existentialists. Wojtyła not only believed in the existence of God and in permanent moral values, but also in the human potential for discovering and implementing God's will through man's thoughts and actions. Wojtyła also believed that "man is not mere consciousness but fulfills himself in action." His books stress the importance of human experience: sensory and intellectual, but also metaphysical. He assigned to humans the responsibility for their actions and stressed solidarity with other men and women. Wojtyła told men and women that instead of existential alienation, they must have a positive relationship to the humanity of others and a sense of community. No individual must be treated as simply a means to an end. The essential feature of the experience of love, according to Wojtyła, is "belonging" or "giving oneself entirely to the beloved."

But while such an idealistic view of love and marriage is certainly appealing to many, it can also be used to justify exploitation of women under the pretext of love by promoting the idea that love requires sacrifices in situations where both partners may not have an equal status to begin with. The problem of unequal status of men and women in marriage, which is quite common in traditional societies, has been brought up consistently by feminists and liberals in criticizing Wojtyła's idealistic philosophy and his theology of love.

Family Counseling in the Kraków Archdiocese

Karol Wojtyła was not only active writing books about love and human sexuality but also devoted a lot of time and effort to marriage and family ministry based on the idea that sex cannot be treated in purely physiological or scientific ways. Catholic marriage counseling was a novelty in Poland after the war, and Wojtyła became its chief promoter and pioneer among the Polish clergy and among his parishioners. The Catholic counselors and volunteers, recruited by Wojtyła in the Kraków Archdiocese to advise couples before and during marriage, were asked "to stress with full determination that erotic experiences cannot be the essential purpose of married life."[42] The purpose of marriage, according to Wojtyła, was to be found in forming a family unit and in deepening spiritual love between the two people. The second order to counselors, most of whom were women, was to let young couples know that contraception leads to abortion. They were to tell them that contraception has the potential of introducing the idea that parents can kill their own unborn children. As early as the late 1940s, Wojtyła rejected the argument that contraception could reduce the number of abortions or, assuming it is still wrong, be allowed as a lesser evil.

Marriage counseling, according to Wojtyła, should be linked with ethics and not with "techniques" in managing human relationships. God, the "Giver of Life," calls upon married couples to cooperate with Him. Only in this context can problems of married life be analyzed and solved. Family counselors were also asked to teach married couples that their love can be developed through both sexual relations and temporary abstinence from sex. Finally, the counselors were to provide married couples with ethical arguments in support of natural birth control methods, but they were also to express concern for the need to assure the survival of the nation through maintaining large families.[43] Women selected for training as family counselors had to be nominated by their parish priests and accepted by Cardinal Wojtyła. They had to be conscientious, discreet, easy to get along with, high-school graduates, and be no older than 45.[44] Training consisted of four one-day sessions of prayers and lectures. From 1969 to 1978, 541 counselors were success-fully trained.[45] Catholic marriage counseling is now well established in many

Catholic Marriage Counseling

Catholic Engaged Encounter
http://www.engagedencounter.org/

Catholic Worldwide Marriage Encounter
http://www.wwme.org/

Retrouvaille
http://www.retrouvaille.org/

Center for Peace in the Family
http://www.peaceinthefamily.org/

Counseling Catholics
http://www.counselingcatholics.com/

countries through such programs as Catholic Engaged Encounter, Catholic Worldwide Marriage Encounter, *Retrouvaille* and others.

A paper entitled *The Mystery of Human Sexual Physiology*, which was found among Wojtyła's documents in Kraków, throws some additional light on his conclusions about sex. Although some doubt exists whether Wojtyła was the author of this paper, it does contain many of his views expressed elsewhere and it has all the characteristics of a lecture which could have been delivered to family counselors being trained under his guidance. The basic premise of the paper comes from Wojtyła's book *Love and Responsibility*. Man, unlike animals, is guided by thinking and has more than just physical and material needs. Animals possess natural instincts which guide them to live harmoniously with nature. Man's life, on the other hand, is full of mistakes, some of which lead to tragedies, as man rarely understands the full truth about himself. The paper's author, who may have been Wojtyła himself or Dr. Wanda Półtawska, takes issue with modern science and medicine for treating human beings as merely bodies without paying sufficient attention to human spirituality. Psychiatrists, for example, want to remove "sin" from human vocabulary, claiming that this outmoded concept causes dangerous neurosis. Sin, however, according to the author, is a God-given concept that allows human beings to determine which actions are good and which can lead to self-destruction. As pope, John Paul II continued to stress this view of sin especially when addressing people in the West, whom he frequently accused of trying to pervert the difference between good and evil by promoting individual morality.

The author argued that religious faith is not an obstacle to science but allows for a better understanding of human life by addressing the spiritual dimension. Medicine can make the mistake of separating the physical and spiritual dimensions of human sexuality. In a human being, sexual drive, according to the author, ought to be organically linked with the spiritual ability to love. Children must be taught this as soon as they begin to discover their sexuality. They should not be punished when caught experimenting with their bodies, but appropriately for their age should be taught that sex must be linked with love and sexual relations are reserved for marriage. Masturbation is a sin because it focuses one's sexual attention on oneself rather than on another person; it is therefore unnatural. The author warns that sexual experiences at a very early age can lead to various sexual deviations in later life and urges that children should be taught chastity and abstinence.

Wojtyła's Contribution to Humanae vitae – Encyclical on the Regulation of Birth

Wojtyła's views on love, marriage, sex and birth control, as developed by him in the 1950s and 1960s, had a greater impact on the Catholic Church outside of Poland than most people realize even today. John Paul II's biographer, Polish-born American journalist Tad Szulc (1926-2001), is one of several authors who reported that Cardinal Wojtyła had been instrumental in convincing Pope Paul VI to issue his 1968 encyclical *Humanae vitae* with its ban on artificial contraception.[46] Apparently on advice from Wojtyła and under his strong influence, Paul VI decided to declare the ban on artificial birth control despite opposition from the majority of mostly Western churchmen and lay experts who were asked by his predecessor, Pope John XXIII, to study the issue. Among those consulted by the commission were Patricia (Patty) Crowley (1913-2005) and Patrick Crowley (d. 1974), a Catholic couple from Chicago who had four children and took care of a number of foster children, one of whom they adopted. Speaking for themselves and other Catholic couples they knew through the Christian Family Movement (CFM), Patty and Pat Crowley pleaded with the commission in 1966 for allowing effective birth control when married Catholic couples want to space births or limit the number of children.

As reported by the *National Catholic Reporter* (*NCR*), a progressive independent weekly Catholic newspaper, liberal author Father Andrew Greeley, a longtime friend of the Crowleys, said that "in terms of lay activism, Patty was the most important woman of her time, and CFM was the most important movement of the preconciliar church."[47]

> *National Catholic Reporter* (NCR)
> http://www.natcath.com/

To Wojtyła, the Crowleys were much different from the Polish couples and women he knew, worked with and respected. Perhaps in his mind, their comfortable middle-class life in Chicago (Pat

Crowley was a lawyer.) did not expose them to the kind of tests that Polish couples he knew had to endure, and therefore they could not understand the need for setting strict anti-contraception and pro-life standards. While he would not accept as valid the reasons offered by this deeply religious American couple for relaxing the Church ban on birth control, other members of the papal commission were sympathetic to their point of view. After the death of John XXIII, the commission reported its findings to Pope Paul VI. Wojtyła, himself a member of the commission, was absent from the meeting in June 1966, during which the majority recommended that the Church should not strictly oppose artificial birth control. Had he been present at the June meeting, however, he would have almost certainly voted against this recommendation. According to Father Maliński, Wojtyła was so deeply disturbed by the results of the discussion in Rome on the issue of marriage and contraception that in January 1967 he organized a three-day conference in Kraków devoted to this subject.[48] Another Polish friend, Father Andrzej Bardecki, also confirmed that Cardinal Wojtyła's efforts played a major role in convincing Pope Paul VI to issue his declaration on birth control. According to Father Bardecki, Wojtyła had given Paul VI the report issued by his special commission of priests and lay experts. Father Bardecki claimed that when he compared the contents of *Humanae vitae* with the Kraków commission report, he found that "at least 60 percent" of the materials were included in the encyclical.[49] Dr. Półtawska was one of the commission's most active members.

Pope Paul VI found in Wojtyła his most faithful ally and an unrelenting defender of his encyclical on birth control. Both shared a negative view of the commercialization of Western life and believed that it was a primary cause of contraception. They both also became convinced that people in the Third World were much more understanding of the Vatican's ban on contraception than people in the West.[50] Public opinion surveys continue to show, however, that while most Western women accept and practice contraception without any guilt, they also show much greater respect for human life than people in other parts of the world and are more likely to agree with John Paul II on such issues as the death penalty. It is also by now a well established fact that the number of abortions in East Central Europe and in some of the Third World countries is much higher than in the West. Wojtyła and Pope Paul VI may have arrived at their decisions about birth control using wrong assumptions about how this issue and other moral questions are viewed in the West and in the Third World.

Did Wojtyła contribute to the most serious crisis within the Church in recent history by encouraging Paul VI to issue his birth control encyclical? Nearly forty years later, Wojtyła's defenders claim that the proposal of the Kraków commission was much more humanistic than what was eventually included in *Humanae vitae*. According to them, missing from the final text of the encyclical was Wojtyła's "emphasis on human dignity and on the equality of spouses in leading sexually responsible lives."[51] According to Wojtyła's defenders, *Humanae vitae*'s sharp focus on sexual acts subjected it to the charge of legalism and pastoral insensitivity, while the Kraków commission's proposal, developed under Wojtyła's leadership, offered a better explanation as to why the Church's position on birth control promoted human dignity, and particularly the dignity of women.[52] But while Wojtyła stressed the element of human dignity, he was also very active in making sure that restrictions on contraception were well understood and uniformly observed by the faithful. He also put a lot of effort and energy into promoting proper birth control techniques. This was not someone who was concerned only with the moral dimensions of contraception but a Church leader who was very much involved in teaching women the practicalities of acceptable birth control methods. Attempts by Wojtyła's Polish friends to disassociate him from the birth control encyclical may have been simply designed to improve his image among liberal Catholics, but liberal American Catholics like Patty Crowley were not persuaded. Writing for the

National Catholic Reporter some 25 years after the publication of *Humanae vitae* while John Paul II was still at the Vatican, she was bitter about the pope's attitude on birth control: "I feel betrayed by the church. The pope continually states that birth control is evil, yet I know that couples must be practicing birth control. One never hears from the pulpit that birth control is intrinsically evil and should not be practiced. Is the church hypocritical? ... I long for a church that is honest about its teachings, that admits its errors and faces the effects of rigidity with openness."[53]

Wojtyła himself confirmed in 1978 that he had sent Paul VI his opinions in writing in 1966, two years before *Humanae vitae* was published. Describing one of his meetings with Paul VI, Wojtyła revealed that the pope immediately brought up with him the subject of birth control. Wojtyła commented that "already at that time he understood the significance of the problem facing Paul VI as the Church's highest teacher and shepherd."[54] Prior to the publication of *Humanae vitae*, Paul VI may have also read Wojtyła's book *Love and Responsibility* in French or Italian translation. In 1967 and 1968 there were also three meetings between Paul VI and Cardinal Wojtyła, during which the two may have discussed Wojtyła's views on contraception. There is strong evidence that the two talked about the issue of birth control and that Wojtyła's ideas were incorporated into the *Humanae vitae* encyclical.

In one of his homilies in 1972, Wojtyła mentioned his frequent meetings with Paul VI as well as the pope's request to him several years earlier to ask "the suffering people" in his archdiocese to pray for him in connection with a decision on a "difficult manner" pertaining to his teaching office.[55] Although Wojtyła was not specific as to the nature of the decision, one can easily assume that it dealt with the birth control encyclical. On another occasion in 1972, Wojtyła revealed that before the publication of *Humanae vitae*, and more frequently after the publication, he had spoken many times with Pope Paul VI, and each time they discussed birth control issues. Wojtyła pointed out that the pope knew of his interest in this issue. Wojtyła also quoted Paul VI as telling him several years after the publication of *Humanae vitae* that "if he had to write it now, after the whole [controversy], I could not have written anything different."[56] There is little doubt that Wojtyła indeed played a major role in helping Paul VI to write the encyclical on birth control, which subsequently led to the alienation of a great number of Catholics throughout the world.

In developing his ideas on contraception, Wojtyła was very much afraid that giving individuals near total control of their sexuality would result in serious abuses of human dignity, with sex becoming an even stronger tool of exploitation for pleasure or profit. Once the divine link, which he perceived between sex and procreation or sex and love, is removed, the sexual act can be viewed as yet another everyday human or even commercial activity, with individuals being free to decide on their own when and with whom to have sex. Wojtyła was afraid that due to powerful emotions linked with sex, individuals cannot be fully trusted with this responsibility without Church guidance, and if left with no outside rules and restraints, are likely to abuse this freedom for exploitation of their sexual partners. It seems that in Wojtyła's mind, allowing artificial birth control would be then the first step leading to the acceptance of sex outside of marriage, including sex between homosexuals and lesbians, and could eventually lead to public acceptance of gay marriages. He was also convinced that allowing artificial birth control would lead to far greater acceptance of abortion, since sex would no longer be viewed as an act protected by God.

At the same time, Wojtyła remained convinced, despite evidence to the contrary, that opposition to the encyclical on birth control originated solely in the United States and in Western Europe. He wrote in 1973, after reading comments from bishops around the world, of becoming convinced that the only center of opposition to *Humanae vitae* exists within the "Atlantic culture," with which Poland is closely linked.[57] He used the term "Atlantic culture" to refer to North America and Western Europe. Wojtyła also criticized the communist authorities in Poland for starting a pro-abortion campaign and accused them of corrupting the meaning of love and responsible parenthood. He pointed out that several years after legalizing abortion in Poland, the same communist authorities became concerned about the dropping birth rate and started to encourage couples to have more children.[58] His point was that only the Catholic Church can offer constant and correct advice on such important matters.

Wojtyła's views on abortion, contraception and women's role in the Church did not change after he became pope. If anything, John Paul II may have become even more conservative and convinced of the correctness of his views. His biographer, Tad Szulc, believed that Wojtyła's opposition to artificial birth control was stronger than ever during his pontificate.

Wojtyła Defends *Humanae vitae*

Immediately after the publication of *Humanae vitae*, Wojtyła engaged a team of experts to write a theological commentary to the birth control encyclical. The commentary was later translated into Italian and published in Rome.[59] Also, soon after the publication of the 1968 birth control encyclical, both Cardinals Wyszyński and Wojtyła sent telegrams to Paul VI expressing their "gratitude for *Humanae vitae*" and declaring that it confirms the viewpoint of the Polish bishops. Cardinal Wyszyński reportedly told the Polish bishops that they had a duty to support the pope on this issue since bishops in some of the other countries opposed the encyclical. Wyszyński reportedly also said that birth control in itself is not the most important issue, but it was being overemphasized by the media and therefore required a response from the Church. According to Wyszyński, the fundamental issue was moral upbringing.[60] Wojtyła also took the same line in stressing the importance of overall sexual morality. At a meeting of the Polish bishops in October 1968, it was Cardinal Wojtyła who conveyed

Pope Paul's thanks to the bishops for their stand on the *Humanae vitae* encyclical.[61]

Wojtyła deliberately took upon himself the role of the chief spokesman of the Polish bishops on the issue of birth control. He shared Pope Paul's concerns about the commercialization of Western life and may have been largely responsible for convincing Paul VI that his encyclical enjoyed a much better reception in the Third World countries than in the West. Throughout the 1970s, he continued to write and speak out in defense of *Humanae vitae* more forcefully than any other Polish bishop and treated it as a *cause celebre* in his archdiocese. Unsatisfied with mere compliance, Wojtyła tried to make sure that all Catholics were not only fully informed about the requirements on birth control but would also suffer consequences if they persisted in disregarding the basic rules. Using his position as the Archbishop of Kraków, he instructed all priests in his archdiocese to refuse forgiveness of sins to any Catholic who violated the Church's teaching on sexual ethics.

Wojtyła also wanted to identify and counsel those Catholics going to confession who were convinced that they were not doing anything wrong by practicing artificial birth control and were not going to discuss this issue with their confessor. Even before the publication of *Humanae vitae*, Wojtyła issued an instruction to priests in 1967, telling them that they must always ask persons seeking forgiveness of sins whether they follow the Church's norms on sexual ethics. The only Catholics exempt from this requirement, according to his instructions, were those of advanced age, those very actively practicing their faith, and persons with obvious nervous disorders. Wojtyła was basically asking his priests to conduct an investigation into sexual habits of Catholics seeking absolution if they themselves chose not to bring up the subject. He instructed confessors to be direct but to ask these questions in the context of showing "interest in the family situation (profession, ages of children, religious upbringing, etc.)." The purpose was to ascertain whether those going to confession were following the Church's teachings on marriage and sex. After becoming acquainted with the penitent's personal life, the confessors were to "formulate delicate questions." As an example, Wojtyła suggested asking "whether [a penitent] has difficulties in reconciling marital relations with the requirements of God's law." The outcome for an unsuspecting sinner could be harsh. Wojtyła instructed his priests to deny forgiveness of sins to those who "stubbornly refuse to accept the principles" and those "who are formal recidivists." Such persons could not receive communion or consider themselves full members of the Church. Under this standard today, the vast majority of women and their husbands in Poland and in the United States could no longer participate fully in the sacraments of the Church. Wojtyła told the priests, however, that even in denying forgiveness of sins, they must try their best not to discourage such people from going to confession in the future and from practicing their religion in other ways.[62]

This 1967 document shows quite clearly that Karol Wojtyła was not going to tolerate the views of those who may see themselves as good Catholics but do not agree with the Church's official teaching. As pope, he would take the same position vis-à-vis Catholics in America and in other countries where the majority of the faithful, including many priests and bishops, rejected his strict rules on contraception and divorce and were willing to show much more tolerance and compassion toward those who did not agree with Rome on these issues. John Paul II always believed, however, that the official position of the Church on sexual ethics should be unambiguously stated and those who do not meet the standards should not be allowed to receive communion. This kind of approach may have worked in Poland forty years ago, but since then it has led to the alienation of millions of Catholics throughout the world. Many Catholics in America and elsewhere have stopped going to confession but continue to receive communion convinced that their more liberal views on divorce, contraception or even abortion do not make them unfit to participate fully in the life of the Church.

As Wojtyła was relentlessly promoting his views on family, marriage, and contraception, he was also formulating new solutions to problems encountered by married couples. In a letter to the priests in 1967, he instructed them that "the possibility of ethical spacing of births through periodic marital continence puts before all of us as pastors new tasks, which we must accept if we are to be faithful to our calling."[63] Wojtyła told the priests that they must not only work on preparing engaged couples for marriage and instructing married couples, but they must also develop the right attitude toward birth control among the older youth. He conceded that lay persons rather than priests should counsel couples in the rhythm method, but noted that they must receive thorough professional and ethical training. Wojtyła appealed to the priests for "full understanding, conviction and uniformity in action."[64]

In 1969, Wojtyła again told the priests in his archdiocese to properly present the content of *Humanae vitae*, but at the same time he instructed them not to discuss the biological details of birth control. This issue was to be left in the hands of lay marriage counselors. In 1969, he also organized in Kraków a conference of Polish theologians on the subject of *Humanae vitae* and once again presented a strong defense of Paul VI's position on birth control. That same year, he told the parishioners in the mountain resort town of Zakopane that marital love "must be focused on a child" and that Polish families should practice love which "does not reject children... our hope on Earth and at the same time the hope and the future of God's Kingdom."[65] He told a group of young married couples in 1972 that "the task of Christian marriages...is to maintain...Christian dignity,...Christian love..., responsibility for [creating] life..."[66] Also as part of Cardinal Wojtyła's efforts to support the ban on contraception, a group of ethicists in Kraków wrote the introduction to the Italian publication of Paul VI's encyclical *Humanae vitae*.[67]

Wojtyła not only preached support for *Humanae vitae*, but also worked hard to recruit lay Catholics to the cause. He created "The Group of *Humanae vitae* Married Couples" whose task was to promote natural birth control and provide support to other Catholics struggling with this issue. Wojtyła wrote a six-point code of conduct for the group, in which he referred to *Humanae vitae* as a document which "anew sets authentically Christian ... requirements for married couples and their pastors." Wojtyła acknowledged that Paul VI had proscribed a difficult rule to follow for Catholics in rejecting artificial birth control. Unlike many other bishops, particularly in the West, Wojtyła was not afraid, however, to encourage the faithful to accept the "great moral requirements" of the encyclical.[68] In a greeting to members of the Church-sponsored association of large families, Wojtyła told them to be proud of their decision to have children: "The world may not understand you, the world may ask why you did not take an easier road, but the world needs your example."[69] Speaking ten years after the publication of *Humanae vitae*, Wojtyła urged married couples to give example to other married couples by "living according to God's law" and by being willing to accept "the blessing of giving life."[70]

Wojtyła was also very concerned that abortion, which was widely practiced in Poland, would undermine the ethical education of new generations of Poles. Soon after the publication of *Humanae vitae* in 1968, the Polish bishops stressed that, despite a dramatic decline in infant mortality, larger families, even under different conditions, were still better for the upbringing of children. The Polish bishops argued that children with many siblings grow up to be braver and less selfish, while a single child is often demanding and has difficulties in getting along with others in adulthood. The bishops pointed out that having children also helps parents to overcome their own selfishness. The bishops were not advocating, however, large families at any cost. In their instructions, they acknowledged that parents must consider their economic situation, but any decision to limit the number of children must have a serious justification and only proper means, i.e. the rhythm method, could be used in practicing birth control. When Cardinal Wyszyński visited Pope Paul VI at the Vatican in November 1968, he presented him with a special letter of thanks for *Humanae vitae*. The letter was signed by a large group of Polish physicians, including those who for many years had been under Cardinal Wojtyła's pastoral care. Among the signatories, there were one hundred university professors. Cardinal Wyszyński also gave Paul VI a second letter signed by more than one hundred large Polish families, some of them with more than a dozen children.[71]

A question that deeply troubled Wojtyła was how parents could teach their children to love if they would opt to terminate an unborn life. In 1975, he told a group of teachers that "one can only love to the end, if one loves from the start." Love, in Wojtyła's mind, started from the moment of conception, and every human being from the moment of conception deserves love for being created in the image of God.[72] Any other approach would be inconsistent with Wojtyła's position that love and marriage represent "a selfless gift of oneself" to the other person, and ultimately to God. Such a selfless gift, Wojtyła told the Poles, must be open to the possibility of a new life.[73]

In November 1975 at the conference on "Threats Facing a Christian Family," Wojtyła delivered a 32 page paper on how Catholic families in Poland could identify and defend against the dangers created by the communist regime and its propaganda. He concluded that the introduction of divorce was the first step toward the secularization of Polish society, followed by, legalization of abortion and promotion of contraception.[74] He attacked the communist program of promoting the model of "a socialist family" through such actions as secular pre-marital counseling, civil wedding ceremonies and non-religious funerals, and stated that the Polish Church was unquestionably opposed to such programs. He also pointed out that the Polish Church took an uncompromising position in support of *Humanae vitae*. He described the contraception ban as a "difficult issue," but concluded that, because of its difficult nature, less than clear positions proved themselves to be the most dangerous.[75]

What Wojtyła may have had in mind was the sexual revolution in the United States and Western Europe brought about by the introduction of the pill. He did not want Poland to follow the same path and believed that the Polish Church might be able to prevent Poles from engaging in premarital sex and sexual experimentation if it succeeded in resisting the introduction of contraception. As in the West, however, Wojtyła's strategy also did not work in Poland. Many Polish women who were able to obtain contraceptives, despite shortages and high prices under the communist economy, were not reluctant to use them. Many women, who could not get contraceptives or were afraid to purchase them because of social disapproval, resorted to secret abortions to avoid unwanted pregnancies.

Coitus interruptus and abortion became the most commonly used contraceptive methods in communist-ruled Poland. The use of more reliable methods was extremely low due to the combination of Church-created social disapproval, lack of sexual education and lack of availability of affordable and effective contraceptives such as the pill. During the communist period, IUD's could only be purchased in foreign currency stores, while limited domestic production and imports of the pill satisfied the demand of only 2.3% of women of the childbearing age in 1978. It was estimated that if the total production of condoms had been distributed equally among all 20 to 59-year-old men in Poland at that time, each person would get no more than three per year.[76] Local production of condoms decreased from 31,404,000 in 1969 to 19,858,000 in 1983. At the same time, the communist authorities made a small number of imported IUDs, about 1 million annually, available only in hard currency stores.[77] Polish feminists suspected that in the 1980s the communist regime may have reached a secret understanding with the Polish bishops to limit the availability of abortion and contraceptives in exchange for a promise that the Church would moderate its criticism of the communist leaders. These rumors could neither be confirmed nor denied.

The influence of the Polish Catholic bishops on the issues of abortion, contraception and sex education became much greater after the fall of communism in 1989. Pro-feminist Polish scholar, Anna Titkow, concluded in the late 1990s that "the negative role of the Roman Catholic Church hierarchy in the process of promoting modern family planning and fertility regulation techniques is extremely significant and consistent."[78] Some Polish bishops approached these issues with similar determination and energy that Karol Wojtyła displayed when he was a priest and bishop in Poland. Ultimately, the Parliament dominated by Right-wing parties outlawed almost all abortions in Poland after the fall of communism.

Wojtyła and Medical Profession

Wojtyła's involvement with the medical profession in Poland dates back to at least the early 1950s. 1956 was the year of the first pilgrimage of the Kraków physicians to the Shrine of Our Lady of Jasna Góra in Częstochowa. It was also the year of the legalization of abortion by the communist authorities in Poland. Since then, there would be hundreds more retreats, pilgrimages and workshops for physicians and nurses from the Kraków Archdiocese, many of them organized by Wojtyła himself or under his close supervision. Wojtyła's contacts with female-nurses were perhaps more numerous and prolonged than with any other group of women, including nuns. The purpose of these meetings, conferences, seminars, retreats, and pilgrimages was to prepare a cadre of medical professionals who would uphold the Church's teachings on birth control and abortion and who would assist women and men in making the right decisions.

St. Florian Church in Kraków (2007).

Wojtyła's work with health care workers started during his early years as a priest in Kraków's St. Florian's parish, where he organized meetings and lectures for doctors on professional ethics. About 250 doctors participated in a retreat led by Wojtyła in 1957. The same year, the pastoral care unit was organized within the Kraków Curia with responsibilities for working with the health care professionals and organizing marriage courses for engaged couples. The vast majority of instructors were lay women.

Soon after Wojtyła became the Archbishop of Kraków in 1964, he created the position of the family counseling instructor who was in charge of the Church-run counseling centers throughout the archdiocese. The first person chosen for this position was a professional midwife whose task was to recruit other women for work in counseling centers outside of Kraków. In response to Wojtyła's suggestions, part of their job was to teach Polish women the rhythm method of birth control. The potential counselors were themselves required to be trained and had to take an exam before being allowed to assume their duties. The counselors continued to attend additional meetings and training sessions, some of which were held at Wojtyła's invitation at the archbishop's palace in Kraków. Wojtyła gave lectures and took part in some of the discussions. One such meeting of marriage counselors, during which natural birth control methods were discussed, was called by Cardinal Wojtyła in

May 1967. Another one, which also included a lecture on the rhythm method, was held in January 1968. There were many others to follow.

In 1968, Cardinal Wojtyła created in Kraków a special unit for pastoral care of families. At that time he was already trying to get doctors and nurses involved in marriage counseling efforts. This was important since one of the main jobs of the marriage instructors was the maintenance of fertility charts for women in the archdiocese. The main instructor for the archdiocese, a woman appointed by Cardinal Wojtyła, visited parishes to help with the preparation of rhythm method charts and interpretation of the more difficult ones. She also ensured that natural birth control methods were taught during meetings with engaged couples. Another part of her job was to seek cooperation from doctors and nurses in the archdiocese to make sure that "at the very least, they would not interfere."[79] The marriage instructors also worked with nursing and medical school students. Under the archbishop's patronage, 82 family advice centers were established, 25 of them in Kraków.[80] Wojtyła also called on the parish priests in the Kraków Archdiocese to initiate special meetings with married couples and insisted that such meetings become a regular part of his visits to various parishes.[81]

Cardinal Wojtyła also arranged for the publication in Poland of Ch. E. Rendu's book, *Did the Church Deceive Us?*, which provided

---

Natural Family Planning Web Sites

Couple to Couple League
http://www.ccli.org/

Couple to Couple League (GB)
http://www.cclgb.org.uk/

Feminist Women's Health Center
http://www.fwhc.org/birth-control/fam.htm

Family of the Americas
http://www.familyplanning.net/

billings LIFE
http://www.woomb.org/

CreightonModel.com
http://www.creightonmodel.com/

Open Embrace
http://www.openembrace.com/

arguments in defense of *Humanae vitae*. Wojtyła concluded that the book's focus on married couples using natural birth control methods represented an important proof of Catholic morality. He wanted the book to be widely available.[82]

In the 1970's, Wojtyła started to organize joint conferences of physicians and theologians to deal with moral dilemmas of family life. Contraception was the topic of the very first joint conference held in Kraków in February 1975. The second joint conference of physicians and theologians the following year also dealt with contraception, and the third conference focused on chastity before marriage.[83] Cardinal Wojtyła used these conferences to enlist the help of Catholic physicians in promoting his view that each conceived life represented a "great good" and any attempt to prevent conception or destroy life be described as a "great evil."

Apparently, most Polish physicians and other experts who participated in these conferences were in agreement with Wojtyła's point of view. Based on their input, he concluded that contraception produced negative psychiatric and demographic consequences.[84] Some of the experts, including Dr. Wanda Półtawska, agreed with him that women using contraception experienced negative psychological effects. The same experts also reinforced his view that limiting population growth is bad for the nation.

In his speeches to nurses and doctors, Wojtyła frequently appealed to their patriotism in urging them to support his anti-abortion campaign. In 1974, he made a passionate appeal to a group of nurses asking them to protect unborn life as a patriotic duty. He told them that Poland had lost its independence in the 18th century because Poles had committed terrible sins. He warned that it could happen again if abortion in Poland remained unchecked:

> I think that the greatest tragedy of our society, our nation, is the death of persons who have not yet been born: conceived and unborn. And, I do not know how before history we will pay for this horrible crime. But, it is obvious that this [crime] cannot be

without consequences.[85]

In a 1975 presentation on the dangers facing the Christian family, Wojtyła talked about a twenty-year effort by the Polish Church to win the cooperation of the medical profession, especially medical doctors, in the fight against abortion and contraception. In 1975, he sponsored in Kraków a conference of physicians and theologians from all regions of Poland under the title "Special Aspects of the Problem of Abortion." Again he appealed to their patriotism, telling the participants to approach the subject as Christians and Poles.[86]

Wojtyła's involvement with the medical profession was also designed to increase efforts on behalf of women who were in need of material assistance. The more usual approach among the Polish clergy and Polish families and communities was to condemn and ostracize women who became pregnant outside of marriage. It was not rare for families, particularly fathers, to force their pregnant daughters to leave home and to refuse them any contact or help. This drove many desperate girls and women to seek secret abortions or to self-induce abortions at a great risk to their lives. Wojtyła was aware of these facts and wanted to provide help and emotional support to these women while at the same time trying to convince his parishioners to change their attitudes. At a conference for physicians in 1957, Wojtyła called on the priests to work closely with doctors in providing material help to women who request abortions but are persuaded to give birth. Wojtyła urged doctors to work for the good of another person and to take responsibility for their patients' welfare. The doctor's job—he told the physicians—was not only to save an unborn baby but also to become involved with the priests and the community in helping young women who had found themselves without any means to care for their babies.

Wojtyła's concern was not limited only to the unborn children threatened with abortion. He was well aware of the various abuses under the communist health care system. While ostensibly health care in Poland was free for everyone, access to medical care was based on privilege and bribery, with many doctors openly demanding money to supplement their inadequate salaries. Wojtyła often also discussed these issues in retreats and conferences organized specifically for Polish doctors. Abortion remained, however, the primary focus of Wojtyła's involvement with the medical profession.

Wojtyła also called on doctors to help priests in providing sex education for young couples preparing for marriage. Referring to physicians as "an operational group for the Church," he told them that priests are not competent to advise young people on all aspects of married life.[87] He compared the respective roles and importance of physicians and priests and concluded that both groups were capable of either building or destroying God's kingdom on earth. Using Christ's words: "who is not with me is against me," Wojtyła told the doctors that it is their moral duty to actively discourage and oppose abortion"[88]

Wojtyła's efforts to win over the medical profession in Poland were largely successful. In August 1996, the Polish Parliament, controlled at that time by the former communists and their allies, liberalized briefly the 1993 law which denied abortions on demand. Yet while abortions once again became legal for a brief period, many Polish doctors refused to perform them citing religious, moral or professional objections. According to *The Los Angeles Times* report, all regional associations of Polish physicians declared abortion unethical and, in the words of one such declaration, "against the very essence of the profession of a doctor."[89] Many hospitals turned away women requesting abortions because the medical staff refused to perform them for reasons of conscience.

Wanda Nowicka (b. 1956), director of the Federation for Women and Family Planning in Warsaw, complained that doctors in Poland are "afraid of Catholic priests and even of orderlies and nurses who may inform on the doctor."[90] Some Catholic doctors also followed Wojtyła's advice on the permissible methods of birth control. Polish feminists believe that the views of doctors on abortion and contraception prevent them from being responsive to the needs of most women and couples in Poland.[91]

While feminists may be appalled by such behavior, this is exactly the kind of reaction that Wojtyła expected from his friends among the medical professionals in Poland with whom he had worked for many years on reducing the number of abortions and the use of contraception. In his mind, they were involved in saving human lives and that is exactly the kind of doctors and nurses he wanted to practice medicine. Social pressure to conform can be very strong in Poland and is used by Polish priests who often openly identified and condemned abortion providers. With the groundwork set by Wojtyła, the Polish Church is continuing a campaign of protests designed to put pressure on anyone who might support abortion. So far, no violent attacks against abortion providers in Poland have been reported, but the level of rhetoric on the part of the more extreme anti-abortion activists is quite high.

Opposing the Catholic Church in this kind of environment is not easy for the nascent feminist organizations in Poland. Ms. Nowicka claims that many Polish Catholic women are among the strongest supporters of legalized abortion, although historically Polish women have been largely silent on such issues. Ms. Nowicka was hopeful, however, that feminist groups in Poland will eventually be able to mobilize women in defense of their rights against the positions taken by the Catholic Church.[92] So far, it has not happened. Many Polish women may not agree with John Paul II's positions on birth control and legalized abortion, but they are not willing to speak up, especially if it would mean opposing or criticizing Poland's most famous son. Most women, it seems, consider it a private matter.

This attitude is not surprising since for nearly 50 years communist censors effectively banned media reporting and open discussion on a variety of sensitive issues, including abortion. One of the many media censorship rules with regard to the Catholic

Church was a prohibition against "demagogic criticism of the law permitting abortion."[93] Another directive for communist censors was to stop any information about Catholic family life instructors and counselors (natural birth control) from reaching the mass media. Such information could only appear in Church publications, which had very limited circulation due to restrictions imposed on Catholic media.[94] The censors also blocked the publication of *Pastoral Work Among Parents,* a book by an East German author Erwin Heretsch discussing ways of strengthening family life through religious education for parents and children.[95] Publication of Cardinal Wojtyła's sermons and those of all other bishops and priests was also subject to censorship.[96]

After the fall of communism, John Paul's access to information

Catholic Youth Web Site	**Jesus Crowd**
	http://www.jesuscrowd.com/index.
Omegarock.com	cfm
http://www.omegarock.com/	**Revolution of Love**
True Girl Magazine	http://www.revolutionoflove.com/
http://www.truegirlonline.com/	**Youth Apostles Online**
Love One Another Magazine	http://www.youthapostles.com/
http://www.loveoneanother-magazine.org/	**Fr. Phil Bloom**
	http://www.geocities.com/Heartland/2964/
Saint Maria Messenger	
http://www.saintmariasmessenger.com/	**The Catholic Youth Foundation**
	http://www.catholicyouth.org/
Pure Love Club	**Catholic Christian Outreach Canada**
http://www.pureloveclub.com/	http://www.cco.ca/
Life Teen	**NET Ministries of Canada**
http://www.lifeteen.org/	http://www.netcanada.ca/
Jesus Youth	**Fellowship of Catholic University Students**
http://www.jesusyouth.org/main/index.php	http://www.focusonline.org/

and media products for and about youth and women may have been somewhat limited to allow him to make well-informed judgments about what was the current state of reporting on women's issues in the West and even in Poland. According to Father Maliński, John Paul II was only getting papers and magazines sent to him by the Vatican's Office of the Secretary of State. On one occasion in 1993, Maliński brought to the pope a number of youth magazines published in Poland, including such titles as *Bravo*, *Popcorn*, and *Girl*. He wanted to prove to the pope that secular media knows how to appeal to young readers through attractive designs and pictures with limited use of text. He explained that these most popular weekly magazines in Poland were unfortunately promoting Western models of behavior and morality, particularly those originating in Germany and the United States. Father Maliński also pointed out to the pope that the magazines deal almost exclusively with two topics, sex and music, while Catholic publications in Poland are not able to compete with these magazines because they lack good design and are not properly targeted. Father Maliński also warned the pope that the mentality of young people in Poland had changed since the fall of communism. John Paul II looked through the magazines several times and finally urged Father Maliński to publish his own magazine aimed at the Polish youth.[97] In the United States, and in Great Britain, also there are also very few magazines and electronic media products for young Catholics that can compete with what secular commercial media can offer.

Help for Single Mothers

One of Cardinal Wojtyła's appeals addressed to the priests in the Kraków archdiocese called for "saving each conceived child, providing immediate help to all needing support, guaranteeing discretion."[98] Wojtyła realized, without stating it publicly, that the Church in Poland was largely responsible for creating the atmosphere of hostility toward unwed mothers. In his appeal, he also called for the involvement of the health services and the religious sisters, while the priests were asked to work with the parish communities and families were encouraged, whenever possible, to open their household to single mothers. Wojtyła stressed that the initiative would "confirm that we not only teach and judge the consciences of unfortunate mothers and fathers, but also want to help them from the bottom of our heart."[99] The Sisters of Nazareth started to accept single mothers in their special quarters in 1974 and four years later the Diocesan Home for Single Mothers was opened in Kraków. Unwed mothers were given medical care and access to adoption services. Spiritual care was also provided, but the home was opened to all women regardless of their religious background.

The initiative was financed through gifts from parishioners and from other funds provided by Cardinal Wojtyła. Collection boxes with signs: "for saving lives of unborn children" were placed in churches throughout the Kraków Archdiocese. In four years, from 1974 to 1978, "Cardinal Wojtyła's SOS" program helped 127 mothers.[100] This was a small number that did not significantly reduce the incidence of abortion, but it was an accomplishment in light of the severe constrains imposed by the communist authorities on the Church in Poland at that time. In 1975 alone, there were 138,600 officially registered abortions in Poland, but the total number was even higher because many abortions performed by private physicians were not reported.[101] At the beginning of Wojtyła's SOS initiative, there were only six slots available to women in a home for single mothers run by religious sisters in the Kraków Archdiocese. While organizing a massive recruitment effort would have been difficult under communist rule, the small number of mothers who received assistance may be an indication that the Polish society was not ready to provide such help. Unwed mothers continued to be condemned and ostracized by their families and neighbors. In this case, Wojtyła was not very successful in providing practical solutions to problems affecting women or in adjusting his ideas to real life situations. Despite opposition and harassment from the communist authorities, he was much more successful in getting strong public support for building new churches. In Western countries, on the other hand, efforts to help single women faced with unwanted pregnancies and contemplating abortions are more widespread and more successful. Many crisis pregnancy centers (CPCs) or pregnancy resource centers (PRCs), run as nonprofit organizations, are active in the U.S., but the UK and other Western countries also have similar centers and homes for mothers. Care Net is the largest network of CPCs in North America, with 1,100 centers advising over 350,000 women annually. Heartbeat International is

CPCs/PRCs

Care Net
http://www.care-net.org/

OptionLine
http://www.optionline.org/

Heartbeat International
http://www.heartbeatinternational.org/

Birthright International
http://www.birthright.org/

CAREConfidential
http://www.careconfidential.com/

Life (UK)
http://www.lifecharity.org.uk/

associated with over 1,000 centers, and Birthright International has over 400 affiliates. The largest UK organizations are CAREConfidential and LifeUK. A group of pro-choice Democrats in the U.S. Congress has accused some centers of giving false information on abortion. These Democrats charged that centers, which receive grants of federal money from the U.S. government, were in some cases telling women that abortions cause an increased risk of breast cancer, infertility and deep psychological trauma.[102]

After Wojtyła had left Poland permanently for Rome, his successor as the Archbishop of Kraków Cardinal Franciszek Macharski implemented the plans for extending help to single mothers unable to cope alone with their pregnancies. During the trip to Poland in 1999, John Paul II thanked the Kraków Archdiocese and Cardinal Macharski for opening the Home for Single Mothers (*Dom Samotnej Matki*) in his hometown of Wadowice. Noting that the home was named after his mother, Emilia Kaczorowska Wojtyła, John Paul II described it as a place where women, who despite sacrifices and obstacles want to guard their gift of motherhood, can find refuge and help. John Paul II referred to the initiative as a "great gift of ...love for the human being and concern for life" and expressed that his mother, Emilia,

"who brought him into the world and brought love to his childhood" is a good patron for this project.[103]

Wojtyła's initiatives to help unwed mothers when he was still the Archbishop in Kraków were combined with intense pastoral activities in which emphasis was placed on promoting pre-marital chastity. In a 1978 pastoral letter, Wojtyła warned that "violating premarital chastity often brings with it tragic consequences" when teenagers may begin their lives by "destroying a conceived life" as a result of "not preserving chastity before marriage [and] wedding."[104] At the same time, he blamed the pressures of secularism and communist-promoted atheism for causing a decline of moral norms among Polish women. One of his frequent appeals to nuns for prayers included a statement that "*niewiasty* (an old Polish word for women, meaning "one who does not know," which is now rarely used but is not perceived in Poland as having any negative connotations) "and female youth [are] strongly threatened by negative forces of modern civilization."[105] Cardinal Wojtyła was

Emilia Wojtyła Home for Single Mothers in Wadowice.

Organizations Helping Women	AfterAbortion.org
	http://www.afterabortion.org/
Scottish Women's Aid	**Feminists Choosing Life**
http://www.scottishwomensaid.co.uk/	http://www.feministschoosinglife.org/
Rape Crisis England and Wales	**Women Affirming Life**
http://www.rapecrisis.org.uk/	http://www.affirmlife.com/index.cfm
The Fawcett Society	
http://www.fawcettsociety.org.uk/	**Media Watch**
Object – women not sex objects	http://www.mediawatch.com/
http://www.object.org.uk/	**Coalition Against Trafficking in Women**
Womankind	
http://www.womankind.org.uk/	http://www.catwinternational.org/
Rights of Women	**Stop Violence Against Women**
http://www.rightsofwomen.org.uk/	http://www.stopvaw.org/
Anti-street Harassment UK	**Pro-Life Alliance of Gays and Lesbians**
http://www.anti-harassment.ik.com/	http://www.plagal.org/

also appealing to male pride calling on men to take responsibility for conceived children:

> Man is called to be the beloved [...], becoming the beloved he must always remember that he is 'a friend of the Beloved [...]. Man must be a servant [...]. Woman in a marriage is a servant of life [...]. Maleness, which has its natural drive toward domination, must be balanced by a willingness to serve.[106]

Cardinal Wojtyła also realized that lack of new housing for young married and unmarried couples was contributing to the growing number of abortions in communist Poland. In 1957, he became involved with a project to build apartments for young married couples. As with the establishment of homes for unwed mothers, the project of building apartments was also largely utopian, but it illustrated Wojtyła's determination and desperation in dealing with the issue of abortion. Plans were drawn up and another priest offered to donate land belonging to his parish in the suburbs of Kraków, but due to the economic difficulties and enormous obstacles posed by the communist bureaucracy, the housing project never moved beyond the planning stage.[107] Danuta Rybicka, one of the female students in Father Wojtyła's group who observed the planning of the unrealized housing complex, referred to it as "The Love Settlement."[108] Sister Klawera Wolska, who worked with homeless girls and troubled youth in Kraków, also reported that Father Wojtyła helped young couples find apartments. He also gave his own money to help the sisters pay various bills.[109] In 1960, he loaned a large sum of money to two of his female students so that they could pay a bribe to secure the right to rent a state-owned apartment. The amount of money requested was so large that he told them to return for it the next day and urged them to be very careful so that they would not be cheated. The girls returned the money three years later. Wojtyła did not want to accept the money at first but finally took it saying that he could use the funds to help someone else.[110]

Despite some setbacks, Wojtyła continued his efforts to help his young friends, many of them women and couples, with their most pressing problems. Even before he became a priest, he tried to help young couples in need. While working in a factory during the Nazi occupation, he agreed to take over the night shift from a fellow worker, whose wife had a difficult birth, so that he could spend more time with his wife and their newborn baby. After the birth of her child, the young woman, whom Wojtyła had never met before, found him and gave him as a thank-you present a pair of new shoes, which he in turn quickly gave to another needy person.[111]

Wojtyła's hopes to change the attitudes within the Polish Church toward unwed mothers have been largely unsuccessful.

Ecofeminism Web Sites

Women's Voices for the Earth
http://www.womenandenvi-
ronment.org/

Women's Environmental Network
http://www.wen.org.uk/

ecofem.org
http://www.ecofem.org/

ecofeminism.net
http://www.ecofeminism.net/

EVE ONLINE
http://eve.enviroweb.org/

The pope's vision of America as country of selfish individuals who need to be re-evangelized or introduced anew to Christian values does not find much support in the results of surveys measuring religious practice and voluntary service in the United States. Father Andrew Greeley countered the pope's view of America by pointing out that 47% of Americans volunteer on the average four hours a week, more than people in any other country in the Western world, or for that matter in Poland or in other countries in Eastern and Central Europe. Moreover, younger Americans are more likely to volunteer than those born immedi-

ately after World War II. Father Greeley attributed much of the difference between voluntarism in the U.S. and in other countries to the higher level of religious practice among Americans, but religious practice is even stronger in Poland, where voluntarism had been very low until the fall of communism and even now is not very strong.[113] In 2003, only 24 percent of survey respondents in Poland declared that during a past year they had done some voluntary work for their community, their church or private individuals, while 76 percent had not engaged in any charitable activities.[114] The number of feminist NGOs, both pro-choice and pro-life, as well as NGOs devoted to other causes such as domestic abuse, ecology and animal rights, is very high in the U.S., the UK and other Western countries. There are also countless feminist web sites and blogs. Some of the ecofeminist organizations declare a spiritual dimension with links to pagan religions. But despite their concern for life of the environment, ecofeminist organizations usually do not claim to be pro-life when it comes to abortion. On the other hand, the number of both pro-life and pro-choice organizations helping women who are pregnant is large and growing. Pregnancy outside of marriage is no longer viewed in most Western countries as an unforgivable moral failing. Jerzy Turowicz was right in predicting that Wojtyła's vision of Catholics working together to extend help to women and children would be implemented more effectively and on a larger scale in Western countries than in his native Poland. Liberal societies exhibit more tolerance and more willingness to help those who fall short of strict moral standards.

Despite his appeals, many Polish priests and Polish Catholics are still hostile or indifferent toward single mothers and more willing to condemn their promiscuity than to offer help. Wojtyła's friend from Kraków Jerzy Turowicz, the late editor-in-chief of the Catholic weekly *Tygodnik Powszechny*, observed in a 1996 interview that single mothers, who decide to give birth, are often turned away by parish workers and priests in Poland Jerzy Turowicz accused the Church administrators and priests of being indifferent to the plight of single mothers and contrasted their behavior with the attitudes of Western countries. While observing that such countries are becoming secularized and de-Christianized, Jerzy Turowicz was not afraid to admit that they are probably showing more sensitivity to those in need than the people of Poland.[112] This was a significant statement by the pope's Polish friend, considering Wojtyła's frequent condemnations of the secularized West as a poor example for the rest of the world to follow.

As a priest in Poland, Wojtyła found it difficult to change negative social attitudes toward unmarried women who became pregnant. He wanted families and communities to offer help to such women in order to dissuade them from getting abortions, while at the same time he continued to strongly condemn premarital sex and contraception. The severity of his message against premarital sex tended to diminish the possibility of success in his other campaign of extending help to women who were considering terminating their pregnancies. Even though on a personal level, Wojtyła was a deeply caring person, his views on abortion were so strong that he came across, at least on this issue, as unable to empathize with women. In his mind, abortion was a terrible crime, not only against God, but also against a defenseless human being. He also saw abortion as a crime against human dignity and against the family. Finally, he perceived abortion as directed against one's own nation, which is made strong by having strong and large families. These religious and cultural assumptions made it difficult for John Paul II to moderate his stand on contraception and abortion or to develop a message for helping unwed mothers that could be more successful. Always concerned with the welfare of the Church worldwide and support among conservative Catholics, particularly in Poland and in the Third World, it was never very likely that John

Liberal Feminist Blogs and Web Sites	Bitch Ph.D.
	http://bitchphd.blogspot.com/
	Angry Black Bitch
feminist blogs	http://angryblackbitch.blogspot.com/
http://feministblogs.org/	
feministe	**Reappropriate**
http://www.feministe.us/blog/	http://www.reappropriate.com/
feministing.com	**Feminist Allies**
http://feministing.com/	http://feministallies.blogspot.com/
Alas! A blog	**Girlistic**
http://www.amptoons.com/blog/	http://www.girlistic.com/
the f word	**Feminists for Animal Rights**
http://www.thefword.org.uk/index	http://www.farinc.org/

Paul II would introduce any drastic changes in his anti-contraception and anti-abortion message to make it more understandable and more acceptable to women in the West.

CHAPTER SIX

Women-Priests

Familiaris consortio — On the Family

In his 1981 apostolic exhortation, *Familiaris consortio* (*On the Family*), Pope John Paul II acknowledged the existence of "a widespread social and cultural tradition" which limits "women's role to be exclusively that of wife and mother, without adequate access to public functions, which have generally been reserved for men."[1] He concluded that "the equal dignity and responsibility of men and women fully justifies women's access to public functions."

According to John Paul II, women should try to "harmoniously" combine their roles at home and at work "if we wish the evolution of society and culture to be truly and fully human." He did not at the same time call on men to combine their professional and family obligations or to make similar sacrifices. As always, John Paul II also called for giving recognition and respect for the

> *In the name of liberation from male "domination," women must not appropriate to themselves male characteristics contrary to their own female "originality."*
>
> *In calling only men as his Apostles, Christ acted in a completely free and sovereign manner.*
>
> *The Church <u>has no authority whatsoever</u> to confer priestly ordination on women and that this judgment is to be definitely held by all the Church's faithful.*
>
> Pope John Paul II, *Ordinatio sacerdotalis*, May 22, 1994
>
> *No one has been a better priest than our Lady. The role that a woman has no man can fill. Every woman has something special.*
>
> Mother Teresa, 1994

"irreplaceable" value of women's maternal and family role. He did not give up the idea that women rather than men are better suited for domestic work, and he still considered it to be in women's best interest to stay at home:

> While it must be recognized that women have the same right as men to perform various public functions, society must be structured in such a way that wives and mothers are not in practice compelled to work outside the home, and that families can live and prosper in a dignified way even when they [women] themselves devote full time to their family.
>
> Furthermore, the mentality which honors women more for their work outside the home than for their work within the family must be overcome. This requires that men should truly esteem and love women with total respect for their personal dignity, and that society should create and develop conditions favoring work in the home.

While John Paul II wanted women's work at home to receive full recognition and respect from society, it was still his position that men are primary breadwinners and that women should seek employment only after their primary duty at home is done. He called on men and society to respect women's work at home, implying that a woman is naturally a domestic worker, but that domestic workers should be respected. John Paul II concluded that men and women have different vocations, which is something that the Church should take into account in promoting "as far as possible the equality of rights and dignity." The document *On the Family* contains a warning for women not to renounce their femininity or try to imitate the male roles. Women, according to John Paul II, should try to express "the fullness of true feminine humanity."[2]

Mulieris dignitatem — Dignity and Vocation of Women

A major document, in which John Paul II had attempted to defend his and the Church's position on women, was his 1988 Apostolic Letter *Mulieris dignitatem* on the dignity and vocation of women, published on the occasion of the Marian Year. [3] It was probably the first document in the history of the papacy devoted entirely to women. But instead of satisfying feminists, it raised even more questions in the West about Wojtyła's traditional view of gender roles. As usual in such documents, John Paul II started out by quoting from other Church pronouncements and from statements by his predecessors to show that the Catholic Church was facing up to the growing role of women outside of the home — a point often disputed by feminists. It is important to note that John Paul referred to both women's dignity and vocation. What many feminists object to immediately is the right of the all-male Church hierarchy to determine unilaterally not only what may threaten the dignity of women but also what constitutes the right vocation for women — both subjects, as John Paul II noted in the opening statement, of "exceptional prominence in recent years."[4]

First of all, John Paul II wanted to show that the Catholic Church was aware of the growing emancipation of women and that among all the world's religions it has been in the forefront of defending women's rights — again statements seriously questioned by his critics who see mainstream Protestantism as being much more sympathetic toward women. Even some early Polish feminists in the 19th century were convinced that Protestant churches, especially in Northern Europe, were more progressive in their treatment of women than the Vatican and the Catholic Church. John Paul II started out by quoting from the 1965 Second Vatican Council *Message to Women* which declares that: "The hour is coming, in fact has come, when the vocation of women is being acknowledged in its fullness, the hour in which women acquire in the world an influence, an effect and a power never hitherto achieved."[5] John Paul II also noted that Pope Paul VI conferred the title "Doctor of the Church" upon Saint Teresa of Ávila and Saint Catherine of Sienna (1347-1380). He also quoted from the 1976 speech by Paul VI in which his predecessor noted that: "Within Christianity, more than in any other religion, and since its very beginning, women have had a special dignity, of which the New Testament shows us many important aspects..."[6]

After discussing a number of Old and New Testament references to women and men and their respective roles, John Paul II took issue with the feminist argument that the Bible is full of examples of male domination over women. While rejecting such arguments as misinterpretations or a human violation as a result of sin, particularly in the biblical injunction to women in the Book of Genesis: "Your desire shall be for your husband, and he shall rule over you" (Gen 3:16), John Paul II nevertheless reminded women not to forget about the natural differences between the sexes:

> Consequently, even the rightful opposition of women to what is expressed in the biblical words, "He shall rule over you" (Gen 3:16) must not under any condition lead to the "masculinization" of women. In the name of liberation from male "domination," women must not appropriate to themselves male characteristics contrary to their own female "originality." There is a well-founded fear that if they take this path, women will not "reach fulfillment," but instead will deform and lose what constitutes their essential richness.[7]

John Paul II's words underscored that the personal potential of women is not inferior to the personal potential of men, but that they are merely different. Masculinity and femininity are an expression of the "image and likeness of God." The biblical words: "Your desire shall be for your husband, and he shall rule over you" were, according to the pope, a result of sin and represented an "evil inheritance" which must be overcome by both men and women acting in accordance with the original relationship between man and woman. This ideal relationship, in John Paul's view, is threatened whenever the dignity of a person is undermined: "For whenever man is responsible for offending a woman's personal dignity and vocation, he acts contrary to his own personal dignity and vocation."[8] It is clear, however, that for John Paul II vocations were differently defined for men and women.

Catholic Web Sites for Mothers and Families	Defending Holy Matrimony http://www.defendingholymat-rimony.org/
Catholic Mom http://www.catholicmom.com/	Catholic Parenting http://www.catholicparenting.com/
Catholic Moms http://www.catholicmoms.com/	Holy Family Institute http://www.vocations-holyfamily.com/
Women for Faith & Family http://www.wf-f.org/	
Catholic Modesty http://www.catholicmodesty.com/	One More Soul Canada http://www.canada.omsoul.com/
Canticle Magazine http://www.canticlemagazine.com/	Domestic-Church.com http://www.domestic-church.com/
Gift Foundation http://www.giftfoundation.org/	Family Facts http://www.familyfacts.org/

To bolster his arguments in defense of different roles for men and women, John Paul II stressed a much larger and more difficult role women must assume when they become pregnant:

Parenthood—even though it belongs to both—is realized more fully in the woman, especially in the prenatal period. It is the woman who "pays" directly for this shared generation, which literally absorbs the energies of her body and soul. It is therefore necessary that the man be fully aware that in their shared parenthood he owes a special debt to the woman. No program of "equal rights" between women and men is valid unless it takes this fact fully into account.[9]

In John Paul's view, motherhood is the most important vocation for women. Speaking to the faithful in July 1995, the pope noted that the need for properly appreciating woman in every area of her life can never be sufficiently stressed. He added, however, that "among the gifts and tasks proper to her, her vocation to motherhood stands out particularly clearly."[10] John Paul II also believed that women have been assigned by nature "the greater part of parenthood."[11] As a result of pregnancy and motherhood, John Paul II considered women to be more empathetic than men. They are, in his opinion, better able than men to understand and pay attention to another person. Women, according to the pope, are also more natural parents, better suited to raise and educate children. Men, on the other hand, have to learn parenthood from women, and while both parents must make a contribution, the role of a mother, in the opinion of the pope, is decisive in developing a child's personality, including his education and moral upbringing. John Paul II based these assumptions mainly on the belief that the Bible assigns such a role to women, particularly in God's choice of the Virgin Mary as the mother of Jesus Christ. Therefore, he argued, Mary is more holy than all men and comes before the male Apostles who, as he pointed out over and over again, were the only ones to be called to ministerial priesthood. He concluded, however, that in the eyes of God, both men and women are equal. They all, in different ways, according to Wojtyła, share in what the Second Vatican Council had recognized as "the universality of the priesthood."[12]

John Paul II continued that both men and women are equal before Christ, as expressed by St. Paul's words: "There is neither male nor female; for you are all one in Christ Jesus" (Gal 3:28), both are redeemed by Christ, and both are called to be the "Bride" of Christ—a female symbol of submission. John Paul II also notes that

Christ is the Bridegroom and a male who "emphasized the originality which distinguishes women from men."[13] The pope then took issue with the feminist argument that by choosing only men to be priests, Christ was simply acting according to the customs of his times. Such a behavior, according to John Paul II, would have been totally uncharacteristic of Christ—the only human being capable of truthfully teaching the way of God:

> In calling only men as his Apostles, Christ acted in a completely free and sovereign manner. In doing so, he exercised the same freedom with which, in all his behavior, he emphasized the dignity and the vocation of women, without conforming to the prevailing customs and to the traditions sanctioned by the legislation of the time. Consequently, the assumption that he called men to be Apostles in order to conform with the widespread mentality of his times does not correspond to Christ's way of acting.[14]

This was a very important point in Wojtyła's thinking about Christ and the role of women. The Gospels do not include any direct comments from Christ on the dignity of women but show that in most cases he treated women with greater respect than was customary during his times, the same way he treated beggars and other social outcasts. John Paul II assumed that Christ never assigned any teaching and leadership roles to women. This may or may not be true. He also assumed that if Christ indeed did not chose women as his Apostles, he was not motivated by the customs of his times but wanted to make a statement on the unsuitability of women for priesthood for the entire future human history. Many liberal Catholics do not share this view and believe that Christ could not have possibly made such a rule.

Elżbieta Adamiak, a female Polish theologian who has studied Wojtyła's views on women, observed that "the Pope looks at femininity from a male perspective and provides women with a specific vision of femininity as model [and] norm."[15] Janusz Poniewierski, a Polish journalist and author of an otherwise very positive book on Wojtyła's papacy, noted that many Catholic women, who want more than just one model focused on motherhood, interpret the pope's position as denying them the right to pursue a variety of ways to express their femininity.[16]

Cardinal Dziwisz, Wojtyła's closest friend, observed that John Paul II had realized women throughout the world were being treated with less and less respect and viewed mostly as objects of desire.[17] He was probably thinking largely of the Western world. But it was in the West, where the feminist movement had started and where most of the calls for the ordination of women are being heard. Most feminists believe that thanks to their movement respect for women in the West has increased, which is not necessarily the case in some of the more traditional societies in the developing world. According to Cardinal Dziwisz, John Paul II saw, however, that women were being denied respect and wrote *Mulieris dignitatem* to bring back their dignity and underscore their important role in society.

Ordinatio sacerdotalis — Reserving Priestly Ordination to Men Alone

Other than birth control and abortion, no other issue has been more controversial in recent Church history than the ban on ordination of women as priests. For many feminists this topic has become the symbol of discrimination against women by the Catholic Church, a mark of the establishment's contempt for women's spirituality and intellect, as well as a device to insure their wellbeing through consigning half of the flock to the caste of worker-bees. Feminists saw Pope John Paul II as the main culprit. For most Catholics in Wojtyła's Poland, however, ordination of women-priests has always been a non-issue. As one Polish priest observed recently, to this day even those few Catholics in Poland, who are critical of the Church hierarchy on various issues, have not called for allowing women to become priests or questioned the cult of the Virgin Mary.[18] In defending Wojtyła's position on this issue, Cardinal Dziwisz pointed out that John Paul II had always defended the Church's stand by saying that "Jesus could have done it differently [making women his Apostles], but he had not done this. And we are faithful to what Jesus had said and done."[19]

Karol Wojtyła, first as the Archbishop of Kraków and later as pope, consistently opposed the idea of the ordination of women. When shortly after his election to the papacy, a woman journalist asked him what he intends to do about allowing women into priesthood, his immediate reply was "The Virgin preferred to stand at the foot of the Cross."[20] This should have been a clear signal that the new pope's vision of the role of women would prevent him from even considering allowing women near the altar. "Woman at the foot of the Cross" was, by the way, the motto of the Polish bishops' letter on the occasion of the International Women's Day in 1969. For Wojtyła, priesthood represents a sacred bond between man (in this case, a male) and God, and between a priest and Christ.[21]

Theologians, who have researched arguments advanced by various churches against the ordination of women, point to three main reasons churchmen give for not allowing women become priests. Some church leaders argue that a woman in front of the altar could become an object of sexual attraction for the male members of the congregation. Another argument is that woman should not exercise authority over men or be in a position of leadership. The ultimate argument, however, has been that Christ himself was male and chose only men as his twelve Apostles, therefore only men can properly represent Christ as priests.[22] John Paul II obviously accepted the last argument, but he never commented directly on the first two. If we assume, however, as true that Christ specifically excluded women from priesthood — something John Paul II strongly believed in — then the logical conclusion is that Christ did not consider women as suitable for leadership roles in the Church. With many Catholics questioning the authority of the Vatican on this issue, John Paul II finally decided in the fifteenth year of his pontificate to make his position absolutely clear. On May 22, 1994, while recovering after the hip-replacement operation, the pope signed on the hospital bed the highly controversial Apostolic Letter *Ordinatio sacerdotalis*.[23] In it he declared that "the Church has no authority whatsoever to confer priestly ordination on women and that this judgment is to be definitely held by all the Church's faithful."[24]

It was a relatively short document, but it was bound to have tremendous impact on the future of the Catholic Church and the attitudes of women worldwide. By declaring that his judgment "is to be definitely held" by all Catholics, John Paul II seemed to have tied the hands of his successors on this crucial issue. Peter Hebblethwaite (1930-1994), the late author of several books on the recent popes, at one time a Jesuit priest and a strong critic of John Paul II, described the letter as "clear, peremptory, brutal and decisive."[25] For Peter Hebblethwaite, it was highly significant — even if it could not be proven — that John Paul II signed the letter in the hospital, acting out of "a sense of mystical urgency" to prevent any further consideration of this issue if anything should happen to him.

In many ways, the publication of *Ordinatio sacerdotalis* is reminiscent of *Humanae vitae* encyclical on birth control issued in 1968 by Pope Paul VI with active encouragement from Wojtyła. As was the case with *Humanae vitae*, John Paul II decided to ignore the advice of many Western theologians. Just like Paul VI on the issue of birth control, John Paul II wanted to settle the issue of female priests once and for all and to remove any doubts.[26] In both cases, the end result was quite different from what the popes had wanted to achieve. Instead of settling the issue of women-priests, *Ordinatio sacerdotalis* stimulated a storm of protests and discussions. The document may have also undermined papal authority and alienated a large number of Catholics. Peter Hebblethwaite argued that Pope Paul's encyclical on birth control involved issues of personal liberty. According to him, the same is true for John Paul's decision on the ordination of women-priests. With the spread of democracy, liberal ideas and market economies, issues of personal liberty have become extremely sensitive in the late 20th century, with increasing number of people around the world demanding more personal freedom. Many women, especially in the West, believed that Paul VI and John Paul II denied them rights, which they thought were rightly theirs.

The main argument advanced by John Paul II in *Ordinatio sacerdotalis* is that Jesus Christ chose his Apostles only from among men. In presenting this argument, John Paul II quoted Paul VI, who made the same point while unsuccessfully opposing the proposal to ordain women in the Anglican Church. The document is, in fact, full of excerpts from previous Church statements, showing Wojtyła's intimacy with traditional Catholic teaching and practice on this issue. He quoted from Pope Paul's letter that excluding women from priesthood has been "the constant practice of the Church, which has imitated Christ in choosing only men."[27] John Paul II failed to mention the findings of the Vatican's Pontifical Biblical Commission, which in a report to Pope Paul VI submitted in 1976, had concluded that there was no evidence that Jesus specifically forbade the ordination of women. Neither Paul VI nor John Paul II was persuaded by the arguments of some of the Vatican's own biblical scholars who had argued that ordaining women might not necessarily go "against Christ's original intentions." The whole commission, however, left the question unsettled, presenting arguments both against and in favor of the ordination of women:

It does not seem that the New Testament by itself alone will permit us to settle in a clear way and once and for all the problem of the possible accession of women to the presbyterate.

However, some think that in the scripture there are sufficient indications to exclude this possibility, considering that the sacraments of Eucharist and reconciliation have a special link with the person of Christ and therefore with the male hierarchy, as borne out by the New Testament.

Others, on the contrary, wonder if the Church hierarchy, entrusted with the sacramental economy, would be able to entrust the ministries of Eucharist and reconciliation to women in light of circumstances, without going against Christ's original intentions.[28]

The Vatican's biblical scholars could not make up their mind in the 1970s; there was too much ambiguity in the Scripture and too much at stake for the future of the Catholic Church. The wording of the 1994 John Paul's *Ordinatio sacerdotalis* is much more striking: "the Church has no authority whatsoever...". John Paul II was fully convinced of the correctness of his views and chose to ignore doubts expressed by the Vatican's scholars. In an apparent effort to show that his hands are really tied on this issue, he instead quoted from the Congregation for the Doctrine of the Faith Declaration *Inter insigniores* that the Church "does not consider itself authorized to admit women to priestly ordination."[29] Still, despite his firm position, the pope seemed to appreciate its potential to alienate women and even for encouraging discrimination against them. He must have sensed the vulnerability of his position, for in *Ordinatio sacerdotalis* he devotes nearly half of the text defending his stand as non-discriminatory. The substance of the argument is the example of Virgin Mary as proof that there can be no talk of discrimination in the sense of unjust treatment since even she was not given the same role as the Apostles and was not chosen for ministerial priesthood. Rather than finding this a reflection of the lack of accurate historical records or a result of the prevailing custom—the arguments advanced by feminists and more liberal scholars—John Paul II called it "faithful observance of a plan to be ascribed to the wisdom of the Lord of the Universe."[30]

Ordinatio sacerdotalis shows nevertheless that John Paul II seemed bothered by the argument that Christ simply did not consider women ready to become his Apostles because of the cultural and social restrictions of his time. Ultimately, he rejected this view as inconsistent with the historical record of Christ's defiance of many prevailing social customs and Jewish laws, even though Christ, who spoke about slavery did not specifically condemn it in the Gospel, and neither did the Catholic Church for many centuries afterwards. Yet in his 1993 encyclical *Veritatis splendor*, John Paul II declared slavery to be "intrinsically evil" together with "any kind of homicide, genocide, abortion, euthanasia and voluntary suicide; ... mutilation, physical and mental torture (there is no approval here for even mental coercion of terrorist suspects by the Bush Administration) and attempts to coerce the spirit; ...subhuman living conditions, arbitrary imprisonment, deportation, ... prostitution and trafficking in women and children; degrading conditions of work which treat laborers as mere instruments of profit." He defined "intrinsically evil" acts as being always evil regardless of historical circumstances and the intentions of the person or persons involved because such acts are by their very nature incapable of being ascribed to God and "radically contradict the good of the person made in his image."[31] Interestingly, in this passage of *Veritatis splendor*, John Paul II did not comment on the fact that the Catholic Church has changed its view numerous times over the centuries as to what acts are "intrinsically evil," and he said nothing about the possibility that denying women certain rights and freedoms simply because they are women could fall into this category. A year later, he dealt with this problem by pointing out in *Ordinatio sacerdotalis* that Christ "emphasized the dignity and the vocation of women."[32] In stressing this point, John Paul II seemed to be making a conscious and deliberate effort not to appear insensitive to the concerns of modern women and to avoid charges of historical hypocrisy. He called the role of women in the Church as "absolutely necessary and irreplaceable."[33] At the same time, he had a very clear idea what this role should be, and it was not one placing women with significant skills and interests in positions of leadership and authority over men within the Church. Women are to be "witnesses to Christ in the family and society...the holy martyrs, virgins, and the mothers of families...bringing up their children in the spirit of the Gospel."[34]

The official *Catechism of the Catholic Church*, approved by John Paul II two years earlier, repeats the assertion that "the ordination of women is not possible," because the Church "recognizes herself to be bound by this choice made by the Lord himself." [35] Neither John Paul II nor anyone else responsible for writing the Catechism would admit that there is in fact no clear record of Jesus ordaining anyone, male or female. The Catechism, (the word means "instruction") described by John Paul II as "a sure norm for teaching the Faith," confirms the established legal position of the Catholic Church that "'Only a baptized man (*vir*) validly receives sacred ordination.'"(*Codex Iuris Canonici*, ca. 1024).[36] The Lord Jesus chose men (*viri*) to form the college of the twelve apostles, and the apostles did the same when they chose collaborators to succeed them in their ministry."[37]

Feminist scholars point out, however, to strong evidence that before men reasserted control and removed women from positions of authority in early Christian churches, women served as deaconesses with some of their functions comparable to those of today's priests. John Paul's letter did not say anything about ordaining of women to the diaconate. This was interpreted by some at the time as a tiny ray of hope, but in September 2001, John Paul II officially stated his opposition not only to ordaining deaconesses but even to the idea of training women for the possibility of serving as deacons in the future. The declaration made public by the Congregation for the Doctrine of the Faith, signed by Cardinal Joseph Ratzinger, the future Pope Benedict XVI, and approved by Pope John Paul II, stated that courses directly or indirectly aimed at the diaconal ordination of women "are lacking

a solid doctrinal foundation" and "can generate pastoral disorien-
tation." Bishops around the world were urged "to diligently apply
the above-mentioned directives." The Congregation defended its
position by asserting that the teachings of the Church, and specifically the teachings of Pope John Paul II, open to women other
ample opportunities for service and collaboration.[38]

The opponents of preparing women for the diaconate claim that
the historical evidence on women-deacons is weak. Some Catholic
priests opposed to the ordination of women question whether
deaconesses in the early Church had any functions relating to
priesthood, and some have even suggested that the term
"deaconess" may have been used only to describe wives of
deacons. What seems clear from the historical record is that the
institution of priesthood, as it is known today, was not yet
developed at the time of the first Apostles. It is also clear that after
a brief initial period of relative equality of sexes, the early male
Church leaders, of whom Saint Paul is a prime example, saw the
high visibility of women in Christian churches as an obstacle to the
further growth of Christianity. By removing Christian women from
public roles and assigning them to the domestic sphere under the
control of males, they made Christianity much more attractive to
many more people in patriarchal societies which they wanted to
convert. Since men occupied the positions of authority in the
ancient world, they were the ones that needed to be persuaded that
Christianity would not undermine their power and influence. But
even with the new restrictions placed on women by early Christian
Church leaders, Christianity as a religion still offered some women
far greater freedom than most pagan religions. For one thing,
Christianity did not allow men to divorce their wives at will and
granted women more dignity by acknowledging that the first
woman was created by God. Early Christian male leaders made
sure, however, that women understood their subservient position
vis-à-vis men. These attitudes began to change significantly only
after the Industrial Revolution freed some women from economic

dependency on men and humanistic ideas started to take hold in the West. The Catholic Church has split on this issue, with Wojtyła and other conservative leaders insisting that God sees women as being substantially different from men, and liberal Catholics denying the existence of substantial gender differences and demanding equal rights and equal roles within the Church for both sexes.

In Wojtyła's view, women should not aspire to have the same ambitions and public roles as men for such aspirations would be inconsistent with God's plan for women. In *Ordinatio sacerdotalis*, John Paul II reassured women that there was nothing demeaning in being excluded from priesthood because becoming a priest should not be seen not after all as the most important or the most desirable goal in life. He concluded this argument by quoting from an earlier Church document that "the greatest in the Kingdom of Heaven are not the ministers but the saints."[39] In his Apostolic Letter, John Paul II conceded that some might still think of priestly ordination of women as open to debate. He obviously felt strongly that there should be no further discussion on this issue. He described his reason for writing the letter as wanting to remove all doubt "regarding a matter of great importance":

> I declare that the Church has no authority whatsoever to confer priestly ordination on women and that this judgment is to be definitively held by all the Church's faithful.[40]

It is clear from the Apostolic Letter that despite its definite conclusion, John Paul II was rather defensive about his position on non-ordination of women. He went into great lengths in trying to portray himself to potential critics as a defender of women's dignity and their rights. That is, of course, as long as they are willing to give up the idea of becoming priests. On this point, Wojtyła was not prepared to give in, although it also seems rather clear judging by the way he argued in support of his position that this very traditional yet sensitive Church leader was ridden by guilt.

Since John Paul II spent almost all of his adult life defending human rights, one can sense from his statements a serious concern that the ordination of women should not be seen as a human rights issue. This was a real concern for John Paul II who was very familiar with numerous groups, both in his homeland and abroad, seeking his protection and assistance in fighting for human rights. This could also explain why Hillary Rodham Clinton, always looking for ways to defend her feminist pro-choice positions against criticism from the Vatican and the Catholic Church, said at the 1995 Beijing conference on women that it was no longer acceptable "to discuss women's rights as separate from human rights." It may have been an indirect way of pointing out to the Vatican representatives at the conference that women do not enjoy full human rights within the Catholic Church and should not be treated differently from men in terms of their rights as spiritual human beings. While John Paul II was always eager to listen to any oppressed class of people, there was no real dialogue between Catholic feminists, or feminists in general, and John Paul II on this issue. There was no attempt on his part to include feminist complaints in the category of human rights violations because it would risk elevating their cause and perhaps raise questions about discrimination of women in the most obvious places: within the Church and within families. Some of feminists' demands were so alien to his view of the true nature of woman that even if he shared many of their concerns, he was not willing to embrace their cause for greater justice and equality, preferring instead to offer his own version of conditional "new feminism."

After a few futile attempts to enter into a dialogue with John Paul II at the beginning of his papacy, feminists realized that the Vatican was not interested in being identified with their causes as they defined them. Always willing to embrace almost any oppressed people, John Paul II also did not want to be seen as coming to the defense of a group, which in addition to demanding ordination of women also advocates access to contraception and liberal abortion and divorce laws. John Paul II admitted that throughout history women have been victims of male oppression, but he consistently rejected out of hand any suggestions of approaching female ordination as a question of justice within the Church.

Conservative and Liberal Arguments on Women-Priests

John Paul's attachment to the Church and her tradition was so great that he found it very difficult to accept blame for many historical acts of Church injustice and discrimination against women. To do so would meant renouncing a multitude of traditional Church teachings and practices for which he was not psychologically prepared even if he understood them to be wrong. It was much easier for John Paul II to admit that the Church was wrong in denouncing the teachings of Galileo (1564-1642) and Darwin (1809-1882), but these were not very complex cases involving Church sanctioned rules of appropriate behavior which affect whole societies. In the case of women, there is almost 2000-year of tradition on top of culture. Wojtyła's ideas of what women should want, as opposed to what they really want now, were shaped by his experiences growing up in a very traditional society with a traditional family and Church environment. In May 1992, after the visit of Dr. George Carey (b. 1935), the then Archbishop of Canterbury, during which he and John Paul II discussed the impending decision by the Anglican Church to allow the ordination of women, the Vatican spokesman announced that "the Catholic Church, for fundamental theological reasons, does not believe it has the right to authorize such ordination."

In November 1992, members of the General Synod voted 384 to 169 for women to be ordained as priests in the Church of England. This move caused some defections of Anglicans, including Anglican priests, to the Catholic Church. Dr Carey told the Synod

The Right Reverend Barbara Clementine Harris b. 1930
Consecrated as bishop: February 11, 1989

The Most Reverend Katharine Jefferts Schori b. 1954
Elected the Presiding Bishop of the Episcopal Church in the United States of
America: June 18, 2006
http://www.episcopalchurch.org/presiding-bishop.htm

The Right Reverend V. Gene Robinson b. 1947
http://www.nhepiscopal.org/bishop/bishop.html

Anglican and Episcopal Web Sites in the U.S. and UK

The Church of England
http://www.cofe.anglican.org/

The Anglican Communion
http://www.anglicancommunion.org/

The Episcopal Church of the United States of America
http://www.episcopalchurch.org/
Episcopal life online
http://www.episcopalchurch.org/ens/

The Episcopal Diocese of San Joaquin
http://sanjoaquin.anglican.org/

The Episcopal Diocese of Quincy
http://dioceseofquincy.org/

The Episcopal Diocese of Fort Worth
http://www.fwepiscopal.org/

before the vote that women must be ordained to the priesthood if the Church of England is to keep its credibility. In 1995, Dr. Carey also had another meeting with John Paul II during which he asked him to state his objections to the ordination of women. According to Dr. Carey, the pope's blunt answer was "Anthropology!" He understood the pope's comment to mean that women cannot be priests simply because they were women, but as mentioned earlier, John Paul II's command of English was not perfect.[41] Anthropology may have been the bottom line, but John Paul II's theological reasoning was more sophisticated. It centered on Christ not selecting women as his apostles — a conclusion which nevertheless has been challenged by many biblical scholars and theologians. Dr. Carey retired as the Archbishop of Canterbury in 2002 and was succeeded by Archbishop Rowan Williams (b. 1950) who has been supportive of the Church's liberal policies on women.

The Anglican Church is now struggling with the issue of homosexual bishops and gay marriages — issues which, in addition to the ordination of women, John Paul II desperately wanted to avoid for consideration within the Catholic Church. Most of the opposition to women-priests and gay-priests and bishops comes from Anglican churches in the Third World, some of which have voted to separate from the Anglican Communion. A few conservative Episcopal congregations in the United States are also considering breaking their ties with the Episcopal Church in the United States, also part of the Anglican Communion, over the issue of women-priests and blessing of same-sex unions. First women-priests in the Episcopal Church ordained in Philadelphia, Pennsylvania in 1974 and the practice was legalized at the General Convention two years later. In 1989, the U.S. Episcopal Church consecrated an African American woman Barbara Clementine Harris as its first female bishop and in 2006 elected Dr. Katharine Jefferts Schori as its presiding bishop. Dr. Jefferts Schori is the first and only female national leader in the Anglican Communion. The first openly homosexual Episcopal bishop, Gene Robinson, was elected on June 7, 2003 at St. Paul's Church in Concord, New Hampshire. In response to these developments, the Convention of the Diocese of San Joaquin in California, regarded as one of the most conservative Episcopal dioceses in the United States, voted to start the process of withdrawing from the Episcopal Church and affiliating with another Anglican church. Some members, however, actively oppose the proposed secession. Responding in December 2007 to Bishop Schori's letter on the issue of the current litigation, the Bishop of San Joaquin, The Right Rev. John-David M. Schofield, used the example of the Catholic Church and other more conservative churches to support his position against the ordination of women and pointed out that contrary to Bishop Schori's suggestion he does not feel isolated: "My understanding of the authority of the Holy Scriptures, as well as Catholic Faith and Order are shared by the Roman Catholic Church, Eastern Orthodox Churches and by some 60 million faithful Anglicans worldwide." The Diocese of Quincy in Illinois, the Diocese of Fort Worth in Texas and some Episcopal parishes in Virginia are also considering seeking a different pastoral oversight over the issue of women-priests and gay bishops.

"Fundamental theological reasons," to which the Vatican spokesman referred in 1992 in rejecting the Anglican Church's plans for ordination of women as theologically unsound, in the opinion of a conservative American Catholic thinker Michael Novak (b. 1933), boil down to the simple argument that Christ, himself a man, did not ordain any women as priests, and himself used gender differentiated terms, such as "Our Father" and the "Son of God." What feminists use to prove that Christianity is biased against women, such as non-gender neutral terms in the Bible, can just as easily be used by conservative Christians as God's argument against women-priests. As Novak pointed out, God could have revealed himself by sending a female Messiah but instead chose a Jewish man, Jesus Christ. Even though pre-

Christian societies had women clergy, Novak maintains that the demand for women-priests is a relatively recent phenomenon associated with the development of Western liberal culture. He believes that until recently, most women and men alike did not see anything wrong with exclusively male priesthood. In that respect, he is still right about a significant segment of women.

When I asked a number of first-generation and second-generation Russian-American women, who are active members of the Russian Orthodox Church but have rejected many of the strict rules on sexual morality including birth control, whether they would go to confession to a woman-priest, all of them said no. However, when I talked to their daughters, now in their late twenties, they saw nothing wrong with women-priests. (According to a 1996 survey analyzed by Father Andrew Greeley, more American Catholic men favor ordination of women-priests than American Catholic women, although women are more liberal on other issues.[42]) While Michael Novak can be described as conservative on moral issues, he is a strong supporter of human rights and free market economy. In Novak's analysis, it was the social and economic advancement of women, helped by freedoms and rights made possible by the development of Western liberal democracies and capitalism, which brought with it growing awareness of the injustice in denying women the opportunity to become priests.[43]

With social justice very much on John Paul's public agenda, the only way that the Catholic Church can argue its position against women-priests now, without explicitly attacking women as a group, is to point out the maleness of Jesus Christ

First Things

http://www.firstthings.com/

and the apparent lack of any evidence of women Apostles. Despite this argument, as Michael Novak observed in an article published in *First Things*, an ecumenical journal devoted to conservative critique of contemporaty society, "the Catholic Church will seem to be at fundamental odds" with the Western liberal culture. If John

Paul II or his successors would give in to the growing demands for equal treatment of men and women within the Church and allow the ordination of women, then, as Novak noted, "the Catholic Church will have adapted itself to the practices of contemporary Western culture."

Knowing Wojtyła's views and background, it would have been unreasonable to expect that such a dramatic change could have happened during his pontificate. First of all, John Paul II would not have broken with tradition. He would not have given in to demands which he perceived to be largely the product of Western secular liberalism, for which he had little respect and a great deal of hostility. He was also convinced, despite some body of evidence to the contrary, that Catholics in the Third World overwhelmingly reject demands for the ordination of women and agree with his position on contraception. Finally, John Paul II believed that even though Jesus did not choose women as his Apostles, women are not inferior to men. As long as the equal value and dignity of men and women is asserted, John Paul II believed that different roles could be assigned to each gender, especially if Christ's own words and actions could be used to support such distinctions.

Feminist and liberal Catholics do not believe that Jesus would have excluded women from priesthood. Had he done so, then according to liberal American Catholic theologian, Richard P. McBrien, Jesus would have been guilty of concluding that women are fundamentally inferior to men. The exclusion of women from priesthood by Jesus would have meant that they "do not have the same capacity as men to approach the throne of God and to make intercession on behalf of us all." Richard P. McBrien also points out that "since every human being is made in the image and likeness of God, and since God is masculine," the exclusion of women from priesthood by Jesus would mean that "women are less godly than men." If Jesus indeed forbade the ordination of women, it would mean that they "are incapable of the priestly work of mediation between God and ourselves."[44] Professor McBrien noted that he does not believe women are less godly than men or incapable of God's ministry.

What seems obvious to Western liberals was not at all convincing for Karol Wojtyła. For someone who grew up in a traditional society with clear division of roles for women and men, women can be asked to find their fulfillment in motherhood and in non-leadership roles in society and in the Church without being considered second-class citizens. This is especially true if women are otherwise valued and honored by their families and their communities for fulfilling their gender role. It is even truer if they are not outwardly discriminated against and if they do chose certain public roles which society considers appropriate for them. Finally, if women are working in solidarity with men on such important goals as national independence, religious freedom and human rights, then there can be little doubt that women are indeed equal, perhaps even better in some areas than men. Karol Wojtyła believed all of these statements to be true and that is how he could justify to himself his position on women-priests.

While throughout his papacy John Paul II continued to insist that Christ did not want women to be ordained, he tried hard to soften the harsh reality of his conclusions by arguing that the presumed decision by the founder of Christianity did not in any way indicate that women are inferior to men. When challenged about his position, John Paul II almost always referred to Christ as the final arbiter on this issue and gave the example of the Mother of Christ as proof that women can enjoy equal status and dignity without being priests. In an interview with French journalist, André Frossard, John Paul II gave answers to questions posed to him during his trip to France in the early 1980s as to why women cannot be ordained, whether the Church will always be run by men and whether women will always have a secondary role. The pope suggested that men and women should learn what Christ actually taught and what he did and to look at the example of the Virgin Mary. John Paul II said that in Christ one can find "unfathomable treasures of wisdom and intelligence."

> The experience of two thousand years teaches us that in the mission of the whole People of God there is no difference in principle between man and woman. Both, in accordance with their own vocations, become this new human being who lives for others and is therefore the glory of God. Although it may be true that it is the successors of the Apostles, and hence men, who govern the Church from the hierarchical point of view, there can be no doubt that in the charismatic sense the influence of women is no smaller; perhaps it is even greater. I beg you to think often of Mary, the Mother of Christ.' [45]

Arguments against the ordination of women advanced by John Paul II can become quite theological and complex, but ultimately they can be reduced to a simple assertion that no female can fully represent a male Christ. As one feminist writer noted rather crudely, this can only mean that the main qualification for becoming a Catholic priest is the possession of male genitalia. Following the same logic, only Jewish, circumcised males should be ordained as priests in the Catholic Church, since all of the original twelve Apostles were Jewish men. These comments from feminists may be designed to shock, but apparently this line of reasoning on the proper gender of priests had resulted in some absurd or perhaps not so absurd practices, depending on how seriously one views the whole issue. According to historical accounts, a special chair was used to test the sex of newly installed popes during the Middle Ages. This special papal throne, known as the *sedia stercoraria*, or the "pierced chair," allowed one of the junior cardinals to discretely touch the testicles of any chosen candidate before his election could be verified.[46] I could not confirm the validity of this account given by an author who claims that persistent rumors of a female pope who pretended to be a man are true. Feminists claim that even the mere existence of these rumors proves that perhaps there is something ridiculous about selecting priests on the basis of gender.

According to a medieval legend, a female pope may have been more than a mere fantasy, although there is no definite historical proof that the so-called Pope Joan was ever elected. The story, whether true or not, is, however, quite fascinating and has interesting links with John Paul II's homeland. According to the historical chronicle of Martinus Polonus (Martin of Poland), also known as Martin of Opava, a woman of English heritage from Germany pretended to be a boy to receive education in Athens and came to Rome continuing her deception. Because of her great learning and skills, she became a close collaborator of Pope Leo IV. When he died in 853, she was elected pope, taking the name of John VIII. She managed to hold the office for two and a half years until 855, when she gave birth to a child as she was going through the streets of Rome. According to this account by a medieval church historian, published in 1265, Pope Joan died after the delivery. Other accounts tell the story of her and her baby being stoned to death by the angry crowd. Still other accounts report that she was allowed to live out her life in a convent.

The official Catholic Church line is that the stories of Pope Joan are the work of Protestant enemies of Catholicism. Martinus Polonus's chronicle *Chronicon pontificum et imperatorum* predates any Protestant attempts at embarrassing the Catholic Church, but most modern scholars dismiss Pope Joan as a medieval legend and a fabrication. Far from being a historian sympathetic to the woman-pope, by including the account of Pope Joan in his chronicle, Martin Polonus was trying to disclose and condemn a shameful error on the part of the Church in the hope that it would never happen again. Martinus Polonus or Martinus Oppaviensis, also known in German as Martin von Troppau and in Czech as Martin z Opavy, was a Dominican priest born in the Czech Silesian town of Opava who studied in Prague and was active in Poland. He then left Poland for Rome, where he became a senior churchman, lawyer and a respected writer of Church history. In 1278, Pope Nicholas III (1277-1280) named already 70-years-old Martin the Archbishop of Gniezno in Poland, but the Polish prelate died before he could reach his homeland.[47]

John Paul II, who frequently mentions almost every famous figure in Poland's history, from Nicolaus Copernicus (Mikołaj Kopernik 1473-1543) to Father Kolbe, never made any references to Martinus Polonus. The historical truth of his account cannot be authoritatively proven, but if a woman-pope did exist, it would have had serious implications for the Catholic Church. There is no specific objection to women-priests in Scripture. John Paul II bases his ban on considering the ordination of women on the uninter-rupted tradition of the Catholic Church of selecting only male priests. Since the church believes that the Holy Spirit guides those who are selecting a pope, the election a woman-pope would mean a highly symbolic break of tradition.

Another legend, for which there is no historical proof, is that of Saint Eugenia (d. c. AD 258), the daughter of the pagan judge, Philip, during the reign of Roman Emperor Valerian. She is believed to have fled her father's house and, after being baptized, entered a monastery pretending to be a man. Because of her abilities she was elected as abbot. After being accused of adultery by a woman, whom she had cured of sickness and whose advances she had resisted, she was taken to her father's court, where she proved her innocence by opening her robe and revealing her real sex. She converted her father and her mother to Christianity and later died in Rome as a martyr for her faith. Her feast day is celebrated on Christmas Day, December 25th. One of the carved capitals in the 12th century Basilica of Mary Magdalene in Vezelay, France, shows Saint Eugenie standing between her disappointed accuser and her astonished father.[48]

But even if the legends of Pope Joan, Saint Eugenia and Nawojka are factually false, the very fact of their existence testifies to a popular desire to reflect, for whatever reason, the Church's marginalization of women. These stories also prove that according to the popular opinion in the Middle Ages, women could and actually did function in roles reserved by the Church for men only. They also point to an early realization among some Christians that the reason for women not holding these positions was the objections of men who did not want to see them in roles of leadership and authority rather than any intellectual and leadership deficiencies on the part of women. John Paul II would probably respond that not everything people think and do is always right and that is why Catholics need to seriously consider the official teachings of the Church. Some of these teachings, of course, turned out to be wrong and unjust.

The Infallibility Argument

Ordinatio sacerdotalis, the 1994 Apostolic Letter on reserving priestly ordination to men alone was one of many documents and statements from Pope John Paul II and the Vatican in recent years designed to counter feminist influences within the Church and to quiet demands for ordination of women-priests. In October 1995, the Vatican's Congregation for the Doctrine of the Faith issued a letter signed by its Prefect, conservative German cardinal Joseph Ratzinger, a close friend of John Paul II charged with keeping doctrinal discipline among Catholics who was later rewarded for his orthodoxy by being elected the next pope. In the letter, Cardinal Ratzinger amplified, explained and defended papal arguments against the ordination of women by stressing the constancy of the Church's tradition and teachings on the subject from the very beginning of Christianity.

Cardinal Ratzinger explained that while John Paul II did not invoke papal infallibility, his ban on the ordination of women should nevertheless be considered as infallible because it is based on the infallibility of the "ordinary magisterium" of all the bishops agreeing with a particular Church teaching. At the same time, Cardinal Ratzinger repeated the argument used by John Paul II

> *I think that a certain contemporary feminism finds its roots in the absence of true respect for woman.*
>
> John Paul II, *Crossing the Threshold of Hope*

that the denial of priesthood to women can only be properly understood in the context of what the Church teaches about "the equal personal dignity of men and women" — as exemplified by the role of Virgin Mary, who was not selected by Jesus to be an Apostle or a priest. In Cardinal Ratzinger's words, "diversity of mission in no way compromises equality of personal dignity." In an attempt to diffuse the claim of male domination within the Church, Cardinal Ratzinger also argued that the ministerial priesthood is "not a position of privilege or human power over others."

Whoever, man or woman, conceives of the priesthood in terms of personal affirmation, as a goal or point of departure in a career of human success, is profoundly mistaken, for the true meaning of Christian priesthood, whether it be the common priesthood of the faithful or, in a most special way, the ministerial priesthood, can only be found in the sacrifice of one's own being in union with Christ, in service of the brethren.

Cardinal Ratzinger, now Pope Benedict XVI, may indeed be right that ministerial priesthood is a sacrifice, but so is being a nun. As one feminist asked, if nuns were to be ordained priests, who was going to do the laundry? The main purpose of Cardinal Ratzinger's letter, however, was to point out that while the pope's original letter *Ordinatio sacerdotalis* was not presented as infallible — papal declarations presented as infallible have been very rare in recent history — the prohibition against women-priests does have the definitive and infallible basis and "belongs to the deposit of the faith of the Church." As long as John Paul II did not claim infallibility himself, there could have still been some doubt whether Cardinal Ratzinger's interpretation was correct. John Paul II finally revealed his own views, when losing his patience with the German bishops in 1999 over the issue of pre-abortion counseling; he told them that his statement on women-priests did indeed represent infallible teaching:

> When the individual Bishops, "even though dispersed throughout the world but preserving among themselves and with Peter's Successor the bond of communion, agree in their authoritative teaching on matters of faith and morals that a particular teaching is to be held definitely and absolutely, they infallibly proclaim the doctrine of Christ."[49]

Liberal Catholics argue that there are serious problems with this argument. First of all, not all Catholic bishops were in agreement with the previous pope on this issue and not all of them had been consulted. Some bishops are known to strongly disagree with John Paul's ban on discussing the ordination of women. They are, however, in the minority.

Women and Priests in the Third World

The publication of *Ordinatio sacerdotalis* was the final blow to those Catholics who were still hoping for some liberal changes during John Paul II's pontificate. Some may have hoped that he would become overwhelmed by doubt and guilt once he realized the enormous injustice and humiliation felt by many women. They did not understand that John Paul II was not a man with a Western liberal perspective on women's rights or someone who changes his mind easily and is willing to experiment with tradition. His attachment to history and tradition, being one of the products of his Polish education, was too great to allow for any drastic break with the Church's past. There is also evidence that toward the end of his pontificate John Paul II was becoming even less tolerant of any dissent within the Church on this issue. In January 1997, the Vatican excommunicated Father Tissa Balasuriya, a Sri Lankan priest who in his book *Mary and Human Liberation* spoke out for equal rights for women in the Catholic Church and promoted the idea of the women's ordination.[50] It was significant that the first theologian since the Second Vatican Council to be excommunicated for doctrinal disagreement was a Third World priest whose primary interest was the liberation of women and the Asian interpretation of the image of God. It was an embarrassing reminder for the Vatican that the idea of women's rights within the Church was spreading even in the Third World. The excommunication of the Sri Lankan Oblate priest without giving him a fair hearing drew international protests forcing the Vatican to reconsider its decision. After difficult negotiations involving the Roman Curia, the Archbishop of Colombo and Father Balasuriya, the excommunication of the 73 year old priest was finally rescinded, in January 1998.

There is little doubt that the pope settled the whole matter himself in order to avoid further embarrassment. We Are Church, the international movement of

We Are Church
http://www.we-are-church.org/

liberal Catholics opposed to the Vatican's current policies on women and other issues, which started in Austria and has spread to over twenty countries on all six continents, greeted Father Balasuriya's rehabilitation as an encouraging success for the realization of human rights for Catholics within the Church.[51]

While John Paul II could easily dismiss criticism of his positions coming from the West as evidence of materialism and secularization, it was painful for him to deal with challenges from Catholics in the developing world, particularly on the issue of women's ordination. John Paul II convinced himself that the vast majority of Catholics living in Latin America, Africa and Asia are opposed to the ordination of women and that their cultures would not tolerate such a drastic move. Because of his Polish experience, he claimed to have a better understanding of what the Catholics in the developing world want from the Church. A challenge from a Sri Lankan priest was an uncomfortable reminder that the opposition to the Vatican's treatment of women was not limited to the United States and Western Europe and that not all Third World Catholics are socially conservative, although the vast majority of them most likely have much more conservative views on women than Catholics in the West.

The controversy over Father Balusuriya was also not the first time John Paul II learned that at least some priests in Asia, Africa and Latin America do not necessarily share his ideas of what role women should be allowed to play in the Church. Some of the criticism was coming from priests and bishops in countries where women still face far more severe discrimination than women in Poland. They realized that the Church must set an example if it wants to affect change in the regions of the world where such change could bring greater prosperity and dignity to both women and men. They seemed less afraid of Western solutions to gender relations than John Paul II, perhaps because their countries had a far longer and a more difficult road to travel in improving the situation of women than Poland and other countries in East Central Europe. At the Synod of African Bishops in 1994, Congolese bishop Ernest Kombo (b. 1941), challenged the pope with a strong recommendation that the highest positions within the Church hierarchy should be open to women. Addressing John Paul II, Bishop Kombo even proposed that the Church consider selecting women as "lay cardinals."[52] The final Synod document, approved by the African bishops, expressed "horror [at] the discrimination and marginalization to which women are subjected in the Church and society." The practical impact of the letter was, however, minimal.

Despite Bishop Kombo's appeal, many priests and bishops in the developing world and even in countries such as Poland continue to promote anti-Western and anti-modernization themes. They may believe in them or see such themes as useful in strengthening local churches and attracting followers, or both. Such attitudes are not surprising considering that for several decades the pope and the Vatican have reinforced these themes on a regular basis. And while some Third World Church leaders doubt the wisdom of the Vatican's position on women's ordination, they may still be in the minority. In fairness to John Paul II, it must be pointed out that he put a stop to the most extreme version of anti-Western and anti-American propaganda found in Liberation Theology. He did that, however, not because he did not believe that the West was responsible for much of the suffering in Latin America and that adoption of Western models would be dangerous for the local population and the local Church, but because he saw the movement as being both violent and under the influence of Marxism. These two elements, violence and Marxism, were for him even more dangerous than heartless capitalism.

Ludmila Javorová — First Ordained Catholic Woman-Priest

The possibility that some women may have already been ordained as priests in the Catholic Church would be a disturbing news to the conservatives in the Vatican. But it did happen in Wojtyła's backyard, in communist-ruled Czechoslovakia, where Catholic bishops had secretly ordained many priests in order to keep the Church alive and functioning as it was being forced to go under-ground. Understandably, there was very little record keeping or coordi-nation among the bishops whose identities were also sometimes kept secret. After the fall of communism, it became known that some of the Czech and Slovak candidates for priesthood had studied secretly in Kraków under Wojtyła's super-vision.[53] If his attempts to help the underground Church in Czechoslovakia were to be discovered by the communist author-ities, he could have been arrested. Wojtyła ordained some of the

> **Ludmila Javorová** b. 1932
> Ordained as priest: December 28, 1970
>
> **Bishop Felix Maria Davídek**
> (1921-1988)

male priests who then worked underground in Czechoslovakia.

But a different type of ordination took place in the 1970s, during the peak of the post-Prague Spring communist oppression. Despite the official Church ban on such ordinations, a valid Roman Catholic bishop, approved by the pope, apparently ordained a number of women to perform priestly functions in the clandestine Church. One of the women-priests was Ludmila Javorová, a Slovak woman from Brno in the present-day Czech Republic. So far, she was the only woman who went public with the news of her ordination, although four or five other women are also believed to have been ordained. When the clandestine Church debated the issue of ministering to women in communist prisons, it was decided that only other women could bring sacraments to women-prisoners without raising suspicions among communist guards that they were in fact priests. Male priests simply could not perform such functions under these circumstances. Bishop Felix Maria Davídek, a linguist and a medical doctor who had been consecrated as a bishop with the Vatican's approval to serve the underground Church in Czechoslovakia, called a secret synod of bishops, priests and laity to consider the issue of ordaining women. Despite a heated debate, his point of view prevailed, and on December 28, 1970 Bishop Davídek ordained Ludmila Javorová, the first woman Roman Catholic priest in modern history. She served as Vicar General of the underground Church for 20 years.

After the Velvet Revolution of 1989, Ludmila Javorová communicated to the Vatican on the activities of the underground Church and her ordination. She apparently received no response from the pope. Instead the Vatican invalidated the ordinations of women and forbade them to perform priestly functions. The ordinations of about 50 celibate men were recognized by the pope. Married men, who had also been secretly ordained in the underground Church, were given the option of joining the Byzantine Slavic Rite Church which recognizes the pope's authority but allows married priests. A declaration by the Congregation for the Doctrine of the Faith,

The Danube Seven

In 2002, Argentinean Catholic Bishop Rómulo Antonio Braschi, who was no longer in communion with the Vatican, ordained seven Roman Catholic women from Germany, Austria and the United States. The women: Christine Mayr-Lumetzberger, Adelinde Theresia Roitinger, Gisela Forster, Iris Muller, Ida Raming, Pia Brunner and Angela White became known as the Danube Seven since the ordinations were performed on a cruise ship on the Danube River. When they refused to repent, the women were excommunicated. Bishop Braschi orders are recognized as "valid but illicit" by the Roman Catholic Church, but the Vatican does not accept the sacramental validity of the ordination of women, which is forbidden by the Cannon Law and was declared "impossible" by Pope John Paul II in *Ordinatio sacerdotalis*. Bishop Braschi now heads the Catholic Apostolic Charismatic Church of "Jesus the King," which has followers in several European and Latin American countries, as well as in the United States and the United Kingdom. One of the Danube Seven women is Christine Mayr-Lumetzberger, a former Benedictine nun who had married a divorced man. She confirmed that she herself and another Danube Seven woman, Gisela Forster, had been ordained bishops in a secret ceremony in 2003. The name of the ordaining bishop is not known and it is not clear whether he was in communion with the Vatican. The Catholic Church does not recognize these ordinations.

Catholic Apostolic Charismatic Church of "Jesus the King"

http://jesustheking.20fr.com/

issued in February 2000, does not mention the women who had been secretly ordained in the underground Church in Czechoslovakia. The Congregation claims to have been guided by "an attitude of respect and waiting" in looking for "the solution of a most delicate problem of conscience" affecting persons "who had suffered a long time in the dark years of communism." But as far as the Vatican was concerned, there has never been any question about the lack of validity of the ordination of women-priests in the underground Czechoslovak Church, so the whole issue was completely ignored in the official document. The Congregation for the Doctrine of the Faith did single out Bishop Davídek as being responsible for ordinations which raise "serious doubts."[54] Cardinal Joseph Ratzinger, Prefect of the Congregation, decided not to address directly the issue of women-priests in the Czech Republic.

If a Catholic bishop in the communist-ruled Czechoslovakia felt that he could ordain a woman-priest, John Paul's argument that the Church has never accepted women as priests becomes somewhat weaker. Ludmila Javorová, a humble woman without any bitterness about her treatment by the Vatican, did not challenge the pope's right to prevent her from functioning as a priest, but she insisted that her ordination remains valid.[55]

Women Clergy in Poland: Felicja Kozłowska

John Paul's opposition to the ordination of women may have been influenced by yet another unusual event, this time in his own country. A schism in the Polish Catholic Church developed in the early 20th century over the issue of ordaining women and male priests submitting themselves to the authority of a woman. Ironically, the conflict within the Polish Church arose largely due to the unusually strong devotion to the Virgin Mary among Catholics in Poland. In 1883, Felicja Kozłowska, a Polish nun, had a vision that the Polish Church was in danger because of what she perceived to be severe moral shortcomings among its male priests. In her vision, God instructed her to help the priests organize into congregations in which they would

> **Felicja Kozłowska** 1862-1921
>
> **Mariavite Churches**
>
> http://www.mariawita.pl
>
> http://www.groups.msn.com/Maria viteCatholicChurch

work on their spiritual renewal by focusing on the veneration of the Blessed Sacrament and praying to the Virgin Mary. When the word of this unusual initiative began to spread, some priests were so impressed by this extraordinary woman that they willingly accepted her spiritual authority. By 1892, they organized themselves into an order under her direction, calling her "Little Mother" (*Mateczka*), "Mama" and also "Maria." They also accepted her idea of spiritual marriages between nuns and priests.

The Mariavites (*Marjawici*), as the new order of nuns and priests began to be known, hoped that they would win acceptance from Rome, but they were quickly condemned by both the Polish bishops, who felt threatened by the movement, and by the Vatican. Pope Pius X (1835-1914), the author of the famous 1907 encyclical against modernism, *Pascendi Dominici Gregis* ("On the Modernists"), was not the one to tolerate such unconventional behavior and excommunicated the order in 1906.[56] Pius X described the Mariavites as "a kind of pseudo-monastic society" of "Mystic Priests," especially among the junior clergy, but he focused most of the criticism on the female founder of the group. She is referred to as "a certain woman," to whom the priests "did not hesitate to entrust themselves without reserve, and to obey her every wish."[57] All the clergy, with the exception of Mama Kozłowska's confessor, were ordered not to have any contacts or dealings with her under any pretext.[58] This led to the formation of a separate Church which, despite great hostility from the Catholic Church in Poland, allowed nuns to give communion, accepted clerical marriage, regarded sexuality as means to advancing spirituality and eventually began to ordain women.

After Mama Kozłowska's death in 1921, Father Jan Maria Michał Kowalski, the leader among the Catholic priests who joined the Mariavite Church, promoted her cult within the Mariavite community. Her photographs were displayed on the altar of Mariavite churches and she was referred to as "the bride of Christ the Lamb" and as bride of the still-living Bishop Kowalski. The bishop introduced public marriages of nuns and priests. In 1928, the Mariavites began to ordain nuns as priests, but the majority of the congregation rejected the leadership of Bishop Kowalski over his expanded veneration of Mama Kozłowska, whom he began to regard as the Third Person of the Trinity. A small group of about three thousand remained loyal to Kowalski. Within this group, there has been a steady growth of the number of women-priests and most of its priests are now women. (11 out of 17 in 1998.) The smaller of the two Catholic Mariavite Churches in Poland also allows marriages between female and male priests. The majority of Mariavites in Poland, numbering in 1998 about twenty-six thousand faithful, continue to worship as a separate Church.[59] Mariavites also claim adherents in Western Europe, Canada and the United States, but their numbers are difficult to estimate.

From the very beginning, the Mariavites in Poland experienced severe harassment from the official Catholic Church and from the Catholic population. They were subjected to ridicule and derision over the special status accorded to women. A book published in 1930 to celebrate ten years of Poland's independence after World War I, referred to the Mariavites as a proof that Poles are not willing to join religious sects. The author claimed that before Poland regained her independence, the Russian government favored the Mariavites in order to weaken the Catholic Church. The author also blamed the appearance of new sects on foreign missionaries, mainly from the United States.[60] Even as early as the 1930s, conservative Catholics in Poland perceived the United States as a source of dangerous religious innovations. During World War II, the Nazis persecuted the Mariavites as purely Polish Church. Bishop Kowalski suffered and died in the Dachau concentration camp, but the Mariavites were able to claim that the ordination of women helped them to save their Church after their male priests had been arrested and killed.

Wojtyła was undoubtedly familiar with the issues surrounding the separation of the Mariavites from the Catholic Church. We can speculate that he was determined not to allow a similar schism to develop as a result of any uncertainty about the role of women within the larger Catholic Church which, by its very claim to be a universal Church, has an increasingly difficult job of functioning under the same rules, in the United States and Western Europe and in the least developed countries in the Third World. Perhaps because of the schism over this issue in the Polish Church, John Paul II's statements on women-priests were absolutely clear, leaving no doubt about his position either then or in the future. The experience of Mama Kozłowska may have convinced him that it is better to be strict and unequivocal rather than to raise any false hopes among women and nuns who may want to be priests.

Polish National Catholic Church

Another similarly unusual case of religious schism occurred, not in Poland but among Polish immigrants in the United States at the turn of the 20th century. Small groups of Polish-Americans became profoundly dissatisfied with the Catholic hierarchy, particularly with Irish-American bishops and priests, whom they perceived as hostile to Polish national culture. They formed a number of breakaway Catholic churches, which were eventually consolidated into the Polish National Catholic Church under Father Franciszek (Francis) Hodur, one of seven children of a poor peasant family in the Austrian-ruled part of southern Poland who immigrated to the United States. Hodur was not only born in the same general region as Wojtyła, but his social background and early life in Poland were

---

Franciszek Hodur 1866-1953

Polish National Catholic Church (PNCC)
http://www.pncc.org/

Kościół Polskokatolicki w RP
http://www.polskokatolicki.pl/

Polish National Catholic Church of Canada
http://www.pnccofcanada.com/index.html

Union of Utrecht of the Old Catholic Churches
http://www.utrechter-union.org/

remarkably similar to Wojtyła's. As a teenager, he became fascinated with the theatre convinced that he could serve his country by helping to educate Polish peasants through didactic folk drama. He soon became disillusioned with the middle class theatre world in Kraków and felt discriminated against because of his poor social origins. At about the same time, he developed a deep interest in issues of social justice, trying to reconcile socialism with Catholic doctrine. Like Wojtyła, Hodur decided to become a priest in order to better serve his people and studied for priesthood at the Jagiellonian University in Kraków some forty years before Wojtyła entered the same school.

Even though his professors described Hodur as an exceptional student, he interrupted his studies and left for the United States on the last day of 1892, probably as a result of his involvement in a seminary students' strike for better food and living conditions. After his arrival in the United States, he finished his religious education and was ordained priest in 1893 in Scranton, Pennsylvania. He soon became known in the Polish-American community in Scranton as a Catholic priest defending Polish parishioners' rights against their Irish bishops.[61] His calls for the creation of a "National Church," appointment of Polish bishops, parochial ownership of property, and selection of parish pastors by parishioners, finally led to his excommunication in 1898. With no hope for reconciliation with Rome, Father Hodur affiliated his denomination with the Union of Old Catholic Churches in Holland and was consecrated as bishop in 1907 at the Cathedral in Utrecht.

The Polish National Catholic Church continued its association with the Utrecht Union of Old Catholic Churches, but in 2003 the Union expelled the Church since the PNCC did not accept the validity of ordaining women to the priesthood, which most other Utrecht Union churches began doing. The PNCC also forbids abortion and homosexual behavior, but in other areas is more liberal than the Catholic Church. It allowed artificial birth control and permits remarriage after divorce. The PNCC does not recognize the doctrine of papal infallibility. According to its 2006 report to the National Council of Churches, the Polish National Catholic Church has 126 parishes in the United States and Canada with 60,000 members.

In its early years, Bishop Hodur's church grew moderately in the United States and even started a mission in Poland, where it lent its support to the liberal regime of Marshall Piłsudski. But the Polish-American missionaries were strongly opposed by the mainstream Polish Catholic clergy and never managed to attract a large number of followers despite their appeals to patriotic and nationalistic themes, which otherwise would have been quite popular with the Polish population. Some of the criticism of their missionary activities in Poland was focused on their American origin. The vast majority of Poles in Poland, as in the United States, preferred to stay with the traditional Catholic Church that served them well during periods of foreign occupations of their native country. In 1998, the Polish National Catholic Church claimed only 21,730 members in Poland.[62]

While some see the creation of the Polish National Catholic Church as a classic case of nationalism, it seems to be just as much, if not more, the case of a small group of Polish immigrants, led by an activist priest with socialist leanings, falling under the influence of the dominant American Protestant culture which encouraged parish democracy and self-government. Ultimately, it was a conflict over control of church property and parish self-management. The vast majority of the Polish-American Catholics (well over 90 percent), however, remained faithful to Rome, although many were undoubtedly upset with Irish priests and bishops, whom they perceived as indifferent to their demands for more autonomy for Polish parishes.

Solutions proposed by Father Hodur and his followers were remarkably liberal, reflecting more the democratic spirit of American Protestantism than the hierarchical system of Roman Catholicism. Members of the Polish National Catholic Church wanted to own their own churches, be able to select their priests and bishops, be allowed to celebrate mass in their native language rather than Latin, and to give their clergy freedom to marry. Liturgy reform was eventually accepted by the Second Vatican Council. But one reform, which neither the Polish National Catholic Church nor the Vatican have accepted to this day, is the ordination of women. In 1978, the Polish National Catholic Church terminated a formal agreement with the Episcopal Church when the latter accepted women into priesthood. At least in that respect, the Polish National Catholic Church is now much closer to the Catholic Church in Rome then to those Protestant churches that have accepted women-priests. In recent years, in response to strong encouragement from Pope John Paul II, there has been a dialogue between Rome and the Polish National Catholic Church, which in 1996 produced a "limited inter-communion" arrangement between the two churches. Defections of Roman Catholic priests to the PNCC have been, however, a source of contention together with different views on the role of the pope and democracy in church governance. The PNCC's Prime Bishop Robert M. Nemkovich attended the funeral of Pope John Paul II at St. Peter's Basilica in Vatican City in 2005 and was greeted by Cardinal Joseph Ratzinger.

While still in Poland, Wojtyła became very familiar with the case of Bishop Hodur and the Vatican's and the American bishops' inability at the turn of the 20th century to deal effectively with expressions of Polish nationalism. Both as the Archbishop of Kraków and later as pope, he met with representatives of the Polish National Catholic Church, expressing deep regret over the schism and his desire to see reconciliation. He also seemed to place much of the blame for the separation of Bishop Hodur's church from Rome not on excessive nationalism of Polish-American parishioners but rather on the insensitivity of the Catholic hierarchy in the United States. It seems, however, that the creation of a national Polish church was a result of the clash of at least three cultures: one that was deeply influenced by Polish nationalism, the culture of highly centralized Catholic Church unable to respond to demands for parish autonomy and national expression, and the American culture of democracy and individual choice derived largely from Protestant traditions. It was an important lesson for Wojtyła as to what can happen when a deeply felt desire for expressing patriotic sentiments is ignored. The experience of the Mariavites in Poland, while somewhat similar in nature, apparently did not convince John Paul II that ignoring women's desire for leadership positions in the Catholic Church can have equal if not much greater consequences. It should be remembered, however, that the issue of women's equal rights within the Church was not nearly as dominant in Poland during Wojtyła's youth and early adulthood as it became later in the United States and in Western Europe.

Letter to the Beijing World Conference on Women

Despite his insistence on promoting traditional roles for women and denying them opportunity to become priests, John Paul II was clearly tormented in the later years of his papacy over the Church's treatment of women. His letter to the U.N. sponsored Fourth World Conference on Women, which took place in Beijing in 1995, reflected his tortured approach to this issue. In a truly revolutionary statement for a Roman Catholic pontiff, John Paul II condemned exclusion of equal opportunities for women. He also condemned violence against women in the area of sexuality and praised "those women of good will who have devoted their lives to defending the dignity of womanhood...at a time when this was considered extremely inappropriate, the sign of a lack of femininity, a manifestation of exhibitionism and even sin."[63]

After a long list of injustices suffered by women, John Paul II tried to tackle the most sensitive subject of the Church's responsibility for oppressing women. This was obviously a painful task for Wojtyła because of his great attachment to tradition and his love for the Church. He wrote that "simply saying thank you" to women "is not enough." But he was not ready to blame the Church outright. To lessen the responsibility, he noted that "we are heirs to a history, which has conditioned us to a remarkable extent." John Paul II would like everyone to believe that it is "historical conditioning," and not necessarily the Church's teachings, that "has been an obstacle to the progress of women." Wojtyła then moved toward the admission of guilt on the part of the Church, but he did it only with the greatest reluctance and ambiguity. First he noted that assigning blame is not easy, "considering the many kinds of cultural conditioning which down the centuries have shaped ways of thinking and acting." Only then, he issued the crucial, but not quite complete and only conditional apology:

> And if objective blame, especially in particular historical contexts, has belonged to not just a few members of the Church, for this I am truly sorry.

Although weak and conditional, this was a remarkable admission of guilt by the pope, especially considering his love for the Church as an institution. This is also the first such acceptance of blame by the Catholic Church's highest religious figure. In this respect, Wojtyła went further than any of his predecessors, even though many conservative Catholics consider the questioning of the teachings by the Church leaders as very dangerous for the authority of the Papacy and the Church itself. This was doubly difficult for Wojtyła because of his deep attachment to tradition and to the authority of the Church and his concern that any criticism of the Church could alienate conservative Catholics and Catholics in the Third World, on whom John Paul II based his hopes for the future. He certainly deserves a lot of credit to making such a statement. But his apology did not come anywhere close to a full acceptance of blame or to being satisfactory to most feminists and many women. He did not say that the Church or its teachings were to be blamed but assigned blame to only "not just a few members of the Church." To admit guilt on the part of the Church or its theology would mean taking necessary actions to rectify the wrongs. This Wojtyła was not prepared to do, even if he realized that such action may be necessary at some point in the future. At the time, he limited himself to calling for a dialogue on this issue.

Other than a brief mention in the letter to the Beijing Conference, John Paul II was generally silent about the Church's historical treatment of women, although he was not afraid to refer from time to time to various other errors and transgressions on the part of the Church not related to women. In the earlier Apostolic Letter *Tertio Millennio Adveniente*, issued in 1994 in preparation for the start of the new millennium, the pope called for the examination of sins committed in the name of religion, including the disunity of the Christian world, religious intolerance and particularly the use of violence in religious wars.[64] He also wrote at length about the martyrdom of Christians, both during the first centuries of the Church as well as today, and about current violations of human rights. There was, however, no specific mention of any Church-inspired violence or other crimes against women.

Hillary Rodham Clinton's assessment of Pope John Paul II's plans for the Beijing Conference was that "the Vatican, vociferous on the subject of abortion, joined forces with some Islamic countries, concerned that the conference would become an international platform to promote the women's rights they opposed."[65] In her speech at the conference, Hillary Clinton, who was the First Lady at the time, said to strong applause from the audience that it was no longer acceptable "to discuss women's rights as separate from human rights." She wrote in her autobiographical book *Living History* that "even the delegate from the Vatican commended me for the speech."[66] President Bill Clinton's later claim that Pope John Paul II was one of the two most impressive world leaders he had met during his presidency (the other was Israeli Prime Minister Yitzhak Rabin) seemed unusual in light of his and Hillary's strong opposition to the papal agenda for women. As journalist Carl Bernstein pointed out in his book *A Woman in Charge*, Bill and Hillary profoundly disagreed with the pope's views on women's rights, abortion, and birth control.[67] Bernstein describes both Bill and Hillary as genuinely religious, which merely confirms that many religious Americans have vastly different ideas about religion, morality and women's rights than John Paul II.

John Paul II messages on his vision of women cannot be easily categorized. He often offended feminists with his choice of words and concepts to describe women and their concerns. At the same time, however, he made a number of appeals on behalf of women's rights with which most feminists would wholeheartedly agree. Since most of these appeals came rather late into his papacy, they may represent the proof that he was, somewhat belatedly, responding to the criticism from feminists and other activists for women's rights. Engaging in an argument with feminists over women's rights and role in society was not an issue for which he was prepared by his experiences in Poland. In the later years of his papacy there was, however, a significant rise in the number of his public comments and statements addressed to women, perhaps as a result of his exposure to the issue in the West.

Considering his relative lack of interest in women's rights during the first fifteen years of his papacy—the period devoted largely to travels, political changes in the Soviet block and efforts to stop Marxist influence in Latin America—John Paul II made a rather remarkable speech in August 1995 to the members of the Vatican's delegation to the Fourth World Conference on Women in Beijing. In his appeal to the members of the delegation, John Paul II called on the Catholic Church to focus its attention on the needs of girls and young women, especially from the poorest countries. Calling his appeal "an option in favor of girls and young women," perhaps for the first time in his life, Wojtyła made a specific observation about the oppression of women in today's world:

It is disheartening to note that in today's world the simple fact of being a female, rather than a male, can reduce the likelihood of being born or surviving childhood; it can mean receiving less adequate nutrition and health care, and it can increase the chance of remaining illiterate and having only limited access, or none at all, even to primary education. Investment in the care and education of girls, as an equal right, is a fundamental key to the advancement of women.

Compared with Wojtyła's numerous statements on human rights of practically every other group, including industrial workers, Jews, American-Indians and many others, this statement on women, even though it came late into his papacy, was revolutionary for a Roman-Catholic pontiff. Still, liberal women viewed it as rather short and weak. For John Paul II, it was another major break with the past. In the same speech, he called on "all men in the Church to undergo, where necessary, a change of heart and to implement, as a demand of their faith, a positive vision of women." This is yet another significant statement for John Paul II who before had almost never said anything critical about the Catholic Church. He qualified his statement by appealing only to "all men," not the whole Church, and asking for change "where necessary." Nevertheless, it was a remarkable admission of guilt and a call for action.

John Paul II also asked men in the Church "to become more and more aware of the disadvantages to which women, and especially girls, have been exposed and to see where the attitude of men, their lack of sensitivity or lack of responsibility may be at the root." John Paul II called on all educational institutions linked to the Catholic Church, including the universities, to give girls equal access to education and, more interestingly, "to educate boys to a sense of women's dignity and worth." Catholic universities were asked to insure that "in the preparation of future leaders in society, they acquire a special sensitivity to the concerns of young women." He also made similar appeals for giving girls and women equal access to Catholic-run health care, charitable programs and development organizations. He asked the religious sisters, but significantly not the religious brothers, to become more involved with the disadvantaged girls and young women. Considering his experiences in Poland, where most schools and organizations of his youth were segregated by gender, this was not unusual, although many women in the West see such gender-restricted organizations as denying girls opportunities for growth and advancement. In the same speech, John Paul II also made a short reference to violence against women — a topic which he rarely addressed during his papacy. "As followers of Jesus Christ, who identifies himself with the least among children, we cannot be insensitive to the needs of disadvantaged girls, especially those who are victims of violence and a lack of respect for their dignity." Feminists saw it as a rather short, indirectly phrased and weak statement, considering that violence against women is a major problem throughout the world, not excluding the pope's native Poland and other predominantly Catholic countries.

John Paul II was apparently deeply hurt by all the accusations coming from feminists that he was insensitive toward modern women. He genuinely believed that his statements about the need to preserve the dignity of women adequately proved that he was their ally in trying to alleviate their suffering and discrimination. He once expressed his bewilderment and sorrow to his ex-student of philosophy from Poland, Sister Zofia Zdybicka, assuring her that he had a great respect for and a high opinion of women.[68] According to her account of their conversations, as reported by Carl Bernstein and Marco Politi in their 1996 biography of the pope and repeated in an interview with me in 2007, John Paul II would often assure her that he was aware of the enormous potential of women for doing good and the unfortunate fact that this potential cannot be yet developed because of cultural constraints.[69]

Bernstein and Politi also included in their book a controversial account of the 1994 meeting between John Paul II and Nafis Sadik, undersecretary of the U.N. Conference on Population and Development.[70] Ms. Sadik, a native of Pakistan, provided the authors with a glimpse of the pope that was not very complementary, at least not in her account of their conversation. She reported that the pope had voiced his objections to homosexual and lesbian families and was apparently unmoved by her statements that women in the developing world, who are in no position to defy their husbands, cannot effectively practice natural birth control methods. According to Ms. Sadik, the pope also suggested that the irresponsible behavior of men might be caused by women.[71] It is highly doubtful, however, that if John Paul II said something to that effect, he meant to put the blame on women.

While the comment about women being responsible for the transgressions of men seems totally out of character for John Paul II, who frequently blamed men, not women, for violence and sexual aggressiveness, his other reported comments to Ms. Sadik were similar to his usual public pronouncements on these topics. He reportedly described birth control as the product of American feminism and the destructive cultural imperialism of the Western materialistic societies, where the family is disintegrating and ethical values have been destroyed. Ms. Sadik felt compelled to challenge the pope's claim that the people in the poorer countries accept the Church's teachings on birth control and abortion. She reportedly told the pope that illegal abortions are actually performed at the highest rates in the poorer Catholic countries, where women have no easy access to contraceptives.[72]

John Paul II and the Vatican officials would frequently reject such arguments as either false or irrelevant. Father Thomas J. Euteneuer, the president of Human Life International, confirmed in an interview with *The National Catholic Register*, the oldest national Roman Catholic newspaper in the United States which usually reflects tradi-

Thomas J. Euteneuer b. 1962

Human Life International
http://www.hli.org/index.html

tional Church teaching, that John Paul II considered distribution and promotion of condoms in the Third World by Western nations as a proof of "contraceptive imperialism."[73] The conversation with Ms. Sadik must have been painful for the pope because he was dealing with a Third World rather than Western feminist. While feminists insists that contraception helps to prevent AIDS, empowers Third World women, and enables them to provide better living conditions and education for their children, the official position of the Vatican on this issue is quite different.

The National Catholic Register
http://ncregister.com/

ZENIT
http://www.zenit.org/

Catholic News Service
http://www.catholicnews.com/

Catholic Information Network (CIN)
http://www.cin.org/

Catholic.net
http://www.catholic.net/

The actual behavior of women in the Third World, whether it is caused by Western influences or not, seems in any case to run counter to John Paul II's expectations. Demographers have been surprised that more and more women in the largest developing countries are making decisions to have fewer children. *ZENIT*, a nonprofit news agency which informs how the world is seen from the Vatican, reported that in his interview in *The National Catholic Register*, Father Euteneuer merely repeated John Paul's firm beliefs on the issue of contraception in the Third World. According to Father Euteneuer, the Western nations and international organizations, such as the United Nations Population Fund, "are introducing the sin of contraception and its denial of God's plan for love and the family; they are force-feeding the culture of death and its inevitable products — disease, immorality, promiscuity, abortion, and the dissolution of the family — to uneducated, unsophisticated and innocent people; and they are robbing these countries of their single most important resource—people."[74]

Women's health and family planning organizations insist, however, that women in the developing world are themselves making decisions to have fewer children. Many experts were surprised to learn that the decline in the birthrates in some of the most populous developing countries started even before women could fully benefit from family planning programs, higher standards of living and better education. It seems that some Third World women decided not to wait for economic progress before deciding to reduce the number of children. Some experts attribute this not so much to government-supported family planning policies but to decisions of individual women who, after being exposed to more information through the media and other sources, are beginning to seek greater economic opportunities and becoming more assertive within their families. Family pressure on women in the developing world to have more children may have also weakened due to urbanization.[75]

The Vatican's position on Western efforts to convince women in the developing world to have fewer children is not much different from what conservative Islamic clerics have been saying about the United States and the West or what some evangelical Christians are saying in criticizing the U.N. In a program on the *al-Jazeera* satellite television network during the U.S. attack on terrorists in Afghanistan, an Egyptian Islamic cleric, Sheik Yusuf Qaradawi (b. 1926), stated that "the problem with Western culture represented by the United States government, a unipolar power, is that it calls for immoral ethics based on monetary beliefs and sexual liberation. And that is against our values." The host of the *al-Jazeera* program fully agreed with his quest. The program's title was "Globalization: The New Face of Occupation."[76] Immorality, consumerism, and loosening of sexual ethics—the three most frequent criticisms John Paul II made against the West—were repeated by a Muslim cleric using almost the same language. Media and government officials in the Muslim world also widely discussed former President Clinton's sexual behavior, pointing out that in light of the Monica Lewinsky scandal, the United States has no moral authority to criticize their countries for human rights violations or to offer its system of government as a model. I personally heard this comment from a high level official of one of the most repressive regimes in Central Asia. The dignity of women—these critics argue—is better protected in more religious Islamic societies. It is difficult to say how much John Paul II would agree with this statement, but it can be safely said that in his view women in Poland and in other more traditional societies enjoyed more dignity and respect than women in the West.

Appeal to Women for Forgiveness

On March 12, 2000, the first Sunday of Lent, Pope John Paul II presided over a solemn ceremony, in which, for the first time in the history of the Catholic Church, the Roman pontiff asked forgiveness for the past and present sins of "the children of the Church." John Paul II had promised such an act during pre-Millennium preparations and it was long awaited by women, Jews, Muslims, and other groups which had suffered persecution from the Catholic Church. Many of them, however, became disappointed when they realized that the promise made by John Paul II in his Apostolic Letter *Tertio Millennio Adveniente*[77] did not meet their expectations. This was particularly true for women who felt that they have been oppressed by the Church almost since the beginning of Christianity and may have expected a special apology addressed only to them.

Preparations for the admission of faults were left to the International Theological Commission working under the direction of its president, Cardinal Joseph Ratzinger, Prefect of the Congregation for the Doctrine of the Faith, now Pope Benedict XVI. The commission produced a document titled, "Memory and Reconciliation: the Church and the Faults of the Past," which was approved by Cardinal Ratzinger and published in December 1999. The document mentioned several specific categories of sins committed by Christians, such as the separation and mutual distrust among Christians, the use of force in the service of truth and the persecution of Jews. What the document did not mention at all was the oppression of women. Much of the document was on the other hand devoted to making sure that the recognition of faults was not based on reinterpreting history according to today's standards. The commission was also concerned that its report would not perceived as one-sided or be "exploited by the Church's detractors."[78] Those who expected a full apology to women did not find it in the document produced in response to the pope's appeal for an admission of sins before the Third Millennium.

As expected, during the ceremony at the Vatican, John Paul II did not accept blame on behalf of the Church as an institution or blamed Christianity for inspiring acts of persecution and oppression. The pope merely acknowledged "the faults committed by the children of the Church"; the Church itself is blameless because it is holy and has Christ as "her Head and Spouse" and "the Blessed Virgin and the saints" as "her most authentic expression." While Jews were mentioned separately as a group which had suffered persecution from Christians, women were put together with victims of racial and ethnic discrimination. During the ceremony at the St Peter's Cathedral in Rome, Nigerian Cardinal Francis Arinze (b. 1932), president of the Pontifical Council for Inter-Religious Dialogue, asked for confession of sins against the dignity of woman and the unity of mankind:

> Let us pray for all those who have suffered offences against their human dignity and whose rights have been trampled; let us pray for women, who are all too often humiliated and emarginated [sic], and let us acknowledge the forms of acquiescence in these sins of which Christians too have been guilty.[79]

After a silent prayer, John Paul II spoke of the non-acceptance of equality between men and women, but he blamed it not on the Church or Christian tradition but on acts of individual Christians and mentioned offenses against women together with other forms of discrimination:

> Lord God, our Father, you created the human being, man and woman, in your image and likeness and you willed the diversity of peoples within the unity of the human family. At times, however, the equality of your sons and daughters has not been acknowledged, and Christians have been guilty of attitudes of rejection and exclusion, consenting to acts of discrimination on the basis of racial and ethnic differences. Forgive us and grant us the grace to heal the wounds still present in your community on account of sin, so that we will all feel ourselves to be your sons and daughters. We ask this through Christ our Lord.[80]

Feminists were offended by the weakness of the apology and claimed that in apologizing, John Paul II was actually justifying different treatment of men and women by stressing that God is the architect of gender differences. In mentioning together gender, racial and ethnic discrimination, John Paul II also opened himself to criticism of inconsistency in his treatment of women. If gender differences, designed by God, call for different treatment of men and women, as for example in the case of Catholic priesthood, then racial and ethnic differences should also require different treatment of various racial and ethnic groups. Yet, race or ethnic origin does not disqualify men from becoming priests. The prayer for forgiveness of sins against the Jews did not mention the Holocaust—something many Jews found objectionable.

Catholic theologians supportive of the pope rejected this type of criticism. Auxiliary Archbishop Rino Fisichella of Rome, a former professor of theology of the Pontifical Gregorian University, pointed out in an interview with the Italian newspaper *Il Giornale* that one must not judge history by applying today's standards. He explained that in making his apology general "John Paul II wanted to give a complete, global vision, making references to circumstances of the past, but without focusing on details out of respect for history." Defenders of the pope's position claim that an objective evaluation of the history of Christianity and the Catholic Church would reveal that Catholics and other Christians have been responsible for much more good than evil, also with regard to the treatment of women. Archbishop Fisichella noted that "the Church is not the one who has sinned; the sinners are Christians and they have done so against the Church, the Bride of Christ." He also rejected the criticism that the Church's *mea culpa* was insufficient by stating that "some were hoping we would ask for forgiveness for the very fact that we exist, but we cannot do this. Thank God, not only do we exist, we also enjoy good health. With every passing year, the Church's face becomes more beautiful and young."[81]

Many feminists and women critics of John Paul II would strongly disagree with this statement, but they may not be entirely right either. The population of Europe is indeed getting older,

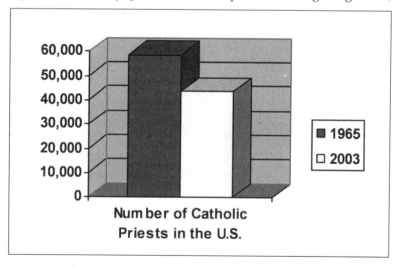

Source: Georgetown University's Center for Applied Research in the Apostolate.

largely because Europeans are not following John Paul II's advice on contraception, but birth rates in the Third World and the

FutureChurch

http://www.futurechurch.org/index.htm

United States are much higher and have produced an overall increase of the number of Catholics during John Paul II's papacy. This says nothing, however, of the quality of their faith or their ethics. Much of the violence during the last two decades has been in the Third World. The number of priests has decreased during John Paul II's papacy and Islam has surpassed Catholicism by becoming the world's number one religion. In 1965, 994 new Catholic priests were ordained in the United States. In 2000, that number dropped to 442, while the American Church grew by 14.3 million and added 1,599 parishes.[82] The median age of a Catholic nun in the United States is now 69.[83] FutureChurch, an organization founded in 1990 in Cleveland, Ohio, has been waging a campaign to convince the Catholic hierarchy to accept women and married priests in response to the growing shortage of priests in the United States and worldwide. Keeping women and married men out of priesthood may mean that Catholics in many areas will be left without priests. On the other hand, much progress was made under John Paul II's leadership in interfaith dialogue, communism fell in East Central Europe and in the Soviet Union, the number of democratic countries greatly increased, and the Roman Catholic Pontiff for the first time in history spoke at length on the status of women and women's rights. It is not clear, however, whether the Catholic Church can remain a viable global institution without a sufficient number of priests and religious sisters.

"Different but Equal" and American Slavery

All recent papal pronouncements on women in seem to be promoting the "different but equal" concept. A similar idea, "separate but equal", was discredited in U.S. history as an attempt to justify discrimination against African Americans in education and other areas. In the 19th and early 20th century, white American legislators in the Southern states tried to perpetuate racial segregation by claiming that African Americans were being given equal access to social services such as public education, but that it was provided to them separately from the white population. The Supreme Court of the United States rejected the "separate but equal" concept as blatantly discriminatory.

John Paul II claimed that women within the Catholic Church enjoy the same dignity, if not the same privileges, even if they were being denied certain important religious functions and positions of authority and responsibility. Man occupying these positions, which are being denied to women, can have a great impact on women's lives. For feminists, this amounts to classic segregation, in this case based on gender rather than race or ethnic origin. James Carrol (b. 1943), an American writer and a former Paulist priest, believes that for the Catholic Church to refuse to ordain women is no different than if the Church also refused to ordain people of color. Carrol called it equally indefensible and equally outrageous.[84] For the majority of people in the United States and in most other Western countries, but not necessarily in Poland and in most of the developing world, the denial of ordination to women is now seen almost with the same disbelief and distaste as racism and racial discrimination—something John Paul II apparently did not fully realize. He was aware, however, that in many cultures he knew, a woman would not enjoy sufficient authority and respect to be able to serve as an effective moral and spiritual leader to large groups of people.

Early American feminists Elizabeth Cady Stanton and Susan B. Anthony, who were also active in the anti-slavery movement, attacked the "different but equal" argument as just another attempt to justify male dominance. Speaking in 1848 at the Seneca Falls women's rights convention, Elizabeth Cady Stanton, argued that the people who claim that there is no superiority or inferiority but merely a difference between the two sexes, upon closer examination "soon run this difference into the old groove of superiority."[85] As to the argument that all of the Apostles, chosen by Christ, were men, feminists point out once again that all of them were also Jewish, yet the Catholic Church does not require priests to be converted Jews.

End of Dialogue?

Particularly objectionable to Catholic feminists was John Paul II's decision to close the issue of female priests to any further discussion. The attempt to stifle dialogue among Catholics on this particular topic was an unusual position for John Paul II to take in light of his background. He was always an ardent supporter of dialogue with all the critics and opponents of the Church, including even communists. In 1966, using some of Marxist terminology, Wojtyła told a gathering of Polish bishops that "dialogue ... is a method of [organizing] human life, especially [for allowing people] to live together—in many various situations, starting with two people (for example, as in a marriage) and finishing with broad correlation of forces in international relations." Wojtyła was pointing out the advantages of dialogue to the Polish bishops, but ultimately also to the Church's religious opponents and political foes, including communists. He was always trying to convince Catholics and everyone else to accept peaceful dialogue as an alternative to hatred-producing conflict. He did that by pointing out that "dialogue always takes the struggle into the realm of the mind, and with that, into the realm of ideas, concepts, [and] principles. Such a transformation sublimates the struggle, cleanses it from negative feelings, from hatred, [and] from desire to destroy a person who is the opponent."[86]

Significantly, however, Wojtyła also stated that a dialogue does not mean that the Catholic Church should compromise on its basic principles or to give in to unfair demands of its opponents. He described dialogue as peaceful seeking of truth or justice, but noted that it can also include elements of struggle, as long as its ultimate goal is to safeguard a person's dignity, freedom and wellbeing. This remained Wojtyła's position in later years. While many of his statements may have suggested a willingness for a dialogue and reconciliation, it should not be forgotten that Wojtyła was a student of Cardinal Wyszyński's highly successful tactics. Wyszyński knew how to engage communists in a dialogue but would never compromise on the basic principles.

By banning any further dialogue in the Church on the issue of ordination of women, John Paul II must have felt very strongly about the correctness of his position. He could still claim that he is a person of dialogue, since the ban can only apply to Catholics and did not affect those who did not recognize his authority on such issues. Ironically, in this case Catholics who disagreed with his position were not treated with the same tolerance that while still in Poland Wojtyła was willing to grant to communists and other adversaries. He pointed out in his 1966 speech that "dialogue is, as we know, the opposite of monologue." He was also arguing that "dialogue can not only be the calm and peaceful way of pursuing truth and justice, but also allows at certain times for contradictions, and even struggle, [to emerge] among its participants."[87] On the issue of female ordination, John Paul II was so certain of the correctness of his position that he would not allow Catholics even the possibility of continuing to seek truth and justice for women by discussing the ordination of women to priesthood. Obviously, he believed that dialogue within the Church and dialogue with the outside world must be conducted according to different standards. For dialogue within the Church, the standards and the limitations are set ultimately by the pope himself. This attitude may have been indicative not only of his growing conservatism but also, in this case, of his conviction that by confusing the faithful, the Catholic and non-Catholic proponents of the ordination of women posed a grave danger for the Church. Otherwise, it would be very difficult to explain how this supporter of peaceful dialogue, even with the

Church's worst enemies, and someone who had personally experienced demeaning and demoralizing effects of communist press censorship, would himself impose censorship on his own co-believers.

Some history may illustrate why John Paul II took such a drastic position. Speaking in 1965, Wojtyła made a distinction between a dialogue with authentic atheists and a dialogue with political atheism as it was practiced by communists.[88] In the case of political atheism, Wojtyła was advocating "creative silence" on the part of Catholics until there will be changes in the communist doctrine. He had no doubt that individual communists will change and that their doctrine will change with them. He seemed to be applying the same reasoning in his dealings with feminists and feminism. Just as the Catholic Church was willing to have a dialogue with communist regimes but rejected the communist ideology that denied the existence of God, John Paul II was willing to have a dialogue with feminists but rejects what he perceived to be the anti-Christian and anti-Church trends in Western feminism.

One can say, however, that Wojtyła's dialogue with atheist Marxists was much more vigorous than his attempts to enter into a dialogue with feminism. The Polish Church under Wyszyński and Wojtyła tolerated very little dissension within its own ranks as it was being subjected to infiltration and blackmail by communist secret agents. At some point, John Paul II must have decided that leaving radical Catholic feminists any doubt or any room to maneuver on the issues of priestly ordination and abortion would only lead to greater confusion and more problems for the Church in the future. Since many of the same women also supported the legal right to abortion, he must have concluded that it might be better if they leave the Church altogether. They could, of course, always return if they changed their views.

Still, when speaking about women's rights within the Church, John Paul II tried to be as diplomatic as possible, but sometimes he did reveal his strong views, particularly when he was unable to contain his exasperation with American and West European liberals. This was the case in December 1999, when he reminded the German bishops of their duty to follow the official Church teachings on a number of issues, including the ban on discussing the ordination of women:

> Without doubt, the dignity of women is great and must be more and more appreciated! However, too little consideration is given to the difference between the human and civil rights of the person and his rights, duties and related functions in the Church. Precisely for this reason, some time ago, by virtue of my ministry of confirming the brethren, I recalled "that the Church has no authority whatsoever to confer priestly ordination on women and that this judgment is to be definitively held by all the Church's faithful" (*Ordinatio sacerdotalis*, n. 4).
>
> As the authentic Pastors of your Dioceses, you have the duty to reject contrary opinions put forward by individuals or organizations and to encourage that open and clear dialogue in truth and love which Mother Church must foster regarding the future of her daughters. Do not hesitate, then, to emphasize that the Magisterium of the Church has taken this decision not as an act of her own power, but in the knowledge of her duty to obey the will of the Lord of the Church herself.[89]

John Paul II was telling the German bishops that they should in fact limit discussion over this issue, even though he referred to "open and clear dialogue." He qualified it, however, by saying that it must be conducted "in truth and love which Mother Church must foster regarding the future of her daughters." One of those who saw the irony of John Paul's position and disagreed with him on the issue of free debate and dialogue within the Church was former Archbishop of Vienna and Wojtyła's old friend, Cardinal Franz Koenig (1905-2004). This retired at the time and highly respected cardinal, who helped to elect Wojtyła to become pope, found banning free debate among Catholics to be a very disturbing phenomenon. Expressing his support for a petition drive by Austrian Catholics, which called for reforms within the Church, Cardinal Koenig said that "We have to be willing to listen to everyone. Freedom of expression in the Church, even by the laity, is of tremendous importance."[90]

Since the publication of the pope's letter calling for the end of any discussion among Catholics on the question of ordaining women, the Vatican has been waging a publicity campaign designed to present John Paul II's positions on women as being even more radical and more pro-women than what many feminists would advocate. At the same time, the Vatican has been trying to convince the public opinion that the ordination of women is irrelevant to the issue of women's rights and women's liberation. In a 1999 interview with Vatican Radio, Cardinal Ratzinger referred to the statement of the conservative Archbishop of Toronto, Cardinal Aloysius Ambrozic (b. 1930), that there are "various points in common between feminism and the Catholic Church."[91] Cardinal Ambrozic asserted in the interview that "women could not find an ally more clearly determined than the Church to recognize and defend their dignity."[92] In commenting on Cardinal Ambrozic's statement, Cardinal Ratzinger, now Pope Benedict XVI, also asserted that it would be incorrect and even absurd to consider the ordination of women to the priesthood as one aspect of the liberation of women. Following John Paul II's lead, the conservative Church leaders are trying to convince women that the Church respects their dignity while denying them the opportunity to serve their fellow human beings in a priestly function. While being a celibate priest can be seen as a sacrifice, women are asked instead to make sacrifices as mothers and wives.

To see John Paul's views on this issue in full, it is best to listen to some of his less publicized statements, particularly when he would allow himself to become more open in his criticism of Western societies and their Catholic churches. This is what John

Paul II told the German bishops in November 1999:

> The Church needs ordained priests who in sacramental celebrations act "in persona Christi" and represent Christ the bridegroom in relation to the Church as bride. In other words: the ordained pastors, who are members of the one Body of the Church, represent its head, who is Christ. Therefore, any attempt to clericalize the laity or to laicize the clergy must be rejected. It does not correspond to the mysterious ordering of the Church as willed by her Founder. Nor are tendencies that eliminate the essential difference between clergy and laity of any use in attracting vocations. I ask you, dear Brothers, to keep alive in your parish communities a deep desire for ordained priests. Even a long period of waiting, due to the current shortage of priests, should not lead a community to accept an emergency situation as a rule.[93]

Women may enjoy full human and civil rights in society, but as John Paul II reminded the German bishops, the Church is an institution established by Christ himself. Regardless of what some liberal Austrian, German or American bishops may think, John Paul II was willing to put his reputation on the line that Jesus Christ did not want women to be priests.

The Congregation for the Doctrine of the Faith (CDF), which through its members and Cardinal Ratzinger invariably reflected the views of the pope, has implied among other things that allowing women to become priests could undermine the Church's current position on the complementarity of the sexes and lead to the neutering of society. CDF Secretary, Bishop Tarcisio Bertone (b. 1934), told the Vatican Radio in January 2000 that "human race feminism," poses serious threats to the Catholic faith by treating human beings as though they were neuter. Bishop Bertone explained that regarding gender as neither masculine nor feminine and allowing individuals to "identify with whatever is preferred" runs against the complementarity of the sexes. In other words, the Church still wants to reserve for itself the right to determine the proper gender roles for women and men. The fact that the Congregation for the Doctrine of the Faith dealt with "human race feminism" at one of its rare plenary sessions indicates the importance John Paul II attached to this issue. It was one of the three major topics discussed by the Congregation at the Plenary Assembly in January 2000, which was addressed by the pope. The primary purpose of the Congregation is to safeguard the orthodoxy of the Christian message. Commenting on the issue of sexual complementarity, Bishop Bertone warned that legislation being proposed in some countries, including Italy, allowing each person to "choose the type of his/her life according to his/her sexual orientation" runs against "God's original creative plan."[94] This Church position has practical implications for gay marriages, adoptions and many other life issues.

In November 2001, John Paul II confirmed in an address to the Vatican Congregation for the Clergy that "the priest celebrates the sacrifice of the Mass and administers the sacraments 'in persona Christi." By insisting that a priest must physically resemble Christ, the previous pope again reiterated that "the title of pastor is reserved specifically for the priest." John Paul II insisted a male priest celebrating the Mass will never be replaced. As to the current dramatic shortage of Catholic priests, the pope said that it would be a fatal error to be resigned in face of the current difficulties by preparing for a future Church deprived of priests. Also nuns will not be able to fulfill the role of priests. John Paul II pointed out that collaboration of those who are not representing Christ as ordained priests is "desirable and often necessary," but he warned the clergy to be on alert against any practices that tend to diminish the authority of parish priests.[95]

John Paul II offered "the theology of woman" and "Catholic feminism" as alternatives to secular or anti-religious feminism. In one of his pronouncements he called it "the authentic theology of woman."[96] However, feminist critics complained that, unfortunately, John Paul II had very little to present as an explanation of what theology of woman meant in practical terms. It is rather clear that unlike his numerous statements on human rights, this was a subject on which John Paul II had not written or said anything specific beyond stating that "the spiritual beauty, the particular genius, of women is being rediscovered."

He did not say what he meant by the use of the word "particular," but it was obvious that at least for him it meant that talents and gifts, and therefore the social roles of women, were different from those of men. John Paul II simply concluded in the page and a half chapter on women in his autobiography, that "the bases for the consolidation of the position of women in life, not only family life but also social and cultural life, are being redefined."[97] The language of this last statement was somewhat official and offered no specific guidance. It may have been an indication that John Paul II was not really certain where the women's emancipation movement was going, but he did offer one advice: the Virgin Mary and devotion to Mary as "a powerful and creative inspiration" for today's women.[98]

What about women who never become mothers, never marry or remain virgins? John Paul II presented Mary as a perfect model for them as well. Mary was not only a mother but, according to the Catholic tradition, also a virgin. John Paul II pointed out that Mary wanted to remain a virgin "in order to achieve an even deeper intimacy with God," and called virginity "a higher order of motherhood" or "a motherhood according to the Spirit." Mary's virginity in John Paul's view was not, however, only spiritual or symbolic but also physical. In a series of talks during general audiences in 1996, John Paul II defended the concept of Mary's virginal conception as a biological fact and the concept of her perpetual virginity, "before, during and after giving birth." He specifically rejected interpretations that explain the virginal conception of Jesus as symbolic, metaphorical, or mythological.[99]

Dan Brown's Official Web Site

http://www.danbrown.com/index.html

Jesus Decoded – U.S. Bishops' Web Site on *The Da Vinci Code*

http://www.jesusdecoded.com/

Opus Dei **Response to** *The Da Vinci Code*

http://www.opusdei.org/art.php?w=32&p=7017

The Da Vinci Hoax

http://www.ignatius.com/books/davincihoax/

With so much focus on virginity in John Paul II's comments about Christ's family, it is no surprise that the Vatican and conservative Catholics reacted passionately to Dan Brown's imaginary story in *The Da Vinci Code* (2003) in which the American author describes Christ's supposed marriage to Mary Magdalene. The book also outlines the alleged conspiracy in which the Vatican and *Opus Dei* members try to maintain male control of the Church by protecting the secret of Christ's marriage. Scholars generally agree that the book contains numerous historical and factual inaccuracies, but its impact on popular culture and how it could shape attitudes about virginity, ordination of women as deacons in the early Church and their role vis-à-vis the male-dominated hierarchy today was a source of considerable worry for conservative Catholic leaders. In response to the book's publication, the U.S. bishops launched a multi-language web site *Jesus Decoded*, where they rebut the various claims in the novel. *Opus Dei* reacted to the suggestion in *The Da Vinci Code* that women *Opus Dei* members are "forced to clean the men's residence halls for no pay" and are otherwise accorded lower status than men. In a statement on its web site, *Opus Dei* rejected these and other claims in the book as untrue: "Like the Church in general," their statement reads, *Opus Dei* "teaches that women and men are of equal dignity and value." The statement further explains that "women members of *Opus Dei* can be found in all sorts of professions, those which society views as prestigious and those which society today tends to undervalue, such as homemaking or domestic work." For those who wanted to learn more, the web site recommended *The Da Vinci Hoax*, a non-fiction book written by Carl E. Olson and Sandra Miesel who reject various claims in *The Da Vinci Code* and assert that it is based on elements of feminist ideas.

John Paul II also defended the concept of Mary's virginity after the birth of Christ by arguing that the reference to Jesus as "firstborn" in the Gospel (Lk 2:7) literally meant that he was "a child not preceded by another" and the mention of "brothers of Jesus" was actually a reference to his cousins. He pointed out that there is no specific word in Hebrew and Aramaic to express the word "cousin" and therefore the terms "brothers" and "sisters" would be used to indicate several degrees of kinship.[100]

For feminists, such a strong focus by John Paul II on Mary's virginity is yet another example of the male-dominated society trying to use religion to control women's sexuality by promoting virginity mostly for women. Feminist scholars point out that the Catholic Church does not devote nearly as much attention to Jesus' virginity and does not have as much to say about virginity for men. Neither does the Church nor the pope pay as much attention to presumed virginity of Mary's husband, although John Paul II devoted a short lecture to this topic at a general audience in 1996. In his talk, the pope disagreed with those theologians who suggested that Joseph was advanced in age and should be considered more as Mary's guardian than her spouse. John

Web Sites for Single Catholics

Catholic Singles
http://www.catholicsingles.com/
Single Catholics
http://www.singlecatholics.com/
The Catholic Unattached Directory
http://www.cathud.com/

Paul II concluded that Joseph's spousal relationship with Mary was based on "virginal affection" and that the two had an understanding at the time of their betrothal about Mary's plan "to live as a virgin."[101]

John Paul's frequent reflections on Mary's virginity, according to his feminist critics, do not respond to the needs and motives of the growing number of modern women who prefer career to motherhood, want to postpone pregnancy or simply do not want to have children. Many modern women, who are not ready to get married, want to have loving relationships and opt for using effective birth control methods, such as the pill. Feminists believe that John Paul II does not have much to offer to such women. If they want physical love and use hormones or barriers, he would brand them unhesitatingly as sinners. For many feminists, presenting Mary as a perpetual virgin also has a strong symbolic significance, since it tends to shape how societies, and particularly male celibate priests, would like to view and treat women.

While for John Paul II Mary's virginity may have been an ideal toward which both men and women should aspire but which—he believed—should be constantly emphasized, for the German feminist Uta Ranke-Heinemann (b. 1927) the doctrine of "virginity at childbirth" is a "monstrous product of neurotic sexual fantasy." She accuses the Church's celibates of robbing Mary of her motherhood and trying to paint a picture of her that has nothing to do with normal women. In her opinion, by insisting on virginal birth of Christ rather than seeing it as an intellectual symbol, John Paul II "finds himself in a growing shambles of outdated ideas." According to Uta Ranke-Heinemann, those who wanted a more truthful image of Mary as a real mother "have been cheated and deprived by the doctrine of an incomprehensible and therefore existentially meaningless natural wonder." Many Christians who think likewise, particularly liberal men and women, find it impossible to see perpetually virgin Mary as their concrete religious model. In her book *Eunuchs for the Kingdom of Heaven*, the German feminist argues that celibate Church theologians who will not allow Mary to have anything in common with female sexuality are not exalting the greatness and dignity of a woman—as John Paul II would assert—but rather "crush what constitutes feminine dignity in particular (Mary) and in general (all women)."[102]Uta Ranke-Heinemann lost her position as a professor of Catholic theology at the University of Essen for interpreting Mary's virginal birth symbolically rather than biologically.

Wojtyła's Theory of Gender Complementarity and Equal Dignity

Both Wyszyński and Wojtyła embraced the more modern theory of complementarity between the genders, according to which men and women are equal in dignity even if they have different abilities which are equally important and complementary. The traditional view that women were intellectually inferior allowed Church leaders for centuries to simply ignore or even encourage all forms of discrimination against women. But the second theory, which is a much more recent development as far as the Catholic Church is concerned, did not originate within the Church. It started to be accepted by more progressive priests only under pressure from social changes taking place in more liberal Western societies. In the mid-20th century, the emphasis among some Church leaders shifted from stressing the intellectual unsuitability of women for priesthood and other leadership roles to emphasizing the concept of "different but equal"—which while not meeting Western standards of equality—seemed more suitable in a world concerned with human rights. Gender complementarity still allowed the Church to justify treating men and women differently and to continue the ban on the ordination of women. This is the theory that John Paul II embraced and promoted.

A contemporary Polish feminist writer, Maria Ciechomska, contends that the theory of complementarity and equal dignity fails to explain why the dignity of a woman would be offended if she became a priest while being a priest does not offend male dignity. She also noted John Paul's 1994 letter to bishops, in which he stated that sainthood is much more important in Christianity than hierarchical Church positions, so that ultimately it is not important whether women become priests. This led Ciechomska to wonder why John Paul II believed it is so very important for men to want to become priests.[103]

The answer can be found throughout John Paul's writings, in which he states and restates his view that Christ deliberately chose men to be priests because he knew that they are better suited for this purpose, while women should aspire to be mothers. Wojtyła accepted this justification, although even he refrained from stating it so flatly for fear of offending women. In any case, John Paul II stressed over and over again that being a mother or a nun was just as important as being a priest. If most people in the West do not see it that way and consider priesthood to be somewhat higher on the social scale than motherhood or even female religious orders, Wojtyła argued that this represents a failure to understand Christ's real intentions and different plans for men and women.

Polish Friends Defend Wojtyła's Views on Women, Family and Feminism

A long-time close friend of Karol Wojtyła, Father Tadeusz Styczeń who teaches philosophy at the Catholic University in Lublin (KUL) and was one of his Polish friends present at his death, defends the pope against accusations that he was trying to Polonize the Church. Father Styczeń explains that the tragic experience of his life in Poland under Nazism and communism made Wojtyła aware of what violations of human dignity can mean in practice. The former Nazi concentration camp at Auschwitz, located in Wojtyła's former archdiocese and not too far from his hometown, was one example of the affirmation of a person through race, rather than his or her basic humanity. Another example was the communist idea that only members of a certain social class are worthy of exercising political control. As Father Styczeń pointed out, the communists soon developed their own ruling class that practiced dictatorship over the proletariat, forcing the Polish workers to rebel on numerous occasions. These experiences made John Paul II particularly committed to the idea that every human being possesses dignity and made him opposed to any attempts to undermine it through the use of violence.[104] Very early into his priesthood in Poland, Wojtyła developed an argument, specifically in opposition to Marxism, that no person can be deprived of life and liberty by any authority, whether secular or religious, since each individual is born in the image of God. Later, this idea helped to launch the Solidarity trade union and led to the fall of communism. As for abortion, John Paul II believed that this was one of the worst possible forms of violence against a person because it was directed against the most vulnerable and the most defenseless. Father Styczeń also pointed out that both communism and Nazism were products of Western thought—a point that John Paul II made on numerous occasions.

Another Polish priest, Maciej Zięba, accuses the media of being obsessed with any papal statements having to do with sex or abortion, while ignoring the basic message behind statements focusing on the defense of life and human dignity. In his book, Father Zięba refers to John Paul's II pronouncements on women's issues as a great achievement of his pontificate and credits him with creating a special form of "Christian feminism." He argues that Catholicism, because of its devotion to the Virgin Mary, can claim to be especially pro-feminist. At the same time, Father Zięba provides perhaps the best explanation as to why John Paul II persisted in advocating different roles for men and women in public life. As with many other positions and attitudes adopted by the pope, the reasons can be found in his earlier life under communism. "Christian feminism" rules out what Father Zięba calls "ideological feminism," which according to the Marxist interpretation assumes the existence of an irremovable antagonism between the sexes. According to this Marxist interpretation, all relationships between men and women can be seen as a form of conflict similar to the class struggle between the proletariat and the bourgeoisie.

John Paul II was a firm believer in social solidarity at all levels, whether it is between labor and management or between men and women. He was extremely uncomfortable with the antagonistic relationship between social classes, as defined by the Marxists, or with the competition for resources between groups and individuals in capitalistic societies, where the rules of the competition are decided in a democratic process. Even such competition can be unfair, if the more powerful or the majority use democracy to gain advantage over the weaker minority. Abortion became for John Paul II the clearest proof that such abuses can occur even in a democracy. Just as he successfully resisted the communist call for class struggle, Wojtyła was unwilling to accept and resisted the idea of an antagonistic relationship between men and women. Instead, he wanted to promote solidarity of both men and women in their common struggle for greater human dignity, but he wanted to see it happen on his own terms and according to his own cultural expectations.

The view that Western commentators focus too much on the pope's statements about sex, feminism and related issues but ignore his underling message in defense of human dignity is shared by former Polish dissident and now a newspaper publisher in Poland, Adam Michnik (b. 1946). Despite his liberal views on sexual ethics and other moral questions, Michnik became one of Wojtyła's many admirers when the future pope was still the archbishop in Kraków. In a 1988 interview, as a member of the underground Solidarity movement Michnik expressed surprise that people in the West were becoming overly concerned with the sexual ethics promoted by the Catholic Church but not with the violations of human rights in Soviet-type systems. Although this was not a direct reference to demands for women's rights, there is a clear implication in Adam

Michnik's statement that violations of human rights occurring in the Soviet block were much more important to him than complains from Western feminists. One Catholic intellectual described the Church's role before 1989 as providing a "breathing space" for both believers and non-believers in Poland. Simply by its own existence, the Church offered something different from the uniform communist system. When freedom came, opinions started to diverge and the society created its own institutions, making the Church less necessary as a defender of freedom and human rights.[105] *Gazeta Wyborcza* and other liberal media in Poland opposed the ban on abortions, restrictions on the sale of contraceptives and other Church-supported political and social measures. The Polish Church was no longer portrayed in the liberal Polish media as an ally in promoting human rights but as an obstacle to building a modern society. Mild criticism of John Paul II and sharp condemnations of the Polish Primate, Cardinal Józef Glemp, and other conservative Polish bishops were becoming more frequent on the pages of *Gazeta Wyborcza*.

In the 1988 interview before all these changes, Michnik defended the Church's strict position on divorce and sexual ethics, pointing out that societies need conservative institutions capable of upholding traditional values. In his opinion, and undoubtedly also in the opinion of John Paul II, "the world has no need of a Church which instantly proclaims everything people want."[106] The question that needs to be asked is to what degree the Church can ignore the views of the faithful without becoming irrelevant. The Protestant churches resolved this issue by splitting into numerous denominations, each one and practically each church representing the consensus of their communities. The Catholic Church wants to be a universal, worldwide institution with the same rules for everyone. But what appeals to liberal Catholics in North America and Western Europe may not go well with conservative Catholics in Poland or in Latin America. As the head of a world religion, the pope also has to consider the Church's relations with the Christian

Orthodox churches and Islam, both of which have an even more restrictive view of women's role in religion. The ultimate question is whether the Catholic Church can keep central control and survive as a global institution in an increasingly democratic and pluralistic world with growing numbers of educated women and men wishing to exercise their religious faith according to their personal preferences. The Vatican may have two choices: maintain control and see a continuing decline of loyalty to the pope among the more educated and more liberal Catholics or make the Church more democratic and more pluralistic and lose the support of the most loyal and most active conservative groups.

Feminists and others working for the ordination of women in the Catholic Church have a difficult task in front of them. If they want to achieve major reforms, they would have to fight for them within the Church. However, the tendency among more liberal Catholics has been to leave the Church with which they find themselves less and less in agreement. If this tendency continues, the Catholic Church is likely to become even more conservative in the future.

The Polish dissident said in 1988 that he would like to live in a country with liberal laws on sexual ethics, but in which the Church offers very strict rules for people to follow. This observation describes the current situation of the Catholic Church in many countries, and the response of Benedict XVI may very well be along the lines predicted by Adam Michnik. Michnik also stated that a world without tradition would be "nonsensical and anarchic." It was Michnik, who in his book *The Church, the Left, and Dialogue*, published in the West in 1977, argued that the Catholic Church, because of its support for human rights, should be seen not as an enemy of liberalism but as an ally of Left-wing intellectuals like himself who were trying to replace communism with democracy. Wojtyła, known for his willingness to talk with people of different opinions and different backgrounds, had long discussions on this subject with Michnik and other Left-wing dissidents in Poland.

After the fall of communism in 1989, Adam Michnik became the editor of *Gazeta Wyborcza*, the largest circulation newspaper in Poland. Many conservative Catholics in Poland who listen to Radio Maryja see Michnik and his paper as major enemies of the Church. Despite many disagreements, Adam Michnik still considers John Paul II a great man, but the previous alliance between Left-wing liberals and the Catholic Church in Poland has long disappeared. In later years of his papacy, John Paul II did not try to re-establish a dialogue with secular humanists in the West or in his own country. If anything, he must have concluded that the Church's strength was in its conservative base in the West and in the Third World. These conservative Catholics would see such a dialogue as a betrayal of their loyalty to the pope and his strict moral standards. Considering the fragmentation of the liberal Christian churches in the West and their declining membership — while conservative churches seem to be thriving — John Paul II's strategy may not have been entirely wrong as far as the interests of the worldwide institution that is the Catholic Church are concerned.

Wojtyła's "New Feminism"

In later years of his pontificate, John Paul II referred to his positions on women as "new feminism" — a term later promoted by those Catholics, including women, who share his views. He launched "new feminism" in his 1995 encyclical *Evangelium Vitae* (*The Gospel of Life*) dealing with abortion, euthanasia, and the death penalty:

> In transforming culture so that it supports life, *women* occupy a place, in thought and action, which is unique and decisive. It depends on them to promote a "**new feminism**" which rejects the temptation of imitating models of "male domination," in order to acknowledge and affirm the true genius of women in every aspect of the life of society, and overcome all discrimination, violence and exploitation.

Lucienne Salle of the Pontifical Council for the Laity described as the greatest novelty in Wojtyła's thinking on women the absence of the spirit of rebellion on the part of women and confrontation between the sexes. In her opinion, the old type of feminism is based on confrontation and fails to respond to women's expectations as it puts women in a confrontational position vis-à-vis the love of their husbands and the need to care for their children. At an international conference in Rome in May 2000, Lucienne Salle repeated Wojtyła's statement that the vast majority of women want to be wives and mothers.[107] She also expressed the pope's views that "new feminism" must consider the nurturing nature of women by being associated more with motherhood, either physical or spiritual. In May 2000, John Paul II called for the promotion of "new feminism" that "without falling into the temptation of pursuing 'macho' models, can recognize and express the authentic feminine genius." The word "macho" when used in this context by the pope implied a criticism of those feminists who insist that there are no basic differences between women and men and that women should adopt male models of behavior. As he often stressed, also in this statement John Paul II placed emphasis on the protection of the unborn by insisting that "women have a singular, and perhaps determinant place for thought and action" on behalf of "cultural

---

Mary Ann Glendon b. 1938

Professor of Law at Harvard University Law School

First female president of the Pontifical Academy of Social Sciences appointed by Pope John Paul II, January 19, 1994.

Nominated by President George W. Bush as U.S. Ambassador to the Holy See, November 2007.

Quote: "What is clearly 'old-fashioned' today is the old feminism of the 1970s — with its negative attitudes toward men, marriage and motherhood, and its rigid party line on abortion and gay rights."

http://www.glendonbooks.com/

change in favor of life."[108]

According to Mary Ann Glendon, a law professor at Harvard University who represented John Paul II at the 1995 U.N. World Conference on Woman in Beijing, "new feminism" must defend the dignity of woman in all its dimensions, especially with regard to the weakest—a clear reference to unborn children and women who would consider having an abortion. Mary Ann Glendon linked "new feminism" with John Paul's often stated need for new evangelization and saw it as a proposal directed especially to the old feminists.[109] The objective is to convince women that the element of confrontation in feminism is counterproductive and should be replaced with solidarity and love. Mary Ann Glendon accused old feminists of promoting a negative attitude toward men, marriage and motherhood. For this American law professor, feminism should focus instead on defending the rights of mothers and families. In an article published by *Commonweal*, a liberal Catholic journal of opinion in the United States, she pointed out that young single women in the United States without any children have almost equal job opportunities with men but women raising children are clearly disadvantaged in the workplace.[110] Orthodox views on women and feminism are more likely to be found, however, in conservative Catholic magazines like *The Wanderer*.

Commonweal
http://www.commonwealmagazine.org/

Another Catholic woman who restated John Paul's views on "new feminism," Jo Croissant, the wife of the founder of the new Community of the Beatitudes in France, pointed out at the same conference in Rome that "one of the errors of feminists' claims was to place woman's liberation strictly in her relation to man." She made a claim that traditional feminism offers women only domination of man as the only alternative to submission.

The Wanderer
http://www.thewandererpress.com/

Ministry to Persons with a Homosexual Inclination – US Conference of Catholic Bishops

http://www.usccb.org/dpp/Ministry.pdf

Many gay, lesbian, bisexual and transgender Catholics in the United States and elsewhere disagreed with John Paul II's views on homosexuality. Their American organization, DignityUSA, has been working to win official Church acceptance for combining spirituality with gay and lesbian sexuality. Dignity Canada is doing similar work, but neither organization is recognized as an official entity within the Catholic Church in North America and both are prohibited from using church facilities. In 1997, Dr. Jeannine Gramick, a Roman Catholic nun, and Fr. Robert Nugent, a Roman Catholic priest, co-founded New Ways Ministry, an organization providing ministry and support to gay and lesbian Catholics in the United States. In 2000, the Congregation for the Doctrine of the Faith under the leadership of Cardinal Joseph Ratzinger disciplined both Gramick and Nugent and ordered them to stop writing and speaking out on issues of homosexuality. Gramick rejected the order and transferred from the School Sisters of Notre Dame to the Sisters of Loretto, which support her in her ministry on behalf of lesbian and gay people. After being silenced, Father Nugent remains a priest in good standing. In 2005, New Ways Ministry raised concerns about the election of Cardinal Ratzinger to the papacy: "Cardinal Joseph Ratzinger's record at the Vatican has been marked by decisions to end discussion on important questions and issues facing Catholics and the world. His hard-handed tactics of silencing theologians and using language that offends rather than heals have caused much alienation and anger....His record on lesbian/gay issues has been notoriously insensitive. Instead of listening to the voices of the laity, or even of other bishops, he has been the architect of documents and policies that reveal a tremendous lack of understanding of homosexuality and of the experiences of lesbian/gay people." A conservative Catholic web site, OurLadyWarriors.org describes New Ways Ministry as "militant advocate of homosexuality which also demands ordination and ministry for homosexuals."

New Ways Ministry

http://mysite.verizon.net/~vze43yrc/index.html

Sisters of Loretto

http://www.lorettocommunity.org/

Instead of relating to man from a position of strength, Jo Croissant, urged women to find the right manner of relating to man "by establishing the relation of woman with God" and seeing herself as "a daughter of God," then "spouse," and finally "mother." The French speaker urged women to free themselves from "complexes" and "old wounds." According to Croissant, only by rediscovering her profound identity as a daughter of God, spouse, and mother—a woman can become genuinely free "without feeling threatened or crushed, and without crushing the other." Jo Croissant restated Wojtyła's view that woman's dignity is not found in confrontation with man. According to her, "woman's dignity is intimately linked to the love she receives because of her femininity and, in addition, the love that she herself gives."[111]

John Paul II's Views on Homosexual Marriages

As part of his vision for Christian families and efforts to counter Western secular cultural trends, John Paul II was strongly opposed to any efforts to treat people who choose to live together on the same level as marriage. In 1998, he told a group of European politicians and legislators attending a conference at the Vatican on family issues that legalizing informal unions of two people and making them equivalent to marriage can only be prejudicial to the institution of the family and would violate the natural law. While marriage, according to John Paul II, was based on its principles other forms of co-habitation derive from the arbitrary will of persons.[112] Such a definition automatically excludes homosexual couples, couples living without marriage, or single individuals wanting to adopt children. John Paul II wanted the Catholic Church to actively oppose any attempts to grant official recognition to non-traditional family units. He saw demands for giving tax and other legal benefits to non-traditional families as undermining families and morals in Western societies. He specifically warned in his December 1999 messages that today's families need "a special protection from the government, which is not infrequently put under pressure by special interest groups in order to legislate certain rights that are in reality the fruit of an individualistic subjective mentality."[113]

In November 2006, the American Catholic bishops adopted new guidelines for pastoral care of gay men and lesbians. The guidelines welcomed gay people to participate fully in the life of the Church while affirming core Catholic teachings that homosexual inclinations are "inherently disordered." The official position is that having such inclinations is not sinful, but sexual activity is. The U.S. bishops reaffirmed the Church's official teaching that persons with a homosexual inclination "must be accepted with respect, compassion, and sensitivity." The document adopted by the American bishops also condemned all forms of scorn, hatred and violence, whether subtle or overt, directed against homosexuals. These positions were strongly supported by Pope John Paul II. The bishops even admitted that many persons with a homosexual inclination "feel themselves to be unwelcome and rejected" by the official Church, but they were not going to change any basic policies. DignityUSA expressed disappointment with the new guidelines. This and similar organizations have been unable to produce a drastic change in how the Vatican and the Church hierarchy in the U.S. view gay men and lesbian Catholics who are sexually active. Benedict XVI does not want gay men and lesbians to adopt children or have the same rights as heterosexual married couples, and neither did Pope John Paul II. These organizations have been successful, however, in promoting greater tolerance and understanding toward their community in North America.

Poland—Practical Applications of John Paul II's Ideas for Women

Having lived under two totalitarianisms, Pope John Paul II, according to former Solidarity leader and former Polish President Lech Wałęsa, would never try to impose his views on anyone. He did instead try to persuade others to accept values, which, in his opinion, could have helped the world avoid new dangers to humanity. John Paul II's supporters in Poland, however, are much less reluctant to use coercive customs and laws to force compliance from those who do not share their values. Poland is a good example of a country in which John Paul's ideas had been translated into specific legislation and government policies that feminists who disagreed with the pope view as highly discriminatory and restrictive. The Vatican's public relations team tried hard to present John Paul II as someone who merely persuades rather than imposes his point of view on others. His official spokesman, Joaquin Navarro-Valls declared that in the realm of ideas, the pope "is not interested in winning but in convincing."[114] These are subtle distinctions, since in the final analysis the pope's views have very real effect on women in many countries around the world.

It is clear that on a personal level, Wojtyła deeply respected each person's dignity, autonomy, and freedom to make moral choices. His positions are well known: total opposition to abortion, rejection of artificial contraception, support for motherhood and family, unacceptability of divorce, and promotion of traditional roles for women. There is little doubt, however, that the pope was also motivated by his concern for preserving women's dignity and was fully opposed to most forms of discrimination against women. His views on women were almost always expressed in compassionate terms, but they were not always interpreted in compassionate ways by some of his most ardent supporters in Poland and elsewhere.

Conservative Catholics everywhere, who would like to see women reject most of the recent advances in personal freedom achieved in the West such as easily available contraception and legal abortion, are convinced that they had John Paul's full approval and support. This was particularly true in Poland where Catholic politicians, supported by the Catholic Church, have passed in recent years a number of restrictive laws affecting women's rights and opposed a number of initiatives designed to combat discrimination against women. Pro-feminist Polish scholar, Anna Titkow, noted that that Catholic politicians in Poland "created the impression that their principal political, strategic, and personal goals were to corral Polish women into the world of 'Church, Kitchen, and Children'"[115] The Polish Catholic Church, Catholic politicians, and the organizations and political parties, which claim to represent the pope's views on these issues, see their role quite differently and claim to speak for the majority of the Polish people, even despite a major defeat for the Right-wing coalition in the October 2007 parliamentary elections.

The controversy as to who should speak for Polish women in democratic Poland goes back to the years immediately after the fall of communism. A Polish coalition of pro-life organizations withdrew its representative from the committee preparing a report for the Fourth World Conference on Women in Beijing in 1995 charging that the Polish delegation was dominated by recently formed extreme pro-feminist groups with very few members. The Polish Federation of Pro-Life Movements claimed to represent the views of a much greater number of Polish women. The Federation felt that these views were being ignored by a group of extreme feminists who had taken over the lead in preparing a report on the situation of Polish women to be presented at the Beijing conference.

These views of pro-life Catholic activists in Poland are not much different from positions taken by conservative evangelical Christians in the U.S., except that the Catholic Church in Poland

and Catholic politicians have had in recent years even more influence over government policies than the conservative Christians in the U.S. The Polish Federation of Pro-Life Movements claimed that contrary to what a tiny group of Polish feminists would like the world to believe, Polish women do not want "safe abortions" on demand in state hospitals. (According to a 2007 survey, 50 percent of adult Poles agree that a woman should have the right to abortion during the first weeks of pregnancy.[116]) The Federation of Pro-Life Movements was also opposed to state subsidies for the sale of contraceptives and to sex education in schools, which—in the organization's view, was focused on biological aspects of sex and promoted early sexual activity and promiscuity. The pro-life movement also expressed its opposition to the idea of accelerated no-fault divorces.

On the sensitive issue of spousal abuse, the Federation accused Polish feminists of a one-sided approach designed to break up families while ignoring the real causes of violence against women. As an example, the group cited violence and pornography in the media, although violence against women was equally common in Poland during the communist rule when there was relatively little violence or pornography on television or in the press. Pro-life organizations in Poland also complained about feminist-supported changes in textbooks for school children designed to promote equality between men and women. They charged that under the pretext of equality, these changes were actually designed to undermine the role of the mother. Groups of extreme feminists in Poland were accused of promoting hedonistic views which destroy families and cause antagonism between women and the rest of the society.[117] The appeal of the pro-life movement was reported in the Catholic press under the title, "In Defense of Woman's Dignity." There can be very little doubt that the views represented by the Pro-Life Federation closely resembled those promoted by John Paul II.

How Wojtyła's positions on contraception, abortion, and divorce are interpreted and applied by Catholic politicians and parish priests in Poland has a much more direct impact on countless women than his philosophical and theological writings in support of moderate forms of Catholic feminism. Very often, elements of compassion, moderation and tolerance disappear as soon as some Polish Catholic priests, political leaders and legislators try to promote practical policies, which — at least in their minds — are closely based on the pope's teachings. Poland is a good example of a country where Wojtyła's ideas have affected women in significant ways, sometimes contrary to the spirit in which they were first proposed by the pope, but nevertheless in line with his basic opinions.

Kazimierz Kapera, at the time a 55 year old dentist, married with six children, named in 1997 to head the Polish government's office for family affairs, made news by his statement that he would oppose an abortion for a hypothetical twelve-year-old victim of rape. His response, actually fully in agreement with the pope's position on abortion for rape victims, was that the girl or her parents should have no say in the matter. What had to be considered, according to Dr. Kapera, was "the beginning of a new life that cannot be punished for the rape with destruction."[118]

Just as John Paul II, Dr. Kapera was against discriminating women in the workplace, considered Poland to be a country in which women enjoy great respect, and saw nothing unusual if a woman becomes a university president or a government minister. But asked to define his comments about "natural role for women," Dr. Kapera responded that it is above all motherhood and raising children together with a husband without necessarily closing off the possibility of self-realization through a career outside of the home. He was in favor of a partnership between wife, husband and older children in performing household duties, thus allowing a woman to work if she wants to, although he was convinced that women who want to work full time represent a very small minority. He was personally against artificial birth control and opposed any government subsidies for birth control drugs. He considered using tax revenues for this purpose an immoral act in light of other health care needs in Poland. He also opposed using condoms as a protection against AIDS and described HIV infection as a consequence of homosexual acts, which he considered a "perversion." He stopped a government program designed to raise public awareness of domestic violence out of concern that it would encourage hate between women and men. He believed that it is easier to raise children in large families and would not allow adoptions by non-traditional families.

Dr. Kapera most controversial comment was made in a radio interview in July 1999 when he asserted that there is no need to worry about feeding people worldwide. Noting that the population growth in Europe is on the downturn, Dr. Kapera observed that "it is important to make sure that the Europeans, that is the white race, have some say in the future." Polish government spokesman described this comment as a "most unfortunate statement."[119] Democratic Union of Women in Poland called on Prime Minister Jerzy Buzek to dismiss Dr. Kapera in view of his "white race" statement, but he was allowed to keep his job.

Dr. Kapera also opposed divorce as incompatible with Catholic faith and proposed instead legal separations as the only alternative to the indissolubility of marriage. He opposed a liberal bill on equal rights, which was passed by the Polish Parliament dominated at the time by Catholic deputies, on the grounds that it violated the natural roles of men and women and their mutual complementarity in marriage. Pointing out that men cannot breastfeed or give birth, Dr. Kapera expressed reservations about the concept of equality for all women under all conditions.

While not identical, his views were very close to those of John Paul II. The practical and legal consequences of these views for Polish women have been significant. In recent years, however, Dr. Kapera's political career has been less successful. He was defeated in the 2001 elections to the Polish *Sejm* (lower house of the National Assembly) and in 2002 failed in his bid to become the mayor of

Kraków as a candidate of the League of Polish Families, a Right wing Catholic party. This party, which was once a powerful member of the Right-wing coalition and tried to ban abortions even in the case of rape and incest, did not win the required minimum of votes in the 2007 elections. It no longer has any deputies in the *Sejm*. Several years earlier, Dr. Kapera formed a new party called Family-Fatherland. In 2005, he was the new party's candidate for a seat in the Polish Senate but again suffered an electoral defeat. Since 1993, he is president of the Polish Federation of Catholic Family Organizations.

The communist regime gave Polish women the right to legal abortion in 1956. The 1956 law allowed abortions on social grounds for women faced with difficult material conditions or difficult personal situations. In practical terms, the communist era law permitted abortion on demand. In 1993, the Polish parliament, dominated by pro-Church deputies, passed the law de-legalizing such abortions. The only allowed exceptions were in the case of rape, incest, or danger to mother's life. During the debate that preceded the vote, some priests and Catholic politicians called for punishing women for obtaining illegal abortions. Typical argument was that taking a human life cannot go unpunished. "People are alive even if we can't see them or even if they are [only six months old]. It is still the same—they are people and nobody can kill people without punishment"—argued a graduate student at the Catholic University in Lublin (KUL) and an activist in the Christian-National Alliance.[120] But most Catholic politicians realized that demanding punishment for women who obtain illegal abortions would be going too far and could jeopardize the outcome of the vote. As Bishop Bronisław Dembowski explained, the Polish bishops insisted that abortion must be declared a crime, but even though it is a crime, "an unfortunate woman cannot be punished."[121] John Paul II never commented directly whether women who obtain abortions should be punished, but it can be safely assumed that he was against such punishment. His close personal friend, Bishop Józef Życiński, described calls for punishing women as "irrational." But according to Jarosław Gowin, a Polish sociologist and a Catholic priest, the idea of seeking punishment for women who resort to abortion was dominant among the Church circles in Poland, even if the issue of legal sanctions against women was not their highest priority.[122]

After the vote in the Polish parliament banning most abortions, women wanting to terminate an unwanted pregnancy were forced to resort to an illegal operation at the cost from $400 to $800, a sum equal to at least a monthly professional wage. There has been also a legal but often more expensive alternative. Depending on their financial means, Polish women have a choice of participating in the so called "abortion tourism," by traveling to one of the former communist countries on Poland's eastern or southern borders or getting an abortion in Western Europe at a higher cost but under better medical conditions. Some of the countries, which have experienced "abortion tourism" from Poland, include the Czech Republic, Slovakia, Ukraine, Belarus, Russia, Lithuania, Germany and Austria. This practice has been described by the critics of the Catholic Church's position on this issue as exporting Poland's abortion problem to other countries. Ireland, the only other European country — also predominantly Catholic — has also been transferring its abortion problem abroad. There are no reliable figures how many Polish women obtain illegal abortions in Poland or terminate their pregnancies in neighboring countries. According to government sources, only 200 legal abortions were performed in Poland in 2006. But Wanda Nowicka, head of the Federation for Women's Rights and Family Planning told Reuters that the number of illegal abortions performed in Poland is closer to 200,000 annually and that many more Polish women travel abroad to have abortions in Belarus and Ukraine.[123] The number of Irish women who travel to England each year seeking abortions has been estimated to reach 7,000 annually. Over the years, approximately 100,000 Irish women have made this journey to England.[124]

Public opinion surveys have shown over the years that the vast majority of Poles, 84% in 1996, attach the highest value to the family and see it as the ultimate goal in life.[125] The highest percentage of such views was among the people of Wojtyła's generation, while only 66% of students chose family over career as the most important value.[126] This suggests that the traditional view of the overriding importance of the family may have started to change. Individual autonomy and freedom, characteristic of the Western societies, are becoming more attractive to the younger generations of the Poles, who may prefer to delay marriage and are satisfied with smaller families. In 1999, for the first time in its recent history, Poland experienced negative population growth. Many Polish women now feel that they can barely afford to raise one child. This is, however, not John Paul II's preferred family model. In the post-communist Poland, the Polish bishops followed his example by trying to encourage women to devote themselves primarily to childcare. But since most Polish women had to work, this was hardly a realistic proposition. In previous years, Polish women could count on the help from their mothers in taking care of their children, but Polish grandmothers who were educated under communism seem now less and less willing to devote themselves entirely to childcare. At a meeting in 1989 focused on education, the Polish bishops still concluded that "young girls should be prepared above all for their roles as wives and mothers without emphasizing their intellectual aspirations."[127]

Research shows that even today Polish women perform the vast majority of household tasks, especially shopping, cooking and cleaning. They are also primarily responsible for all the tasks connected with raising children. Despite of this heavy burden, Polish women have accepted their outside of the home careers as worthwhile beyond the economic benefits and are not willing to give up their jobs at the earliest opportunity despite of what some Catholic clergy and politicians are trying to suggest.[128] In fact, Polish women are beginning to assign less value to traditional female pursuits such as raising children and maintaining a home.[129] This trend is particularly strong among students and young career women who are becoming more and more like their Western counterparts. Family life and having children as goals in life have become relatively less important for college-bound high school students and young men and women from educated families.[130]

John Paul II was convinced that most women would choose to stay at home if men could earn enough money to maintain large families. Contrary to what most conservative Church leaders may think, this is not what most Polish women want. The traditional view of marriage, in which the wife stays at home, is shared by nearly 50% of Polish men; but only 31% of Polish women want to be full time housewives. A marriage based on a partnership, in which both husband and wife work outside of home and each devotes the same amount of time to household tasks, is preferred by 44% of Polish women and 30% of Polish men.[131] The traditional model of marriage largely appeals to the older generation, to those with only elementary education and to the most religious individuals.

Education also has a significant impact on women's views on marriage. Only 10% of the Polish women with higher education prefer the traditional model as opposed to 39% of women with only elementary education.[132] Polish men have similar expectations of their future partners as men in the West. They are looking for love and mutual attraction, but they also have three additional requirements that make them somewhat different from Western men. They want their Polish wife to have the same religion, to be neat and to cook well.[133] The Polish weekly newsmagazine *Wprost* concluded in 1996 that with the high cost of eating out in Poland, the Polish family is largely a cooking and cleaning service. Women do the vast majority of the work at home. The magazine points out, however, that changes are taking place — 99% of women-managers in a Western company in Poland are unmarried. None of them, according to the magazine, think that not having a husband makes them less attractive.

Polish women, however, are not embracing most of the ideas which Western feminists consider important. One can easily see the influence of John Paul II's teachings in the attitudes of a significant segment of Polish women who question for example the need for special legislation protecting women's rights. They say that they oppose such legislation because they see themselves first and foremost as "human beings" rather than women or feminists. According to the Polish newsmagazine *Wprost*, most Polish women sociologists and psychologists interviewed for the article were convinced that the only women being discriminated against in Poland are those who allow it to happen. They accuse feminists of proposing special legislation that only proves that women are not sufficiently talented, intelligent or ambitious. Such legislation is also viewed as a reminder of primitive communist propaganda extolling the virtues of women-workers.

A well-known Polish actress thought that some feminists may have forgotten that women are also part of the human race composed of both men and women. She considers masculine women to be their own worse enemies. Another Polish woman accused feminists of hypocrisy in trying to obtain all the rights belonging to men while holding on to all the privileges which Polish women enjoy. She advised women to accept gender differences and learn to live with them. Another woman said she prefers to differentiate people according to their abilities rather than their gender. Some successful professional Polish women, according to the *Wprost* article, are concerned about the negative impact of public campaigns for greater gender equality supported by feminists. They feel fully qualified to do their jobs and fear that such campaigns will sow doubts about qualifications of all women in the workplace.

Many women interviewed for the article expressed disdain for women who do not appear feminine. Polish sociologists consulted by *Wprost* expressed the view that women must realize that no legislation will be a substitute for qualifications and skills. Another Polish woman interviewed for the article believes that some of the discrimination against women is caused by women themselves and not by flawed legislation. In the opinion of some of the women quoted in the article, if a woman is certain of her worth as a professional and can strongly defend her position, she will not be discriminated against and will not have to complain. They see feminists as women who dress as males and hate all men.

Some Polish women simply call for allowing women a free choice between work at home or a professional career on condition that either choice is respected. A Polish actress described herself as unemancipated and full of admiration for her husband with whom she shares household duties. Proposals to guarantee women a 40 percent representation in the Polish parliament were dismissed by the interviewees as "ridiculous" and compared with the affirmative action legislation in the U.S. The interviewees reacted the same way to proposals for granting women preferential points in employment, stressing that women should be judged by their professionalism, not by their gender. Some of them expressed views very similar to those advocated by John Paul II, calling for cooperation rather than competition between men and women. They want men and women to find "a common language, without denigration, hate and aggression against another human being."[134]

Polish women, interviewed for the *Wprost* article, represented the intellectual elite in Poland. The article did not mention such common problems in Poland as spousal abuse, sexual exploitation and pornography, sexual harassment, unequal division of household work or even the position of the Catholic Church on abortion, contraception and the ordination of female priests. The women interviewed for the article readily referred to "the feminist trap" and the need to turn against it, without realizing that feminism in its Western form has not even arrived in Poland and that Western feminism has many currents, from the most radical to quite conservative and even religious. In some respects, John Paul II may have been more progressive on women's rights than the majority of Polish women today. Even he seemed more willing to condemn sex discrimination in public life, except, of course, when it comes to gender discrimination within the Church itself. He also showed compassion for women who are less skilled and less qualified for the job market because of past discrimination.

Many Polish women have strongly negative views of feminists. Asked to name people they would not want to live with, Polish women placed a feminist in the third place after an HIV carrier and a former member of the secret police.[135]

Havel, Gandhi and Alternative Views of Western Feminism

There was not much support for feminist ideas among the anti-communist opposition in Poland and in other former Soviet-block countries. Even the most humanistic opposition figures in East Central Europe grew up in highly patriarchal societies and families and all of them considered communism a much greater threat to human rights than gender discrimination. If they thought about feminism at all, most of them, found it at least strange if not ridiculous.

Václav Havel b. 1936
http://www.vaclavhavel.cz/Index.php?setln=2

Mahatma Gandhi 1869-1948

Václav Havel, who after 1989 became president of Czechoslovakia and later president of the Czech Republic, had the courage to admit in 1985 that he knew little about feminism, although he was "prepared to believe that it is far from being the invention of a few hysterical women, bored housewives or cast-off mistresses." He described how most of his women-friends in the dissident movement in Czechoslovakia refused to sign a human rights petition, proposed to them by two young feminists visiting from Italy, because "it seemed to them ridiculous that they should sign something as women" or try "to reinforce their civic opinion by stressing their defenseless feminism."[136]

Havel's female dissident-friends dismissed an opportunity to join the international feminist movement, even though in 1985 the position of women in Czechoslovakia was, by Havel's own admission, "incomparably worse than in the West." At that time both in Poland and in Czechoslovakia a much greater fight for human rights was underway. Feminism in Havel's mind, and most likely also in Wojtyła's mind at that time, would have been associated with something "ridiculous." In describing the atmosphere among the Central Europeans prior to the fall of communism, Václav Havel wrote about "strange, almost mysterious horror of anything overstated, enthusiastic, cynical, histrionic or overly serious." Feminism, he concluded, would have been incompatible with the spiritual culture of life under communist dictatorship.

If individuals with such strong humanistic and liberal views as Václav Havel perceived feminism as something that may appear ridiculous, it can be attributed not only to their upbringing and culture under which they grew up but also to political conditions they had to face in their countries. Havel has apparently changed his views about feminism, but one can only read his letters to his late wife Olga, written from prison in 1979, to see that he, just like Wojtyła, was a product of traditional upbringing. In a letter written from a prison cell in November 1979, Havel told his first wife that her "cultural, domestic and social life should keep you so occupied that you won't feel the need for a regular job."[137] Havel gave his wife detailed instructions on how she should take care of their household, encouraged her to follow his advice, and suggested that if she really wanted to work, she should consider ushering in a theatre, which — as he reminded her — she used to enjoy.

Václav Havel is one of the most liberal, pro-Western politicians in East Central Europe who strongly supports pro-choice legislation and equal employment opportunities for women while at the same time promoting respect for life and human rights around the world. He seems not to be overly concerned, as John Paul II certainly was, that giving women a legal right to abortion, while still perceiving abortion as morally wrong, would so greatly undermine respect for life and human rights that it could eventually produce much more fatal abuses resulting in the destruction of civilization. Obviously, Havel and others have more faith in democracy, their own countrymen, and even the West than John Paul II ever did. It should be noted, however, that John Paul II experienced and observed the genocides of World War II and the cruelest period of communist rule in Poland, while Václav Havel, who is younger, did not, although he was imprisoned and suffered under the communist regime in Czechoslovakia in later years.

Other public figures, widely admired in the West for their moral courage and concern for the oppressed, are now also viewed by some feminist scholars as patriarchal and conservative on gender issues. In her book, *Women and Human Development*, American scholar Martha C. Nussbaum asserted that any reader of *Autobiography* of Mahatma Gandhi (1869-1948) "is likely to be struck by the strange combination of a rare moral depth and radicalism…and attitudes toward his wife that are extremely traditional and male-centered."[138] Wojtyła read Gandhi's books and was an admirer of his positions on non-violent resistance to colonialism as well as his traditional views on religion, abortion and contraception. On the larger issue of balancing rights of individuals and community interests, he would also be in agreement with Gandhi's statement that "all rights to be deserved and preserved came from duty well done." Gandhi claimed to have learned this from his "illiterate but wise mother."[139] Reflecting their respective societies' primarily agrarian social mores, both Gandhi and Wojtyła shared a deep attachment to community and a much greater emphasis on the duties rather than the rights of individuals.

In the 1950s, Wojtyła studied the writings of the Indian independence leader about his advocacy of non-violent overthrow of the British rule.[140] When visiting India as pope in 1986, John Paul II stopped to pray at Raj Ghat, the place where Gandhi's body was cremated, and throughout his trip to India he made frequent references to Gandhi's statements. Significantly, one of Gandhi's statements the pope quoted during his visit was that procreation should not be limited by immoral and artificial means but through discipline and self-control. In an apparent attempt to shame the West and court support in the Third World and among non-Western religions, John Paul II stated that on this issue Gandhi was more Christian than many of those who call themselves Christians.[141] The primary theme of the pope's speech in Raj Ghat, where he planted a memorial tree in honor of Gandhi, was, however, not birth control but Gandhi's larger legacy as a "hero to humanity" who advocated non-violence in resisting oppression.[142] John Paul II described the Indian leader as someone who preached "the need for mutual understanding, acceptance, and collaboration between religious groups in the pluralist society of modern India and throughout the world."[143]

CHAPTER SEVEN

What to Expect from the New Pope

American Catholics and the New Pope

Speaking in 1978 after the death of Pope Paul VI, American Catholic priest and author Father Andrew M. Greeley suggested that the crisis, in which the Catholic Church found itself, required a new pope who would be "a man of holiness, a man of hope, a man of joy." He described such a pope as "a holy man who can smile."[1] In a subsequent discussion, Father Greeley said that he would not be personally opposed to a female pope and added that "a papessa could not make more mess of the Church than we men have over the last 1900 years."[2] Cardinal Albino Luciani, Patriarch of Venice (1912-1978), who was elected after the death of Paul VI and took the name of John Paul I, was indeed famous for his smile, but he died after only thirty-three days as pope, thus opening the way for the election of Karol Wojtyła.[3] After John Paul II death in 2005, Father Greeley was not optimistic that the new conclave

---

Joseph Alois Ratzinger – Pope Benedict XVI

Born: April 16, 1927, Marktl am Inn, Bavaria, Germany

Quote: "Faced with the abuse of power, the answer for women is to seek power. This process leads to opposition between men and women, in which the identity and role of one are emphasized to the disadvantage of the other, leading to harmful confusion regarding the human person, which has its most immediate and lethal effects in the structure of the family."

http://www.vatican.va/holy_father/benedict_xvi/index.htm
http://thepopeblog.blogspot.com/

would elect a pope who would focus on the worldwide sexual and social abuse of women, but expressed some hope that ultimately the Church hierarchy will discover the fundamental equality of women. He added, however, that such a discovery will come "perhaps later than sooner."[4]

In 1996, after nearly two decades of Wojtyła's papacy, American Catholics were asked in a survey what they would expect from a new pope. A large majority wished for a pope who would radically democratize the Church. For example, 65 percent of the respondents hoped that a new pope would allow the ordination of women. Slightly more Catholic men were in favor of ordination than Catholic women, but the difference was not statistically significant. Catholic women in the U.S. who participated in the 1996 survey were, however, more likely to support radical changes than men, particularly on the issue of greater democracy and decentralization of power within the Church. Support for reforms increased with the level of education. American Catholics, who have grown accustomed to electing and rejecting political candidates for over 200 years, find it difficult to tolerate bishops or priests whom they may not like and on whose selection they were not consulted. Sixty-nine percent of the respondents

---

Official Catholic Web Sites

Vatican

http://www.vatican.va/

Catholic Church in Australia

http://www.catholic.org.au/

Canadian Conference of Catholic Bishops

http://www.cccb.ca/

Catholic Church in England & Wales

http://www.catholic-ew.org.uk/

Catholic Communications Office – Ireland

http://www.catholiccommunications.ie/

Catholic Chuch in New Zealand

http://www.catholic.org.nz/

Bishops' Conference of Scotland

http://www.bpsconfscot.com/

U.S. Conference of Catholic Bishops

http://www.nccbuscc.org/

would prefer a pope who would permit married priests. Support for married priests was seven percent higher among women than among men. Educated women were most likely to overwhelmingly support greater pluralism and other reforms within the Church. Sixty-five percent of the respondents expressed hope that a new pope would allow the laity and clergy to choose their own bishop. In the past, priests and people within their own diocese elected bishops, but currently all Catholic bishops are appointed by the pope.[5] American Catholics also wanted a pope who would be more concerned about the lives of ordinary people and would like him to choose more lay advisors to reflect this concern.

Dismissal of Western Liberalism

His liberal critics have argued that John Paul II did not seem to fully understand the crucial link between Western liberalism and the unprecedented expansion and protection of human rights, including the rights of women. Women enjoy more freedoms, greater educational and job opportunities, less discrimination and greater economic prosperity in precisely those countries which have embraced the liberal ideas of the primacy of constitutionally guaranteed individual rights over group rights. These countries are also much more likely to have a successful free market economy, albeit with strong elements of social protection and social services. Most of these countries belong to the so-called Western world. According to Polish feminists, women in Poland and in some of the other countries, where outward manifestations of popular religiousness are much stronger than in the West, are not necessarily better off, neither with regard to their social nor economic status. Wojtyła did not accept this analysis as valid, may have overlooked it or did not consider it sufficiently important.

While John Paul II claimed to be able to understand the Third World much better because of his Polish roots, he did not accept the link between the lack of liberal democracy and the lack of economic opportunities for women. He saw capitalism and

Western exploitation of smaller, weaker and poorer nations with traditional cultures as far more significant for explaining poverty and violence in the world. But not all weak and small nations are poor. As it turns out, some of the smallest nations in the world, most of them in Europe but also some in Asia, happen to be most prosperous by benefiting from free market economy and globalization. It is also true that some of the smaller and less developed nations with traditional cultures often become violent and aggressive toward their ethnic or religious minorities or their neighbors. Some of the recent examples are Somalia, Rwanda, Afghanistan and Sudan.

In his public statements, John Paul II was much more likely to condemn secular humanists and liberals than religious fundamentalists and nationalists, although he himself strongly opposed all forms of forced religion and any kind of ethnic prejudice. In his views on economic and social systems, John Paul II was much closer to those on the Left of the political spectrum, although he rejected their views on religion and personal morality. He also believed that too much of a welfare state can stifle creativity and initiative. He saw communism as the worst example of such an economic and political system, but he did not reject all aspects of communism, just as he did not reject all aspects of capitalism.[6] Ultimately, however, he was in favor of a highly regulated and socialized economy and usually talked about capitalism as it existed fifty or even a hundred years ago. In an interview with Radio Free Europe/Radio Liberty shortly after the death of John Paul II, Mikhail Gorbachev recalled that during their meeting at the Vatican, the pope told him: "I criticized communism but, I want you to know, that I also criticized all the vices of capitalism."[7]

Probably as a legacy of communism and communist propaganda, most people in Poland strongly agreed with John Paul II's view of the advantages of the welfare state and of government regulation of the economy. In a survey conducted in 2003, the vast majority of Poles (81%) expressed support for welfare state policies and more than two thirds wanted the government to play a strong role in regulating the market and slowing down the pace of privatization of state-run enterprises.[8] Interestingly, members of the Catholic-dominated The League of Polish Families (*Liga Polskich Rodzin, LPR*) — the most conservative Polish political party on religious and moral issues, which strongly supports John Paul II's moral agenda, including a total ban on abortions — are overwhelmingly in favor of expanding welfare state policies (81%). On economic policy issues, members of the Right-wing Catholic party hold similar views as supporters of the former communist party who are in favor of re-legalizing abortions in Poland. While true in Poland, however, this is not the case in the United States, where evangelical Christians and other conservative Christians are strong supporters of less regulated free market capitalism. Liberal Christians in the U.S., on the other hand, generally support welfare state solutions to social and economic problems. No doubt that one of the main reasons John Paul II favored welfare state solutions was his belief that under such a system more women can afford to stay at home and families can have more children thanks to government-provided support and subsidies.

With the fall of communism in Central and Eastern Europe, John Paul II may have thought it was his duty to warn against the abuses of the capitalist system. He may have also seen that Central and East Europeans government and business leaders were using capitalist solutions without sufficient social restraints and government regulations. It is also possible that his view of modern capitalism and market economy was distorted to some degree by the influence of communist era propaganda, views of his conservative Polish friends and the lack of sufficient first-hand knowledge of social and economic structures and institutions in the West. John Paul II also seemed convinced that liberalism and capitalism without a strong religious element carried with it the danger of yet another genocide. He disregarded most of the evidence that liberal democracies have been the most successful in protecting all categories of individual rights. One of the few and the most critical exception for protection of rights in liberal democracies are the rights of the unborn, and that may have convinced John Paul II that despite its scientific and economic achievements, the materialistic civilization based on liberal and free market ideas is particularly dangerous.

In his interpretation of recent history, Wojtyła seemed to have overlooked the fact that it was the democratic West that eventually defeated both fascism and communism; and even though fascism was born in the West, so was modern liberal democracy. While Stalin had to switch sides after being betrayed by Hitler and became the West's reluctant ally against Nazi Germany, in all likelihood the Soviet Union would not have been able to win the war on its own without American help, and Hitler would not have been defeated without a determined effort by Great Britain and the United States. Still, Poland did not become independent after World War II, while the West enjoyed freedom and economic prosperity despite the Cold War. Wojtyła and many Poles rightly saw this as a moral betrayal of Poland by her Western allies.

Franklin Delano Roosevelt (FDR)
1882-1945
Winston Churchill 1874-1965
Joseph Stalin 1878-1953

While Americans consider Franklin Delano Roosevelt one of the greatest American presidents, many Poles see him largely as an unprincipled leader who at the conference with Stalin in Yalta agreed that Poland should be part of the Soviet sphere of influence in Europe. FDR knew or should have known that Stalin, whom he called "Uncle Joe," had no intention of keeping his promises about democratic elections in Poland. He and Winston Churchill also assigned to Stalin Poland's eastern territories without seeking agreement from the Polish government, their loyal wartime ally. These historical events may have also affected John Paul II's view of the liberal West.

Some pro-Western Poles of Wojtyła's generation expected the U.S. and Great Britain to protect Poland's independence even if it meant going to war with the Soviet Union. They were gravely disappointed. After five years of fighting, neither the Americans nor the British were willing to go to war with the Soviet Union at the end of WWII. Washington, however, did keep up the pressure on the communist regime in Moscow throughout the Cold War until the Soviet Union collapsed on its own destroyed by its failed ideology. And despite tremendous population losses and suffering during WWII, Poland's historical record of dealing with her neighbors and ethnic minorities was also far from noble. In 1938, the interwar Polish government occupied the Zaolzie region in Czechoslovakia (Czech: České Těšínsko) as that country was being dismembered by Hitler. Only a year later, Poland herself was attacked and partitioned by Hitler and Stalin.

John Paul II seemed to have accepted the Romantic notion that Poland was a weaker, suffering nation that was somehow more tolerant, less aggressive and morally superior to all Western nations. When Wojtyła visited the West shortly after the war, he was appalled by the empty churches and the lack of religious fervor. He was highly suspicious of most liberal ideas coming from the West, including radical fem-inism, and was trying to offer women an alternative model of Christian feminism based on his own interpretation of Scripture more in line with his Polish experience. Family played an extremely important role in recent Polish history by

Hans Küng b. 1928

Books: *On Being A Christian, My Struggle for Freedom: Memoirs*

Quotes: "If you cannot see that divinity includes male and female characteristics and at the same time transcends them, you have bad consequences."

"We must fight the patriarchal misunderstanding of God."

The Global Ethic Foundation

http://weltethos.org/dat_eng/index_e.htm

protecting religion, national customs and national identity. Wojtyła tried to offer this model of family life to a rapidly changing world.

In the four decades since Vatican II, most of the appeals for equal rights of women in the Catholic Church have come from feminists, Western theologians and lay Catholics in the West. One of the most prominent Catholic theologians, Hans Küng, a Swiss Catholic priest whose license to teach Catholic theology was revoked by the Vatican on orders from John Paul II but who remains a priest in good standing, continued to call on the Church to grant women the same dignity, freedom and responsibility which they enjoy in Western societies. Women, according to Küng, should have equal rights in Church law, in the Church's decision-making bodies, and they should be able to study theology and be ordained.[9] Only "complete legal equality up through the ordination of women" can counter what Hans Küng calls "the silent mass exodus of women from the Church."[10] In an interview with *Newsweek* magazine in 1991, Küng said that "Rome and Cardinal O'Connor base the exclusion of women priests on the idea that God is the father and Jesus is his son, there were only male disciples, etc. They are defending a patriarchal church with a patriarchal God." Like many other liberal Catholic theologians in the West and in the developing world, Küng also called for the election of popes by a body consisting of bishops and laypeople. Unlike the College of Cardinals, nominated only by the pope, such a body would be representative of the whole Church. Küng is president of the Global Ethic Foundation which promotes inter-cultural and inter-religious education and dialogue.

Echoing some radical feminists, Hans Küng described John Paul's pontificate as misogynist.[11] Halina Bortnowska, a Catholic journalist in Poland who in the past had criticized some of Wojtyła's positions, believed, however, that John Paul II may yet be appreciated in the West as a great ethical and social thinker. What made him great, according to Bortnowska, was his overwhelming concern for human rights of all those who are on the very margins of civilization and can be described as the most "excluded" and without any protection. That is how Halina Bortnowska explained and justified Wojtyła's concern for those "whom parents deny the right to be born."[12] If John Paul II will be viewed as a great human rights pope, however, Bortnowska believes that it is more likely to happen first in the West than in his native Poland.

Wojtyła is already perceived in the West as someone who was a great moral figure and an effective leader in the peaceful struggle for human rights in Eastern Europe and throughout the world. With the exception of some religious conservatives, few in the West, however, saw his campaign against contraception as a major human rights issue. Even evangelical Christians in the United States seem to be practicing artificial birth control. Because of his stand on the role of women, Western liberals and secular feminist women in the West perceived John Paul II as being opposed to equal rights, primarily for women who want ordination to priesthood. They also blamed him for not supporting equal treatment and equal rights for divorced Catholics, former Catholic priests, homosexuals and others who did not meet his strict criteria for full Church participation. Many Catholics in the West and even in developing countries do not consider the right to conception to be as important as a woman's legal right to control her body and her fertility.

John Paul II believed otherwise and, at least, in some of his opinions he enjoyed strong support from other Western religious leaders. The Rev. Billy Graham (b. 1918) believes that John Paul II will go down in history as "the greatest of our modern Popes" and described him as "the strong conscience of the whole Christian world."[13]

Because of his deep religious faith and his belief in the supernatural, John Paul II was a very difficult figure to understand by non-religious liberal humanists who put their faith in rational thought, a scientific approach to life and a flexible moral code. The fact that he was highly educated makes him even more incomprehensible to many less religious and non-religious Westerners. John Paul II apparently believed in the literal sense in the virginal birth of Christ, although he was a strong supporter of science and, unlike some evangelical Christians, accepted Darwin's theory of evolution as scientifically valid.

How to Evaluate John Paul II and Benedict XVI

Cardinal Wyszyński, Cardinal Wojtyła and other Polish bishops were largely successful in enforcing uniformity and conformity within the Church in Poland, at least in outward appearances if not in actuality. But the communists made it easy to accomplish this by managing to alienate most Poles and drive them even closer to the Church. Enforcing moral and doctrinal uniformity in democratic and pluralistic societies that are becoming even more pluralistic requires a different set of skills. Wojtyła's success in Poland convinced him, however, that he could be equally successful following a similar path in managing the universal Church. But a religious leader, operating in a more democratic, pluralistic and a more tolerant environment, must understand that he can be successful only if he achieves at least some of his goals without creating a schism or driving too many people away. John Paul II was partly aware of this dilemma, but when choices had to be made,

> **Citation for the U.S. Medal of Freedom Presented to Pope John Paul II by President Bush, June 4, 2005**
>
> *A devoted servant of God, His Holiness Pope John Paul II has championed the cause of the poor, the weak, the hungry, and the outcast. He has defended the unique dignity of every life, and the goodness of all life. Through his faith and moral conviction, he has given courage to others to be not afraid in overcoming injustice and oppression. His principled stand for peace and freedom has inspired millions and helped to topple communism and tyranny. The United States honors this son of Poland who became the Bishop of Rome and a hero of our time.*

he made sure that he did not alienate the Church's conservative base. He compromised far more in favor of the ultra-conservative part of the Church than in favor of more liberal and more tolerant Catholics, although in interactions on a personal level he himself was highly sensitive, tolerant, one could say even liberal.

Ultimately, as the leader of a global institution with a 2000 year history, he may have been correct that putting the Catholic Church on a more conservative path would not only preserve its future role but would also help ward off most attempts to split it apart. The conservative base in any church or religious organization is much more likely to be loyal, supportive, committed and more likely to back a strong conservative leader. He assumed, perhaps correctly, that a loose coalition of liberal Catholics would not be able to save the Catholic Church as a global institution in the face of any serious threats.

Many problems, however, remain unresolved, the biggest being the shortage of male priests and the departure of Catholic women from the Church. If Wyszyński and Wojtyła were correct and the future of the Church depends more on the faith of women rather than men, then the Church, as it exists now, may be in big trouble. If women continue to abandon the Catholic Church and the number of Catholic priests continues to decline, the Church will either become smaller and even more conservative, or new popes will have to find creative solutions to bring women back.

Any church that is interested in large global membership needs a leader who knows how to enforce moral and doctrinal uniformity by presenting a powerful but sufficiently general message that unites rather than divides the faithful. John Paul II's experience in Poland taught him how to micromanage the lives of the believers, largely with their enthusiastic support and acquiescence, although without general adherence to his moral teachings, especially on birth control and abortion. It is doubtful that any future pope can be successful in a democratic and pluralistic world if he chooses to focus so much attention on telling highly educated women and married couples which birth control methods they should use.

Like any leader, the pope must set priorities, and he cannot set too many of them without risking failure. John Paul II may have been trying to achieve too many goals. By focusing on less important ones, such as birth control, he may have undermined his efforts in pursuing more important ones, such as protecting lives of the unborn, securing world peace and economic progress for the poor, and making the Catholic Church more dynamic and more united. On the political side, his instinctive anti-capitalist, anti-Western and anti-American attitudes may have resulted in far more harm than good for the very people he was trying so hard to help. One could argue that if it were not for the perennial criticism of American interventionism from the liberal Left in the United States and in Europe, as well as from the Vatican and the American bishops, the Clinton Administration might have been persuaded to intervene in Rwanda to prevent the genocide which claimed hundreds of thousands of innocent lives. Prior to the genocide, John Paul II's messages to Rwandan Catholics focused on birth control and the dangers of Western materialism rather than the threat of extreme nationalism and tribalism. John Paul II may have left a legacy of unreasonable anti-Americanism within the Catholic Church that may be harmful to global peace and to the poor nations of the world if it is not understood and reversed.

John Paul II was a product of his nation and culture, just as any new pope brings with him to the Vatican his own cultural heritage. Qualities that had helped Karol Wojtyła survive and defeat fascism and communism did not necessarily equip him well to deal with pluralistic and democratic societies. Self-righteousness and unwillingness to compromise on principles worked well in dealing with Nazi and communist dictators. This experience tended to reinforce the idea that positions supported by the Church hierarchy were the only ones acceptable on practical and moral grounds. Poland's tragic history also tended to reinforce the idea that as pope John

Paul II was called by God to help his country and the world in overcoming internal and external threats. National culture that any new pope brings with him to the Vatican may have a tremendous impact on how he deals with women's issues. No one should expect radical and rapid changes in a conservative and global institution such as the Catholic Church, but a different style and approach to the concerns of educated and independent women may determine whether they stay in the Church or drift away.

As life becomes safer and more predictable and educational levels of the population continue to increase, church attendance and outward religiousness tend to decline. The Catholic Church and other churches will have to come up with new formulas for increasing their own relevance. If the Catholic Church wants to maintain its influence and encourage women to have children, it could provide daycare facilities in every church and Catholic institution, but it seems that taking care of children is not something religious sisters with advanced college degrees are eager to do, and neither are male priests and deacons. Engaging in cultural wars with non-believers can be an effective way of attracting and keeping the most committed followers. This strategy is likely to limit Church membership to a smaller number of dedicated and conservative Catholics, but it may be one of the few strategies that can keep the Church alive and dynamic in the post-modern world. This may have been the direction in which John Paul II was taking the Catholic Church. This strategy also seems to be working well for evangelical churches in the United States as well as in other countries.

Encouraging hostility toward capitalism, globalization, the West and the United States may also work in the short-run in some developing nations as a way to gain followers for the Catholic Church, but in the long-run this approach is likely to produce more poverty, more victims and greater oppression of women. John Paul II's intention was to help the poor and the disfranchised, but by promoting doubts about Western models of development, he may have delayed reforms that could have helped some of the poorest nations overcome their poverty and customs that oppress women.

The new pope and any future popes may also choose a different strategy that would make religion more inclusive, more tolerant, more democratic, friendlier toward women and more focused on real needs of individuals rather than the needs and interests of nations, large groups and institutions. This strategy may work in democratic countries and countries striving for democracy, but it may result in creating a variety of different liberal churches with far smaller memberships and with few common links and traditions found in conservative churches. Such a strategy might also weaken the power and influence of the papacy and the Vatican and produce an even greater pluralization and loosening of the Church's moral and social message. Whether Catholicism can survive under this strategy as a universal world religion with a common set of beliefs and moral standards which would be the same for the West and the developing world is highly uncertain. Even if the Roman Catholic Church could function well as many separate churches loosely united by very broad religious and moral principles, a more democratic and tolerant Church might not survive as a single, powerful entity.

Conservative, elements which due to Pope John Paul II's influence now dominate the Catholic Church, are not likely to accept such a strategy, just as they are highly unlikely to accept women-priests or welcome homosexuals and lesbians who want to practice same-gender sex and seek sacramental marriage. They would not want to be part of such a church and would separate from it, as some conservative Catholics did on a much smaller scale following the reforms of Vatican II. Mutual misunderstanding and ideological hostility is likely to derail any attempts to bridge the gap between radically liberal and radically conservative Catholics. A dialogue between more moderate elements, however, is sorely needed. Benedict XVI can encourage such a dialogue to strengthen the Church and its mission, particularly in Western Europe and in the developing world.

It is doubtful, however, that Benedict XVI, the former enforcer of John Paul II's vision of morality and gender relations, will adopt a style in dealing with women much different from his predecessor's. He may have a somewhat more realistic view than Wojtyła on the limits of the Church's influence over women's private behavior. If he thinks in more practical terms about what independent women are likely to tolerate in messages from their male priests and bishops, his future pronouncements may reflect this and may facilitate greater dialogue and some compromises between more moderate liberals and conservatives within the Church. But Benedict XVI's decisions affecting women, if there are any, are more likely to deal with the nuances of the basic views on the role of women within and outside the Church rather than with the Church rules themselves. These rules, especially the ban on ordaining women-priests, are not likely to change under this new pope. In her book *From Pope John Paul II to Benedict XVI*, Sister Mary Ann Walsh quoted a young American woman from San Francisco as saying after the inaugural mass of Pope Benedict XVI that she would like the Catholic Church to include women and allow priests to marry, "but those are pipe dreams with this pope."[14]

Prospects for a dialogue between the Vatican and more radical Catholic feminists, as opposed to "new feminists" who accept the teachings of Pope John Paul II, also do not look promising under Pope Benedict. In his 2004 Letter to the Bishops on the Collaboration of Men and Women in the Church and in the World, Cardinal Ratzinger blamed radical feminism for overemphasizing the subordination of women and forcing them to seek power, although he did not specifically use the words "feminism" or "feminists" in the letter. This tendency, according to Cardinal Ratzinger, leads to competition between sexes with "lethal effects in the structure of the family." He also blamed radical feminism for minimizing and obscuring the differences between the sexes. In Cardinal Ratzinger's view, this kind of reasoning makes "homosexuality and heterosexuality virtually equivalent" and calls into question the role of "the family in its natural two-parent structure of mother and father."[15] The document was approved by Pope John Paul II.

There is strong resistance to radical feminism, homosexual marriages, legalized abortion, contraception and ordination of women-priests among conservative Catholics who applauded Cardinal Ratzinger's election as pope. At the very beginning of his papacy, John Paul II also put his faith in this group of dedicated religious conservatives. At that time, he was strongly encouraged and supported by Cardinal Ratzinger. Radical feminist and liberal Catholics have lost much of their 1960s and 1970s enthusiasm, significance and influence. This was partly a result of John Paul II's deliberate policy of encouraging theological and moral conservatism and opposing liberal Catholics and radical feminists on almost every issue they considered critical. Many early feminists, including some Catholic nuns, have left the Church as a result.

There were also major setbacks during John Paul II's papacy as far as his vision for women was concerned. The number of Catholic nuns in the United States has dropped from 180,000 in 1965 to about 73,000 in 2005, but orders which still attract younger women today are those that have kept strict rules and original religious habit.[16] As the late Cardinal Krol reported in 1978, a few months after Wojtyła was elected pope, John Paul II always strongly favored such a traditional dress for religious women.[17] While the influence of more radical Catholic feminists continued to diminish during his papacy, personal attacks on John Paul II's conservatism became less frequent and his stature as a major religious and moral figure continued to grow. Still, one of the feminist nuns in Chicago admitted to journalist Cheryl Reed that she had been praying for a "happy death" for John Paul II for a long time. "Nothing's going to change until the death of the current guy," she said prior to John Paul II's death.[18] The vast majority of American Catholics, however, had a more positive opinion of John Paul II even if they disagreed with him on many issues. According to a telephone poll conducted in April 2005, 88 percent of U.S. Catholics thought John Paul II was a great pope and 71 percent believed he would be made a saint.[19]

Peggy Noonan, the bestselling author, conservative columnist and former speechwriter to President Ronald Reagan, titled her 2005 book *John Paul the Great.* But even she admitted that when U.S. bishops went to Rome to ask the pope for permission to summarily

Peggy Noonan b. 1950
http://peggynoonan.com/main.php

remove priests accused of abusing children, John Paul II did not respond as the seriousness of the problem required. He expressed pain for the victims but ultimately called for compassion and warned against submitting to media sensationalism. This did not erase John Paul II's greatness in Noonan's eyes and she offered an insightful explanation. The pope was "a Pole of another era" who could not imagine or categorize this kind of massive abuse and cover-up involving American priests and bishops. Noonan wrote that in Poland men worshiped alongside women, but priesthood was "a masculine and manly institution" composed of noble and heroic men who risked their lives to defend the people from the Nazis and communists[20] We now know that about 10 percent of Polish priests became secret police informants, but the Polish Church led by Wyszyński and Wojtyła ultimately won its heroic struggle with totalitarianism because of their courage and unwillingness to compromise on the principles of religious dogma and morality. They also managed to preserve the Polish Church as a strong institution. Noonan was probably right to conclude that "the very heroism of the pope's life—the courage that his life demanded in fighting communism, atheism, Nazism, paganism, the culture of death—tended to blind him to the new menace." Whether dealing with sexual abuse by priests or with the demands of feminists and liberal Catholics, John Paul II still applied the

Wicca and Other Pagan Web Sites

Witches' Voice

http://www.witchvox.org/

The Celtic Connection

http://www.wicca.com/

Covenant of the Goddess

http://www.cog.org/

The Pagan Federation

http://www.paganfed.org/

Pagan Dawn

http://www.paganfed.org/pd-curr.php

The Pagan Federation International

http://www.paganfederation.org/

As for religious sisters who might hope for a radical change under the new pope, Benedict XVI is likely to disappoint them. In her journalistically objective book about the diverse but shrinking world of American nuns, *Unveiled: the Hidden Lives of Nuns, The Chicago Sun-Times* reporter Cheryl Reed concluded that most feminist nuns became much less vocal during the later years of John Paul II's papacy and have given up on the male-dominated Church. Reed quotes a radical feminist nun as saying that the pope means nothing to her. "Let those guys go over there and stay in Rome and not have abortions," she told the journalist and added, "You know a woman should have the right to choose."[21] The sister also described how the study of Hinduism, Buddhism, Wicca and other religions enriched her spiritual life and her understanding of Christianity. Many radical nuns and former nuns have stopped attending Catholic Mass celebrated by male priests. They participate instead in Woman-Church ceremonies or experiment with New Age religions and spiritual movements. The number of such nuns is difficult to estimate but they are a small minority within the community of Catholic religious sisters.

lessons of Polish history and Polish customs and traditions. A more precise explanation may be that John Paul II realized the seriousness of the charges about the sexual abuse of minors by priests—he was after all a very smart man and such abuse was not unknown in Poland—but his love for the Church as an institution and a strong desire to protect its reputation combined with the lack of any strong tradition of internal Church criticism in Poland may have resulted in his ambivalent response.

It is highly unlikely Benedict XVI would change any of the basic Church rules regarding women to satisfy radical feminists or even women who desire moderate reforms. He may be, however, less inclined to engage in wholesale criticism of the West. Early in his papacy, in a speech at the University of Regensburg in Germany, Pope Benedict XVI quoted a 14th century Byzantine Christian emperor's views about religious violence in historical Islam. He was severely criticized in the Islamic world and by some non-Muslims for making these comments. Subsequently, the Secretary of State of the Holy See issued a declaration that "the Pope's option in favor of inter-religious and inter-cultural dialogue is equally unequivocal." Benedict XVI later offered an apology for offending the sensibility of Muslims. Pope John Paul II, with his strong support of traditional religions and cultures, especially in the developing world, would have been more careful in speaking about Islam.

Benedict XVI also seems less reluctant than John Paul II to criticize New Age religions and secular post-modern movements, fearing perhaps correctly that they offer a competing and easy alternative to the heavy moral demands and obligations of traditional Catholicism. In what can only be described as an indirect rebuke of former U.S. Vice President and Nobel Peace Prize winner Al Gore, Pope Benedict XVI said in a papal message at the end of 2007 that ecological concerns, such as those promoted by anti-global warming activists, should be taken seriously but not to the point of making lives of animals and plants more important than the protection of human life and the general interests of mankind. This may have been an indirect and delayed punishment for Al Gore's earlier activism in supporting the Clinton Administration's pro-choice policies during the 1994 Cairo UN Conference on Population and Development when the Vice President became involved in a major fight with Pope John Paul II over abortion and birth control. Benedict XVI's message suggested that the anti-global warming movement may be engaging in propaganda of fear and confrontation to push forward its liberal ideological agenda, just as radical feminists—Marxist and post-Christian—used ideas developed by Marxist thinkers to weaken religion and the Catholic Church without any serious intellectual challenge from Western academics or Church theologians. In fact, many Catholic theologians accepted and used these ideas for several decades until Pope John Paul II and Cardinal Ratzinger intervened.

Benedict XVI's message on global warming implied the existence of a similar threat that needs to be confronted earlier rather than later: "It is important for assessments in this regard to be carried out prudently, in dialogue with experts and people of wisdom, uninhibited by ideological pressure to draw hasty conclusions, and above all with the aim of reaching agreement on a model of sustainable development capable of ensuring the well-being of all while respecting environmental balances." By suggesting early that global warming theories may be to some degree flawed, Benedict XVI has challenged Western liberals on yet another front.

Benedict XVI is also unlikely to emphasize greater involvement of the laity in running the Church, greater participation of women in Church administration, more transparency, more accountability on the part of bishops and priests, greater compassion toward those who fall short of the Church's strict moral standards, as well as more openness in dealing with such issues as violence against women and sex crimes involving priests. If he resists reforms favored by liberal Western women and men, he is likely to please many Catholics in the developing world, where John Paul II saw the future strength of Catholicism. Sister Mary Ann Walsh quoted a statement by Archbishop Raphael Ndingi Mwana'a Nzeki of Nairobi, Kenya that Pope Benedict would "continue to [be a] champion for the poor in society," and work to fight "the raging poverty and suffering of Africans." More significantly for women, however, Archbishop Onaiyekan of Abudja said, "Pope Benedict XVI has been there with the late pope, and he will toe the same line on the issues of female ordination, homosexuality, use of contraceptive devices …There is no cause for alarm."[22]

Dr. Pia de Solenni, a moral theologian in the United States and one of the leading proponents of new feminism, also does not believe that Benedict XVI will change John Paul II's approach to women's issues. Commenting on the 2004 Vatican document "On the Collaboration of Women and Men in the Church and in the World," signed by Cardinal Ratzinger and approved by Pope John Paul II, Pia de Solenni wrote that "sex differences are an essential component of human identity."[23] She was hopeful that "Benedict XVI will continue the conversation to more fully explore the unique feminine gift that only women can provide to the Catholic Church." Like most new Catholic feminists, she believes that the Church's ban on ordination of women represents the core teachings of Catholic faith and is not necessarily a sign of discrimination. She also suggested that conservative and liberal labels may not appropriate for evaluating religious leaders such as John Paul II and Benedict XVI, whose duty is to defend the core beliefs of their faith. She accurately observed that Wojtyła was viewed as a liberal university professor and later as a conservative pope. "His thinking has not changed substantially, but the perceptions of him have. We can rest on the perceptions that others have created, or we can encounter him for who he really is," de Solenni wrote. Indeed, John Paul II's thinking on many important issues was puzzling to most Westerners and, in fact, to many Poles. In 2001, Pope John Paul II presented Dr. de Solenni the Award of the Pontifical Academies for her doctoral work on feminist theories in light of the anthropology and theology of St. Thomas Aquinas.

Theological analyses exploring the sacramental significance of Christ's masculinity for the ordination of women may be important, but ultimately the impact of historical events and cultural backgrounds of religious leaders and their followers seems far more decisive. It is no accident that feminist ideas originated among educated classes in countries with liberal traditions and were most strongly opposed in countries with more traditional and less democratic cultures. Prominent theologians of new feminism, such as Michele M. Schumacher and Pia de Solenni, may offer persuasive theological arguments that being denied ordination does not necessarily offend the dignity of women.[24] It seems far more significant, however, that many Christian denominations have been ordaining women for quite some time with the support of millions of liberal Christians. It is no surprise that this is happening mostly in Western countries, especially those with traditions of religious pluralism and liberal democracy.

In addition to dealing with the demands of feminist women and the Catholic churches in the developing world, Benedict XVI also faces the unenviable task of trying to stem the growth of secularization and religious indifference in the West, particularly in Western Europe. Most experts and journalists agree that Catholic teachings on birth control and gender roles have contributed significantly to the alienation of women from the Church and the growth of religious indifference among educated Catholics. It will be interesting to see whether Pope Benedict will try to accomplish a reversal of this trend without making the Catholic Church more democratic and more tolerant. While it is almost certain that he will not compromise on the principal values of Catholicism, especially on the sanctity of life and abortion, he has the option of declaring a truce on the ideological war with the West and perhaps even using some of the Western secular ideas and concepts to benefit all Catholics, particularly those in the developing world. To be more effective, while still upholding the basic principles, he also may want to avoid the mistake of Paul VI and John Paul II of expressing an unequivocal and detailed opinion on almost every issue dealing with women's lives and bodies, especially birth control. There is no doubt, however, that Benedict XVI fully shares John Paul II's deep fear of "the culture of death," or, as he described it in his praise of John Paul II's encyclical *Evangelium vitae*, "an anti-culture of death," which "reinvents the business of killing, in abortion and euthanasia, as though it were a boon for mankind."[25]

Cultural origins and early intellectual interests of the new pope may give some indication whether he is more likely to be more conservative and uncompromising or more generous and compassionate, but they do not necessarily determine views and behavior of every person. There are always individuals who are able to overcome cultural influences from their past and who learn to understand and accept new ideas from other cultures. One should

Catholic Blogs

romancatholicblog.com
http://romancatholicblog.typepad.com/roman_catholic_blog/
Orthfully Catholic
http://orthfullycatholic.blogspot.com/
British Catholic Blogs
http://britcat.blogspot.com/
Extreme Catholic
http://www.extremecatholic.blogspot.com/
Happy Catholic
http://happycatholic.blogspot.com/
The Curt Jester
http://www.splendoroftruth.com/curtjester/archives/008565.php
Catholic and Enjoying It!
http://markshea.blogspot.com/
Bashing Secularism
http://bashingsecularism.blogspot.com/
American Papist
http://www.americanpapist.com/blog.html
The Recovering Dissident Catholic
http://therecoveringdissident-catholic.blogspot.com/
Mirror of Justice
http://www.mirrorofjustice.com/mirrorofjustice/
Modestly Yours
http://blogs.modestlyyours.net/

look at all candidates to any leadership positions in the Church to see whether they understand not only their own culture but also other cultures and traditions that may offer better solutions to some of the problems affecting women. One can try to evaluate their statements to see whether they are more likely to give encouragement to strongly conservative forces in the West and in the developing world or whether they will encourage them to learn from liberal-democratic models that helped to produce freedom, tolerance, prosperity, and greater opportunities for women.

John Paul II's appointment of 231 mostly conservative cardinals (plus one secret nomination *in pectore*), the majority of whom selected Benedict XVI and will select the next pope, will definitely put a conservative stamp on the Catholic Church for a long time. The Catholic Church is not an institution where change is easy or fast, but each new pope can always make a fresh start and still has enough authority to implement his own vision for the Church if it happens to be different from that of his immediate predecessors.

John Paul II considered the conservative nature of the Catholic Church to be one of its virtues, particularly in a fast changing world, in which it is sometimes difficult to distinguish between good and bad ideas or to fully comprehend all of their final implications. He was undoubtedly concerned that ordination of women-priests could split the Catholic Church into two camps: the affluent and liberal West and the underdeveloped Third World, where women will continue to be oppressed. His view, however, may have been overly pessimistic, and he may have been underestimating the universal desire of women to break away from the old cultural barriers of gender discrimination. Without the change in emphasis by Benedict XVI and future popes, women everywhere, but particularly in the Third World, may continue to suffer. Again, this assumes that John Paul II was wrong about Western democracies and their propensity for self-destruction through moral relativism, excessive individualism and what he perceived as unreasonable demands that ignore real differences between men and women.

John Paul II spoke repeatedly in defense of women's rights, but somehow this message was overshadowed by his conservative agenda on birth control. While he was still alive, some of his strongest critics were liberal Catholics who wanted greater rights for women and more democracy within the Church. While they disagreed with him on women's rights and sexual morality, these liberal Catholics were much closer to John Paul II than his conservative supporters on such important issues as religious and ethnic tolerance, social reforms, universal access to socialized medicine, the death penalty and the need for apologies for various crimes committed in the name of the Church and Christianity. The most vocal anti-feminist, anti-Western and nationalistic groups within the Catholic Church considered John Paul II to be their moral authority and sometimes their closest ally. Obviously, his limited pro-woman message did not reach these groups, and they ignored his calls for tolerance and dialogue. Despite his condemnations of anti-Semitism, some of his strongest supporters in Poland, particularly those associated with Radio Maryja, continue to make anti-Semitic statements almost on a daily basis.[26] John Paul II was not able to get them to accept his views on the issue of ethnic and religious tolerance.

John Paul II was also not able to convince feminists that he was pro-woman, although in many ways he was. He seemed to have failed to make his message clear to conservative Catholics and failed to bring liberals closer to his point of view. Despite his best intentions, he may have left a perception, if not a legacy, of opposing women's rights. His opposition to artificial birth control started in the specific cultural and historical context of an intense struggle with the communist regime to preserve moral values and the tradition of large Catholic families. What at that time seemed still achievable in Poland, namely introducing natural birth control methods, had already been rejected by men and women in the West, and ultimately it was never widely accepted by Polish

Catholic Women's Organizations

Council for Australian Catholic Women
http://www.cacw.catholic.org.au/
Catholic Women's League of Canada
http://www.cwl.ca/
Catholic Women's League of England & Wales
http://www.catholicwomensleague.org/
Association of Catholic Women (UK)
http://www.associationofcatholicwomen.co.uk/
National Council of Catholic Women (US)
http://home.catholicweb.com/NCCW/index.cfm
CatholicWomen.com
http://www.catholicwomen.com/index.htm
Sisters of Life
http://sistersoflife.org/

couples. Wojtyła may not have been even fully aware how much resistance his views on this issue encountered among women in his own country because they would not contradict him in public or in private, as women in countries with long democratic traditions are much more likely to do. With the help of Dr. Półtawska, other Polish women and his conservative Polish friends, he was, however, successful in convincing Pope Paul VI to accept his point of view on contraception. But neither Paul VI nor John Paul II were able to explain successfully to the majority of lay Catholics their idea about the link between contraception and preserving marital love and women's dignity.

It could be said that in Wojtyła's relationship with women, the critical moment was his decision, made in Poland sometime in the 1950s, to actively engage the Church in the opposition to artificial birth control. By making a distinction between "natural" and "artificial" birth control methods, Wojtyła put himself and later the whole Catholic Church past the point of no return. His conservative Polish friends, particularly Dr. Wanda Półtawska, encouraged him to adopt this view. According to Dr. Anna-Teresa Tymieniecka, another one of his close friends and collaborators but a longtime resident in the United States, this group of Wojtyła's Polish friends had very limited knowledge of Western women and life in the West in general. Some critics consider Dr. Półtawska's distinction between natural and artificial contraception as nothing more than a verbal trick, since it could be argued that the ultimate intention of both is to prevent conception and in a way to deceive God. This issue affected almost all of Wojtyła's other decisions dealing with women, since he steadfastly refused to change or modify his initial position. John Paul II failed to convince even the majority of Catholics in Poland that artificial contraception used by married couples who have a loving relationship is offensive to God and human dignity or that it necessarily leads to abortion or sexual promiscuity, much less to abortion or genocide. Few agreed with John Paul II that using the rhythm method of birth control is acceptable, but using other, more reliable methods, is not.

As the historical record of Wojtyła's pivotal role in convincing Paul VI to issue the birth control ban encyclical becomes clearer, his legacy may be that of a leader who helped to alienate many women from the Catholic Church. He invested so much intellectual energy in developing arguments against contraception that he was not able to change or modify his position and win greater approval and understanding for his many other campaigns in defense of human rights and human dignity. It would have taken enormous courage for John Paul II to admit that he and Pope Paul VI had made a mistake. It would have required also a lot of courage to declare that many saints, popes, and his male teachers and mentors were equally wrong in some of their views on women.

Throughout most of his life, Karol Wojtyła had first-hand knowledge of only three political systems: semi-authoritarian and nationalistic government of interwar Poland, fascism and communism. As an adult, he became convinced that only Christianity can help individuals and societies avoid the abuses of human rights associated with secular ideologies. He was highly successful in opposing communism and developed effective skills in dealing with the highly aggressive and cruel political system and communist bureaucracy. Whether he could have used the same skills just as effectively in dealing with pluralistic societies seems less certain. The Catholic Church, which Wojtyła served in Poland under communist rule, was by necessity closed to dissent and plurality of views. Cardinal Wyszyński expected and received nearly total obedience and respect from his bishops. Even if they disagreed with him, they would not admit it in public. The Polish Church equipped Wojtyła with outstanding abilities to peacefully confront enemies and to prevail in face of extreme danger. This made John Paul II the most effective world leader in opposing and defeating communism with nothing but words and the spiritual power of the Church. It is much more difficult, however, for a religious leader from a country without a long tradition of pluralism and democracy to be successful in dealing with growing numbers of people who, in the post-communist world, accept pluralism and freedom of choice, even in religion, as their natural rights.

There is nothing to suggest that this trend toward more freedom and religious choice will not continue. The Catholic Church is already losing ground to evangelical and other Protestant Churches in Latin America and among Latinos in the United States. Thanks to the spread of liberal democracy and prosperity created by free market economics, more and more individuals want to and are able to choose their own religion, and for Catholics, their own version of Catholicism.

Many of Wojtyła's assumptions about women can be traced back to the specific conditions under which he grew up and worked as a priest in a country of strong religious, patriotic, and patriarchal traditions and values. One should be careful, however, in drawing any final conclusions about John Paul's legacy as the first non-Italian pope in nearly 500 years. Perhaps his personal experience of World War II and communist oppression made him more qualified to see potential future dangers to humanity, which his promotion of conservative values may have helped to avert or diminish. If John Paul II was right, we may still see a much more vigorous conservative religious revival in reaction to the excesses of Western individualism and secular liberalism.[27] Western liberals find it hard to imagine, however, that women could experience more protection and less discrimination if the Catholic Church and the rest of the world accept Karol Wojtyła's notions of perfect womanhood and reject the Western secular tradition of tolerance for different views on morality and personal fulfillment. While individuals often do overcome their early cultural conditioning through exposure to new ideas, the knowledge of how women have been treated by the society that yields a new pope for the Catholic Church may give at least some

Catholic Information Web Sites

Catholic Answers
http://www.catholic.com/
cath.com
http://www.cath.com/
catholic-pages.com
http://www.catholic-pages.com/start/
Catholic Community Forum
http://www.catholic-forum.com/index.php
Catholic Online Forum
http://forum.catholic.org/
insidecatholic.com
http://insidecatholic.com/
CatholiCity
http://www.catholicity.com/
Catholic Australia
http://www.catholicaustralia.com.au/
catoliCanada
http://catholicanada.com/web/index.php
CatholicIreland.net
http://www.catholicireland.net/pages/index.php

clues as to how he will view and treat women.

Historical upheavals, Polish traditions and Polish women played a significant role in shaping Karol Wojtyła's life and his views about women, family, marriage and feminism. He was neither an extreme conservative nor an extreme liberal. He tried hard to understand and to overcome some of the more oppressive customs and traditions relating to the treatment of women. He made a number of revolutionary statements in support of women's rights. But John Paul II never abandoned his traditional view of women and gender roles, which the Polish women he knew accepted and encouraged. They became his most loyal allies and supporters of his pro-life and pro-family agenda. Ultimately, he concluded that while some feminist and liberal ideas were good and should be embraced by the Church, he saw many others as misguided and dangerous. More liberal in his younger years, he ultimately sided with the conservative elements within the Catholic Church. He accepted their assessment of the moral and religious state of Western societies. His initial inclination toward dialogue turned to strong criticism of the West. At the same time, he was reluctant to criticize ultra-conservative Catholics, even when they totally disregarded his far more moderate positions on some of the religious, social and political issues. He was unable to bridge the differences between his views and those of liberal women, both secular and religious.

But regardless of whether Pope John Paul II's assessment of the West and the women's rights movement is proven right or wrong, religious and non-religious moderates need to engage in a dialogue on how to advance human dignity and respect for human life while promoting social and economic opportunities for men and women. The first step should be to recognize and understand the value of liberal traditions for protecting human freedom and hopefully reconcile them with Christian values of moral responsibility for individual behavior and duty toward others. Without a great degree of individual freedom, respect for human rights and at least some economic security, Christian values and morality will fail, as they did in Hitler's Germany and in many other nations. A right combination of liberalism and Christian compassion (or any other religious or spiritual altruism) seems to offer the best chance for humankind to achieve peace, justice and prosperity. Societal changes brought about by the Industrial Revolution and the tradition of individual freedom and tolerance mixed with Judeo-Christian values helped to launch the modern feminist movement in Britain and America, while models based only on strict individualism or idealization of class, race and encouragement of group conflict turned out to be historic failures. John Paul II tried to put a human person in the center of the debate over the meaning of human dignity, but he may have underestimated the importance of individual freedom for preserving the ability of individuals and nations to make moral choices in favor of life while protecting life and dignity of others. The evidence of history did not support his strong criticism of liberal traditions or his linking of liberalism with fascism and communism. Historical evidence also did not support Marxist and radical feminist attacks on liberalism and capitalism and their fascination with collectivist solutions to social problems without respect for human rights and wishes of individual men and women. But in the spirit of his famous speech "Be Not Afraid—Swing Wide the Gates to Christ," inaugurating his pontificate in 1978, John Paul II was right to call attention to numerous assaults on human life and dignity and to criticize models of behavior that may enslave rather than free women from discrimination.[28]

Contrary to his belief, the traditional Polish model of gender relations was too inflexible to be appropriate for the entire world. The work of Wojtyła's women was needed in a country where women who wanted to lead a moral life had very few choices. Their choice deserves respect, even if most women now do not share John Paul II's views on birth control and disagree with some of his views on what constitutes ideal womanhood. These views were based partly on his reading of the Scriptures but also to a large degree on Polish traditions and the example set by Polish women before World War II and shortly thereafter.

Without the acceptance of tolerant respect for at least some diversity of opinion on gender issues, it will be difficult to reconcile different expectations of various cultural and national groups that make up the Catholic Church. If Catholics and feminists committed to the idea of freedom and tolerance are unwilling or unable to participate in a dialogue on the future of the Church and the status of women, more radical elements within the Church and the feminist movement will try to impose their own agenda. If history is any guide, radicals on both sides will offer simplistic theories with far-reaching but often dangerous consequences. To have the influence they deserve, John Paul II's passionate appeals for protecting human life and his calls for human solidarity need strong traditions of freedom of expression and tolerance found in liberal societies.

APPENDIX

Sources and Communist Spy Scandal
at the Vatican

As I was putting finishing touches on my book, some of the sources used in my research became the subject of a heated controversy in Poland related to most recent communist history. Polish media published reports and excerpts from official documents showing that the communist secret police had recruited a number of priests, including some of Karol Wojtyła's closest friends, and turned them into informants who spied on him and other Polish Church leaders. Most of the priests who were named in the documents vehemently deny these accusations, claiming they had been forced to meet with secret police officers but never revealed any sensitive information. Father Mieczysław Maliński, one of the accused priests who maintain they were victims of the communist regime rather than collaborators, was especially close to the pope and wrote numerous books about Wojtyła's early life in Poland.[1] Over the years, he has been a major source of information for numerous papal biogra-

Father Mieczysław Maliński b. 1923

http://www.malinski.pl/

Quote: "I was never a SB (communist secret police) agent."

Father Isakowicz-Zaleski b. 1956

http://www.isakowicz.pl/index.php

Saint Albert Chmielowski Foundation

http://www.albert.krakow.pl/

Poland's Commissioner for Civil Rights Protection (Civil Rights Ombudsman)

http://www.rpo.gov.pl/index.php?s=3

phers. Some of his accounts are by far the most revealing of Wojtyła's personality and his attitudes toward women and sex. I was able to confirm nearly all of Maliński's information by consulting other independent sources and felt confident that retaining it was justified as part of the historical record.[2]

Much of the information about Father Maliński was made public by another Polish priest, Father Tadeusz Isakowicz-Zaleski, who studied the secret police files and published a book in 2007 based on his analysis of the documents. His work on the spy scandal has generated, however, a lot of controversy within the Catholic Church in Poland. In 2006, John Paul II's friend and personal secretary, Cardinal Stanisław Dziwisz, ordered Father Isakowicz-Zaleski to refrain from public comments about some of the accused priests and suggested that the issue requires a more careful and scholarly evaluation. Dziwisz created a special commission to study the secret files.

During the communist period, Isakowicz-Zaleski was a priest in the underground Solidarity labor movement and was twice severely beaten in 1985 by unknown assailants assumed to be secret police operatives. When he started his historical research in 2005, his Church superiors either ignored his questions or tried to discourage him from revealing compromising information. In September 2007, the head of Poland's official Civil Rights Ombudsman's Office awarded Father Isakowicz-Zaleski a special medal "for his courage in defending basic truths and values even in the face of contrary majority opinion and opposition." Father Isakowicz-Zaleski is of Armenian descent and is a special pastor to the Armenian community in Poland. He has been active in publicizing information about the early 20th century genocide of ethnic Armenians by Turkish nationalist forces, which the Turkish government denies took place. In 1987 he co-founded the Saint Albert Chmielowski Foundation. The foundation runs a home for handicapped persons in Radwanowice near Kraków and has 26 other facilities throughout Poland.

When I contacted Father Maliński in May 2007 to get his response to Father Isakowicz-Zaleski's accusations, he would only say that he was working on his autobiography. It was published in late 2007 and included numerous refutations of Father Isakowicz-Zaleski's claims. At the time, Father Maliński referred me to his statement posted on his web site, in which he strongly denies being a communist secret police agent.[3] He insists that he never signed any document promising to deliver information, and that John Paul II knew about his encounters with communist functionaries but had no objections. Since John Paul II never questioned Father Maliński's information about him, and their friendship continued until the pope's death in 2005, I saw no reason to omit Maliński's information from my book, but I included notes alerting readers to alternative interpretations.

At this time, it is impossible to know the whole truth about the spy scandal. For obvious reasons, most priests who had been involved with the communist secret police are now trying to minimize the extent of their cooperation and the possible harm it produced. It is unlikely that Father Maliński's dealings with the communist security services can be fully uncovered, explained and assessed. We know that secret police surveillance of Wojtyła started as early as 1949 when he was a young priest. An internal communist party document issued in November 1963 stated that "despite appearances of compromise and flexibility in relations with the state authorities, he is a very dangerous ideological enemy."[4] The regime, however, agreed for Wojtyła to become a bishop, viewing him as a possible challenger to the more conservative Cardinal Wyszyński, who was Poland's Catholic Primate. Their agents at the Vatican and in Poland told them that Wojtyła was close to Pope Paul VI—a relationship that the regime thought could be used to undermine Wyszyński's position. The communists in Warsaw always preferred to deal with the Vatican and liberal Western Church leaders rather than with the Polish bishops. Communist-era files show that in his contacts with the secret police, Father Maliński expressed great admiration for Wojtyła and told secret police officers that Wojtyła was a progressive priest, which was essentially true. Eventually, the secret police realized that despite his progressive social views and respectful manner, Wojtyła's sermons and activities became a major ideological threat to the regime. They continued to keep him under close observation, even inquiring about such things as to who was buying his underwear.[5]

The documents I examined show that while some of the priests who were informing on Wojtyła were indeed active collaborators, others were not. Reports about their alleged recruitment may have been exaggerated by their secret police handlers and could ruin the reputations of innocent individuals. Some priests claim that, with the knowledge of their bishops, they became double agents trying to influence the communist regime or, as Father Maliński insists, they attempted to evangelize communist officials and treated them with understanding and respect—a way of dealing with ideological enemies practiced by the pope himself. Unfortunately, in most cases of priests close to the pope who had frequent contacts with the secret police we cannot be sure of the true motives, circumstances and possible effects of these contacts. We can safely assume, however, that Karol Wojtyła, the Catholic Church and the Polish and Western media were targets of numerous disinformation campaigns orchestrated by communist secret services.

Spying on the Church leaders was part of a larger effort to undermine religion in Poland through media propaganda campaigns as well as media censorship. In an attempt to weaken the Church, communist propagandists focused heavily on women's issues and religion but their strategy did not produced desired results in Poland, as it did in the Soviet Union, where religion had been largely eliminated from public life and the hierarchy of Orthodox Church brought under the control of the KGB. The vast majority of Polish women (and men) remained loyal Catholics. Pope Paul VI's ban on artificial birth control offered an ideal opportunity for propagandists to promote further dissention within the Church, but while the communist media discussed the birth control issue to some extent, this also did not turn Polish women away from the Church. Even though the majority of Polish women ultimately ignored the papal ban on contraception, they did so quietly and did not publicly question the authority of male priests and bishops.

I have not come across any documents showing that the communist secret police and intelligence services actively tried to manipulate Wojtyła's and Dr. Półtawska's interest in birth control issues. They could have anticipated that Pope Paul VI's 1968 anti-contraception ruling for Catholics might lead to a crisis within the Church, but I found no information about any secret campaign to exploit this particular issue. The communist-era files show that the secret police were far more interested in Wojtyła's activities among students and workers than his collaboration with women in promoting natural birth control training. Still, the crisis within the Catholic Church produced by the *Humanae vitae* encyclical, especially among Western women, has been far greater than any damage done by communist secret police surveillance and disinformation activities.

John Paul II was certainly aware that some of the priests close to him were spying for the secret police, but he may not have known which ones. He was also a target of numerous disinformation campaigns and provocations orchestrated by communist spies to cover up

Father Stefan Filipowicz SJ b. 1934

Director of Vatican Radio Polish Service 1973-1980

Voice of America Religious Commentator 1983-1990

Quote: John Paul II: "Filipowicz, perchè mi hai tradito?" ("Filipowicz, why did you betray me?")

Filipowicz: "Santità, non L'ho tradita mai!" ("Holy Father, I never betrayed you!")

their activities and to embarrass the pope and the Catholic Church. One Polish Jesuit priest whom I knew, Father Stefan Filipowicz, claims he was an innocent victim of one such provocation when he was removed in 1980 from his position as the director of Polish programs of Vatican Radio. As many other Polish priests, he had contacts with the secret police, which he now describes as unavoidable but not harmful. Communist-era files show that he had never signed a declaration to become an agent. They also show that while he passed on some general information, he later refused to continue meetings with his handlers and warned them that he was reporting their conversations to his Church superiors.

Father Filipowicz now suspects that when he refused to comply with persistent demands for sensitive information, the secret police fabricated evidence showing that he was an informant and passed it on to someone close to the pope. This, he believes, resulted in his removal from his position at Vatican Radio. According to Father Filipowicz, on March 1, 1980, shortly after his dismissal from his radio job, John Paul II approached him during a public prayer and asked him in Italian, "Filipowicz, perchè mi hai tradito?" ("Filipowicz, why did you betray me?") Father Filipowicz says he was surprised by the question and responded also in Italian, "Santità, non L'ho tradita mai!" ("Holy Father, I never betrayed you!")

I met Father Filipowicz in the early 1980's after his Jesuit order had sent him to Chicago. Without knowing the circumstances of his departure from Rome but aware of his journalistic radio experience and contacts at the Vatican and among Polish bishops, I recruited him as a commentator for Voice of America's coverage of papal visits to Poland and other countries, a position he held for several years. I did not learn about the controversy surrounding his role at the Vatican until the Polish media recently published some of the secret police files.

In responding to these media reports, Father Filipowicz said that at the time he had no idea what was behind the pope's unusual question. In an article in the Polish church journal *Horyzonty Wychowania* (May 2006), Filipowicz wrote that initially he did not realize there may have been a link between his removal from Vatican Radio and the secret police attempts to recruit him as an active agent. Later, he began to suspect that a person of Polish descent claiming to represent the German Episcopate, who had befriended earlier a number of Polish priests at the Vatican, was in fact a Polish secret police agent with enough contacts and influence to have him removed from his radio position.[6] Father Filipowicz categorically denies that he was an informant and now suspects that the pope's remark resulted from a secret police provocation, in which other persons close to John Paul II may have been involved.

Recently published Polish secret police files seem to confirm that such provocations did occur, but I saw no information on what caused Father Filipowicz to lose his job at Radio Vatican or could explain John Paul II's most unusual question delivered in Italian in a public setting to the Polish Jesuit priest. The files

> **The Polish Institute of National Remembrance**
>
> http://www.ipn.gov.pl/portal/en/

show that Filipowicz had never signed an agreement to become an agent. He also said that he had always informed his superiors about his meetings with the secret police. Professor Ryszard Terlecki, since 2007 a member of the Polish Sejm (Parliament) and previously an independent scholar of the Polish Institute of National Remembrance, reviewed Filipowicz's files. He concluded that Filipowicz was a "reluctant" secret police collaborator who gave mostly information which he considered harmless. Terlecki also said that the priest never signed any recruitment documents and at the end made vigorous efforts to break his contacts with the secret police. Father Filipowicz considers the current controversy an assault on his good name and character. He also sees it as an ironic act of the previous communist regime's final revenge against priests like himself who spent their entire lives fighting communism in Poland.

Some Polish priests thought they could outwit the secret police without harming anyone while also securing some benefits for themselves, such as getting a permission to travel abroad or an official approval to publish a book or a magazine, which in any normal country would not be a privilege but a basic right. It is clear from reading the secret police files that the pope could never be certain who among his friends might have been reporting to the Polish intelligence or the KGB, as it was not certain in some cases whether individuals listed as agents were real agents or simply priests or lay persons trying to survive under extremely difficult conditions. Also, some of the Western media coverage of John Paul II's papacy — whether it was on international politics, relations with Washington and Moscow, or on women's issues — was almost certainly influenced to some degree by communist intelligence services and other intelligence organizations, including the CIA. The Polish secret police collaborated closely with the KGB in Moscow to gather information on the pope and his close friends, including Dr. Wanda Półtawska, and the KGB was known to have cultivated "friendly" journalists in the West.

But despite their best efforts, communist secret police officers, who spied on Wojtyła, were frustrated by the lack of any information that could be used to blackmail him or ruin his reputation. To cast doubt on his moral character among Western journalists when he was already at the Vatican, they decided to engage in a bit of forgery. They knew that in the 1960s the Archbishop developed a close personal relationship with middle-aged Polish widow, Irena Kinaszewska, who worked for the Catholic weekly *Tygodnik Powszechny* and was employed by Wojtyła to organize his letters and documents. The Archbishop apparently gave her this job to earn some extra income, as she was a single mother raising a young son. Based on the information received from one of their agents at *Tygodnik Powszechny*, the communist secret police suspected that during a trip to Italy Mrs. Kinaszewska carried messages between

Wojtyła and Pope Paul VI. Their informants also suggested that the Archbishop might have been romantically involved with Mrs. Kinaszewska, although even some of their agents discounted it such a possibility.

In a book published in 2006, Polish journalist Marek Lasota reported that in 1983 the secret police unit in Kraków created a fictitious diary made to look as if it had been written by Mrs. Kinaszewska. Police agents then planted the diary in the apartment of Wojtyła's friend, Father Andrzej Bardecki (1916-2001). The plan was to find the diary during a subsequent police search of Father Bardecki's apartment and leak it to the media in order to embarrass John Paul II. By distracting his elderly housekeeper, two female secret police agents managed to place the diary in Father Bardecki's apartment during his absence After this successful operation, the agents got drunk and were involved in a major car accident. Their plan, however, was thwarted when the woman in charge of Father Bardecki's apartment alerted him to the unusual visit by unknown individuals. Suspecting a secret police action, the priest searched his apartment, found the diary and destroyed it. A police search of his apartment two days later turned up nothing.[7] Had there been any real romantic affairs with women during Wojtyła's years as a priest and bishop in Poland, the secret police, who kept him under close surveillance, would have probably known about them and would not have had to resort to forgery and provocation.

But when recruitment efforts and provocations failed, the secret police often employed intimidation tactics and physical violence to achieve their aims. After leaving a meeting with Cardinal Wojtyła in 1977, the same priest was so severely beaten by unknown assailants that he became nearly unconscious and required hospitalization. Wojtyła said at the time that his friend was beaten instead of him. The beating may have been retaliation for Father Bardecki's refusal to become a secret police informant. The Polish security services were particularly interested in recruiting him because of his close friendship with Wojtyła, as was apparently the Soviet intelligence, according to the documents smuggled to the West by a senior KGB archivist Vasili Mitrokhin.[8] The beating of the cardinal's friend may have also been a warning from the secret police and the communist regime that they were unhappy with Wojtyła's support for *Tygodnik Powszechny*.[9] While subject to government censorship, the paper, where Father Bardecki served as the Church advisor, was not as pro-regime as the communists wanted it to be. Its editors frequently took risks and tried to outwit the censors while refusing to sufficiently praise the achievements of communist leaders. After Father Bardecki's death in 2001, Pope John Paul II wrote that his friend gained respect of "the generation which had struggled with the lie of the ideology aimed against God and man."[10]

As the pope's popularity and influence grew, the KGB became even more obsessed with trying to collect information on him from his friends and close associates. In order not to arouse suspicion, the Soviets used agents who had covers as West German or Canadian citizens. Some of John Paul II's friends approached by these individuals probably had no idea they were talking with Soviet agents. The KGB also relied on the Polish security and intelligence services to send to Moscow up-to-date information about the pope' opinions and activities. The day after Wojtyła's election as pope in October 1978, the KGB chief in Warsaw sent to Moscow an assessment prepared by the Polish security service which concluded that "Wojtyła holds extreme anti-Communist views."[11] In June 1980, the KBG mission in Warsaw reported that their Polish "friends" have "experienced agents, towards whom John Paul II is personally well disposed and who can obtain an audience with him at any time." The KGB mission in Warsaw also reported that the Polish security services have access to Vatican Radio and the pope's secretariat.[12]

One of the stated aims of the KGB's cooperation with the Polish security service (*SB*) was to gain the pope's support for the policy of peaceful co-existence while at the same time intensifying "disagreements between the Vatican and the USA, Israel and other countries."[13] One way to discredit John Paul II among the liberal circles in the United States and in other Western countries would have been through leaked media reports stressing his Polish conservatism and his conservative positions on women's rights. It is more than likely that some such media reports were inspired by the KGB and intelligence services of other communist regimes. Unlike the CIA, communist operatives used the information gathered from their sources at the Vatican and in Poland to undermine and weaken the pope's influence and the power of the Catholic Church. When some of the pope's friends refused to become collaborators, the communist secret police tried to discredit them in his eyes by spreading disinformation.[14]

The CIA, on the other hand, was concerned with winning the pope's support for covert financial assistance to the independent Solidarity trade union and for pressuring the communist regime in Warsaw. The CIA also wanted greater understanding from the Vatican for the Reagan Administration's policies in Latin America and its tough stand against the Soviet Union. But John Paul II was not happy about appearing to be too close to Washington and its international policy. Always mindful of public opinion and wanting to put as much distance as possible between the American administration and John Paul II, the pope's personal secretary Stanisław Dziwisz categorically denies even now that the Vatican provided material support to Solidarity. He describes reports of any financial aid from the Vatican as "pure fabrications" and "lies" by some Western media outlets. According to Dziwisz, John Paul II's support for Solidarity was enormous but limited to its moral dimension, such as numerous papal calls for respecting the people's right to freedom and human rights.[15]

William Casey (1913-1987), the CIA director in the Reagan Administration who developed a personal friendship with John Paul II, was the U.S. official who, apparently with the pope's knowledge and approval, initiated financial assistance to Solidarity, occasionally using the Church channels. Dziwisz may be therefore technically correct in saying the material assistance did not come from the pope and the Vatican. Casey also wanted to find and publicize information that the KGB was behind the assassination attack on the pope by the Right-wing Turkish nationalist Mehmet Ali Ağca, even though the KGB's possible involvement in the May 13, 1981 attack in the St. Peter Square was disputed by Moscow and some of Casey's own CIA analysts.[16] By an interesting although totally unrelated coincidence, on the morning of the assassination attempt which nearly ended his life, John Paul II met with Dr. Jérôme Lejeune (1926-1994) and his wife. Dr. Lejeune was a French pro-life physician, a close friend and advisor to the pope on the rhythm method of birth control for women.[17] (The pope attributed his recovery after the assassination attempt to a miracle performed by the Virgin of Fátima.)

The Vatican spy scandal only proves how difficult it is to uncover the full truth about John Paul II and his papacy. As someone who had lived the first sixteen years of his life in Poland and later as a journalist working in the United States, I was well aware of the constant efforts by the Polish communist regime to undermine the Catholic Church and to find collaborators among priests and journalists. Polish diplomats representing the regime in Warsaw and intelligence officers posing as newspaper reporters tried several times to recruit me as their agent because of my journalistic work at the Voice of America. I rejected these attempts and treated them as a minor annoyance, but priests and journalists in Poland who were too outspoken or refused to cooperate risked being harassed, fined, imprisoned or beaten up by unknown assailants.

> **Father Jerzy Popiełuszko** 1947-1984
> *To Kill a Priest* a movie by Agnieszka Holland
> http://www.imdb.com/title/tt0096280/

Communist security services were implicated in murders of a number of patriotic priests. Solidarity priest Father Jerzy Popiełuszko was killed in October 1984 by three secret police officers who abducted and brutally tortured him. While he was unconscious but apparently still alive, they dumped his body in the Vistula River reservoir. Their actions were discovered only because Father Popiełuszko's driver managed to escape and alerted the Church authorities.[18] According to historians who have studied the communist security police files, another Polish priest, Biblical scholar and former co-president of Poland's Council of Christians and Jews, Father Michał Franciszek Czajkowski, was providing information to the secret police on Popiełuszko and a number of other opposition activists. After the spy scandal became public in 2006, Father Czajkowski at first denied these charges but later issued an apology and admitted his 24-year-long collaboration with the secret police while questioning some of the information in his file. He ended his cooperation with the secret police after Father Popiełuszko's murder.

I also found out recently from three of my former journalist colleagues at the Voice of America that before coming to VOA they were blackmailed into becoming secret police informants while they were still living in Poland or elsewhere in Europe. These journalists told me they broke off their contacts with the secret police as soon as it was relatively safe to do and were not active agents in the United States. In some cases, their family members had been threatened with imprisonment or loss of jobs, while others simply wanted to

Vatican Radio (Radio Vaticana)

http://www.radiovaticana.org/index.html

Voice of America

http://www.voanews.com/english/portal.cfm

Radio Free Europe/Radio Liberty

http://www.rferl.org/

BBC

http://www.bbc.co.uk/

escape from communist Poland and study in the West. They all insist that they had never provided the secret police with any useful or harmful information, but they did not reveal their former secret police ties to me or their other colleagues at the Voice of America until many years later.

Communist attempts to influence the flow of information from American radio stations to listeners in Poland go back to World War II. Socialists and communists with pro-Moscow sympathies worked in the Polish section of the Roosevelt Administration's Office of War Information (OWI), the precursor of the Voice of America.[19] They suppressed information about Stalin's responsibility for the Katyń massacre of Polish military officers and supported Soviet territorial demands against Poland. These positions, however, were at the time generally in line with the policy of the Roosevelt White House and the State Department. Actor John Houseman (1902-1988), a British-Jewish refugee from Romania best known for his role as a law professor in the film *The Paper Chase*, was the first Voice of America director. He alluded in his memoirs to the issue of how VOA reported Polish news during the war by questioning why the Poles working at the Voice of America were "obsessed by mad dreams of a 'Greater Poland.'" He also accused them of being anti-Semitic."[20] He was able, however, to to impose the official Roosevelt Administration line on the Polish question in VOA radio programs. Houseman's job could not have been too difficult since one of the key persons in charge of Polish broadcasts in Washington during the war was Stefan Arski (Artur Salman 1910-1993) who in 1947 returned to Poland, joined the communist party and became a leading communist journalist publishing anti-American propaganda.[21]

After the war, the Polish communist intelligence service managed to infiltrate a few agents into the staff of Radio Free Europe and recruit a few more agents among journalists who already worked there. The station, based at the time in Munich, Germany, was initially under the control of the CIA, although professional journalists ar RFE generally managed to preserve their independence, especially in the Polish Service. Even though the U.S. Congress had ended CIA's involvement with Radio Free Europe in 1971, the regime in Warsaw continued to view the work of RFE with particular concern because, like VOA and BBC, its radio broadcasts exposed communist propaganda lies and weaknesses of the communist system. A few communist agents who were active while working at RFE represented a tiny number among thousands of Polish émigré journalists. Despite the regime's efforts at jamming of shortwave radio signals, Polish media in the West managed to provide uncensored news and information to millions of listeners in Poland and significantly contributed to the fall of communist dictatorship.

Both the Polish Catholic Church and Wojtyła understood the importance of Western radio broadcasts for listeners in Poland. Polish-language Western radio programs regularly included reports on Cardinal Wyszyński's and Cardinal Wojtyła's sermons and their activities in defense of human rights. A Catholic priest, who had access to priests and bishops in Poland, was assigned permanently to the Polish Service staff at Radio Free Europe in Munich. Cardinal Wojtyła also met secretly with RFE journalists, briefing them on issues which were of particular concern to him and the Polish Church. It was his way of getting the information to the people in Poland, but these secret meetings during his trips to Italy in the 1970s were also designed to influence RFE reporting.

As bad as the spy revelations may appear for some individual priests and for the Catholic Church in Poland, they must be seen from a proper historical perspective. In fact, the number of priests who were involved, estimated to be only about 10 to 15 percent (this number may have been higher in major cities), was quite small compared to some other groups active in public life in Poland under communism. After World War II, the majority of writers, artists and journalists who stayed in Poland became in one form or another supporters of the communist regime and promoted, at least initially, its many agendas. Some did it out of conviction and many simply because they wanted to survive and did not want to work in less attractive and less paying jobs. Later many switched sides, but the regime never managed to corrupt the Catholic Church as an institution. From the very beginning Polish priests and bishops opposed communism as an ideology and a political system designed to deny the Polish people freedom of religion and other basic human rights. These events, I believe, prove how difficult and complicated life was for Karol Wojtyła and for many other Poles of his generation. In this book I try to bring their perspective on life closer to those who have not experienced such moral challenges and attacks on human dignity. I also try to explain how these experiences may have influenced their opinions and how they judged actions of others.

Family and Professional Sources and Personal Observations

I was helped in my understanding of the tragedy of war and communism by the stories I heard from my grandparents, my parents and a few patriotic teachers and by listening to shortwave radio programs. These stories, my own experience of living under a dictatorship, as well as books by Holocaust survivors and witnesses of communist repression, helped me understand and appreciate Wojtyła's deep concern with protecting human dignity and human life. In my later professional career as a Voice of America reporter, I was also fortunate to be able to cover human rights issues in Poland and to report on the papacy of John Paul II.

Although slightly younger than Karol Wojtyła, my parents experienced some of the same horrors of the Nazi occupation and communist rule as he did as a seminary student and a young priest. Even as a ten-year-old child living in a German occupied town in southern Poland, my mother became a witness to genocide. Her parents' house was located next door to the Gestapo headquarters where Poles were tortured and killed. She told me that sometime in

1942 her dad heard rumors of Nazi plans for a mass execution of the town's Jews and that she overheard her parents arguing what they should do with this information. She knew enough of what was happening and begged them to warn the family of her Jewish girlfriend so that their lives would be saved. Her parents were afraid, however, that the Gestapo would kill them if the Germans found out who passed on the warning to the Jewish neighbors, as such a warning would likely be spread within the Jewish community. My mother went alone to the house in which the young Jewish family lived, telling them to leave and seek shelter with the partisan forces operating in the nearby forests. But there was not enough time for the family to escape, they may have not believed the information given by a small child or they simply saw no way out of the impending tragedy. The Nazis murdered the entire family together with nearly a thousand other Jews from the town and the region—men, women and children. All the Jewish victims were lined up naked against ditches and shot.

My father did not have a similarly terrifying experience, but he used to tell me how German soldiers forced him to dig anti-tank trenches, and he remembered World War II as a time of constant hunger and danger. The Nazis took as a hostage one of his cousins, Józef Znachowski, and, under the principle of collective responsibility, shot him in retaliation for partisan attacks. They also took my father's brother John Lipień and sent him to Germany to do forced labor. Eventually liberated by American soldiers, my uncle came to the United States. Thanks to him, my parents and I were also able to emigrate from Poland and establish new lives in Chicago.

My maternal grandfather, Jan Maciaszek, like so many other Poles, was also a victim of both Nazi and communist repression. During the war, he refused to declare himself an ethnic German, which would qualify him for privileged treatment. (One of his grandmothers was German.) Since he did not claim his German ancestry, the Nazis took him from his home in the middle of winter and forced him to build military fortifications. Because of hard work, lack of food and cold, he contracted TB and died after the war. Before his death, the communists confiscated his small private shoe making business he was managing with my grandmother.

Fate and geography also forged a few not particularly significant but interesting links between my home town, my family and Karol Wojtyła. We lived in the same region in southern Poland. When he was a bishop in Kraków, Wojtyła visited my parish church several times. One of our neighbors, Mrs. Zofia Abramowicz-Stachura, was one of Wojtyła's former students. His close friend, Father Mieczysław Maliński, was my mother's religion teacher. He and the future pope spent a lot of time together and for six years in the early 1950s Maliński invited Wojtyła to give religion lessons for students in a high school attended by my mother. At that time the communist authorities were still not quite finished removing priests and nuns from all schools. My mother had a vivid memory of young Karol Wojtyła commenting on the meaning of life and impressing young women with his kindness and sophistication. Later, she came close to being denied her high school diploma when she laughed in class after a teacher told the students to have a special celebration in honor of Stalin's birthday. Soon after she graduated, communists closed down her Catholic school.

My mother's problems at school were just a small example of the power of the communist regime to destroy people's lives. As a priest and bishop, Wojtyła had to deal with much more serious attempts at intimidation and persecution under communism, but eventually he triumphed over his former enemies when, with his help, democracy returned to Poland in 1989. Before the fall of communism, he himself became the victim of an assassination attempt, which his personal secretary and closest friend for many years believes was probably ordered by the Soviet KGB. According to Cardinal Dziwisz, John Paul II was convinced that the Right-wing nationalist Turkish assassin Mehmet Ali Ağca (b. 1958) could not have acted alone.[22]

I grew up with the stories of the suffering and sacrifices of the people who lived through World War II and communism—a series of the most terrible tragedies in recent human history. During this time of horrific crimes against human dignity, many women showed remarkable courage in the face of tremendous suffering. I think of Halina Stabrowska, a devoted assistant to the underground Polish Home Army chief, who did not betray him despite being brutally tortured by the Gestapo. She paid with her life for her service to the cause of freedom and human solidarity. Another woman, Sophie Scholl, was a member of the White Rose group of university students in Nazi Germany practicing non-violent resistance during the war. She dared to condemn Hitler's inhuman policies when most Germans were either silent or too afraid to speak out. For distributing anti-Nazi leaflets at the University of Munich, Sophie Scholl, her brother Hans Scholl and another student Christoph Probst, were executed by beheading. Their arrest and trial are depicted in an Oskar-nominated 2005 German film *Sophie Scholl – the Final Days* written by Fred Breinersdorfer and directed by Marc Rothemund. Most of the male members of the group were medical students, and some, including Sophie's brother, had fought with the German army in Russia.

Joseph Ratzinger, the current pope, who was six years younger than Sophie and did not participate in the White Rose activities,

---

Halina Stabrowska d. 1943

Stanisława Leszczyńska 1896-1974

Clemens August Graf von Galen 1878-1946

Sophie Scholl 1921-1943

Hans Scholl 1918-1943

Christoph Probst 1919-1943

Sophie Scholl – the Final Days (*Sophie Scholl – Die letzten Tage*) http://www.sophieschollmovie.com/

Hitler Youth/*Hitler-Jugend*

http://en.wikipedia.org/wik

i/Hitler_youth

The League of German Girls

in the Hitler Youth

http://www.bdmhistory.co

m/research/main.html

was also drafted into the German army at the end of the war even though he was studying to be a priest. He had no sympathy for the Nazi cause but did not engage in active resistance against fascism. Like Sophie's brother Hans, the current pope was also a member of Hitler Youth/*Hitler –Jugend*, a paramilitary organization of the Nazi party, but membership in Hitler Youth was made mandatory for German children in 1936. When international media reported this fact, the current German government responded that compulsory membership of the *Hitler-Jugend* had little bearing on the pope's religious convictions or on his ability to lead the Roman Catholic Church. Ratzinger deserted from the German army shortly before the end of the war[23]

According to some accounts, Sophie Scholl, who was Lutheran, and her Christian friends were inspired to start their anti-Nazi activities by the Catholic Bishop of Münster, Clemens August Graf von Galen, who in a July 1941 sermon denounced the Nazi killings of mentally handicapped persons.[24] The students were also protesting the killing of Jews, Poles and others groups considered subhuman by the Nazis.[25]

I am also reminded of the story of Stanisława Leszczyńska, a Polish midwife and a prisoner at the Auschwitz concentration camp who made every possible effort to deliver and save babies in defiance of the Nazi orders to have them killed. Out of more than 3,000 babies she helped to deliver at Auschwitz-Birkenau, only about thirty survived.

These women were braver than most men and showed through their courage and leadership that narrow theories of male domination and oppression are not as descriptive and ultimately not as important for the understanding of the common history of men and women as are much broader concepts of human dignity, human freedom and human solidarity. But I also realized after living in the United States for some time how difficult it is to explain to younger Americans my own perceptions and understanding of this period. I believe John Paul II faced the same problem, except his difficulties in communicating effectively his concerns to feminists, liberal Catholics, and women in general are still having enormous impact on the Catholic Church and on the situation of women worldwide. And even if he did manage to explain his concerns, they may not have seemed entirely relevant to people who have never experienced similar historic tragedies and now feel sufficiently protected by their sense of freedom from dangerous ideologies and human rights violations. They, of course, cannot also agree what constitutes a human rights violation, as demonstrated by pro-choice and pro-life positions on abortion or arguments in favor of or against women-priests. John Paul II and most feminists definitely could not agree on these points.

One lesson I learned from these women and others who had lived through the horrors of World War II and communism is that under conditions of severe suffering, humiliation and oppression, only very few individuals are capable of behaving with honor, compassion and heroic human solidarity. Under such conditions, only very few individuals can resist discriminating against and oppressing others on the basis of ethnicity, religion, race, class and moral or political convictions. Examples of noble and tolerant behavior are also relatively rare in societies that have not yet reached the critical stage of cruelty and tyranny but live under strong pressure to conform to the demands of a single dominant ideology or religion that does not tolerate dissent and severely punishes lack of conformity. Liberalism based on rational individualism needs to be taken seriously as a system of ideas and principles that allow dissent, including moral dissent, to emerge and challenge real or potential threats to human life and dignity. History has shown that best results for nations and individuals are

Jan Karski (Jan Kozielewski) 1914-2000

"It was easy for the Nazis to kill Jews, because they did it. The Allies considered it impossible and too costly to rescue the Jews, because they didn't do it. The Jews were abandoned by all governments, church hierarchies and societies, but thousands of Jews survived because thousands of individuals in Poland, France, Belgium, Denmark, Holland helped to save Jews. Now, every government and church says, 'We tried to help the Jews,' because they are ashamed; they want to keep their reputations. They didn't help, because six million Jews perished, but those in the government, in the churches — they survived. No one did enough." *The Diary of Hannah Rosen: Europe's Jews and America's Response, 1937-1945 by Elizabeth S. Rothschild.*

http://www.remember.org/educate/hrdiary.html

achieved when women and men are free to merge liberal ideas with Judeo-Christian or other religious and non-religious ethical values and traditions.

Yet many people living in liberal-democratic societies still find it extremely difficult to imagine the evil of totalitarian ideologies and the oppression brought on by extreme nationalism and religious fundamentalism. Many Western liberals and early 20th century feminists were fooled by communist propaganda claims about the status of women and the treatment of minorities in the Soviet Union and in developing countries experimenting with Soviet-style socialism. Even some Western journalists became apologists for the Soviet regime if not its active agents. One such journalist, British-born Moscow correspondent for *The New York Times* Walter Duranty (1884-1957), has been accused of deceptive reporting and relying on Stalinist propaganda in his dispatches about the 1932-1933 Ukrainian famine, which took millions of lives.

News reports of massive human rights violations in the Soviet block were viewed with a great deal of skepticism by liberal opinion makers in the West, just as initial reports of Nazi crimes

Voice of America Headquarters in Washington, D.C.

against Jews and other groups were also met with disbelief. I am reminded of Jan Karski, an emissary of the Polish underground army sent during the war from Nazi-occupied Poland to Great Britain and the United States, where he met with British foreign secretary Anthony Eden, President Roosevelt, Jewish leaders and journalists. Karski's accounts of Nazi atrocities against the Jews were largely dismissed as propaganda by American and British political leaders and the media. Laurel Leff's book, *Buried by the Times*, presents a devastating record of how one of America's most important liberal newspapers failed in its coverage of the fate of European Jews from 1939 to 1945. *The New York Times*, despite being owned by a prominent Jewish family, reported nothing about Karski's mission and his accounts of the Holocaust.[26]

Many of the skills used in writing this book I learned at the Voice of America, a U.S. taxpayer-funded station which broadcasts overseas from Washington, D.C. VOA is a great American institution whose work unfortunately remains largely unknown in the United States.[27] VOA journalists helped to bring down the Iron Curtain with nothing more than the peaceful power of ideas and words—a way of solving human problems so strongly favored by

Karol Wojtyła. They continue to provide news and information to those who still lack full freedom or seek to know more about America. As many countries, including some of America's closest friends and allies, question and criticize American values and intentions, international broadcasting and other public diplomacy efforts to increase understanding between different nations, religions and cultures deserve much greater recognition and support.

As a supporter of independent and objective journalism, I was certainly aware that VOA—a media outlet financed by the U.S. Congress and part of the U.S. government—has been accused of spreading propaganda. But this was generally not what I personally experienced at the Voice of America as a journalist while preparing radio broadcasts to Poland. Since 1976, VOA has had a Congressionally-approved legal charter guaranteeing its journalistic independence and protecting their journalists from interference with the news by U.S. administration officials. In the 1970s and 1980s, I did a lot of reporting on Pope John Paul II and his historic travels to Poland, as well as on pro-human rights activities of Polish priests and bishops, without experiencing any major attempts at interference from U.S. government bureaucrats. In their book *His Holiness* about Pope John Paul II, Carl Bernstein and Marco Politi wrote that Radio Free Europe (another U.S.-financed international radio station) and the Voice of America became primary conduits of the Reagan Administration policy of separating the Poles from the Warsaw Pact.[28] The authors further claim that the Voice of America was used to send coded messages to the underground Solidarity activists about deliveries of equipment for *samizdat* publishing activities and other matters. The authors pointed out that sending coded messages in VOA programs would constitute a violation of U.S. law.[29] If such messages were sent, I was not aware of them as the person in charge of radio broadcasts to Poland. They could have only been sent without my knowledge in Voice of America editorials, a three-minute daily presentation of the views of the U.S. government over which VOA journalists had no control and regarded them as a black mark on our reputation as a news organization. I worked at the Voice of America Polish Service in Washington, D.C. from 1973 until 1993 and was in charge of radio broadcasts to Poland during the period of the suppression of the Solidarity labor union and the imposition of the martial law by General Wojciech Jaruzelski (b. 1923). During this admittedly sensitive time for U.S. policy makers, I experienced no more than three or four significant attempts by low and mid-level government officials to interfere with our reporting. In all cases, I was able to resist or ignore their requests.

One of the most bizarre attempts at interference with VOA reporting occurred during the martial law in Poland in the early 1980s. What made this attempt strange were arguments made behind the scenes by the State Department diplomats that contradicted public statements from the White House. Using informal communication channels, State Department diplomats tried to discourage me from conducting telephone interviews with Solidarity leader Lech Wałęsa (b. 1943), who at the time was under constant secret police observation. They argued privately that broadcasting such interviews would be provocative, could lead to police reprisals and might harm their secret negotiations with the Jaruzelski government. When we ignored their requests, they tried to question through diplomatic back-channels whether Wałęsa was really the person we interviewed by phone. It was a silly argument obviously aimed at exerting pressure, but already at that time U.S. government diplomats could no longer make public requests to force VOA journalists to comply with their peculiar demands. At least for me, their interference was a nuisance but not a major problem.

Another case of attempted censorship occurred in the 1970s when a comment by a Polish writer, who had accused Stalin of ordering the Katyń massacre of thousands of Polish military officers during World War II, was briefly eliminated from a VOA news report. During the Cold War, the State Department and the White House never officially blamed the Soviet Union of this crime and tried to keep silent on this issue. The Soviets always insisted that the murders had been committed by the Nazis. After consulting with the Polish Service journalists, VOA corrected its news report by restoring the accusation against the Soviet Union and noted that Moscow still denies any responsibility for the massacre.

The Voice of America gave me a unique opportunity to influence the course of recent history, in which John Paul II played such a significant role. On separate occasions, both he and Solidarity leader Lech Wałęsa expressed to me their appreciation for the work done by VOA journalists in keeping the people in Poland informed during the several decades of communist rule. The pope knew that millions of Poles were listening to the Voice of America, Radio Free Europe, the BBC, Radio France Internationale, Vatican Radio, Deutsche Welle and other Western radio stations.[30] After retiring from VOA in 2006, I founded FreeMediaOnline.org, a San Francisco-based non-profit organization, which uses its informational activities to support press freedom worldwide and to assist independent journalists who struggle with censorship and government repression. The FreeMediaOnline.org web site has information on how journalists and news consumers can overcome the effects of censorship and propaganda. Our web site also features a special page with news about the role of media in reporting on issues of concern to women. My personal web site, TedLipien.com, has additional material about John Paul II, his papacy, and his views on women and feminism.

TedLipien.com
http://www.tedlipien.com/

FreeMediaOnline.org
http://www.freemediaonline.org/

Women & Media
http://www.freemediaonline.org/
womenandmedia.htm

SELECT BIBLIOGRAPHY

Accattoli, Luigi. *Karol Wojtyła: Człowiek końca tysiąclecia.* Wrocław: Wydawnictwo Sw. Antoniego, 1999.

Allen, John L. Jr. *All the Pope's Men.* New York: Doubleday, 2004.

Andrew, Christopher and Mitrokhin, Vasili. *The Mitrokhin Archive: the KGB in Europe and the West* London: Penguin Books, 2000.

Ascherson, Neal. *Black Sea.* New York: Hill and Wang, 1995.

Beauvoir, Simone de. *All Said and Done.* New York: G.P. Putnam's Sons, 1974.

————. *The Second Sex.* Translated and edited by H. M. Parshley. New York: Alfred A. Knopf, 1989.

Bernstein, Carl. *A Woman in Charge.* New York: Alfred A. Knopf, 2007.

Bernstein, Carl and Marco Politi. *His Holiness - John Paul II and the Hidden History of Our Time.* New York: Doubleday, 1996.

Bliss Lane, Arthur. *I Saw Poland Betrayed.* Belmont: Western Islands, 1965.

Bogucka, Maria. *The Lost World of Sarmatians.* Warsaw: Polish Academy of Sciences, Institute of History, 1996.

Boniecki, Adam. *Kalendarium życia Karola Wojtyły.* Kraków: Wydawnictwo Znak, 1983.

Bór Komorowski, Tadeusz. *The Secret Army.* Nashville: The Battery Press, 1984.

Briggs, Kenneth A. *Holy Siege: The Year That Shook Catholic America.* San Francisco: HarperSanFrancisco, 1992.

Byrne, Lavinia. *Woman at the Altar: The Ordination of Women in the Roman Catholic Church.* Collegeville: The Liturgical Press, 1994.

Christian Feminism. Weidmann L., Judith. San Francisco: Harper & Row, Publishers, 1984.

Ciechomska, Maria. *Od matriarchatu do feminizmu.* Poznań:

Wydawnictwo Brama.

Clinton Rodham, Hillary. *It Takes a Village*. New York: Simon & Schuster, 1996.

_____. *Living History*. New York: Simon & Schuster, 2003.

Cornwell, John. *The Pontiff in Winter: Triumph and Conflict in the Reign of John Paul II*. New York: Doubleday, 2004.

Curran, Charles E. *Loyal Dissent*. Washington, D.C.: Georgetown University Press, 2006.

Daly, Mary. *Beyond God The Father: Toward a Philosophy of Women's Liberation*. Boston: Beacon Press, 1973.

_____. *Pure Lust: Elemental Feminist Philosophy*. Boston: Beacon Press, 1984.

_____. *The Church and the Second Sex*. New York: Harper Colphon Books, 1975.

The Dark Side of the Moon. London: Farber and Farber Limited, 1946.

Davies, Norman. *Europe: A History*. London: Pimlico, 1997.

_____. *Heart of Europe: A Short History of Poland*. Oxford: Oxford University Press, 1986.

Dembińska, Maria. *Food and Drink in Medieval Poland: Rediscovering a Cuisine of the Past*. Philadelphia: University of Pennsylvania Press, 1999.

Dobroszycki, Lucjan. *Reptile Journalism: The Official Polish-Language Press under the Nazis, 1939-1945*. New Haven and London: Yale University Press, 1994.

Dorbritz, Jürgen and Fleischhacker, Jochen. "The Former German Democratic Republic." *From Abortion to Contraception: A Resource to Public Policies and Reproductive Behavior in Central and Eastern Europe from 1917 to the Present*. Edited by Henry P. David. Westport, Connecticut and London: Greenwood Press: 1999.

Dworkin, Andrea. *Intercourse*. NewYork: Free Press Paperbacks, 1987.

_____. *Life and Death: Unapologetic Writings on the Continuing War Against Women*. New York: The Free Press, 1997.

Dyduch, Jan. *Kanoniczne wizytacje parafii Kardynała Karola Wojtyły.* Kraków: Wydawnictwo Sw. Stanisława BM Archidiecezji Karakowskiej, 2000.

Dziwisz, Stanisław and Svidercoschi, Gian Franco. *Swiadectwo w rozmowie z Gian Franco Svidercoschim.* Warszawa: TBA Komunikacja Marketingowa Sp. Z o.o., 2007.

Ebon, Martin. *The Soviet Propaganda Machine.* New York: McGraw-Hill, 1987.

Filipiak, Maria and Szostek, Andrzej. *Obecność Karola Wojtyły na Katolickim Uniwersytecie Lubelskim.* Lublin: Redakcja Wydawnictw KUL, 1987.

Filipowicz, Stefan. "'Santita, non L'ho tradita mai—Ojcze Święty, nigdy Cię nie zdradziłem'" Jedna ze stron mojego życia." *Horyzonty Wychowania,* May 2006.

Flynn, Ray with Robin Moore and Jim Vrabel. *John Paul II: A Personal Portrait of the Pope and the Man.* New York: St. Martin Press, 2001.

Fox-Genovese, Elizabeth. *Feminism Without Illusions: A Critique of Individualism.* Chapel Hill: The University of North Carolina Press, 1991.

Friedan, Betty. *The Feminine Mystique.* New York: W. W. Norton and Company, Inc., 1963.

Frossard, Andre. *"Be Not Afraid"* translated by J.R. Foster. New York: St. Martin Press, 1984.

Gasidło, Władysław. *Duszpasterska troska Kardynała Wojtyły o rodzinę.* Kraków Wydawnictwo "CZUWAJMY", 1996.

Gaustad, Edwin Scott. *A Religious History of America.* San Francisco: HarperSanFrancisco, 1990.

Greeley, Andrew M. *Making of the Pope 2005.* New York: Little, Brown and Company, 2005.

Grossman, Vasily. *A Writer at War: A Soviet Journalist with the Red Army, 1941-1945.* Edited and Translated by Antony Beevor and Luba Vinogradova. New York: Vintage Books, 2005.

Halecki, Oskar. *A History of Poland.* Chicago: Henry Regnery

Company, 1966.

Hampson, Daphne.*Theology and Feminism*.Oxford: Basil Blackwell Ltd, 1990.

Hebblethwaite, Peter. *The Years of Three Popes*. Cleveland: William Collins, Inc., 1979.

Houseman, John. *Unfinished Business*. New York: Applause Theatre Books, 1989.

Held, Virginia. *Feminist Morality*. Chicago and London: The University of Chicago Press, 1993.

Horowitz, Daniel. *Betty Friedan and the Making of "The Feminine Mystique": The American Left, the Cold War, and Modern Feminism.* Amherst: University of Massachusetts Press, 1998.

Isakowicz-Zaleski, Tadeusz. *Księża wobec bezpieki*. Kraków: Wydawnictwo ZNAK, 2007.

Janion, Maria. *Kobiety i duch inności*. Warszawa: Wydawnictwo Sic!, 1996.

John Paul II. *Crossing the Threshold of Hope*. New York: Alfred A. Knopf, 1994.

_____. *Gift and Mystery*. New York: Doubleday, 1996.

_____. *Jan Paweł II do Kościoła w Polsce: 20 lat papieskiego nauczania*. Selected and edited by Fr. Zdzisław Wietrzak SJ Kraków: Wydawnictwo WAM, 1998.

_____. *Jan Paweł II w Polsce: 2-10 VI 1979, 16-23 VI 1983, 8-14 VI 1987 Przemówienia i homilie*. Warszawa: Instytut Wydawniczy PAX, 1991.

_____. *Memory and Identity*. New York, Rizzoli International Publications, 2005.

_____. *Przemówienia do Polonii i Polaków za granicą, 1979-1987*. Katolicki Ośrodek Wydawniczy, Veritas, 1988.

_____. *Rise, Let Us Be on Our Way*. New York: Time Warner Book Group, 2004.

Karol Wojtyła jako biskup Krakowski. Pieronek, Tadeusz and. Zawadzki, Roman M. eds. Kraków: Wydawnictwo Sw. Stanisława BM Archidiecezji Karakowskiej, 1988.

Klehr, Harvey, Haynes, John Earl, Frisov, Fridrikh Igorevich. *The Secret World of American Communism*. New Haven and London: Yale University Press, 1995.

Kłoczowski, Jerzy. *Dzieje chrześcijaństwa polskiego*. Paris: Edition du Dialogue, 1991.

Kluszyńska, Dorota. *Co Polska Ludowa dała kobietom*. Warszawa: Książka i Wiedza, 1950.

Küng, Hans. *On Being a Christian*. Translated by Edward Quinn. New York: Doubleday, 1984.

Kwiatkowska, Halina. *Wielki kolega*. Kraków: Oficyna Wydawnicza KWADRAT, 2003.

Kwitny, Jonathan. *Man of the Century: the Life and Times of Pope John Paul II*. New York: Henry Holt and Company, 1997.

Lackorońska, Karolina. *Michelangelo in Ravensbrück*. Cambridge: Da Capo Press, 2006.

Lasota, Marek. *Donos na Wojtyłę*. Kraków: Wydawnictwo ZNAK, 2006.

Leftwich Curry, Jane. *The Black Book of Polish Censorship*. New York: Vintage Books, 1984.

Leff, Laurel. *Buried by the Times*. Cambridge: Cambridge University Press, 2005.

Liberty for Women: Freedom and Feminism in the Twenty-First Century. McElroy, Wendy, ed. Chicago: Ivan R. Dee, 2002.

Lieblich, Julia. *Sisters: Life of Devotion and Defiance*. New York: Ballantine Books, 1992.

Lukas, Richard C. *Forgotten Holocaust: The Poles under German Occupation 1939-1944*. New York: Hippocrene Books, 1997.

Mansfield, Stephen. *Pope Benedict XVI: His Life and Mission*. New York: Jeremy P. Tarcher/Penguin, 2005.

Maliński, Mieczysław. *Ale miałem ciekawe życie*. Kraków: Wydawnictwo WAM, 2007.

————. *Dwa dni z życia Karola Wojtyły*. Kraków: Wydawnictwo ZNAK, 1998.

————. *Wezwano mnie z dalekiego kraju*. Wrocław:

Wydawnictwo Wrocławskiej Księgarni Archidiecezjalnej TUM, 1996.

_____. *Życiorys Karola Wojtyły*. Warszawa/Struga—Kraków: Wydawnictwo Michalineum, 1987.

Micewski, Andrzej. *Cardinal Wyszyński: A Biography*. San Diego: Harcourt Brace Jovanovich, Publishers, 1984.

Michalenko, Sophia. *The Life of Faustina Kowalska*. Ann Arbor: Servant Publications, 1999.

Michnik, Adam. *Letters from Freedom*. Berkley and Los Angeles: University of California Press, 1998.

Morawski, Zdzisław. *Watykan bez tajemnic*. Warszawa: Książka i Wiedza, 1997.

Noonan, Peggy. *John Paul the Great: Remembering a Spiritual Father*. New York: Viking, 2005.

Nowak-Jezioranski, Jan. *Polska wczoraj, dziś i jutro*. Warszawa: Czytelnik, 1999.

Nussbaum, Martha C. *Women and Human Development*. Cambridge: Cambridge University Press, 2000.

O'Brien, Darcy. *The Hidden Pope: The Untold Story of a Lifelong Friendship That Is Changing the Relationship between Catholics and Jews*. New York: Daybreak Books, 1998.

Olson, Lynne and Cloud, Stanley. *A Question of Honor: The Kosciuszko Squadron*. New York: Vintage Books, 2004.

Oppenheim, Bohdan W. Logs for the film *The Polish Cross*. Los Angeles: Marymount Institute, 1993.

Penn, Shana. *Solidarity's Secret: The Women Who Defeated Communism in Poland*. Ann Arbor: Michigan University Press, 2005.

Philosophy of Women. Mahowald Briody, Mary ed. Indianapolis: Hackett Publishing Company, 1983.

Pigozzi, Caroline. *Życie prywatne Ojca Świętego*. Warszawa: Prószyński i S-ka, 2001.

Półtawska, Wanda. *And I Am Afraid of My Dreams*. London: Hodder & Stoughton, 1979.

_____. *Stare rachunki*. Warszawa: Czytelnik, 1969.

Poniewierski, Janusz. *Pontyfikat.* Kraków: Społeczny Instytut Wydawniczy ZNAK, 1999.

Pospieszalski, Antoni. *O religii bez namaszczenia.* Kraków: Zaklad Wydawniczy NOMOS, 1997.

Przez Podgórze na Watykan. Cholewka, Marek ed. Kraków: Wydawnictwo "Czuwajmy," 1999.

Puddington, Arch. *Broadcasting Freedom: The Cold War Triumph of Radio Free Europe and Radio Liberty.* Lexington: The University Press of Kentucky, 2000.

Radford Ruether, Rosemary. *Sexism and God-Talk: Toward a Feminist Theology.* Boston: Beacon Press, 1993.

Ranke-Heinemann, Uta. *Eunuchs for the Kingdom of Heaven.* London: Penguin Books, 1991.

Ratzinger, Joseph. *The Legacy of John Paul II: Images and Memories.* San Francisco: Ignatius Press, 2005.

Reconciling Catholicism and Feminism. Barr Ebest, Sally and Ebest, Ron, eds. Notre Dame: University of Notre Dame Press, 2003.

Reed, Cheryl L. *Unveiled: The Hidden Lives of Nuns.* New York: Berkley Books, 2004.

Reproducing Gender: Politics, Publics, and Everyday Life after Socialism. Gal, Susan and Kligman, Gail, eds. Princeton: Princeton University Press, 2000.

Rowbotham, Sheila. *Woman's Consciousness, Man's World.* London: Penguin Books, Ltd, 1973.

Schüssler Fiorenza, Elizabeth. *Discipleship of Equals.* New York: The Crossroad Publishing Company, 1993.

Sheehan, Timothy P. "Supplementary Statement by Mr. Sheehan," *Reprinting of House Report No. 2505, 82nd Congress, Concerning the Katyn Forest Massacre, Committee on House Administration, United States House of Representatives.* Washington, D.C.: U.S. Government printing Office, 1988.

Steichen, Donna. *Ungodly Rage: The Hidden Face of Catholic Feminism.* San Francisco: Ignatius Press, 1992.

Stanford, Peter. *The She-Pope: A Quest for the Truth Behind the*

Mystery of Pope Joan. London: Arrow Books Limited, 1998.

Stein, Edith. *The Collected Works of Edith Stein*. ICS Publications, 1987.

Styczeń, Tadeusz and Balawajder, Edward. *Jedynie prawda wyzwala: rozmowy o Janie Pawle II*. Rome: Polski Instytut Kultury Chrzescijanskiej, 1987.

Suenens, Leo Jozeph. *The Nun in the World*. Westminster: The Newman Press, 1962.

Tazbir, Janusz. *Kultura szlachecka w Polsce*. Poznań: Wydawnictwo Poznańskie, 1998.

The Dark Side of the Moon. London: Farber and Farber Limited, 1946

Theorizing Black Feminisms: the Visionary Pragmatism of Black Women. James, Stanlie M. and Busia, Abena P.A., eds. New York: Routledge, 1993.

Titkow, Anna. "Poland" in *From Abortion to Contraception: A Resource to Public Policies and Reproductive Behavior in Central and Eastern Europe from 1917 to the Present*. Henry P. David, ed. Westport, Connecticut: Greenwood Press, 1999.

Tong, Rosemarie. *Feminist Thought: A Comprehensive Introduction*. London: Routledge, 1995.

Tymieniecka, Anna-Teresa. *Phenomenology and Science in Contemporary European Thought*. New York: The Noonday Press, 1962.

Walsh, Mary Ann, RSM. *From Pope John Paul II to Benedict XVI*. Lanham: Rowman & Littlefield Publishers, Inc., 2005.

Wieruszewski, Roman. *Równość kobiet i mężczyzn w Polsce Ludowej*. Poznań: Wydawnictwo Poznańskie, 1975.

Wills, Garry. *Papal Sin: Structures of Deceit*. New York: Doubleday, 2000.

Wojtyła, Karol. *The Acting Person*. Translated by Andrzej Potocki. Boston: D. Reidel Publishing Company, 1979.

_____. *Aby Chrystus sie nami posługiwał*. Kraków: Wydawnictwo Znak, 1979.

_____. *Człowiek drogą Kościoła*. Fundacja Jana Pawla II, Osrodek Dokumentacji Pontyfikatu, 1992.

_____. *Kazania 1962-1978*. Kraków: Wydawnictwo ZNAK, 1979.

_____. *Love and Responsibility*. Translated by H. T. Willetts. New York: Farrar, Straus and Giroux, 1994.

_____. *Nauczyciel i pasterz*. Michał Jagosz, ed. Rzym: Ośrodek Dokumentacji Pontyfikatu Jana Pawła II, 1987.

_____. *The Way to Christ – Spiritual Exercises*. San Francisco: Harper, 1994.

_____. *Wykłady lubelskie: człowiek i moralność III*. Lublin: Wydawnictwo Towarzystwa Naukowego Katolickiego Uniwersytetu Lubelskiego, 1986.

Women in Christ: Toward a New Feminism. Schumacher, Michele M., ed. Grand Rapids: Wm. B Erdmans Publishing Co, 2004.

Wyszyński, Stefan. *Godność kobiety*. Warszawa: Instytut Wydawniczy Pax, 1998.

_____. *Z rozważań nad kulturą ojczystą*. Warszawa: Instytut Wydawniczy Pax, 1998.

Zawacki, Edmund. "The Polish National Spirit" in *Poland*. Edited by Bernadotte E. Schmitt. Berkeley: University of California Press, 1947.

Zdybicka, Zofia. "Prawdziwy i fałszywy feminizm" in *Roczniki Filozoficzne*, Tom LI, zeszyt 2, 2003.

Zapis Drogi: Wspomnienia o nieznanym duszpasterstwie księdza Karola Wojtyły. Kraków: Wydawnictwo Sw. Stanisława BM Archidiecezji Karakowskiej, 1999.

NOTES

NOTES FOR INTRODUCTION

[1] http://www.vatican.va/holy_father/john_paul_ii/index.htm is the official Vatican web site for Pope John Paul II. Also see: http://www.tedlipien.com.

[2] Stanisław Dziwisz and Gian Franco Svidercoschi, *Świadectwo w rozmowie z Gian Franco Svidercoschim* (Warszawa: TBA Komunikacja Marketingowa Sp. Z o.o., 2007), p. 228-229. Karol Wojtyła's personal secretary and his closest friend, Cardinal Dziwisz, thought it was highly significant that John Paul II's last words were spoken to a woman.

[3] Some argue that there was nothing unique about Wojtyła's moral and gender agenda and that he and the Polish women who assisted him were simply following and implementing the Church's official teachings. In fact, Wojtyła and his women associates were far more liberal on issues of gender and sexual morality than nearly all Polish priests and bishops, but by the 1960s they were far less liberal than most Catholic women and Catholic theologians in the West.

[4] For information about Betty Friedan's secret Marxist past see: http://www.salon.com/col/horo/1999/01/18horo.html and Horowitz, Daniel. *Betty Friedan and the Making of the Feminine Mystique: the American Left, the Cold War and Modern Feminism.* Amherst: University of Massachusetts Press, 1998. Also see: http://www.greatwomen.org/women.php?action=viewone&id=6 2.

[5] Betty Friedan, *The Feminine Mystique* (New York: W. W. Norton and Company, Inc., 1963) quoted in *History of Ideas on Woman: A Source Book*, Rosemary Agonito, ed. (New York: G.P. Putnam's Sons, 1977), p. 384.

[6] Author's interview with Sister Zofia Zdybicka, May 24, 2007.

[7] My assistant's phone conversation with Dr. Wanda Półtawska,

May 24, 2007.

[8] For Aristotle's comments on women, including his observation that "their nature is very similar to that of children," see: http://home.myuw.net/jjcrump/courses/medWomen/aonwom en.html.

[9] Polish literature from the 16th through the 19th century is full of misogynist comments, although there was at least one writer who demanded that women be given access to education. Andrzej Gabler wrote in the 1530s that Polish men were afraid to educate girls "lest they should overtake them with brain power." According to this writer, "the girls' constitution is very subtle and their ability to learn and understand all things is sharp and quick." But a more popular writer of the same period, Andrzej Frycz Modrzewski, presented a strongly anti-feminist viewpoint, arguing that females, "whom God has put under the rule of males," should not be admitted to public affairs. He pointed out that the Roman laws also barred women from holding public offices. According to Polish historian Maria Bogucka, the movement to emancipate women, which was in progress in Western Europe starting with the Renaissance, "was barely noticeable in Poland."

[10] Polish Protestant Arians, also known as the Polish Brethren, were expelled from Poland in 1658 after being charged as collaborators of the invading Protestant Swedish armies. They found refuge in countries like the Netherlands and England, where their liberal social views (equality of all people, non violence, tolerance and rational religion) influenced the thinking of later philosophers of the Enlightenment. One of them was John Locke, the father of Western liberalism, who called for educating women and expanding their rights in marriage and society. Ideas brought to Western Europe by Polish Arians also contributed to the spread of Unitarianism and theological concepts now embraced by some Evangelicals (God as a single person). Through their connection to the thinkers of the Enlightenment, the Polish

Brethren philosophers also had an intellectual impact on political and religious beliefs of the Founding Fathers of the United States, especially James Madison and Thomas Jefferson (who claimed to be a Unitarian). Their liberal ideas, however, never had much influence in Poland.

[11] Even Russia had German-born Catherine the Great who took a leading role in the partitions of Poland, for which she was hated by generations of Poles. The last Polish king Stanisław August Poniatowski, whom she put on the Polish throne and later deposed, was one of her many lovers. Austria had Maria Theresa who was also the Holy Roman Empress. This powerful Catholic ruler had sixteen children including Marie Antoinette, the queen beheaded during the French Revolution. Polish magnates would not tolerate in a Polish queen extravagance reminiscent of Maria Theresa's daughter, but then no Polish queen was ever executed. (Male Polish Sarmatian magnates, on the other hand, took pride in their extravagant behavior.) As for Maria Theresa, her Catholic religion did not stop her from also participating in the First Partition of Poland, which led to the eventual loss of Poland's independence in the late 18th century. Another great European female monarch, England's Elizabeth I, was not only a powerful queen but also the head of the Church of England. The Polish nobility genuinely hated two of Poland's Western European queens: the Italian Bona Sforza d'Aragona (1494-1557), and the French Marie-Louise Gonzaga (1611-1667), both of whom, instead of devoting themselves to good works and prayers, became involved in politics and wanted to force reforms designed to strengthen their husbands' power. The Polish nobles were not accustomed to queens playing politics and did not look favorably on Western women trying to introduce new ideas that challenged the patriarchal order. Sophia Copolla's 2006 film *Marie Antoinette* has references to Maria Theresa, Marie Antoinette and the Partition of Poland; see:

http://www.sonypictures.com/homevideo/marieantoinette/inde

x.html..

[12] For information about the Jagiellonian University and Queen Jadwiga see: http://www.uj.edu.pl/dispatch.jsp?item=uniwersytet/historia/historiatxt.jsp&lang=en#narodziny.

[13] Jerzy Wolny, "Sesje historyczne w okresie pasterzowania Kardynała Karola Wojtyły" in *Karol Wojtyła jako Biskup Krakowski* (Kraków: Wydawnictwo Sw. Stanisława BM Archidiecezji Krakowskiej, 1988), pp. 472-473.

[14] Karol Wojtyła, *Nauczyciel i pasterz*, Michał Jagosz, ed.,Ośrodek Dokumentacji Pontyfikatu Jana Pawła II, (Rzym, 1987), pp. 515-516.

[15]The young queen may or may have not been unhappy in her marriage to Jagiełło, but she was definitely passionate about food and lavish entertaining. She imported large quantities of exotic ingredients, such as almonds, and introducing Western cuisine at the Polish court. See: Maria Dembińska, revised and adapted by William Woys Weaver, *Food and Drink in Medieval Poland: Rediscovering a Cuisine of the Past* (Philadelphia: University of Pennsylvania Press, 1999), p. 134.

[16] The 2003 U.S. State Department report on human rights practices noted that in a public opinion poll, conducted the previous year, 12 percent of Polish women identified themselves as victims of domestic violence, while 7 percent reported to had been beaten multiple times. Also, 43 percent of respondents stated that they knew at least one woman who was physically abused by her husband. In 1996 the police registered more than one million cases of domestic violence in Poland. Eighty percent of the cases were in the homes of alcoholics, with women and children being the vast majority of the victims. Women's organizations cited by the U.S. State Department describe the violence against women in Poland as "surrounded by taboos and accompanied by shame and guilt, particularly in small towns and villages." See The U.S. Department of State, *Country Report on Human Rights Practices for 2003*. The State Department Report for

2006 did not show that much progress has been made in protecting Polish women and their rights. Domestic violence against women continued to be a serious problem. According to authorities, 36,534 people reported domestic violence during the year, an increase from 2005. Women's organizations believed the number of women affected by domestic abuse was underreported. According to NGOs, courts often treated domestic violence as a minor crime, pronounced lenient verdicts, or dismissed cases. The NGO Center for Women's Rights believed that sexual harassment was also a serious and underreported problem. Many victims either did not report abuse out of shame or fear of losing their job or withdrew their claims in the course of police investigations. Social awareness of the problem continued to increase, however, as more cases of sexual harassment were reported by the media. The country was also a source, transit point, and destination for trafficked persons, primarily women and girls but also, to a lesser extent, boys. Internal trafficking for the purpose of sexual exploitation also occurred. Persons were trafficked to and through the country, primarily from Ukraine, Bulgaria, Romania, Belarus, and Moldova. A relatively high number were members of the Turkish minority in southern Bulgaria and from the Romani population in Romania. Destination countries included Germany, Italy, Belgium, France, the Netherlands, Austria, Denmark, Sweden, and Australia.

[17] Andrew M. Greeley, *Making of the Pope 2005*, (New York: Little, Brown and Company, 2005) p. 244.

[18] *CIA World Factbook, 2007.*

[19] Joseph Ratzinger, *The Legacy of John Paul II: Images and Memories*, (San Francisco: Ignatius Press, 2005), p. 20.

[20] Ibid., p. 12.

[21] Ibid., pp. 20-21.

[22] In the mid 19th century, a group of upper middle class Polish women, know as *Entuzjastki* ("Enthusiasts"), began to advocate limited educational reforms and called for women's access to

education. At a congress of Polish women, which was held in Warsaw in 1907, a special committee was created to study the issue of equal rights for women and men. The delegates demanded full social and political rights for women, including access to higher education, the right to choose one's profession and the right to work at equal pay. The delegates also formed the Polish Society for the Emancipation of Women.

[23] For more information about individualist feminism, ifeminists and other libertarian feminists see: http://www.ifeminists.net/e107_plugins/enews/enews.php; http://alf.org/; http://www.womensfreedom.org/.

[24] For more information about Opus Dei see: http://www.opusdei.org/. For more information about Radio Maryja and Father Rydzyk see: http://pl.wikiquote.org/wiki/Radio_Maryja.

[25] The American Jewish Committees web site, http://www.ajcarchives.org/main.php?GroupingId=6060, has a large archive on Father Coughlin, including contemporary pamphlets.

[26] *The Warsaw Voice*, "Rydzyk under Fire," September 12, 2007.

[27] ZENIT News Agency, "Terrorism Profanes Name of God, John Paul II Says," *Daily Dispatch*, September 24, 2001.

NOTES FOR BRIEF OUTLINE OF POLISH HISTORY

[1] I used some of the material from the U.S. State Department's publication "Background Note: Poland." I supplemented it with information about the role of the Catholic Church, the Polish Romantic movement, the situation of Polish women, and the controversy over U.S. policy toward Poland at the end of WWII. See: http://www.state.gov/r/pa/ei/bgn/2875.htm.

[2] Timothy P. Sheehan, "Supplementary Statement by Mr. Sheehan," *Reprinting of House Report No. 2505, 82nd Congress, Concerning the Katyn Forest Massacre, Committee on House Administration, United States House of Representatives* (Washington,

D.C.: U.S. Government printing Office, 1988), p. 15.

[3] The successful destruction of the democratic opposition by the communist regime is described in the book by the U.S. Ambassador to Poland Arthur Bliss Lane, *I Saw Poland Betrayed* (Belmont: Western Islands, 1965).

NOTES FOR SHORT BIOGRAPHY OF KAROL WOJTYŁA

[1] I consulted the biography issued by the Holy See Press Office and included additional references to events and documents dealing with women. For the Vatican's official biography of Pope John Paul II see:

http://www.vatican.va/news_services/press/documentazione/d ocuments/santopadre_biografie/giovanni_paolo_ii_biografia_bre ve_en.html.

[2] Halina Kwiatkowska, *Wielki kolega* (Kraków: Oficyna Wydawnicza Kwadrat, 2003), p. 62.

[3] George Weigel, *Witness to Hope: The Biography of John Paul II* (New York: Cliff Street Books, 1999), p. 71.

NOTES FOR CHAPTER ONE – CARED FOR BY WOMEN, EDUCATED BY MEN

[1] John Paul II, Rise, *Let Us Be on Our Way* (New York: Time Warner Book Group, 2004), p. 59.

[2] Weigel, *Witness to Hope*, p. 58.

[3] Roman Antoni Gajczak, *Wadowice: miasto papieskie* (Marki-Struga: Michalineum, 1995), p. 89.

[4] Gajczak, *Wadowice: miasto papieskie*, pp. 70-72.

[5] Weigel, *Witness to Hope*, p.30.

[6] John Paul II, *Gift and Mystery* (New York: Doubleday, 1996), p. 20.

[7] http://www.vatican.va/holy_father/benedict_xvi/.

[8] Gajczak, *Wadowice: miasto papieskie*, p. 70.

[9] PBS *Frontline* program, "John Paul II: The Millennial Pope," PBS

Online and WGBH/Frontline, 1999.

[10] http://www.newadvent.org/cathen/03659d.htm.

[11] Gajczak, *Wadowice: miasto papieskie*, p. 31.

[12] Weigel, *Witness to Hope*, p. 32.

[13] Ray Flynn with Robin Moore and Jim Vrabel, *John Paul II: A Personal Portrait of the Pope and the Man* (New York: St. Martin Press, 2001), p. 26.

[14] Gajczak, *Wadwice, miasto papieskie*, p. 70.

[15] Ibid., p. 8. For more information about Wadowice and the Papal Museum see:
http://www.it.wadowice.pl/index.html?lang_id=UK;
http://www.wadowice.pl.

[16] http://www.uj.edu.pl/index.html;
http://www.uj.edu.pl/index.en.html.

[17] Władysław Kopalinski, *Encyklopedia "drugiej plci"* (Warszawa: Oficyna Wydawnicza Rytm, 1995), p. 332.

[18] Gajczak, *Wadwice, miasto papieskie,*p. 28.

[19] Ibid., p.73.

[20] Ibid., p. 75.

[21] Ibid., p. 86.

[22] Kwiatkowska, *Wielki kolega*, p. 44.

[23] John Paul II, *Gift and Mystery*, p. 6.

[24] Father Maliński strongly emphasized in his books Wojtyła's pacifism and their mutual decision not to join the underground armed struggle against the Nazis. I could not confirm whether information in Maliński's books has any links to the revelations in Father Tadeusz Isakowicz-Zaleski's book about priests who spied on Wojtyła for the communist secret police: *Księża wobec bezpieki*, (Kraków: Wydawnictwo ZNAK, 2007) pp. 228-293. Father Isakowicz-Zaleski also reports in his book about another well-known Polish cleric, Archbishop Stanisław Wielgus, whom Pope Benedict XVI had nominated to become the archbishop of Warsaw. Wielgus was forced to resign in 2007 before he could assume his duties. Polish media revealed that he had been a

communist secret police informant—a charge Wielgus categorically denies. Interestingly, the communist secret police was far less successful in recruiting Polish nuns as informants and spies. Only a handful of nuns collaborated with the regime. Nuns may have been much more resistant to blackmail because they had less influence and fewer privileges than priests, including less frequent travels abroad. Consequently, the secret police was less interested in recruiting nuns. Lay women connected with the Church were, however, some of the more effective agents. For Father Maliński's response see comments in the Appendix and his personal web site: http://www.Maliński.pl/. The Appendix also has more information about the communist spy scandal involving Polish priests with links to John Paul II.

25 Ibid., p. 43.

26 John Paul II, *Gift and Mystery* (New York: Doubleday, 1996), p.5.

27

http://hektor.umcs.lublin.pl/~mikosmul/slowacki/index2.html.

28 Adam Boniecki, *Kalendarium życia Karola Wojtyły* (Kraków: Wydawnictwo Znak,1983), p. 65.

29 Mieczysław Maliński, *Przewodnik po życiu Karola Wojtyły*, (Kraków: Wydawnictwo Znak, 1977), p. 13.

30 Maliński, *Przewodnik po życiu Karola Wojtyły*, p. 50.

31 *Kalendarium*, p. 58.

32 Wojtyła, *"Aby Chrystus sie nami posługiwał"* (Kraków: Wydawnictwo Znak, 1979), p. 25.

33 Michał Szafarski, "Jan Tyranowski: kierownik duchowy Karola Wojtyły" in *Przez Podgórze na Watykan*, Marek Cholewka, ed. (Kraków: Wydawnictwo "Czuwajmy," 1999), p. 161.

34 Ibid.

35 Mieczysław Maliński, *Wezwano mnie z dalekiego kraju*, (Wrocław: Wydawnictwo Wrocławskiej Księgarni Archidiecezjalnej TUM, 1996), p. 29.

36 Wojtyła, *"Aby Chrystus sie nami posługiwał"*, p. 20.

37 Maliński, *Wezwano mnie z dalekiego kraju*, p. 19.

[38] Maliński, *Przewodnik po życiu Karola Wojtyły*, p. 38.

[39] http://www.myss.com/news/archive/2007/022307.asp.

[40] Matthew Fox, "Some Reflections on the Recent Papacy of JPII," 2005, http://www.matthewfox.org/sys-tmpl/htmlpage8/.

[41] Matthew Fox, "The Emperor Has No Clothes: How this 'Not-Ready-For-Prime-Time-Pope' Puts his papal foot in his mouth and starts a Holy War between Islam and Christianity," http://www.matthewfox.org/sys-tmpl/theemperporhasnoclothes/.

[42] Marek Cholewka, ed., *Przez Podgórze na Watykan* (Kraków: Wydawnictwo "Czuwajmy," 1999), pp. 254-255.

[43] Maliński, *Wezwano mnie z dalekiego kraju*, pp. 80-81.

[44] Weigel, *Witness to Hope*, p. 32.

[45] Isakowicz-Zaleski *Księża wobec bezpieki*, p. 417-419.

[46] Mieczysław Maliński, *Ale miałem ciekawe życie* (Kraków: Wydawnictwo WAM, 2007), p. 170.

[47] Maliński, *Wezwano mnie z dalekiego kraju*, p.77.

[48] Isakowicz-Zaleski *Księża wobec bezpieki*, pp.288-297. For Father Maliński's response see: http://www.Maliński.pl/ and comments in the Appendix.

[49] Maliński, *Ale miałem ciekawe życie*, p. 187.

[50] Ibid., pp. 326-330.

[51] Ibid., p. 335.

[52] http://diecezja.pl/index.php?page=dziwisz.

[53] Wojtyła, *"Aby Chrystus się nami posługiwał"*,p. 102.

[54] Karol Wojtyła, *Tygodnik Powszechny*, No. 51-52, 1970.

[55] Margarite Fox, "Susan Sontag, Social Critic with Verve, Dies at 71" in *The New York Times*, December 28, 2004.

[56] Maliński, *Wezwano mnie z dalekiego kraju*, p. 340.

[57] Zdzisław Morawski, *Watykan bez tajemnic* (Warszawa: Książka i Wiedza, 1997), p. 290.

[58] Darcy O'Brien, *The Hidden Pope: the Untold Story of a Lifelong Friendship that is Changing the Relationship between Catholics and Jews* (New York: Daybreak Books, 1998), p. 193.

[59] Ibid., p. 250.

[60] *Kalendarium*, p. 40.

[61] Ibid.

[62] Edwin Scott Gaustad, *A Religious History of America* (San Francisco: HarperSanFrancisco, 1990), p. 238.

[63] Ibid., p. 239.

[64] O'Brien, *The Hidden Pope*, p. 124.

[65] Piotr Poźniak, "Obdarzeni przyjaźnią" in *Przez Podgórze na Watykan*, Marek Cholewka, ed. (Kraków: Wydawnictwo Czuwajmy, 1999), p. 147.

[66] Maria Poźniak, "Dawne dzieje" in *Zapis drogi*, p. 187.

[67] Maliński, *Wezwano mnie z dalekiego kraju*, p. 61.

[68] Richard C. Lukas, *The Forgotten Holocaust: The Poles under German Occupation 1939-1944* (New York: Hippocrene Books, 1997), p. 31.

[69] *Kalendarium*, p. 111.

[70] Ibid., p. 218.

[71] *Zapis Drogi*, pp. 340-343.

[72] Ibid., 387.

[73] Jadwiga Kozłowska, "Po latach…" in *Zapis drogi*, p. 105.

[74] Maliński, *Wezwano mnie z dalekiego kraju*, p.323.

[75] Ibid., pp. 326-328.

[76] Jacek Fedorowicz, "Garść wspomnień z okresu tworzenia się kręgu przyjaciół księdza Karola," in *Zapis drogi*, p. 75.

[77] Janusz Rieger "Moje i mojej rodziny spotkania z Wujkiem i Srodowiskiem" in *Zapis drogi*, pp. 194-195.

[78] Danuta Rybicka, "Całe bogactwo" *Zapis drogi*, p. 204.

[79] Janusz Rieger "Moje i mojej rodziny spotkania z Wujkiem i Srodowiskiem" in *Zapis drogi*, p. 194.

[80] Karol Wojtyła, "Listy to redakcji w sprawie campingu" ("Homo Dei" nr 3 (81), maj – czerwiec 1957) in *Zapis Drogi*, p. 14.

[81] Karol Wojtyła, *Love and Responsibility*, translated by H. T. Willetts (New York: Farrar, Straus and Giroux, 1994), p. 189.

[82] Karol Wojtyła, "Listy to redakcji w sprawie campingu" in *Zapis*

Drogi, p. 14.

[83] Ludwik Jacek Broel Plater, "Moje spotkania z Wujkiem" in *Zapis Drogi*, p. 170.

[84] Karol Wojtyła, *Love and Responsibility*, p. 192.

[85] Danuta Rybicka, "Całe bogactwo" in *Zapis Drogi*, pp. 203-221.

[86] Maliński, *Wezwano mnie z dalekiego kraju*, p. 328.

[87] Danuta Ciesielska, "Ze wspomnien najistotniejszych" in *Zapis drogi*, p. 57.

[88] Danuta Rybicka, "Całe bogactwo" in *Zapis drogi*, p. 212.

[89] Author's interview with Danuta Ciesielska, May 23, 2007.

[90] Joanchim Gudel, "Duszpasterz" in *Zapis drogi*, p. 83.

[91] *Zapis Drogi*), p. 272.

[92] Ibid., p. 61.

[93] Maria Filipiak and Andrzej Szostek, eds.,*Obecność: Karola Wojtyły na Katolickim Universytecie Lubelskim* (Lublin: Redakcja Wydawnictw KUL, 1987), p. 107.

[94] *Przez Podgórze na Watykan*, pp. 210-212.

[95] *Obecność Karola Wojtyły na Katolickim Uniwersytecie Lubelskim*, p. 138.

[96] *Kalendarium*, p. 147.

[97] Ibid., p. 159.

[98] *Obecność Karola Wojtyły na Katolickim Uniwersytecie Lubelskim*, p. 136.

[99] Ibid.

[100] George Weigel, *Witness to Hope*, p. 139.

[101] *Obecność: Karola Wojtyły na Katolickim Uniwersytecie Lubelskim*, p. 168.

[102] Ibid., p. 171.

[103] Zofia Abrahamowicz-Stachura, "Zawsze z Wujkiem," in *Zapis drogi*, pp. 32-35.

[104] Ibid., pp. 28-29.

[105] John Paul II, "List Ojca Świętego do Środowiska," in *Zapis drogi*, pp. 324-325.

[106] *Kalendarium*, p. 160.

[107] *Obecność Karola Wojtyły na Katolickim Uniwersytecie Lubelskim*, p. 170.

[108] Marta Podlaska, "Niezapomniane lata z Wujkiem i Rodzinką" in *Zapis Drogi*, p. 181.

[109] Author's interview with Professor Zdybicka, May 24, 2007.

[110] Zofia Zdybicka, „Prawdziwy i fałszywy feminizm" in *Roczniki Filozoficzne*, Tom LI, zeszyt 2, 2003.

[111] Danuta Rybicka, "Całe bogactwo" in *Zapis drogi*, pp. 206-207.

[112] Ibid., p. 208.

[113] Teresa Życzkowska, "Od Beskidów i Bieszczad do Watykanu" in *Zapis Drogi*, p. 317.

[114] O'Brien, *The Hidden Pope*, p. 393.

[115] Ibid., p. 252.

[116] Karol Wojtyła, *The Way to Christ — Spiritual Exercises* (San Francisco: Harper, 1994), p. 53.

[117] Wojtyła, *Kazania: 1962-1978*, p. 200.

[118] Wojtyła, *The Way to Christ – Spiritual Exercises*, p. 53.

[119] Ibid.

[120] Ibid., p. 54.

[121] Wojtyła, *Kazania: 1962-1978*, p. 200.

[122] Wojtyła, *The Way to Christ — Spiritual Exercises*, p. 54.

[123] Wojtyła, *Kazania: 1962-1978*, p. 200.

[124] Wojtyła, *The Way to Christ — Spiritual Exercises*, p. 52.

[125] Wojtyła, *Kazania: 1962-1978*, p. 203.

[126] Ibid.

[127] Ibid., p. 485.

[128] Ibid.

[129] Ibid.

[130] Wojtyła, *The Way to Christ — Spiritual Exercises*, p. 33.

[131] Ibid., p. 35.

[132] Ibid., p. 35.

[133] Wojtyła, *Kazania: 1962-1978*,

[134] Ibid., p. 186.

[135] Wojtyła, *The Way to Christ — Spiritual Exercises*, p. 36.

136 Wojtyła, *Kazania: 1962-1978*, p. 187.

137 Wojtyła, *The Way to Christ — Spiritual Exercises*, p. 37.

138 *Kalendarium*, p. 146.

139 Ibid., p. 202.

140 John Paul II, Rise, *Let Us Be on Our Way*, p. 96.

141 Maliński, *Wezwano mnie z dalekiego kraju*, p. 199-201.

142 Maliński, *Przewodnik po życiu Karola Wojtyły*, p. 34.

143 Wojtyła, *Nauczyciel i pasterz*, p. 230.

144 Ibid., p. 308.

145 Maliński, *Wezwano mnie z dalekiego kraju*, p. 46.

146 Ray Flynn with Robin Moore and Jim Vrabel, *John Paul II: A Personal Portrait of the Pope and the Man* (New York: St. Martin Press, 2001), p. 132.

147 Mother Teresa Ewa Potocka (1814-1881) founded the Congregation of the Sisters of Our Lady of Mercy in Poland in Warsaw on November 1, 1862 when she took over a home for girls who were prostitutes. This was the first "Mercy House". http://www.sisterfaustina.org/.

148 M. Beata Piekut, "Moje wspomnienia o Ojcu Świętym Janie Pawle II" in *Przez Podgórze na Watykan*, Marek Cholewka, ed. (Kraków: Wydawnictwo "Czuwajmy," 1999), p. 216.

149 Ibid., p. 219.

150 For the authorized biography of Sister Faustina see: a book by Sister Sophia Michalenko, C.M.G.T.: *The Life of Faustina Kowalska* (Ann Arbor: Servant Publications, 1999).

151 John Paul II, *Rise, Let Us Be on Our Way* (New York: Time Warner Book Group, 2004), p. 194.

152 ZENIT News Agency *Daily Dispatch*, April 30, 2000.

153 Ibid.

154 Bohdan W. Oppenheim, Logs for the film *The Polish Cross* (Los Angeles: Marymount Institute, 1993), p. 44.

155 Jan Dyduch, *Kanoniczne wizytacje parafii Kardynała Karola Wojtyły* (Kraków: Wydawnictwo Sw. Stanisława BM Archidiecezji Krakowskiej, 2000), p. 74.

[156] Maciej Krobicki, "Przygody bieszczdzkie," in *Zapis drogi*, p. 115.

[157] Ibid., pp. 183-184.

[158] Maliński, *Przewodnik po życiu Karola Wojtyły*, pp. 194-196.

[159] Dziwisz and Svidercoschi, *Świadectwo*, p. 5.

[160] Caroline Pigozzi, *Życie prywatne Ojca Świętego* (Warszawa: Prószyński i S-ka, 2001), p. 20.

[161] Dziwisz and Svidercoschi, *Świadectwo*, pp. 230-231.

[162] Pigozzi, *Życie prywatne Ojca Świętego*, p. 11.

[163] Ibid., p. 106.

[164] Ibid. pp. 26-28.

[165] Ibid., p. 11.

[166] Ibid., p. 26.

[167] Mary Ann Glendon, "The Pope's New Feminism," *Crisis Online*, March 1997.

[168] John Paul II, *Jan Paweł II w Polsce: 2-10 VI 1979, 16-23 VI 1983, 8-14 VI 1987 przemówienia i homilie* (Warszawa: Instytut Wydawniczy PAX, 1991), p. 104.

[169] Ibid., p. 99.

[170] Urszula Perkowska, "Kariery naukowe kobiet na Uniwersytecie Jagielońskim w latach 1904-1939" in *Kobieta i kultura*, Anna Zarnowska and Andrzej Szwarc, eds. (Warszawa: Wydawnictwo DiG, 1996), p.139.

[171] Ibid., p. 143.

[172] *National Catholic Reporter*, Oct. 19, 1979.

[173] John Paul II *Pilgrimage of Peace: The Collected Speeches of John Paul II in Ireland and the United States* (New York: Farrar Straus Giroux, 1980), p. 157.

[174] Richard P. McBrien, *Report on the Church: Catholicism After Vatican II* (San Francisco: HarperSanFrancisco, 1992), p. 127.

[175] Madonna Kolbenschlag, "John Paul II, U.S. Women Religious, and the Saturnian Complex" in *The Church in Anguish: Has the Vatican Betrayed Vatican II?* (New York: Harper & Row, Publishers, Inc., 1987), p. 253.

[176] Sisters of Mercy of the Americas, Press Release "Twenty-five Years Ago," 2004 News in http://www.sistersofmercy.org.

[177] Carl Bernstein and Marco Politi, *His Holiness - John Paul II and the Hidden History of Our Time* (New York: Doubleday, 1996), pp. 516-517.

[178] Ari L. Goldman, "2 Nuns Quit Order in Battle With Vatican on Abortion," *The New York Times*, July 22, 1988.

[179] "The List" *National Catholic Reporter*, February 25, 2005. See: http://ncronline.org/NCR_Online/archives2/2005a/022505/022 505h.php.

[180] Patricia Hussey and Barbara Ferraro, "Communities of faith; When people of faith sit still, they support injustice," Charleston Daily Mail, February 29, 2004.

NOTES TO CHAPTER TWO: MARXISM, SECOND SEX AND WOJTYŁA'S FEMINIST PHILOSOPHY

[1] Camille Paglia, "Libertarian Feminism in the Twenty-First Century" in *Liberty for Women: Freedom and Feminism in the Twenty-First Century* (Chicago: Ivan R. Dee, 2002), p. 27.

[2] Simone de Beauvoir, *The Second Sex*, translated and edited by H. M. Parshley (New York: Alfred A. Knopf, 1989), p. 126.

[3] Sheila Rowbotham, *Woman's Consciousness, Man's World* (London: Penguin Books, Ltd, 1973), p. xvi.

[4] Rosemary Radford Ruether, *Sexism and God-Talk: Toward a Feminist Theology* (Boston: Beacon Press, 1993), pp. 224-225.

[5] Daphne Hampson, *Theology and Feminism* (Oxford: Basil Blackwell Ltd, 1990), p. 1.

[6] Mary Wollstonecraft's books can be viewed online at Project Gutenberg: http://www.gutenberg.org/browse/authors/w#a84; http://www.gutenberg.org/etext/16199.

[7] Woolf, Virginia. "The Four Figures," http://etext.library.adelaide.edu.au/w/woolf/virginia/w91c2/c hapter13.html.

[8] *The Women's Bible* can be downloaded from Project Gutenberg:

http://www.gutenberg.org/etext/9880.

[9] In the introduction to *The Woman's Bible*, Elizabeth Cady Stanton attacked the Biblical portrayal of women as evil and inferior: "The Bible teaches that woman brought sin and death into the world, that she precipitated the fall of the race, that she was arraigned before the judgment seat of Heaven, tried, condemned and sentenced. Marriage for her was to be a condition of bondage, maternity a period of suffering and anguish, and in silence and subjection, she was to play the role of a dependent on man's bounty for all her material wants, and for all the information she might desire on the vital questions of the hour, she was commanded to ask her husband at home. Here is the Bible position of woman briefly summed up." Elizabeth Cady Stanton disagreed with the view of some of her Christian friends in the feminist movement who argued that Christianity was responsible for helping women secure more rights for themselves in the Western world. She attributed such advances mostly to the power of reason helped by secular political action. Educated and financially secure, she did not see religion as particularly helpful to women in dealing with life's tragedies and difficulties, although she acknowledged the importance of those passages in the Bible and other religious books which teach "love, charity, liberty, justice and equality for all the human family…" Overall, Elizabeth Cady Stanton concluded that, as far as woman is concerned, "all the religions on the face of the earth degrade her, and so long as woman accepts the position that they assign her, her emancipation is impossible."

[10] Elżbieta Adamiak, "Czego Kosciół powinien nauczyć się od teologii feministycznej," in *Więź*, 1(471), January 1998, p. 94.

[11] See the analysis of Barbara Welter in the introduction to *The Original Feminist Attack on the Bible* (New York: Arno Press, 1974), p. xiii..

[12] Barbara J. MacHaffie, *Her Story: Women in Christian Tradition* (Philadelphia: Fortress Press, 1986), pp. 88-91.

[13] Elizabeth Fox-Genovese, *Feminism Without Illusions: A Critique of Individualism* (Chapel Hill: The University of North Carolina Press, 1991), p. 244.

[14] Elisabeth Schüssler Fiorenza, "Feminist/Women Priests – An Oxymoron?," *New Women, New Church*, Fall 1995, p. 18.

[15] Deirdre Bair, *Simone de Beauvoir* (New York: Summit Books, 1990), p. 555.

[16] Martin Ebon, *The Soviet Propaganda Machine* (New York: McGraw-Hill, 1987), pp. 128-130.

[17] See: Rosemarie Tong, *Feminist Thought: A Comprehensive Introduction* (London: Routledge, 1995), pp. 195-216.

[18] Bair, *Simone de Beauvoir.*, p. 609.

[19] Simone de Beauvoir, *All Said and Done* (New York: G. P. Putnam's Sons, 1974), p. 449.

[20] For more information about the Vatican's Index of Forbidden Books (*Index Librorum Prohibitorum*) see: Tom Heneghan, "Secrets Behind the Forbidden Books" in *America*, February 7, 2005.

[21] Bair, *Simone de Beauvoir*, pp. 456-457.

[22] Tom Heneghan, "Secrets Behind the Forbidden Books."

[23] Elizabeth Schüssler Fiorenza, *Discipleship of Equals* (New York: The Crossroad Publishing Company, 1993), pp. 144-145.

[24] Simone de Beauvoir, *All Said and Done*, p. 462.

[25] Sally Quinn, "The Death of Feminism," *The Washington Post National Weekly Edition*, January 27-February 2, 1992.

[26] Center for the Advancement of Women, 2003, http://www.advancewomen.org/.

[27] Schüssler Fiorenza, *Discipleship of Equals*, pp. 314-316. Dr. Schüssler Fiorenza also argues that feminist should recognize that some traditional family values dealing with children, home, and religion "are also important for emancipatory movements."

[28] Leo Jozeph Suenens, *The Nun in the World* (Westminster: The Newman Press, 1962), pp. 15-16.

[29] Weigel, *Witness to Hope*, pp. 336 and 343. For more information about George Weigel see:

http://www.eppc.org/scholars/scholarID.14/scholar.asp.

[30] http://www.womenpriests.org/scholars.asp.

[31] Charles E. Curran, *Loyal Dissent* (Washington, D.C.: Georgetown University Press, 2006) pp. 184, 218-219, 240.

[32] Dave Eberhart, "Red Army Raped Every German Woman, Says Author," in *NewsMax.com*, May 2, 2002. Antony Beevor, author of *The Fall of Berlin 1945*, described how a Soviet journalist Natalya Gesse, a close friend of the scientist Andrei Sakharov, observed the behavior of Red Army soldiers in 1945: "The Russian soldiers were raping every German female from eight to eighty. It was an army of rapists." The Red Army soldiers also raped non-German women. Many of them were Jewish, Russian, Ukrainian, Belarusian and Polish women who had been slave laborers and concentration camp prisoners. Some were also Nazi collaborators who had escaped to Germany before the Red Army advance. See: http://archive.newsmax.com/archives/articles/2002/5/2/80440.shtml. and http://www.telegraph.co.uk/news/main.jhtml?xml=/news/2002/01/24/wbeev24.xml&sSheet=/news/2002/01/24/ixworld.html.

[33] Some U.S. soldiers were guilty of raping German women, but these appeared to be isolated incidents. According to one first-hand account from a German woman, "After having been 'liberated' by the Russians and lived under Soviet occupation for about three months, the U.S. military were greeted like *saviors and gods* by us." See: Elfrieda Berthiaume Shukert and Barbara Smith Scibetta, *War Brides of World War II* (Novato: Presidio Press, 1988), pp. 124-125. For other first-hand accounts of rapes of women by Red Army soldiers see: Vasily Grossman, *A Writer at War: A Soviet Journalist with the Red Army, 1941-1945* Edited and Translated by Antony Beevor and Luba Vinogradova (New York: Vintage Books, 2005).

[34] Vittorio Messori's interview with Cardinal Joseph Ratzinger in *Jesus*, November 1984.

[35] Wojtyła, *Nauczyciel i pasterz*, pp. 651-652.

[36] http://www.freemediaonline.org/wojtyla_lipien_voa_
interview.htm.

[37] Simone de Beauvoir, *The Second Sex*, p. xxii.

[38] Julia Lieblich, *Sisters: Life of Devotion and Defiance* (New York:
Ballantine Books, 1992), p. 14.

[39] Mary Daly, *The Church and the Second Sex* (New York: Harper
Colophon Books, 1975), p. 220.

[40] Lieblich, *Sisters*, p. 111.

[41] Patricia Lefevre, "Margaret Traxler lived her passion for justice:
teacher marched in Selma, carried a banner in St. Peter's Square –
Appreciation," *National Catholic Reporter*, March 1, 2002.

[42] Cheryl L. Reed, *Unveiled: The Hidden Lives of Nuns* (New York:
Berkley Books, 2004), pp. 74-93.

[43] The order was founded by a Polish nun, Mother Mary Angela
Truszkowska, who was beatified by Pope John Paul II in 1993.
The sisters minister to Polish Americans since their arrival from
Poland in 1874. They still wear their traditional religious garb.

[44] For more information about Polish American women see:
http://www.prcua.org/news/ladieshistory.htm.

[45] Lieblich, *Sisters*, p. 121.

[46] Ernest Tucker, "Nun keeps fight alive after disbanding
women's group," *The Chicago Sun Times*, May 26, 2000.

[47] Martin Browne, "Women Raise Their Voices," *The Tablet*, July
11, 2001.

[48] Hampson, *Theology and Feminism*, p. 46.

[49] Ibid., p. 89.

[50] John Paul II, Papal Letter of John Paul II to the Women of the
World, July 10, 1995.

[51] Hampson, p. 15.

[52] Ibid.

[53] Ibid., pp. 92-93.

[54] Donna Steichen, *Ungodly Rage: The Hidden Face of Catholic
Feminism* (San Francisco: Ignatius Press, 1992), p. 160.

[55] Mary Daly, *Pure Lust: Elemental Feminist Philosophy* (Boston:

Beacon Press, 1984), p. 56.

[56] Ibid.

[57] Ibid.

[58] Schüssler Fiorenza, *Discipleship of Equals*, p. 7.

[59] Ibid. p. 315.

[60] Rosemary Radford Ruether, "American Catholic Feminism: A History" in *Reconciling Catholicism and Feminism?*, Sally Barr Ebest and Ron Ebest, eds. (Notre Dame: University of Notre Dame Press, 2003), pp. 3-12.

[61] For more information about Jane Sullivan Roberts see: http://www.feministsforlife.org/news/jsroberts.htm.

[62] "Not Everybody Loves Patricia," *The New York Times*, December 31, 2006.

[63] See "Call to Action History: Rooted in Church Teaching," http://www.cta-usa.org/index2.php?dest=history.html..

[64] Greeley, *Making of the Pope 2005*, p. xxii.

[65] John Paul II, *Talks of John Paul II* (Boston: St. Paul Editions: 1979), p. 15.

[66] John L. Allen, Jr., *All the Pope's Men* (New York: Doubleday, 2004), p. 377.

[67] Vatican Information Service, Ninth Year - N. 15, January 25, 1999.

[68] Michele M. Schumacher, ed., *Women in Christ: Toward a New Feminism* (Grand Rapids: Wm. B Erdmans Publishing Co, 2004).

[69] Greeley, *Making of the Pope 2005*, p. 11.

[70] John T. Noonan, Jr., *A Church Than Can and Cannot Change: The Development of Catholic Moral Teaching* (Notre Dame: University of Notre Dame Press, 2005), p. 202.

[71] Andrea Dworkin, *Life and Death: Unapologetic Writings on the Continuing War Against Women* (New York: The Free Press, 1997) p. 243.

NOTES FOR CHAPTER THREE: POLISH ROOTS

[1] Jerzy Kłoczowski, *Dzieje chrześcijaństwa polskiego* (Paris: Edition

du Dialogue,1991), p. 49.

2 ZENIT News Agency, *Daily Dispatch*, January 24, 2000.

3 Edmund Zawacki, "The Polish National Spirit" in *Poland*, edited by Bernadotte E. Schmitt (Berkeley: University of California Press, 1947), p. 336.

4 Inertia.pl, Urlopy rodzicielskie, December 6, 2001.

5 Zawacki, p. 246.

6 Antoni Dunajski, *Chrześcijańska interpretacja dziejów w pismach Cypriana Norwida* (Lublin: Redakcja Wydawnictw Katolickiego Uniwersytetu Lubelskiego, 1985), p. 37.

7 Ibid., p. 127.

8 Zawacki, p. 329.

9 Zawacki, p. 338.

10 Halecki, p. 243.

11 Wikimedia Commons has media related to Black Madonna of Częstochowa and National Shrine of Our Lady of Częstochowa. See:
http://commons.wikimedia.org/wiki/Cz%C4%99stochowa#Jasn a_G.C3.B3ra_Monastery.

12 *Kalendarium*, p. 766.

13 Kłoczowski, *Dzieje chrześcijaństwa polskiego*, p. 69.

14 Maria Janion, *Kobiety i duch inności* (Warszawa: Wydawnictwo Sic!, 1996), p. 96.

15 Ibid., p. 97.

16 Ibid.

17 József Mindszenty, *The Mother* (Radio Replies Press, 1949), Chapter One.

18 Anna Goliszek, "Idea Narodowa w neoromantyzmie," in *Charakter Narodowy i Religia*, Kazimierz Wilinski, ed. (Lublin: Wydawnictwo Uniwersytetu Marii Curie-Skłodowskiej, 1997), p.47.

19 Ibid. p. 52.

20 Adam Podgórecki, Polish Society (Westport: Praeger Publishers, 1994) p. 78.

[21] Ibid., p. 78.

[22] Oscar Halecki, *A History of Poland* (Chicago: Henry Regnery Company, 1966), p. 69.

[23] Wojtyła, *Nauczyciel i pasterz*, pp. 515-516.

[24] Jerzy Wolny, "Sesje historyczne w okresie pasterzowania Kardynała Karola Wojtyły" in *Karol Wojtyła jako Biskup Krakowski* (Kraków: Wydawnictwo Sw. Stanisława BM Archidiecezji Krakowskiej, 1988), pp. 472-473.

[25] Maria Dembińska, revised and adapted by William Woys Weaver, *Food and Drink in Medieval Poland: Rediscovering a Cuisine of the Past* (Philadelphia: University of Pennsylvania Press, 1999), p. 134.

[26] Wojtyła, *Nauczyciel i pasterz*, p. 71.

[27] Maria Bogucka,*The Lost World of Sarmatians* (Warsaw: Polish Academy of Sciences, Institute of History, 1996), pp. 53-54.

[28] Maria Ciechomska, *Od matriarchatu do feminizmu* (Poznań: Wydawnictwo BRAMA), p. 99.

[29] Ibid., p. 100.

[30] Bogucka, p. 59.

[31] Boleslaw Klimaszewski, ed., *An Outline of Polish History* (Warsaw: Interpress, 1984), p. 84.

[32] Janusz Tazbir, *Kultura szlachecka w Polsce* (Poznań: Wydawnictwo Poznańskie, 1998), p. 42.

[33] Neal Ascherson, *Black Sea* (New York: Hill and Wang, 1995), p. 236.

[34] Bogucka, p. 40. Maria Bogucka points out that from the end of the 16th century the custom of hand-kissing became obligatory "towards every older or more important person."

[35] Ascherson, *Black Sea*, p. 240.

[36] Rev. Wiesław Al. Niewęgłowski, *Moje spotkania z Janem Pawłem II* (Warszawa: Wydawnictwo Salezjanskie, 1995), p. 31.

[37] Ibid. p. 31.

[38] John Paul II, *Crossing the Threshold of Hope*, p. 120.

[39] Centrum Badania Opinii Społecznej (CBOS), "Konkubinat par

heteroseksualnych i homoseksualnych," Warszawa, 2002.

[40] Maliński, *Wezwano mnie z dalekiego kraju*, p. 29.

[41] John Paul II, *Crossing the Threshold of Hope*, p. 119.

[42] Ibid., p. 119.

[43] Ibid., p. 120.

[44] Norman Davies, *Heart of Europe: A Short History of Poland* (Oxford: Oxford University Press, 1986), p. 383.

[45] Karol Wojtyła, *Wykłady lubelskie: człowiek i moralność III* (Lublin: Wydawnictwo Towarzystwa Naukowego Katolickiego Uniwersytetu Lubelskiego, 1986), p. 277.

[46] The Alan Guttmacher Institute cites these figures from Jones RK, Darroch JE and Henshaw SK, "Patterns in the Socioeconomic Characteristics of Women Obtaining Abortions in 2000-2001," *Perspectives on Sexual and Reproductive Health*, 2002, 34(5):226-235. On the abortion figures worldwide see The Alan Guttmacher Institute (AGI), *Sharing Responsibility: Women, Society and Abortion Worldwide*, (New York: AGI, 1999). Of an estimated 46 million abortions annually worldwide in 1995, 20 million were obtained illegally. In 54 countries representing 61% of the world population abortions were legal in 1995. In 97 countries, which account for 39% of the world population, abortions were illegal. The number of induced abortions declined worldwide between 1995 and 2003, from nearly 46 million to approximately 42 million. About one in five pregnancies worldwide end in abortion. The decline in abortion incidence was greater in developed countries, where nearly all abortions are safe and legal (from 39 to 26 abortions per 1,000 women aged 15-44), than in developing countries, where more than half are unsafe and illegal (from 34 to 29). It appears that the transition to democracy and capitalism to Eastern Europe produced a significant drop in abortions. Although abortion rates and ratios (the number of abortions for every 100 births) in Eastern Europe have fallen significantly in recent years, they remain higher than in any other region. In 2003, there were more abortions than births in that

region (105 abortions for every 100 births).

[47] Norman Davies, *Europe: A History* (London: Pimlico, 1997), p. 1328.

[48] John Paul II, *Letter to Families*, #13.

[49] Dziwisz and Svidercoschi, *Świadectwo*, p. 75.

[50] Ibid. p. 76.

[51] Roman Wieruszewski, *Równość kobiet i mężczyzn w Polsce Ludowej* (Poznań: Wydawnictwo Poznańskie, 1975), pp. 111-112.

[52] Marian Tadeusz Medrala, "Arcybiskup – Proboszczem," p. 232.

[53] Stefan Wyszyński, *Godność kobiety* p. 33.

[54] Ibid., p. 29.

[55] Ibid., p. 29.

[56] Ibid., p. 169.

[57] Główny Urząd Statystyczny, *Sytuacja społeczno-zawodowa kobiet w 1983 r.* (Zarząd Wydawnictw Statystycznych i Drukarnii, 1984), p. 105.

[58] Ibid., p. 98.

[59] Dorota Kluszyńska, *Co Polska Ludowa dała kobietom* (Warszawa: Książka i Wiedza, 1950), p. 9.

[60] Jane Leftwich Curry, *The Black Book of Polish Censorship* (New York: Vintage Books, 1984), pp. 180-186.

[61] *Kalendarium*, p. 265.

[62] Ibid., p. 269.

[63] Ibid., p. 281. For more information about Pope Paul VI see: http://www.vatican.va/holy_father/paul_vi/index.htm.

[64] Vincent C. Chrypinski, "Church and Nationality in Postwar Poland," in *Religion and Nationalism in Soviet and East European Politics*, Pedro Ramet, ed., (Durham and London: Duke University Press, 1989), p. 247.

[65] *Pielgrzymka do Polski*, p. 219.

[66] John Paul II, *Jan Pawel II do Kosciola w Polsce*, p. 174.

[67] *Kalendarium*, p. 392.

[68] Ibid., p. 46.

[69] Ibid., p. 32.

[70] Tadeusz Pieronek and Roman M. Zawadzki, eds., *Karol Wojtyła jako biskup Krakowski* (Kraków: Wydawnictwo Sw. Stanislawa BM Archidiecezji Krakowskiej, 1988), p. 516.

[71] *Kalendarium*, p. 130.

[72] Ibid., p. 131.

[73] Ibid., p. 134.

[74] Karol Wojtyła, *Nauczyciel i pasterz*, p. 388.

[75] *Kalendarium*, p. 780.

[76] Ibid., p. 771.

[77] Ibid., p. 167

[78] John Paul II, Address to the Faithful in Gniezno, June 3, 1979.

[79] Ibid.

[80] John Paul II, Homily During Mass at the Airport in Masłow, June 3, 1999, Kielce.

[81] Stefan Wyszyński, *Z rozwazań nad kulturą ojczystą* (Warszawa: Instytut Wydawniczy Pax, 1998), p. 115.

[82] Interview with Prof. Stefan Swieżawski, http://www.kaipl/bedziesz.

[83] Jonathan Kwitny, *Man of the Century: the Life and Times of Pope John Paul II* (New York: Henry Holt and Company, 1997, p. 223.

[84] John Paul II, *Przemówienia do Polakow za granicą*, p. 22.

[85] Kwitny, pp. 265-266.

[86] http://www.smu.edu/theology/people/curran.html.

[87] Many liberal Catholics saw the removal of Father Curran and the earlier papal action against dissident theologians Hans Küng as proofs of John Paul's authoritarian style of leadership and his desire to stifle debate and impose censorship within the Church. This image of Wojtyła is, however, far different from how he was remembered by his Polish friends in Kraków. Jerzy Turowicz, the late editor of the Kraków Catholic weekly *Tygodnik Powszechny*, told an interviewer that in his position as the archbishop, Wojtyła had never requested that the paper not publish something or change its editorial analysis. According to another *Tygodnik Powszechny* staffer Halina Bortnowska, Wojtyła had no problems

working with people he did not always agree with. It seems that while he was still in Poland, Wojtyła was tolerant and not eager to impose his own view on his friends and associates within the Catholic community. This changed dramatically when he became pope. One can only suppose that what some Catholics in the West consider to be legitimate topics of theological debate, for John Paul II they were absolutely off-limits because of their potential to create confusion among the faithful. See Weigel's, *Witness to Hope*, p. 212.

[88] Jeffrey Weiss, "Biographer Had Unprecedented Access to John Paul II, Papers" in *The Dallas Morning News*, October 16, 1999.

[89] Vatican Information Service, Ninth Year - N. 15, January 25, 1999.

[90] Lynne Olson and Stanley Cloud, *A Question of Honor: The Kosciuszko Squadron* (New York: Vintage Books, 2004).

[91] John Paul II also strongly opposed the first Gulf War. In this case, there were interesting analogies between Poland being attacked in 1939 by Hitler and Stalin and Kuwait being invaded and occupied also by a much stronger and aggressive neighbor. In 1939, Poland's allies, Great Britain and France, did not come to her defense. A coalition led by the United States liberated Kuwait. John Paul II believed, however, that the risks of a military intervention in Kuwait were too great. He also suspected the U.S. of being motivated by a desire to keep control of the oil resources in the Middle East—a views shared by many Left-wing West European and American liberals.

[92] Bohdan W. Oppenheim, Logs for the film *The Polish Cross* (Los Angeles: Marymount Institute, 1993), p. 195.

[93] *Kalendarium*, p. 302.

[94] Czesław Miłosz, *Native Realm*, trans. Catherine Leach (Garden City, N.Y.: Doubleday, 1968), p. 82 cited by Adam Nowotny in "Fortress Catholicism: Wojtyła's Polish Roots" in *The Church in Anguish: Has the Vatican Betrayed Vatican II?* (New York: Harper & Ro, Publishers, Inc., 1987), p. 23.

NOTES FOR CHAPTER FOUR – SIGNIFICANT WOMEN, WAR, GENOCIDE AND ABORTION

[1] For Dr. Półtawska's views about women and their role in society see: "Rola kobiety - Strażniczki Życia" by Wanda Półtawska, http://www.tezeusz.pl/cms/tz/index.php?id=647 (in Polish).

[2] In his book *Księża wobec bezpieki*, Father Isakowicz-Zaleski also charges that Archbishop Paetz may have been an informant of the communist secret police. As with many such accusations, it is difficult to assess the real nature of contacts between priests and communist secret police officers. Archbishop Paetz denies these charges.

[3] Giacomo Galeazzi, "Preti pedofili, il segreto di Stanislao: Il cardinale Dziwisz accusato di aver taciuto gli abusi sessuali dei preti polacchi," *La Stampa*, February 22, 2007.

[4] John L. Allen Jr., "Polish Prelate Accused of Sexual Abuse: Archbishop Once Worked in Papal Household," *National Catholic Reporter*, March 15, 2002.

[5] Tadeusz Isakowicz-Zaleski, *Księża wobec bezpieki*, (Kraków: Wydawnictwo ZNAK, 2007) pp. 271-276.

[6] Wanda Półtawska, *And I Am Afraid of My Dreams*, translated by Mary Craig, (New York: Hippocrene Books, 1989), p. 11.

[7] Kwitny, p. 154.

[8] Władysław Gasidło, *Duszpasterska troska Kardynała Wojtyły o rodzinę* (Kraków Wydawnictwo "CZUWAJMY", 1996), p. 107.

[9] Ibid., p. 18.

[10] Kwitny, p. 164.

[11] Wanda Półtawska, "Priestly Celibacy in the Light Of Medicine and Psychology."

[12] Ibid.

[13] Ibid.

[14] Ibid.

[15] Frank M. Rega, "The famous cure of Bishop Karol Wojtyła's good friend Dr. Wanda Półtawska through the intercession of the

Saint of the Gargano: Rumors that Padre Pio had predicted that the Polish Bishop would be Pope are denied," cited in http://www.frankrega.com, 2005.

[16] Weigel, *Witness to Hope*, p. 153.

[17] ZENIT News Agency, "3 Canonizations May Draw Huge Crowds" in *Daily Dispatch*, February 26, 2002.

[18] http://fatherpiodevotions.com, "Short Biography of Father Pio," 2005.

[19] Wanda Półtawska, "Padre Pio: The Saint of Our Time," *Lay Witness*, October 1999. Also see: Weigel, *Witness to Hope: The Biography of Pope John Paul II*, p. 153.

[20] Kwitny, p. 219.

[21] Gasidło, *Duszpasterska troska Kardynała Wojtyły o rodzinę*, p. 32.

[22] Ibid., p. 47.

[23] Ibid., p. 60.

[24] Ibid., p. 59.

[25] Ibid., p. 74.

[26] Ibid., p. 57.

[27] Ibid., p. 103.

[28] Ibid., p. 105.

[29] Wojtyła, *Love and Responsibility*, pp. 282-285.

[30] Dr. David Kingsley, "The Combined Oral Contraceptive Pill: Abortifacient and Damaging to Women," Respect Life Publications.

[31] Maria Ryś, „Narodzenie i zagrożenie" in *Pukam do drzwi Waszych domów I pragnę się z Wami spotkać* (Warszawa: Instytut Wydawniczy PAX, 1994), p. 138.

[32] Wanda Półtawska, "Priestly Celibacy in the Light of Medicine and Psychology."

[33] Kwitny, p. 155

[34] Ryś, „Narodzenie i zagrożenie"in *Pukam do drzwi Waszych domów i pragnę się z Wami spotkać: Rozważania na temat Listu do Rodzin Ojca Świętego Jana Pawła II*, pp. 135-138.

[35] http://www.dobreksiazki.webpark.pl/poltawska.htm.

36 Kwitny, p. 156.

37 Półtawska, *And I Am Afraid of My Dreams*, translated by Mary Craig, p. 11.

38 Ibid. pp. 84-98.

39 Ibid. p. 99.

40 Sarah Helm, *A Life in Secrets: Vera Atkins and the Missing Agents of WWII* (New York: Anchor Books, 2007), p. 329.

41 Wanda Półtawska, *And I Am Afraid of My Dreams* (New York: Hippocrene Books, 1989), p. 112, quoted by George Weigel in *Witness to Hope: The Biography of Pope John Paul II* (New York: HarperCollins Publishers, Inc., 1999), p. 53.

42 Półtawska, *And I Am Afraid of My Dreams* , p. 137.

43 Ibid., p. 58.

44 Karolina Lackorońska, *Michelangelo in Ravensbrück* (Cambridge: Da Capo Press, 2006), p. 259.

45 Eva Hoffman in *Michelangelo in Ravensbrück*, p. xv.

46 Półtawska, *And I Am Afraid of My Dreams*, p. 15.

47 Ibid., p. 74.

48 Ibid., p. 175.

49 Wanda Półtawska, *Stare rachunki* (Warszawa: Czytelnik, 1969).

50 Półtawska, *And I Am Afraid of My Dreams*, p. 191.

51 Bogna Lorence-Kot, *The Sarmatian Review*, January 1995.

52 Ibid.

53 Wanda Półtawska, "Rola kobiety - Strażniczki Życia," http://www.tezeusz.pl/cms/tz/index.php?id=647.

54 Wanda Półtawska, *And I Am Afraid of My Dreams* (London: Hodder & Stoughton, 1987), p. 144.

55 Lucjan Dobroszycki, *Reptile Journalism: The Official Polish-Language Press under the Nazis, 1939-1945* (New Haven and London: Yale University Press, 1994), p. 168.

56 Stanisław Krajski, Radio Maryja (Warszawa: Wydawnictwo Sw. Tomasza z Akwinu, 1998), pp. 152-153.

57 During a visit to West Germany in 1974, Wojtyła's friends suggested that he take a walk in a district where shops selling

pornography could be seen. He came back revolted but what he had seen and told his friends that while he wrote in his book *Love and Responsibility* about three aspects of sex: physiological, psychological, and ethical — "the West focuses only on physiology." It was a sweeping conclusion to be made based on a short walk through the streets of a red-light district in a West German city. A look at a magazine rack at any gas station in Poland twenty years later would have shown that certain people, even in an overwhelmingly Catholic country, are attracted to pornography. Pornography did not have to be brought to Poland from the West. I saw a locally-owned sex shop located not too far from Wojtyła's former residence in Kraków.

58 Norbert Wójtowicz, "Ojciec Kolbe nie demonizowal," in *Bez uprzedzeń*

59 Michnik, p. 198.

60 Karol Wojtyła, *Nauczyciel i pasterz* (Rome: Ośrodek Dokumentacji Jana Pawła II, 1987), p. 421.

61 Tomasz Gołąb, "Swięty numer 16670," in *Gość Niedzielny* 36/2000.

62 Wojtyła, *Nauczyciel i pasterz*, p. 130.

63 Ibid., pp. 415-417.

64 Jonathan Luxmoore and Jolanta Babiuch, *The Vatican and the Red Flag: The Struggle for the Soul of Eastern Europe* (New York: Geoffrey Chapman, 1999), p. 147.

65 John Paul II, Homily at the Former Concentration Camp, Auschwitz-Birkenau, June 7, 1979.

66 Gajczak, *Wadowice: miasto papieskie*, p. 93.

67 *Kalendarium*, p. 74.

68 PBS *Frontline* program, "John Paul II: The Millennial Pope," PBS Online and WGBH/Frontline, 1999.

69 ZENIT News Agency, *Daily Dispatch*, March 23, 2000.

70 Darcy O'Brien, *The Hidden Pope:The Untold Story of a Lifelong Friendship That Is Changing the Relationship between Catholics and Jews* (New York: Daybreak Books, 1998), p. 272.

[71] PBS *Frontline* program, "John Paul II: The Millennial Pope," PBS Online and WGBH/Frontline, 1999.

[72] Antoni Pospieszalski, *O religii bez namaszczenia* (Kraków: Zakład Wydawniczy "NOMOS," 1997), p. 150.

[73] The Main Commission for the Investigation of Crimes Against the Polish Nation. The Institute of National Memory and the Polish Society for the Righteous Among the Nations, Those Who Helped: Polish Rescuers of Jews During the Holocaust, Part II (Warsaw: 1996), pp. 48-132, as quoted in Richard C. Lukas, *The Forgotten Holocaust: The Poles under German Occupation 1939-1944* (New York: Hippocrene Books, 1997), pp. 310-337.

[74] Gisela Bock, "Equality and Difference in National Socialist Racism," in *Beyond Citizenship: Equality & Difference*, Gisela Bock and Susan James, eds. (London and New York: Routledge, 1992), p. 96.

[75] While women play an important role in nearly all nationalistic and totalitarian ideologies, surprisingly, Hitler and other Nazi leaders did not take the opportunity to fully mobilize German women for the war effort. They refused to send German women into combat even when there were not enough German men to fight the advancing Russian and Western armies. Unlike the Americans and the Russians, the Nazis did not make a special effort to employ German women in the war industries. Millions of forced laborers from Poland and other countries were brought to Germany so that German women could stay at home.

[76] Jürgen Dorbritz and Jochen Fleischhacker, "The Former German Democratic Republic" in *From Abortion to Contraception: A Resource to Public Policies and Reproductive Behavior in Central and Eastern Europe from 1917 to the Present*, edited by Henry P. David (Westport, Connecticut and London: Greenwood Press: 1999), p. 134.

[77] Michael Berenbaum, *The World Must Know* (Boston: Little, Brown and Company, 1993), p. 65.

[78] Gisela Bock, "Racism and Sexism in Nazi Germany:

Motherhood, Compulsory Sterilization, and the State" in *Different Voices: Women and the Holocaust* (New York: Paragon House, 1993), p. 172.

[79] Nikolaus Wachsmann, "Annihilation through Labor: The Killing of State Prisoners in the Third Reich," in *The Journal of Modern History*, Volume 71, Number 3, September 1999, p. 625.

[80] David Bonetti, "Revisiting a Scientific Horror Story in Art," *San Francisco Chronicle*, July 27, 2001.

[81] Lukas, *Forgotten Holocaust: The Poles under German Occupation 1939-1944*, p. 22.

[82] Anika Rahman, Laura Katzive and Stanley K. Henshaw, "A Global Review of Laws on Induced Abortion, 1985-1997" in *International Family Planning Perspectives*, Volume 24, No. 2, June 1998.

[83] Vatican Information Service, Eighth Year N. 180, October 27, 1998.

[84] Daniel Johan Goldhagen, "What Would Jesus Have Done?," *The New Republic*, January 21, 2002.

[85] Gisella Perl, "A Doctor in Auschwitz" in *Different Voices: Women and the Holocaust* (New York: Paragon House, 1993), pp. 113-114.

[86] Karolina Lackorońska, *Michelangelo in Ravensbrück* (Cambridge: Da Capo Press, 2006), pp. 231-232.

[87] Helm, *A Life in Secrets:*, p. 326.

[88] Dougals Martin, "A Nazi Past, a Queens Home Life, an Overlooked Death," *The New York Times*, December 2, 2005.

[89] Lackorońska, *Michelangelo in Ravensbrück*, p. 269 and 329.

[90] "End of an Era," *The Warsaw Voice*, No. 23, August 2002.

[91] John Paul II, *Jan Paweł II do Kościoła w Polsce: 20 lat papieskiego nauczania*, selected and edited by Fr. Zdzisław Wietrzak SJ (Kraków: Wydawnictwo WAM, 1998), p. 175.

[92] For accounts of the treatment of women in Soviet prisons and camps during World War II see *The Dark Side of the Moon*, pp. 86-87.

[93] Alina Gryglowska's memoirs can be found in the KARTA

Foundation Archive: "Telling the Story of Dissent." See http://microformguides.gale.com/Data/Download/9056000C.rtf

[94] Alina Gryglowska, "Wspomnienia spotkań z Ojcem Świętym Janem Pawłem II" in *Zapis drogi*, p. 79.

[95] Jerzy Zapadko Mirski, "Zapiski powstańcze," *Zwoje* (*The Scrolls*), 7 (11), 1998.

[96] Tadeusz Bór Komorowski, *The Secret Army* (Nashville: The Battery Press, 1984), pp. 59-60.

[97] Tadeusz Bór Komorowski, p. 252.

[98] Gisella Perl, p. 114.

[99] http://www.phenomenology.org/index.html.

[100] Weigel, *Witness to Hope*, pp. 174-175.

[101] Karol Wojtyła, *The Acting Person*, translated by Andrzej Potocki (Boston: D. Reidel Publishing Company, 1979) p. ix.

[102] Bernstein and Politi, *His Holiness*, pp. 129-134.

[103] Anna-Teresa Tymieniecka, *Phenomenology and Science* (New York: The Noonday Press, 1962), p. 64.

[104] Marek Lasota, *Donos na Wojtyłę*, p. 83.

[105] Maliński, *Wezwano mnie z dalekiego kraju*, pp. 231-233.

[106] Quoted by Kenneth A. Briggs in *Holy Siege: The Year That Shook Catholic America* (San Francisco: HarperSanFrancisco, 1992), p. 474.

[107] Author's interview with Dr. Tymieniecka, May 27, 2007.

[108] Kwitny, p. 332.

[109] Kwitny, pp. 341-342. Pope John Paul II's personal secretary, Cardinal Dziwisz, confirmed in his book *Świadectwo* that this was indeed the pope's assessment. According to Dziwisz, John Paul II knew that the Soviet Union would eventually fall, but he did not expect that it would happen soon.

[110] Bernstein and Politi, pp. 142-145.

[111] Author's interview with Dr. Tymieniecka, May 27, 2007.

[112] 3WCAX-TV News, "Local Couple Friends with Pope," Hanover, New Hampshire, April 2, 2005. See:

http://www.wcax.com/Global/story.asp?S=3159580

[113] Kwitny, p. 342.

[114] Vatican Information Service, Eighth Year - N. 170, October 12, 1998.

[115] ZENIT News Agency, *Daily Dispatch*, May 19, 2000.

[116] Edith Stein, "The Separate Vocations of Man and Woman According to nature and Grace" in *The Collected Works of Edith Stein* (ICS Publications, 1987), Volume Two "Essays on Woman."

[117] For a discussion of individualism in the feminist thought see Elizabeth Fox-Genovese's book *Feminism Without Illusions* (Chapel Hill: The University of North Carolina Press, 1991).

[118] Edith Stein, "The Significance of Woman's Intrinsic Value in National Life" in *The Collected Works of Edith Stein* (ICS Publications, 1987), Volume Two "Essays on Woman."

[119] *Pielgrzymka*, p. 102-103

[120] Ibid. p. 103.

[121] Michael G. Smith, "The Public Policy of Casey v. Planned Parenthood," Leadership U., 1997.

[122] Mother Teresa, *Life in the Spirit*. Edited by Kathryn Spink. Quoted in *Wise Women*, edited by Susan Cahill (New York: W.W. Norton & Company, 1996), pp. 192-193.

[123] Mother Teresa, "Notable and Quotable," Wall Street Journal, 2/25/94, p. A14.

[124] Kenneth A. Briggs, *Holy Siege: The Year that Shook Catholic America* (San Francisco: HarperSanFrancisco, 1992), p. 473.

[125] John Cornwell, *The Pontiff in Winter: Triumph and Conflict in the Reign of John Paul II* (New York: Doubleday, 2004), p. 130.

[126] Hillary Rodham Clinton, *Living History* (New York: Simon & Schuster, 2003), pp. 417-419.

[127] Dziwisz and Svidercoschi, *Świadectwo*, pp. 156-157.

[128] Cornwell, *The Pontiff in Winter: Triumph and Conflict in the Reign of John Paul II*, p. 70.

[129] Flynn, *John Paul II*, p. 114.

[130] Bernstein and Politi, p. 528.

131 Flynn, *John Paul II*, p. 117.

132 Ray Flynn with Robin Moore and Jim Vrabel, *John Paul II: A Personal Portrait of the Pope and the Man*, p. 117.

133 Ibid.

134 Bernstein and Politi, p. 529.

135 *The New Republic*, "Pat Robertson v. America, Round II," January 21, 2002.

136 James C. Dobson, "Why Boys Are So Different," FocusonYourChild.com. *Focus on the Family*, 2001.

137 ZENIT News Agency, "Terrorism Profanes Name of God, John Paul II Says," *Daily Dispatch*, September 24, 2001.

138 Marc Champion, "In Book, Thatcher Urges UK To Consider EU Withdrawal," *The Wall Street Journal Europe*, March 19, 2002.

139 Karol Wojtyła, "Wychowanie do prawdy i wolności," in *Człowiek drogą Kościoła* (Warszawa: Fundacja Jana Pawła II, 1992), p. 79.

140 John Paul II, *Letter to Families* #14.

141 John Paul II, edited by Cardinal Achille Silvestrini, *A Pilgrim Pope: Messages for the World*, p. 168.

142 Tadeusz Styczeń and Edward Balawajder, *Jedynie prawda wyzwala: rozmowy o Janie Pawle II*, (Rome: Polski Instytut Kultury Chrześcijańskiej, 1987), p. 38.

143 John Paul II, *Letter to Families* #14.

144 For English text of *Slavorum apostoli* see: http://www.vatican.va/edocs/ENG0220/_INDEX.HTM.

145 Alexander Solzhenitsyn's Commencement Address to the Harvard University Class of 1978, June 8, 1978. For the full text see: http://www.columbia.edu/cu/augustine/arch/solzhenitsyn/harvard1978.html.

146 ZENIT News Agency, *Daily Dispatch*, July 12, 2000.

147 Helmut Juroś, ed., *Europa i Kościół* (Warszawa: Fundacja Akademii Teologii Katolickiej 1997), pp. 8-9.

148 ZENIT News Agency, "Pope Warns Poland to Guard its National Identity," *Daily Dispatch*, December 3, 2001.

[149] Vatican Information Service, Twelfth Year – N. 38, "John Paul II: Europe Must Conserve Its Christian Heritage," February 25, 2002.

[150] Jan Nowak-Jeziorański, *Polska wczoraj, dziś i jutro* (Warszawa: Czytelnik, 1999), pp. 262-263.

[151] ZENIT News Agency, *Daily Dispatch*, July 12, 2000.

[152] Radio Maryja, "Potrzeba narodowej dyskusji, a nie propagandy!," November 30, 2001.

[153] POLITIKAonet.pl, December 2001.

[154] Rafał A. Ziemkiewicz, "Ucieczka do Europy," *Wprost*, November 25, 2001.

[155] See comments by Artur Zawisza in "Notes for the Film *The Polish Cross*," Bohdan W. Oppenheim, ed. (Los Angeles: Marymont Institute, 1993), pp. 141-143.

[156] *Wprost*, "Antyeuropejski katalog Antoniego Maciarewicza," November 25, 2001.

[157] Radio Maryja, October 27, 2000.

[158] Radio Maryja, December 9, 2000. For more information about Lillian Hellman and her alleged support of the Moscow Trials in which Stalin had purged the Soviet Communist Party of members who were then liquidated see: http://en.wikipedia.org/wiki/Lillian_Hellman. Lamont, Corliss, Hellman, Lillian, et al., "An Open Letter to American Liberals," *Soviet Russia Today*, March 1937.

[159] Radio Maryja, February 11, 1997.

[160] John Paul II, edited by Cardinal Achille Silvestrini, *A Pilgrim Pope: Messages for the World*, p. 169.

[161] John Paul II, "Message for the Celebration of the World Day of Peace," January 1, 2000.

[162] Ibid.

[163] Andrzej Pelczar and Władysław Stróżewski, eds., *Servo Veritatis II* (Kraków: UNIVERSITAS, 1996), p.60.

[164] Ibid. p. 61.

[165] Bohdan W. Oppenheim, Logs for the film *The Polish Cross* (Los

Angeles: Marymount Institute, 1993), pp. 178-181.

[166] John Paul II, *Jan Paweł II do Kościoła w Polsce*, p. 79.

[167] Wojtyła, *Nauczyciel i pasterz*, pp. 674-675.

[168] Libor Stloukal, "Understanding the 'Abortion Culture' in Central and Eastern Europe" in *From Abortion to Contraception: A Resource to Public Policies and Reproductive Behavior in Central and Eastern Europe from 1917 to the Present*, Henry P. David, ed. (Westport, Connecticut: Greenwood Press, 1999), p. 29.

[169] Henry P. David, "Overview" in *From Abortion to Contraception: A Resource to Public Policies and Reproductive Behavior in Central and Eastern Europe from 1917 to the Present*, Henry P. David, ed. (Westport, Connecticut: Greenwood Press, 1999), p. 8.

[170] Stloukal, p. 34.

[171] Ibid., p. 37

[172] Ibid., pp. 97 and 127.

[173] The Alan Guttmacher Institute citing Henshaw SK, "Unintended Pregnancy in the United States," *Family Planning Perspectives*, 1998, 30(1):24-29 and 46.

[174] Susan A. Cohen, "New Data on Abortion Incidence, Safety Illuminate Key Aspects of Worldwide Abortion Debate," *Guttmacher Policy Review*, Fall 2007, Volume 10, Number 4.

[175] Wojtyła, *Nauczyciel i pasterz*, p. 341.

[176] John Paul II, *Jan Paweł II do Kościoła w Polsce: 20 lat papieskiego nauczania*, pp. 81-83.

[177] Domosławski, p. 163.

[178] ZENIT News Agency, "'Question Abortion' Campaign in U.S. Colleges," *Daily Dispatch*, August 24, 2000.

[179] *The New Internationalist*, January 1996.

[180] ZENIT News Agency, "NCCB Statement on Catholics for a Free Choice," *Daily Dispatch*, May 12, 2000.

[181] See http://www.blackgenocide.org for more material in support of the "Black Genocide" argument. The lowest abortion rates are in the most developed countries of Western Europe. In most of the developing countries and in many East European

countries, women who have had at least one birth account for the
majority of abortions. By contrast, unmarried women are more
than four times as likely as married women to obtain an abortion
in the United States. In some countries, in which the majority of
population is Muslim, Muslim women have lower abortion rates
than Christian women, but abortion rates for Turkish-born
women living in the Netherlands were much higher than for
native Dutch women. See The Alan Guttmacher Institute,
"Worldwide, Women of All Backgrounds Choose Abortion," New
York and Washington, 1999. Another study of the Alan
Guttmacher Institute, which promotes lower population growth,
confirms that overall abortion rates, including both legal and
illegal, in developed and developing countries are similar, even
though the developing countries have far more restrictions against
legal abortions. See Stanley K. Henshaw, Susheela Singh and
Taylor Hass, "The Incidence of Abortion Worldwide,"
International Family Planning Perspectives, Volume 25, Supplement,
January 1999.

[182] Loretta J. Ross, "African American Women and Abortion:
1800-1970," in *Theorizing Black Feminisms: the Visionary Pragmatism
of Black Women*, Stanlie M. James and Abena P.A. Busia, eds. (New
York: Routledge, 1993), pp. 141-159.

[183] Published in *The New York Times* and reprinted in *The
International Herald Tribune*, January 23, 1998.

[184] ZENIT News Agency, "Bush's Phone Call to Pro-lifers at
Washington Rally," January 23, 2002.

[185] Carl Brown, "Our Nuremberg?" in *USA Today*, July 31, 2000.

[186] Zbigniew Nosowski's 1992 interview with Rabbi Byron L.
Sherwin, Vice-President of the Spertus College of Judaica in
Chicago, *Więź*, Special Issue, "Under One Heaven: Poles and
Jews,"1998, p. 164.

[187] Jarosław Gowin, *Kościół po komuniźmie* (Kraków: Instytut
Wydawniczy Znak, 1995), p. 136.

[188] ZENIT News Agency, *Daily Dispatch*, June 1, 2000.

[189] Gowin, p. 136.

[190] ZENIT News Agency, *Daily Dispatch*, August 24, 2000.

[191] Alissa J. Rubin, "Support for Abortion Rights Eases," *The Los Angeles Times* Service as reprinted in *The International Herald Tribune*, June 19, 2000.

[192] Gary Langer, "Poll: Support for Civil Unions Rises, Yet Sharp Divisions Remain," ABC News Polling Unit, November 8, 2007. http://abcnews.go.com/PollingUnit/story?id=3834625&page=1. "Opinie na temat Aborcji," CBOS, Warszawa, October 2007. http://www.cbos.pl/SPISKOM.POL/2007/K_152_07.PDF; http://www.cbos.pl/SPISKOM.POL/2007/K_051_07.PDF.

[193] Hillary Rodham Clinton's remarks to NARAL, Washington, D.C., January 22, 1999.

[194] LaTonya Taylor, The Church of O," *Christianity Today*, April 1, 2002.

NOTES FOR CHAPTER FIVE – CONTRACEPTION VERSUS LOVE – AGENDA FOR POLISH WOMEN 1947-1978

[1] *Kalendarium*, p. 226.

[2] *Obecność: Karola Wojtyły w Katolickim Uniwersytecie Lubelskim*, p. 152.

[3] Maliński, *Wezwano mnie z dalekiego kraju*, p. 143.

[4] Wojtyła, *Nauczyciel i pasterz*, p. 527.

[5] Maliński, *Przewodnik po życiu*, p. 186.

[6] Maliński, *Przewodnik po życiu*, p. 120.

[7] Lukas, *The Forgotten Holocaust: The Poles under German Occupation 1939-1944*, p. 27.

[8] Ibid., p. 4.

[9] Wojtyła, *Nauczyciel i pasterz*, p. 239.

[10] Ibid.

[11] *Duszpasterska troska*, p. 108

[12] Ibid. p. 161.

[13] *Kalendarium*, p. 810.

[14] Wojtyła, *Nauczyciel i pasterz*, p. 359.

[15] Ibid., p. 361.

[16] Ibid., 392.

[17] Ibid., p. 352.

[18] Duspasterska troska , p. 164.

[19] Wojtyła, *Nauczyciel i pasterz*, p. 365.

[20] Duszpasterska troska, p. 112.

[21] *Kalendarium*, p. 311.

[22] Wojtyła, *Nauczyciel i pasterz*, p. 239.

[23] Ibid., p. 721.

[24] *Duszpasterska troska*, p. 108.

[25] Ibid. p. 109.

[26] *Kalendarium*, p. 470.

[27] Ibid., p. 470

[28] Ibid., p.730.

[29] Interview with Neal Ascherson for PBS program *Frontline*, PBS Online and WGBH/Frontline, 1999.

[30] Bernstein and Politi, p. 135.

[31] Author's interview with Dr. Tymieniecka, May 27, 2007.

[32] Wojtyła, *Love and Responsibility*, p. 27.

[33] Ibid., p. 35.

[34] Ibid., p. 39.

[35] Ibid., p. 41.

[36] Ibid., p. 42.

[37] Ibid., p. 56.

[38] Interview with Eamon Duffy for PBS *Frontline* program, PBS Online and WGBH/Frontline, 1999.

[39] Wojtyła, *Love and Responsibility*, p. 273.

[40] *Karol Wojtyła jako bisku* p. 233.

[41] Ibid., p. 83.

[42] Ibid., p. 97.

[43] Ibid., p. 97.

[44] Ibid., p. 99.

[45] Ibid.

[46] Tad Szulc, *Pope John Paul II: The Biography* (New York: Scribner, 1995), p. 255. For the text of *Humanae vitae* encyclical see: http://www.vatican.va/holy_father/paul_vi/encyclicals/docum ents/hf_p-vi_enc_25071968_humanae-vitae_en.html.

[47] Robert J. McClory, "Patty Crowley, giant of Catholic laity, dies at 92," *The National Catholic Reporter*, December 9, 2005.

[48] Mieczysław Maliński, *Zyciorys Karola Wojtyły* (Warszawa/Struga—Kraków: Wydawnictwo Michalineum, 1987), p. 154.

[49] Bujak, Rożek, *Wojtyła*, p. 165.

[50] Jonathan Kwitny, *Man of the Century*, p. 220.

[51] Weigel, *Witness to Hope*, p. 209.

[52] Ibid.

[53] Robert J. McClory, "Patty Crowley, giant of Catholic laity, dies at 92," *The National Catholic Reporter*, December 9, 2005

[54] *Kalendarium*, p. 826.

[55] Ibid., p. 444.

[56] Ibid., p. 472.

[57] Ibid., p. 478.

[58] Ibid.

[59] Maliński, *Zyciorys Karola Wojtyły*, p. 154.

[60] Peter K. Raina, Collector. Photocopy of secret Polish government document, dated September 22, 1968, in the Hoover Institute Archives.

[61] Andrzej Micewski, *Cardinal Wyszyński: A Biography* (San Diego: Harcourt Brace Jovanovich, Publishers, 1984), p. 293.

[62] Wojtyła, *Nauczyciel i pasterz*, p. 208.

[63] Wojtyła, *Nauczyciel i pasterz*, p. 211.

[64] Ibid.

[65] *Kalendarium*, p. 325.

[66] Ibid., p. 447.

[67] *Duszpasterska troska*, p. 38.

[68] Ibid., p. 307.

[69] Ibid., p. 154.

70 Ibid., p. 208.

71 Micewski, *Cardinal Wyszyński: A Biography*, p. 294.

72 *Kalendarium*, p. 648.

73 Ibid., p. 676.

74 Ibid., p. 665.

75 Ibid., p. 666.

76 Anna Titkow "Poland" in *From Abortion to Contraception: A Resource to Public Policies and Reproductive Behavior in Central and Eastern Europe from 1917 to the Present*, Henry P. David, ed. (Westport, Connecticut, 1999), p. 180.

77 Ibid., p. 179.

78 Ibid., p. 189.

79 *Duszpasterska troska*, p. 33.

80 Władysław Gasidło, "The Church in Kraków in the Service of the Family During the Ministry of Archbishop Karol Wojtyła" in *Karol Wojtyła jako Biskup Krakowski* (Kraków: Wydawnictwo Sw. Stanisława BM Archidiecezji Krakowskiej, 1988), p. 552.

81 *Kalendarium*, p. 181.

82 Ibid.

83 Maliński, *Wezwano mnie z dalekiego kraju*, pp.248-249.

84 Ibid., p. 248

85 *Kalendarium*, p. 560-561.

86 Ibid., p. 625.

87 Ibid., p. 151.

88 *Kalendarium*, p. 151.

89 Dean E. Murphy in *The Los Angeles Times*, February 19, 1997.

90 The International Planned Parenthood Federation, "Abortion in Poland: Women Made to Suffer in God's Backyard," March/April 1997 (1997/2); http://www.oneworld.org.

91 Anna Titkow, "Poland," p. 189.

92 Wanda Nowicka, "One Step Forward, Two Steps Back: Wanda Nowicka on Abortion Rights in Poland," http://www.iwhc.org/poland.html.

93 Jane Leftwich Curry, ed., *The Black Book of Polish Censorship*

(New York: Vintage Books, 1984), p. 284.

94 Ibid., p. 286.

95 Ibid., p. 305.

96 Ibid., p. 314.

97 Maliński, *Przewodnik po życiu Karola Wojtyły*, p. 215-216.

98 *Duszpasterska troska*, p. 109.

99 Ibid., p. 109.

100 Ibid., p. 114.

101 Anna Titkow, "Poland" in *From Abortion to Contraception: A Resource to Public Policies and Reproductive Behavior in Central and Eastern Europe from 1917 to the Present*, Henry P. David, ed. (Westport, Connecticut: Greenwood Press, 1999), p. 194.

102 Marc Kaufman, "Pregnancy Centers Found to Give False Information on Abortion," *The Washington Post*, July 18, 2006.

103 John Paul II, Homily in Wadowice, June 16, 1999.

104 *Duszpasterska troska*, p. 112.

105 Wojtyła, *Nauczyciel i pasterz*, p. 723.

106 *Duszpasterska troska*, p. 113.

107 *Kalendarium*, p. 151.

108 Danuta Rybicka, "Całe bogactwo," *Zapis drogi*, p. 218.

109 Sister M. Klawera Wolska, "Pasterz i ojciec Zródlarzy," in *Przez Podgórze na Watykan* (Kraków: Wydawnictwo "CZUWAJMY", 1999), pp. 210-211.

110 Maria Bucholc, " Nade wszystko ucieczka w kazdej potrzebie..." in *Zapis Drogi*, p. 47.

111 *Kalendarium*, p. 89.

112 Domosławski, p.232.

113 Andrew Greeley, "Religion After 2000," posted in http://www.agreeley.com.

1144 Centrum Badania Opinii Społecznej (CBOS), "Czy Polacy są społecznikami?", Warszawa, February, 2004.

NOTES FOR CHAPTER SIX – WOMEN-PRIESTS

1 http://www.vatican.va/holy_father/john_paul_ii/apost_exhor-

tations/documents/hf_jp-ii_exh_19811122_familiaris-consortio_en.html.

[2] John Paul II, *Familiaris consortio* ("On the Family"), #22-23.

[3] http://www.vatican.va/holy_father/john_paul_ii/apost_letters/documents/hf_jp-ii_apl_15081988_mulieris-dignitatem_en.html.

[4] John Paul II, *Mulieris dignitatem*, #1

[5] Ibid., #1.

[6] Ibid., #1.

[7] Ibid., #10.

[8] Ibid., #10.

[9] Ibid., #18.

[10] John Paul II, *Angelus*, July 16, 1995.

[11] Ibid.

[12] John Paul II; *Mulieris dignitatem*.

[13] Ibid., #25.

[14] Ibid., #26.

[15] Janusz Poniewierski, *Pontyfikat* (Kraków: Spoleczny Instytut Wydawniczy ZNAK, 1999), p. 186.

[16] Ibid.

[17] Dziwisz and Svidercoschi, *Świadectwo*, p. 149.

[18] Jarosław Govin, *Kosciól po komunizmie* (Kraków: Społeczny Instytut Wydawniczy Znak, Fundacja im. Stefana Batorego, Warszawa), p. 260.

[19] Dziwisz and Svidercoschi, *Świadectwo*, p. 151.

[20] Carl Bernstein and Marco Politi, *His Holiness: John Paul II and the Hidden History of Our Time*, New York: Doubleday, 1996), p. 183.

[21] *Kalendarium*, p. 377.

[22] Barbara J. MacHaffie, *Her Story: Women in Christian Tradition* (Philadelphia: Fortress Press, 1986), p. 140. Also see Paul Jewett, *The Ordination of Women* (Grand Rapids: Wm. B. Eerdmans, 1980).

[23] http://www.vatican.va/holy_father/john_paul_ii/apost_letters/documents/hf_jp-ii_apl_22051994_ordinatio-sacerdotalis

_en.html.

[24] John Paul II, "Apostolic Letter on Reserving Priestly Ordination to Men Alone," (*Ordinatio sacerdotalis*).

[25] Peter Hebblethwaite, *The Next Pope* (San Francisco: HarperSanFrancisco, 1995), p. 164.

[26] Peter Hebblethwaite, *The Year of Three Popes* (Cleveland and New York: William Collins, Inc., 1978), p. 19.

[27] John Paul II, *Ordinatio sacerdotalis*.

[28] The Pontifical Biblical Commission, 1976.

[29] John Paul II, *Ordinatio sacerdotalis*.

[30] Ibid.

[31] John Paul II, *Veritatis splendor*, #80. For an in-depth discussion of the changing nature of the Catholic Church's moral teachings see: John T. Noonan, Jr., *A Church Than Can and Cannot Change: The Development of Catholic Moral Teaching* (Notre Dame: University of Notre Dame Press, 2005).

[32] John Paul II, *Ordinatio sacerdotalis*.

[33] Ibid.

[34] Ibid.

[35] *Catechism of the Catholic Church* (New York: Doubleday, 1995), p. 440.

[36] http://www.vatican.va/holy_father/john_paul_ii/apost_constitutions/documents/hf_jp-ii_apc_25011983_sacrae-disciplinae-leges_en.html.

[37] Ibid., p. 439. Also see: http://www.vatican.va/archive/ENG1104/_INDEX.HTM.

[38] Vatican Information Service, "Notification on the Diaconal Ordination of Women," Eleventh Year – N. 155, September 17, 2001.

[39] John Paul II, *Ordinatio sacerdotalis*.

[40] Ibid.

[41] John Cornwell, *The Pontiff in Winter: Triumph and Conflict in the Reign of John Paul II* (New York: Doubleday, 2004), p. 133.

[42] Andrew Greeley and Michael Hout, "American Catholics and

the Next Pope: A Survey Report," ARCC Temple University web site, http://astro.temple.edu/~arcc/greels.htm.

[43] Michael Novak, *First Things*, April 1993, p. 32.

[44] Richard P. McBrien, *Report on the Church: Catholicism After Vatican II* (San Francisco: HarperSanFrancisco, 1992), p. 135.

[45] Andre Frossard, *"Be Not Afraid!"* translated by J.R. Foster (New York: St. Martin Press, 1984), pp. 121-122.

[46] Peter Stanford, *The She-Pope: A Quest for the Truth Behind the Mystery of Pope Joan* (London: Arrow Books Limited, 1998), p. 11.

[47] Ibid., p. 19.

[48] Hugues Delautre and Jaqueline Greal, *Vezelay: Basilica Sainte Madeleine* (Villeurbanne: Lescuyer Societe Nouvelle, 1999), p. 22.

[49] John Paul II, "Address to the German Bishops on the Occasion of Their *Ad Limina* Visit," November 20, 1999.

[50] *The Times*, London, August 25, 1997. Also see: http://www.pax-romana.org/templDB.cfm?pgurl=icmica/tissa.html.

[51] International Movement *We Are Church* Press Release concerning the lifting of Fr. Tissa Balasuriya's excommunication.

[52] Bernstein and Politi, p. 508.

[53] Kwitny, p. 220.

[54] Declaration of the Congregation for the Doctrine of the Faith *On Bishops and Priests Ordained Secretly in the Czech Republic*, February 11, 2000.

[55] Andrea Johnson, *New Women, New Church*, Winter 1997-98.

[56] For the text of the encyclical see: http://www.vatican.va/holy_father/pius_x/encyclicals/documents/hf_p-x_enc_19070908_pascendi-dominici-gregis_en.html.

[57] For more information about the Mariavite Church see: http://www.mariawita.pl/.

[58] Pius X, Encyclical *Tribus Circiter* on the Mariavites or Mystic Priests of Poland, April 5, 1906.

[59] Główny Urząd Statystyczny, *Rocznik Statystyczny Rzeczypospolitej Polskiej: 1998* (Warszawa: Zakład Wydawnictw Statystycznych, 1998), p. 109.

60 Władysław Abraham, "Stosunki wyznaniowe" in *Dziesięciolecie Polski Odrodzonej* (Kraków, 1930), p. 363.

61 Joseph W. Wueczerzak, "History and Origin of the Polish National Catholic Church," www.pncc.org.

62 Główny Urząd Statystyczny, "Niektóre wyznania religijne w Polsce w 1998 r.," www.stat.gov.pl.

63 John Paul II, Papal Letter of John Paul II to the Women of the World, July 10, 1995.

64 http://www.vatican.va/holy_father/john_paul_ii/apost_letters/documents/hf_jp-ii_apl_10111994_tertio-millennio-adveniente_en.html.

65 Hillary Rodham Clinton, *Living History* (New York: Simon & Schuster, 2003), p. 299.

66 Ibid., pp. 305-306.

67 Carl Bernstein, *A Woman in Charge* (New York: Alfred A. Knopf, 2007), p. 297.

68 Bernstein and Politi, *His Holiness - John Paul II and the Hidden History of Our Time*, p. 514.

69 Ibid.

70 http://www.un.org/News/dh/hlpanel/sadik-bio.htm.

71 Bernstein and Politi, p. 521.

72 Ibid., p. 523.

73 http://www.hli.org/president_hli.html.

74 ZENIT News Agency, *Daily Dispatch*, February 20, 2001.

75 Barbara Crossette, "Birthrates Declining in Developing Countries," *The New York Times* report in *The International Herald Tribune*, March 11, 2002.

76 Sharon Waxman, "Arab TV's Strong Signal," *The Washington Post*, December 4, 2001.

77 http://www.vatican.va/holy_father/john_paul_ii/apost_letters/documents/hf_jp-ii_apl_10111994_tertio-millennio-adveniente_en.html.

78 International Theological Commission, "Memory and Reconciliation: the Church and the Faults of the Past, December

1999.

[79] ZENIT News Agency, *Daily Dispatch*, March 12, 2000.

[80] Ibid.

[81] ZENIT News Agency, *Daily Dispatch*, March 13, 2000.

[82] The Georgetown University's Center for Applied Research in the Apostolate, "Priest Shortage Statistics in the U. S. and Worldwide," FutureChurch.org, 2007.

[83] John J. Fialka, *Sisters* (New York: St. Martin's Press, 2003), pp. 15 and 331,

[84] Interview with James Carroll for PBS *Frontline* program, PBS Online and WGBH/Frontline, 1999.

[85] Elizabeth Cady Stanton, "Address Delivered At Seneca Falls," July 19, 1848 quoted in *The Elizabeth Cady Stanton – Susan B. Anthony Reader: Correspondence, Writings, Speeches*, Ellen Carol DuBois, ed. (Boston: Northeastern University Press, 1997), p. 31.

[86] Karol Wojtyła, *Człowiek drogą Kosciola*, Fundacja Jana Pawla II, Ośrodek Dokumentacji Pontyfikatu, 1992, pp. 96-97.

[87] Ibid. pp.96-98.

[88] Karol Wojtyła, „O dialogu wewnątrz i zewnątrz Kościoła" in *Człowiek drogą Kościoła*, p. 90.

[89] John Paul II, "Address to the German Bishops on the Occasion of Their *Ad Limina* Visit, November 20, 1999.

[90] Ingrid H. Shafer, "Reading the Signs of the Times: Reflections on the Global Church in October and November 1995," Ingrid Shafer's Columns and Commentaries, http://astro.temple.edu.

[91] Vatican Information Service, Ninth Year - N. 37, February 25, 1999.

[92] Vatican Information Service, Ninth Year - N. 29, February 15, 1999.

[93] John Paul II, "Address to the German Bishops on the Occasion of Their *Ad Limina* Visit," November 20, 1999.

[94] ZENIT News Agency, *Daily Dispatch*, January 25, 2000.

[95] ZENIT News Agency, "Only an Ordained Priest Can Be a Pastor, Pope Insists," *Daily Dispatch*, November 23, 2001.

96 Ibid.

97 Ibid.

98 Ibid.

99 John Paul II, General Audience, July 10, 1996.

100 John Paul II, General Audience, August 28, 1996.

101 John Paul II, General Audience, August 21, 1996.

102 Uta Ranke-Heinemann, *Eunuchs for the Kingdom of Heaven: Women, Sexuality and the Catholic Church* (New York: Penguin Books, 1991), pp. 344-347.

103 Ciechomska, p. 239.

104 Tadeusz Styczeń and Edward Balawajder, *Jedynie prawda wyzwala: rozmowy of Janie Pawle II* (Rome: Polski Instytut Kultury Chrzescijanskiej, 1987), p. 86.

105 See interview with Jacek Woźniakowski in "Logs for the Film *The Polish Cross*," Bohdan W. Oppenheim, ed. (Los Angeles: Marymont Institute, 1993), p. 182.

106 Adam Michnik, *Letters from Freedom* (Berkley and Los Angeles: University of California Press, 1998), p. 109.

107 ZENIT News Agency, *Daily Dispatch*, May 22, 2000.

108 ZENIT News Agency, *Daily Dispatch*, May 19, 2000.

109 ZENIT News Agency, *Daily Dispatch*, May 22, 2000.

110 Mary Ann Glendon, "Feminism and the Family an Indissoluble Marriage," *Commonweal*, February 14, 1997.

111 ZENIT News Agency, *Daily Dispatch*, May 22, 2000.

112 Vatican Information Service, Eight Year - N. 178, October 23, 1998.

113 Ibid.

114 ZENIT News Agency, *Daily Dispatch*, June 1, 2000.

115 Anna Titkow "Poland" in *From Abortion to Contraception: A Resource to Public Policies and Reproductive Behavior in Central and Eastern Europe from 1917 to the Present*, Henry P. David, ed. (Westport, Connecticut, 1999), p. 183.

116 40 percent were opposed to legal abortions. Of the 50 percent who approved of legal abortions, however, less than half said that

the right should extend to abortions on demand for any reason. See: Michał Wenzel, "Opinie na temat aborcji," CBOS, Warsaw, October, 2007. Another survey showed that Polish women accept Catholic moral teachings in greater numbers than Polish men. See: Rafał Boguszewski, "Polacy wobec różnych religii i zasad moralnych katolicyzmu," CBOS, Warsaw, June 2006.

[117] Zródło, "W obronie godności kobiety," July 16, 1995.

[118] Trybuna, February 4, 1998.

[119] The Warsaw Voice – News No. 30 (561), "Kapera's White Power," July 25, 1999.

[120] Bohdan W. Oppenheim, Logs for the film The Polish Cross (Los Angeles: Marymont Institute, 1993), p. 144.

[121] Ibid. p. 210.

[122] Jarosław Gowin, Kościół po komunizmie (Kraków: Społeczny Instytut Wydawniczy Znak, 1995), pp. 127-128.

[123] Gabriela Baczynska, "Catholic Poland mulls tighter abortion laws," Reuters, December 13, 2007.

[124] Brian Lavery, "Irish Narrowly Reject A Tighter Abortion Law," The New York Times in The International Herald Tribune, March 8, 2002.

[125] Ibid., p. 51.

[126] Ibid.

[127] Maria Janion, Kobiety i duch inności (Warszawa: Wydawnictwo Sic!, 1996), p. 325.

[128] Główny Urząd Statystyczny, Rocznik Statystyczny Rzeczypospolitej Polskiej: 1998 (Warszawa: Zakład Wydawnictw Statystycznych, 1998), p. 53.

[129] Ibid.

[130] Ibid., p. 51.

[131] Ibid., p. 54.

[132] Ibid., p. 56.

[133] Wprost, January 14, 1996, p.43.

[134] Monika Kazimierczyk, Wprost, March 8, 1998, p. 57.

[135] Ciechomska, p. 2.

[136] Václav Havel, *Open Letters: Selected Prose 1965-1990*, Paul Wilson, ed. (London and Boston: Farber and Farber, 1991), p. 308.

[137] Václav Havel, *Letters to Olga: June 1979-September 1982* (New York: Henry Holt and Company, 1989), p. 46.

[138] Martha C. Nussbaum, *Women and Human Development: The Capabilities Approach* (Cambridge: Cambridge University Press, 2000), pp. 247-248.

[139] Quoted by Cass R. Sustein, "Rights of Passage" in *The New Republic*, February 25, 2002, p. 38.

[140] Kwitny, p. 244.

[141] Janusz Poniewierski, *Pontyfikat* (Kraków: Społeczny Instytut Wydawniczy ZNAK, 1999), p. 147.

[142] John Paul II, edited by Cardinal Achille Silvestrini, *A Pilgrim Pope: Messages for the World* (Kansas City: The K.S. Giniger Company Inc., 1999), p. 126.

[143] Ibid., p. 127.

NOTES FOR CHAPTER SEVEN – WHAT TO EXPECT FROM THE NEW POPE

[1] Peter Hebblethwaite, *The Years of Three Popes* (Cleveland: William Collins, Inc., 1979), p. 49.

[2] Ibid.

[3] http://www.vatican.va/holy_father/john_paul_i/index.htm.

[4] Greeley, *Making of the Pope 2005*, p. 96 and p. 254.

[5] *American Catholics and the Next Pope: a Survey Report* by Andrew Greeley (The University of Chicago) and Michael Hout (The University of California, Berkley).

[6] See Dziwisz and Svidercoschi, *Świadectwo*, p. 169.

[7] Interview with Mikhail Seergeevich Gorbachev conducted by Radio Free Europe/Radio Liberty correspondent Irina Lagunina. The interview was published in RFE/RL's *Russian Political Weekly*, Volume 5, Number 14, April 8, 2005.

[8] Centrum Badania Opinii Społecznej (CBOS), "Poglady elektoratow partyjnych na temat istotnych kwestii

spoleczno-politycznych," Warszawa, May, 2003.

[9] Hans Küng, *On Being a Christian*, translated by Edward Quinn (New York: Doubleday, 1984), pp. 526-527.

[10] Hans Küng, "On the State of the Catholic Church or Why a Book Like This is Necessary" in *The Church in Anguish: Has the Vatican Betrayed Vatican II?* (New York: Harper & Row, Publishers, Inc., 1987), p. 15.

[11] Ibid., p. 7.

[12] Halina Bortnowska, *Znak*, No. 503, April 1997.

[13] John Christensen, "John Paul II: Conscience of the World," CNN.com, 1999.

[14] Sister Mary Ann Walsh, RSM, *From Pope John Paul II to Benedict XVI* (Lanham: Rowman & Littlefield Publishers, Inc., 2005), p. 120.

[15] For the full text of the Letter to the Bishops on the Collaboration of Men and Women in the Church and in the World see: http://www.vatican.va/roman_curia/congregations/cfaith/docu ments/rc_con_cfaith_doc_20040731_collaboration_en.html.

[16] Reed, *Unveiled*, pp. 6-7.

[17] John Paul II, *Talks of John Paul II* (Boston: St. Paul Editions, 1979), p. 16

[18] Reed, *Unveiled*, p. 99.

[19] Walsh, *From Pope John Paul II to Benedict XVI*, p. 2.

[20] Peggy Noonan, *John Paul the Great: Remembering a Spiritual Father* (New York: Viking, 2005), pp. 173-175.

[21] Reed, *Unveiled*, p. 91.

[22] Walsh, *From Pope John Paul II to Benedict XVI* , p. 166.

[23] Pia de Solenni, "Our Role in the Church," *The Washington Post*, April 24, 2005.

[24] Michele M. Schumacher is the editor of *Women in Christ: Toward a New Feminism* (Grand Rapids: Wm. B Erdmans Publishing Co, 2004).

[25] Ratzinger, *The Legacy of John Paul II: Images and Memories*, p. 30.

[26] For some of the quotes from Radio Maryja programs, as well as John Paul II's comments about the station, see:

http://pl.wikiquote.org/wiki/Radio_Maryja.

[27] Such a revival seems to be limited largely to radical Islam and evangelical Protestants in the United States and in the developing world. It is also happening in Russia and some of the other republics of the former Soviet Union. I have seen no evidence of any significant revival of religious faith in Western Europe, except among some of the European Muslims.

[28] John Paul II said: "Be Not Afraid! Open up, no; swing wide the gates to Christ. Open up to his saving power the confines of the State, open up economic and political systems, the vast empires of culture, civilization and development.... Be not afraid!"

NOTES FOR COMMUNIST SPIES AND SOURCES

[1] On his personal web site, http://www.Maliński.pl/, and in his latest book, Father Maliński categorically denies that he had been an agent of SB or UB (communist secret police organizations).

[2] Father Maliński's books publicized bits of information that could potentially damage John Paul II's reputation among some readers. His emphasis on Wojtyła's pacifism during WWII could have been used by the communist regime against Wojtyła as part of the regime's anti-Church and anti-German propaganda. Maliński's books also included details about Wojtyła's lack of interest in romantic relationships with women during student years, the insular network of Kraków priests and the future pope's anti-liberal attitudes on several hot-topic issues. Such information, if read in a certain way, could alienate either liberal or conservative Catholics as well as secular Leftists. Anyone who knew Wojtyła personally and was aware of his remarkable integrity would know, however, that these details could not support any wild suspicions and speculations. Father Maliński's reasons for emphasizing this information remain unclear. He was more of a religious liberal than Wojtyła and a maverick priest. As a writer, he enjoyed publicity and contacts with Western journalists. He may have been simply responding to Western

media interest in such topics. I never came across any indication that John Paul II objected to what Father Maliński was writing about him.

[3] Father Maliński's email to the author, May 24, 2007.

[4] Marek Lasota, *Donos na Wojtyłę* (Kraków: Wydawnictwo ZNAK, 2006), p. 44 and p. 106.

[5] Ibid., p. 240.

[6] Stefan Filipowicz, "'Santita, non L'ho tradita mai – Ojcze Święty, nigdy Cię nie zdradziłem'" Jedna ze stron mojego życia" in *Horyzonty Wychowania*, May 2006 (10), pp. 207-255.

[7] Lasota, *Donos na Wojtyłę*, pp. 165-170.

[8] Christopher Andrew and Vasili Mitrokhin, *The Mitrokhin Archive: the KGB in Europe and the West* (London: Penguin Books, 2000), p. 351.

[9] Weigel, *Witness to Hope*, pp. 212-213.

[10] John Paul II's letter, dated Sept. 29, 2001, published in *Tygodnik Powszechny*.

[11] Andrew and Mitrokhin, *The Mitrokhin Archive*, p. 662-663.

[12] Ibid., p. 669.

[13] Ibid., pp. 669-670.

[14] Lasota, *Donos na Wojtyłę*, pp. 322-323.

[15] Dziwisz and Svidercoschi, *Świadectwo*, p. 132.

[16] For more information about the assassination controversy and accusation of CIA disinformation see: Bernstein and Politi, pp. 305-306.

[17] Ibid., p. 293.

[18] For more information about this and other communist era crimes in Poland see: The Institute of National Remembrance - Commission of the Prosecution of Crimes against the Polish Nation (IPN) web sites: http://www.ipn.gov.pl/portal/en/ (English) and http://www.ipn.gov.pl/portal/pl/ (Polish). Also see: Grażyna Sikorska, *Jerzy Popiełuszko: A Martyr for the Truth* (London: Fount Paperbacks, 1985).

[19] Harvey Klehr, John Earl Haynes, Fridrikh Igorevich Frisov, *The*

Secret World of American Communism (New Haven and London: Yale University Press, 1995), p. 281.

[20] John Houseman, *Unfinished Business* (New York: Applause Theatre Books, 1989), p. 249.

[21] Jarosław Jędrzejczak, *58 lat sekcji polskiej Głosu Ameryki 1942-2000 Nowy Jork, Monachium, Waszyngton* (Włocławek: 2001). Unpublished manuscript.

[22] Dziwisz and Svidercoschi, *Świadectwo*, pp. 123-127.

[23] As a devout Catholic, Ratzinger's father was a bitter enemy of Nazism. In 1941, one of Ratzinger's cousins, a 14-year-old boy with Down syndrome, was killed by the Nazi regime in its campaign of eugenics.

[24] For the texts of the White Rose leaflets see: http://www.jlrweb.com/whiterose/leaflets.html.

[25] Vicky Knickerbocker, "Study Guide for Sophie Scholl: The Final Days," The Center for Holocaust and Genocide Studies, University of Minnesota.

[26] Laurel Leff, *Buried by the Times* (Cambridge: Cambridge University Press, 2005), p. 213.

[27] VOA web site, http://www.vonews.com/, posts news, information, audio and video in multiple languages. For information about saving VOA from budget cuts see: "America's disarmament in the war of ideas" on http://www.freemediaonline.org/america_disarms_in_the_war_of_ideas_112264.htm and http://www.petitiononline.com/tl1122/petition.html.

[28] Bernstein and Politi, *His Holiness*, p. 265.

[29] Ibid. p. 382.

[30] Bernstein and Politi, *His Holiness*, p. 341.

INDEX

Abortion, 9-10, 15, 20-21, 27-29,
35, 40, 42, 48, 55, 109-111,
113, 117, 120-121, 125-126,
141, 144-145, 147, 151, 159,
162-163, 168, 170-171, 175,
177-178, 184, 191, 195, 198-
199, 201, 203-205, 207, 212-
213, 238, 240, 242-244, 251-
253, 257, 259, 265-266, 268,
272-273, 275, 280, 284-285,
288, 290-291, 297-302, 307-
309, 311, 315, 321, 325-330,
332, 335-336, 338-339, 343,
346, 359-366, 368-369, 378,
380-381, 383-385, 389-424,
430, 437-438, 441-445, 448-
452, 455, 458-459, 461, 469,
474, 479, 491, 501, 506-507,
510-511, 521, 532-533, 536-
538, 542-545, 547-548, 552,
555, 567, 572, 576, 578-579,
583, 609, 616, 622, 639, 647,
651, 655-656, 661-663, 666-
667, 673-674
Abramowicz-Stachura, Zofia,
107-108, 606
African Americans, 89, 177, 188,
327, 398-400, 518
African American women, 399,
662
AfterAbortion.org, 457

Alas! A blog, 461
Albert Chmielowski
Foundation, 589-590
Albertine Brothers, 81
Albertine Sisters, 81
Albright, Madeleine, 173
AlterNet, 372
American women, 9, 13, 21, 24,
32, 129, 152, 160, 167, 240,
350, 361, 398, 399, 406, 483,
643, 662
Anarcha, 370,
Anarkismo.net, 370
Anglican Communion, The, 480
Angry Black Bitch, 461
Anti-Semitism, 28, 88-89, 197,
258, 283, 313, 318, 320, 322,
324, 352, 417, 581
Anti-street Harassment UK, 457
Applebaum, Anne, 169
Arendt, Hannah, 82-83
Ascherson, Neal, 235, 423-424,
615, 646, 664
Auschwitz, also Auschwitz-
Birkenau Nazi extermination
camp, also Oświęcim
33, 42, 143, 285, 288, 303,
309-310, 316-319, 322, 328,
331, 334-335, 338, 351, 353,
404, 423, 424, 531, 608, 654,
656

Balasuriya, Tissa, 491-492
Bardecki, Andrzej, 434, 597-598
Batka, Marian, 323
Beauvoir, Simone de, 9, 149-150, 155-159, 162, 176, 189, 353, 639, 641, 643
Beer, Regina, 88-89
Benedict XVI, Pope, also see Ratzinger, Joseph, 22, 31, 44, 52, 71, 136, 165, 171, 173-174, 475, 490, 513, 523, 535, 541, 557, 566, 570-571, 574-580, 619, 622, 630-631, 676,
Benedictine Sisters of Erie, The, 179-180
Bennett, William J., 367
Bernstein, Carl, 76, 143, 342, 347-349, 365, 426, 507, 509, 612, 615, 639, 657-659, 664, 668, 670-671, 678-679
Biberaj, Elez, 4
Biden, Joe, 410
Billings LIFE, 447
Birth Control, 12, 17, 21-22, 24, 27, 29, 40-41, 55, 80, 85, 95, 122, 154, 162, 190, 195, 198, 202-203, 226, 247, 252-253, 257, 259, 268, 276, 280, 287, 288, 289, 290, 294-299, 325, 348-349, 359, 362, 364, 373, 387-390, 393-394, 399, 409, 418, 421, 424-425, 427, 429, 431, 433-439, 441-443, 445-448, 451-452, 469, 471-472,

483, 501, 507, 510, 529, 545, 556, 565, 567-568, 576, 578-579, 581-583, 587, 592-593, 600
Birthright International, 455
Bitch Ph.D., 461
Black Genocide, 398-399, 661
Black Madonna, The, 60, 128, 214-216, 261-262, 287-288, 335, 445, 645
BlackGenocide.org, 398-399
Blackwell, Antoinette Brown, 150, 152-153
Bloom, Phil Fr., 452
Boff, Leonardo, 146
Boniecki, Adam, 79, 615, 632
Bortnowska, Halina, 396, 564-565, 676
Bosnia, 172, 226, 369
Bosnian women, rape of, 395-396
Braschi, Antonio, 496
Braun-Gałkowska, Maria, 103
Broadsheet, 372
Brown, John H, 4-5
Brownback, Sam, 410
Browne, Martin, 180
Brunner, Pia, 496
Bruskewitz, Fabian, 196
Brzezinski, Muska, 350, 351
Brzezinski, Zbigniew, 173, 345, 350, 351
Buchanan, Pat, 367
Bush, George W., 147, 177, 197,

278, 367, 402-403, 474, 537, 566
BushTelegraph, 372
Byrne, Lavinia, 185, 615

California Catholic Women's Forum, 194
Call to Action, 193, 196, 644
Canticle Magazine, 466
Cardinal Wojtyła SOS, 41, 423, 454
Care Net, 455
CAREConfidential, 455
Cassidy, Edward, 322
Catholic Apostolic Charismatic Church of "Jesus the King", 496
Catholic Culture, 158
Catholic Information Network, 511
Catholic Mom, 466
Catholic Moms, 466
Catholic News Service, 511
Catholic Order of the Humility of Mary, The, 142
Catholic Parenting, 466
Catholic University in Lublin (KUL), 2, 39-40, 103-106, 139, 374, 415, 531, 547
Catholic Youth Foundation, The 452
Catholic.net, 511
Catholic-Pages.com, 158
Catholics for a Free Choice, 192, 193, 397-398, 661

Catholics Speak Out, 188
Catholics United for the Faith, 145-146
Celtic Connection, The, 574
Center for Lesbian and Gay Studies in Religion, The, 187
Centrum Jana Pawła II in Kraków, 3
Chicago Catholic Women, 179, 192-193
Chittister, Joan, 179-181
Chmielowski, Albert Adam, Saint Albert, 81-82
Chopra, Deepak, 413
Christian Coalition of America, 366
Christian Family Movement, The, 192-193, 433
Christian-Universalism.com, 151
Church of Christ, Scientist, 151
Church of England, The, 480
CIA, 21, 278, 345, 596, 599-600, 602, 628, 678
Ciechomska, Maria, 232-233, 531, 615, 646, 673-674
Ciesielska, Danuta, 1, 100-101, 103, 635
Ciesielski, Jerzy, 1, 68, 78-80, 100
Clinton, Bill, 327, 363-365, 568, 576
Clinton, Hillary Rodham, 361-363, 394, 400, 408-409, 478,

506, 616, 658, 671

Coalition Against Trafficking in Women, 457

Coitus interruptus, 298-299, 391, 444

Colin, Margaret, 195

Commonweal, 538

Complementarity, gender, 8, 11, 14, 162, 191, 524-525, 530, 546

Concerned Women for America, 192, 194, 366-367

Consumerism, 16, 19, 28, 47, 171-172, 229, 239, 243, 271, 315, 321, 512

Contraception, 12, 17, 21-22, 24, 27, 29, 40-41, 55, 80, 85, 95, 122, 154, 162, 190, 195, 198, 202-203, 226, 247, 252-253, 257, 259, 268, 276, 280, 287, 288, 289, 290, 294-299, 325, 348-349, 359, 362, 364, 373, 387-390, 393-394, 399, 409, 418, 421, 424-425, 427, 429, 431, 433-439, 441-443, 445-448, 451-452, 469, 471-472, 483, 501, 507, 510, 529, 545, 556, 565, 567-568, 576, 578-579, 581-583, 587, 592-593, 600

Coughlin, Charles E., 28, 315, 629

Couple to Couple League, 447

Courtois, Stéphane, 169

Covenant House, Charleston, WV, 145

Covenant of the Goddess, 574

Creation Spirituality, 71

CreightonModel.com, 447

Culture of death, 191, 321, 389, 400, 402, 511, 573, 579

Culture of life, 191, 389, 400, 411, 554

Curran, Charles, 146, 165, 276, 616, 642, 649

Da Vinci Code, 527-528

Da Vinci Hoax, The, 527

Dads.org, 262

Daly, Mary, 9, 175-177, 186, 189, 342, 616, 643

Danube Seven, The, 496

Davídek, Felix Maria, 494-495, 497

Davies, Stuart, 4

Death Penalty, 27, 42, 165, 191, 195, 230, 272, 326, 365, 368-369, 396, 398, 407-408, 410-412, 419, 435, 536, 581

Defending Holy Matrimony, 466

Deskur, Andrzej Maria, 77

Different but equal, 11, 153, 190-191, 199, 517-518, 530

Dignity Canada, 539

DignityUSA, 539, 541

Dobson, James C., 366-367, 659

Domestic-Church.com, 466

Dworkin, Andrea, 203-205, 616, 644
Dziwisz, Stanisław, 28-29, 76-77, 80, 136, 244-245, 286, 362, 469-470, 590, 599-600, 606, 617, 624, 633, 638, 648, 651, 657-658, 668, 675, 678-679

E5men, 262
Ecofem.org, 459
Ecofeminism.net, 459
Eddy, Mary Baker, 150-152
Effective Fathers Ministries, 262
EMILY's List, 409
ENDOW, 192, 194
Engel, Barbara, 143
Episcopal Church of the United States of America, The, 480
Episcopal Diocese of Fort Worth, 480
Episcopal Diocese of Quincy, 480
Episcopal Diocese of San Joaquin, 480
Episcopal Life Online, 480
Euthanasia, 42, 110, 191, 242, 243, 321, 324-326, 329-330, 369, 378, 383, 400-402, 412, 416, 424, 474, 536, 579
Evangelical Christians, 27, 160, 197, 272, 327, 365-369, 412, 512, 543, 561, 565-566, 569, 584, 677
Evangelium Vitae, 7, 42, 199, 389, 394-395, 536, 579
EVE ONLINE, 459

Falwell, Jerry, 366-367
Familiaris consortio, 42, 202, 462, 668
Family Facts, 466
Family of the Americas, 447
Father Pio, da Pietrelcina, 40, 294-295, 652
FatherDaughterDance.com, 262
Faustina, Saint, 41, 43, 112, 129-132, 620, 637
Fawcett Society, The, 457
Federation of Christian Ministries, 188
Federation of Poles in Great Britain, 174
Felician Sisters, 178
Fellowship of Catholic University Students, 452
Female genius, 11, 113, 191, 226
Female orgasm, 290-291, 428
Femina, 372, Feminist.com, 372
Feminine Mystique, The, 8-9, 207, 617-618, 624
Feminism and Nonviolence Studies Association, The, 192, 194
Feminist Allies, 461
Feminist Blogs, 461
Feminist Majority Foundation, 368
Feminist Theologians

Liberation Network, 187
Feminist Women's health
    Center, 447
Feministe, 461
Feministing.com, 461
Feminists Choosing Life, 457
Feminists for Animal Rights,
    461
Feminists for Life, 192, 194-195,
    396, 405,
Ferraro, Barbara, 145-147, 639
Ferraro, Geraldine, 144
Filipowicz, Stefan, SJ, 2, 593-
    595, 617, 678
Firley, Zofia, 126
Florek, Józefa, 39
Flynn, Ray, 57, 363-364, 617,
    631, 637, 658-659
Focus on the Family, 366-367,
    659
Forster, Gisela, 496
Fox, Matthew, 71, 146, 633
Fox-Genovese, Elizabeth, 153,
    189, 617, 641
FreeMediaOnline.org, 3, 614,
    643, 679
French, Marilyn, 169
Friedan, Betty, 8-10, 182, 367,
    617-618, 624
Friends General Conference
    Library, 151
Future Church, 188
F-Word Ezine, The, 372

Galen, Clemens August Graf
    von, 326, 607-608
Gandhi, Mahatma, 553-556
Gebara, Ivone, 146
Gebert, Konstanty, 322
Genocide, 10, 55, 110, 172, 175,
    203-205, 243, 284, 302, 329,
    330, 339, 359, 369, 381, 393,
    398-400, 403, 405, 408, 474,
    561, 568, 583, 590, 604, 651,
    661, 679
Germana, Sister, 137-138
German women, 169, 325-326,
    356, 642, 655
German women, rape of, 642
Gift Foundation, 466
Girlistic, 461
Giuliani, Rudolph, 410
Glendon, Mary Ann, 42, 138,
    537-538, 638, 673
Global Ethic Foundation, The,
    563
God of Desire, 164
God Talk, 188
Goldszmit, Henryk, 323
Gorbachev, Mikhail, 346, 560,
    675
Gore, Al, 363, 575
Graham, Billy, Rev., 565
Grail, The, 192-193
Gramick, Jeannine, 146, 539
Gravel, Mike, 411
Grażyna, 218-219
Greeley, Andrew M., 196, 433,

459, 483, 557, 617, 628, 644, 667, 669, 675

Gryglowska, Alina, 40, 336, 338, 657

Gutiérrez, Gustavo, 144, 146

Halter, Marek, 319

Hampson, Daphne, 149, 181-184, 618, 639, 643

Harris, Barbara Clementine, 480

Havel, Václav, 553-555, 675

Heartbeat International, 455

Heaton, Patricia, 195

Hodur, Franciszek (Francis), 500-503

Hoffman, Eva, 306, 653

Holocaust, 89, 203-205, 319, 321, 325, 339, 352, 404-405, 515, 604, 611, 619, 634, 655-656, 663, 679

Holy Family Institute, 466

Hoover Institution, 3

Horodyska, Jadwiga, 92

Horowitz, Daniel, 9, 618, 624

Huckabee, Mike, 412

Humanae vitae, 12, 40-41, 162, 287, 296, 433-439, 441-444, 448, 471, 593, 665

Hunt, John 4

Hunt, Mary E., 187

Hunter, Duncan, 412

Hunthausen, Raymond, 146

Hussey, Particia, 145-147, 639

Individualism, 8, 23, 66, 85, 153, 163, 190, 236, 275-276, 355-358, 370-371, 374-375, 380, 580, 585, 587, 609, 617, 641, 658

Institute of the Blessed Virgin Mary, The, 185

Institute of Women Today, The, 176-177

Iraq, 21, 27, 146, 168, 177, 197, 278

Isakowicz-Zaleski, Tadeusz, 76, 96, 589-590, 618, 631, 633, 651

Islam, 29-30, 172, 198, 278-279, 359, 364-365, 513, 517, 535, 575, 633, 677

Jadwiga, (Hedwig), Queen, Saint, 18-20, 42, 226-231, Jadwiga, Sister, (Wojtyła's secretary), 135

Jagiellonian University in Kraków, 38-39, 59, 61, 63, 74, 88, 140, 229-230, 297, 316, 342, 429, 501, 627

Javorová, Ludmila, 494-497

Jesus Crowd, 452,

Jesus Decoded, 527

Jesus Youth, 452

Jews, Judaism, 23, 28-29, 33, 47, 58, 88-89, 91, 117, 123, 171-172, 182, 188, 205, 282, 285, 309, 312-328, 330, 351-352,

356, 358, 365, 408, 424, 508,
513-515, 519, 601, 605, 608,
610-611, 620, 633, 654-655,
662
Jodko, Marta, 92
John of the Cross, Saint, 70, 72
John Paul II, Short Biography
of, 38-43

Kaczorowska, Emilia, 38, 47-50,
456
Kane, Theresa, Sister, 41, 141-
143
Karski, Jan, 610-611
Kasperkiewicz, Karolina, 40,
105
Katyń, 34, 602, 613, 621, 629
KEPHA, 262
Keyes, Alan, 410
KGB, 31, 34, 386, 592, 596, 598-
600, 606, 615, 678
Kinaszewska, Irena, 596-597
Kissinger, Henry, 173
Kissling, Frances, 397-398
Kler-Med, 297
Kluger, Jerzy, 88, 322
Kolbe, Maximilian, Saint, 309-
318, 321-324, 488, 654
Kolbenschlag, Madonna, 142,
638
Korbońska, Zofia, 4
Korboński, Stefan, 4, 91-92
Korczak, Janusz, 323
Kotlarczyk, Mieczysław, 65, 67-

68, 73-74, 86-87, 260
Kotlarczyk, Zofia, 64, 73, 86-87,
260
Kowalska, Faustyna, Sister,
Saint, 41, 43, 112, 129-132,
620, 637
Kozłowska, Felicja, 497, 499-500
Krol, John, 196, 572
Królikiewicz, Halina,
Kwiatkowska, 38-39, 62, 87, 630
Kucinich, Dennis, 410
Küng, Hans, 146, 563-564, 619,
649, 676
Kwitny, Jonathan, 76, 288, 296,
298-299, 301, 343, 345, 348,
350, 619, 649, 651-653, 657-
658, 665, 670, 675
Kydryńska, Aleksandra, 39, 90

Lackorońska, Karolina, 305-306,
332-334, 619, 653, 656
LaHaye, Beverly, 366
Lasota, Marek, 597, 619, 657,
678
Latoś-Kasprzyk, Teofila, 2
Lay Missionaries of Charity,
360
Leadership Conference of
Women Religious, The, 141,
192-193
Lesbian Gay Bisexual
Transgender Religious
Archives Network, 187
Leszczyńska, Stanisława, 42,

334-335, 339, 607-608
Lewaj, Jadwiga, 39, 92
Liberalism, 9, 23, 29, 66, 85, 93,
    113, 161, 163, 167, 170, 199,
    236, 239, 241-243, 246, 248,
    280, 282, 284, 315-316, 330,
    338, 355-356, 370, 371-372,
    378, 383, 386, 388, 429, 484,
    535, 559, 561, 585, 587, 609,
    625
Liberation Theology, 82, 144,
    218, 494
Library of Congress, 3
Life (UK), 455
Life Teen, 452
Likoudis, James, 145-146
Lipien-Rohrer, Leokadia (Lodi),
    1
Lipien, Ted, iv
Lipień, Helena Maciaszek, 1
Lipień, John, 605
Lipień, Marek, 2
Lipień, Stanisław Bolesław, 1
Living Rosary, 69, 72-73
Lobcom.org, 370
Lorence-Kot, Bogna, 308
Loreto Sisters, 185
Love and Responsibility
    Foundation, 164
Love and Responsibility, 7, 40, 79,
    93, 98-99, 108, 111, 164, 191,
    289, 290-292, 299, 339, 394,
    424-426, 428, 432, 436, 623,
    634-635, 652, 654, 664

Love One Another Magazine,
    452

Maciaszek, Justyna, 2
Maciaszek, Marta, 2
Maliński, Mieczysław, 63-64,
    67, 70, 72-77, 80, 86, 91, 100,
    128, 135, 202, 238-239, 274,
    323, 342-343, 416-418, 434,
    453, 589, 590-591-592, 606,
    619, 633-635, 637-638, 647,
    657, 663, 665-667, 677-678
Mały Dziennik, 312
Mansour, Mary Agnes, 146
Maria Shelter, 176-177
Mariavites, 498-504, 670
Martinus Polonus, 487-488
Marxism, 9, 25, 66, 84, 93, 113,
    148, 154, 156, 160, 162-163,
    168-169, 218, 236, 240, 246,
    314, 346, 353, 370-372, 494,
    532, 639
Matylda, Sister, 137
Mayr-Lumetzberger, Christine,
    496
McCain, John, 411-412
Media Watch, 457
Michnik, Adam, 533-536, 654,
    673
Mickiewicz, Adam, 65, 208-210,
    213, 217-220
Militia of the Immaculate, The,
    313
Millett, Kate, 156-158

Miłosz, Czesław, 283, 314, 650
Ministry at Pacific School of
Religion, 187
Ministry to Persons with a
Homosexual Inclination, 539
Missionaries of Charity
Fathers, 360
Missionaries Under The Sun,
158
Modjeska, Helena, also Helena
Modrzejewska, 82-83
Modrzejewska, Helena, also
Helena Modjeska, 83-83
Molla, Gianna Beretta, Saint,
396-397
Monfort, Louis Marie Grignion
de, 80
Mother Teresa – The Path of
Love, 360
Mother Teresa of Calcutta
Center, 360
Mother Teresa, Agnes Gonxha
Bojaxhiu, 5, 10, 43, 55, 284,
359-362, 462, 637, 658
MS Magazine, 368
Mszana Dolna, 107
Mulieris dignitatem, 42, 464, 469,
668
Muller, Iris, 496
Myss, Caroline, 71

Nancy, Snow, 4-5
NARAL Pro-Choice America,
368

National Association of
Evangelicals, 366
National Catholic Register, The,
511
National Coalition of American
Nuns, The, 176-177
National Fellowship of
Catholic Men, 262
National Organization of Men
Against Sexism, 372
National Organization of
Women (NOW), 368
NET Ministries of Canada, 452
Neu, Diann L., 187
New Age, 71, 181, 413, 574-575
New feminism, 7, 10-11, 26, 42,
153, 162, 187, 189-192, 194,
199, 352-353, 478, 536-538,
577-578, 623, 638, 644, 676
New Ways Ministry, 539-540
No Status Quo, 370
Noonan, Peggy, 573, 620, 676
Nostra Ateate, 320
Nowicka, Wanda, 450-451, 548,
666
Nowojka, 61, 488
Nugent, Robert, 146, 539
Nussbaum, Martha C, 555, 620,
675

O'Brien, Darcy, 117, 322, 620,
633, 654
O'Reilly, Jane, 147
Obama, Barak, 399, 409-410,

413
O-Books, 5
Omegarock.com, 452
One More Soul Canada, 466
Open Embrace, 447
Oprah, Winfrey, 413
OptionLine, 455
Opus Dei, 28, 198, 363, 371, 527,
    629
Order of Our Lady of Mercy in
    Łagiewniki, 3, 133
Ordinatio sacerdotalis, 42, 462,
    469, 471-474, 477, 489-491,
    496, 522, 668-669
Our Lady's Warriors, 158

Paetz, Juliusz, 286, 651
Pagan Dawn, 574,
Pagan Federation International,
    The, 574
Pagan Federation, 574
Paglia, Camille, 148, 639
Paul VI, Pope, 12, 35, 40-41,
    257, 276, 287, 295-296, 320,
    348, 433-439, 442-443, 464-
    465, 471-472, 557, 579, 582-
    583, 591, 597, 648, 665
Paul, Ron, 412
Personalism Library, The, 164
Personalism, 10, 163-164, 191,
    375
Piekut, M. Beata, 130, 637
Pietrzyk, Basia, 304
Pigozzi, Caroline, 136-137, 620,

638
Planned Parenthood, 368, 658,
    666
Plater, Emilia, 218-219
Poland, Brief Outline of
    History, 32-37
Polish American Congress, 174
Polish Information & Culture
    Center in Dublin, 174
Polish National Catholic
    Church of Canada, 500
Polish National Catholic
    Church, 17, 500-503, 671
Polish Roman Catholic Union
    of America, 178-179
Polish women, 7-8, 11-13, 17,
    20-21, 24, 32, 35, 48, 53, 68,
    91-92, 106, 111-112, 117, 129-
    130, 171, 216-220, 222-223,
    225-226, 232-233, 240-241,
    244, 246-251, 253-254, 256,
    258-259, 261, 266-267, 284,
    298, 302, 304-305, 307, 327,
    328, 334-338, 367, 384, 395,
    414, 444, 446, 451, 456, 543-
    544, 546-553, 582, 586, 588,
    592-593, 624, 627-629, 642,
    663, 674
Politi, Marco, 76, 143, 342, 347-
    349, 365, 426, 507, 509, 612,
    615, 639, 657-659, 664, 668,
    670-671, 678-679
Polski Dublin, 174
Poole, Myra, 180

Pope Joan, 487-488, 612, 670

PornNoMore.com, 262

Półtawska, Wanda, 10, 12-13, 40, 55, 80, 215, 285-286-289-303, 305-309, 311-312, 329-330, 339, 344, 348-349, 428, 432, 434, 448, 582-583, 596, 620, 624, 651-653

Positivism, 240-241, 244

Późniakowa, Zofia, 39

Probst, Christoph, 607-608, 679

Pro-Life Alliance of Gays and Lesbians, 457

Promise Keepers, 366-367

Pure Love Club, 452

Quinn, Donna, 179, 181, 184

Quinn, Sally, 160

Radical Women, 370

Radio Maryja, 28-29, 243, 382-383, 385, 536, 581, 629, 653, 660, 676-677

Rahner, Karl, 146, 202

Raming, Ida, 496

Ranke-Heinemann, Uta, 529, 621, 673

Rape Crisis England and Wales, 457

Ratzinger, Joseph, also see Benedict XVI, 22-23, 44, 52, 71, 146, 165, 171, 188, 198, 418, 475, 489-490, 497, 503, 513-514, 523-524, 539, 557, 571-572, 577, 607-608, 621, 628, 642, 676

Ravensbrück Nazi Concentration Camp, 40, 302, 304-306, 308, 311, 332, 333, 619, 653, 656

Reappropriate, 461

Redstockings, 370

Reed, Cheryl L. 178, 572, 574, 621, 643, 676,

Religious Coalition for Reproductive Choice, 368

Remember the Women Institute, 205

Revolution of Love, 452

Rhythm Method, 120, 247, 253, 298, 390, 429, 441, 443, 446-447, 583, 600

Richardson, Bill, 410

Rights of Women, 457

Roberts, Jane Sullivan, 195, 644

Roberts, John G., 195

Robertson, Pat, 366-367, 659

Robinson, V. Gene, 480

Roe v. Wade, 175, 284, 361, 366, 410, 412

Rohrer, Chloe, 1

Rohrer, Douglas, 1

Roitinger, Adelinde Theresia, 496

Roman Catholic Womenpriests, 166-167

Romney, W. Mitt, 411

Rosen, Hannah, 610

Rothschild, Elizabeth S., 610
Rowbotham, Sheila, 149, 621,
   639
Ruether, Rosemary Radford,
   149, 192, 194, 621, 639, 644
Rybicka, Danuta, 94, 100, 114-
   115, 458, 634-637
Rydzyk, Tadeusz, 382, 629
Ryś, Maria, 301, 652

Safir, Enver, 4
Saint Maria Messenger, 452
Sapieha, Stefan, 39, 68, 74-75,
   84, 91
Sartre, Jean-Paul, 155, 429
Schillebeeckx, Edward, 146
Scholl, Hans, 607-608, 679
Scholl, Sophie, 607-608, 679
School Sisters of Notre Dame,
   The, 176-177, 539
Schori, Katharine Jefferts, 480
Schumacher, Michele M., 190,
   199, 342, 578, 623, 644, 676
Schüssler Fiorenza, Elizabeth,
   154, 157-158, 161, 172, 184,
   187-188, 621, 641, 644
Scottish Women's Aid, 457
Second Sex, The, 9, 24-25, 148-
   149, 156-159, 175-176, 207,
   615-616, 639, 643
Sinsinawa Dominican Sisters,
   176, 179
Sisters of Mercy, The, 141, 639
Sisters of Notre Dame de

Namur, 145
Solzhenitsyn, Alexander, 376-
   378, 659
Sontag, Susan, 82-83, 633
Southeastern Pennsylvania
   Women's Ordination
   Conference, 188
Southern Baptist Convention,
   366
Spiritus Christi Church, 188
Stabrowska, Halina, 337, 607
Stanton, Elizabeth Cady, 150-
   151, 518, 640, 672, 672
State Department, U.S., 34, 278,
   373, 602, 613-614, 627
Steichen, Donna, 184, 189, 621,
   643
Stein, Edith, Saint, 318, 351-358,
   622, 658
Stop Violence Against Women,
   457
Stucky-Schaller, Magrit, 143
Styczeń, Tadeusz, 106, 531-532,
   622, 659, 673
Suchocka, Hanna, 380
Suenens, Leo Jozef, 162, 622,
   641
Susan B. Anthony List, 192, 194
Szczepańska, Helena, 41, 49-50,
Szkocka, Irena, 39, 90-91
Szulc, Tad, 76, 433, 438, 665

Tarnowska, Maria, 102-103
Teresa of Ávila, Saint, 70, 352-

353, 465

The Acting Person, 2, 13, 41, 164, 168, 292, 339-340, 622, 657

The f word, 461

Theology of the Body International Alliance, 164

Theology of the Body Times Square Discussion Group, 164

Theology of the Body, 16, 164, 203

These Last Day Ministries, 158

Thompson, Fred, 412

Tobiana, Sister, 6, 43, 137

Tradition in Action, 99

Traxler, Margaret, 176-177, 181, 184, 643

True Girl Magazine, 452

Turowicz, Jerzy, 388-389, 460, 649

Tygodnik Powszechny, 79, 257, 317, 388, 460, 596, 598, 633, 649, 678

Tymieniecka, Anna-Teresa, 2, 13, 41, 168, 277, 339-344, 347-351, 426, 583, 622, 657, 664

Tyranowski, Jan, 68-74, 78, 632

U.S. Holocaust Memorial Museum, The, 205

Union of Utrecht of the Old Catholic Churches, 500

Unitarian Universalist Association of Congregations, 151

University of California at Berkley, 3

University of Fribourg, 342

Utilitarianism, 244, 429

Vanzant, Iyanla, 413

Vatican Council II, 40, 167, 196, 201, 320, 415, 417-418, 464, 467, 492, 503

Vatican Radio, 2, 523-524, 593-595, 598, 601, 614

Vladimiroff, Christine, 180

Voice of America (VOA), 4, 34, 593, 600-602, 604, 611-614

Waldheim, Kurt, 324

Walewska, Maria, 218, 224

Wanda, Princess, 218, 220-222

Wanderer, The, 538

Ward, Mary, 185

Wasser, Hedwig, 143

WATER (Women's Alliance for Theology, Ethics, and Ritual), 187, 192

Weber, Anka, 88

Weigel, George, 76, 164, 276, 277, 366, 630-631, 633, 635, 641, 652-653, 657, 665, 678

White, Angela, 496

Wicca, 574

Wikipedia, 3, 608, 660

Williamson, Marianne, 413

Witches' Voice, 574
Wojtarowicz, Teresa, 106
Wojtyła, Edmund, 38, 48, 52, 55
Wojtyła, Karol (Pope John Paul II), Short Biography of, 38-43
Wojtyła, Karol, Sr., 38, 45-48
Wojtyła, Olga, 38, 48
Wolska, Klawera, 103-104
Wołoszyn, Maria, 3
Woman's Bible, The, 152, 640
Womankind, 457
Women Affirming Life, 192, 194, 457
Women for Faith and Family, 192, 200, 466
Women of the Third Millennium, 192, 194
Women priests, 16-17, 29-30, 101, 112, 182, 193, 199, 202, 279, 343, 361, 402, 462, 469, 471-472, 479, 481-483, 485, 488-491, 495-497, 499-500, 503, 564, 570-572, 580, 609, 641, 667
Women's Alliance for Theology, Ethics, and Ritual, 187, 192
Women's eNews, 372
Women's Environmental Network, 459

Women's Justice Coalition, 188
Women's Ordination Conference, The, 187-188, 192-193
Women's Seminary Quarter, The, 192
Women's Voice for the Earth, 459
Women-Church Convergence, The, 192-193
Women-Church, 155, 184, 192-193
WomenPriests.org, 166
Wyszyński, Stefan, 35, 246-248, 252-256, 267, 438, 443, 520-521, 530, 566-567, 573, 584, 591, 620, 623, 648-649, 665-666

Youth Apostles Online, 452

Zachuta, Feliks, 319
Zanussi, Krzysztof, 278, 281
Zdybicka, Zofia, 2, 40, 106-108, 111, 114, 285, 509, 624, 636
ZENIT, 511
Zirer, Edith, 319-320
Zukav, Gary, 413
Żarnecka, Zofia, 87-88
Życzkowska, Teresa, 115-116, 636